A COUPLE'S T

ACROSS CANADA

A COUPLE'S TRAVELS

ACROSS CANADA

Li-Chen Campbell

For any request, contact Li-Chen Campbell, 32292 Pineview Ave. Abbotsford, British Columbia, Canada v2T 1R5. Or email to blcm@telus.net.

Cover Design: ASM Printing Design, Canada

Printing and Bounding: Bookmasters, US

Library and Archives Canada Cataloguing in Publication

Campbell, Li-Chen, author

A couple's travels across Canada/Li-Chen Campbell – First edition.

Issued in print and electronic formats.

ISBN 978-0-9948737-1-2 (paperback).–ISBN 978-0-9948737-0-5 (ebook)

1.Campbell, Li-Chen – Travel – Canada. 2. Canada – Description and travel. I. Title.

FC76.C34 2015 917.04'73 C2015-906067-2

C2015-906350-7

TO THE CANADIANS

LIKE IT OR NOT

IN ONE WAY OR ANOTHER

YOU HAVE CONTRIBUTED TO THE BIRTH OF THIS BOOK

ACKNOWLEDGEMENT

I would like first to express my deep gratitude to my husband's unwavering support for me to write and publish this book and his painstaking proofreading for the book. Because of some criticisms in this book, we have received harassment and attacks. Bruce had never shown any fear of those hostilities but concerns for my health, and he had tried his best to give me his loving care.

This book has waded into Canada's historical, political, cultural, economical and social situations. I have based the facts and records in those fields on the writings of other writers, historians and statisticians. For the fluidity of the writing, I have paraphrased or used my own words to fit those facts and records into the book. But the readers should consider them all quoted. I have listed some books I used in the References at the end of the book. Quite some facts and records come from the introductions, illustrations and documents of different museums, galleries and public and historical sites my husband and I had visited throughout the country. The country's natural, geological and geographical conditions and features are all based on different books of other writers and introductions of different natural museums and reserves. Whether their names and books are mentioned or not in the References, all those writers deserve the full credits. I did not create those facts and records; those writers did all the work in collecting the information and bringing them in the forms of books and museum displays to serve the public.

The criticisms, opinions, views and comments in the book are my own. If some of them coincide with those of other writers, they are not my intentional copying. In this world, only Adam and Eve could be sure that when they said something, nobody else had already said them.

PREFACE

Mark Twain dedicated his The Celebrated Jumping Frog of Calaveras County, and Other Sketches to John Smith, saying, "It is said that a man to whom a book is dedicated always buys a copy. If this is true in this instance, a princely affluence is about to descend upon the author."

Every writer, if she or he intends to have his or her book published, will wish or even dream that the book will be bought by many people. But not this writer. Though I have dedicated this book to all the Canadians, I know that I can neither wish nor dream that every Canadian will buy a copy of this book. Because of some criticisms in the book, even when I was writing the book, I and my family had already received harassment and attacks and our life had become difficult, I cannot foresee what will happen when the book is printed and presented to the public. Still, everyone can wish for miracles. No exception for me on this. Even though I have received the threat that my book, if it comes into being, will be shredded, I still wish that it will be received kindly by the Canadians. Anyone with a sound mind, after reading this book, will see that the author's intention of writing this book is for the country to be healthier and stronger.

Constructive criticisms, especially criticisms on racism, are like bitter medicine for personal or collective illnesses. For the medicine to work for the affected people, those people have first to see that they need this medicine. If those people don't even see that they have the illnesses, they, of course, will refuse the bitter medicine and be angry with the ones giving the medicine. If my criticisms have hurt some personal or collective pride, I hope the hurts will prompt them to change their ways, instead of letting their anger with the bitter medicine push them to retaliate and to beat down the criticiser. I am not too much concerned about the fate of this book. Even if not a single Canadian dares to buy a copy, I am determined to finish writing the book, to have it printed and to present it to the public, just to prove a point, to promote the freedom of thought and expression which is vital to intellectual progress and progress of the country.

A Couple's Travels Across Canada has been based on the travelling my husband and I had conducted throughout Canada in recent years, but the book has also talked extensively about different things concerning the country, its history, past and present economy, tradition, culture, religion, politics, political and social systems, achievements, problems and so on. Each province or territory my husband and I had visited has been individually dealt with about its past and present situations, including some of its specialities and prominent products. Canada is a large country with varied geologic and geographic features, the descriptions about the appearance of the country cannot be comprehensive but limited to what we had seen and known, but those descriptions are heartfelt and efforts have been put in to give a true picture of the country's natural beauty.

If the readers try to categorize this book into a certain genre, their efforts will be wasted. From the start, I have had no intention to put the book into a certain frame. I have put in whatever I think necessary to bring the country and its different places into full being, alive, understandable and believable. This endeavour comes from the experiences and feelings of a traveller. Merely going through different places of a country can only have surface impressions. To really see and understand a country, one must get to know as many aspects of the country as possible. People will be surprised that, after knowing different things about certain places, they can see the country in a new light with colour, flesh and blood. Travelling through Canada has been a learning process especially for me to better understand and appreciate the country. This learning experience has resulted in this book gathering all sorts of information about the country and its provinces and territories and trying to put them into a very limited space of one book. The background information about the country and its different places cannot be in full detail and specific, but general and representative. The only purpose of them being brought up in this book is for the readers and myself to see and know the country better.

A book about travelling cannot miss the main topic. Detailed descriptions are for our travelling experiences, where we have been, what we have seen, heard and encountered, and how we have felt. I have tried to show a truthful personal travelling experience throughout the country. For some rich and powerful people, their travelling experiences might be totally different. They fly to different locations and spend their holidays or vacations in villas or grand hotels. Being able to give people favors or businesses, they will meet pleasant smiles and receive the best services, all the conveniences and comforts. They will, of course, see the country in a golden pink colour. As for us, we had just upgraded our camping from tenting to RVing. Though satisfied with the luxury of a small trailer, compared with the real luxury travellers, we are just the baseline wanderers, staying on campgrounds and Walmart parking lots. Yet, we are the ground travellers and we see more than those sky travellers. We have seen the country from a different angle that reveals not only the grand, the beautiful and the shining, but more of the true full picture of the good and bad, the ordinary things and people with some unordinary characteristics, and the daily life activities of the country.

Most places we have been, we have received the normal helpful courteous services like the other ordinary people. But in our present life situation, we have encountered more bad things than other ordinary people. We had been harassed and attacked by some people who came out or were sent out to us on some hostile missions. On certain location and in a slow traffic, our van's front windshield had been shattered by an on-coming tractor-trailer shooting out large rock; we had a narrow escape with our lives. In a midnight at another location, our trailer had been blasted by eggs. Then a four inch long nail had been driven into our tire in a quiet country location. Following this and with a busted tire, we had to handle a small pothole-ridden country road suddenly strewn with dead porcupines. Besides these, we had to face constant harassments, mostly noise attacks, on most campgrounds and Walmart or some other store parking lots, hard to get some decent sleep. I don't believe that many travellers can boast such a difficult adventure through hostilities and hatred in traveling across the free democratic modern Canada.

I have recounted those ugly incidents with sharp criticisms. This has further offended or hurt the delicate sense of pride of some Canadians. They might cry out that it was impossible that this kind of things could have happened to an ordinary couple traveling through Canada; those incidents must be fictional. I have absolutely no demands on my readers. They can have whatever opinions or judgements on this book. There is no absolute truth, but relative truth in the world. I can tell the readers that every word about what we had encountered in our travels across the country is true, exactly as how things had happened to us, but it will not change an iota of some people who have made up their minds to think that they are fictional. This kind of things is quite normal to writers. If they write a fiction, many things in the story will be spotted as true life incidents; if they write a non-fiction, some people will think it fictional. So, I will let the readers decide about the truth or false of all those descriptions about the harassments, attacks and abuses we had received in our life and our travelling, instead of me talking until my face turning blue to convince them of the truth. If they feel too much displeased, offended or hurt, they are welcome to think whatever way they like to ease some of those bad feelings.

Quite some comments and criticisms in this book are about racial discrimination in this country. Those comments and criticisms are not only based on our own life experinces, but also coming from our observations on the conditions of the coloured and native peoples through our traveling and getting information from different channels. Because of our own situation, we had paid close attention to the conditions of the visible minorities along our way, how many of them appear residing in the cities, how many are working, how well their businesses are doing, and how many are participating in leisure and recreational activities. We found that the situation is very varied in different cities and regions, better in large cities than in small cities, and generally better in the west than in the east. From people's attitudes towards us, an interracial couple, we could have a rough view about how the coloured Canadians were treated in different places. Unfortunately, we have come to the conclusion that racism is still a wide spread problem in the country.

I may have overstressed the topic of racism by repeatedly coming back to it in the book. This may come from the habit of my former teaching career; to drive an important point into the receivers' minds, repeated hammering is needed. This repetitive hammering, however, may be seen by some people as insensitive, jamming into their throat the very thing they want to avoid. I can only wish that those people can understand that my only intention is for the good of the country, and they will see that the general visible minorities are at the receiving end of racism and racial discrimination is their daily life reality; the coloured Canadians generally wish to see the situation change, so that they can be treated as equal human beings and enjoy equal opportunities and an equal quality life.

Many other things have been talked about in the book. I believe that many travellers will agree with me on this: when we come across certain things or people, beautiful cities or majestic scenery in our travelling, we will not be dumfounded with a blank mind. Those stood-out things, people or nature scenes always prompt certain relevant thoughts and feelings in us. Many things or scenes in our travelling across the country had just this catalyst effect on us; they prompted certain thoughts and emotions in us. Besides describing what we had encountered in our travelling, I have recorded those thoughts and feelings generated by those different things and scenes in the forms of comments and opinions. This has resulted in many things such as life, death, human nature, environme-nt, national and international situations and so on, being talked about in the book, which might have given the book a Hodge Podgy free style. However, the main line of the book has been maintained; it is the travelling across Canada, from the west to the east and from the south to the north. This Hodge Podgy style may have made the book colourful and interesting just like our travelling.

Although we had encountered some unpleasant, dangerous or harmful things instigated by some hostile people on our way, we have learnt to switch our minds quickly away from them to see the beautiful and interesting things and people. Gaining this quality has enabled us to enjoy immensely our travels across the country. If we had let those negative things dwell in our minds and get hold of us, we could not have continued the journey and would have missed many amazing beautiful things that the country had offered. Life, as a matter of fact, is just like travelling. Whether we are poor or rich, fortunate or unfortunate, in privileged or underprivileged class or race, going through life, we will meet all sorts of things and people; we all have to learn to focus our minds on the positive to help us to move on and to enjoy life.

I hope that the readers will read this book with an open mind to see both the positive and the negative sides of the country. I am sure that, in spite of the candid descriptions of some unpleasant ugly things and sharp criticisms, they will find many positive, interesting and enjoyable things in the book. So, come along, let's travel across Canada through reading, learning to understand, to enjoy and to appreciate the country.

Enjoy the reading!

Li-Chen Campbell
Abbotsford
June, 2015

CONTENTS

CHAPTER ONE

GETTING STARTED

Travel has been one of the important human activities since the humans started to exist. In the beginning, travel was a necessity for survival. The humans had to travel outside their caves to hunt and to find food. Then when their brains had been a little more developed, they moved away from their caves to live in more open areas. With the changes of their shelter arrangement and more development of their brains, human beings traveled further. However, for tens of thousands of years, humans had traveled on foot. Their two legs carried them to places they wanted to go and distances they wanted to cover. With further developments of their brains and intelligence, human beings had gradually traveled and spread all over the earth; this, however, had taken them many thousands of years. In fact, they have conquered not only distances but also all other living beings on earth. They have made and used all other living beings and non-living materials to serve their needs and wants. Their living quarters and living conditions have gone from convenient to snug and luxurious. Their travelling methods have gone from by-foot to by all kinds of motor devices.

While the human beings have been accomplishing amazing wonders for themselves, they are becoming more selfish and greedy. Their usages of other living beings and non-living things have gone amazingly excessive. Their insatiable hording habits and wastefulness have caused the destructions of some other living species, natural resources and natural environment. To satisfy all their desires, they have created countless gadgets and machineries to make their life more comfortable and luxurious. They have dug low and deep everywhere on earth to draw fossil fuels to run those gadgets and machines. Within about one hundred years, the smokes puffed out by their gadgets and machineries have been quickly ruining the atmosphere of the beautiful planet. Quite some human beings have realized that if they keep their abominable habits to live the highly selfish life, they will soon destroy the place they live on. Those people have started to put in efforts to change the situation, to educate people and to prevent further damages done to the earth. Still, quite some people will not or cannot change their habits and are determined to live the life they have always known. Like every other small or large fights between the human beings since they started to exit, this big fight to save or to destroy the planet has been and will be a long lasting and hard one.

Besides those horrendous environmental damages human beings have been doing to their home planet because of their bad habits, they have another dirtier habit that is even worse. They are habitually aggressive, violent and warlike. For thousands of years, they have fought among themselves unceasingly, first with sticks and stones and then with knives, spears, swords, bows and arrows. In the recent few centuries, with the development of their science and technology, their weaponry have gone to the extreme height; they have now got not only guns, cannons and missiles, but also nuclear weapons that can destroy the whole world in a very short time.

Nonetheless, when inspired or fired up by some lofty ideas, human beings can become the most noble and pure spiritual beings. Their altruism can go to the highest extend. They will work hard and strive selflessly to build a better life for others, and they will sacrifice everything including their own lives for love and for serving their ideals or beliefs. Countless of their creations and works in human history have been out of their best intentions to serve the mankind and the world. Unfortunately, sooner or later some of those unselfish achievements have been turned to serve the ends of greed and selfishness. There is no doubt that the human race and its world have progressed steadily and rapidly in the recent few centuries. The sad thing is that, with the progress, the danger of all being destroyed has also increased in the same scale. It seems that the human race will never fully metamorphose to perfection. After all those tremendous achievements they have made, their survival on the planet earth has remained precarious.

With many critically dangerous situations going on in the modern life of human beings, life goes on as it has always been. Even if the whole world is going to crumble to pieces, most of human beings concern only about their lives today, about how they are going to solve the immediate problems that will inevitably impact their daily life and how to live or enjoy life to the fullest their capacities can reach. Travel, of course, is one of the human activities to be carried on just as it had been carried out from ancient time. Only the modern-day travel has gone to such a grand scale that the cave man could never have dreamt about.

Man has traveled on foot for eons. In the recent centuries, they have started first to travel by horse drawn carts, wooden boats and then motor-driven devices on land, on water and in skies. Their traveling speed has gone way passed that of all other animals. With their aeroplanes, they can fly from this side of the globe to the other side in less than a day. They have traveled to the space and to the moon with their rockets or spaceships that are faster than the sound. They have also traveled with their motor devices deep into the ocean where many ocean-dwellers can never go.

With this kind of capabilities, human beings are growing intolerably arrogant. They consider the world their oyster; they can eat it whichever way they want. Their brutal ravishments on the oyster have started to bring sands into their own teeth and hurts into their own stomachs. After all, the oyster is much tougher than they are. By the time when they are extinct, the oyster will still survive for a much longer time.

While the human beings becoming highly mobile in the modern time, the frequency of traveling by large quantity of people has sky-rocketed. Every day, millions of people travel all over the world by the motor devices of their choices. People go to different places to work, to communicate, to fight in a war, to make money in doing businesses with others, to study different subjects from others, to enjoy themselves by seeing other places and other peoples, to go on missions to teach other people what they have learnt and believed in, to help other people who need their help, to escape from some unpleasant or life-threatening situations or for all other kinds reasons, large or small.

According to the popular belief, human minds can be broadened by traveling. Unfortunately, the facts or reality say differently. Not all human minds can be broadened by traveling. Some minds are impossible to change because of their set convictions, beliefs or ways of thinking. For some people who don't like certain things, certain countries or peoples, no matter how far or how long they travel; nothing they see, hear, smell and taste can change their rigid minds. When going to strange places and encountering different peoples, they can always find things in those places and peoples to fit their already formed thoughts and beliefs about them. In their hearts or minds, they will say to themselves with the satisfaction, "Aha! Just like what I have always thought about them! They are indeed far below us. How can they carry on their lives in this way and in this kind of places?" If they see other people doing well in their well-built places, they will still say, "Okay! So what? There are always better things and people in the world than them." This kind of people's formed and set minds are very hard to be moved or impressed. They are closed-in like an iron box without a door. Not a breath of fresh air or a fly can get in to cause a little disturbance. Those people are bores in human societies.

They live a boring life no matter what they do or where they go. They bore not only others but also themselves.

On the other hand, there are people who have never traveled much or far, but they can keep an open mind to other places and other peoples. In the old time, those people had accomplished this open-mindedness by reading books to know different places and different peoples. In the modern time, in addition to more books, the communication devices have been greatly advanced. People, sitting in their own homes, can see different places and different peoples from their TV screens. Anything happens in any corner of the world can be broadcasted and shown to the whole world in just a few minutes. People with open minds and compassionate hearts, whether they sit at their own homes or travel to other places, can always find positive things in other places and other peoples to appreciate, to understand, to sympathize and to love. This kind of people lives a rich and valuable life. They are a joy to be held.

Almost everybody in his or her life has considered and done some traveling for one reason or another. Like everybody else, there was this ordinary couple living in the small city Abbotsford in Canada, who had one day started thinking of taking a long trip across the country. It would be indeed a long journey for them. Canada is a second largest country in the world, land wise. It is a large portion of the North American continent and bound by three oceans. To its east, there is the Atlantic Ocean, to its west, the Pacific Ocean, to its north, the Arctic Ocean and to its south, the United States. The couple's journey would be starting from the coast of Pacific Ocean to reach the coast of Atlantic Ocean and then from the south to some distance into the north. Still, the journey would be considered as transcontinental or trans-Canada. This was not the first time that the couple had traveled thus; they had traveled across the country four times before. With their motor vehicles, they had never encountered much trouble for such a journey. In today's world, even a transcontinental journey would be thought as a common trip. Only their former trips had never been for pleasure and never included the province of Newfoundland, a large island at the east end of Canada, and cities in the north. This time they were going to take more time to see a bit of the country and to go to the famous remote province of Newfoundland and the northern cities.

The couple, Mr. and Mrs. Duihne were in their fifties, not a young age. James Duihne was a disabled retired military veteran and his wife Meilin was a Chinese Canadian who had no job and did some writing at home. They had all the time to take such a trip. But the main reason for their decision to take such a long trip was to escape the unpleasant situation in their present life. The ordinary couple could have lived a very peaceful life, as Jim's pension had provided that they could spend their later life time without financial worries. Unfortunately, hell had suddenly broken lose in their life. By pointing out some wrong doings of some services, a small thing some people might say, a tremendous storm had risen around them and threatened to engulf them at any moment. Rumours and slandering were spread around to cause people to become hostile to them. Loud noises were constant in their neighbourhood, trying to drive them away from the city. Their lives had been threatened, some attempts had been made to frame them and they a totally lost the peace of life.

The couple were bewildered and confused beyond their lives. Canada has been a free peaceful democratic country since its birth in 1867. Normally people can complain and criticize without having to suffer consequences. What had happened that would cause this kind of hostilities and hatred towards this couple? The couple speculated and guessed in many different ways and about many different things. They could not find an accurate answer. One thing seemed sure that racism was involved in this case and there might be some in-fights between powers of the country and the couple were caught in. As the couple were ordinary folk and at the bottom of the society, they became the victim of the racism and some power struggles. The couple could have many wild speculations and guesses, but they could not do anything to change the situation, but suffer whatever fell upon their heads.

When the couple thought that things could not get any worse in the situation, they did get worse. They found out or realized that they had been watched and listened into twenty-four hours a day. Some people might say that this was an incredible technological wonder to happen in human life. Just think if this kind of technology being used to survey suspicious people, potential criminals or terrorists, to find out what they were going to do and to prevent them from doing those bad things ahead of time, the world might be more peaceful. But most decent people might say that using this kind technology on ordinary people was an outrageous invasion on human beings' private life, certainly a violation of human rights and the whole society would be turned upside down by countless law suits.

Modern technology is a two edged sword. It can be used for the welfare and wellbeing of the world, and it can also be used to destroy the world. This is no longer a new knowledge, as the world has already been greatly impacted by this double edged sword for quite a long time. However, it looks that the innocent ordinary people are more vulnerable of being hurt by the bad edge of this sword. Jim and Meilin, a very ordinary couple, had been cut by the sharp edge of the modern technology; they had no way of finding out how and why this sword was thrusting into and damaging their life. Facing this kind of injustice and violation to their rights, the couple could do nothing. They could not launch a law suit, as they were unable to find who is behind all these injustices and unable to act with their shallow financial condition. To face the difficult situation, Jim had turned a blind eye to everything that was happening around them in order to keep on living a peaceful life. Meilin, on the other hand, had put some efforts in her writing. She thought that if she wrote about the things that had happened in their life and let people know what was going on; people might stop doing those bad things to them and let them return to their peaceful life. She could not have been more wrong with her wishful thinking. Soon, whatever she was writing at home had been a public reading. She thought again, "Well, if more people know about the truth, more people might help to stop this injustice."

Meilin was wrong again. Her writing had exposed some bad things in the society. The wide publicity of her writing had offended more people and some of them truly wanted the couple's blood now. The situation and their inability to change it had frustrated and infuriated the couple. Then the couple thought, "Wait a moment, perhaps we can turn this kind of publicity to our own advantage and to the advantage of the people on the lower level of the society, who have seldom a voice in the public!"

The couple did just that; they spoke and Meilin wrote whatever were in their minds and in their life. Of course, their talks and writing included more complaints and more criticisms which exposed more of the bad things they had seen and heard in the society. The couple had always lived in the lower end of a city and were bound to see some of the social ills. They had lived in two other cities before and had never noticed much of those bad things. Now in this city, because of their present situation, quite some shady people jumped out to attack them. This had quite opened their eyes, as they started to pay close attention to what were going on in their surroundings. They saw the problems of narcotic drug users, traffickers and dealers around them. They highly suspected child pornographic problems going on close by. They thought that they had seen more because they lived in the lower end of the city where the crimes might be more concentrated; the problems might not be so serious in the whole society. Still, they were stunned to see that quite some people were under the control of the crime organizations and the underground society had so much power and could reach so far and wide.

To be more discreet, Meilin wrote those bad things they saw or suspected in the form of a novel. She had also written about the problem of some city police being corrupted by the crime organizations and getting involved with some underground activities. The couple's outspokenness and Meilin's writing had very much offended the city and its police force. Abbotsford is a small city with many churches. People are proud of their religious community. Unfortunately, the religious background does not make the city absolutely clean and pure. Later on, the TV media reported the break of the cases that a policeman of this very city had been working for the crime organization with large marijuana-grow-operation and a young man was involved with child pornography. Things were just like what Meilin had written in her novel. Still, the proud and religious people of this city could not forgive the ordinary couple for exposing the bad things and causing the city to lose face.

In addition to the crime organizations, the city and its police force that had set their minds against the ordinary couple, some political leaders in powerful positions seemed also getting mad with them. Politicians in high positions are used to respects and prestige that come with their power positions. Their heads are normally high above the clouds and they have long formed strong pride for themselves and the country. Even if they know that it is just an illusion to think and ask others to think that everything is going great in the country and people are living a grand life in the paradise, they prefer to hold the illusion tight and turn a blind eye to the reality which sometimes can be quite grim. Maybe, in this way, their political life and career can go much smoother. Now this small meddlesome veteran and his Chinese wife had dared to point out some unpleasant things in the country and what they had talked and written about had been publicized everywhere. This offensive action of the small couple had hurt their pride and made them feel that this whole thing had made the country lose face. No matter what had caused the couple to do the things they were doing, their action had disturbed the comfort of some big honchos' peace and it was downright unforgivable in their eyes.

As for the couple, the event had forced them to protect themselves and to tell the truth in spite of the cost of their life. They had no regret for what they had done. If the whole country could not face the reality, they were certainly not the ones to blame. The bad things for them were that they had to face the constant harassment and attacks from all kinds of people. To release some of the tensions and to keep on living their own life, the couple decided to take this long trip across the country. They thought that travelling would help them to escape the present situation for a while and moreover they could have a closer look at the country. They started immediately imaging seeing the wonders created by the Canadian people, the gardens of Eden and the numerous rivers and mountains of the vast country. They thought that by travelling, they could escape all the troubles, the frets, the worries and even themselves; they could just emerge into whatever would be along the way; they could do, feel, think and, above all, taste the water of life freely. Wasn't travelling supposed to mean all these? At this moment, they had no idea that the harassments and attacks would be waiting for them in most of the places they were going to visit. Even if they had a little anticipation of them, they knew that travelling would provide a best fencing system against those bad encounters.

When people are travelling, the unpleasant things they may encounter at certain places will soon pass and be forgotten. The places, people and sceneries for the travellers change fast. Their minds wonder from place to place and from one attraction to another, never stop and are always being refreshed or renewed. Nothing much will be strongly retained in the travellers' minds at any moment. Only later, when they come back home to take a long rest from the travelling, they can sort out their memories and to see or to be more amaze at what they have gone through. Travellers are like the wind; they are blowing through places, keep on going and never get attached or entangled with anything they come across on the way. This characteristic of the free wind must be the most attractive aspect of travelling.

The couple had always enjoyed the sense of freedom when they were driving on the highway. The road stretched on in front of them. They were constantly moving forward, leaving everything behind. At those moments, they had absolutely no care about and no attachment to anything. In their situation now, they knew well that this sense of freedom was highly illusive. Still, they would like to hold this illusion for whatever brief moments they could get and to taste this precious free feeling. Perhaps, the whole human life is an illusion. If we do not have any illusion, we might not have a life at all.

Canada, with its vast land and closeness to the North Pole, is a country that has large portion of its land under severe cold weather conditions. To survive in a more comfortable natural environment, the country's cities, towns and villages are mostly located along the south side. This residential arrangement is of course not only for comforts, but largely a necessity for survival. The arable land for agriculture is situated along the south, many industries are located towards south and Canada's main economical partner, the United States, is in the south. The journey Jim and Meilin were going to take would be across the country through the trans-Canada highway which is almost parallel to the border with the United States. They would go through almost all the ten provinces of the country and visit most of the major Canadian cities. Though their journey this time was only latitude crossing the country, the distance would not be short. If they took some short excursions from the main track, they would drive for over seven thousand kilometres to reach the east end and then over seven thousand kilometres to come back. Later on, they would take one or two longitude trips to visit the northern part of the country. They would drive again thousands kilometers for those trips.

If the couple had to cover such long distances by foot like the ancient travelers, it would take them years to accomplish such a stunt. In their age and health condition, they might never reach their final destination. Luckily, they lived in the modern time and most travelers in a rich country today, if they prefer, are carried by motor vehicles. Though not rich, Jim and Meilin had possessed some small luxury equipment for comfortable traveling. They had a van and a small trailer. Their van was capable to tow the small trailer. Their trailer, though only sixteen feet long and about seven feet wide, had everything to satisfy their needs for modern living. In the trailer, there were a stove with three burners and an oven, a microwave stove, a fair-sized fridge, a small heating furnace, a small hot-water-tank, an overhead air conditioner, a small fan and even a roof-top antenna to receive signals from TV stations. Some appliances were run by propane fuel, but the fridge could be turned on by either the propane or electricity; the air conditioner, the microwave stove and the fan were run by electricity only. For sleeping, there were a double bed and a single bunk bed on top of it. Besides the beds, the two small couches could also be turned into a small bed. There was a small table, though it had to be tucked away most of the time to leave a little space for them to turn around in the trailer. There was also a small bathroom with a tiny bathtub, a showerhead and a seat-toilet. In the tiny kitchen and sitting area, there were plenty of overhead cupboards and by the stove, there was a small counter with a sink. The bathtub and the kitchen sink were both equipped with faucets. For entertaining, there was a stereo with two speakers and a radio, and when the cable system had not been in place, watching TV in the trailer was possible. The trailer was well equipped to use the city water or carry some water in its water tank. It had a sceptic system enabling the couple to let all the liquid waste drain out. On top of all these, there were plenty of electric light fixtures to light up the inside and outside of the trailer when the trailer was empowered. A canopy that could be rolled out to one side of the trailer provided a shady spot when they were camping.

Compared with those monster luxury motor-homes running on the highways everywhere today, Jim and Meilin's trailer was tiny, but they were content and happy with it. Though so many things were compacted and cramped into a very limited space, they felt at home in it. They had everything to satisfy their needs and wished for nothing more.

Towards the end of their planning and preparing, the couple felt a bit restless with their anticipations for the trip. Jim had grown up in the east and Meilin had studied in the east for years. The couple met and got married in the east. Both of them had cherished beautiful memories of that part of the country. Many years had gone by, since they came to and lived in the west. Would those beautiful familiar places be the same? How about the people there? Were they the same or changed? Jim was anxious to see his relatives. His two brothers, a sister and quite some other relatives were living in the east, whom he had not contacted for many years. The couple planned to visit the grave of Jim's father who had passed away before Jim met Meilin. Expecting that the trip might not be all smooth sailing because of their present situation did not dampen their enthusiasm for the journey. No matter what would happen along the way; they were determined to try their best to enjoy the traveling.

CHAPTER TWO

BRITISH COLUMBIA

Jim and Meilin's journey would start from British Columbia, the province at the west end of the country. They were living in this province and had already visited many scenic places here. British Columbia is indeed a beautiful province; people here lovingly describe it as "super natural". Most part of the province is covered by the Coast Mountains and the Rocky Mountains. Those tall mountains have blocked the severe coldness from the Canadian north, making the province the warmest coastal place of the country. Many mountain peaks are snow capped year around and some valleys are with glaciers. Close to the coastal area, the land receives plenty of rains annually. This kind of natural conditions has made trees cover almost all the province, and some trees here can live hundreds of years long and grow into gigantic sizes. Deep in the mountains, huge ancient trees are still existing and lush plants and vegetations are thriving. Through the mountainous terrains, numerous canyons and spectacular waterfalls have been formed by rivers. Along the coast of the Pacific Ocean, some areas and islands are hauntingly beautiful and unforgettable to visitors. There are not only several national parks, but also quite some large provincial parks in this province. In those parks, the pristine beauty of the land has been preserved for visitors to enjoy and a viable natural environment has been maintained for the benefit of all living beings.

Agriculture is not the mainstay of this province. Being a large province, British Columbia has only a little more arable land than the small province of Prince Edward Island. The planting of grains, fruit trees, grapes and berries is carried out mainly in the flat land of the three large valleys. However, the province produces one thirds of the country's fruit. Fishery, mining, lumbering, shipping, tourism and some other industries have more prominent positions in people's lives here.

Like other places in North America, the natives are the first people who came here before others. The evidence of the aboriginal peoples' existence here could be physically traced to at least nine thousand years ago. Then in the fifth century, it is believed that some Chinese landed at the coast of British Columbia. During the 1570's, Sir Francis Drake might have sailed along the same coast. But in 1774, Spain took possession of the whole North American coast. In 1778, England's Captain James Cook reached Vancouver Island. Britain objected Spain's rights to the region and in 1792, dispatched Captain George Vancouver to survey, to take possession for Britain and to explore the Northwest coast. Today, both Vancouver Island and Vancouver city are named after this captain. While Captain Vancouver is taking possession from the sea, Simon Fraser travelled through the Columbia River and reached the Fraser River which is named after him. David Thompson too explored deeper through the mainland. Thomson River today bears his name.

Before 1866, British Columbia was two British colonies, the Vancouver Island and the mainland named British Columbia. Because of running into high debt, the two colonies combined into one and retained the name British Columbia which has remained as the name of the province. In 1871, British Columbia joined Canada, as the federal government was going to assume the colonial debt and to build a railway to the Pacific, which would connect the isolated British Columbia to other parts of the country.

Two major things in history boosted British Columbia's population and economy. The first thing was the gold discovery in the Fraser River valley. At first, the Hudson's Bay Company tried to discourage the gold seekers in order to protect its trade monopoly. By royal charter, the Vancouver Island was ceded to the Hudson's Bay Company in 1849. Then, in 1857, the news of gold discovery broke out and thousands of gold-hungry people rushed into the Fraser River sand bars from California. Later on, quite some other gold discoveries along other rivers had also been made. In 1856, Vancouver Island's population was only 450. With the sudden influx of people for gold, the second colony British Columbia had to be created on the mainland. The birth of British Columbia came thus from the gold-rush.

The second major thing that had pushed British Columbia forward was the Pacific Railway which had been built to the Pacific coast in 1885. The railway had brought about the settlements along the gold-bearing rivers. When it branched out, numerous settlements sprung up with the arteries. With the railway, British Columbia's rich nature resources like fish, lumbers and minerals could reach other parts of Canada and other parts' specialties could come here. Before the railway came into being, Vancouver was already a port city, but the railway confirmed its port status and made it one of the largest ports in the country. Vancouver port today is a major import and export portal of the country. On the whole, the railway had set the province on the way to become the third largest industrial province of the country.

With the economic development, the population of the province has grown swiftly in the twentieth century. In the fur trade era of the nineteenth century, there were only a small number of white men coming from the British Isles, who normally married the native women here. During the gold-rush time, quite some Americans came. Then immigration has gone steadily in a grand scale. People of all colours, nationalities and creeds have come here.

Mentioning the province of British Columbia, the Canadians will first of all think of its large Asian population. Vancouver city has the largest Chinese community in North America, next only to San Francisco. One thirds of the city's population speak Chinese. However, Asians or any other immigrants are more evenly spread through the whole country today. Vancouver has received more Asians not only from China, but also from other Asian countries through history. The impression of British Columbia as an Asian prevalent province has been set into the Canadians' minds; it seems unlikely to change very soon. Asian immigrants like to choose British Columbia to settle down, as the province is warm and its climate was close to that of the countries they came from. But the concentration of the immigrants in large cities can only be explained by the country's own habitation tradition. Canada has long grown from an agriculture country to an industrial one, and therefore from a rural country to an urban one. Over eighty percent of Canadians today dwell in cities. In order to find jobs, the immigrants coming to Canada will naturally choose cities to settle down.

Most Asian immigrants coming to this province have chosen to settle down in Vancouver and its vicinities. During the 1990's, quite some rich people from Hong Kong had come here to set up their homes. The reason of their coming was that China was going to take over Hong Kong in 1997 when the 99 years lease of the place to Britain expired. The rich people in Hong Kong were afraid that the Communists were going to take over the things they owned, so they fled that island. With their wealth, they were welcomed by the rich countries and settled down mainly in Britain, the United States and Canada. When they came to Canada, they chose Vancouver and its vicinity cities and especially Richmond to live. Richmond has a good name and might bring good luck for their future life here. Very soon, because of this inflow of rich Hong Kongnese to Vancouver, the Canadians gave Vancouver a nickname – Hongcouver. The Chinatowns in Vancouver and Richmond have boomed. The booming businesses here might have come from many years of hard work by the large Asian population here, but the rich Hong Kong people seem to have given the Chinatowns more wealthy lustre.

After China took over Hong Kong, the Chinese government encouraged that life and businesses there go on as usual. The rich Hong Kongnese had feared for nothing and some went back to Hong Kong to carry on their businesses there, leaving their families to live in those countries they had fled to. Anyway, those rich countries have gained by accepting the rich Hong Kongnese. They have brought in a lot of money to create businesses here. Their continuing to do businesses in Hong Kong and have their families to spend money in the rich countries is a win-win situation for the countries they have settled in.

In addition to the rich Hong Kongnese, British Columbia has also received quite some affluent East Indians. When the big ethnic conflict broke out in Indian, quite some Sikh people fled that country. Some of those Sikh people had been doing well in India, residing on the fertile land and generating wealth through agriculture and businesses. When those rich Sikh people came to Canada, they too chose British Columbia to continue their farming and businesses.

British Columbia has been very much benefited by the inflow of Asian immigrants in its economical developments along the history. From the very beginning, the Chinese and Japanese had greatly contributed to the province's prosperity by building the Pacific Railway. Then through different periods of time, the Asians had put tremendous amount of money and labours to make the province rich, mostly from the businesses and enterprises created by them. However, through history, this province had bore a strong anti-Asian sentiment. In times of economic recession or depression, this anti-Asian sentiment would flare up to a dangerous degree. Whenever jobs got scarce, there would be some demonstrations of the white people, demanding different things and the exclusion of the Asians. By 1923, there was even exclusion laws passed against the Asians.

Today, the situation has improved considerably. Some political leaders have seen the contributions the Asian Canadians have made to the prosperity of the province and also the importance of involving the Asians as equal citizens politically and economically; they have put some efforts in bringing the Asian Canadians to the same social level as the white citizens. The efforts have resulted in an Asian mayor of Victoria, the capital of the province, an Asian lieutenant governor, an Asian police chief of Vancouver and some other prominent positions held by Asian Canadians.

Those great achievements in bringing equal rights to all the Canadian citizens are definitely not reached easily. The opposing force has been strong all the time. It tries very hard and sometimes desperately to maintain the old social order of the whites on top and the coloured below. Some of the political leaders belong to this backward force. Thus, the struggles of pushing this province forward or dragging it backward have been lastingly fierce.

The backward politicians are mostly opportunists for votes from the white folks who bear anti-Asian sentiment. In the beginning, the Asians coming here were almost all labourers who worked on building the railway, in the mines, lumber mills and farms. Even when they got into some service work, they had been kept on the lowest level. Still the white folks had tried hard to push them out of the province or to stop any more from coming. The Asians had survived the harsh living and working conditions and the rampant racial discriminations from the white society. After many years of struggles, their hard-working and industrious qualities have brought them some success mainly in their own businesses here.

Today, though some of the Asian Canadians have gained higher social status and better jobs or positions in the society, they are but a very small portion of the Asian population. Even in Vancouver and its vicinities, most Asian Canadians are not rich or in any kind of prominent positions. They work mainly in those Asian owned businesses or companies. Quite some white folks are still trying their best to keep them away from their society.

The anti-Asian sentiments are like the waves of the Pacific Ocean, up and down, and never entirely cease. Now and then, there are still some rallies put on by some white people and led by some backward politicians, trying to put the Asian Canadians down. Not long ago, there was a pamphlet issued by the provincial government, suggesting the change of the voting system so that some people from other ethnic groups could have more chances to be elected into the political leadership. Some Asian names had been printed on the pamphlet to give an example. This pamphlet had aroused a big rally from the public; the white folks roared, saying that they did not want any more politicians. But the whole thing could be understood as that the white folks actually disliked having any more Asians in the political leadership. The pamphlet scheme might come from the good intention of the forward-pushing politicians, but it might also come from the bad intention of the backward politicians who just wanted to give the white folks a chance to roar and to show that they did not want to see the Asians getting higher than themselves. This kind of white people had despised the Asians when they were poor. Now they have seen some rich Asians; they are even more intolerant to the Asians being wealthy. Either way, they seem to have determined to dislike the Asians being here.

Another situation had happened in recent time. Quite some white folks felt sore when the Canadian government had finally readdressed a historical wrong in putting a head tax on the Chinese people who wanted to immigrate to this country. This head tax for the Chinese had been carried out about a century ago. The Canadian government today promised to reimburse those Chinese families whose ancestors had paid this tax. But to claim this reimbursement, those Chinese families had to produce some evidence that this tax had indeed been paid by the family. Things had happened so many years ago, most people who had paid this tax had long gone. Even some of them had left some descendents; the offspring might not all be able to produce any evidence to make the claim. Still, the whole thing did not sit well with the white folks who bore anti-Asian sentiment. When the prime minister came to pay a visit to the Chinese community in Vancouver at a Chinese Spring Festival, another big rally had happened. The prime minister and his host had been shut in the Chinese community hall for several hours. On the surface, the roar from the white folks this time was to protest against the government's withdrawing some support to the drug addicts, but the rally could also be understood as that the white folks here had given the prime minister a warning or a threat, telling him not to get too smitten with the Asians.

Well organized rallies large or small do happen now and then in the province. Some are truly out of good intentions to push some issues to be resolved in order for the society to move forward; some can be seen used by some people for other purposes, although those rallies will all have the very right claims or slogans. The opportunistic politicians are quite smug about their abilities in playing this double edged political sword.

The Asian Canadians can only wish that the white people and especially the political leaders will see clearly the world situation today. What makes a country wealthy and strong have been shifting from rich natural resources to rich human resources. Any clear minded people and especially leaders who are patriotic will treasure and develop their country's human resources. Canada, a country becoming diversified, multi-cultured and multi-coloured, will have a good future only if the country will treasure its human resources and treat all its different citizens equally; racial discriminations, exclusiveness and oppressiveness should be gone not only from practice but also from people's minds.

Jim and Meilin were now living in this beautiful province with this kind of political climate. Being an interracial couple, life was not easy for them here. When hell broke loose after they pointed out some wrong doings in services and especially after they had totally lost their privacy, their life became gravely difficult. To the backward politicians and the white folks with anti-Asian sentiment, this bold Chinese woman simply had a death wish, who dared to poke and criticize the whites and their grand society by speaking out and even writing a book. Even without any prompt of some crime organization, actions would be taken swiftly to handle her and her supportive husband for breaking the rules here.

Meilin had written truthfully about her life here in Canada. Belonging to the coloured race, she had experienced the lack of equal opportunities in the job market and had also seen that large number of people like her had suffered the same difficulties in finding suitable jobs. As she and her husband had been watched and listened into day and night now, and her writing on the computer was publicized, she had received support and sympathy from not only coloured people, but also some white people. The backward politicians and those white people with anti-Asian sentiment got scared. They considered Meilin a rebel and called her a communist. This was quite laughable. If Meilin were a communist, then Jesus Christ would be the first and the biggest communist. There had been numerous people along the history who had called for equal rights and equal opportunities for all the ordinary people; they would all be communists. Those white people with anti-Asian sentiment tried every way to put the couple down and to turn people and even the coloured people against them. Soon they had succeeded in gaining support from quite some local whites. They then coerced the coloured people, especially the Chinese Canadians, to show their hostilities towards the couple. Though the situation was turning from bad to worse for the couple, they still felt some sincere support from some people.

The dirty tricks and schemes pulled by those racially discriminatory whites and their followers were numerous. They did not even let an international event go by without thrusting their sword for some cuts. When the Winter Olympic Game was held in Vancouver in 2010, some facilities had been built in Richmond. Among them was a huge indoor stadium. The building was shaped like a boat and in blue colour. Jim and Meilin went there especially to have a look. To them, the stadium seemed to symbolize Noah's Ark. The large beams inside were built by countless small wood pieces linked together. The intricate wood work looked indeed an amazing architecture stunt. But the cement floor of the building had already started cracking just after the completion of the facility. It was reported that the stadium was built on a piece of wet land and the structural damages were expected to happen. With the religious implication of the building's shape, the art decoration outside the stadium, on the contrary, looked like a political symbol. The gigantic blue boat had two big red fishing nets hanging over two small ponds. The implication here seemed to show that some red elements, communists of course, were trying to fish here. Apparently, the artist had a different set of mind than the architect. If this whole thing were pointing to Meilin, she would feel flattered, but she had absolutely no power and no ambition to go fishing anywhere. If this were pointing to some real red power trying to fish here, the whole thing would be even more laughable. Nowadays, the communists in the whole world have turned their attentions to economical developments and gone into capitalism. Richmond is a pond too small indeed for them to go fishing in.

This newly built stadium and its art decoration outside were somewhat ambiguous in indicating anything, but there was another big piece of artwork placed in downtown Richmond for this Olympic Game, which was more explicitly political. Three gigantic human heads carved from tree roots and in red colour had been placed under the newly-built sky-train mono railway. Each of the heads was about ten feet high and five feet wide. They were an Asian woman's head upside down and full of long spikes, a white man's head lying sideway and a squashed Asian man's head. The new mono railway ran right over and through the Chinatown. Of course, it was said to have been built for the Olympic Game and for the prosperity of Chinatown. However, it was quite hard to explain this odd and threatening piece of artwork lying under the mono railway for this big occasion of Olympic Game. The Asian woman's head seemed very likely pointing to Meilin who was now a well known rebel and a threat in the eyes of the racially orientated white folks with strong anti-Asian sentiment. It looked that her sharp-tongued criticisms had duly earned her a head full of spikes. The other two men's heads would be pointing to her supporters and sympathizers.

It looked that Meilin's writing had scared those backward people so much that they wanted to cut her head and her supporters' heads off and have the trains to run over them. The main purpose of this political art display was, of course, to warn and threaten others not to follow or do the same kind of things as this Asian woman had done or was doing.

People can still all remember how the ancient powerful people had done to any of those who were against them. They would cut off the rebels' heads and hung them over the city gates or some other public places to warn and threaten others. Nowadays, people in power cannot do this kind of things anymore, at least not openly anyway. However, nothing can prevent them from using some artwork to try to achieve the same result.

To Jim and Meilin, this kind of political art show was quite barbaric. In order to influence the immigration policy, the backward people were the ones who had often been crying the loudest that the Asians were difficult to assimilate. It was hard to tell what the racially orientated people wanted the Asians to assimilate to. Assimilate to their narrow mindedness, their barbaric behaviours, their hostilities or their hatred? Jim and Meilin, an ordinary couple, had spoken and written at their own home. Most of their talks and writing were meant to make the country better for every citizen; they were trying to contribute to the cause of a strong and harmonious society. They could not figure out why their little action would be so threatening to some white folks here. Those folks had been so proud of their superior culture, but their actions and displays had shown their inferiority.

Whenever the word inferiority is mentioned, some racist fanatics will go bunkers and fight violently to protect their race. Those fanatics flatter themselves too much as to think that they can represent their race. Compared with the good, loving, modest and great people in their race, the racist fanatics are much too inferior to take the representative position for their race.

The couple could not comprehend at all why or how their talks and Meilin's writing would scare so many people. It was understandable that some crime organizations would fear being exposed, but hard to understand why so many others would work so hard in trying to put them down. What Meilin had talked about and asked for in her writing, equal rights and opportunities for the coloured people, are given by the laws of this country and clearly written in the constitution and the charter of rights and freedom. Plenty of good politicians had worked hard along the history to carry out the set laws in the life of this country, so that all the citizens disregarding their different colours, nationalities and creeds could enjoy equally a good life here. Those good politicians had worked hard, trying to bring all the people together to build a strong country. Why would those backward people totally disregard the rules of democracy and the laws of this country and try to drive fears into the hearts of the ordinary people in order to shut them up? What they were doing was clearly dividing the people and weakening the country for their own gains. Using the event of Olympic Game for wrongful political purpose was a political hate crime in the eyes of the couple. Olympic Game is the event and occasion to promote peace and harmony among all kinds of peoples in the world. It definitely should not be used for promoting racism, fear or hatred.

In view of giving equal rights and opportunities to all the citizens, there is a distance between the reality and the ideals dreamt about and written into the laws of Canada. Many efforts and achievements have been made in the recent decades in shortening this distance. The situation for the coloured people today is much better than that just half a century ago. But the work is not finished and should not be stopped mid-way or even go backwards. As for Jim and Meilin, they were disgusted and tired of the constant harassment and attacks showering down on them. The situation for them now was like a whirlpool that was pulling them down deeper. Yet they were determined to pull themselves out and distance themselves from the whole thing. They had no desire to get into those struggles which seemed futile to change anybody or anything. However, they knew it would not be easy to pull out with their present condition when they had no privacy at all and whatever they did or said would offend some people. Anyhow, they still had to try. This journey across Canada would be one of their efforts in trying to get some peace.

Jim and Meilin packed up their trailer. Every detail had to be considered and covered for the preparation. It would be a long trip. Even with their good van and well equipped trailer, it would not be easy. Though their journey would start from the west end of the country, they did not and had no intention to go to Vancouver in the starting point to touch the water of the Pacific Ocean. That kind of act might be highly symbolic to some other travellers, but had no significance in their minds.

Vancouver is one of the largest cities in Canada, a leading industrial, commercial and shipping centre of the western part of the country. Like other metropolitan cities, Vancouver has plenty of showy skyscrapers and attractions. Living in a vicinity city, Jim and Meilin had visited Vancouver quite a few times and knew the megacity well. They had enjoyed the city's museums, galleries and gardens. What impressed them most was the city's Stanley Park. Vancouver is a coastal city. The large Stanley Park is situated as a small peninsula. The Park is mostly surrounded by the ocean and has its own hills, forest and lake. From the highest point of the park, the visitors can overlook part of the Vancouver city with a drop of the magnificent mountains in a distance. There are trails through the park's rain forest for hikers to enjoy. By the lake or the pond, the ancient trees will take several people stretching their arms to hold each one of the tree trunks. Native people's artworks, the totem poles, stand on a prominent spot of the park. The park has a large Aquarian with all kinds of ocean living beings, a zoo, an amphitheatre, quite a few golf courses, sports grounds, swimming pool and several beaches. All along the shore and circling the peninsula, the seawall is also a paved walkway providing a scenic route for visitors and joggers to enjoy. City parks normally show the city status. Stanley Park shows well the large city status of Vancouver. On the other hand, Stanley Park has also shown the natural beauty of British Columbia with plenty of trees, varied land features and by the ocean. The only thing missing is the numerous tall mountains that have covered most part of the province.

Vancouver, though the largest city in British Columbia, is not the capital of the province. Victoria on Vancouver Island occupies this position. Jim and Meilin had also visited Victoria quite a few times. They had spent their first wedding anniversary in Victoria. That was the first time they had visited British Columbia. At that time they were living in Alberta and Jim was still serving in the military. The couple were deeply impressed by the beautiful Victoria and the Vancouver Island. In the following years, they had taken a few more trips to visit the island and the whole British Columbia. The couple loved Victoria and the island mainly because of the abundant flowers and the beautiful Pacific coastal scenery. They were in Victoria in spring and summers and overwhelmed by the numerous gardens blooming with all kinds of flowers. The cultivated flowers were not only in parks, but also in people's private gardens, shops and any public places.

In the nineteenth century, the English settlers on Vancouver Island built the city in the image of their hometown in England and they named it after Queen Victoria. The city soon became a government and commercial centre. In 1868, Victoria was chosen to be the capital of British Columbia. The city deserves indeed the title of garden city, as it is in bloom everywhere almost all the seasons. But besides flowers, the city has quite some other significant culture characteristics. The large provincial museum is here in a big modern glass building. The Thunderbird Park beside the museum hosts the native people's art works. Victoria is not a big city with skyscrapers; its most eye-catching uniqueness has to be its being in full British style. The buildings, the shops, the streets, the double-decker buses, the red public phone booth and almost everything here make the place a copy of a British city. The

Empress Hotel occupying a whole city block looks like an English palace. The legislative buildings are massive structures of English or Romanesque palace style. People have no need to go to England to see an English city; Victoria can well satisfy their desire or curiosity for the purpose. The imitations of a British city have gone into every detail; the gardens, the green ivy covered buildings, the tearooms, the china-shops and many more are typical British. The city gives the visitors a strong impression that the people here live an unrushed, cultured and genteel life just like those well-to-do Brits.

So many years later, Jim and Meilin were now residents of British Columbia. For the preparation of the cross-country trip, the couple went to Richmond only. They needed some of those canned sweet soups made by oatmeal, beans, peanuts and some other goodies. Those canned soups were good for traveling; they were ready to serve and had no need to be cooked. Richmond Chinese stores sold those soups; the couple went there to get some for the trip.

Richmond is probably the most prosperous Chinatown in Canada. There are several streets that have Chinese stores lined along or doted; those stores are of good buildings and full of different goods. More importantly, Richmond Chinatown has not only Chinese grocery stores and restaurants, but also almost everything for a modern community. There are Chinese banks, law offices, medical and dental clinics, herb stores and warehouses, auto shops and dealerships, stores of furniture and all kinds of other goods and even some language, music and dance schools. The most striking difference of Richmond Chinatown from other Chinatowns of the country is that all the Chinese stores and businesses here seem doing smashing good businesses and having plenty of Chinese customers. Though the local white folks seldom visit those Chinese stores, the Chinese merchants do not care, as they are quite satisfied with the large quantity of Chinese customers.

Jim and Meilin did their shopping quickly in a Chinese shopping mall and enjoyed a Chinese lunch in the mall's food court afterwards. Along the street of Richmond Chinatown, there are several Chinese malls and strip malls. Some of the malls are two stories high and host large Chinese grocery stores, food courts and all kinds of other stores. Whenever the couple came to shop in Richmond, they would not miss the chance of having a delicious Chinese meal in the mall's food court. There are not only Chinese restaurant stalls in those food courts, but also restaurant stalls of some other different Asian countries. Besides Chinese food, people can taste the Korean, Japanese, Thailand, Malaysian,

Vietnamese food and so on. Sometimes, a stall of bubble tea, coffee or fruity drinks will pop up among all the restaurant outlets. Inside the Chinese grocery stores, there are all kinds of fresh or cooked food; there are meats, fish, vegetables, tofu, snacks, cakes, deserts, spices, dry goods, frozen goods, live goods and what not. The combination plates of cooked food in the grocery stores or in the food courts of the malls here might be the best tasting Chinese food in the lower price range of the whole country. If people want to try the specialty Chinese food or any other type of Asian food, Richmond Chinatown has plenty of high rank Asian restaurants to satisfy their taste buds.

Of course, the street of Chinatown is still a Canadian street. There are also other Canadian stores including large department stores and Superstore along this street. For the restaurants, Burger King, Wendy's, White Spot and so on will not miss out the good business here. Also on this street is the large Richmond city hall, a modern glass building of many stories high with all its beautiful gardens and waterfall fountains. The main Chinatown street is of four lanes with a planted isle running in the middle. The lanes are narrow and the street looks rather crowded. In the recent time, the sky train mono railway runs through the street over one side of the pedestrian walks. The railway is built on cement pillars over twenty feet high. This additional modern structure has made this street look even more crowded and ever busier.

The main condition for the existence of the prosperous Richmond Chinatown is the city's large number of Chinese and other Asian Canadians. White folks here almost never visit the Chinese stores. A sky-train mono railway built over the four-lane Chinatown street looks conspicuous and strange. It makes one sense that this might be out of some alternative motive of some power who did not like to see the Chinese Canadians doing well individually or community wise, and they had to do something to exert their power over the yellow race's little achievement. This reality is of as much British Columbia as the country that, in quite some white people's minds, the coloured people, especially the Asians here, should not be allowed to have the equal rights and opportunities as the whites and to soar freely as the whites. Those racially discriminatory people don't feel good to see the coloured people doing well. Still, Richmond Chinatown has defied the odds and presented an image of a small hustling bustling cosmopolitan community that is doing well.

The couple's preparation for the trip was soon finished. Another family member who would go with them was their small dog. Vixy was a fifteen year old poodle-terrier who had been with them since he was a pup. Through the years, the dog had given the couple plenty of joy; they loved him dearly. Only the recent two years had been a difficult time for them and Vixy. Ever since the veterinarian put Vixy under anaesthesia twice and pulled out all his teeth, he had not been himself. He started peeing and pooping in the house, falling down the stairs and not even recognizing Jim and Meilin some times. It was a heart-ranching situation for the couple to watch Vixy's condition deteriorating. They strongly suspected that what the veterinarian had done to Vixy was under the instruction of some power that were behind the harassment and attacks to them. Vixy was a healthy dog; not all his teeth needed to be pulled out and especially he should not be put under anaesthesia twice. One dose of anaesthesia could do a lot of damages to a small dog, let alone a double dosage.

Anything could happen in Jim and Meilin's life now. If their own lives had been in danger, their dog's life would be even more so. Their home had been broken into numerous times. Because nothing was missing, they did nothing about the break-ins. They knew that even if they had called the police, there would be no help. The police were mighty mad with them now, as the couple's talks and Meilin's writing had criticised some local police. When the couple first moved into this small city, they had received constant police visits. The police would come pounding at their door and asking for somebody the couple had no idea of. When the couple got fed up and wrote a complaining letter to the police chief here, the police visits stopped. Since the start of the harassment and attacks to them, the couple got threatening phone calls and visits from some suspicious people. Those people would come pounding at their door now, not only at day time, but also in the middle of the nights or wee hours of mornings. Jim had called the police quite many times for those problems and also for some loud fighting in a neighbour's house or loud noises night after night in the neighbourhood. The police either hung up on Jim's calls or if they answered his calls and promised to send somebody to check, there would be no sign of the police showing up afterwards. Finally, two policemen came to their door one night after one of their neighbours came to their door to threaten them. The couple thought that the police would do something this time, but what the police did was telling them that they should not call the police any more. The situation had led to the conclusion in the couple's minds that some of the local policemen were corrupted and had connection with some dark force of the society, and those police might be very much behind the harassment and attacks to them too. How could the couple expect the police to solve the problems they might have partially created and certainly supported? The couple shut down the ringer of their phone, turned a deaf ear to the knocks or poundings at their door and stopped calling the police.

More serious things had happened than the police shovelling. Their family doctor refused service to them and the auto shop could no longer be trusted. Then, Meilin was being abused when she went to the hospital for some emergent problems. As for the alarms going on or the obscene callings from the microphones whenever they walked into some shopping stores, the couple ignored them; they could only be counted as minor problems now. The most annoying thing was that anywhere they went; they were bound to meet some hostile people coming out to give a show. Though some of those shows were highly ridiculous juvenile pranks, the vile intentions were obvious. The couple tried to be calm and thought, "Oh, well, things happen in life. We have to find some way to deal with them or get used to them in order to keep on living."

The atmosphere was getting intense and stifling. The couple suffered many sleepless nights because of the loud noises in the neighbourhood. In the early June, they were on their way for this cross-country trip to escape the situation and to gain some peace back to their life. A neighbour agreed to mow their lawn and look after their house while they were gone. They had also contacted the citizens' patrol office that would also keep an eye on their property. So they had no worries about their home while they were gone. In this fine summer morning, their van and trailer started moving. The same neighbour and his wife who would look after their house dressed all in black waved their goodbyes to them. A gigantic airplane hovering over the place was giving out prolonged thundering noises which turned the whole place into a boiler room. As soon as the couple got on the highway, a fleet of yellow school buses passed them by; each had the large word "Lynch" on the side. Jim was quite happy that they had finally started the trip; he was oblivious of what was going on around. Meilin sensed that they had been notified that they were marching to their own funeral or something. She had long been used to this kind of threats now; this grand rowdy sinister send-off did not rattle her either.

There is an old saying: the wise always keeps death in sight. Every living being has to die sooner or later. People should try their best to keep themselves from harm's way, but if it is their time to leave this world, there is no need or use to kick and scream. They should consider death another adventure, the biggest one, and exit this life with peace. Who knows? On the other side, things might turn out to be better. Though Jim and Meilin were not that wise, they had always kept a sight of death. They felt that to live a peaceful fulfilling life, they had not only to embrace life, but also to know that death was the shadow of life, close and unavoidable. To be afraid of death was to let the shadow dominate life and not to fully enjoy life, no matter how long or how short life would be.

Under Meilin's watch and urge, Jim drove slowly, at the speed of eighty kilometres per hour. Having all the time to relax and enjoy the trip, they had no need to rush. With the van towing the trailer, it was much better to drive slowly. Still, they soon passed Hope, a small city that started the mountainous terrain. By noon, they reached Merritt, another small city in the deep of the mountains. From here, they were going to start serious mountain climbing. At home, they had thought and worried about the steep highway which would start just after they had passed Merritt. They were not sure whether their van could pull the trailer up to the top of those high mountains.

Arriving at Merritt, the couple decided to rest in Merritt for the afternoon and night and start the hard climbing tomorrow. They found a campsite in Merritt, which was almost fully occupied by campers. However, the office of the campground assigned lot forty-four for them to set their trailer on. This was no surprise. For quite some time now, the number four or forty-four or even four four four had followed them everywhere. The indication was clear that there was a wish for them to fall, as "four" sounded like "fall". For what the couple had done and what had happened to them, this wish was unreasonably malicious, clearly racist and ridiculously childish. Right now they were situated at the bottom of the society. Jim was retired and Meilin had no job. Where would they fall to, while they were already on the ground level?

Merritt was a small city just like many other small cities in Canada. People lived a good and peaceful life with their rather new good houses. There were a few not so large apartment buildings, sufficient shopping stores and other public facilities. This city seemed proud of their country singers, as there were quite some posters of those public figures along the streets. Apparently, there were not many people living here; the streets looked quite empty. Coloured people were very few and that might be one of the reasons for the cold treatment Jim and Meilin had received here.

Towards night, Jim and Meilin had found out the big problem of their lot on the campground. Not far from their campsite, there was a big lumber mill which was running some big machines to cut the trees into lumbers. Those machines were running by the energy generated by burning wood. The spot where Jim and Meilin's trailer was situated was the closest spot to the loud noises of the machines and the smokes from the huge chimney. When the dark night fell, they could see the flames shooting out of the big chimney with smokes thick and fierce. The loud cutting and rumbling noises from the machine continued and seemed to go on for the whole night. With this kind of loud noises and the pungent smell of fire and smokes, it was impossible for Jim and Meilin to sleep. They got up in the middle of the night, pulled up their trailer and drove out of the campground. The campground was at the skirt of the city. They drove into the small city and parked their van and trailer in a parking lot of a strip mall. Though they could still hear the running of the machines, the noises were not that invasive anymore and they were no longer suffering the smell of the smokes. They had a half night's sleep on the parking lot.

Next morning, having had a simple breakfast of cereal with milk, banana and juice, they started moving on. Though the noises and smokes had stopped from the lumber mill now, the small city no longer looked peaceful or admirable. The couple wondered how people here could allow such a mill operating close by their city and how people living around the lumber mill could have endured this kind of noises and smokes. They also wondered how the campground could have been fully occupied by all those campers. Were those people all deaf or had they all lost their sense of smell? Perhaps people living here had long been used to this kind of condition, but to Jim and Meilin, the drop-in visitors, the lumber mill looked an abomination to the beautiful natural environment and a health hazard for the people living here. To get out of the small city, the couple had to negotiate with some big lumber trucks. The workers had started their working day early. Large tractor-trailers with full loads of lumbers filled up the street that connected the small city to the highway.

British Columbia is an industrial province. It has had many saw mills, pulp and paper mills, mines and even a large aluminum smelting plant through the history. In recent years, it has built quite some hydroelectric plants, oil refineries and manufacturing plants. British Columbia is among the rich provinces of the country. Its wealth is built mainly on exporting primary and secondary resources. It has exported nationally and internationally lumbers, minerals, fish and wheat through the history. In recent years, it has added natural gas, oil and hydroelectricity to its exporting list.

Jim and Meilin knew the general situation of the province economy. They were surprised to see a saw mill powered by burning wood in Merritt. In their minds, this kind of mill operation was ancient and long obsolete. They hoped that many other mills and plants in this province were modern and not using the same power system. For the ordinary people like them, they could only hope that, in the modern economic developments, the government, the economical and political leaders and the developers would have a keen sight of protecting the natural environment and the sustainability of the natural resources. The old ways of extracting and exploiting the earth should be abandoned, as they are killing the goose that lays the golden eggs and will eventually kill Mother Nature and human beings themselves as well.

Leaving Merritt, the couple hoped that the situation of the antique lumber mill of the city would soon change. A short distance away from Merritt, the mountain climbing started. The steeply sloped highway was indeed a challenge to their van. Though a rather new vehicle, the van soon started panting. Loud hoarse sound came out of the engine to let them know that it was working very hard. The speed of the vehicle dropped as low as twenty kilometres per hour sometimes. On their right side, the valley was becoming deeper. Some clouds started floating beneath them in the valley. The neighbouring green mountain tops were gradually in level view. On the left side, the highway was against or on the side of the mountain they were climbing. They could see some side-trails on this side. Those tails were running upwards the mountain for some distance. Those side trails were the paths for the run-away trucks and other vehicles. When going down on this sharply steep highway, some drivers, especially the drivers of heavy trucks, might lose control of the breaks. Those unfortunate drivers would certainly be happy to see those sidetracks. They could run their vehicles to those upwards paths to save their own lives and the lives of other travellers who happened to be on the way. Along this dangerously steep highway, the couple could imagine that some emergencies might have happened for those life-saving trails to be used and especially in winter times when the road turned icy.

With strenuous efforts, their van had finally pulled the trailer up to the mountain top. The highway ran quite some distance on top of the mountains. On a spot, a sign was saying that the peak was 1,500 metres above sea level. For the highway to be built so high up to the mountain tops was quite amazing to the couple. Driving on top of the mountains was absolutely one of the highlights for every trip Jim and Meilin had gone through here. They would drive with their vehicle windows open; it gave them an exhilarating feeling. When the weather was fine and the sun was shining, they could indeed feel on top of the world. This kind of feelings could not be gained by sitting in an airplane as passengers. Even though the airplane could fly much higher, inside a container, one could not feel so physically high up in the air. It was at this moment, they could well understand why those mountaineers were so attracted or even addicted to mountain climbing.

Jim and Meilin traveled mainly for travel's sake. The destination and visiting certain places were more of secondary. They enjoyed just driving on the highway. Driving on top of the mountains was indeed the high moment of enjoyment in travelling. At this kind of moments, nature had dominated their minds. The troubles they had encountered in the human world and the struggles they had to go through in their life were entirely forgotten. All the worldly matters appeared utterly insignificant when facing nature in Her full presence and power. On top of the mountains, the sky seemed brighter and closer. Because of the high altitude, the trees on top of the mountains were not so big and tall. The woods were not dense. This had made the space look wide open.

The euphoric bliss the couple had felt on top of the mountains might very well have something to do with the gravity, the higher the altitude, the less the gravity pull. Plus the air on top of the mountains was absolutely clear and fresh, though the oxygen level might be a little lower. They felt that their bodies had less dragging-down feeling, their heads seemed lighter and their minds were clear of all those rubbish thoughts. This light feeling quite easily made them think of the belief that all the human troubles and sufferings came from the human possession of their physical bodies. They toil and struggle to serve their bodies and to serve the senses that come with their bodies. So many troubles they have gone through to satisfy not only their physical senses, but also emotional senses such as desires, cravings, pride, ambition, jealousy, hatred and so on. If the human existence is only spiritual, what kind of changes will that make!? Well, perhaps after life, death will give the humans a pure spiritual existence. Many religions have speculated about this since the humans started having religious thoughts. Still, many humans may not like the pure sterile spiritual existence, as they have appreciated highly the gratifications to their physical bodies and all the senses related to their bodies.

Enough for those far-fetched reveries; the enjoyment for Jim and Meilin on top of the mountains ended. Even though driving slowly, they had gradually left the mountainous area and then passed the whole terrain of the Coastal Mountains. They were soon going to reach the Rocky Mountains. As they did not have a good night's sleep, the couple decided to stop in the early afternoon and camp in a provincial park by the highway. Tomorrow, they would tackle the Rocky Mountains where the border of British Columbia and Alberta stretched through.

For those who own a recreational vehicle which is called RV in Canada, there are many campgrounds they can set their RVs on. Those campgrounds provide all the services to RVs. On the camping lots, the RV owners can hook up their RVs to water supply, to electricity and even to a sewer drainage outlet. The campers can enjoy the modern living with all the modern facilities in their RVs. The only problem with this kind of campgrounds is that they are normally located at the edge of the town or the city, and not at the natural scenic places. There is another type of campgrounds which are normally provided by the national or provincial parks. Those campgrounds are located in the beautiful parks and near some spectacular natural scenery. However, those campgrounds will have fewer services. On the camping lots, there are no electrical plug-ins and no sewer drainage outlets. Water taps will be the community ones shared by all the campers, so are some public washrooms or outhouses. For some large parks, there will be well equipped bathrooms with showers and flush toilets.

Jim and Meilin's small trailer could still be called a RV. The campgrounds they liked had normally been those ones in the parks. The couple had been camping in summers for quite many years. In their early camping years, they had used a tent. Only in recent three years, they had this modern trailer. After so many years of roughing it in a tent, the couple figured that their old bones deserved some pampering. Besides, Jim's arthritis caused by his old injuries could not stand the tenting any longer. Even though there were fewer services in the park campsites, Jim and Meilin, with their modern trailer now, still preferred the parks over those fully serviced campsites. For them, camping was to be close to nature. The park campsites had nature at hand; the fully serviced campsites normally had only full home comfort.

After many years of quiet camping, Jim and Meilin had experienced a boom in the camping of recent years. In summer time now, the campgrounds near the cities in British Columbia would be full. The number of people coming out to camp in warm seasons had dramatically increased. With more campers, the tranquility in camping was disappearing fast.

The pace of modern life has been increasing rapidly. The stress generated from living in today's world has driven many people to the verge of nerves' breakdown. As a matter of fact, the number of insanity cases has soared in an alarming rate. People are living in a more and more aggressive and hostile social environment created mainly by their drives to get ahead. Human beings have never felt so poignantly that they need to get away from it all at least for some period of time; away from the human society, away from their stressful daily lives and works, and away from all the cares and worries that come with the modern living. The problematic modern living has resulted in the boom of camping. More and more people have realized that nature offers the best cure for their hurts and wounds sustained in their life's struggles and the best tranquilizer for their overstrained and tattered nerves. In order to live a normal life with their mental health intact, human beings need to be close to nature sometimes to gain that precious inner balance and peace; they need to feel that they are just part of nature, not the master of nature or the centre of the universe, and they need to see that their desperate struggles for the petty things are insane or insignificant when compared with the powerful, yet beautiful and harmonious nature.

The Canadians are lucky, as there is still quite some wilderness left in this country. The parks have preserved and conserved the vast wilderness in the best scenic places and there are campgrounds provided for people to stay a few days in those beautiful spots. More and more people flock to those parks during their vacations, holidays or just weekends. Most are seeking the inner peace and mental balance by merging themselves with the beautiful nature. Yet, there are a number of campers who are just there because they want to follow the trend or fashion of time. If many people are doing the camping thing nowadays, they must do it too. There might not be the slightest idea in those people's minds why the others are so much taking in to camping.

Those fashion campers have brought quite some bad things to camping. They are not there to be close to nature; they have brought whatever they are doing at home to the campgrounds. They will have their loud music; their gatherings will be night long chatting, laughing, drinking and some other rowdy amusements. This kind of camping parties is mostly held by some yet-to-be civilized youngsters who are spoiled and have absolutely no considerations for others. The campers who happen to be close to this kind of groups can kiss any peace goodbye and consider their camping trip a total loss.

Then there are some campers who have to have a bonfire whenever they camp. The bonfire is a traditional thing. Camping without a bonfire is not camping at all to them. Nothing is more strong or unshakable than a tradition. Those campers do not care about the smokes which will accompany them and the other campers around them for their whole camping duration. Watching their small children playing in the thick smokes seems only giving them pleasure. There are some forest fires started by those careless campers who have left their campfires continue to burn after they vacated the site. Those disastrous happenings will never have any effect in changing the strongly traditional minded campers; they love their bonfires and will not even think of camping without a bonfire.

Then there are the modern campers with their big RVs, who sometimes also choose the parks' campsites. Some of them can never live a night or a day without electricity, so they have brought their portable generators to make electricity. The cranking-up of just one of those generators can send a vibrating rumbling through the whole campground. The other campers can forget their idea of seeking inner peace in nature. The woods of the campground with the resonant booming of the generator will turn out to be worse than their own homes. Even if those modern campers have the latest and quietest generators, the continuous purring of their equipment will still drive other campers crazy.

In Jim and Meilin's present situation of being followed by harassment wherever they went, they had long found that whichever campground they visited, they would meet some people deliberately making noises or create smoky environment around them to ruin their enjoyment. They had felt deeply this loss of tranquility in their camping ventures. On this cross country trip, they knew that the noises and smokes might also follow them on the campgrounds they pulled in. They had dreaded this happening. They were escaping from the noises at their hometown. Would they have to face them all along this long trip? Now when they were approaching this provincial park with a campground, they could only pray that this campground would be noise and smoke free. In the very dry period of summer, there would be a ban on campfires in the parks to prevent forest fires caused by some careless campers. They wished that the fire ban was on now, so that the smoky situation would be eliminated.

This park campground the couple were driving to was close by the highway. After a few minutes' drive away from the highway, they had entered the dense woods. The campground was nestled in the woods and by Thomson River. In British Columbia, the park campsites were normally among large trees. Each camping lot would be surrounded by tall trees that formed a private cove. Though there would be plenty of space for each lot, the campers would still feel and hear their neighbours lodging in the other coves around. The roads on the campgrounds were smooth, well maintained and passable for two vehicles. There would be hiking trails around the campgrounds for the campers to venture into the wilderness to enjoy the mountains, valleys, rivers, canyons, lakes, creeks, waterfalls or even glaciers.

When Jim and Meilin drove into this campground, they felt disappointed. Before they entered the camping area, they could hear the booming noise of a generator and saw a trail of thick smoke rising up from the woods. Obviously, the fire ban was not on. They quickly decided to go to the picnic area by the campground and at the riverbank. They had camped here before and knew that the picnic area would surely be quiet and smoke free at night.

The couple drove to the picnic area. Though it was still early afternoon, the area had no visitors. They parked their van and trailer in the shade of the large trees of the parking lot and got out of the vehicle. The place was perfect. They could hear the birds chirping in the woods and the river gently murmuring under the river bank. There were two outhouses nearby for visitors, which they could use for the night. They had the propane stove to cook a hot meal for supper. The only thing they needed from the campsite was some water. They had two water jars for getting water from the campground's community water taps. The camping area was not far; it would not be a problem for them to carry some water from there. They heaved a long relief and felt happy. If the harassment had already been prepared, waiting for their arrival, it looked that they had escaped the ill-attempt and were going to have a quiet camping night at this beautiful spot.

The couple walked around a bit, stretching out to release the fatigue from the long drive. The picnic tables with fixed seats were in the woods on the river bank. There was nobody in sight. The wide Thomson River was flowing quietly below with waves smiling in the sun. Any clouds in the couple's minds were cleared away by such a beautiful and peaceful scene. At about five o'clock, they decided to fetch some water and to get their supper going. Vixy would of course go with them for a stroll. He was always happy and anxious to go out for a walk. Even with his present weak physical condition, he would not turn down an offer for an outing. Hearing the jingle of his collar, he immediately jumped up, ready to go.

It took about seven or eight minutes walk for them to reach the nearest water tap on the campground. They filled up the two water jars and started to walk back. Half way on their return trip, Vixy's long thin legs started wobbling and then he fell down on the road. Jim and Meilin were shocked; Vixy had never done this before. Jim handed the water jars to Meilin and bent down to pick up Vixy. Vixy's body and limbs were soft, as if all the strength had left him. The couple walked quickly back to the trailer; Meilin carried the water and Jim carried Vixy in his arms.

In the trailer, Vixy lay in his small bed quietly and paid no attention to the water offered to him. Jim and Meilin hastily finished their own supper and washed up. After their own things done, all their attention was focused on Vixy who still had no response to food, water or any of their care. The couple were scared and worried, and did not know what to do. After seemingly a long wait, Vixy started snoring loudly with his eyes wide open. He stared with the blank eyes and snored horribly. Obviously, he was not sleeping. Jim and Meilin were at their wit's end. What could they do? It seemed that Vixy was having a stroke or something.

When the couple were worried sick about Vixy's horrible condition, they heard a truck coming into the parking lot. Jim went out and Meilin also peeked through the window to see who was coming. It was the park warden's truck. After the truck was parked, a woman warden came out and walked towards their trailer. It was seven o'clock in the evening. Before Jim asked any question, the warden said, "Sir, this is a picnic area. You cannot stay here overnight. You have to move your trailer to the campground."

"Sorry, mum. Our dog is having a stroke or a heart attack right now; we cannot move," answered Jim firmly.

Jim was of soft characters. Normally, he observed strictly all the rules and regulations. If being pointed out that he was in any way out of the line, he would immediately obey the order to correct it. This kind of absolute obedient habit might have come from years of being a soldier in the military. But right now, he stood firm and said no to the warden. To show the warden that he was telling the truth, he invited the warden to have a look at the dog.

The woman warden was in her late thirties. She looked through the open door of the trailer and saw the dog lying in his small bed on the floor with the terrible staring eyes and the loud snoring. Sympathy came to her eyes and voice. She asked, "Oh... what happened?"

"He just collapsed on the way when we were having a walk," said Jim. Then he asked, "Do you know if there is a vet nearby we can call for him to come to have a look at our dog?"

"No, but I'll check it for you," said the warden. Then she left with her truck.

Vixy remained the same after the warden left. Time crawled slowly while Jim and Meilin watched and waited for any changing sign of Vixy. At about nine o'clock, the warden showed up again. She brought the news that there was no vet around. Then she told the couple that they could stay here in this parking lot for the night.

Jim and Meilin were disappointed, but could do nothing. They thanked the warden before she left and did not know what they could do for the night. It was impossible for them to sleep while Vixy was in such a terrible condition. They felt sick with worries and scares. The live of their dog they had loved for so many years seemed slipping away in such a horrible way. Even with an open mind about death, when death seemed near, they felt it hard to handle. At about ten o'clock, Meilin asked Jim to try again, giving some water to Vixy. It seemed a miracle that Vixy responded a little this time. Then Jim tried more urgently. Vixy drank some water with difficulties. After a while, Vixy quieted down. Finally he closed his eyes and seemed gone to sleep. Jim and Meilin felt a great relief. Now they could get some sleep too. They decided that tomorrow, as soon as they got to Hinton, the first city after they crossed the border to Alberta, they were going to take Vixy to a veterinarian.

CHAPTER THREE

ALBERTA

Next morning, Vixy seemed feeling better and had his breakfast. However, he was becoming more difficult to handle. Jim and Meilin could not touch him. Before they left for the trip, they had Vixy groomed by a professional pet groomer. For quite some time now, Jim could no longer groom Vixy. With his thick fur coat off, Vixy looked naked and his thin legs looked exceptionally long. Traveling through the mountains, the couple found that the temperature was cool even in June. At night, Jim and Meilin had to sleep in their sleeping bags. Vixy would not even let them throw a blanket on him, though he was shaking from the coldness. It looked that Vixy would have a very hard time on this long trip. Jim and Meilin decided that when they took Vixy to see the veterinarian, they would ask the vet's opinion about what they should do with Vixy. It would be very hard to part with Vixy, but his present condition forced the couple to see that it might be better to let Vixy sleep and part with this life, otherwise Vixy would go through more sufferings in the days ahead.

The couple and their dog got up after the uneasy night and started moving early next morning. They were gradually leaving the winding mountainous road with steep slopes up and down. The closer they came to the border to Alberta, the more the land was levelled-out. Soon they were approaching the Rocky Mountains on the Alberta side.

The range of the Rocky Mountains starts from the north of Alaska and ends in the middle of New-Mexico. It spans almost the whole North America and is regarded as the spine of this continent. The immense expanding of the magnificent Rocky Mountains through the two provinces, British Columbia and Alberta, has resulted in four spectacular national parks; they are Kootenay and Yoho in British Columbia, and Banff and Jasper in Alberta. Jim and Meilin had visited all the four national parks before. They found that the Rocky Mountains along the border close to or in Alberta were different than those in the west side of British Columbia. Close to Alberta, the trees on the mountains were smaller and there were rarely rain forests in the valleys like those in British Columbia. This condition might mainly be the result of the much drier and colder climate in Alberta. Except for the Rocky Mountains along the border area, Alberta has mostly the prairie land. Without the protection of the high mountains, Alberta has to face the severe coldness from the Canadian north. However, the Rocky Mountains close to or in Alberta look more rugged and magnificent. The sharply jagged or pointed peaks of the mountains thrusting so high into the sky are often accompanied by drifting white clouds. Those peaks are bare rocks; nothing can grow on that kind of high altitude in the cold climate.

Being one of the three prairie provinces in the country, Alberta's agriculture is more prominent than that of British Columbia. The province has been traditionally a large wheat grower and exporter of the country. Its large cattle ranching industry has also been prosperous. But what has put this province in a very important position in recent years is its oil and natural gas industry. Alberta is naturally privileged with the largest oil deposits of the country. Oil in this province was first found by the native peoples who had used the crude oil as remedy for the ailment of rheumatism. In 1947, Alberta struck a major oil discovery near Leduc about twenty kilometers away from Edmonton. Following this discovery, there were quite some other larger oil fields being found. Then there were the natural gas and oil sands discoveries in the province. It is estimated that from the oil sands alone in the Athabasca River valley to the north of Fort McMurray, 300 billion barrels of oil can be extracted; it is one of the richest oil reserves in the world.

Today, Alberta produces almost ninety percent of the country's oil. With the development of the oil and natural gas industry, other manufacturing industries have sprung. The petroleum and natural gas provide raw materials for refinery plants and then the by-products of the refineries lead to the manufacturing of plastics, chemicals and fertilizers. When the price of oil and gas was soaring high, the economy of this province was doing well. Alberta is the only province that has no provincial sales tax and the low-income families there can enjoy almost free use of natural gas for their home heating. But when the price of oil has dropped in the recent few years, Alberta's economy has been hit hard.

Jim and Meilin had lived in Edmonton, Alberta for ten years before they moved to British Columbia. They knew rather well the situation of Edmonton, if not the whole province. The two big cities, Calgary and Edmonton of this province seemed to have a rivalry going on. Calgary is bigger, rough-neck and aggressive type and very proud of being the oil province of the country. Edmonton is rather the quiet type, though no less assertive. Being the capital of the province with more government offices, Edmonton has often played the gentleman. The Edmontonians, on the other hand, are less reserved in claiming that Calgary is a less pleasant place, much colder in winter and hotter in summer.

Calgary's rough-neck image might have come from their large annual rodeo which is called the Calgary Stampede. The famous festival has all kinds of shows and contests related to the early western life a century ago. Today, Calgary is becoming one of the largest cities in the country. Although Edmonton is still regarded as the oil capital of the country, the oil industry, especially the oil sands industry seems to have been more around Calgary. In good times, more people came to the area to find jobs, which made Calgary a large financial and administration centre. The city has grown rapidly in recent years.

Edmonton was started by the Hudson's Bay Company in 1795 as a fur trading post called Fort Edmonton on the banks of North Saskatchewan River. The trading settlement followed suit and the place became the main resting-point for people to go on to the north and the pacific. The first boom of the city came at the gold rush era. Lots of people went through Edmonton to reach the Klondike gold rush. Having been unsuccessful by digging gold, many prospectors came back to Edmonton to settle down, trying to get rich slower and in more steady ways. Edmonton developed with the population boom. The second boom of the city came with the discovery of the oil in Leduc. Later, more oil fields had been discovered within the forty kilometer perimeter of the city. People flocked to the area to get jobs in the petroleum industry. Since the starting time, Edmonton has been the Gateway to the North. It is the transportation and supply or distribution center for the north. In early times, the bush planes started from Edmonton, transporting medicine, food, mails and all kinds of materials to Yukon and Yellowknife. From there, those supplies went to remote northern areas. The city played an important role in the construction of the Alaska Highway and the development of the Canadian north. In 1905 when Alberta was formed, Edmonton was elected the capital of the province. Today, Edmonton is the location of government offices and still the transportation and supply centre for the north, and it has a large oil refinery and some other manufacturing plants.

The couple knew well that the situation for the coloured people in Alberta was not any better than that in British Columbia. If the white folks have harboured anti-Asian sentiment in British Columbia, the white folks in Alberta are just indifferent to the coloured folks. There are not many equal opportunities in the job market for the coloured people in Alberta just like that in British Columbia. Living in Edmonton for ten years, Meilin had tried very hard to find a job suitable for her academic credentials and abilities, but failed miserably. With a master degree in

English from a reputable provincial university in Canada and teaching experiences, she could only find baby-sitting or housekeeping type of jobs in Edmonton. Jim had worked hard in the military for almost seventeen years, but he had been kicked out three years before his retirement. Jim had experienced a cruel and heartbreaking releasing procedure in the Edmonton military base, and the couple could not exclude that the whole thing might be partially caused by his being married to a Chinese woman. Ten years life experiences in Edmonton had given the couple the right to say that racial discrimination in Alberta was no less a problem than that in British Columbia.

Today, the population of the coloured people in Alberta may not be much smaller than that in British Columbia. There is a Chinatown and a large Asian community in Edmonton. Though the Chinatown in Edmonton is smaller than those in Richmond and Vancouver, it seems also doing good businesses. In recent years, some Buddhist temples have been erected in Edmonton, and the biggest among them is a traditional-styled temple built by the Vietnamese community. Still, the biggest Buddhist temple in Edmonton cannot compare with the two large Buddhist temples built by the Chinese community in Richmond. There are also churches erected by the Asian and black communities in Edmonton. Jim and Meilin had been very much impressed by the music presented in a black church there. They went to that church often while living in Edmonton. That was the first time in Meilin's life in Canada to see a fair-sized black community in a city. Though there are some Asian medical doctors and lawyers practising in Edmonton, there are almost no Asians in prominent political positions there. For the Chinese Spring Festival, the premier of the province may come to join the Chinese new-year celebration; the Buddhist temple may have a MP come to give a talk in their function. This kind of political gestures, concerns and kindness cannot generate much substantial benefits for the ordinary Asian folks. The good jobs and positions with higher social status seldom go to them.

In Edmonton, Jim and Meilin had the chance to get to know some native peoples. As Jim could not keep a job because of his injuries sustained in his military service and Meilin could not find a decent job because of her Asian origin, in order to survive, the couple had a small rental business. Their rental property was of the basic housing type in the lower end of the city; they could only have the tenants who were at the bottom of the society. They had some native families who had answered their advertisement to rent their places. They rented out two and sometimes if they were lucky, three suites to different families. The living conditions of the native peoples they had seen were way below that of the other Canadians. All their native tenants had no jobs, were on welfare and had almost nothing. In addition to these, the couple had watched the TV news reporting a case of police brutality towards a native man causing his death. The native peoples have not caused this kind of conditions entirely by themselves, as there are facts to show that giving the native peoples equal opportunities, they can do well just like other non-native people. In Alberta, the very province where some native peoples have been abused, a man of Métis origin and a man of Cree origin have gained high provincial political positions and entered the leadership rank of Alberta.

Having lived in Edmonton for ten years, the couple now chose to go through Edmonton instead of Calgary on their way for this cross-country trip. They knew the streets of Edmonton well; it was easy for them to move around the city. Besides, they wanted to have a look again at their old places. Having crossed the border, the first Alberta city they were going to enter on this route would be Hinton. First of all, they had to take Vixy to a veterinarian. Hinton was a city and an ideal place to find a good doctor for Vixy. The couple had never entered this small city before. Passing by Hinton quite a few times on their way from or to Edmonton, they had often dreamt of owning a small piece of land in this place. It would be wonderful if they could put their small trailer on a piece of land to enjoy the beautiful place whenever they wanted. Hinton is at the east end of Jasper National Park and near a hot spring; it has all the characteristics of the beautiful national park. The range of the Rocky Mountains is in the view and the air is absolutely clean and fresh. Hinton city is sitting on high ground with grand views of the magnificent mountains around. The place is not right in the deep of the mountains; one has no feelings of being overpowered or oppressed by the tall mountains.

When Jim and Meilin came close to Hinton, they saw a large sign directing the travellers to a RV Park. They followed the sign and pulled their trailer into the campground which was on a piece of higher ground at the edge of the city. The RV Park was not big and could only receive about a dozen big RVs, but it offered full service. There were already four large brand new RVs occupying the good shady spots, and their cables and hoses were all hooked up. Jim parked their trailer and van on a partially shaded lot. Before they could settle down, they went to the office to register. The owner of the RV Park had a large new house with an add-on office in front. When Jim and Meilin walked into the office, there was nobody around. But the house door connected to the office was wide open.

They could see that the house was a four split type and the sitting room was several steps higher than the office. Upon their ringing of the bell; the owner came down from the house. He was a short bulky man in his fifties. While he was receiving the couple's payment and doing the paper work, he chatted with Jim easily, though his breathing was laboured. It looked that the owner was a heavy smoker; his office and home were filled with the stale smell of cigarette smoke. His difficult breathing and deeply creased earlobes showed that he was suffering from some heart problem.

"So, are you passing by or planning to stay for a few days?" the owner asked friendly.

Jim answered, "Our dog has suffered a heart attack; we have to stay here a day or two to have the vet check him up. We thought he was a goner last night, but he pulled through. We are going to go across the country. He might not be able to endure the trip..."

"Oh... I'm sorry to hear it," the owner said with some interest and then he started talking about his own dog, "I had a small dog before. The dan thing drank some coolant leaked out from the car and got seriously ill... the vet said that he could put the dog to sleep and had it cremated for four hundred dollars... I turned him down. I just took the dog to the backyard and shot it with my shotgun..."

Jim and Meilin winced, finished the registration for one night and left the office. They did not like the way the owner talked about his late dog. Coming back to their trailer and van, the couple started to set things up for the night. The afternoon was still young. After everything was settled, they took Vixy out for a walk. Though the RV Park was not big, there was a large lawn for people to roam about. The mountains in a distant looked beautiful and peaceful. The couple felt relaxed. Vixy was weak. Normally he would be very excited and happy for any kind of walks, but now he seemed not that interested in walking too much. Jim thought that they had to stay out a bit longer and let Vixy do all his toilet things.

While the couple and their dog walked on the lawn, another RV pulled in. It was a large trailer that looked like a big shining tin-can and pulled by a large new truck. Soon after the tin-can settled, a petite woman in her fifties came out with two small dogs that were the same size as Vixy. The woman walked her dogs on the lawn and soon met Jim and Meilin with their dog. A friendly conversation was struck between them. Of course, the talk would be about their dogs. Jim offered the information about Vixy's condition and his last night's ordeal, and the woman talked about her dogs.

"The eagle had picked up my dog three times and dropped it three times," said the woman innocently, but her information sounded not that convincing.

Her dog looked weighing eleven to fifteen pounds. It must be a sight to see an eagle picking it up to the sky and drop it three times! The woman had no expression to show that the experience was an ordeal for her dog or herself. Very likely, she was saying this thing to hint something else.

In Jim and Meilin's present situation, it was not unusual to meet some people who were under some instruction to come to harass or attack them. Because of the outspokenness and the publicizing of what they had said and Meilin had written, they had lost not only their privacy, but also a peaceful life. Attacks and harassment were constantly pouring down onto them in different ways. Quite some people were scared that the Americans might side with the couple and make things worse, and some were jealous that with the Americans' support, the couple might move up in the society and get benefited in some way. If this petite woman was under some instruction to harass or humiliate the couple, her hinting was, of course, about the Americans' involvement in this situation. Whenever the eagle is mentioned in any kind of political talks, it is unmistakably implying the US. Very likely, the woman was instructed to hint that the couple were two dogs that had been picked up by the eagle US three times and dropped three times. This must be the most absurd and funny thing coming up in this large scaled harassment to the couple so far. It must have come from some people's mixed feelings of jealousy, fear, gloating and hatred.

Ever since the Nine Eleven event, the eagle seemed to have suffered a nerves breakdown. It needed some pickup remedy to fly normally and calmly again. It would never pick up a pair of underdogs to fly in the sky. The ordinary couple would be lucky, if the eagle would not pluck their eyeballs out just for fun. As a matter of fact, the eagles, the crows or any other high flying birds in the world are pretty much profit-driven nowadays. No bird would pick up an ordinary couple to fly, as there is absolutely no profit to be made in such an endeavour. This being said, the couple were not at all the lap or running dog type; they were incapable of finding any way to suck up to the powerful and to present themselves available for a pickup by any kind of high flying birds. Those jealous or afraid Canadians were scaring themselves for nothing.

The night in the RV Park was uneventful. The couple had a good sleep. Vixy too had a sleep. Next morning, they all had their breakfast. Jim unhooked the van from the trailer and they drove into the part of Hinton that was easy for them to reach. It was the small part, probably the old section of the city. Small houses were closely linked together and lined up along the small streets. The couple had no problem to find the shopping mall, as it appeared to be the only one in this area. The strip mall had different stores and a large grocery store around a parking lot. An animal clinic was among the stores.

When the couple and their dog walked into the clinic, there were no other customers. The receptionist, a young girl, was friendly. She talked amicably and offered precise information. Vixy sensed that he was in trouble and had refused to enter the clinic at first. Most time at home, when Vixy was well, he stuck closely to Jim and was mainly Jim's pet. But when he was sick or in trouble, he would stay close to Meilin. This behaviour of his had given some comfort to Meilin who thought that Vixy had chosen her as his protector.

The clinic was warm inside. While they were waiting to see the doctor, Vixy started shaking and stuck close to Meilin's legs. Meilin rubbed his back gently and comforted him. Soon they were called into the doctor's office. The doctor was a man in his late thirties, who looked kind and intelligent. His clothes under the white uniform were plain and he wore a pair of rubber garden shoes. Obviously, he was not the owner of the clinic and not rich. Jim and Meilin talked about Vixy's condition, starting from all his teeth being pulled out and his being put under anaesthesia twice for that operation in an animal hospital.

"Ever since then, his condition was deteriorating and he pooped and peed in the house. We now could not touch him anymore. The day before yesterday, he had suffered a heart attack or stroke. He just collapsed while we were taking him out for a walk," Jim offered all the information he could think of at this moment.

The doctor tried to pick Vixy up to the table for the examination; Vixy would not let him. Then the doctor squatted down and checked him on the floor.

"There might be two possibilities," the doctor talked gently. "Either the dog is going blind or there is a tumour growing in his brains."

The couple had suspected that losing all his teeth and being twice under anaesthesia might have done great damages to Vixy. It looked that the doctor would not say anything that would do damages to his unknown colleagues. Then the doctor continued, "There are ways to find out whether there is a tumour in his brains, but it will be expensive. Your dog is fifteen years old now. It would be better just to wait. Let him be.

Eventually, he will fall down or something and break his bones. Then we'll have to put him to sleep..."

Meilin actually felt some relief, as the doctor did not give Vixy a death sentence. She said, "Well, we'll just wait for the last straw to fall then. In the mean time, the dog has to endure the suffering and the last straw will bring more suffering." Later, she had regretted very much that she had mentioned the suffering at this moment.

When the couple thought that the clinic visit was finished and they were going to take Vixy back to the trailer, the doctor seemed to have changed his mind. He said with a more serious tone, "If somebody calls me in the middle of a night, asking me to put their dog to sleep, I will never do it. But your dog is fifteen... his condition... well, let's have another look."

The doctor approached Vixy again, trying to pick him up; still he could not do it. Vixy was trying to bite him and would not let him near. Then the doctor put on a pair of heavy gloves that were covering up to his elbows. Meilin offered that Vixy had no teeth and was in no way dangerous, but the doctor would not handle him with his bare hands. He must have been bitten quite a few times by other dogs. After several tries, the doctor resigned to letting Vixy stay on the floor. He then produced a small cotton ball and started testing Vixy. He shot the cotton ball a little way from Vixy to see if there was any response coming from him. Vixy was so nervous. Several times the cotton ball was flying in front of him; he never paid any attention to it.

The small cotton ball had decided Vixy's fate. The doctor said with a resigned tone, "Well, if you decide to let the dog sleep, I have no objection."

Jim and Meilin came to the clinic to ask for the doctor's opinion about what they should do with Vixy. They thought that Vixy's fate would be decided by the doctor, not by them. But now it seemed that the final decision was still theirs. It was too hard a decision to make in Meilin's mind. She believed that Vixy was just too nervous to see the cotton ball. She hoped that Jim would say that they would take the dog back and wait. But Jim said with a resigned tone also, "Well, it would be better to let Vixy sleep..."

Soon the nurse or the vet's helper came into the office with a form and asked the dog owners to sign. While Jim read the form, Meilin talked to him, "Jim, don't be hasty. Think carefully before you do anything."

In her mind, it was a life that they were handling, a life that they had loved for so many years, and the decision should not be so hastily made. After some time pondering, Jim signed the form. Now Vixy was going to die by euthanasia and his body would be cremated. The coffin, a small cedar box, for his ashes was chosen. Soon, the doctor came in with the injection. Vixy received the injection quietly without objection; he seemed also resigned to his own fate. After the injection, the doctor and the nurse left the office. Jim and Meilin thought that the injection would be given slowly by intravenous dripping, but in the small place, euthanasia was instant death. In just a few second, Vixy vomited all the food he ate for his breakfast. The nurse came in and quickly cleaned up the vomit. Then in the next few seconds, Vixy collapsed to the floor. He was lying peacefully at Meilin's feet. Jim lay down also on the floor beside Vixy and started crying. Meilin was heartbroken and said to Jim with a choked voice, "Let's put Vixy on the table... he should not die on the floor...."

They lifted Vixy up to the table. His body was soft and warm, but his pulse had already gone. Meilin could no longer hold her tears; she bent down close to Vixy with tears streaming down and whispered, "You know we love you... you know it... we love you..."

The doctor came in and showed his sincere concern and sympathy. Meilin asked for a moment longer alone with their dog. The doctor said, "No problem... take your time..."

After some time of saying goodbye to Vixy, Jim and Meilin had to leave the office. They knew that Vixy was no longer in that body. He was gone and so suddenly.

During this moment of ordeal for the couple and their dog, the clinic seemed to have been informed who this couple were. Whether the doctor was also informed about the couple or not, his attitudes towards the couple and their dog did not change; he remained kind and did his best in this difficult situation. A middle-aged woman had shown up in the middle of this procedure. Her specially coloured costume and attitudes showed that she was coming to show some hostility to the couple, the enemies of the state. When the couple went to the receptionist counter to pay the fee, they could see that the receptionist had been duly informed who they were. The young girl had changed into a different person. Her face had no longer smile on it and her talk was no longer amicable. The couple paid the fee of seven hundred dollars and received four dollars of loonies back. Except the doctor, the clinic staff turned deadly cold towards the couple. For Jim and Meilin, all they had felt at that moment was the sickening paradoxical emptiness and heaviness of their hearts. The clinic staff's attitudes were absolutely nothing to them. Vixy's death was so sudden and they were in no way prepared for it. They had always thought that they could keep an open and calm mind towards death. Now when death hit so suddenly to a life so dear to them, the open and calm mind could not be found. Their hearts were filled with heavy sad feelings, yet there was that sickening emptiness that could only be described as death.

They were informed that Vixy's body would be sent to Edmonton to be cremated. The couple had asked that his body be cremated separately and they would come to the clinic to take his ashes about a month later. More than a month later, on their way back from their trip, the couple came to the clinic to pick up Vixy's ashes. The clinic told them that they had just received Vixy's ashes from Edmonton. The couple took the cedar box with Vixy's ashes in. On one side of the box, there was a metal plate with Vixy's name engraved on. Vixy died on June 5, but the date of his death on the paper was marked as June 13. The couple had no idea what this June 13 meant. The box was sealed and there was no way to open it. Holding this rather heavy small box in their hands, the couple had very much doubted whether this box had actually contained Vixy's ashes. All the terrible thoughts had popped up in their minds about what had been done to Vixy's body. They could do nothing about it, but take the box and leave the place.

At the moment after Vixy's death, when Jim and Meilin walked out of the animal clinic, they felt difficult to move on immediately. The sky turned darker; a drizzle had started at the time when they were in the clinic and was still going on. At the time when they arrived here, the parking lot was almost empty. Now it was filled with large heavy vehicles. It looked like a power showdown to the couple by the town's people. The couple felt, before they could move on, they had to take a breath and to alleviate some of this dark heaviness caused by Vixy's death. They decided to check out the grocery store to divert their minds. They walked in the grocery store. It was no use. They came out quickly without buying anything and drove away. Along the highway that was cutting the city into two parts, there were some large department stores. Maybe, with more things going on in those stores, they could have some success in lighten up their minds and hearts. They went to the Wal-Mart and walked around. Still, it was useless. Coming out of the store, they decided to check out a real estate office which was nearby. They had dreamt of buying a small piece of land here before. Maybe such a big thing could finally turn their minds away from Vixy's death.

When they walked into a real estate office, a good looking middle-aged woman received them. The couple talked about what they had wanted and the woman presented a few options to them. They were shocked to see how expensive a small piece of land was here. They were informed that they could not actually own a small piece of land here, but only rent or lease it in a peculiar way. On top of almost half million dollars they would have to pay to "buy" the small piece of land, they would have to pay several thousand dollars more each year for rent or strata fee as the woman put it. The woman saw the couple's stunned expressions and said with a smile, "The land here is mostly crown land. Just by the national park... you know... all quite expensive..."

The information had thoroughly waked the couple up from their dream. Actually, they had no desire for land here anymore as Vixy had died here. Visiting the real estate office was mainly to divert their minds. Still, they did not need this shock. After a short conversation about the land, Jim started talking about Vixy, his dilemma and his death. Jim was an extravert person; talking about sufferings and receiving sympathy from others could help him to alleviate some pains.

The woman showed her sympathy, but commented, "People don't regard their pets as their family members. My ex-husband had an animal clinic before. I know this..."

The woman did not say what she thought people were regarding their pets as, but she had offered the information to the wrong persons. At this moment, Jim and Meilin had felt from the depth of their heart and soul that they had just lost a dear family member. When the couple walked out of the real estate office, they realized that nothing could ease the pains they had felt and they could not stay one minute more in this place where Vixy had died. They had to run away as fast as they could.

They went back to the RV Park and quickly hooked up the trailer. There were still the three grocery bags of Vixy's food they had bought for the long trip; now Vixy could no longer enjoy them. Vixy had long been on soft food diet. Jim and Meilin bought the best dog food from Superstore for him. They were mostly soft meaty food in small sealed pouches. The couple decided to give them to the woman with two dogs. If her dog had really been picked up by an eagle three times, the dog definitely deserved some good food for his ordeal. Before they started moving, Jim took Vixy's food to the tin-can trailer. After he came back, the couple started pulling away from the RV Park immediately.

When their vehicles were moving, the petite woman ran out from the tin-can trailer to meet them. She talked to Meilin sitting on the passenger side of the van, "I'm very sorry about your dog. It is very kind of you... all those dog food. Here, please accept this money..."

The woman stretched out her hand to Meilin with a twenty dollar bill. Her face was full of an uneasy expression.

"No," Meilin turned it down and said, "Our dog would like your dogs to have the food."

Jim chipped in too, "Yes, please take them and thank you for your concern."

The couple drove away while the petite woman waved goodbye to them. Soon they were on the highway. Driving for a long time, the couple were silent and both were thinking about Vixy. Then Jim started shedding tears again. In order to comfort him, Meilin started talking.

"Vixy's soul is in heaven now. He is better off than us, enjoying a different life without any suffering," said Meilin, trying hard to convince Jim and herself.

"Yes, it is better for him now. He will never make the trip. It will just be more sufferings for him..." Jim answered and tried hard to justify the situation.

"According to Buddhist belief, at the time of their death, animals' consciousness will transgress to other new-born living beings. If the death coincides with the birth of a new-born baby, an animal can very well be reborn as a human. Nobody can tell.... Vixy might have been reborn as a human baby at the moment of his death..." said Meilin again, feeling a little better by her own words.

"Yes, let's hope so," agreed Jim, a smile coming up on his face.

The couple were interested in the reincarnation belief, but they had never believed that humans could reborn as animals and animals could reborn as humans. They thought that even if reincarnation were true, humans would only be reborn as humans and animals as animals. However, at this moment of painful loss, they desperately needed the universality of this belief to lighten their minds and hearts. It seemed that only the thought of Vixy being in heaven or reborn as a human baby could help in the present situation. The couple talked and felt better. Not long after they left Hinton, the landscape started opening up. The mountains were left behind and the prairie became more of the land feature. The driving was becoming easier and they felt a bit relaxed. Soon they came to the four-lane highway which meant that they were not very far from Edmonton. In a few more hours, they could arrive in that big city. However, they had decided to go to Wabamun Village before entering Edmonton. They had owned a small acreage there before and loved the place. They would like to have another look at it.

With the harassment situation going on in their life, they did not have much peace in the place they were living now. The noise attacks were constant. Though their dream to buy a piece of land in Hinton evaporated, they still wished to buy a small piece of land and use it as a refuge from this hideous harassment. Wabamun would be ideal, if the land there was still cheap. The couple had very much regretted that they had sold their three acre land with a mobile home in Wabamun. Now their home was troubled and they had no other place to run to. The real estate prices had sky-rocketed in recent years. It would be very hard now for them to get a place that was not too expensive and not too far from their home.

The whole afternoon while they were driving on the highway, the rain never stopped. Normally, in traveling long distance, they would encounter different weathers along the way; some places would have rains and some other places would enjoy sunshine. It seemed a bit unusual to have such a large area covered by rains this day. When the couple entered Wabamun Village, the rain was still on. It was almost evening; they had no heart to find a campground. They parked their van and trailer on a parking lot of a church. Nobody would need the church parking lot for the night; they were going to spend the night here. Perhaps, they could have a quieter night by the church than on a campground.

After supper, they went to the gas station to get some gas and also some information about land or properties for sale around. They did not get much information, but found a realtor's advertisement. It looked that they had to use a realtor if they wanted to get any information about a piece of land here. They called the number; a woman answered the phone and said that she could see them tomorrow morning at ten. After this settled, the couple went back to the trailer to sleep. It was a very hard day for them. Vixy's sudden death had weighed heavily, and the rains all along the way had not helped. Even with the talks and efforts to lighten the situation, they still felt depressed.

When the dark night started blanketing the place, the rain was getting heavier. The couple sat in their trailer with a small battery-powered light on. Jim shed some more tears, missing Vixy. Then they went to bed. Though very tired, Meilin felt impossible to fall asleep. She was an introvert person; things normally went in her deeper and harder for her to work them out. The pains, regrets and heavy empty sad feelings were gnawing her relentlessly. She felt that she had failed Vixy who had chosen her to be his protector; she did nothing to prevent his death.

Human emotions are irrational, wild, absurd, mystic and very hard to control and direct. The rational mind knows well that all living beings will die and death is as natural as birth, but emotions will not let death win or let a close loved one go easily. The rational mind will normally be totally vanquished by irrational emotions. Human emotions will try everything and every way to deny death's supreme victory; they simply will not accept that death means total annihilation of the living beings.

The rains never stopped, pouring down heavily the whole night. In addition to the tumultuous rainstorm, a heavy truck had been booming through by the church parking lot every half an hour. The forceful angry rushing of the engine sounded from the same truck. This was not new anymore. In most places the couple went to, they would encounter some people who were sent out to harass them by making loud noises through their vehicles. Vehicles and especially large vehicles could do more efficient job in making noises. This truck driver seemed the worst of them all. Perhaps the bloody beefsteaks and loads of beers had boosted his energy and got him going non-stop the whole night.

The heavy rains were beating down on the small trailer violently. In the peak of the storm, they sounded like the urgent war drumming or bullets showering down on the metal roof. In this terrible dark stormy night, Meilin felt no fear, but despair and the strongest wanting in her life. She wanted more than anything else in the world that Vixy was still alive and sleeping with them in the trailer. She knew that if it were possible, she would have given up everything she had in exchange for Vixy being alive. The emotion was so strong that it shook her. She had never experienced such a deep longing and never wanted something so badly in her whole life. She knew that this kind of longing would enable her to do something drastic if there was any slight possibility that she could accomplish it. Only, no matter how bad she wanted and longed, she could not bring Vixy back from death. So the strong longing worked on her despair and made her spend the whole night in the miserable sufferings of dark hopelessness.

The rains stopped in the morning. When the sun came out, there was not a thread of cloud in the blue sky. It was hard to believe what a turbulent wild night had just passed. The bright sunshine and the blue sky started an entirely new day. Even after a terrible sleepless night, Meilin felt better, could let Vixy go now and start anew. It is a mystery how quickly and drastically the human mind can change and adjust with the changes of emotions, and the changes of emotions can be triggered by a simple change of the weather. Jim looked refreshed and was immediately busy at repairing the trailer taillight which was damaged by the last night's rainstorm. The couple got up early and had plenty of time to do the repairs and have their breakfast before going to see the realtor.

Near ten o'clock in the morning, they found the realtor's house in the small village. The house was a big sturdy wooden structure by the railway. A few minutes before the appointment time, the couple walked up to the door; the realtor was ready for them. A stately woman in her fifties came to let them in; she introduced herself as the realtor. Later, the couple got to know that she was divorced and lived alone in the big house. But it looked that she had rented out part of her big house. When Jim and Meilin were sitting in her office and talking with her, they could hear that a family was in other part of the house. The large office was close to the entrance door and a nice large bathroom was beside the office. The interior of the house was tastefully decorated. Upon Jim and Meilin's praising about her interior decoration, the realtor said that she had been an interior designer. After the couple told her what they had in their minds, the realtor started her computer and soon pulled out quite some information. She produced quite a few properties for sale in coloured brochures. It looked that the prices of the land and properties here had gone up considerably than the time when Jim and Meilin had owned the acreage in this area, but they were still much lower compared with the real estate prices in British Columbia. Soon Jim and Meilin had spotted a few places that were interesting.

"Could you show us these places?" Jim asked hopefully.

"No problem, but the field trip has to be tomorrow," the realtor answered readily.

The couple were thankful. Looking for a piece of land in the countryside was not an easy job. Without a realtor's help, it would be almost impossible to find those places in a large area where there were not many people living around. As for having to wait another day, the couple knew that they could not push and had to be patient. The realtor might have a previous engagement; besides, in a small place, things were normally moving slowly. After leaving the realtor's house, the couple had almost a full day to look around and to find a campground. They decided to check out the village first, have a look at their old acreage and then go to locate the campground.

Wabamun Village is a small place. It has about fifty households in the village centre and some other residences with acreages spreading in a rather large area around the Wabamun Lake. In a small place, facilities normally go singly. The village has one post office, one school, one church, one community hall with a library in the basement, one office of Credit

Union acting as a bank, one senior citizens' residence, one fire hall, one gas station, one hotel, one restaurant and one grocery store. The couple walked along the clean paved streets which were not long and had little traffic. Along the streets, there were some bungalows and two storey houses side by side with some small mobile homes. Obviously, the housing regulations or rules were relaxed in a village. In cities, mobile home parks were separated from other housing areas and normally tucked away in the city skirt or some not so prominent corners. It appeared that Wabamun Village had very little change since the last time they were here; that was years ago. The only thing new in the village was a grocery store which was bigger than the old one and fuller of goods. The old grocery store was still operating right on the opposite side of the new one. Another new thing was at the entrance of the village. A decorative art piece had replaced the old welcoming board; it was a large metal dragonfly perched on a ten foot metal pole, with wings spanning ten foot wide.

The couple had lived in this area before. They had never seen many dragonflies around, let alone big dragonflies. They wondered about the appearance of this big dragonfly ornament here. It seemed that some people here might have read Meilin's books. Like most people, they did not like the Chinese woman's writing. If the small place had been mentioned by some white writer of British or European origin, the villagers might have felt very much honoured; some other token might have been put up to show their pride and appreciation. Since the place had been mentioned by a Chinese woman in her abominable writing, the people here must have felt only indignation, as if their place had been degraded or marred by her. Even though what the Chinese woman had written about this place was mostly good, the villagers would never be pleased to have been mentioned by a Chinese woman, most probably a red alien in their eyes. Something had to be done to show their anger or mockery towards this bold yellow woman. As the woman had come from China which was symbolized by dragon, a dragonfly was appropriate to mark her intrusion to this place of theirs. Quite some white Canadians living in small villages or towns were prejudiced towards the coloured people, as those villages or towns were predominantly occupied by the whites. Their prejudice often went to the extent of narrow-mindedness or close-mindedness towards different peoples and different cultures as a whole. It was much harder for the coloured Canadians to live and work in small places than in large cities of the country.

The world has very much changed and is still changing. In the recent decades, the Asians in the world have become less political and more practical; they have concentrated their minds on economical developments. China and quite some other Asian countries are developing fast and presenting some marvellous qualities and merits for the western countries to learn from. The wise will learn from anybody. Confucius once said, "If I walk with even only two people, one of them must be my teacher." Unfortunately, the rise of Asia has caused some jealousy from the west and brought some dangerous situations to that continent. As for some Canadians, especially those living in small places, the changes in the world seem to have hardly touched them; they seem to have become more political and less practical. Their minds are stuck fast to the belief or conviction of white superiority. Their views about the Asians and their countries have remained the same as those given by some old writings they had encountered many years ago. They are indeed like the frogs in the bottom of a well; the size of the sky to them is the size of the well's opening. And for the live of them, they will not jump out of the well to see the broad sky. They refuse to come up into the modern world, change with the time and be benefited by the changes in the world.

It did not take long for Jim and Meilin to have a good look at the small village. From last night's booming noises of a truck and now the art display of a dragonfly, Meilin could see that they were not going to have a peaceful life here like before. If they had acquired a piece of land here, the harassment would follow them. They could only afford a small piece of land, which meant that they might not be able to escape the noise attacks from the neighbours. However, the appointment had been made with the realtor lady and Jim seemed still highly interested. Meilin thought that she might as well go along and see what would come up.

The couple then went to their old acreage which was about seven or eight minutes drive from the village. They were surprised to see that their old place had changed greatly. The old mobile home was gone. A brand new house stood in its place. The marsh area had been all cleaned up and turned into a large lawn. A family with children were living here now. The couple could see some children's toys on the lawn. It was a nice change for their old place. They felt good to see it. Now they could move away from this place with a good last impression. Only the couple wondered, with the trees, bushes and marsh area gone, whether the deer, the hare, the field mouse and the mallard would still visit this spot. However, the surroundings still looked beautiful and peaceful; trees and bushes were still the main inhabitants around. Not far from their old place, the couple saw a small acreage with a small house for sale. The price marked on the for-sale sign was over three hundred thousand dollars! Jim and Meilin were astounded. Less than two decades ago, they had bought the three acre land here for five thousand dollars and sold the land with the mobile home for twenty-nine thousand dollars. The high price jump scared them. They thought that if they had kept their old acreage, they might be rich now.

Having looked around, the couple drove back to the highway towards a provincial park. They knew there was a campground in the park. Wabamun Lake is a fair sized lake. A power plant is sitting at the lake's west side. Wabamun Village is located at the north side of the lake and the provincial park is at the east side of the lake. Before oil and gas were discovered, coal mining was the main mining industry in Alberta. Today, coal mining is still an important part of the mining industry in this province. Wabamun area has a large coal mine and is still producing well. Wabamun power plant generates power by burning coal, which reminds people of the existence and importance of the coal mining industry. The couple wondered that with Alberta being the king of oil in the country now, how long Wabamun power plant was still going to burn coal.

Fossil fuels have been damaging the natural environment since the start of Industrial Revolution. It looks that the human dependency on fossil fuels will continue for a long time yet into the future. Human population in the world is rapidly increasing, and all peoples need and deserve a good life. Increasing demands for more economical developments are inevitable. Those developments will need more energy and more fossil fuels, which will result in more damages to the natural environment. Will the human beings be able to curb the ever increasing needs for fossil fuels or to find alternative energy sources in time to save the natural world which all the living beings depend on? This is a big and urgent question. The good sign is that quite some people of the world have seen the danger the planet is facing, and they have been trying to lower down the emissions from burning fossil fuels, to limit other kinds of pollutions and to repair some of the damages already done. Alberta has the heavy industry of extracting and distributing oil, gas and coal. It has a heavier task in the protection of natural environment. It is visible that the province has paid greater attentions and taken greater measures in this direction in recent years.

After about fifteen minutes drive, the couple arrived at the provincial park and found the campground. They had never camped here before and were surprised to see a large and well equipped campground.

The road around the campground was wide and smooth. Quite many camping lots were spreading in the woods and a big modern bathroom was on top of a hill. The couple drove around and found a lot they liked. But soon after they set their trailer on, they had to change site. The neighbour of this lot appeared quite noisy. Now on any campground, as soon as the couple saw potential dangers such as noises or smokes, they would move away to a different spot right away. There was no need to wait until the middle of the night to remedy the situation.

After things settled and they felt rested, the couple took a short trip to check out the park which was connected with the campground. Though the size of this Alberta provincial park could not compare with the large size of a provincial park in British Columbia, Wabamun Lake Park had been very much improved in recent years. A long boardwalk and a washroom had been built on the east bank of the lake. On the wide boardwalk, there were quite some benches for people to sit down and enjoy the lake. Two new long docks were stretching a long way into the water. While the couple were walking towards the lake, they saw flocks of seagulls flying over or playing on the lake. Among the seagulls, there were some cranes. The couple could not remember that they had ever seen cranes here before. Meilin took out the camera and started taking pictures. When the cranes had enough of the place, they took off together. Their taking-off motion looked so elegant and graceful. The couple were glad to see Wabamun Lake clean and well. A few years ago, there was a train derailment by the lake. While living in British Columbia, they had watched in dismay the news about the disaster on TV. Hazardous chemicals from the derailed train cars had leaked into the lake and caused environmental damages here. People must have taken tremendous efforts to clean up the lake and to restore it to the present condition. Now it looked that all were well, birds still coming and fish still living in the water.

It was quite relaxing for the couple to sit on the bench and watch the birds flying over the lake and a few men fishing on the docks. The serene lake under the blue sky was a needed remedy for yesterday's grave trial from Vixy's death. In a fine day, it was much easier to bear the grief and to think with a more rational and positive mind. Vixy was finally released from the end sufferings of his life and they should feel glad for him.

The couple had a good day and a good night's rest. Their mental condition was considerably improved. Next morning they went to the realtor's home at ten o'clock. The realtor lady was ready for them. The three immediately started. Jim and Meilin offered to take their van, but the realtor turned it down. She knew the roads better and was going to drive. She invited the couple to sit in her car; she would take them to the places they were interested in. The stylish and motherly woman looked capable and was easy to talk to. Soon the couple got to know that she had two sons and was already a grandma. She sometimes took her grandchildren to go fishing in Wabamun Lake and their fishing was sport type.

"A few days ago, I caught a big jackfish. My grandkids were jumping in joy. We released it back into the lake," the woman talked joyously.

From her easy and continued talk, the couple got to know that the lady was a believer of the New Age stuff. It was quite unusual for a woman at her age and living in a small place to have kept a wide open mind towards new and different things. She even knew the ancient Chinese way of Feng Shui, the methods of harmonizing or using the positive energies of the universe for living and well-being. This knowledge might have come along with her former trade of interior design.

It took more than half an hour drive for them to arrive at the first place. The drive was very pleasant. Alberta's countryside was wide open. The roads through the vast farm fields were all straight. The farm fields were separated into large square sections by straight lanes. The chequered fields were green or golden according to the crops planted and the stages of their ripening. The vast view of the fields looked beautifully colourful and orderly. Alberta's oil fields are everywhere, but they are not as predominant as the farm fields. Large areas of land have been cultivated for farming. Along long stretches of highways and country roads, the most prominent scenes are vast farming fields; some of them were reaching to the horizon.

The first piece of land they were going to see was a three acre property in a developed residential area. It meant that the acreage would have access to a public road, hydro power and natural gas. It was the same kind of acreage the couple had owned here before. When they arrived at the place and got out of the car, they had a look at the site. It was a piece of flat land without trees. The view was far reaching and the neighbours were clearly to be seen. The couple started planning that if they got this piece of land, they would plant some trees. However, they realized that they could plant trees and change the landscape, but they could not change the neighbours. While they were checking, a man was cutting big trees down with a chainsaw on a site opposite to this one. Unlike this piece of bare land, the neighbour's land was full of trees. The place was quite far from the highway, but the price for these three acres was sixty thousand dollars, much higher than the five thousand dollars they had spent in buying the three acre land near the highway years ago.

The second place they went to was also the same type of residential acreage. It was a one acre land with a cabin. The owner asked for ninety thousand dollars. Upon looking at this property carefully, they found many more problems. The small cabin looked to have been abandoned for years and was in a grave condition. The neighbours were very close. On one side, there were no trees to separate this property from a neighbour's mobile home close by. The owner of that mobile home had a big dog chained to a tree at the entrance between his property and this cabin property. The dog yanked his chains ferociously and gave a fiercely loud welcome to the three approaching strangers. The mobile home site had a huge pile of ready cut firewood that was stacked larger and higher than the mobile home. Obviously, all the trees around had gone into that gigantic pile of firewood. It was quite obvious why and how long ago, the owner of the cabin had fled from this place.

The following two places were farm land; each had five acres. The brochures for these two properties must be written by a professional writer; the scenery of the properties was breathtakingly depicted. The couple were almost drooling for the land when they read it. The owner asked fifty thousand dollars for each of the five acres. When they had arrived at the places according to the direction of the brochures, they could not decide which exact piece of land was for sale, as there were no for-sale signs. One five acre land looked far from what was described in the brochure, and the other did have a grand view. The realtor lady had tried several times to contact the sellers' realtor who was also a woman, but failed. The three waited by the road for quite some time. Finally, their realtor reached the seller's realtor. It turned out that the brochure had given a false advertisement for the land. The five acres for sale had no view; the land beside it which was not for sale did have the beautiful view. It must be the one not for sale that had aroused the passionate description of the brochure writer.

After all the running around, checking and waiting, they went to the last site. It was a ten acre land and looked ideal. The land was flat, among those large farm fields and with a vast country view. There was a lane of mature trees at the back of the property, acting as the divider between this land and the neighbour's fields. Through the lane of trees, there was a small dried up brook. Probably in spring, the brook would be alive with water. The owner asked for sixty thousand dollars for the land. Jim and Meilin liked the land, but were very much doubted that the owner had the right to sell it to people who were going to use it for residential purpose. The land was obviously a piece of prime farmland; the crops had just been harvested and the stubs were still in the field.

The whole morning and a large part of the afternoon, the three were either on the road, waiting or checking the land for sale. The distances from one property to another were far and they had covered a large area to find those places. They had missed their lunch. Fortunately, Meilin had brought some chocolate bars with them. They shared the bars with the realtor lady while on the run. After they finished and came back to Wabamun Village, the couple thanked the realtor lady sincerely. Without her, it would be impossible for them to find even one of those places. The couple told the realtor lady that they would think over all the places they had visited, and when they came back from their trip, they would come to see her and give her their decision. In the meantime while they were away, they wished that the realtor lady would keep an eye for them when there were some new properties coming up for sale, the similar ones to those they had already looked at. The realtor lady promised to continue to do her best.

"Hopefully by then, we will have something you will really like," said the lady good-naturedly.

More than a month later when Jim and Meilin returned from their trip, they called the realtor lady immediately after they set up their trailer in the park campground. The attitude of the lady had changed drastically. She did not ask whether they had decided to buy a piece of land they had already looked at or make an appointment to let them see her. She sounded scared of even talking to them. It was quite unusual for a realtor to refuse a promising buyer. There was only one possible explanation: the realtor lady had been reprimanded for treating the couple the same way as her other clients and was told not to sell anything to them. The changed attitude of the realtor did not upset the couple much. By this time now, the couple's wish to buy a piece of land had diminished. From the trip, they could see that wherever they went, the harassment would follow them, and Wabamun area would be no different than their hometown now.

Right now, the couple spent another night at the campground before they moved on to Edmonton. Next morning, the drive was easy. The distance between Wabamun and Edmonton was only about sixty kilometres. The scenery along the four-lane highway was the same. The wavy land was spotted by dairy farms, some residences, grass land, woods, lakes and pounds. They had driven on this piece of highway many times when they lived in Edmonton and had the acreage in Wabamun. The familiar scenery brought back a lot of sweet memories. The couple wondered what the blazes had made them do the things to change their life to the present one. Well, what had been done could not be undone. Laugh or cry; they had to live their life the best they could in whatever present or future conditions would be. Perhaps, it would be better to laugh. Hadn't they have learnt that what kind of life they would live mainly depended on their own mental conditions?

The couple pulled their trailer to a RV park with full service at the skirt of Edmonton. After they set up their trailer on a lot, there was still almost a full day for them to go into the city to check around. Jim unhooked the van from the trailer and they drove into the city. They checked their old houses which they had sold just before the real estate prices soared. The old houses looked the same. The new owners did nothing to improve them. Then they drove around to see the familiar places around. Edmonton seemed still their city. They knew it well and could move around freely and easily.

Edmonton is a beautiful city with many interesting sites and facilities. Though there are a large oil refinery and a cement plant at the city skirt, ample attentions have been paid to keep sufficient green spaces for the residents. The city has the largest urban park area in North America. Its river valley park covers miles of green land along the river and through the city. Fort Edmonton, the start point of the city, has been well kept, renovated and built into one of the largest historical sites in the country. It has been turned into a historic theme park depicting the main historical periods the city had gone through. There are buildings of different time periods with relevant old furnishings. People in old time costumes were strolling in the park, making old time food, doing some smith work and showing the realities of the old time. There were model buildings of the native peoples' encampment, the white people's settlement and the developing business community. The park is quite big. There is farm field with seasonal planting and a small steam-engine train for the visitors to go through the whole park.

Another important attraction in Edmonton is the famous West Edmonton Mall. It is believed to be the largest shopping and entertainment centre in the world. The enclosed mall has three levels of shopping and entertainment areas hosting over 800 stores and services, over 100 eateries, 13 movie theaters, several hotels and nine major entertainment attractions. There are amusement park with all kinds of rides, water park where seals give performances and a genuine large ancient battleship is in display, huge swimming pool with ocean waves, ice palace of a year round skating rink, miniature golf courses and some other recreational facilities; all in the giant mall.

The couple knew well all the attractions in Edmonton. They did not revisit them this time, instead they went to the military base where they lived and Jim worked for over a year. Things changed considerably there. The section of the military base which had been in this city spot had moved out of the city to join the main section outside the city boundary. When this section of the military base was built decades ago, it was outside the city. Now the city had expanded so much; the residential houses and facilities had caught up and passed the military base. The military base had to retreat further away from the city. Perhaps some years later, the city would catch up with that section of the military base again. Where would the army move to then?

The Personnel Married Quarters, including the one where Jim and Meilin had lived in, were vacated by the military families and rented out to civilians. The couple checked with the office in charge of the rental business and found out that the rent was quite reasonable for those small houses or suites in the townhouses. Part of the land of the military base had been sold. A civilian housing project was well on its way. Quite some luxury houses had already been built along some newly paved streets on the land. With the budget cuttings on military spending, the army looked to have become industrious in managing their finances or businesses.

Jim and Meilin checked the military community garden where they had enjoyed their vegetable planting before. The garden was still there, thriving with vegetables and flowers. A large new section of the garden had been added to the old one. It looked that more military personnel and their families had taken to gardening. The visit to the military base did not arouse bad feelings in the couple's minds. The turbulent sad ending of Jim's military career seemed long ago history. Though some memories remained, the couple could review them calmly now and try to filter the bad things out and preserve the good things.

The improvements of human life and human society largely depend on human beings' ability to learn from their past experiences and then move on to a newer and higher level of existence. Human life and human society are multi-faceted. Both negative things and positive things happen in people's lives and in society. People have to be able to learn from them all. However, dwelling in the past mistakes, wrongs or hurts and agitating the scars of old wounds to keep negative emotions will interfere or prevent people from moving forward. Many people have spent their lives in trying to improve human life or human society. They study or teach in the fields of religion, philosophy, history, literature, political science, social science and so on. All those fields are closely related to and reflective of the multiplicity of human life and human society, and they do indeed help. However, they can become theoretic and abstract. When they entirely lose touch of the multi-sided reality, they lose their value and usefulness in human life.

Injustice had happened to Jim at the end of his military career. The couple had fought back and exposed some problems. What had they learnt from this experience? They learnt that life could sometimes throw a hard ball at them. No matter how unexpected, unprepared or unequipped they were, they were forced to face and deal with the seriously difficult situation. They felt great indignations in facing injustice and felt that the situation was entirely out of their control at the time of the happening. Only afterwards they learnt that the most important thing in such a situation was to remain calm and patient; anger and other negative emotions would only complicate things and damage their own health. In those miserable days when they thought that they could no longer go on, they should have seen that no matter how bad things went, all would eventually pass; when they hit the bottom, if they did not give up the fight for their own rights, the only way afterwards would be up. So many years had passed since the grave trial hit them. Now this visit to the military base showed that they had entirely gotten over what had happened to them and had moved on with their life. They no longer felt those negative emotions. After the storm, the sky cleared up. All had passed and what was left had been kept as important memories.

After the visit to the military base, it was lunch time. The couple had their lunch in their favourite Chinese restaurant in Chinatown. Edmonton Chinatown had also some changes. A new gate had been built to give the place a more Chinatown accent. The large grocery store in Chinatown had some Chinese art or culture displays in front the store. There was a new Chinese superstore opened in the Chinatown area. There was also another large Chinese grocery store opened in West Edmonton Mall. Those Chinese stores were full of goods and customers. The couple even spotted some white customers in those Chinese grocery stores. It looked that the Edmonton white people had moved ahead of the Vancouver white people; they became less prejudiced towards different people and different cultures.

The touring of the city was quite pleasant. When the couple came back to the campground, they had a nice shower. The campground had been very much enlarged and improved from the last time they saw it. More lots had been opened for large RVs and the bathroom was upgraded a bit. Jim and Meilin thought that they could have a good night's sleep after running around the whole day. They went to bed early, as tomorrow would be another full driving day for them. They were aiming at crossing the border and entering Saskatchewan tomorrow.

To their dismay, immediately after they went to bed, the noises started. The camping lots were not big here and the RVs were closely lined up. Two middle-aged couples sat around a picnic table right beside their trailer and started chatting loudly in the dusk. The four were like putting on a show, talking and laughing non-stop. With only a few feet of space separating the lots and no trees between them, Jim and Meilin could hear every word of their chatting. Besides the noises, the two couples had started their campfire and the smokes soon filled up Jim and Meilin's small trailer. Sleeping was impossible for them and changing site was also impossible. The campground was fully occupied now. There was no other way but wait patiently until the four got tired of their gossiping and went to bed. The wait was long; the break finally came in the middle of the night. The four stopped chatting and went to their large trailers. After the noises stopped, Jim and Meilin found that the smokes did not dissipate. Jim got up and went out to check their fire pit. He soon came back and got the water basin with some water.

"They left the fire going on. It was mainly the smouldering smoke now. I'm going to put it out," Jim informed Meilin before going out with the water basin.

He poured water on the neighbours' fire pit and made sure that the fire was totally out. After all these frustrations and efforts, the couple finally had a little sleep in the end part of the night. Next morning, they were greeted by a bright sunny day. Even after a bad night's sleep, it seemed not too much problem for them to move on in such a beautiful day. They soon pulled their trailer out of the campground and started driving towards Saskatchewan. In no time, they were on the highway. The highway first ran a distance in the section of the northern part of the city. The traffic on the highway was already heavy in the early morning. When the moving traffic line slowed down, the couple had some leisure to look around. Large billboards along the multi-laned highway were advertising different things. One was especially large and eye-catching; it was voicing the city people's strong objection to the city's intention to sell the municipal airport.

Canada has a history of people struggling against the few rich elites trying to monopolize or control the country's economy. However, those brave fighters seem to have been losing their ground in recent years. Some Canadians seem to have been on a selling mode. The business people have been selling their businesses, the entrepreneurs selling their enterprises, the land owners and farmers selling their land, the sports company even selling their star hockey player who was practically the nation's idol and now the cities selling their airports. A large portion of the country's businesses and industries has already been foreign-owned, mainly American-owned. No matter how large a country is, piece by piece, it can be sold out. When others control the country's economy, they can control the policy making and practically control the country. To keep up with the Joneses and to live an American dream, the Canadians will soon find out what a steep price they will have to pay. By the time when the Canadians sell the last piece of their properties, their national identity will be worth nothing.

The economists are not concerned. According to their economic science, all are well. Yet ordinary people like Jim and Meilin still have concerns for the country's situation. Their concerns mainly come from their life experiences. It seems to them that the public owned facilities privatized or sold to private owners, domestic or foreign, quite often turn out to go downhill for the consumers. The prices tend to go up and services go down. Human beings have the tendency to be greedy. No matter how many efforts some rich people and their servants put on to beautify themselves, the facts often turn out to show their greed. Sooner or later, the orientation of their businesses or corporations turns more to gain profits than to serve. It is understandable that every business has to gain profits to survive, but to serve should still have some weight or priority. Putting the service as the priority of their work, the business owners and their employees will remain decent human beings and their work will be not only building up wealth, but also fulfilling social and moral obligations to their fellow human beings.

Gandhi once said that the whole world would not be enough for one man's greed. He had indeed seen the dark side of human nature. For some people, the more they have, the more they want. Their minds are set on the gaining mode and the whole world indeed will not satisfy them. Money and power tend to corrupt people. To the ordinary people, the economy of the country might be better off controlled by democratic, public and cooperative ways, and not by a few rich elite. Those ways can keep the poor and the ordinary people from being taken advantage of and keep the rich to be morally and spiritually safe from corruption. Though Canada is a country built on the principles of capitalism, it has also been practicing socialism. This has ensured its people to enjoy social welfare, universal health care, unemployment insurance, public pension and old age pension. However, from time to time, this kind of practices has been threatened by some mal-managements, worries about the country's future financial condition or some radical capitalist reformers. Of course, any perceived danger approaching those social benefits will arouse great concerns from the people. No doubt, the Canadians will do their best to protect what they have fought and worked so hard to achieve.

Last night's noises and this morning's billboard's warning of the danger of Edmonton city airport being sold had agitated the couple. They started talking on their way.

"Here too!? They are going to sell the city airport too! What's next?" said Jim with irritation.

"They might probably sell their wives and children next," answered Meilin jokingly.

"For the right amount of money, they might probably do that," Jim agreed with a sneer.

Jim was not a sarcastic person. The couple had suffered the noise attacks from the planes at their home. Jim, even with his soft characters, had been pushed to the limit.

"They might even sell their mother," he added.

"For less money probably," Merlin said more wryly

The couple chatted while trying to get through the heavy traffic and to get onto the highway outside the city. In their present situation, their conversation might be like pouring oil onto a fire, bringing them more troubles. They did not want to care much of the consequence. If they could not talk to themselves, they might as well give up their life entirely.

CHAPTER FOUR

SASKATCHEWAN

The highway through the prairie land was all level and straight, but it was not an easier drive than on the mountainous road. The wind was much stronger on the plain, as there was not much higher ground to block it. It took more energy for the vehicle to move forward against the strong wind. Judging by more fuels their van had consumed, Jim and Meilin concluded that the prairie drive, though safer, was harder for the vehicle. Still, the couple soon crossed the border and went on to the highway of Saskatchewan. Their feelings on the wide open land devoid of high mountains were different. The sky seemed closer to the ground, but the mind was more elevated, purged of trifling thoughts and becoming more open and natural. Though the highway was straight and reaching far to the horizon, the land along the road was not at all flat. The earth waved gently with ups and downs; a vast view of the prairie rolling land could only be achieved on a higher ground which was hard to find. Along the highway, there were hardly large bodies of water to be seen.

However, Saskatchewan is known for its large number of lakes. Eons ago, a large part of Saskatchewan was the bottom of the sea. During the last Ice Age, the whole province was covered by glaciers. Today, this province and Alberta are the only two provinces of this country, which have no border touching the salt water of an ocean. After the glaciers gone, the land had been strewn with boulders and sills that had been carried here by ice. When large areas of lakes dried up, they became good farmland. Still the drainage of the land today is not that good. Many lakes don't drain and large area of the prairie land is rather dry and some sand dunes remained.

More than one third of Saskatchewan is within the Canadian Shield, a vast hard ancient rock terrain that has covered almost half of Canada. The rocky shield is rich in minerals, but impossible for agriculture. The shield areas in Saskatchewan have numerous deep swamps and bogs; mining is very difficult. Still, Saskatchewan is the province next to Alberta that produces the most petroleum in the country and has a developed potash industry. It has the most deposits of potash in the world and produces one quarter of world's potash. Its uranium, other mineral and non-metallic mineral productions have been up in recent years. Yet Saskatchewan is mainly an agriculture province. Its vast prairie farmland has been wheat fields since the start of the European settlements. The province is one of the largest wheat growers and exporters of the world. With the world's situation changing more towards industrialization or high-tech industries, agriculture cannot bring great fortune. Saskatchewan is not among the rich provinces of Canada. The province has putting quite some efforts to diversify in recent years. The economical developments have started putting more stress on mining industries

Canadians owe the province of Saskatchewan for some good socialistic policies. In 1923, Saskatchewan farmers were the first in North America to form the largest cooperative organization, the wheat pool, to stabilize wheat prices by collective selling and planned marketing. The organization had protected a large number of farmers' livelihood and profits. This cooperative system had then been extended to dairy, livestock and poultry productions. When the economy was doing well, the province went further in carrying out socialistic measures. Saskatchewan is the first province that has provided free hospital care, social welfare and quite some other social benefits to its citizens. Canadian universal healthcare, pension plan and other social welfare have been modeled from Saskatchewan's early socialistic system. However, for a good system to remain to be a good system, it depends on not only its establishment, but also on its management and development. Like everything else in the world, the Canadian good socialistic system needs to develop and renew with different times and different situations. Otherwise, a good system can become stagnant, obsolete and problematic. The management of the health-care system needs to improve. New methods, rules or principles have to come up to date to ensure that the system runs more smoothly and more efficiently. The Canadians have been worried whether their good system of health-care and pension plan can last, as the cost has gone out of control. Beefing up the management and attending to the development, the system should be running better and last as long as people wish it to last. Neglecting the management and the development, the system can deteriorate and collapse. The Canadian government and all levels of administrations have a rather difficult task to make sure that the system functions in a healthy good condition and to have a long life span for the future generations.

Saskatchewan is a province that had gone through an important historical event of this country. The well-known Métis rebellion had happened in this province in 1885 when Canada was just a newborn baby. Métis are a people of mixed blood of natives and whites. They were started by the early European fur traders and settlers who had married the local native women. Historians have written and talked a lot about the Métis rebellion with different views and different opinions. Most of them agree that the cause of this rebellion is mainly the government's neglect and indifference to the grievances of the Métis and the native peoples. Those grievances were largely about the land issues. The extensive white people's settlements had turned large areas of the prairie land into farm fields. The growing farmland had encroached on the hunting grounds and depleted the games of the native peoples and the Métis. Then the reroute of the trans-Canada railway was far away from the land of the native peoples and the Métis, which rendered it impossible for them to develop and prosper. Also, a few years later after the native peoples signed some treaties with the government, the buffalos, their main food source, disappeared. The government did not keep their promise which was signed in the treaty to help the starving native peoples with food. In addition to these, the Indian commissioner appointed by the government dispersed the large concentrated native residences into smaller communities, afraid that the native peoples' gathering together would pose threats towards the whites. This was also breaking the treaty that gave the native peoples the right to establish their reserves.

Years before the rebellion became the armed fights in 1885, the rebellious moods and movements had already begun. In the beginning, it was in a much larger scale. The historians believe that they were the struggles between the North-West and the central Canada, the native peoples and the whites, the French Canadians and the English Canadians and the Protestants and the Catholics. When the struggles were becoming more serious, the white settlers in the North-West, who had been in the fight from the start, dropped out, and then the Catholic clergy who had been supportive to the Métis and the North-West people withdrew their support. In the end, the armed fighting was carried out only by the Métis and the native peoples. Their leader was Louis Riel, a Métis of French native descent.

This civil war in Canadian history was played out on the prairie land of Saskatchewan. It did not last long. The government dispatched the army through the newly built trans-Canada railway and defeated Riel's army. But the real reason for this war to have ended so fast was that the native peoples had kept their promise in the treaty that they would not rise up in arms against Canada. There was only four percent of the native peoples joined the armed fights and the two native leaders in the rebellion gave themselves up in the end. If the natives had broken their promise in the treaty, the war would have turned into a guerrilla war and lasted much longer.

After the war, the punishment to the natives was much more severe than to the Métis. Forty-four of the native fighters were executed by hanging. The leader, Louis Riel, was also sentenced to death by hanging. In spite of many French Canadians, some Americans, British and French people voicing strong objections to Louis Riel's death sentence, the leader was executed and became a martyr in Canadian history. The Canadian government had learnt a lesson from this early event. Immediately after the war, the government shipped sufficient food to the starving native peoples in the famine areas. Canada has learnt a lesson from this event; the country has no capital punishment today.

Jim and Meilin were traveling in this prairie province, very peaceful now. It was hard for them to imagine the battles that had been fought on this rolling land more than a century ago. What they saw was the endless grain fields. The only thing breaking the vast flatness of the landscape was an occasional tall grain-elevator that completed the prairie scenery. Further into this land, the couple could see some large black cylindrical containers standing here and there in the fields. Most probably, they contained petroleum. It looked that the development of petroleum industry in this province was well on the way.

The strenuous pulling by the engine against the strong wind soon resulted in the drain of the fuel. The couple were worried whether they could reach a gas station before they were totally out of gas. The gas stations seemed too sparsely located along the highway on this vast prairie land. Luckily, when the needle of the fuel indicator dropped dangerously low in the red area, a gas station and a small village appeared in view. The couple heaved a relief, feeling fortunate. If they were stranded on this long stretch of highway, there was no telling how long they had to wait before being rescued.

While gassing up their van, the couple found that the protective metal flap over the front window of their trailer was almost torn off by the strong wind. They had to slap themselves, as they had forgotten to close that flap when they started this morning. Now they had to repair it before they could move on. It took some time for the couple to straighten the bent metal and force the flap to close. This was the best they could do now; a good repair had to wait until they were home.

After the couple left the gas station and went on their way, they noticed that they got company. The traffic on the long stretch of highway was light. Occasionally they would come across some other vehicles. A companion traveller would of course have all their attention. A small man dressed in red was riding a small red scooter type motorcycle in the ditch between the four-lane highway. He must have come out from the village at the time when the couple left the gas station to get on the highway again. It would be impossible for someone to last on such a long drag of highway by means of a scooter, if he did not come from nearby. The land was dry and the ditch was fairly bare of grass or plants; there was no problem to ride a scooter, a motorcycle or even a car in it. The man rode on his red scooter in a high speed. The tiny machine gave out a loud buzzing noise and had a tail of dust behind it. For quite some distance, the man and his tiny loud scooter were accompanying Jim and Meilin, sometimes a little ahead and sometimes a little behind. It looked quite comic and gave the couple a break on the monotonous long drive.

In the couple's present situation, it was highly possible that the man was sent out to ridicule or humiliate them. His red costume and tiny red scooter, of course, were the indication of the couple, red, tiny and loud. Unfortunately, the show only generated a hearty laugh and not hurt feelings from the couple. Nonetheless, the couple had not expected that this kind of show would be put on in Saskatchewan. Of all the provinces, Saskatchewan should be the last to have much qualms or hard feelings towards the communists. During the 1960s, the province's economy was in a dire situation. The price of the wheat was so low; large quantities of wheat of the province could not be sold. Fortunately, China and some other communist countries bought large volumes of wheat from the province at a fair price. At that time, China was in a bad situation, a large famine was broken out from the natural disaster of three years continued drought. Saskatchewan's wheat had saved quite some lives of the starving people in China, and in the meantime, the trade with the communist countries had saved Saskatchewan's economy.

The world situation is such: if countries are friendly to and help each other, all the peoples will benefit and the world will be more peaceful; if the countries are hostile and bear hatred to each other, all the peoples will suffer and the world will experience more disturbances and conflicts. Politics should be very much secondary in the relationships between countries. Human beings are all the same everywhere; their welfare and safety should come first before all the political games. Let the big boys play their games, but the food and shelters of the peoples should be much more important than their games and should never be allowed to be harmed or destroyed by their games.

The man and his tiny scooter ran a long while beside the couple's vehicles. Finally, they ran out of steam and dropped out; probably the scooter was out of gas or battery power. If the man's scooter was totally out of power, he would have a long way to walk back to the village. Further on to another populated place, the distance would be even greater for him. Along the prairie highway, there are mostly vast farm fields and the farm houses were few. As for Jim and Meilin, they returned to the long unaccompanied drive and started talking about their next camping site. By now, they knew that wherever they went, the harassing shows and noises might come to them. They decided that their next camping site should be the one most convenient for them to reach. They were not going to spend efforts to find a campground any more. If they could camp on some parking lot of some big store near the highway, they would be happy. They had seen some large RVs camped on some Walmart parking lots. If other people with fancy RVs could do it, they should have no problem to do it too.

The fees for camping had increased considerably in recent years. Years ago, the couple had paid six dollars per night to camp in the national or provincial parks. Now they had to pay from over twenty to over thirty dollars per night for the same camping sites in those parks. To stay in the RV Parks with full services, the fees would be over thirty dollars and a few places even reached forty to over fifty dollars per night. On a cross-country journey, the cost for camping was quite high for the couple. If they had to spend so much money for their nights on campgrounds, they expected that their money be well spent and they could get some decent rest and sleep. Now this seemed out of their reach. The reality was that they were spending good money to receive harassment on some of those campgrounds. They knew that they could very well be harassed when they camped on some stores' parking lots or some other places, but they would at least not have to pay for them.

Not very far into their cross-country trip, the couple had realized that the trip was going to be much more costly than they had anticipated. Not only the camping fees, but also the cost of the fuel for their vehicle was very high. They would spend from one hundred to two hundred dollars on fuels per day, according to the distances they drove and the gas stations they happened to visit. Some places had a bit lower prices for gas and some had higher prices. All the prices had passed a dollar per litre and some could go as high as a dollar and thirty or forty cents per litre. The couple had been living a very thrift life through all those years. After Jim was released from the military, in order to survive, they had to be very careful in spending every penny. Because of their frugal habit, they had weathered the most difficult financial crises in their married life. Now Jim had gained a decent pension and they could afford such a long trip. Still, every sense from their old frugal habit was against large spending and especially when the spending did not get them the value which was due to them. Naturally, their thoughts would turn to alternative ways to save money on this cross-country trip and especially the ways that might also beat the harassment.

In the afternoon of this day's travel, the couple reached Battleford. Battleford is a small city, one of the oldest communities in Saskatchewan. It had been the capital of the Northwest Territories in the old time when Saskatchewan was not separated from the territories to become a province. When the couple were approaching the city skirt, they were happy to spot a Walmart not far from the highway. They decided to camp on the store's parking lot for the night. After a few minutes of drive on a side road away from the highway, they pulled their trailer into the large parking lot of Walmart. This Walmart was a little way from the small city. Almost all around it were low hills with gentle round tops. The land was covered with green grass and small bushes; large trees were hard to be spotted. The couple parked their van and trailer at the edge of the parking lot where few customers parked their vehicles.

When they got out of their van, they heaved a breath of relief from the strenuous long drive. The gentle landscape soothed their minds and they felt that the prairie view was taking a nice hold of their imagination. Walking around the parking lot and looking at the natural scenery, they could picture some scenes of a battle that had gone on in this place in the old time. They could see in their mind's eye some fighters on horseback suddenly appearing on top of those round hills. Battleford, though not the major battle fields in the Métis rebellion like some other places close by, had experienced the war. Riel's army had fought here and the place was taken over by the official army in the early stage. A major battle ground had been in Fort Battleford about forty kilometers away from here, where the headquarters of North West Mounted Police was established in 1876 to enforce law and order. Today Fort Battleford is a national historical site and visitors can have guided tours around the place to experience history.

After stretching themselves and relaxing for a while, the couple stabilized their trailer and got ready for the night's stay. The place was clean and had the beautiful prairie view, looking absolutely ideal for camping. Satisfied with the settlement, the couple went to the Walmart. The advantage of camping at Walmart was that they could do some shopping and use the washroom of the store. They had a nice walk in the store and bought some drinking water, food and snacks. When they were leaving the store with the things they bought, a funny scene was playing out at the store entrance. A boy about nine or ten years of age triggered the alarm system at the doorway. The alarm was beeping so loud and causing quite a few customers to focus their attentions on the boy. The security guy, an old gentleman, came up and searched him with a hand-detector. The boy had about a dozen of small toys and some other knick-knacks hiding under his T-shirt. The customers around could not help laughing. What was the silly boy thinking of? Did he really think that he could hide those things under his T-shirt and take them out of the store?

All this time, the old security man looked strict and performed his duty without any smile. His hand-detector beeped wildly all over the boy. The boy smiled and gave up all the things he took. He looked not at all silly or dumb, but quite smart. There was no shame or any other expressions on the boy's face; the whole thing seemed just a show from him. This had put some suspicion in the couple's minds. Ever since the harassment started on them, they had experienced many absurd dumb shows put on in the public places where they happened to be. Whether those shows were put on deliberately to attack, humiliate, ridicule or degrade them or the coloured people, they had never paid too much attention to them. They knew if they felt hurt or upset, the people behind those stupid shows won. They had long learnt to brush those ridiculous dumb things off like the unpleasant dirt. Because of their outspokenness at their own home, the couple had suffered the worst insinuations and slanders aiming at smudging them. They had gone through fire and high water and were able to face anything now. If this show of the boy shoplifting was another of those dumb shows instigated by the harassers for the couple to see, they did not even bother to think about what it meant. They had a good laugh like the other customers and enjoyed the show.

Jim might have seen a few shoplifters being caught in his life. Meilin had been in Canada for more than twenty years. This was the first time that she had seen somebody being caught for shoplifting. She had always been very much impressed by the Canadian shopping system. In stores, all the goods were displayed on the shelves along some aisles. Customers could check them, pick them and bring them in their carts to pay at the cashers' counters in the front of the stores. This kind of shopping system could be possible only in the condition that the general public were honest decent human beings and stealing was a rare happening. Some shops and stores had complained about shoplifting problems, but they were not at all a serious general problem, otherwise, during the more than twenty years of life here, Meilin could have seen quite a few of the shows as this one put on by the boy.

Coming back to their trailer, the couple soon started to cook their supper. Though they were tired, they would rather cook in the trailer instead of going to the restaurant. Whether it was because home cooking could save money or the food could be more nutritious and less fatty, they could not decide, but most of time they cooked their own food. Once in a while, a restaurant meal was still a treat to them and especially to Jim who had strong attachment to restaurant food. After supper, the couple had a walk around the parking lot and then came back to the trailer to relax with some music. Then they turned on the radio, curious about what the local station was offering. They got a local native peoples' radio station. Two reporters, a male and a female, were discussing the provincial development in uranium mining. Their voices were crisp clear. There was plenty of confidence and assurance in their tone. It looked that the native peoples here had assumed their identity as the masters of the land. They not only were concerned about, but also knew their duty and responsibility to the development and prosperity of this place they had called home for thousands of years. It was quite clear that they were aware that Canada's well-being was their own well-being.

Canada's treatment towards her aboriginal peoples has been steadily improving, but there are still a lot of things to be done. Quite some white folks still consider that the native peoples are not up to their level and not their equals. Because of their improved conditions, the native peoples, on the other hand, are having more confidence in themselves and want to be an equal partner in all aspects of the country. They have placed a challenge to the white folks to come up to their mental level and to accept them as equal partners of this land.

Over the radio, after the two reporters talked for a while, some native country singers took over. Both the male and female singers sang superbly. The music, the lyrics and the way the singers were handling the art with their skills and emotions were all of high quality. Those singers could very well compete with and surpass quite some other singers in the country.

In judging the civilization level of a nation, its culture should be the first and most important yardstick. Contrary to some people's views that the native peoples are below them, the first nations are well civilized. For thousands of years, the native peoples have developed their own unique ways to live with their own inner beings and the natural world. Their intelligence has developed in an unique way. Putting down the misconceptions and silly pride, other peoples can very well learn something from the native peoples. The environmental problems the world is increasingly facing show that the native peoples are more civilized and compatible with the natural world. It is clear now that it is not for the native peoples to join up the mad race in accumulating wealth and power, but for other peoples to learn something from the native peoples to live a more natural, environmentally friendly and not too intrusive life with Mother Nature. Economic developments will undoubtedly go on, but they should be carried out with a view of protecting the natural environment and the sustainability of the natural resources. Only in this way, can the human race and the planet have the chance to last for a much longer time.

Jim and Meilin had a good night's sleep on the parking lot. The whole parking lot was almost deserted at night. Besides their vehicles, there were a few cars parked at the back of the parking lot. Those cars must belong to the Walmart workers who were on night shift. There were also two other RVs took the advantage of camping on this parking lot. They had parked in the front part of the parking lot, far away from the couple's trailer. It was a quiet night for the couple. Since they had started the trip, quiet nights were hard to come by; they very much appreciated the ones that gave them a decent sleep.

Next day, they drove only a short distance to reach Saskatoon, a big city in Saskatchewan. Regina, not Saskatoon, is the capital of this province. In 1883, the capital of Northwest Territories had moved from Battleford to Regina. In 1905 when Saskatchewan became a province, Regina was chosen as its capital. Regina is a Latin word for queen. The name was given by a governor general's wife who was the daughter of Queen Victoria. Obviously the city name was chosen to honor the princess' mother, Queen Victoria. Jim and Meilin had visited Regina before and were impressed by the city's museums, galleries and other government and culture facilities. Somehow, what had retained most prominently in their memory was a geese sculpture in the city centre. A large white sculpture of several geese stood high in a city centre street. The wings of the geese were spreading wide, showing that they were soaring into the sky. The gentle curves of the geese and their wings were full of elegance and beauty. The pure white colour and the lively flying motion of the birds had enhanced the artistic power to trigger imaginations of all that were good, pure and free in nature. After so many years, the couple could still summon up the beautiful image of this geese sculpture from their memory whenever they thought of Regina. On this cross-country trip however, the couple decided to go through Saskatoon, as it was on the route they were presently taking. They wanted to spend some time touring Saskatoon, the largest city of this province. They had passed by this city before, but never visited it.

The couple found a campground at the city skirt and set up their trailer. They chose this campground, because there was an important first nation's park nearby. Wanuskewin Heritage Park is about ten kilometers away from the campground. It is a large theme park that shows the history, culture and life of the native peoples of the northern plains. Long before they reached Saskatchewan, the couple had already decided to visit this theme park. After they settled on the campground, they went to the camp office for the registration and some information about Wanuskewin Heritage Park. They were informed that the park was closed for renovation. It was a pity. The couple had anticipated to see the more than 6,000 years of history of the native peoples on the northern plains, how they used the land, their summer and winter campsites, their arrangement of medicine wheel by some boulder alignment, their bison hunting skills and so on. Well, the couple could do nothing about this disappointment. The campground looked peaceful. They knew that if they were going to tour Saskatoon, they had to camp on the campground anyway. They had to unhook their van from the trailer to tour the city and could not leave their trailer sitting on some store's parking lot and wander away to enjoy themselves. They were afraid that when they came back, their trailer might not be there waiting for them.

After checking the information in a tour book, the couple chose some spots which looked interesting for them to visit in Saskatoon. Next morning, they drove into the city and started the tour early. The size of Saskatoon cannot compare with that of the mega cities in Canada, but it is fairly large. Saskatoon is known as a city of bridges. There are seven bridges over the South Saskatchewan River, connecting the two parts of the city. To start their tour, the couple first dropped into a large grocery store that happened on their way. For one thing, they would like to compare the prices of food here with the prices of other places and especially their own hometown. The Superstore they went in looked the same, large and full of goods. The couple soon found that the prices of food here were relatively the same as those in their home city. The difference here seemed that there were rarely coloured people around. They did not see any coloured people working as clerks in the store, only one or two coloured people as customers. In the streets of the city too, they spotted only a few coloured people. From news reports, the couple got to know that new immigrants had started choosing Saskatchewan among some other provinces to settle down now. Before, the newcomers' favourite choices were large cities in Ontario, Quebec and British Columbia. New immigrants coming to this country nowadays were mostly coloured people. If the immigration trend was like the reporters' information over TV, the couple did not see much of a reality here. Perhaps, it would still need some time to show the result of the trend, or the province was still not prosperous enough to attract large quantities of immigrants.

The large size and prosperity of a city are normally resulted from the large injection of immigrants and emigrants. The rich provinces of the country, such as Ontario, Quebec, Alberta and British Columbia, all have a large immigrants' population. The large cities of those rich provinces have gotten so big and so prosperous because of the immigrants through different times and they are continuingly to be benefited by the inflow of newly arrived immigrants. The country is built by the immigrants coming here in different times. The old established citizens have to see that accepting the newcomers as equal citizens and giving them opportunities to use their strength and skills will only benefit and strengthen their cities, provinces and the whole country. For the newcomers, with the support and help of the old established citizens, they can fully develop their potentials and become strong contributors to the constructions and developments of the cities, the provinces and the country. Racial discrimination and exclusiveness towards the newcomers will only damage the country.

After leaving the store, the couple went to have a look at the University of Saskatchewan. This university is known for its strong science and agriculture faculties. On campus, there is a Diefenbaker center hosting displays about this Canada's 13th prime minister. The couple drove around the campus twice and could not find a parking space. Having difficulty in finding parking space was normal on any university campus. It looked that University of Saskatchewan was of no exception. The couple had a look at the university while driving through. Quite some large buildings were in pinkish earthen colour, roundly rather than angularly shaped. There were sufficient green lawns. The campus gave them the impression of a fairly new university. As they could not find a place to park, they could not see much. After the two driving through rounds, they left the campus.

The next place the couple headed for was a city park called Saskatchewan Forestry Farm Park and Zoo. They thought that the park must be featuring farms and they had never seen a farm park before. But after they arrived at the park and toured around, they found that it was just like any other parks in any other cities. The landscape did not give much indication of a farm or a forest. However, a large building in the park, which hosted a zoo, looked as a big barn. This perhaps was the reason for the name of Farm Park. The couple walked on the path that led to some flower gardens and a pond. The gardens were beautiful and well cared for. There was a special place for the newlyweds to have their pictures taken. Not long after they had arrived at the park, a gardener working in the park told them that there was a curiosity in the park. A white robin had stayed in a certain spot of the park and never left. Jim and Meiin had never seen a white robin before. They tracked down the place where the white robin frequented. Sure enough, they spotted the white robin. The bird had the same feature as a robin, but its feather was pure white. After watching the bird for a while, they noticed that the bird indeed stayed close to a certain spot and would not fly far off. The place happened to be by a rose garden which was named after somebody called Robin. The person being honoured seemed to be a famous horticulturist. Judging by the gardener's mysterious tone when he described the bird, the couple realized that people here must be thinking that the soul of the honoured person called Robin had gone to this white robin bird or he had reincarnated into the bird. Anyway, the strange white robin that would never leave the beloved garden must have generated quite some imagination and thinking.

Gardening is a human pleasure rarely surpassed by other human pleasures. It is a pure pastime or endeavour that can indeed engage the gardeners in a way that is away from all the worldly struggles. In the Bible, the genesis states that God had put Adam and Eve, the first created humans, in a garden to keep them pure and free from corruptions. Of course, the gardening mentioned here is not profit generating or livelihood maintaining but confined to beautifying the people's living surroundings, giving esthetic feelings and purifying minds and spirits. Watching plants growing and flowers budding and blossoming can indeed give the gardeners the experience of a heavenly pleasure. No wonder that some people will imagine or believe that some souls might be lingering on in their beloved gardens even after their bodies have left this world.

It did not take long for the couple to check out the whole park. When they were leaving the park, it was still morning. While they were driving away from the parking lot, their van suddenly started sounding in a serious problem. The wheel on the driver's side gave out loud clanking noises. This looked strangely suspicious and alarming. When they came into the park, their van was running quietly and smoothly. Now when they were leaving, it sounded like that it was at its last leg and could fall apart at any moment. The park was in the suburb of the city. The couple decided not to call a tow-truck. Gingerly, they drove the clanking van with lots of worries to a busy city street and found an auto repair shop. They waited quite some time for the mechanic to find out what was wrong with the van. The receptionist, a man in his fifties, finally got the result and informed them.

"The cap of the wheel's boot section had almost fallen off. The mechanic who replaced the boot for you before did not put the cap on right," said the man.

This finding had lessened some suspicion in the couple's minds. All the way while they were driving to find the auto shop, they thought that somebody had done damages to their van while they were away in the gardens. They had heard that the crime rate in Saskatchewan was the highest in the country. Now the mechanic's finding about the problem of their van had cleared up some of their suspicion, as they did have the boot of that wheel changed not long ago. That boot was deliberately damaged by the mechanic in an auto shop in their hometown, when he was doing some other work for their van at that time. The couple had found out the damage immediately and had that auto shop replaced the boot. It looked that the wanton mechanic might have still done the shady trick when he was replacing the boot.

Ever since the harassment started on the couple, they had lost almost everything in living a peaceful life. They had lost their privacy entirely and were harassed at home or anywhere they went. They had lost their quality healthcare and auto-care. The harassers needed only to make a few phone calls to have people do damages to them wherever they were. The couple, on the other hand, could not figure out clearly what kind devils were behind and pulling the strings of the people and why so many people would even break the laws to do their biddings.

Jim and Meilin went to the auto repair shop before lunch. They had brought some food with them when they started this morning. At noon, they had a simple lunch from their carry-on bag in the waiting room. Then they y waited and waited for the whole afternoon, reading every piece of magazines in the waiting room and checking every vehicle for sale on the parking lot of the place. The auto repair shop was part of a rather large auto dealership. The long building had the sales department in the front section and the parts and service department at the back. While they were waiting, a few other customers had come and gone. They were the first here in the morning and by half past five in the afternoon, they were the only ones left still waiting in the waiting room. They had no heart to walk into the street to kill time, thinking that the van might be ready while they were gone. Finally, their van was ready just before the shop was going to close for the day. They were informed that the shop had found a second-hand part to put on for their van and the cost of the one hundred and sixty some dollars was a cheap price for them.

This kind of long waiting to be served in an auto repair shop and to be served as the last customer was a norm for the couple now. They had to be satisfied that they had been served at all and to be grateful if there was no more new damages done to their vehicle. From this and other kinds of services they received, the couple could well perceive the hostilities and hatred towards them. All these happenings were the result that they had lost their privacy and people could hear their normal conversations and complaints in their daily life and the criticisms in Meilin's writing. In the society, what the general population had daily talked and complained about were in fact much worse than the couple had done or were doing. This kind of hostilities and hatred coming onto them had to be because Meilin was of Chinese origin and they were an interracial couple. The Canadians had a much lower tolerance ratio towards the complaints coming from the coloured people. To them, the coloured people should be greatly grateful for being allowed into this country and they should keep quiet and do the works that the whites would not like to do. The tolerance of seeing the coloured people in Canada was rising, but hearing from them remained highly offensive to some white people. Therefore, to some whites, the outspoken couple, instead of being the victims of discrimination and persecution, who had never asked for or had any control of the situation, had crossed all the lines set up by the society for the type of people like them, and they should be punished, put down or put away from the society in whatever way they could manage.

As for the couple, they were greatly infuriated by the situation. Now the incident in Saskatoon disturbed their peace of mind in touring the city and triggered fresh anger. They believed that their suspicion about the damages done to their vehicle bore evidence that the treatment they had received from different service providers had crossed the lines set up by the country's law that no service provider should refuse or give altered services to any customer of different colour, culture, creed or religion. However, the couple could not do much, as most of the maltreatments were made as if they were normal happenings. Most ground level service people normally had no idea what was happening to this couple; they gave their altered services to the couple under orders and served the couple or did something to the couple as they were told to do. In such circumstances, what the couple could do was only to defy the hostile force by keeping on doing what they had always been doing, saying whatever they liked to say and living their life as they had always lived. What had happened to their van in Saskatoon might be caused by the damages done by the mechanic in their hometown; it might also be caused by vandalism in the Farm Park; or it might just be a normal mechanic failure of their vehicle. However, the couple could no longer cheat themselves by thinking that what had happened in the auto repair shop was also a normal happening, as this kind of shitty tricks of delaying serving them to the last minute had been pulled on them many times now.

The incident with their van had used up the larger part of their day. The couple had planned to visit the city's library where there was a history room displaying more than 6,000 years' history of this city and Saskatchewan province. After the incident, they had lost interest. Next day, they got up early and headed for Manitoba, the next province on their way. The visit to Saskatoon was not satisfactory. They did not see much

CHAPTER FIVE

MANITOBA

It took some time for the couple to reach the border of Manitoba. After entering the province of Manitoba, the scenery changed. The fields looked greener and the hills taller. Though it was still hard to call those hills mountains, they were bigger and higher than those low hills in Saskatchewan. The couple soon noticed what made this province greener; there were much more water in Manitoba. Large rivers could be spotted along the highway. Because of the taller hills, the wind here was not as strong as in Saskatchewan. The climate in this province must be warmer than that of Saskatchewan. With warmer climate, more water and less wind, the planting in the fields here looked ahead of Saskatchewan.

Manitoba is the most eastern one of the three prairie provinces. Though there are quite some geographic similarities between Manitoba and Saskatchewan, there are some important differences. Manitoba is indeed endowed with a better climate. It does have more rainfalls each year and a longer planting season than Saskatchewan. The three prairie provinces all share some fertile lands of black soil which are ideal for farming. Manitoba, with its wet condition, has maintained well the fertile lands. Saskatchewan, however, with the dry condition, has lost some of the fertile lands through the years; strong wind has swept away the dried soil and turned some fertile farm fields into barren lands. Agriculture has considerable weight in the economy of Manitoba. In the modern time, the province is diversified with its farming endeavours. Besides wheat, other grains and plants are grown. Quite some efforts have been put on cattle ranching, dairying and poultry production. With more rivers flowing and connected with large lakes, Manitoba has a developed hydroelectricity industry. It can not only satisfy the needs of the province, but also export electricity to the United States. Manitoba had started its economy with fishery and fur trade in the old days. It has one of the largest fresh-water fisheries in the world.

Part of Manitoba's northeast border is connected with the Hudson Bay. In 1610, Henry Hudson discovered the bay which was later named after him. But the fur trade had been started by two French fur traders when they found the Hudson Bay route to the interior fur trading country. This finding had started the Hudson's Bay Company, a British trading company. In 1670, Hudson's Bay Company was granted trading rights on all the waters that ran into Hudson Bay. The commercial activities, mainly fur trade, started rolling from the trading posts along the bay. First, there were small trades between the white fur traders and the aboriginal peoples. Gradually, it developed into a gigantic scale of trading and spread all over North America. The initial goal of the Hudson's Bay Company was to obtain furs from North America. The business went very well. The company then grew into a large stock company in the world. Its business soon expanded from trading to other things such as retail and department stores reaching into many countries of the world. The fortune and the commercial power of this gigantic company had lasted for two hundred years.

Hudson's Bay Company had very much been a part of Canadian history and life in the early days. The Company had controlled the fur trade and owned large areas of land along the Hudson Bay for almost two centuries. In 1868, to comply with the Rupert's Land Act, the Hudson's Bay Company transferred all its land and exclusive trading rights to the Dominion of Canada for 300.000 pounds. In 1931, all the Company's business affairs in Canada had been brought under the control of the Canadian Committee at Winnipeg, the capital city of Manitoba.

When Manitoba's commercial activities started with the fur trade of the Hudson's Bay Company, the large trading empire built its first retail store in Winnipeg. With the developments along the history and after the commercial power of the Company being transferred to Canada, Winnipeg has remained to be the trading and financial centre for the prairies. In those early days, the province of Manitoba had generated wealth and power from the fur trade and all other related businesses. Even after the fur trade had gone; its glory and generated wealth had left a shinning mark on Manitoba. As a merchant province, Manitoba was much richer than the farmer province Saskatchewan from the start. Today with the well developed hydroelectricity, manufacturing and mining industries, Manitoba has managed to remain ahead. The Manitobans are very much affected by the wealth and power. They are extremely proud, territorial and fiercely protective of their provincial rights.

The Manitobans regard Louise Riel as the father of their province. This might be partially the result of Riel's famous speech addressing the jury who sentenced him to die. He proclaimed, "I know that through the grace of God I am the founder of Manitoba...."

However, the main reason was that under the leadership of Louise Riel, Manitoba had already been formed as an independent colony before 1870 when Canada confirmed its provincial status by the Manitoba

Act. The early Manitoba was centred on the Red River valley. In the early 19th century, Manitoba was mainly resided by the Métis and the native peoples. The Métis of five thousand strong with bilingual culture and centred at Fort Garry on the Red River had been used to the rule of Hudson's Bay Company and had a good economy based on annual buffalo hunting and a nearly self-sufficient agriculture. Before the second Métis rebellion in 1885, Riel had led the people of Manitoba to form their own state. This first rebellion had met strong resistance from some other settlers and Ontarians. By the time when the government sent a military expedition to crush the rebellion, it was already over. Riel fled the country until he was called back for the second rebellion. For this first rebellion, the government of Canada had granted the rebels most of their demands. Among other things, Manitoba was guaranteed to have the equality of both English and French as official languages and the equalities for both Protestant and Catholic schools. The main grievances of the Manitobans then were the unfair freight rates for shipping goods through the railway system. The fights had also ended in the Manitobans' victory. The federal government had adjusted the rates to be fair to the province. These probably have been the reasons that the Manitobans have honoured Riel. These too have started the Manitobans' fighting spirits for their provincial rights and benefits.

Canada has ten strong provinces. Regionalism sometimes runs high. Each province is concerned whether the province has gotten the fair share of benefits and responsibilities of the country. There is nothing wrong for the provinces to want fair treatments from the federal government. Only those fights should not be too selfish and too extreme. It is reasonable to negotiate with the federal government for the benefits of the provinces, but unreasonable to run the federal government ragged and unable to decide which province to please. The provinces should help each other and put the country in an import position. Like the ten fingers, if all the fingers separate and only protect themselves, the hands will be weakened and become useless; if all the fingers work cooperatively together, the hands can then be strong, useful and able to accomplish endless things.

In recent years, there is a foul wind blowing with the sentiments of provincial rights. Some shady organizations or racist groups have used the banner of fighting for the provincial rights and benefits to gain quite some people and even high rank provincial politicians to their side. This kind of shady people have worked mainly for their own gains. They promote racial discrimination against the coloured citizens and immigrants, claiming that it is not good or beneficial for their particular province to have the inflow of coloured people. Their damaging activities under the banners of fighting for the provincial rights have created quite some hostilities and even hatred towards the coloured Canadians. They can instigate barriers or exclusive policies against the country's coloured people. This kind of separating people according to their colours and preventing the established whites from embracing the coloured people as equal citizens will only do great damages to the provinces politically and economically. The extreme provincial rights they have promoted will eventually weaken and do great damages to the country. People have to see that the efforts of those shady organizations or racist groups under the banner of provincial rights are for their own gains only. Manitoba has suffered from this foul wind. The racial discrimination in this province is rather severe. With this foul wind, the crime rate in this province has dramatically risen in recent years and it has surpassed that in Saskatchewan. Winnipeg today has become the murder capital of the country.

Manitoba is located at the very centre of Canada. Winnipeg is the transportation, commercial and industrial center of the province and a very important gate city connecting the country's west and east. The raw goods of the west and the manufactured goods of the east all go through this city to be distributed over the country. Canadians cannot afford to let things go wrong with this province.

The population of this province has dramatically increased since the inflow of the immigrants formed by Scottish peasants in the 1860s. The early farmer settlers had met armed resistance of the trappers and voyagers. However, more European immigrants came in the later years to settle down on the fertile lands along the rivers. They had pushed agriculture on this land to the prosperous height. Manitoba has known traditionally for its high quality wheat. Winnipeg had been the heart and the commercial centre of the country in the old days. Important federal government offices had stationed in Winnipeg. Even today, after the power of the country has shifted to Ontario, the headquarters of Revenue Canada is still located in Winnipeg. Manitoba is the traditional place to take control of the things involving with money. Manitobans are well aware of this situation and used to this sense of power. There are plenty of efforts made to direct this sense of power to positive ways and to lead the Manitobans to be more tolerant and inclusive to different people who have come to this province in different times. Judging by the rise of the crime rate in this province, those efforts have been hard uphill battles.

Driving on the highway of Manitoba, besides the greener scenery, Jim and Meilin had noticed that the highway of this province was much rougher. They had just come from Saskatchewan and could not help comparing these two provinces in some different aspects. Though the wind in Saskatchewan was strong, the highway there was smooth and comfortable to ride on. Now they were in a rich province, but the highway here was so bumpy. Driving on this highway, they had to hold their teeth tightly together, afraid that the shakes and vibrations might cause them to bite their tongues. Though the highway was wide with four lanes, the surface of the road was hard like the rock. Sometimes, the cracks and potholes on the highway were strewn along for long stretches of the road.

"Ey! Who would have thought that the highway in a richer province would be worse than in a poor province," Meilin complained, wondering how long they had to endure this rocking drive.

"It looks that the road is paved by cement, not asphalt. Cement has no gives as the asphalt; it is hard like the rock," Jim commented knowingly. He had no complaint. On a long distance travel, he knew that they had to be prepared for any kind of conditions from the weather, the road or any other encounters.

Before going to Winnipeg, the couple decided to go to Riding Mountain, a national park in this province. There are not many parks in Saskatchewan and Manitoba. Riding Mountain is a well recommended prairie park in some books that have introduced Canadian parks. The couple had never seen a prairie park before and thought that they should visit this park. They drove forty kilometres off the main highway to reach the park. When they arrived, it was already late afternoon. They pulled their trailer to a RV Park which was located near the gate of the park. They were going to rest for the night; the sightseeing had to wait until tomorrow.

The RV Park was on a fair-sized open ground. There had been some large trailers parked at the skirt of the campground along the trees and bushes. Those trailers looked empty; they seemed belonging to some long-term residents who had used them for holidays and weekends. Jim and Meilin chose a lot on the centre lawn and set up their trailer. Their neighbour was a couple in their thirties, who had a large trailer with a wooden deck built in front of it. Jim soon had a chat with the neighbour and found out that they lived in Winnipeg and spent their weekends and holidays here in their trailer.

Soon after the couple settled down, the RV Park had its worker start mowing the lawn. After the long tiresome drive, the mowing noise was quite annoying, but it did not last too long. It was already supper time; the worker was off work soon. The evening and night in the RV Park were uneventful. The water from the tap here tasted muddy and terrible. Jim complained about the water to the neighbour and they agreed with his comment.

Early next morning after breakfast, Jim unhitched the van from the trailer and the couple drove their van to the park. Not very long after entering the park gate, they reached a large lake called Clear Lake. There were no mountains or even hills around; the lake was surrounded by trees and bushes. Riding Mountain is a plateau on top of a large elevated terrain of the prairie, which might be the cause of its name, the Riding Mountain. Clear Lake is a large lake among several other lakes in this area. The lake looked very open on the vast level prairie land and serenely beautiful under the broad sky. Driving a short distance along the lake, the couple entered the street of a historical resort town called Wasagaming. On one side of the street, there were crafts shops and restaurants in beautiful log buildings. On the other side of the street, there were the woods with large tall trees and the lake was a sling-shot away from the woods. Most visitors had gathered in this area, doing some shopping, going to the restaurants and relaxing by the lake. Some kids were jumping into the lake from a dock stretching a long way into the lake. Their shouting and laughter could be heard far way off.

Riding Mountain National Park had gone through some historical events. During 1930s the Great Depression, unemployed Manitobans had been put to work in this park to build some houses. Then in WWII, the park had been turned into a POW camp to hold the German soldiers who were captured in North Africa. The prisoners worked in cutting wood until being released in 1945. Now the park had returned to its normal function; people can enjoy nature and wild lives can carry on their peaceful existence here.

The couple guessed that to really feel the prairie park, they had to hike around the lake. They did not have the energy to do that and did not want to spend too much time in this bustling tourist town either, so they drove on. Along the road, they soon spotted another lake and stopped their van to have a look. This lake was much smaller than Clear Lake and was called Mirror Lake. The name suited the lake well; it did look like a round mirror. In this sunny day with hardly any wind, the quiet lake was clearly reflecting the blue sky, the green trees and bushes around it. The couple felt at this moment that it was worth their efforts to drive the forty kilometres to come here to feel the peace and serenity radiating from the lake. Unfortunately, they could not stay long by the lake, as the parking space and time were very limited.

Driving along the park road all flanked by trees and bushes again, the couple soon saw a small paved side-road. The road-sign said that it was Pit Run. Since motor vehicles were allowed to drive on Pit Run, the couple turned their van onto it, thinking that a drive on a small road might provide a closer feel of the prairie park. The small road led to a more densely wooded area. The trees along both sides of the road were big and tall. This was the first time that the couple had seen so many big trees on the prairie land. Soon they could see some cottages in the woods. Each cottage had at least three acres of wooded land around. The modern cottages were not like those old plain wooden ones with one or two rooms; they were big and built in all styles of beauty and cozy comfort. The small road stretched through the woods for a long distance and there were some other side-roads branching from it and leading to other parts of the cottage land. The couple were amazed to see such a large area full of luxury modern cottages. It was a treat for them to enjoy the displays of so many beautiful cottages along the road in the quiet woods. Obviously, those cottages belonged to the people who lived and worked in Winnipeg. On such a large wooded cottage land by the lake, there were quite some families that had the privileges to own those beautiful cottages and spend their peaceful leisure time here. This showed that Winnipeg had indeed no lack of families with old or new money.

The tour of the park took the whole morning. When Jim and Meilin came back to the trailer park, it was already afternoon. They spent another night in the RV Park. The second night on the campground was not that peaceful. Starting from the afternoon, loud music was blasting out from a trailer near theirs. Luckily, the music was turned off at about nine o'clock at night. Next day the couple pulled out of the RV Park and headed for Winnipeg. On their way, they spotted a sign showing that Neepawa was ahead. Neepawa was a town where Margaret Laurence, a famous Canadian woman writer, was born. The couple decided to visit and pay their respect to the birthplace of Margaret Laurence.

Though an avid reader, Meilin did not read many works by Canadian writers. When she started her graduate studies in literature, her interest oddly turned somewhat to history and philosophy. She made excuses that she did not read much of the Canadian writers because some of her time and energy had been spent on the books of history and philosophy. However, she knew that Canada had quite some world class writers. During her university days, she did read some of books by the famous Canadian women writers such as Margaret Attwood, Margaret Laurence and Alice Monro. Alice Monro was a short story writer who had won a Nobel Prize in 2013 to become the first Nobel Prize winner in Canadian literature. At the time when Meilin read her short stories, she was very impressed and even thought of translating some of them into Chinese. But with years passing by, she could not remember much of her stories. As for Margaret Laurence, it was a different story. Meilin had encountered the novels of Margaret Laurence when she was working on her thesis for her master degree. The readings came not from the requirement of her courses or her thesis, but from a professor's gift. On her second birthday in Canada, a professor gave her three books of Margaret Laurence as a birthday gift. They were The Diviner, The Stone Angel and A Bird in The House. After reading them, she loved, admired and respected Margaret Laurence's writing. The language of Margaret Laurence was fluid and beautiful. The main women characters portrayed in her novels were strong with fighting spirits for love, independence and a life they wished for.

Margaret Laurence is a realistic novelist. Through her stories, she has shown truthful pictures of the society and people's lives which she was familiar with or knew well. Her successful novels are based on the life stories of herself and the people in a small prairie town called Manawaka. The readers all know that Manawaka is the fictional name Margaret Laurence had created for her novels; the actual place is Neepawa. Her writings are down-to-earth, vivid and convincingly realistic. While she writes about the narrow-mindedness and ugly side of some small town people, she also lovingly, simplistically and beautifully shows the pure good hearts of some people who are at the lower social level and do the lowest and dirtiest work in the town. Margaret Laurence's stories have also narrated truthfully the miserable living conditions of the native people she had encountered in her life. She is a strong believer and promoter that the native peoples are in every sense the equal human beings who deserve the same good life as the whites.

In 1926, Margaret Laurence was born in a lawyer's family in Neepawa. When she was four years old, her mother died. Her father Robert Harrison Wemyss remarried his wife's sister who was a teacher and a librarian. When Margaret was nine years old, her father died. Her step-mother and aunt took her and her brother to live with their maternal grandparents. Margaret started writing when she was very young. Her first professional writing job was with the town's newspaper. In time, Margaret went to the college which is today's Winnipeg University and got her Bachelor of Arts degree. After that, she married John Fergus Laurence, a civic engineer. Mr. Laurence took his wife to England. There they lived for a year and then they went to Africa where Mr. Laurence worked as an engineer. They had two children, a girl and a boy. Years later, they came back to Canada and lived in Vancouver for a while. In 1962, their marriage ended. Margaret took her children to England and lived there for years. Then they came back to Canada. She settled down at Lakefield Ontario and lived there until her death in 1987.

Margaret Laurence had produced quite some first class realistic novels during her life time. The academic world of Canada had heaped honorary degrees and awards on her for her achievements. Several movies based on her novels had been produced. Her books had been translated into quite some different foreign languages. One of her novels had become the best seller in a foreign country. In the later years of her life, Margaret Laurence had worked passionately for the causes of peace, social justice, women's rights and so on. Perhaps her success in the world had been partially the reason that had forced the hand of Canada. For her efforts and achievements, she was honoured as a Companion of the Order of Canada. However, in spite of the enthusiastic academic world about her achievements, the general public of the country are not that warm towards Margaret Laurence and her works. Her novels have shown the dark side of human society and human conditions. Her Manawaka seems to be not only the image of Neepawa, but also the miniature of Canada. It is easy for the readers to sense her sharp criticisms to some people and some things in the society.

Human beings have the tendency to punish criticisms and opinions; even they know it is wrong to do so. In the world history, many truthful realistic writers have been persecuted and even killed in some different countries. Margaret Laurence was lucky to be a Canadian realistic writer. In spite of her sharp criticisms, she had been loved, honoured and respected by quite some people, especially some intellectuals of this country. However, she had also offended some people, especially some people in Neepawa. Some town's people thought that she had betrayed their town by showing the unpleasant side of it. Some others in the general public of the country regarded her as a lefty complainer. Even when she was alive, she had adversaries and she knew well the situation. In her autobiographic novel The Diviner, the heroin, a writer, mentioned that some small-minded people had been gossiping about her "dirty writings".

Nobody in the world is completely praised or completely blamed. It takes a writer to know the true condition of another writer. Meilin is a realistic writer. Her writings have inevitably touched the unpleasant side of the society. Part of human life and human society are unpleasant, ugly and dark. No country in the world is a perfect paradise and immune to them. Being a woman of Chinese origin, Meilin could not get a single publisher to publish her books and not a single literary agent would dare to take the risk in assisting her. Her writings carried sharp criticisms to some bad things in the society and especially to racial discrimination. This seemed a big taboo in the publishing world of this country and a serious problem for a coloured writer to see his or her books published. For the coloured people in Canada, if some have dreamt or have the talent of making it in the literary world, they have to be smart enough to write only their unpleasant lives in their origin countries or anything that will not touch much of their lives here in Canada. If they write their lives here, there should be no criticisms but praises and comparisons to show how much better their lives have been here in Canada. Meilin unfortunately belonged to those stubborn and over literarily minded writers who wanted to write truthfully and write whatever they felt like to write. She would of course have very little chance with the traditionally or conventionally minded publishing world. Nonetheless, now and then people will see some degrading books appearing on the shelves of bookstores. This has brought the recognition that the publishers are not that traditional or conventional, but are afraid of touching some sensitive spots of the nation, such as political issues like racism and maltreatments towards the native peoples and the coloured Canadians.

However, for a freak stroke of luck or irony, Meilin's books had been read by many people who got into her computer while she was working on her books. The most important thing for most writers, if they are not starving, is probably that their writings are read by others. Meilin was happy with this good fortune, even though it meant that she would suffer financial losses from her labour. Samuel Johnson said, "No man but a blockhead ever wrote, except for money." Meilin was one of those blockheads. She believed that there were quite many like her and most of them were poets. Even there were no other gains for her efforts and hard work; writing itself had given her pleasure and enriched her life. When the society or life had failed her, she was lucky to be able to turn to her whiting, the work of art, to learn something, to know herself and to feel what it was to be human. Most importantly, in her present situation, she had probably gained some sympathetic and supportive readers who had followed her writings all this time, and they might not all wanted to get a free reading or ruin her chance of any financial gain. Perhaps in this way, her writings would have some influences and generate some changes in the society. Unfortunately, with this good fortune, came a lot of troubles for her and her husband. They had been attacked by all kinds of people with the basest methods. All kinds of things had been tried to degrade both her and her husband as persons. The constant harassment and the total loss of peace and privacy in their life had made the couple doubt the sanity of their attackers. They could not figure out whether all these hostilities and hatred were coming from people being offended by Meilin's criticisms or because of people's utmost intolerance to see a Chinese woman writing and writing well.

It was not hard for Meilin to discern that those crazy attacks on her and even on her family came partially from people's jealousy. In today's world with the market overfilled with books, not many writers could have a large readership. Many published writers have not had much luck to have their books noticed by the public. In quite many people's eyes, the Chinese woman was a lucky dog, an unexpected upstart who had shamelessly stolen the spotlight that should be on any white writer. The situation had made Meilin see that Margaret Laurence might more or less have suffered the same thing as she was suffering now. Her sharp criticisms must have generated dislikes and even hatred from some people. With all those honorary degrees and awards, she might have encountered even more jealousy. Such thoughts and understanding had made Meilin feel close to Margaret Laurence. However, she knew that there was a big difference between herself and this famous Canadian woman writer. Being white, Margaret Laurence had never had to face racism. The hostilities, hatred and jealousy Meilin had to face came largely from racial discrimination. In some white people's minds, a good Chinese woman here must be a Chinese woman unseen and unheard; she should be unable to write, let alone to criticize.

More than two decades had passed since the death of Margaret Laurence. Had the attitudes or feelings of the people in Neepawa changed towards her? From some tourism information, Jim and Meilin knew there was a museum established in Neepawa in honour of Margaret Laurence. The old home in which Margaret Laurence grew up was purchased and preserved to make this museum. The couple were going to check out this museum and the gravesite of Margaret Laurence. This woman writer was every bit worthy of their respect.

When Jim and Meilin entered the town of Neepawa, they pulled their vehicles to the gas station by the main street. They needed gas. Besides, the best place to get the information of how to get to the museum would be the gas station. When their vehicles stopped at the gas pump, Jim got out of the van and went to the office to pay for the gas and to ask for information. Meilin also got out of the van to stand under the shade of a tree at the entrance. While the summer was advancing, the days were getting hotter. It was better to stand away from the hot vehicles to get some fresh air and to wait until Jim finished gassing the van.

It did not take long for Jim to come out of the office and to fill up the gas tank. When Jim started pulling the vehicles away from the gas pump, Meilin followed the movement of the van. She was going to get in the van when Jim reached her. Suddenly, she noticed something seriously wrong on the ground where the van was going to run right over. A big piece of sharp metal was sticking out of the ground! Meilin waved her hands frantically, telling Jim to stop. But it was too late; the van seemed to have run right over it. When Jim stopped the van and got out, the couple checked. Very luckily, the wheel missed the sharp metal object just by an inch. A little way over, the tire would surely be badly damaged. On a close look, they found out that the sharp metal was a broken piece of the water-main cover, which was lodged tightly in the hole with the sharp point sticking up. There were many those round metal covers on the streets and paved grounds in towns and cities; the large ones were for sewer-mains and the small ones for water or other mains underneath the streets. Those metal covers protected the entrance holes that provided access to those underground channels.

This incident looked suspicious to Jim and Meilin. On this ground of a gas station, a small metal cover for the water-main would be broken and the sharp metal point stuck out so dangerously on the path where all the vehicles were coming and going. It needed a big hammer to break this metal cover and strength to lodge the sharp piece so firmly in the hole. However, the couple were relieved that they had escaped this danger; otherwise an entire tire had to be replaced. It was obvious that a patch-up job would not do for the damage done by such a big sharp metal point. Jim got a hammer and worked on the metal piece, forcing it to lie flat in the hole, so that other drivers would not have the misfortune to run into it. After this done, Meilin asked Jim whether he had got the information about the museum's whereabouts.

"Nobody in the gas station knows where the museum is," Jim answered with some frustration.

While they were talking, a middle-aged man drove in with a car. He looked like a local as he had no traveling gears with him. Jim went to the guy and asked for information about the museum. He came back with his head shaking. The man did not know anything about it either. The couple drove away from the gas station. They were going to drive along the main street to see what would come up. They thought that the town was small and they might bump into the museum. Not far from the gas station, they saw a man walking on the sidewalk. Jim pulled the van up to get hold of the man and started asking for information again. This time, they got the result. The museum was only three blocks away from the gas station and with only one turn.

It took them no time to reach the place. The museum was a large red brick house of two storeys. There was a sign on the front lawn, saying, “Former Home of Margaret Laurence”. The couple parked their van across the street in the parking lot of a grocery store. When they walked to the house and reached the door, they found that the museum was not open. They decided to check out the town and then come back again. Just when they were leaving, a middle-aged woman came and opened the door. She was the guide and probably also the care-taker of the museum.

The brick house belonged to Margaret’s maternal grandparents in the old days. There were some remodelling and renovating done to make it look more up-to-date. On the first floor, the sitting room had been connected with the dinning-room to make it look spacious and another building had been added to the back of the house to function as a big kitchen. The guide’s introductory talk was clear and casual, fitting a home environment. On the walls of the sitting room, there were some old pictures of the grandparents and landscape paintings. On the wall where a staircase was leading to upstairs, there was a picture of Margaret Laurence when she was a young girl. She looked a spirited girl with high expectations. Though the old furniture was only a few in the sitting room, they gave the impression of a well-to-do family in the old time. In the added kitchen, there were some books by Margaret Laurence and by some critics on her works; there were also some crafts and memorabilia for sale.

On the second floor, small rooms in the old days had been changed into just two to be suitable for the museum. There were more displays concerning Margaret Laurence in a large room. A large woven blanket with meaningful pictures and words was hanging on a wall. It was presented to Margaret by the native people. There were some pictures of Margaret Laurence in this room. One of them was a caricature drawing of a small owl with a big head. Margaret’s face with an exaggerated big mouth was the owl's face. The guide said that Margaret liked this drawing when she was alive. At the back of the upstairs, there was the small bedroom which must be used by Margaret and her small brother when they moved into this house to live with their grandparents. In front of the window, there was a small desk with an old typewriter on it; Margaret might have used it for her first writing job with the town's newspaper. Over the chair back at the desk, there was the graduation gown which Margaret wore when she was receiving some honorary degrees from some universities. There were some more ancestors' pictures hanging on the wall of this room. One of them was in an old military colonel's uniform.

Margaret Laurence's graduation gown sitting on the chair at the desk was quite thought provoking. Whatever great achievements, honors, fame, fortune or power some people have gained in their lives, all have to be left behind eventually. A few people, good or bad, will be remembered after they are gone, but whether they know that the living are still thinking of or remembering them after they are gone, that is unknown. Even if the dead kn4w what was going on in the living world, they probably would not care. All those memorial ceremonies, records, memorabilia, museums, monuments and so on are for the living. It is amazing that knowing that we all have to leave everything in this world in the end, quite many people will still do their best to live a meaningful life and to contribute to the society or the world in whatever way they can, while some others will also do their best to gain and accumulate and never feel what they have is enough.

One item in this room had caught the couple's full attention. Below the respectable ancestor's picture and at the corner near the bedroom door, there was a piece of paper pasted on the wall. Looking closely, Jim and Meilin saw that it was a prayer written by Margaret Laurence. The couple read the prayer carefully. This was the first time even for Meilin to read this prayer by Margaret Laurence. After the reading, the couple were deeply moved; the prayer showed what a noble soul this great writer was and what a great ideal she had cherished and worked for in the later years of her life.

The couple took a picture of the prayer which reads:

May our eyes and hearts be opened
To all faiths that praise
And protect life
May our lives be committed
To honouring and saving life

May we struggle all our lives
For lives of us all
For all the children
And may we strive with all our lives
Against destroyers against wars
Against those whose distortions
Have taken and would take again
Beloved children to untimely death
May we oppose those hatreds
With every strength and word
In all our lives as long as life
Shall last, and may at last
Our fears be brave and may we praise
Life given   live lived   with hope
May our symbols of faith
Of caring and respect and love
Become one symbol
As our children are
Our mutual children
As the Holy Spirit
Breath in us all
And may we learn
Not to hurt
May we lean
One upon another
Give and receive loving strength
And may we learn
We are one
People   in our only home
Earth.
AMEN

After reading this prayer, the couple stood and paused at the spot for quite a moment. They believed that those words must have touched every soul that had read them. The museum visit ended with the couple still pondering those words of prayer. They knew that there were many inspiring prayers by some great spiritual or other peoples in the world. The general aspirations of the peoples were race equality, unity of the world peoples, happiness, love and peace. The couple could not understand why with so much powerful thinking, compassion and love, the world was still in constant turmoil and hatred was still prevalent everywhere; Canada was relatively a more peaceful country, but racism and other vices still existed.

With all kinds of questions that could not be easily answered, the couple went to the cemetery to visit the gravesite of Margaret Laurence. From the museum, they got the direction to the town's cemetery and also to the gravesite of Margaret Laurence. It was not hard for them to find the cemetery. They were quite surprised to see such a large grand cemetery for a town. It meant that the town was not small at all. There were paved paths meandering through the gravesites and one of them was wide enough to drive a vehicle through. Quite some large gravestones and even monuments were standing in this cemetery. This seemed to mean that there were some important or rich people who had lived and died here or lived here once and buried here.

The couple thought that they could easily spot Margaret Laurence's gravesite, as she could be counted as an important person in this country. They had a small brochure card of the museum, which had a picture of the museum in the middle, a picture of Margaret Laurence on top, and beside her, there was a statue of a stone lady leaning on a large cross, and on the bottom part of the card, there was a yellow and red lily with the words stating that Neepawa was the lily capital of the world. This brochure card looked partially appropriate, as The Stone Angel was one of the famous novels by Margaret Laurence. But the red yellow lily gave the couple an uneasy feeling. People all knew that different coloured flowers had different meanings. A yellow lily normally meant ingratitude. Were the town's people still unforgiving Margaret Laurence for her showing the world the town's unpleasant side? It was the small town that had given Margaret the first writing job. The town's people probably thought that they had the right to consider the writer ungrateful. The picture of the stone lady beside Margaret had no wings and could not be seen as an angel, but the statue looked solemn and beautiful. The couple thought that this statue must be part of the gravestone for Margaret Laurence and it should be easy for them to find this statue even in such a large cemetery. Finding the statue, they would have found the gravesite of Margaret Laurence.

The couple looked and looked. It was far from easy to find Margaret Laurence's gravesite among so many gravesites. Finally, they spotted the stone lady. It was a small statue on top of a gravestone. They were overjoyed, thinking that they had finally found Margaret's gravesite. But they were immediately disappointed. On a close look, they found out that it was somebody else's gravestone. The couple had to start looking again. They were determined to find the gravesite of Margaret Laurence. Their efforts had finally been rewarded and they found the gravesite at the bottom edge of the cemetery. Not far from this location, the land sank about a hundred feet. A small river or a stream was flowing down there. Margaret Laurence's gravestone was a small pure white stone with a Celtic cross engraved on one side and her name on the other side. There were no other ornaments on or around the gravestone and the gravesite. Her white gravestone was standing on the green lawn, simple and pure. Close by her gravestone, there was a large black gravestone with her father's name Wemyss engraved on. Jim and Meilin liked the simple pure white gravestone of Margaret Laurence. They paid their respect and took some pictures.

Margaret Laurence died at the age of sixty-one. According to the modern standards of life span, she died young. There are no talks about how she had died in any introductory writings about her personal life. Very rarely an odd one or two have mentioned that she was ill. In the very recent year after over two decades of her death, her children suddenly produced a suicide note, claiming that it was written by Margaret Laurence before she committed suicide. The suicide note had all the indication that Margaret Laurence was suffering from a nerves breakdown. This was a very strange shocking outcome for Margaret Laurence's death, as her person and her works had no indication of mental problem or suicidal tendency at all.

To Jim and Meilin, Margaret Laurence looked healthy and was busy with the works she was passionate about in the later years of her life. She passed away just two years after she wrote the prayer the couple had just looked at. Another strange thing was that Margaret Laurence would ask her children to bury her ashes in Neepawa. Since she left the small town to go to the college when she was a young girl, she had never looked back. She lived in Africa, England, Vancouver, and settled in Ontario and died there. Compared with other writers, Margaret Laurence was extremely broadminded. Nobody would expect that she would commit suicide or wanted to be buried in Neepawa, as what she had concerned about was the whole world, the whole Canada and all the different peoples.

After leaving the gravesite of Margaret Laurence, the couple had a walk around the cemetery. The place was peaceful. Many gravesites with large gravestones had patches of pansies planted on sites. In the summer sun, the flowers were blooming vibrantly; the pedals looked like that the dead were peeking out of the ground with glaring eyes. Didn't one of Margaret Laurence's strong women characters disliked and sneered at the pansies? Meilin could not remember clearly. But it was strange that so many people would plant the same flowers on the gravesites of their family members. It was the first time for Jim and Meilin to see the flower beds flourishing with the same kind of flowers all over a cemetery. Wasn't this town the lily capital of the world? The couple did not see a single lily.

The cemetery tour had taken the rest of the whole morning. Jim and Meilin decided to have their lunch and a rest by the cemetery. They had parked their vehicles by the street just outside the cemetery. They were in the shade of large trees along the street and had a good view of the front part of the graveyard. While they were having their lunch, a young man half-naked walked on the cemetery path in their view. The youngster walked on that path back and forth quite some times, staring at their trailer with defiance. One thing seemed clear that he might be sent here to put on a show to the couple, but it was unclear whether he was showing his disrespect to the couple or to the dead, or even to Margaret Laurence. Of course, the town's people knew the couple's intentions and doings in their town. The couple's suspicion was not totally unfounded.

Suddenly, the whole thing seemed clear to the couple. Over two decades after the death of Margaret Laurence, some people in Neepawa had never forgiven her for showing the ugly side of the town to the world. Depressing thoughts set in the couple's minds. The whole thing suddenly seemed meaningless. It was no longer important how Margaret Laurence died and how long she had lived. Everybody had to die. The pansies would have to die, so would the roses, the peonies and the lilies. Even the disrespectful youngster would soon join the people under his feet, sooner than he could imagine. At this moment, the youngster must think and feel that he was an immortal and would live on forever. Margaret Laurence's books would last longer and the effects or influences of her works, if there was any, might last even longer. But death would take them all; the mighty or the insignificant and even the whole human race and the world would be gone in the end.

What is the meaning of all the things? Human beings like continuation, but the definite ending for all is death. The only little hope comes from the expectation or speculation in the human minds that their souls will survive in another realm of reality after their material bodies have gone, but there is very little to back up this hope of theirs. Survival after death remains a permanent mystery. Even with the highly developed modern science and technology, human beings are still far from solving this mystery. The couple imagined that if Margaret Laurence's soul survived her bodily death, she must be laughing right now about the fuss of the living world and the futile struggles of her own mortal life. This thought seemed to have given a little comfort to the couple, as it seemed unnecessary for them to bother too much of how or why such a great woman writer with such noble ideals died a tragic or dubious death at the age of sixty-one.

Most human beings live their lives in fear. The poor fear of starvation and the rich fear of losing what they have; the powerful are the most fearful of losing their power. Yet, the most feared things are changes. To many people, changes are the worst plagues, though they know well that the society cannot move forward without changes and improvements. People sometimes will do all they can to prevent changes. For instance, racism, though a definite culprit preventing society from evolving to a higher civilized level, has been hold fast by many people, because eradicating racism means changing their habitual way of thinking or behaviours, which will shake the whole foundation of their thoughts and beliefs. Besides holding fast their habitual way of thinking and living, the almighty money is the only common language that most people can fully understand and trust, as it gives them security, a pillar to hold on in any kind of storms of life. Human nature is largely dominated by selfishness, noble ideals like the ones given by Margaret Laurence spout very occasionally. Still, countless human beings have fought and even given their lives for those rare noble ideals. Only the systems they have helped to build on those noble ideals often turn foul and the new governments turn to corruption. Human beings are imperfect; they cannot build perfect systems. They can build good systems, but they have to work constantly and vigorously to improve what they have built to prevent them from deteriorating, decaying and falling apart. Unfortunately, the mighty ones once up there are often too conceited to see this, so the maintenance works are often neglected.

The couple were overwhelmed by the depressing thoughts and felt hard to breathe. They had sensed the negativities of the town and were affected by them. After their lunch, feeling impossible to rest here, they took off. Leaving Neepawa behind and with the forward motion of their vehicles, they felt better and even their breathing improved quickly.

The couple were ordinary people in the country. Because of pointing out some bad things in some services, they were besieged by harassment and attacks. In order to invalidate their criticisms, attempts had been made to frame them as the most hideous criminals. It looked that they had unknowingly touched some power; drastic measures and efforts had been made to put the couple down. In order to protect themselves, Meilin wrote done what had exactly happened to them, hoping that when people knew the truth, they would leave them alone to their peaceful life. What a mistake she had made! Her writing had generated more harassment and attacks. Because her writing had mentioned their sufferings from racial discrimination, she had offended more people; the force of their adversaries had enlarged. By simply having a voice, though considered by the couple a truthful voice to express what had happened to them and what they had seen and heard, Meilin had disturbed the order of the society and hurt the sense of superiority of quite some white people. In those people's minds, it was an outrage that a Chinese woman should have a voice to criticize the whites and their society.

With the hostilities and hatred increasing around them, Meilin had several times decided to quit writing. But every time when she stopped writing, the harassment and attacks seemed only heightened even more. Plus whenever she stopped, she became physically sick. It was rather strange that she seemed to have been pushed by a divine force, a creative force or a mystic force from the collective consciousness or unconsciousness. She could not tell. But she might have touched the cord that had the same things needed to be expressed or voiced. It was simply beyond her comprehension why her truthful writing would scare so many people and they would be so desperately wanting to put her down. This showed that there was a strong force that had always tried to suppress or to muffle the kind of expressions and voices which was being blown through this Chinese woman at this moment. Many times in her writing, Meilin tried to tell people that what she and her husband wished for was only a peaceful life. They were ordinary people who had no ambition or desire for anything else. Fame or high positions were nothing to them. At their age and after what they had gone through, they were the last persons who would fight or even give their lives for some lofty causes. To say it a bit condescendingly, their minds had long transcended this sort of struggles.

Meilin's explanations were useless. The couple had been considered as a large threat by God knows who, perhaps some crime organization, some political power or some other; the couple could not tell. They had suddenly become the target of almost everybody. With their totally open situation and being at the bottom of the society, they could be jumped on and kicked around by any kind of dickens. Worse still, some hot-headed or headless hate-mongers started giving them death threats and even attempting to kill them. This situation had infuriated the couple. They were determined to talk whatever they liked to talk about. Meilin would write whatever she felt like to write. She was a human being, equal to any white. Why couldn't she have her own thoughts and her own opinions and why couldn't she express them at her own home? People did not like criticisms from a Chinese woman; she gave them more and especially the criticisms on racial discrimination. She criticized and gave her opinions about not only the small city Abbotsford, but also the country and even the world.

Unlike Margaret Laurence whose vision was blurred by the heaped-up honours and awards and probably never suspected that her life might be in danger, the couple saw clearly the hostilities and hatred of some people and knew that they had to take measures to protect themselves. However, the couple decided that nothing would drive them to hatred. They had seen what hatred could do to human beings and their souls. Hatred has brought inhumanity of man to man in the world, which has created so many miseries, including the miseries of the haters themselves. Hatred breeds dark mentalities which render those haters unable to love and respect even themselves. The couple definitely did not want to become the type of people who were full of hostilities and hatred and doing all those vicious or unlawful things.

In spite of the difficult situation, the couple tried to live a normal life. At this moment under the spell of depressing thoughts, they were determined to pull their minds away from negativities and to look at the good side of things. After all, they were still alive and some people did see the truth. Clear minded, the couple would try their best to keep themselves safe from harms. However, if the haters did succeed, they would leave this life with peace and go to see what was really on the other side. The couple decided that even if the world was going to end tomorrow, they were going to live today meaningfully and to be satisfied with themselves that they had tried their best to live their life as free human beings without too much bondage. Some sunny thoughts had finally squeezed into their minds and lightened their moods. The drive became pleasant again. Not long, they reached Winnipeg. They pulled their vehicles to a campground at the city skirt, as they planned to take a tour of the city. A few times before, they had passed by this city without entering it. This time, they were going to have a look.

The campground was a RV Park with full service. A large building was housing an office, a lounge and a nice bathroom with several shower stalls. A billiard table and some magazines were in the lounge for travellers to have some relaxation time. The land of the campground was flat; each camping lot had a fair-sized space. After setting up their trailer, the couple had a shower. There was not much time left before supper time. When full service was provided on a campground, camping in a trailer was indeed more comfortable. They cooked their supper and enjoyed a hot meal with music. After supper, they had a walk around the campground. There were a large lawn with children's playground and trees along the paths around the campsites. The couple felt peaceful, thinking that they would have a nice night's sleep. After the night fell and when they were in bed, the noises started. Big vehicles were rushing through on the path by their site; every one of them bursting with loud music. Though this kind of happening was expected by the couple now, it was still quite annoying. As the noises did not come from other campers near them, changing site would not remedy the situation. Still, the couple managed to have some sleep. Tomorrow would be a full day for them; they were going to tour Winnipeg.

Winnipeg is a large city sitting at the confluence of the Red River and Assiniboine River. For thousands of years, the native peoples had used this spot for trading. In 1738, French trader and explorer Pierre Gaultier de la Verendrye set up Fort Rouge at this spot. Fort Rouge was then succeeded by Fort Gibraltar built by the North West Company in 1804. Then in 1821, Hudson's Bay Company founded Fort Gary here. In the same year, Lord Selkirk brought a group of Scottish settlers to this fertile land. The European settlements soon started sprawling around. After Manitoba became a province, Winnipeg was elected as the provincial capital. The name Winnipeg came from the Cree words for muddy water. Today, Winnipeg is an important transportation center connecting the Canadian west and east, as all roads and railways had been forced by the Canadian Shield to go through here. The city is an important storage and trading center for grains and livestock of the prairies. Winnipeg now is not only the location of government offices, but also the industrial and manufacturing centre of Manitoba.

The couple started their sightseeing early next morning. The first place they went to was the Royal Canadian Mint, the plant where money was made. There are two mints in Canada; one is in Ottawa and one in Winnipeg. Jim and Meilin had never visited a mint before. Since this trip was for traveling only, they were not going to pass the mint without a look.

So much of human life is involved with money. From the beginning of conscious human life when understanding started germinating in human minds, the importance and power of trade have dominated human life. Trade started from bartering by the primitive man. Through ages, humans gradually found that bartering could not satisfy all their needs for trade. Sometimes, one side needed food from the other side, but the other side might not need animal skins for exchange. At other times, one side needed animal skins, but the other side might not need food at that moment. Innovation or creation was born out of the needs or demands in the scheme of surviving. Crude currency was thus born.

In the very early stage of human development when the humans started more and more realizing the value of trading with each other, they started using shells, barks, pebbles or other kind of material things as currency for trading purposes. In this way, trading could be carried out not only in one small group, but also in a larger group or among groups in an extended area, and it could be done in any time. With the advance of their brains and the development of their communities; humans came to use metal pieces such as gold, silver and coppers as currency for trading, because those metal pieces were not so plenty and so readily available and they looked precious to embody importance and value. When the human population had grown, gold and silver had become inconveniently bulky and rare for large demands and usages in wider and different markets. When paper was invented, humans soon started to use pieces of paper plus pieces of other not so rare and lighter metals to act as currencies for trading. Instead of using the weight of the metal pieces to measure the value, they put symbols, pictures and numbers on pieces of paper and metals to embody the amount or value. Thus, money was born for trading purpose. The paper pieces were bills and the metal pieces were coins. Today, money is inclusive of many things: gold and silver are still hard currency, paper bills and nickel coins are used by people for daily trading of necessities, and there are also all kinds of bonds and numbers written on large or small documents; they all mean money. However, when stripped of the powerful grandeurs, money alone is but a material thing, a token, which is made or produced by human beings for trading purposes. Not many people have seen how those money bills and coins are produced in a factory. This actual production of money probably has much less or no significance to many people, though money as the possession of wealth has the utmost importance and occupies great interests and attentions of everybody.

Still, to satisfy the curiosity of some people, Canada has its mints open to visitors who would like to have a look at the procedure of actual money-making, not in the sense of money-earning or money-possessing. The mint in Winnipeg was by the highway at the city skirt and not far from the campground. The couple soon arrived at the plant. The plant was a large modern glass building that looked like a pyramid with the tip cut off. The ground around the plant was cultivated with lawns, gardens, pond and water fountain, which made the visitors feel like going to visit a luxury manor. Walking into the main door, the couple saw a large hall which contained an indoor garden with plenty of trees and bushes, a pond with a walkway wandering over, an interactive museum and a souvenir shop. They immediately started the tour. In the interactive museum, there was a large bar or brick of the purest gold resting on a stand and guarded by a RCMP officer in a full red uniform with the sandy rimmed-hat. The gold brick was a little bigger than a normal brick and worth over half a million dollars. It was the first time that Jim and Meilin had seen such a big bar of gold. Jim asked the RCMP officer whether he could lift the bar to see how heavy it was. He was allowed to do so. He tried it and could hardly lift the gold!

There were some other interactive displays in the museum for people to learn something about money making and related facts. Another thing interested the couple in the museum was a large board which was shaped and made as a Canadian coin. On this coin board, there was a hole for anybody to put his or her face in to have a picture taken. The only human face on the real Canadian coins is the queen's face. Here, everybody could put his or her face on this large coin and have a picture taken to keep as a souvenir. The couple liked this sense of humour and had some pictures taken with their faces on the large coin. They joked that every dog would have at least one of its days to shine and this probably was their day to have the opportunity to touch a big bar of gold and have their faces shown on a large coin.

The tour of the money-making area was guided. The couple joined a tourist group. The plant proper was in a large hall with all kinds of machines. The visitors could walk through a long corridor half surrounding and high above the workshop. The corridor had glass wall facing the workshop, so the visitors could look down and see the line of money-making machines cutting out pieces from large metal sheet and the metal pieces going through different procedures to become actual coins. The visitors could also see the designers working in their rooms and craftsmen doing some refining works. The guide was a young girl whose talk was formal and clear. She not only talked about the making of the coins, but also some history and special markings left by the money-making craftsmen. The coins with all kinds of pictures, symbols and patterns today are the works of all kinds of craftsmen and artists. In the old time, the looks of money bills or coins would remain the same for long periods of time. Today, money has blossomed with all kinds of designs. Each province has its representative coins, each special event will have special coins for the occasion and still more special coins are made to celebrate special people of the country. Like the human life and everything involved with human life, the modern-day money design has become rich, colourful and diversified.

The Royal Canadian Mint in Winnipeg is one of the most modern mints in the world. The high tech and high speed machines can punch over seven hundred coins per minute. The plant not only produces all the Canadian coins, but also coins for over seventy other countries. They saw not only the round coins being made, but also coins in other shapes. This looked strange to the visitors at first, as the Canadian coins were all round. The guide saw the questions on the visitors' faces and explained immediately, "The mint produces not only coins for Canada, but also for quite some other countries." The couple watched the coin-making, but did not see any bill-making. They thought that the bills must be made in the mint in Ottawa.

After the tour of the workshop from above, the couple went to the souvenir shop. It was a large brightly lit shop. Many souvenirs and expensive coins were for sale. In the old time, gold and silver had been used to make coins that were used as currency. Today, gold and silver are still being used to make coins, only those coins are special and for collection purpose only, and their value depends on their exquisite designs and collectability. Some collectors can make money by their purchases of those coins. The couple chose a little inexpensive souvenir and were given a free coin holder for special coins that might fall into their lap in the future. At the end of the tour, they felt that they had learnt quite something from visiting the mint. Handling money all their life, it was the first time that they had seen how money was made and known something related with money making.

After the mint visit, it was still morning. They drove into the city and went to the city centre. Winnipeg, though could not compare with the size of the mega cities like Toronto or Montreal, was a large city. There were skyscrapers in the downtown area and the traffics on the main thoroughfares were rather heavy. In the heart of the city centre, there was the old confederation building which showed that this important federal government office was here in the beginning of the province. Also in the city centre, the king's and queen's statues stood by the important buildings of the Winnipeg Symphony Orchestra and Ballet Company. With the development of commerce, the culture of Winnipeg had advanced. The couple knew that Winnipeg was the first city to establish a ballet company in the country and the Royal Winnipeg Ballet Company had consistently given world class performances, but the Toronto and Vancouver Symphony Orchestras were known as very good in the country.

Not far from those important buildings, there was the Winnipeg Chinatown. A building of traditional Chinese architecture had unmistakably identified the place. After checking out the statues and some of the downtown important buildings, the couple went to Chinatown. The large red building was in a combined architecture style of both modern and ancient. It was several storeys high and had kept the traditional Chinese tiled roof and the red front pillars, but its main structure was modern. The building was sitting on elevated ground. There were quite some wide cement steps leading up to the main entrance of the building, which gave it the air of a temple. On the ground in front of the building, there was a traditional Chinese garden with two pavilions and stone walkways wandering over two ponds. Only there was no water in the ponds; some black stone slabs in the ponds were symbolizing water.

Jim and Meilin climbed up the steps and entered the building. Inside, the place looked small. The hall was not big and an elevator door was in the centre of the hall. Some rooms were lined on one side. The couple could not see a single soul around. The doors to the rooms were all closed, except one hair-salon with neon lights was open. The hair-salon looked the only business here. It was Asian owned and had no customer. Jim and Meilin checked the direction board and saw that on other floors of this building, the rooms were mainly used by some government offices or agencies. It was strange to the couple, as there were signs in and out showing that this building belonged to the Chinese community, but there seemed no Chinese organizations occupancy here. There was not much for the couple to see in the building. Jim and Meilin then tried to use the washrooms in the building. The washrooms were locked and they could not get in. This showed that the place was rarely used by the public. Luckily, there was a cleaning lady walking by with her cart. The couple asked to use the washrooms. The cleaning lady opened the doors for them. She waited there and then locked the doors of the washrooms again after the couple came out.

Coming out of the building, the couple decided to rest a little in one of the pavilions over the ponds. While sitting down on the rail, they looked around. No Chinese were around, but a group of white young men and women were sitting on top of those cement steps and looking down on them. The youngsters' postures and facial expressions all showed that they were now the occupiers of this place. Under the stares of those youngsters, the couple felt uncomfortable and soon left. After leaving the place, they walked along the Chinatown Street behind the building. There was one Chinese grocery store around. They went in to do some shopping. The store, though with the usual Chinese goods, was not that big and there was not a single customer around. The couple bought a few odds and ends and left. Walking along the street further, they still did not see a Chinese and the pedestrians were only a few white people. The whole Chinatown gave them the impression of a ghost town.

What had happened to the Chinese community here? They must have been doing well in some period of former time, as they had built such a large impressive building. The couple had no way to get an answer for this question. They left the Chinatown and headed for the largest park in the city. The park was called the Forks which was located at the confluence of the two main rivers of the province, Assiniboine River and Red River; both rivers ran through Winnipeg. The Assiniboine River ran right into the Red River, forming a T junction, the city centre was right at this T junction. From the map, the park occupied a large green area.

When the couple arrived at the place, they saw that it was indeed a large urban park close to the skyscrapers and by the river. There were a stylish stone and wooden gate for the park and some metal sculptures in the centre of the entrance, which gave the place a new ancient feeling. Words engraved on the stones were telling the history of the place. The Forks was an important place of historical significance. This very spot had been used as a trading place by the native peoples for thousands of years. The signs of their lives and activities found here could be traced back for over six thousand years. Then in the fur trade era, different peoples had come by the rivers to this spot to do their trading with the native peoples and among themselves. While they gathered here for businesses, they enjoyed themselves with parties and entertainments. Those merry-making gatherings were often accompanied by story-telling, stories about themselves and stories of hearsays. Of course, there were also booze, brawls and fights. With such a history of warm togetherness of different peoples, the couple wondered what had happened to the city today. They could hardly see any coloured or native peoples around and the city had been reported as the murder capital of the country. Later, the couple learnt over some TV reports that Winnipeg and even Manitoba had been the city and province that were most prejudiced towards the native peoples. This was a disturbing situation, as Manitoba had actually been started by the native peoples and the Métis. Coming to the park, the couple had spotted some banners showing some efforts in bringing different peoples together. That was one positive thing they had seen in the place so far.

The couple passed the gate and walked into the large park. There were large lawns and plenty of mature trees in the park. A walkway along the river was stretching far to connect quite some public facilities and the legislative building. On the largest lawn there was a big stage set up on one side. This must be the modern gathering place and it was ready for the coming Canada Day. Not far from the stage, there was a gigantic rocket sculpture. It was hard to tell what material the sculpture was made of. The rocket stood upright more than a hundred feet high with its point thrusting to the sky. There were many thick steel cables fastened to two sides of the rocket, anchoring the rocket to the ground. The cables made the rocket look like having wings. This was indeed an impressive piece of artwork. Besides this, there was a sculpture garden in the park, which looked created much earlier than the rocket. The garden was a large round area built by wide circles of cement steps descending to the base. The center base was a round cement platform with an engraved imprint of a star. The place must also be functioning as an amphitheater. The center base was the stage and the circles of cement steps audience seats. Around the top circle were more than half dozen of sculptures built by bricks, cement and metals. The sculptures looked like ancient devices of telescopes for observing stars. They were the sculptures symbolizing the ancient cultures which speculated and imagined things concerning astronomy. Painted on the bases of those sculptures were ancient stories about people's understanding of astronomy. Those stories were based on the ancient cultures of the aboriginal peoples, the Chinese, the Indians, the Aztecs and some other peoples. Around the base circle were some metal plagues engraved with the ancient European star-chart. It was quite an interesting garden which showed the interests and curiosities of the people here in other cultures and the human thirst to know the universe from ancient time on. The couple wondered whether the people here today were still curious and interested in other cultures and the knowledge of the universe, or their eyes were fixed on the sky now only for the desire to fly high.

All those running around and touring the places had used up their whole morning; the couple had already seen quite a lot. By the time when they reached the indoor-market place of the park, it was already passed one o'clock. Though there were hardly coloured people around, there were a Chinese and a Korean restaurant stalls among some other restaurant stalls in the market. The couple picked the Chinese one to have their lunch. It turned out that they had made a mistake. Things seemed to have been prepared for the couple by some people who knew that they would choose Chinese food. The combination plates served by this restaurant stall were as salty as pure salt. Meilin, a woman of Chinese origin, had never tasted Chinese dishes as salty as this in her life. In the modern days and with people getting more and more conscious of eating healthy food, a Chinese restaurant serving such salty food would never survive. The only explanation left was that this special service was instigated by the harassers to give the couple a special treat. Meilin had a heart condition. This was not the first time that things had been done in attempt of doing damages to her.

After leaving the Forks, there was not much time left for the day. The schedule for the afternoon was simple for the couple. They went to the legislative building to have a look. Legislative buildings could well show the wealth and mentality of different provinces. The legislative building of Manitoba was large and in full grandeur of neoclassic style. It was said that this legislative building was visited every years by many admirers and people who were interested in neoclassic architecture. On top of the tall dome, there was the Golden Boy. In his raised right hand, there was a torch pointing to the north representing progress and the development of the north. In his left arm, there was a sheaf of wheat representing the agriculture of the province. The Golden Boy symbolized eternal youth and prosperity. The statue was sculpted by a French artist in Paris, It was covered by 24 carat gold, over 17 feet tall and weighed more than one and half tons. After a difficult journey during the WW I, it came to stand on this prominent position of Manitoba legislative building. Having viewed the frontal of the building, the couple climbed up the steps to reach the entrance of the building. They passed the large columns on the top landing to enter the big door. In the large front hall, there were many more wide steps in the center leading up to another level. On each side of this grand staircase, there was a live-like black-coloured bull bison sculpture. Again, the bulls must also symbolize prosperity and the province's natural resources. There were quite some halls, corridors and balconies, and they were stuffed with worthy paintings and artworks.

Marble floors, steps and columns with sculpted mythic figures were everywhere. From their cross-country tour, the couple had found that there were not many other legislative buildings that could compare with the legislative building of Manitoba. Of course, the couple might not have seen enough to make this comparison.

The grandeur of the backyard of Manitoba legislative building seemed to have also surpassed that of others. The paved ground was large. There was a gigantic round water fountain in the centre back. The mist from the powerful shooting water had covered quite some surrounding area. Passing the water fountain, there were some steps leading up to the river bank. On top of the river bank, there was the black-coloured statue of Louis Riel holding a roll of document in his hand. Then there were more wide cement steps and terraces descending to the river below. On both sides of the large paved backyard ground, there were big green lawns with abundant mature trees. At this moment, there was an artwork display going on in a wooded area of the ground. Over a dozen of polar bear sculptures were sitting upright on the lawn in the shade of the large trees. The polar bears were live-size and live-like. Each one had beautiful paintings on its body. The paintings were mountains, rivers, city skyscrapers, festivals, children playing and so on. Both the sculptures and paintings must be done by mature artists, as they looked in high quality. Besides the polar bears, there was a permanent artwork standing on one spot of the lawn. It was the Inuit artwork called the Man. A big figure of man was formed by stones and slabs. The couple were familiar with the Man, the famous Inuit artwork. Each time of seeing this piece of artwork, they would think of man in the natural world, lonely but part of nature. It was a simple and seemingly crude artwork, yet powerfully expressive. This piece of artwork had first been created by the Inuit in the Arctic in the ancient time to state their existence in this extremely isolated part of the world. The Canadians today have treasured it, as they too exist around this northern part of the world now. As for the polar bear display, Jim and Meilin had also seen this kind of artwork shows in Edmonton and Vancouver. They were sculptures of cows, bears or pigs in these two cities. This was the first time that they had seen so many polar bears.

It seems that in recent years, some Canadians are getting more fascinated by the polar bears with some sentiments other than concerned that polar bears are becoming an endangered species. They might have liked the indication of white polar bears living close to the North Pole like the Canadians. The actual animal that has been adopted by Canada as the nation's symbol is beaver. To some white people, the beaver seems a lower species, brown and cannot compare with the polar bear, white, big, strong and able to live in the cold north. Those people must be thinking that the polar bear can be a better symbol for their white country. However, others can argue that the beaver may have more good qualities than the polar bear. The polar bear, though large, white and able to endure extreme coldness, is very much confined to live in the cold northern area and at the verge of extinction because of the global warming. The beaver, however, is a humble private creature, diligent builder, and can survive both in water and on land and will probably last as long as the earth. On top of these, Canada is not pure white; the country has her aboriginal peoples and her other colourful children. Manitobans probably have not much rapport with the beaver. During the fur trade era, the trappers had killed all the beavers in this region for their furs. Later on, beavers had to be reintroduced into this province to keep them going again.

The visit to the legislative building ended the couple's Winnipeg tour. They did not go to see the museums and galleries, but felt satisfied with what they had seen. They went back to the campground and spent another night there. Next morning, they started rather late. Though they had planned to cross the border to enter Ontario, the next province, they were tired from yesterday's sightseeing and wanted to take this day easy. Instead of bypassing the city to move on, they drove through Winnipeg city to have another general look. Dragging their trailer through the unfamiliar busy city streets made them feel uneasy. The skyscrapers seemed rather impersonal. Near noon, they turned into a smaller street on their route and pulled their trailer to a parking lot by the Seven Oaks House Museum which was believed to be the oldest house in Winnipeg. The couple decided to have a quick look at this old house and then carry on. They walked to the old house and were surprised to see a large old mansion. The house was built in the 1850's and older than Canada, but the large wooden structure three storeys high and with verandas around was still sturdy and perfectly sound. It must have belonged to a rich family in the old days. The wood works of the building exterior showed great attentions to detailed craftsmanship. Many decorative carvings looked painstakingly done. There were some gardens around the house. Some middle-aged men and women were working in them. They must be the volunteers for the upkeep of the museum.

Unfortunately, the museum was closed to visitors this day. The couple came back to their vehicles and had their lunch in their trailer on the parking lot. Then they started moving on. At the other end of the city, they spotted a Walmart store. As the store was on their route, they pulled their vehicles into the parking lot to do some shopping. This Walmart was rather large. After their shopping and a walk around the store, it was already late afternoon. Coming out of the store, they pulled their trailer to the back of the store where there was a parking lot for the customers who came to the Walmart auto shop for some auto repair work. No vehicles were parked there. Obviously no customers were visiting the auto shop at this moment and the door of the shop was closed. The place was quiet and cool. The large building of the store had cast a nice shadow over the parking lot and a cool draft was blowing through. The couple had a rest at the spot. In the hot summer, a shaded and cool place was very much appreciated.

Jim and Meilin decided to stay in this nice spot for the night. Yesterday was a full busy day; they needed a good rest before going further. The quiet spot by the Walmart was ideal and perhaps they could have a better sleep here. They cleaned up some broken glass pieced on the parking lot, stabilized their trailer and settled down for the rest of the afternoon. Things went pretty well for the time left in the afternoon. The place was quiet and only one car came for the service of the auto shop. As the shop door was closed, the car soon left. Jim and Meilin sat outside their trailer, did some reading and enjoyed the cool wind that was gently drifting through. The enjoyment did not last long. Towards supper time, five young men and four young girls came. The young men started playing football on the large lawn beside the parking lot. The lawn covered the whole area of the store's backyard, but the group stayed close to the parking lot. The young players stood some distance apart, throwing the olive-shaped ball towards each other. The young girls were sitting at the edge of the lawn, watching. With the shouting and laughing from the sportsmen and the girls, it looked quite a jolly game. Only the hard ball forcefully thrown by the young men was sometimes flying so dangerously close to the couple's van and trailer. If the ball hit their vehicles, it might very well do some damages.

Jim and Meilin were alarmed. They stood up in front of their vehicles and stared at the group. The ball sometimes was shooting right at them. They, in due response, threw their displeased and disapproving expressions to the group. Luckily there was no mishap. After about an hour of the rowdy playing, the group left. The couple felt a relief and prepared their supper in peace. The evening and the early night were pleasantly uneventful. The place remained nicely quiet and cool. The couple thought that they were going to enjoy a peaceful free night at this parking lot nobody used. But in the middle of the night while they were in a restful sleep, they were woken by a loud explosion. It sounded like that their trailer had been bombed. The couple jumped up from their beds and had no idea whether they were awake or in a nightmare. After a brief moment, they realized that they were awake and something had just happened to their trailer. They both reached for their flashlights and started checking around. There were no holes on the ceiling or anywhere of their trailer and there was no damage inside their trailer; obviously they were not being bombed by a real bomb.

After a moment of composure and with no more explosions, Jim went outside with his flashlight to check. There was nobody around, but one side of their trailer facing the empty parking lot was covered with running-down eggs. He came back into the trailer to report his finding, "Some rascals had thrown eggs on our trailer! There must be more than a dozen eggs running down on the side of the trailer!"

Meilin was furious. Angry words poured out of her torrentially. "The dogs! Are they mad or just stupid? Who do they think we are!? We are just ordinary people taking a tour, enjoying a free night just like some rich people with luxury rigs. Why do the stupid dogs have to listen to the evil people to treat us like this? We have never done anything to them! The blind, stupid, mad dogs!!"

In the modern-day society, some high-rank politicians or celebrities might sometimes receive some egg-throws from some angry ordinary people who feel being mistreated or harmed by them. Jim and Meilin were ordinary people at the bottom of the society. They had never enjoyed any of the perks the powerful and the rich had enjoyed in their lives and never did any harm to other ordinary people. If anything, their talks and criticisms at their home were aimed at helping in improving the conditions of the people on the lower levels of the society. Now they were suffering this kind of shitty treatments that normally went with the power, fame and fortune. The whole thing was not only utterly unfair, but also highly absurd. The only possibility for this kind of things to happen to them was that some people, especially the youngsters, had been misled and used by some sort of power to abuse the couple and to shut them up. Of course, the main thing to excite and motivate the hooligans against this interracial couple would be racism. It looked that some people with power were very much offended by the couple's private talks and Meilin's writing, which resulted in the couple's entire loss of their privacy and having a very difficult life. But they had the right to live their life just like everybody else and could not suddenly become dumb and mute because of the situation they were in. If their private talks and Meilin's home writing had offended and upset some power, it must be that they had hit them on the right spots and they deserved every bit of the couple's criticisms. The bad thing was that, legitimate or illegitimate, the powerful could motivate and use a large number of people and the couple would inevitably lose their peace in life and their lives would be endangered. However, this egg-throw abuse would not scare the couple to voluntarily give up their life for the comfort and peace of the powerful. Compared with the couple who had to suffer daily the shitty situation with their rights being grossly violated and their lives being threatened, it was nothing at all for the powerful to feel a little disturbed by the couple's private talks.

After ranting out their angers, Jim took a basin of water and went outside to clean their trailer. If the eggs dried up, it would be very difficult to clean them off. It took a long time for Jim to have roughly cleaned up some of the mess. They did not have much stored water and could not use up all their drinking water. After this raucous happening, there was not much time left for the couple to sleep. They tried to go back to catch a little more rest, but were unsuccessful. The event was too upsetting for them to quiet down their minds.

However, if the couple had thought that this was the worst that had happened to them on this trip, they were dead wrong. On their way back and when they were approaching Winnipeg again, the worst had really happened, which had almost brought a real funeral ending like the send-off the couple had received at their trip's start. A month later when the couple came close to Winnipeg to go back home, a long stretch of highway in the area close to the city was under reconstruction. The four-lane highway had been reduced to two lanes and the traffic speed had been limited to sixty kilometres per hour. All the traffic had to go on one side of the highway on the two lanes that were rather closely connected. While Jim was driving the van at the speed limit in a line of vehicles, another line of vehicles were running opposite direction in the other lane. Then the couple could see a large tractor-trailer with double long trailers coming towards them at the speed limit. They did not pay much attention, as there were quite some other big trucks in both lanes. When the tractor trailer was about a metre or two in front of them, they experienced a loud explosion. There was no mistake; their van had been hit by a rock shooting out from the coming-on tractor-trailer.

For a moment, the powerful shot had taken the couple's breath away. By the time, the couple looked at their front windshield; the tractor trailer had already passed by. The rock had shattered the whole lower part of their windshield. Because of the way the windshield was built, the broken pieces of the glass were still stuck together, but a hole was clearly formed in the centre of the stretching lines of the broken window. If the hit had been a little higher, the rock could have penetrated the windshield and hit Jim. The result of that happening was hard to imagine. As such, Jim was quite shaken. Though suffering from memory loss and some other problems from the head injury in the military; Jim had been a well trained soldier who could remain steady in a dangerous critical situation. Under the loud explosion, he had held the steering-wheel and did not lose control. If Meilin were driving, she would surely have lost the control of the vehicle and their vehicles could have collided with other coming-on vehicles or went into the midsection of the big tractor-trailer. Then their death classified as from vehicle accident would have been achieved.

For quite some time after the hit, the couple remained silent, trying to calm down and sort out their thoughts or feelings. Then Meilin started angrily, "This might be an attempted murder! The speed limit is so low, how can a rock be shot out so powerfully from a facing-on vehicle? And the rock hit us just before the tractor trailer came up!"

Jim answered, still a bit shaken, "I'll not go that far, but in my whole driving life, this is the worst!"

Jim had been driving for about forty years and Meilin had been driving for about twenty years. They had both experienced the first rock shot of this scale in their driving lives. In their present situation of suffering from constant harassment and attacks from different people, this rock shot could not be entirely concluded as accidental. Then when they came back to Abbotsford, the same kind incident had happened to them again, which made the scale tip more to agree with Meilin's suspicion.

One day, the couple drove to do their weekly grocery shopping. When they were just going to turn into a parking lot, a car was driving towards them. Both their van and that car had slowed down to no more than thirty kilometres per hour. At about a metre distance between their van and that car, the couple experienced a powerful rock shot from that car. This time, the driving speed was so low, about thirty kilometers an hour; Meilin had seen the rock shooting out from the front of that car. The car sat lower than their van, still the rock did some damage to the middle of their front windshield. After this shot, the car was sped up and soon disappeared in the street. When the couple realized what had just happened to them, the car had long gone. Meilin was agitated and spoke quickly to Jim, "See! You should believe me now. This rock shooting thing is not accidental! Can you believe that a small car driving at the speed of thirty kilometres per hour can splash a rock out from the front of the car to damage our van? And the street is so clean; there are no rocks or pebbles around!"

This time, Jim kept silent, as suspicion also came into his mind. Then Meilin continued, "Next time, if this kind of things happen again, we are going to turn our van around immediately and follow the vehicle shooting the rock. We'll catch the bastard! We are going to check under the hood of that vehicle to see if there are some devices there. With the damage done to our vehicle, we have the right to do so!"

"Yes, we'll do that," Jim agreed, feeling the seriousness of the incidents.

All those things that had happened to the couple when they were just passing through Winnipeg made them wonder. Two things looked clear to them. One was that racial discrimination was a serious problem in this city and province. The Chinatown of Winnipeg becoming a ghost town might not just be their feelings or imagination, but the result of racial discrimination. Quite some coloured people might have been beaten down and driven out from this place. The dark racist power could not tolerate Jim and Meilin, an outspoken interracial couple, even though they were just passing through the place. There probably had never been such precedence in this place that an interracial couple's voice would be heard in the public. The abused or persecuted people here probably had always taken quietly what had been thrown at them or just left to some other places of the country that were more tolerant to their existence. The couple's private yet open talks had often carried sharp criticisms to racial discrimination. In the strongly white orientated society, the couple had to be put down and their "crime" had to be severely punished in the minds of the racists. It looked that Winnipeg had plenty of those dark characters who were powerful and bold.

The second thing the couple realized was that quite some crimes, large or small, were accompanied or started by discriminations. The abuses and persecutions to people of different colour, age, gender, creed, religion or political views would inevitably come to the point that it is, after all, the strong beating down the weak, the majority beating down the minority or the powerful beating down the powerless. Any minor differences from the weak powerless minorities could offend the strong powerful majority and bring troubles and miseries to the weak. At the present time, that Winnipeg had become the murder capital of the country might very well have something to do with or to have been started by racial discrimination. The resentment and dissatisfaction of some whites towards the country's accepting coloured people, though sparks at the start, could enflame into dark vicious violent fire.

Canadians have to hold firm the memories and the profound lessons from the Second World War which was started by racial discrimination. In this War, not only millions of Jewish people had been brutally killed, but also many other peoples had perished by the insane violence of the racists who so strongly believed that their races were superior and other races and weak people should be cleansed from the face of the earth. To oppose this grave injustice and violence, many people, including many Canadian white men and women, had given up their lives to fight in the War. Any decent and sane people in the world would not allow this kind of history to repeat. In Canada, no efforts should be spared in putting down racial discrimination. Everybody, if accepted by the country to be a citizen, should be welcomed, accepted and treated as equal citizens. Though this equality issue has been firmly set up in the constitution of the country, it has sometimes been far away from the minds and agendas of some big or small politicians. Under such attitudes of the politicians, quite some Canadians will not even admit that Canada has a problem of racial discrimination. Yet, the neglect of paying serious attention to this issue and making sure that racial discrimination be gradually eliminated from the Canadian life can lead to grave consequences. This issue is closely related to the country's safety, prosperity and definitely vital for all the Canadians to be able to live a safe, peaceful and happy life.

At this moment after the egg-attack, Jim and Meilin tried hard to calm down and go back to take a little more rest, but sleep or peace of mind had left them. When dawn descended with a little gentle light, they got up and had their simple breakfast. It would be better to start driving in the early hour of the morning. The traffic would be light and more importantly, they could have their minds diverted from this upsetting event. The couple pulled their vehicles out of the parking lot of the Walmart and was in no time running on the street leading to the highway toward Ontario.

Traveling is like life. Staying in the spot where bad things have happened can cause the mind chew the misery repeatedly. Moving forward and leaving the past behind will sometimes be the best way to reset the mental state and to start anew. Of course, in many ways, life cannot be entirely like traveling. We cannot always physically move away from the places where bad things have happened to us. However, human beings have long learnt the best ways to move forward and to leave the bad past behind. Most of those ways depend on their strength and will to control their minds. Though Jim and Meilin had not hewn their strength or will to control their minds to a high degree, they had been trying hard to cultivate and practice this skill. In their present situation, they knew that they very much needed this skill to survive.

The streets of Winnipeg leading to the highway at the early hour of morning were relatively quiet. The couple soon came to the end of the city's east section. They were going through an old section of the city. The buildings along the street were far from pretty. They were one storey high with stucco, wood or metal sidings. With flat roofs, those buildings looked like square boxes, closely linked together and lined up along the sidewalks. It was an old commercial area. All those square buildings housed small businesses.

All the large cities in Canada have their high areas with stunning skyscraper or stylish old tall large buildings, modern museums and galleries, beautiful parks and gardens and all kinds of grand government or public facilities. Yet they all have their low areas with some not so pretty buildings or facilities. In those well developed large cities those low areas are gradually disappearing; those ones still existing are mainly left from history. Some old buildings and old streets have been deliberately preserved; they are the ones that have historical, artistic or architectural values. The oldest house, the couple had seen in Winnipeg was among those ones. In that street where this old house stood, there were some more old large houses in different colours and mainly Victorian style. That street must be the high end of the city in the old time. Now the couple were passing through the low end of city left from the old time. They had seen this kind of low areas almost in every large city; some cities had small low end area and some large. Even in a rich country, the couple knew that they were bound to see different areas in a city. The situation looks going into the future as it is one of the inequality expressions in human society. In modern days, with the rapid enlargement of the middle class, more Canadians are living in two or even three storey houses or nice condos. Still, there are high areas of a city where huge luxury mansions with beautiful gardens will dazzle every passerby. In the low areas however, tiny old bungalows and even tinier apartments will surprise the onlookers. Then even if it is occasional, the rich country will still have some homeless people whose tent dwellings and small shopping carts holding all their possessions will unavoidably depress anyone who happen to encounter them.

The couple drove through the old low end of Winnipeg. The box-like business buildings along the street occupied their feelings and thoughts. Their minds had been pulled away from the upsetting event of last night. Soon they left the city and came onto the highway flanked by broad green fields and occasional rivers and hills. Immediately, they felt better, could let go of the unpleasant night and move on with their trip. Their expectations of seeing wonders and beauty of nature and human cities went up again.

CHAPTER SIX

ONTARIO

Compared with the trans-Canada highways across some other provinces, the trans-Canada highway through Manitoba was the shortest so far. Jim and Meilin soon crossed the border and were running on the highway of Ontario. The trans-Canada highway across Ontario was the longest in the country. The long stretch of the highway through some hilly or mountainous terrains here was mostly of two lanes. Jim and Meilin knew that it would take them a few days just to exhaust the Ontario highway. They were prepared and patient for the long haul.

The land of Ontario is quite varied. There are almost all geographic features, flat land, marshes, hills, mountains, lakes, rivers and the ocean along some of its borders. Still, the rocky Canadian Shield has covered more than half of this province. The other most dominant land feature of Ontario is the gigantic lakes. Of the five great lakes in North America, Ontario shares four of them with the United States; they are Lake Superior, Lake Huron, Lake Erie and Lake Ontario. Only Lake Michigan is entirely in the United States. Ontario is a province of water. The native peoples named the place Ontario meaning Beautiful Lake or Beautiful Water.

Ontario is the richest, most populated and most industrialized province in Canada. It is the political and financial centre of the country today. Over one thirds of the Canadians live in this province. The dominant industry of this province is manufacturing. Ninety-five per cent of the automobile and parts industries of Canada are in this province. Besides the manufacturing, the mining industry in this province is also leading in the country. The province has rich nickel, uranium, copper and other mineral deposits of Canada. Plenty of water for the development of hydroelectricity, sufficient man power, developed transportation system, close to the industrial centers of the United States and above all, the abundant resources have been the foundations for the province to gain the top positions in its pulp and paper, mining and manufacturing industries. Agriculture had played the major role in the old days. Today, though industries have been leading the economy, agriculture has not lost its importance; it is more diversified with the increase of fruit, cattle, dairying, poultry and fresh water fish productions.

Ottawa, the capital of Canada, is in Ontario. Toronto, the capital of Ontario, is the largest city in Canada and one of the largest and culturally most diversified cities in the world. More than 100 languages are spoken by the people and more than 200 ethnic groups reside here. Toronto is a major industrial, commercial, educational and English speaking culture centre of Canada. It has half of the head offices and three quarters of Canadian national business establishments. The Toronto Stock Exchange is next only to the New York Stock Exchange; its annual stock trading is worth billions of dollars. Things are just like a Canadian historian's saying: the power, the people and the money reside here in Ontario.

To the Canadians, Ontario is the province of opportunity. Through the time, people all over the country have come here to seek jobs and to make a fortune. Though the problem of racial discrimination in this province is not much better than other provinces, it is regarded by the immigrants as the ideal place for their settlements in Canada. Compared with other provinces, Ontario has provided more opportunities for the immigrants, and therefore over half of the immigrants coming to Canada choose Ontario to settle down. This continued large inflow of immigrants from the world and emigrants from other provinces has built, boosted and strengthened Ontario economically, culturally and politically throughout history.

Jim and Meilin were aware of Ontario's position in Canada. During their driving on the highway of this province, they paid attention to not only the scenery, but also the people, the farm houses, the villages, the towns and the cities. The population in this province was indeed much higher than other provinces. Along the highway, there were more farm houses and more urban residences. They had definitely no feelings of being in the wilderness here. Though the crop fields here were pocketed and not like those broad ones in the prairie provinces, they could be spotted all along the highway. Some of the farm houses were built by bricks, which were hard to see in other parts of the country. Large plants or factories normally appeared with towns or cities.

The couple spent their first night by the highway. In the late afternoon, they spotted a large restaurant with a spacious parking lot by the highway. They pulled into the parking lot and decided to spend the night there. According to the map, the place was called English River. Around the restaurant, there were a few residential houses and a fire-hall. The houses were in good condition and with large green lawns around them, but the rest of the township was a little distance away and hidden from the view.

Jim and Meilin set up their trailer at the back of the parking lot away from the highway. Besides the paved parking lot, there was another large gravel parking lot at the back of the restaurant. It looked that this place was favoured and frequented by the truckers. The long distance passenger buses also used this place as a resting stop. The coupe soon saw a bus with a full load of passengers pulling into the parking lot and the bus riders leaving the bus to have a meal in the restaurant or using the washroom there. After their own supper, the couple had a walk around and enjoyed some fresh air. The bus with all its passengers had left. The place was clean and quiet. The couple were happy that they could have a nice free night here. After last night's ordeal, they needed a good sleep. They had no idea whether there was a campground around and had no heart to find it. The place looked ideal. Tomorrow morning, it would be convenient for them to pull their vehicles out and immediately run on the highway again.

To their dismay, the restaurant started fixing their roof or chimney not long after the supper. The loud banging and clanking made it impossible for them to rest. They were using the restaurant parking lot for free and had no right to complain. They waited patiently. The noises eventually stopped around nine o'clock at night. They went to bed immediately. Sleeping was no problem when they were tired of the day's traveling after last night's trouble. But in the middle of the night, they were waked up by loud booming noises again. Frustrated, Jim got up and went outside to check what was going on. He came back soon.

"Three big tractor-trailers have parked together on the gravel lot. The drivers have left the engines running. Maybe they will turn them off soon," Jim reported and went to bed, trying to get some sleep.

Well, the place must have always been the truckers' place. The couple had to be patient, wait and pray that the truckers would turn the engines off soon. The noises from the engines of three big tractor-trailers sounded like constant vibrating thundering. It was impossible for them to sleep. They waited and waited. An hour or more had passed; the trucks were continuingly thundering and looked going to go on till morning.

"Why do they have to keep the trucks running in the hot summer?" asked Meilin, very much frustrated and suspecting that this was harassment trick being pulled on them again.

"I don't know. Maybe some truckers cannot sleep without the sound of the engine running," answered Jim.

"They need three trucks running to sleep!?" Meilin was disgusted and then she said, "Jim, we have to move, otherwise it will be another sleepless night."

Jim agreed. Instead of staying here and waiting for the everlastingly thundering trucks to stop, it might be better to venture into the darkness and find another spot to sleep for the little time left. The place had no street lights. Except the lit parking lot, all around was pitch darkness. Jim turned the van lights on and took off the stabilizers from the trailer. When they pulled their trailer out of the parking lot, he had to turn on the van's high-beam to see the road. Meilin remembered that some distance back by the highway, there was a construction site where a house was being built. Quite some space was there. She asked Jim to get their vehicles there.

The couple drove in the utter darkness. There were no other travellers on the road and no lights to be seen in this hour of night. They reached the construction site and parked their trailer there. They did not bother to stabilize the trailer and went to bed immediately for the two hours or so of sleep. Early next morning, they got up and had a simple breakfast. They decided that it would be better to leave the site before the workers came to work.

With very little sleep again for another night, the couple drove a short distance next day. The city of Thunder Bay was near. They turned into the road to reach the city and found a nice campground at the city skirt. It was a large campground with partial service. All the campsites were in woods. The campground had covered a whole hill and a valley with a river running by. The couple set up their trailer on a lot all surrounded by trees and bushes. Ontario is in the central part of Canada. The province starts the eastern regions and part of it reaches further south. Toronto is the most southern mega city in the country and the central heart of the North America Continent. Being partially eastern and southern, Ontario has more broad-leaf trees as well as the tall trees like those in the cold northwest. With lots of water, the trees and bushes were lushly thick here. It was a week day; there were no other campers around. The couple were glad and had their hopes up again, thinking that this time they were going to have a good sleep. They paid the fees for two nights, knowing that they needed a good rest before pushing on further.

Things went pretty well the whole afternoon. The couple remained to be the lone campers and enjoyed a nap with only birds chirping and soft wind rustling through the trees. After the nap, they walked to the river which must be Kakabeka River, as Kakabeka Falls was near. The river bed at this spot was wide. The water was shallow, very clear and running rapidly. The pebbles, stones, boulders and slabs in the water were clearly to be seen and some of them were protruding out of the water. The couple hopped on the stones and slabs and went to the middle of the river. All around them were small waterfalls formed by the stones breaking the way of the flowing water. The only sound here was the sound of flowing water. This was paradise to the couple. They enjoyed to their hearts' content the fresh air, the water flowing sound and the beautiful river with the green river banks; they were fully enchanted by the beauty and peace of nature. At this moment, all the anger, fret and frustration were washed clean from their minds. They were part of nature, pure and peaceful. Somehow, those small waterfalls around them had brought back fresh and clear memory of the giant Niagara Falls. Years ago, the couple had visited the famous Niagara Falls in Ontario. The treasured memory of that visit would probably stay with them for the rest of their life.

Niagara Falls is not only the most treasured natural wonder in Ontario, but also in the country and even in the world. Every year, millions of people come from all over the world to pay their visit and to enjoy the spectacular beauty of this natural wonder. The spot has been especially favored by the newlyweds as their honeymoon destination. Though with tremendous force, the waterfalls seem to be able to generate abundant feelings of beauty, harmony and romance.

There are actually two waterfalls on the Niagara spot, one on the Canadian side and one on the American side. The Canadian Falls is 177 feet high and 2,215 feet wide. There is a concave formed on the crest, shaping the giant waterfalls semi-circular and resulting in the name, Horseshoe Falls. Across the river, the American Falls is straight, 184 feet high and 1,075 feet wide. On the Canadian side, a walkway with a low stone wall for people to view the waterfalls is built along the high river bank and a street is accompanying this walkway. During the tourist season, the tour buses are pouring into the street and visitors filling up the walkway. The splendid view of the waterfalls on both the Canadian and American sides from this walled walkway is perfect and very close. Still, there are fair-sized motor boats called Maids of the Mist running back and forth in the rapidly flowing river, taking visitors even closer to the Horseshoe Falls to feel the tremendous force and the thundering power of the waterfalls. The splash of the waterfalls is so powerful that a permanent mist is formed to shroud the bottom part of the falls. The Maids of the Mist look like tiny spirits flowing in and out of this white mist. In a sunny day, a rainbow will emerge from the mist to make the visitors feel being blessed. The newlyweds aboard those motor boats near the waterfalls will probably feel being baptised and promised a beautiful loving marriage by the touch of such a forceful splashing of water from such powerful waterfalls. Then, there are helicopters taking the visitors to the sky to view the waterfalls and the surrounding area from above. On the American side, a wooden staircase is hanging down on the cliff side by side with the waterfalls. The visitors can go on the stairs to be physically right by the waterfalls. There are two bridges over the river, connecting the two sides. People can enjoy the two waterfalls whichever way they like; of course, they have to be able to pass the hoops of an international border to go to the American side.

Along the river-bank street on the Canadian side; many beautiful modern restaurants, hotels and shops have been built in recent time. At night, coloured lights will illuminate the waterfalls to make them look even more romantic. However, whatever facilities and decorations the humans have been putting around or on the waterfalls and whatever amount of visitors have been pouring into this spot, the natural beauty and force of the waterfalls stand out, untouched, undiminished and incomparable.

Niagara Falls has not only attracted nature-lovers and honeymooners, but also dare-devils who cannot control their urges to fall with the waters from the top to the bottom. The spectacular beauty and harmonious appearance of this natural wonder have the power to mesmerize or intoxicate the visitors that they lose all their fears to the dangers of this powerful natural force. Each year in the old days, there would be some dare-devils jumping over the giant waterfalls; some were encapsulated by barrels or metal containers. A few survived those most daring jumps, and most lost their lives, being pinned down by the tremendous pounding force of the colossal amount of water. Today, jumping over Niagara Falls is illegal. The dare-devils have to be saved by law.

Niagara Falls is about 12 thousand years old. The river is actually a strait, collecting the drainages from the Upper Great Lakes, pouring down tremendous amount of waters from three waterfalls and draining into Lake Ontario. Besides these two waterfalls at the location of Canadian and American cities of Niagara Falls, there is a smaller one called Bridal Veil which is separated from these two giant ones by some small islands. Almost four million litres of waters are pouring down from these three waterfalls per second. The depth of the river at the drop point of the waterfalls is about the same as the height of the waterfalls. The river following the waterfalls is one of the wildest, full of rapids and whirlpools. The flow of the rapids can reach 48 kilometres per hour. Of course, this kind of natural power is harvested for electricity. The flow of the three waterfalls have been diverted evenly to prevent the rapid erosion of the limestone crests and diverted to turn the turbines to produce electric power. On the Canadian side, a power station is built by the Horseshoe Falls. But during the tourist season, the flow diversion is only done in the middle of the night to leave the full beauty and power of the waterfalls for the visitors to enjoy during the day.

The couple felt it a pity that they were not going to revisit Niagara Falls on this cross-country trip. Their present journey was long; they were not going to revisit those famous sightseeing spots that were not on their route. Even they would very much like to see Niagara Falls again; they had to dismiss the idea. They had to concentrate their energy to finish their present endeavour. However, they planned to visit Kakabeka Falls the first thing tomorrow morning. They would not miss the waterfalls that happened to be on their way.

After the river excursion, the couple came back to their campsite, feeling refreshed. When they arrived at their campsite, they saw that they got company. A middle-aged couple with a rented motor home had camped not far from them. Jim and Meilin felt a relief. As long as the neighbours were not large groups of young people, the place would remain safe from loud noises and they could have a good sleep. The evening went quietly and they went to bed early. They soon fell asleep. At about ten o'clock, they were awakened by loud noises. A group of young people came and camped not far from them. Their loud music, shouting and screaming woke the couple from their sweet sleep. The rowdy noises must have also disturbed all the small animals in this thick wooded area and sent them running. Luckily, the noises only lasted for about an hour and then all were quiet down. The whole woods heaved a relief and everybody went back to sleep again. Jim and Meilin had a sound sleep after this interval.

Next morning, when the couple were leaving the campground with their van for the sightseeing of the waterfalls and Thunder Bay, they saw a worker working by the park's road. Jim stopped the van beside the worker. After the morning greetings, he talked about last night's noisy incident, "Some youngsters were so noisy for a while last night, and then they stopped..."

"Oh, that... We asked them to stop when the curfew started; they would not comply, so we drove the rowdy bunch out of the park," answered the worker with a smile.

"Thank you very much for doing that. It's hard to get a decent sleep on a campground nowadays. I hope all the campgrounds will carry out the strict rules and do what you have done," said Jim gratefully.

The couple were indeed grateful for what this campground had done to the inconsiderate youngsters and to preserve a peaceful environment for their normal patrons. If the youngsters were sent out especially to harass the couple, they got some help this time to swat it off. With thankful words and waves of goodbyes, the couple left the worker waving his goodbye with a broad smile.

The couple soon arrived at the Kakabeka Falls. The place was a provincial park. There were abundant trees and bushes around the river and the waterfalls. Though the size of the waterfalls here could not compare with that of Niagara Falls, its beauty and roaring power had touched the couple just as well. The beauty, harmony and peace of nature in large or small scale, all have the power to influence or affect human emotions, moods or mental states. Paying attention, anyone can find something in nature to enjoy, to love and to appreciate.

The couple did not stay long in Kakabeka Falls. They soon left for Thunder Bay. It did not take long for them to reach the city centre. Thunder Bay became a city in 1970 as the result of Fort William and Port Arthur joining together. It is a rather new city, but it has grown rapidly into a medium-sized city. The city is by Lake Superior and has been a large port, a seaport. During the 1950's, Canada and the United States joined forces to build St. Lawrence Seaway. The seaway is a 3,768 kilometer marine highway extending from western shore of Lake Superior to the Atlantic Ocean. St. Lawrence Seaway connecting the Great Lakes with the Atlantic Ocean was opened in 1959. Since then, it has been a vital part of Ontario's economy. It has transformed inland ports such as Thunder Bay, Sarnia, Winsor, Hamilton and Toronto into seaports. Today, Ontario handles about 30% of national and international waterway shipping of the country.

While driving through the main streets of Thunder Bay, the couple could see that the city streets were wide, large new buildings along the streets gave the city a modern appearance and the whole place looked clean and spacious. Jim and Meilin parked their van at the harbour to have a good look at Lake Superior. The lake was vast and looked like the ocean. But at the harbour, there was a long dam separating the harbour from the lake and leaving only a gate to let ships and boats in. The waves of the lake appeared a bit gentler than the ocean waves. Perhaps bearing the knowledge of freshwater lake in mind, people tended to feel the lake more friendly and peaceful. Standing by the shore of the gigantic lake, Jim and Meilin were overwhelmed by its size. It was every bit like the ocean. The wind was sweeping strongly over this immensely open space dominated by water and sky. There were quite some motor boats anchored at the harbour. They looked like boats for pleasures rather than for fishing. The shipping piers and fishing vessels must be in another location. The place they were in was a park. There was a stone bridge over a lagoon here. The lake water was flowing into the lagoon and some water fountains in the lagoon were shooting waters. In this harbour park, there were displays of two large anchors and some other objects concerning navigation. There was also a simple sculpture of sailing boats. Thunder Bay must have some significance in military history, as there was an ancient cannon sitting beside those displays of navigation. The couple knew that the War of 1812 had been fought in this area of Ontario. On the green lawn not far from those displays stationed an original train car in orange and green colours. The couple felt that all those simple displays had well illustrated the city, its history and the things important to the people here.

The War of 1812 is a war fought between the British Colony of Canada called British North America and the United States along the borders between Ontario and some American states. The bloodiest battle happened at Lundy's Lane in Niagara Falls. This fierce battle was the turning point, as the war soon ended afterwards. In 1814, the Treaty of Ghent was signed to reinstate the border line. Two hundred years later, the Canadians generally consider the War of 1812 resulted in a Canadian victory in driving out the American invaders and the Americans generally consider this war ambiguous and resulted in a draw. Thank God, for the following two hundred years and more, there has been peace between the two countries. Following the cities on both sides of the Niagara River, some Canadian cities have formed a bound with American cities to become sister cities. The political and economical relationships of the two countries, though not entirely trouble free, have been closely related.

After viewing the harbour, the couple turned their attention inland. Close to the harbour, there were two large buildings. One was a stylish old building built by red bricks. Along the shore of the lake, there was a railway track parallel with a city street. The old brick building stood by the railway; it might have been a train station or the custom building for the harbour in the old days. The international border with the United States was close by through the lake. Now the old building hosted a large restaurant and some other shops. Across the street, there was another large building. This one was brand new. With a line of big frontal columns, the modern building had an air of a Roman temple. This building belonged to a bank.

While Jim and Meilin were checking around the harbour, loud music was drifting from the inner city. They asked some passers-by for the reason of the music and got the information that a street event was going on in the city. The couple walked some distance to reach the street where the festival was on. They saw that the traffic had been blocked from a wide street. A large stage had been set up in the centre of this street. A band was playing loud music and a male singer was singing on the stage. Along the street, some venders had set up their stands. They were selling crafts and local produces. A street performer was juggling knives and then fire balls in the street. A toy train pulled by a tractor was carrying children and fun-loving adults, running up and down the street. Everything seemed going for a great festival, but as it was not a weekend day, there were not many attendants. Jim and Meilin watched the street performer, rode the toy train and bought some snacks to nibble on. They had attended quite some street festivals in different cities. This one was smaller and had less hustling and bustling than the others.

After leaving the festival street, the couple drove around the city. Without the city map, they could only drive through the main streets and have a rough look. The wide streets and large buildings along the streets gave them the impression of a new well-to-do city. They did a little shopping and then went back to the campground. After the sightseeing, they planned to stay in the trailer to rest for the afternoon and take a walk around the campground after supper.

The place remained quiet and peaceful. They were glad that they could get a good rest here. After the supper and the walk, they settled down to read a book and to relax. With so many lakes, Ontario must have had quite some marshes. The couple found that mosquitoes here appeared more numerous and they had to close their trailer door all the time. While they stayed in the trailer, resting, somebody came to knock on their door. Jim opened the door and saw the neighbour, the middle-aged man from the rented motor home. The man was stubby and had a well-weathered face with a gentle smile.

"Good evening. Sorry to bother you. I would like to ask the direction..."

The man spoke correct English with a strong foreign accent. There was not much space in the couple's trailer; Jim stood at the door and talked with him.

"Good evening. What do you want to know?"

"Which highway should I take to go to Prince Rupert?"

"That's a long way yet from here..." said Jim.

Prince Rupert is a place in British Columbia at the west end of the country by the Pacific Ocean. To reach the place, there are four Canadian provinces yet to cross from here. Practically, Prince Rupert is almost half way across the country from this spot.

Meilin cut in, thinking that she had studied the country's map more thoroughly and could offer some help, "It's simple. You can keep on going this highway until you hit Highway 16, the Yellowhead Trail. Then just follow the Yellowhead Trail west to the end. Prince Rupert is at the end of that highway."

The man thanked them for the direction. Then he looked wanting to have a chat. Jim started asking him questions. The couple got to know that their neighbour came from Germany. The German couple had a friend in Prince Rupert who owned a piece of land there. They heard that the place was beautiful and decided to visit their friend and the place. They took the cross-Canada journey from the east to the west to reach Prince Rupert and did not have a map of Canada!

"Yes, Prince Rupert is a very beautiful place. So, you have started from Halifax! What do you think of Canada?" Jim asked. Like most Canadians, he liked to hear foreigners praising the country.

"It is large and beautiful," said the man sincerely. Then he tried to find more words to say something, but said something else instead, "But don't go to Wawa. We have come from there. Our van... vehicle... is covered by insects. It changed colour of the vehicle..."

The size of Ontario alone can be the size of several Germany. It was obvious that this German man was very much impressed by the size of the country and in the meantime, overwhelmed by the wilderness of some parts of Canada. Most of us like to hear praises for our country, our society, our people, our families and ourselves, but life can never be full of praises. The wise know well that unpleasant things said in good intentions are often more valuable than all the praises. In this case, it was obvious that the man was honest and his intention was to return a favour by giving a warning about the numerous insects in Wawa. Jim and Meilin thanked him for his information. They could well imagine that in the lake area with water all around, insects could raise havoc.

After the man left, Meilin said to Jim, “We have a map of western Canada. We won’t use it. Why don’t you give it to the German couple?”

Jim took the map and went to the motor home. He stayed there quite long and had another chat with both of them. Coming from Germany for a cross-country tour in such a large country, the German couple might have felt lonely and craved for some company. Asking directions might also be a way for them to have a chat with other travellers.

Jim and Meilin had another good sleep on this campground. Next day, they started moving early in the morning. On the south side of Thunder Bay by the highway, they spotted a direction board pointing to a place where a monument in honor of Terry Fox, a Canadian hero, was set up. Terry Fox was a young man, a British Columbia resident, who had suffered from bone cancer when he was 18. One of his legs had been amputated and a stick of steel had been put in its place. Under the heavy burden of such personal sufferings, the young man started a cross-country run in 1980 to raise the awareness of cancer and to promote cancer research in fighting the disease. His courageous and unselfish act had moved and inspired not only the Canadians, but also many people in the world. For two years, all the eyes and thoughts had been focused on this young man and on his Marathon of Hope. Unfortunately, Terry Fox did not finish the run. Cancer stopped him at Thunder Bay. He passed away not long afterwards. However, with one leg and cancer, the young man had run 5,373 kilometres and covered half of the cross-country distance. A monument had been built here at Thunder Bay to commemorate his heroic deeds.

Jim and Meilin turned their vehicles to the side road leading to the monument. They were going to pay their respect to this heroic young man. In a short distance of climbing up a hill, they arrived at the site. There was a large flat open area on top of the hill. A paved parking lot had occupied a large part of the place. A building in red colour and oriental style was by the parking lot. The monument was at the edge of the hill, overlooking part of Lake Superior. There could not be a place more appropriate than this for the monument.

In spite of all the vile and treacheries in the human world, the human spirit can reach the noblest height when inspired by some pure noble ideas. The inspired noble human spirit is indomitable. One of those noble ideas is the idea of fighting against sufferings, which has, time and again, raised human spirit to the unconquerable peak. Diseases are very much part of human sufferings. Many battles against them have been fought during the human history. Terry Fox, the courageous young Canadian man had joined the noble rank in setting up a shining example of the indomitable human spirit in fighting against sufferings for the whole human race.

Jim and Meilin parked their vehicles in the parking lot. They could see the large monument standing high not far. They walked through a path lined up by tall trees on both sides to reach the monument. The grand monument had a large bronze statue of the running Terry Fox on top of a stand, facing the west, the direction he was running to. On the wall of the monument stand, there were the engraved emblems of the ten Canadian provinces and two territories. At the base of the monument, there was a large map of Canada marked by the distance covered by Terry Fox's Marathon of Hope. Around the monument, there was a pool of water. As the whole monument was fenced off by a low iron-rod fence, the visitors could not get too close to the monument. But the couple saw that some visitors had been throwing coins towards the water and the map. This seemed a disrespectful act.

In the whole world, any good things set up by some human beings; some other human beings will try to tear them down. There is no exception in Canada concerning this matter. However, in this case, most people throwing coins towards the monument might have acted out of habit; they might simply want to touch their particular province by their coin throws. In any park, if there was an interesting body of water, people would throw coins to that water. This annoying habit might have started by some wishing-well thoughts. While people were throwing coins, they wished that their throws would bring them some luck if their coins reached a certain spot.

Human habit is the most tenacious thing and very hard to change. People act habitually without thinking most of time. However, the worst kind of habits is the habitual thinking or views about certain things and people, because this kind of habit involves consciousness and thoughts, and it is intentional habit. Even with plenty of facts in life to prove that some habitual views are wrong, some habitual thinkers will never change their views or the way of their thinking. This is why the most difficult thing to change in the world is the human beings who have set up their iron-fisted habits and their habitual ways of thinking and habitual ways of life. Perhaps someday in the future, when human beings are evolved or civilized to the level that they can easily and constantly change bad habits and foster good habits, the world then can be easily changed to the good.

Jim and Meilin looked at the statue of the heroic young man; they knew that it did not matter much that some mindless people would throw coins towards it. Terry Fox had gone and he would certainly not bother about those trifling things. More importantly, this courageous unselfish young man's deeds and spirit would last in people's minds for a long time to come. Looking at the enormous Lake Superior below and beyond, the couple felt that things pure and noble like Terry Fox's spirit were like the lake; they would always be there with human life, co-existing with some bad and ugly things.

After paying respect to Terry Fox, the couple went to the red building to have a look. It was a tourist information office. They did not tarry long there. Soon they were on the road again. After two nights of good sleep, they drove a bit longer this day and reached Sudbury.

Sudbury is a large city in Northern Ontario. It is well known in the world for its mining, smelting and refinery. Its special geographic feature has raised the geographic science in this region to an important position. The geologists have believed that about two billion years ago, a huge meteorite hit Sudbury Basin and made this area very rich in minerals. Leading by rich nickel storage, many other minerals are also abundant here. The rich mineral deposits have not only resulted in the prosperous mining and related industries in this area, but also the efforts in geographic science and the existence of several museums concerning the geography and mining in this area. The most notable museum is the Dynamic Earth in the city, which takes the visitors seven storeys deep down into the earth to see the rock formations of the earth. The museum also shows a 120 year mining history of Sudbury. In 2001, seven surrounding towns had joined Sudbury to make it a large city. The people here today have proudly called their city the Great Sudbury.

Jim and Meilin did not have much detailed information about Sudbury. At the entrance of the city, the couple spotted a large shopping centre. The medium-sized or large cities are quite many in Ontario; they were all spacious and had large buildings. The shops and department stores here looked larger than those in the equivalent cities of other provinces. This shopping centre at the entrance of Sudbury was formed by large new buildings which housed the big businesses such as Superstore, Walmart, Sears, Zellers and so on. There were large parking lots around those store buildings.

It was near supper time. Jim and Meilin decided to spend the night on one of those parking lots, instead of going to hunt for a campground. Pulling into the shopping centre, they were glad to see that quite some other travelers had the same idea. A side parking lot by the Walmart had already been occupied exclusively by quite some campers. Most of them had large luxury motor homes and trailers. Jim and Meilin joined those travellers and parked their small trailer among them. Though some of those travellers with luxury rigs might think the couple's small trailer out of place among them, the couple had never felt that they were intruders in this kind of high society. Weren't they the same in trying to get a free camping night on a parking lot?

After stabilizing their trailer and a little rest, the couple went to the Superstore to buy some ready-made food. They were tired after the day's driving and did not have much heart to cook. Large grocery stores normally served foods such as the roasted chickens, cooked pizza, turkey salad and some other things. The cost of buying those foods was much lower than to eat in a restaurant. Walking into the Superstore here, they had a bit different sensation. The height of the ceilings here doubled those of the other Superstores and the lighting too was doubly brilliant; these gave them the feelings of comfort and luxury. The couple did not spend much time looking around. They bought a roasted chicken, a potato salad and a green salad. They liked this kind of arrangement for a meal. As they had a fridge in the trailer, the chicken would be several meals, and even the potato and vegetable salads could provide another one or two meals.

The supper was effortless and delicious. After the supper, the couple went to the Walmart. They had a walk there and bought some odds and ends for the trailer and snacks for nibbling on the road. When they came back to the trailer to wash up and have some relaxation time, they were annoyed that a neighbouring trailer was still running their generator. Not long after Jim and Meilin set up their trailer among the large luxury travelling rigs on this parking lot, a neighbouring trailer started running their generator. The machine had stood outside the large trailer and the loud noise was constantly booming. The generator kept on rumbling long after supper. It looked that it would go on the whole night. The couple tried to ignore the noise and to have a little rest, but it was difficult to do so.

"Why do they need the generator going on after supper?" asked Meilin, very much annoyed.

"Probably for the air-conditioner or something else, but I'm going over there to talk to them. There are so many people around here; all need some rest and a good night's sleep," said Jim with determination.

Just after the couple pulled their trailer into the shopping centre, a shower had started and the temperature was nicely cooled down. The couple thought that they would have a good sleep here, but now with the generator roaring, it looked that they were going to kiss a nice night's sleep good-bye again, unless they would confront the problem and do something about it. Jim was normally an easygoing person and did not like to have confrontations with others. But after so many bad camping nights, he was resolved to do something now. On this public parking lot, there would be no park-warden coming to see the curfew being observed. Somebody had to do something to make sure that the night would be quiet.

"That's good. You go there and ask them to turn that thing off! People need some rest. It is not that hot now; they don't need to run the air conditioner," said Meilin. She was glad, thinking that when being pushed against the wall with nobody coming to save you, even a lamb like Jim would butt. She wished that Jim would go there like a lion and roar at the inconsiderate people.

Jim went to the noisy trailer and came back quickly with a satisfied smile on his face.

"They are going to turn the generator off," he announced.

Not long, the rumbling machine was stopped. The couple heaved a relief, thinking that they could have a good sleep that night after all. Before the dark night fell, there were some heavy vehicles rushing through the street by the parking lot, but afterwards, things quieted down and they did enjoy another good night's sleep.

Next morning, the couple debated whether they should go into the city of Sudbury to have a tour. From the tour guide book and from what they had seen so far, they knew that there were quite some attractions in Sudbury. Besides the industrial and scientific features, the city and the area had numerous lakes and provided plenty of summer recreation areas for swimming, boating, fishing and hiking. This shopping centre at the city entrance had already given the couple a strong impression of a rich city. The quantity of tourists with luxury travelling rigs had also told them that the city had plenty of attractions and recreational facilities to be able to lure all those well-off people. However, without a city map and having to drag their trailer behind, the couple felt intimidated to venture into a strange city. As they did not have much long to drive to Toronto, they decided to drive on. Ever since they started the trip, they felt the urge to push on and to finish the long journey. However, Toronto, the capital of Ontario, was on their agenda and they would take the efforts to go through. They had been in Toronto twice before, but did not see much, so they were going to pay the mega city another visit. They knew that Toronto was massive and hard for the visitors to get around. This time, they checked the map carefully, decided the route they were going to take and the campground they were going to stay.

Toronto, the monstrous mega star city of Canada, is envied, admired and disliked by quite some Canadians in other parts of the country. It is among the lead giant cities in the world and therefore well-known internationally. People living and working here have come from all parts of the world. They themselves are the most colourful part of the city and have made the city great. They have brought different cultures here to dress up the city in any kind of chichi styles and colours imaginable. The visitors coming to this city are most likely to be dazzled, puzzled or confused.

Like most monstrous cities in the world, besides the brilliance, Toronto has also all the disadvantages of a huge city. First of all, the traffic congestions can be headaches. With the city sprawling to such a large area, it is getting more and more difficult for people to go to work and to attend to different things. The relationships between people are normally more indifferent in large cities. The large number of different people in Toronto will inevitably create some tensions and conflicts. With the increase of population, wealth and different social structures, more social problems will rise. Toronto seems to have been handling both achievements and problems rather well. It is the leading city in Canada to put more efforts in encouraging culture diversities, fostering tolerance and acceptance of different people and giving equal opportunities to the newcomers.

Like all the mega cities, Toronto had a humble beginning. The first European coming to the site of Toronto was a French explorer called Etienne Brule who visited here in 1615. The place was then the aboriginal peoples' trail end where Lake Huron and Lake Ontario linked together. The name of Toronto had a native tribe language origin, meaning Place of Meeting. What a significant name for the modern Toronto! People all over the world have met here today. In 1720, seeing the place an ideal spot for fur trade, the French established a post here. In 1793, the place was chosen to be the capital of the new British Colony of Upper Canada. It was given a name - York. During the War of 1812, York was captured by the Americans. Then the American General Zebulon M. Pike was killed in an explosion in Fort York, which caused the Americans looting and burning the town. This gave the British the excuse to attack Washington D.C. and burn the White House in 1814. When the population increased to about 9,000 in 1834, York was incorporated as the city of Toronto. When

Canada was born in 1867, Ontario was one of the four provinces to form the Confederation. The other three provinces were Quebec, New Brunswick and Nova Scotia. After Ontario became a province, Toronto was elected as the capital of the province. The rise of Toronto as a dominant commercial and manufacturing power started as early as the 1850's. The population of the city had grown steadily. At the turn of 19th and 20th centuries, several surrounding cities joined in and made Toronto a metropolitan city in 1954.

While approaching Toronto, Jim and Meilin felt going into a large fast flowing current. The highway lanes had quickly increased and in some places it became ten or even a dozen lanes. The number of vehicles on the highway had also increased suddenly to fill up all those traffic lanes. Everybody was moving fast and there was hardly any space between vehicles to change lanes. Still, some vehicles were manoeuvring skilfully in the heavy traffic, weaving freely like snakes in this large fast flowing current. Those vehicles must be operated by the people who had been traveling on this highway daily. But for Jim and Meilin, the small-city dwellers, the dizzy fast movement of the heavy traffic had made them all tensed up; every nerve and muscle of theirs was tightly twanged up.

When the traffic current was moving towards the cluster of skyscrapers, the couple thought that they were driving towards the city centre. But after quite some time driving, they found out that they had started moving away from the skyscrapers. The highway did not go into the city centre and was bypassing it. Meilin concentrated on checking the map. There were numerous direction signs and branching-out side roads along the highway. The couple were soon lost in this big traffic current and missed the turn they were supposed to take. Now they were pushed by the current, involuntarily moving further away from the city. After a long way of driving, though it seemed still within the municipal boundary, the couple started seeing suburban residential houses. Then the highway signs started showing that they were heading for Kingston, another city some distance away from Toronto. Now the couple knew that they had definitely missed the turn-off road to reach the campground.

"Jim, we have to get off the highway at the next turn-off road and go back," Meilin suggested.

At the next turn-off road, the couple got off the big traffic current and drove to a side street. They decided that they were going to take the side street to go back, instead of venturing onto the nerve-racking highway again. Driving along the street, they saw that the place was every bit still the city. There were plenty of businesses and residential houses on both sides of the street. Now they could drive more leisurely and stop at some place to ask for direction. They stopped their vehicles at a gas station. After putting some gas into the van, Jim went to the office to pay the bill and to ask for information. He got the direction to the campground without problem. They could take the very street they were on to reach the place.

The distance to go back and to reach the campground was not short. After quite some time driving, the couple decided to stop at a fast food restaurant by the street to have lunch. With all the running around, it was already passed one o'clock in the afternoon. After lunch, they had some rest in the van. It was supposed to be an easy drive today, but turned out to be quite difficult for them. Soon they started driving again. The streets all appeared wide here; shops and houses along the streets were well spaced out and there were plenty of trees and green lawns around. They had to stop twice more to ask directions before reaching the campground.

The campground was situated by a main street that looked like a highway. It had many camping sites and full services. At the back of the campground, there was a large urban park called Park Rouge. Jim and Meilin set up their trailer on a lot and were glad that they could finally rest after the stressful driving and trying to find the place. Not long, it was supper time. After preparing and finishing the supper, they decided to take a walk towards Park Rouge. There was a walking trail into the park by the gate of the campground. They walked a short distance to reach the park trail that started by crossing a bridge over a stream. The park trail stretched and wandered deep into the dense woods; it looked like to go on forever. The park with hills and valleys was massive. Jim and Meilin did not walk too far and soon turned back to the campground. They were quite tired and had no energy for a long distance hiking. However, they were quite impressed by such a large park. All through the trail, they had met only a few hikers. The tranquil woods made them forget that they were in a mega city.

Coming back to the campground, they got some information from the camp office at the gate. They needed the direction information to prepare for tomorrow's trip to reach the city centre. They were told that they could get to the city centre by taking the bus and then the tram, and they could also drive through this main street the campground was on to reach there.

With the problem of traffic congestions getting more and more serious in large cities of the world, almost all those cities have turned to underground or sky for solutions. Subway and sky train systems have boomed in large cities. Tracks have been extensively developed under and above the grounds of cities. Large quantity of people has been moved around faster by the subway and sky train systems. Those city trains are called trams; they are powered by electricity. There is nothing in those subway tunnels and tram tracks over the streets to interfere or obstruct their traffics, so the speed of the trams is getting higher and higher. People taking the trams can get to their destinations quickly; have less danger of getting into an accident or traffic jam and no headaches to find a place to park their personal vehicles, as they carry only themselves. The cities thus receive less street traffics and less polluting emissions from large quantity of personal vehicles. The tram system is indeed a win-win solution for both city transportation and pollution problems. No wonder many large modern cities have jumped to it. Toronto, of course, has long adopted this system to be a veteran. Only the city is now overdue in the maintenance and updating works for this system. Things are getting more and more expensive. The Torontonians are worried about the cost of updating their transportation system.

For Jim and Meilin, taking the tram to visit a huge strange city was scary. They worried whether the stops of the tram would be just at the places they wanted to go, whether they could get off the tram at the correct spot, how they would get around without a vehicle if they got lost in the large city; so on and so forth. After some discussion, the couple decided that they were going to drive to the city centre tomorrow. It seemed to them that driving their own vehicle still gave them a bit more control over any possible situation. The night on this campground was problem free. They had a quiet night and a peaceful sleep. Next morning, they started early. The route they were going to take had been checked and studied carefully last night. Following the map, they thought that they would have no problem to reach the city centre.

Soon the couple were in the traffic flow. Though the traffic stream on this six-lane street was much slower than that of the main highway, it was no less heavy. It looked that many people had chosen this route to go to work or attend to their daily businesses. The vehicles moving in the street were bumper to bumper. With numerous traffic lights along the way at numerous intersections leading to other streets and vehicles turning in and out in every intersection, the speed of the traffic flow was very slow. The speed did not bother Jim and Meilin much. They were tourists and not in a hurry to get to their destination. But for those people who had to get to work or some appointments at certain time, the traffic speed must be maddening. The couple, however, had time to look around and enjoy the street scene. The wide street and other branching-out streets appeared to them not old but new. Along the street they were in, large new buildings for businesses or other purposes had occupied all the ground and nicely spaced out. If they had not gone through this street, they could never have imagined how big the city was. It took about two hours for them to get close to the skirt of the city proper. When they were approaching the city centre, the street seemed becoming narrower. This feeling might largely come from seeing more and more buildings showing up along the street. The buildings, large or small, started lining closely together and standing right to the edge of the pedestrian walks, making the street look crowded. The area they went through at the entrance of the city centre might be one of the old areas in Toronto. The buildings were mostly of wood structure, two or three storeys high and in different colours and old style. Yet they gave the couple the impression of a well-to-do street in the old time.

With the map and following the traffic flow, the couple only made one wrong turn in this trip and had quickly corrected the mistake. Entering the city centre and seeing the skyscrapers and large grand buildings shooting up, they felt a bit overpowered. Their destination was the legislative building today. In their former visits, they had already toured some places of Toronto. They had visited Casa Loma, the famous Toronto castle. Though a young city in the world; Toronto has a big old European castle. The castle was built in1911 to 1914 by the Scottish stonemasons for the Canadian financier, Sir Henry Pellatt. It is a replica of medieval castle in combined Norman, Gothic and Romanesque styles. The ancient-looking castle has 98 rooms, numerous fireplaces, suits of armor, decorated suites, lofty towers, secret passageways, 800 feet underground tunnel and luxury stables. It is in every way a traditional European castle, but has some modern luxury. It had cost 3.5 million dollars to build Casa Loma in the old time, hard to imagine how much it would cost to build such a castle in the modern day. Home is a man's castle; the financier had a real castle for his home. The castle surrounded by flower gardens stands on top of a hill, overlooking Toronto. In their former visit, the couple had also gone to the top of the CN tower, the landmark of Toronto, to view the wide sprawling city. In a sunny day, Niagara Falls about one hundred kilometers away can be spotted from the tower. Even today, CN tower, Toronto's communication and observation tower, is still one of highest buildings or free-standing structures in the world. The tower is 1,815 feet high and the observation deck is at 1,465 feet height. Of course, the couple had seen the water-front Toronto and viewed the unique Toronto city hall, a domed building embraced by two tall tower buildings, like a pearl lying inside a half opening shell. Toronto is a city with plenty of unique modern buildings side by side with some large old stylish buildings and designed by some known architects.

Still, the couple felt that they did not see much of this giant city in their former visits. Now they were going to see Ontario's legislative building. After they entered the city centre, they had no problem to find this government building, but it took some doing for them to find a parking lot. Driving around the massive legislative building for a few times, they had finally found a parking lot in a side street not far from the legislative building. The parking fee was ten dollars for the whole day, a surprisingly good deal compared to some high downtown parking fees in some other large cities.

The Ontario legislative building was a massive group of buildings built by sandstones of reddish earthen colour and sitting on Queen's Park. According to the introduction on the landmark stone, the ground was first leased from King's College, today's Toronto University, in 1859. Queen's Park was established on this spot in 1860. The legislative building was built on this ground in 1892 and the first legislative session was held here in 1893. Also according to the introduction, the style of the building was Romanesque. The standard style of provincial legislative buildings in Canada is normally classic or neoclassic. The buildings have large columns and domed towers, which give the appearance of power, dignity and magnificence. To Jim and Meilin, the lay persons of architecture, this Ontario legislative building looked different from other legislative buildings and it was every bit like a gigantic castle, but no less grand and magnificent.

In front of the legislative building, there was a large ground of green lawns with mature trees and flower beds. The statue of Queen Victoria and some important statesmen of the country were on the ground. The statue of the first Canadian Prime Minister, John A. Macdonald, was standing in the center front of the ground. The statue of Queen Victoria sitting in a chair was at the back among the trees. On one side of the front lawn, there was the native peoples' symbolic artwork of a totem pole. The statues were black stone or bronze sculptures on high stone stands. In Canada, the statues around important buildings are mostly of black colour. Maybe the black colour can endure the weather better, or the black-coloured statues give more sense of power and strength. The couple could not tell. Anyway, the black statues looked strikingly significant on the green lawns in front of the grand important buildings. A street circled all around the Queen's Park, looking like a moat separating the castle-like legislative building and its ground from the city around. Yet, the legislative building in the park was closely facing a thoroughfare stretching forward with large modern buildings on both sides. At the back of the legislative building, there was the campus of Toronto University.

After touring around the outside of the building, the couple went inside the building through the main entrance door. The legislative building was open to visitors. Instead of large columns lining in the frontal of the building, the Ontario legislative building had a lofty peaked front with three large vaulted entrance doors. Over the vaulted doors, there were intricate lavish carvings of flower pattern. The inside of the building could only be described as the interior of some large palace. The couple had never seen the inside of a palace. This might be even grander than the inside of an old palace. Though the buildings were over a hundred years old, the inside looked shinning and brand new. The large entrance hall had very tall vaulted ceiling and a wide staircase in the centre leading up to the second floor. There were large columns with vaults and sculpted patterns supporting wide walkways and corridors. Marbles and stained-glass windows and flower-patterned ceilings were everywhere. Huge oil paintings of some significant historical events were on large walls; they were early 19th and 20th century Canadian art.

Jim and Meilin were awed by this kind of grandeur. It was hard for them to take in all the splendours at once. There were many visitors around. A large group were arranging themselves on the central staircase to have a picture taken. Many others were lined up, waiting to have a guided tour. There was a tour guide showing people around and giving introductory talks. The couple followed a group to listen to the guide. The young woman guide talked about some of the pictures on the wall and the structure of the main hall. Then she led the visitors to the two large side halls. The side halls hosted quite some exhibits of arts and crafts which showed some history, statistics and geography of the province. The other hall had large portraits of the chancellors of different terms on the walls. Those portraits were also valued artworks in different painting styles.

After the guided tour, Jim and Meilin roamed around a bit, had some close look at the place and the exhibits and took some pictures. The guide tried to get people to follow her and to leave space for the next group of visitors. People seemed continuously pouring in. The outside and inside tours of the legislative building took quite some time. After all was finished, it was already afternoon. Coming out of the building, Jim and Meilin decided to walk over the street to pay a brief visit to Toronto University. It turned out that the walk was rather long. The university was so large and had quite some streets on campus. There was a huge lawn bordered by buildings which were of traditional European style, greyish white colour with green metal roofs. The buildings had plenty of domed or peaked towers. There was a clock tower in the centre of an intersection which completed the European architecture style of the campus.

Toronto University is Ontario's provincial university, the largest university in the country. Each year, it enrolls over 40,000 students. It has comprehensive faculties and curricula of arts and science, medicine, law, education, engineering, architecture, applied science, food science, social science, business management, pharmacy, nursing, dentistry, forestry and so on. It is one of the best universities in Canada. The origin of the university, King's college, a Church of England institution, was chartered in 1827 and established in 1843. It was then reorganized and completely secularized in 1849. The university has a long history since its establishment. This kind of seniority has made its traditional European appearance understandable. However, in spite of its conservative look, in modern times this university has given an impression of progressiveness and openness to new ideas and new views in the academic world.

Jim and Meilin decided not to walk too far into the campus. They were tired and hungry. It was already way passed their lunch time. They were impressed and satisfied by what they had already seen. On their way through a small section of the campus, they saw quite some coloured students. Since they came to Toronto, the couple had seen some coloured people working in the restaurant they had their lunch in and the campground they stayed on. In old times, the problem of racial discrimination in Toronto was as serious as in other places of Canada. There were reports of the police shooting the black youth and the difficulties faced by the coloured people who were trying to find jobs here. In recent years, things must have been improved. No serious racial discrimination cases in this city had been heard over the news. From what they had seen, Jim and Meilin were convinced that Toronto had moved forward in battling the problems of racial discrimination. How much improvement had been made by this city and how much was still lacking in this aspect, it was not for the short-time visitors like the couple to see.

When Jim and Meilin got back to their van, they were famished. Though they had some snacks while resting in the leather sofas of the legislative building, some proper food was still needed for lunch. Luckily, they had brought a picnic lunch with them. Sitting down in their van, they wolfed down the canned fish, canned vegetable and bread, and then finished their late lunch with an orange as dissert. After the lunch, the couple had a nap in their van; they very much needed it. When they got up from the nap, it was time for them to drive back to the campground.

Driving back to the campground seemed easier. This seemed normally the case. It might mainly be that the route going back was familiar now and there was no more anxious anticipation. When the couple reached the campground, they saw that there was a large motor home parked beside their small trailer and a campfire had already been started close to their tiny trailer. The couple were dismayed. Normally, the owners of large luxury motor homes would not come out to light up a campfire; they preferred to stay within their cozy luxury zone. The situation looked a bit suspicious to the couple. Fortunately, not long after they came back, a shower started. The campfire was soon extinguished. The fire bugs must feel disappointed, while the couple were pleased that they would have a nice night's sleep free of smoke on this campground for another night. The campground had a nice bathroom with shower stalls and a laundry room. After supper, the couple had a good shower to relieve the fatigue of the day's travelling and sightseeing, and then they did their laundry. They went to bed early afterwards. Tomorrow would be another full day for them.

Next day, they took the long drive to venture into the city centre again. Their schedule for this day was to visit the Royal Ontario Museum. They arrived at the Museum without any problem. The Museum was located at a busy street. Like everything else, the Ontario Museum was very large. It had a modern front which looked like a gigantic piece of abstract art. Different sized glasses or crystals of geometric shapes formed several prisms, some thrusting towards the street and some pointing to the sky. Some of those glass crystals had the quality of mirrors jutting out at all directions and reflecting the street and the sky at different angles. It was indeed an impressive stunt of architecture expressing art, abstract art in this matter. In front of the building, there was a sign made of a large pointed piece of glass crystal. On this sign, there were the words: Michael Lee-Chin Crystal.

Royal Ontario Museum is considered the greatest cultural asset of Canada. The new glass crystal structure added to the front of the old brick museum is designed by architect Daniel Libeskind and named after the Canadian investor and philanthropist Michael Lee-Chin. This glass crystal structure is indeed a bold design liked by some people and disliked by some others. The museum however houses more than 5 million art, archeology and science objects, the largest museum of science and world culture in Canada.

The couple started their tour of the museum immediately. The museum had several storeys; each storey had several large galleries and each gallery was filled with exhibits. The other provinces had also large museums, but the couple were quite impressed by the large quantity of comprehensive and detailed collections of exhibits here. There were numerous fossils of prehistoric animals, stuffed live-like present day lives and other nature specimens. Besides the large collections showing nature history, the museum had quite many galleries showing the world and Canadian cultures. The couple were glad to see the exhibits showing the ancient Greek culture. There were sculptures, metal works and a model showing them as they were in Athens' Golden Age. More interestingly, the museum had an oriental gallery with many valuable exhibits showing the ancient cultures of China, Japan and Korea. There were quite some ancient oriental paintings, artworks and even large sculptures of ancient Chinese warriors with chariot. The European gallery had many arms and armors that were dated from Bronze Age to World War I. Then there were the galleries introducing the culture of the aboriginal peoples in Canada and some decorative and pictorial arts showing the Canadian history and arts. The museum was indeed a large treasure trough. The couple felt it a great treat to be able to view all those treasures here in one museum. Away from China for so many years, Meilin was both surprised and glad to see so many Chinese ancient artworks in display here. What's more amazing was that this large museum was educational. There were interactive hands-on specimens for both adults and children. The museum also offered films, lectures, theatrical performances and some other educational programs.

The tour of the museum took many hours. It was impossible for the couple to check everything carefully. They had to run through quite some galleries to have a glance at so many things in display. By the time when they finished, it was already afternoon. They were quite tired and hungry again. When they came out of the museum, they saw a large cathedral-like building across the street not far from the museum. The cathedral turned out to be a theologian college. There are quite some universities and colleges in Toronto and Ontario affiliated with Toronto University. Some of them are theologian colleges. While in affiliation with Toronto University, Emmanuel College operates under the United Church of Canada, Trinity and St. Michael's are of Anglican and Roman Catholic, Knox College of Presbyterian and Wycliffe College of Anglican.

The couple had no idea which church this college belonged to. They went there to have a look and to find a place to have their picnic lunch. Learning from yesterday's experience, they had brought their lunch again. When you were tired and hungry, the easiest way was to have your own food at hand to serve yourself. Instead of going around and hunting for a restaurant, the couple chose to have their own picnic lunch again. After walking through the beautiful flower beds in front of the college, they went up to the entrance of the college. The college was formed by a group of connected buildings. The outer layer of the college was shaped like a grand cathedral of gothic style with spiked towers. Inside the college, there was a square lawn fully surrounded by the connected buildings. Some small whitish paths on the green lawn gave the ground a beautiful symmetric pattern. The lawn was not large and there were some large mature trees in this closed-in yard. Some benches were set at the edge of the lawn. Though not far from the noisy busy street, the place inside here was secluded and very quiet; the surrounding buildings had entirely blocked away the outside world. Jim and Meilin found a bench in the shade and started their lunch. Besides them, a middle-aged woman was the only other visitor. She was sitting quietly on a bench with a notepad, painting the beautiful lawn and the college buildings. Occasionally, a few college students or staff walked quietly through the lawn to reach a building. The yard was emitting peace and tranquility, an ideal place even for meditation. It might have functioned as a monastery in the old days. The couple were glad that they could have their lunch and a rest here.

In ancient times and especially Feudal Age, quite some young people would go to clergy colleges for a priesthood future. If a young man was not born in an aristocratic family, church was the way for him to raise his social status, to gain a respectable position and to have a good future. Going through a clergy college was sometime the only way for some young men to make something of themselves in the society. Of course, the ambitions of most of those young men were supported by their strong religious belief and faith then. In those old days, church and clergy colleges controlled education system, had great power in all aspects of life and could give their students a good future. In addition to theology, the clergy colleges had taught other subjects such as language, history, philosophy, arts and science; they were the main education institutions of the society then. People who went to this kind of institutions not only learned the theorems of religion, but also some other subjects. Still, the clergy colleges had prepared the young men mainly for a clergy career. Occasionally, some young men of rich families would go to the colleges to learn just for the sake of learning. Like the church, the clergy institutions in the ancient societies had a high position in people's lives and the learning world.

Today, the church has no longer political power and lost its esteemed position in the society and people's lives. Moreover, religious belief is in decline. The clergy colleges have followed suit and lost their importance in people's lives. In the modern day society, if some young people want to raise their social status, to better themselves and to have a good future, they have to go through secular universities or colleges. Those modern education institutions teach arts and science in all aspects practical to modern-day life. Still, like the church, religious colleges have stayed on in societies. There are still some young people going through them to learn theology and some other subjects. But compared with the large number of young people going to the secular institutions today, the young people coming to clergy colleges are a small number. Those few modern-day clergy-college-goers must be truly interested in religion and want to serve God, and to serve others and society in this field. A clergy career is no longer highly esteemed and it does not provide a high social status; those young people getting on this less trodden and unpopular path today have to be truly devoted to religion and spirituality.

Jim and Meilin could see that teaching and learning have been kept on in this religious institution, but the students were few and the future of the college looked not very promising. They knew that the populations of the monasteries and nunneries were also aging and dwindling. The situation could not be changed by anybody or any force. Time has changed. People's way of thinking and way of life have fundamentally changed. Religion is on a slanting slope, declining. The spiritual aspect of human life and thinking is diminishing or going in different directions. What can save the good part of the religious teachings in human life cannot be easily figured out by anybody. Modern science and technology have turned human beings into a new species, more materialistic, cynical, inquisitive and craving for more practical things.

After lunch, the couple had some rest in this peaceful college. They walked around. One side of the college was an old chapel. Another side appeared also ancient and had a side door leading to the outside. Over the door, there was an ancient religious emblem. There was only one side looking like built in later time and being used as a teaching building now. Though the college looked bright outside with new paintings of silver and white, the inside retained some old look, which led the couple to the belief that it was once a monastery.

The couple left the college with some pondering thoughts. On their way back, they passed a Chinatown. Toronto has three large Chinatowns, two little Italys, a Greek town and clusters of Polish, Portuguese, Indian, Korean and so on. It is indeed a cosmopolitan city. The Chinatown the couple came to appeared not the largest. Still, the Chinatown colour had trailed on a long way of the block. A centre isle was running through the middle of the six lane street. On the isle there were small trees and sculptures of red dragons rolling along. The couple parked their van by the street and went to check out some Chinese stores. Like other Chinese stores everywhere, the Chinese stores here had their goods spilled out to the sidewalk. The business of the stores seemed going well. Jim and Meilin found a Chinese supermarket on a side street and bought some canned sweet soups made from several kinds of beans and grains. They had run out of those soups that were indeed good for travelling, already cooked and delicious. Then the couple left the Chinatown. The parking meter fees here were rather high.

Coming back to the campground, the couple decided that the two-day sightseeing was enough of the Toronto tour for them. They knew that there were many more attractions in Toronto. They regretted that they could not visit more of them. The numerous galleries and theaters could only be enjoyed if they lived here for a period of time. They also knew that, like Niagara Falls, the most famous attraction in Ontario was the Shakespeare Festivals in Stratford. Since 1953, Shakespeare's plays have been performed by the North American Stratford-upon-Avon River. This summer culture festival started in tents and now Shakespeare's plays and some other great playwrights' works in original or modern versions have been performed in four large theaters in Stratford City every summer. The Stratford Theater has become one of the three largest English speaking theaters in the world. Once, an American professor asked Meilin whether she had watched a play from the Shakespeare Festivals in Ontario's Stratford, saying that his wife and he had watched plays there quite a few times. Meilin felt sorry that she had to answer, "No". Now she was passing Ontario again with her husband and they were not going to Stratford to watch a play. She felt a great loss. Well, in life, nobody could have it all and we all had to take some losses somewhere sometimes. The couple were now on a cross-country journey; they had to concentrate on achieving this goal. Right now, though they had seen very little of Toronto, the little taste was enough for them. Toronto had given them a strong impression of a gigantic, modern, and well diversified city rich in culture. Tomorrow, they were going to go to Ottawa, the capital city of Canada.

CHAPTER SEVEN

OTTAWA

The couple had another good night's sleep on this campground. Next morning they started early. The distance between Toronto and Ottawa was not that far. By noon, they were approaching the capital city of Canada. They had planned ahead to camp on a campground at the city skirt and had no problem to find the place. The campground was by the highway. They soon pulled their vehicles into the campground and parked them in front of the camp-office for the registration. The Ottawa campground was large. Some camping sites had full service and some partial service. The partial-service ones had electricity and water, but no sewer drainage. Jim and Meilin chose a partial-service site as it was cheaper. They could choose a site near the public bathroom, so that they would not really need to use the toilet in their own trailer. As for showers, they had never used their own shower in the trailer and would use the showers in the public bathroom again. Their trailer's hot-water tank could only be operated by propane and they had not tried to use it yet.

The couple booked for four nights. They figured that the tour of Ottawa would take at least three days and today they would do nothing, but settle down and rest for the rest of the day. From the office, the couple got to know that there was a special bus taking off from the campground every morning; it would take the tourists to the city centre and there, the tourists could mount on a double-deck tour bus to go sightseeing. This was a great arrangement. From their experience of touring Toronto, Jim and Meilin knew that this kind of arrangement would save them a lot of troubles. With the traveling part being taken care of, they could comfortably concentrate on touring the city. The fare for the bus taking them into the city in the morning and bringing them back to the campground in the afternoon was fifty dollars per person for a total three days. This was a great bargain. The couple jumped to it. They bought the tickets and were all set for the three day traveling to the city and back.

After this down, they drove to the campground to find a site. All the camping sites were in the woods. They chose one well shaded and not far from the bathroom. When they had barely settled down, they smelled smokes from some neighbour's campfire. It was early afternoon; some campers had already started their campfire, probably for cooking lunch. The couple immediately pulled up their trailer and moved away from the smoking area. They knew that their small trailer could not handle much smoke. After they resettled, things went well. They cooked and enjoyed their meals in their trailer. For the afternoon, they rested and took a walk around the campground. Towards evening, some noises started around, but things quieted down later at night. Probably, the park wardens had the noisy people under control.

The couple slept well. Next morning at eight o'clock they went to the office area. A bus was already waiting there. After they got on the bus, other two sets of couples came and got on the bus too. The two sets of couples were in their sixties; they looked healthy and dressed comfortably well, and must have worked some white-collar jobs before their retirement. Soon the bus driver came. He was a tall man in his fifties with a well weathered and experienced face.

"Welcome to my bus, folks. I'm Frank. I'll be your driver for the three days. I hope we'll all enjoy it! First of all, I have to tell you the rules. The bus will take you to the city centre where the double-deck tour bus stop is located. At five o'clock sharp in the afternoon, I'll take you back to the campground. My bus will be parked a little way from the tour bus stop. Make sure come to get on the bus before five o'clock." The bus driver rumbled on with an amicable smile. Though he tried to sound serious, he could not very well do so.

"If we miss the bus, we have to walk back!?" an old gentleman asked with a laugh.

"That's right," said Frank and started laughing too.

After a short moment waiting, the bus started moving. Altogether the passengers were six, just the three sets of couples. Frank turned out to be an eloquent talker. He was not a tour guide, but he obviously enjoyed acting like one. Jim and one of the old gentlemen talked to him all the way. Soon the tourist group got to know the bus driver very well. Frank not only talked about himself, but also spoke eloquently about politics and some other things. When he was young, Frank worked as a driver with an international organization that helped people in poor or war-torn countries. He had gone to some of those turbulent countries. He got a bullet wound through one of his knees while he was working within a war zone. The passengers now knew why the bus driver walked with a limp. Frank had married three times. He and his wife now had a small organic farm where they raised a few cattle and chickens. Their farm must be very small and not that profitable, as he had to work on driving this bus every day and his wife was also working with some company, selling some type of herb medication.

As there were only a few passengers, the tourists introduced themselves and got to know each other. The old couples were Mr. and Mrs. Sherman, and Mr. and Mrs. Rayleigh. They were close friends travelling together. Mr. and Mrs. Sherman were both plump and looked a bit spoiled by a good life, self-centred and pleased with themselves. Mr. and Mrs. Rayleigh were the type of old folks who tended to be thinner with the progressing of their years. Mrs. Rayleigh looked rather tense and sensitive towards other peoples' opinions. Mr. Rayleigh was obviously a very reserved man who never talked much. Self-absorbed, Mr. Rayleigh looked oblivious about the things going on around him and was concentrated on the sightseeing. Carrying a big bag of camera equipment, he was engrossed in taking pictures of the scenery outside the bus window. Mr. Rayleigh belonged to the type of old gentlemen who would take care of his house and make his garden the envy of the neighbourhood, but never bothered about what were going on in the neighbourhood.

Frank had a small box not far from his driver's seat. In the box, there was a little seed money. This showed that tips were welcome. During the three day travelling, Mr. Rayleigh turned out to be a generous tipper. Mr. and Mrs. Sherman were small tippers. Jim and Meilin were also small tippers, as their financial situation was just turning a little better and they were very careful about their spending.

The distance between the campground and the city centre turned out to be not short. Frank drove the bus skilfully while chatting with his passengers. The bus first ran on a small country road parallel to the highway. Along this road, there were broad fields on one side. When the bus was passing by a large piece of grassland with a few buildings far away, Frank mentioned with a philosophic tone, "This piece of land used to be owned by Nortel, a giant company. The CEOs of that company would come here to ride their horses. After Nortel crashed, the land was sold. Now we don't know who the new owner of this big land is." Then he added, "How the mighty falls!"

Jim and Meilin agreed with Frank entirely. Nortel used to be a large stock company of telecommunication and equipment which had offices in quite some countries of the world. For some reason, the company crashed and their stocks fell through the bottom. Many investors had lost money. After the company's crash, Jim and Meilin listened to some financial adviser over TV, who said that it was a good time for people to buy some shares of this company, as later on, when the company's stock went up, they would gain. Jim and Meilin bought four thousand dollar worth of shares from this company. The stock actually went up quite some, but after a year or so, it dropped like a dead fly and never came up again. The four thousand dollars the couple put in became a few dollars and then a few cents; the investment was a total loss to them. They realized that they must be among those gullible who had put their contributions in only to compensate some of the old investors. After the old investors gained some money back, the new investors had to wait until the sun rising up from the west to gain their money back. Anyhow, those horse-riding CEOs had earned enough money from their millions of dollars yearly salary and bonuses. There was no loss to them. As for Jim and Meilin, the small investors, this was their first and last venture in buying stocks. At their age, they could not take any more losses like this one. Quite some other people had lost much more and some had even lost their life's savings. Considering this, Jim and Meilin could not complain too much. This was one of the games of capitalism that the couple were far from being qualified to play.

The bus moved on smoothly and was soon on the highway. The traffic was not too heavy. Frank had driven vehicles through shootings and bombings; this kind of drive must be nothing to him. When the bus came to the suburbs of the city, it was running by the Ottawa River. Along this route, there were no residential houses. Everywhere on the waving land, there were large green lawns, plenty of mature trees, shrubs and flowers. With the river along the way; the whole place looked like a beautiful park, very clean and orderly, befitting the capital city of the country.

At some point of the bus ride, Mr. Sherman asked Meilin, "So, where were you originally coming from?"

When people here asked a coloured person where he or she originally came from, you knew that they meant from which country you came. To them, all the coloured people must have come from some other countries. Meilin answered, "I originally came from China."

Upon the mentioning of China, Meilin saw Mr. Sherman's face lit up. Afterwards, the old gentleman's attitudes towards her had changed dramatically. He showed more friendliness, though his courtesy and interest seemed a bit exaggerated and condescending. He looked immensely enjoying his own good manner and kind gesture towards the Chinese woman. His wife soon joined in with the same kind of amusing behaviour. Meilin could almost feel the patting on her back from the couple's good treatment. She was puzzled, but pleased. Anyway, it was not every day and every occasion that she could meet some white people showing this kind of friendliness and kindness to her. She had no objection to receiving them. However, the strange thing was that: the more Mr. and Mrs Sherman were showing their ostentatious good manners to Meilin, the more Mrs. Rayleigh turned indifferent and even cold towards her. Mrs. Rayleigh looked obviously more and more uncomfortable about her friends' flattering attitudes towards the Chinese woman. After a while, Meilin turned her attention away from the old folks to listening the more interesting chatting of Frank and enjoying the beautiful scenery outside the window. There was something going on between the old folks. She was not the one to know what it was and had no interest to know.

When the bus was drawing near the city proper, large magnificent buildings started showing up. Most buildings looked very modern and of typical European style. Ottawa, though a big city, was much smaller than the mega-city Toronto. It was obvious that all the attentions here had been concentrated on beautifying the city to make it a proper capital for a rich country like Canada. Everything looked in careful order, streets were lined with beautiful trees, sidewalks were clean and generously wide, green lawns were meticulously manicured and gardens were everywhere. No industries were around. It was hard to imagine that less than two hundred years ago Ottawa was a tiny inhabited place in the wilderness.

The site of Ottawa was first spotted by Samuel de Champlain in 1613. For centuries afterwards, Ottawa River had been a highway for fur trade. At the site of the city, there is the confluence of Ottawa River, Gatineau River and Rideau River. The water transportation is blocked by the Chaudière Falls where two tributaries join. In the old days, this was the spot where the fur traders, the explorers and the lumbermen met. The first European settlement was made on the north shore of the river, today's Gatineau, Quebec, by Philemon Wright who had brought his family here in 1796. Then in 1800, Nicholas Sparks established a farm here which was today's downtown Ottawa. In 1826, under the charge of Lieutenant Colonel John By, the construction of Rideau Canal started. The canal was originally built for the British gunboats to have a safe passage, but it turned out to be a great commercial venture of the place. The canal reached Kingston, connecting Ottawa River with Lake Ontario. Soon paper and pulp mills started and lumber business boomed here, creating a village that would eventually became Ottawa. The early community was then called Bytown, named after John By. For quite many years, the place had been a foremost centre of timber industry. In 1855, to settle the conflicting claims of Toronto, Montreal and Kingston, Queen

Victoria selected it to be the capital of the United Provinces of Upper and Lower Canada. Bytown was then incorporated into the city of Ottawa. The name of Ottawa had a native tribe origin. When Canada came into being in 1867, Ottawa became the nation's capital.

When the bus arrived at its destination, Jim and Meilin saw that the tour bus stop was at the very heart of the city where the Parliament Hill was nearby. There were several double-deck tour buses lined up at the side of the street, waiting for tourists. On the other side of this street, there was the National War Memorial.

After getting off Frank's bus, the passengers were directed to a booth on the spacious sidewalk. Tickets were sold there for the ride on the double-deck buses. It was fifteen dollars per person for the whole day ride. The tour bus would stop at every important sightseeing spot and would go through the route every hour. The tourists could get off the bus to tour the places they intended to see and then get on the bus again to go to another spot. The tour system here was like the one the couple had experienced in Washington DC. They were glad that things were set up the same way here, which was indeed convenient for the tourists. The couple bought two tickets for the day. After this done, there was still time before the double-deck bus started for today's run. Frank's bus had arrived a bit early. Jim and Meilin saw Frank standing not far, with a cup of coffee in his hand; they went up to thank him and to have a talk with him again. Frank gave them some point for riding the tour bus.

"You can ride the double-deck bus for the whole tour around first to get to know all the spots. There was a tour guide on the bus. You can get the full story. Later on, you can start the sightseeing on individual spot," said Frank kindly.

Meilin could feel that Frank's friendliness was sincere. Normally, when in contact with some strange white people, she could feel that there was a barrier between the white folks and herself. She could sense that they were thinking or feeling that she was different from them and not one of them. Frank seemed to have absolutely no such barrier or differentiation in his mind towards her. This might have come from the life experiences of being exposed to different peoples in his early years. He had risked his life to help those different peoples in miseries or in dangers. In return, he must have received those peoples' sincere gratitude, friendship and respect. This kind of background had conditioned him to regard Meilin as just another human being like himself. For this, Meilin liked Frank. Jim also liked Frank. He talked to him about his injuries from the military service and the consequent pains and problems he was suffering every day. Frank could fully understand and sympathize. He took out his business card for his organic farm and wrote down a different phone number on it.

"This is my wife's phone number. Call her. She can get you on some herb medication. It has helped me a lot," said Frank while handing the card to Jim.

Jim thanked him. Then the two men talked about their injuries, herb medicines and some other things. Jim also liked to talk. When talkative men got together, they could easily beat women in chatting. Soon one of the double-deck buses opened its door. Jim and Meilin left Frank to get on the bus. They mounted on the top deck where they could see more. They chose a front seat, as Meilin would sometimes get motion sickness when riding on a bus. She preferred the front seats which seemed to help some. The two old couples from the campground also got on the top deck of this bus. The old acquaintances met again. Mr. and Mrs. Sherman's charm towards Meilin was again in full display. Mrs. Rayleigh, on the other hand, complained that she did not like to sit in the sun. It happened that Meilin was sitting in a shady spot in the very front. She got up to give her seat to Mrs. Rayleigh. Mrs. Rayleigh accepted and sat down in the shady spot. But after a short moment, she got up and went back to her old seat. Seeing Mr. and Mrs. Sherman so friendly towards his wife, Jim was happy. This was a rare occasion, as his wife was more often treated indifferently or even as an alien by his kinsmen. Jim started talking about his wife's education. "She has gone to the level of Ph.D., much higher than my education," said Jim with a big proud smile.

This information seemed to have the effect of an explosion. Mr. and Mrs. Sherman cooled down immediately. They were like two balloons suddenly lost all the air; they never paid attention to Meilin again. Mrs. Rayleigh, on the other hand, had changed into a different person, especially towards Meilin. All the hurts had gone off her face and there was even joy showing up in her eyes now. She came to sit behind Meilin and started a small talk.

"So, you came from China..." said Mrs. Rayleigh gently. Without waiting for Meilin to respond, she continued, "My son and daughter-in-law have recently adopted a baby girl from China. They are happy..."

Meilin gave some sound of amazed admiration. Now she could see the reason of the drama between the old folks. Mrs. Rayleigh had felt that her friends' exaggerated charm towards Meilin was a mockery to her family adopting a baby from China. She had sensed the discriminatory intention from her friends. As she was not used to this kind of behaviours, she reacted rather intensely. Now Meilin's education had helped her in beating down the sneering of her friends. There was possibility that when her adopted granddaughter grew up, she could achieve the same as this Chinese woman did. Would her friends be able to put down and laugh at a Ph.D. granddaughter though of Chinese origin?

Meilin had gotten a Master Degree here. She did go up to the Ph.D. program, but did not finish it. With Jim being released from the military and some other problems, she had to quit her studies. The reality of her life was totally different from the picture Mrs. Rayleigh was making up now in her mind from Jim's information. With all her education, she could not get a suitable job. What she could have were the lowest level jobs which were for most coloured people here, and those low level jobs were highly unstable and short lasting. If she would tell Mrs. Rayleigh the truth, she would probably dash the old lady's hope for her adopted granddaughter. Though Meilin's education did not bring her any substantial benefit, she felt that, at this moment, it had helped this old lady to love her adopted granddaughter and to brace herself against racial discrimination which she would inevitably face because of this new family addition. Meilin decided to keep the bad part to herself. She was glad that her education had at least benefited this old lady at this moment.

The tour bus started moving. There were quite some tourists on bus. The tour guide was a young woman. She soon started the guiding talk. For the three day tour rides, the tour guides had changed several times. Some were better than the others. Today the guide sounded clear and fluent. Her talk was not only descriptions of different places, but also comments and even criticisms of political colour blended with humour. From Frank to some tour guides, people in Ottawa seemed more open. They appeared to know the essence of democracy. They knew their rights and would not hesitate to think and to say what were in their minds. This kind of attitudes had created a healthy democratic atmosphere here which was rare in some small places in Canada. In small places such as the small city the couple resided in, ordinary people normally would not openly express themselves; they watched and followed the authorities closely. This kind of behaviours had ensured that they would go with the flow and have a peaceful life, but it had gradually made them lose the ability to think and to express themselves.

The bus first went through Wellington Street where most important buildings were located. There were the Parliament Buildings, the Bank of Canada, the Supreme Court of Canada, The Library and Archives of Canada, the Nation's War Museum, and a significant Anglican

Cathedral. Again, the couple were impressed by the very clean, spacious and orderly city. The important large buildings all looked magnificent. The wide street was flanked by wide sidewalks and lined up by beautiful trees. There were plenty of spaces between some of those important buildings. Green lawns and mature trees were everywhere. Jim and Meilin had been in Ottawa three times before; twice they were just passing by and once they had a brief visit to the Parliament Buildings and the National War Memorial. They were glad that they were taking this systematic tour now.

The bus soon went across the bridge over Ottawa River to the other side where Gatineau was. Ottawa, Ontario is located on the south side of Ottawa River and Gatineau, Quebec is on the north side of the river. The border between the provinces of Ontario and Quebec runs through the Ottawa River, but the national capital looks formed by both Ottawa and Gatineau. To Jim and Meilin, this situation of Ottawa looked quite representative of the situation of the country which was formed mainly by the English and the French. The guide soon pointed out the old European settlement and a paper mill site in Gatineau. The first European settler in Gatineau however was a New England Puritan with his family.

Canada is formed mainly by two forces of people; the English speaking people, one force and the French speaking people, the other force. From the beginning of the European settlements on this land, there have been conflicts between these two forces. Through the years, the English force has grown bigger and stronger. Today nine provinces of the country are mainly resided by English speaking people, and only one province, Quebec, is mainly resided by French speaking people. Anyway, the solidarity of the country very much depends on the two main forces getting along and living together harmoniously and peacefully.

In recent decades, there has been a third force growing in this country, which is formed by the newcomers, mainly the coloured people. The third force has every potential to strengthen and hasten the development of the country and to help it to soar. However, this possibility very much depends on the country, especially the established Canadians to have the vision and broad mind to tap into this new force and to help it to develop its full potentials. Pressing this force down or keeping it at the bottom of the society, the country will lose part of its own rich human resources. The negative result will of course affect the country's development and prosperity. Though Canada is a developed country, there is no country in the world that does not need constant improvement and development. The whole human world is developing in an amazing speed in just a few centuries. Any country that would remain in the old time and not change with the changing world will inevitably suffer all kinds of dangers.

There is still another force in Canada which is easily ignored by most people. It is the force of the native peoples. With the increase of native peoples' population in recent years, this force also has the potential to contribute to and strengthen the country. This also largely depends on the country to help this force to develop. Keeping this force down, it will become the burden of the country which some white people are already complaining about today. Historically, the country had been afraid of the native peoples getting strong and some policies had been carried out to keep them down and weak. Now Canada is reaping its own mistakes made in the past. There are still two ways before the country today, keeping the old ways of treating the native peoples and bearing the burdensome consequence, or correcting the old mistakes and helping the native peoples to become strong.

The tour bus moved on smoothly. The tour guide never stopped talking. In Gatineau, the bus went to two places, Canadian Museum of Civilization and Casino du Lac-Leamy. The two places stood close to each other. The casino was a huge modern building accessible by bus through two long lanes lined up by beautiful trees and flowerbeds. The guide asked if any tourists wanted to stop here. Nobody did. It looked that everybody had the same idea of going around the whole route for the first run. Jim and Meilin decided that they would come to visit the Canadian Museum of Civilization later. The bus turned around in front of the casino and left the sightseeing sites in Gatineau.

When the bus was passing through the street along the Ottawa River, the guide pointed out the residences of the prime minister and the governor general across the river. Both important residences were located on top of the Rockcliffe Mountain. When the bus was facing the residence of the prime minister on the other side of the river, the trees around the Prime Minister's home were blocking the view. The tourists could only see part of the top section of the building. Still, the guide said with a sunny manner, "The prime minister must be having his coffee now. He might be looking at our bus from his window. Let's say good morning to him. 'Good morning, Stephen Harper!'" Some tourists followed her and said good morning to the country's prime minister. As for the Rideau Hall, the residence of the governor general, it could not be spotted from this side of the river. However, the bus soon went back to the south side of the river and passed the Sussex Street where these two important residences were located. From the street, the two residences could not be seen at all. The prime minister's home was entirely blocked off by abundant trees; the visitors could only see the iron-rod fences and the guard house at the perimeters of the premises. Rideau Hall was not far from the prime minister's place, but from the street, the tourists could only see the iron-rod fence with a guarded gate. However, Rideau Hall was open to visitors, Jim and Meilin planned to pay a visit to it later on.

Rockcliffe Park occupies a large part of Ottawa city. Rockcliffe Mountain is part of this large park. The bus moved slowly through the park. Everywhere the tourists looked; there were well trimmed green lawns and large mature trees. Along the road and on some higher points of the mountain, there were lookouts for visitors to enjoy the scenes down below. The sceneries in the nation's capital looked more beautiful, clean and orderly. This effect might mainly come from the good weather and the clean air. It was a sunny day. There was not a thread of cloud in the sky. The sun seemed shining more brilliantly, the sky looked bluer and the trees and lawns greener. All the things under the sun here looked sharply clear and bright. The air was fresh, clean and very clear. This kind of clean natural atmosphere was getting more and more difficult to be seen or experienced in large cities of the world. Ottawa was endowed or privileged to have such clean air by having no industries around. It was a city of federal government. Most people here were employed by the government.

At one point, the bus was passing by a small building in the Rockcliffe Park. It was a lone building; no other buildings were around in this part of the park. The building stood not far from the road and looked a bit odd. Soon, the guide talked about this building. "This building is a bathroom built especially for the queen. It was prepared for the emergency situation if the Queen on her visit here wanted to use a bathroom while she was having a walk around the Rockcliffe Park. Six million dollars had been spent on building this bathroom, but the queen never used it. The bathroom has always been locked up. Perhaps it will still serve its purpose in the future," said the guide with a laugh.

Jim and Meilin decided not to come to visit this bathroom which seemed a tourist attraction now, as it was far away from a bus stop. If they came to have a close look at this special bathroom, they had to take a long walk. The bus left the Rockcliffe Park and was passing by a large open green land with a few one level buildings. The guide introduced that the place was the Royal Canadian Mounted Police Stables. On the green meadow, the RCMP officers and their horses practiced their famous Music

Ride, a ceremonial equestrian display. Some days, the lucky visitors could see the officers and horses in training. Today nobody was around.

When touring Ottawa on a tour bus, the embassies of different countries would of course be on the agenda. The bus passed by some beautiful embassy buildings. When it was passing by a particular one, the guide pointed out the Embassy of Saudi Arabia and said, "It is the most expensive embassy in Ottawa. Over thirty million dollars has been spent on its construction." The building looked not that grand; it was only one or two storeys high, but with plenty of windows. When the bus was passing by the American Embassy, the guide said enthusiastically, "The American embassy is built the strongest. It is bullet proof!"

"Probably nuclear bomb proof too," one of the tourists remarked with a laugh; he was echoed by some other tourists.

The American Embassy looked an ordinary concrete modern building, greyish colour and five or six storeys high. All along the way, while watching the beautiful sceneries and listening to the interesting talk of the guide, the tourists laughed, gave their ohs and ahs; some of them would put in their own smart remarks. The bus tour turned out to be quite cheerful and relaxing. Meilin never felt any motion sickness. The bus was now passing through Sussex Drive. Besides the embassies and government offices, some important attractions were also along this drive. They were the Royal Canadian Mint, the National Gallery of Canada and the Notre-Dame Cathedral Basilica. Jim and Meilin decided that they would come to visit the Gallery and the Basilica later. As for the Mint, they had already visited one in Winnipeg; they were going to skip this one here.

Further on, the bus was running by the famous Rideau Canal. Both Ottawa River and Rideau Canal ran through Ottawa City. Rideau Canal looked like a river; only its banks were perfectly straight which gave away its man-made status. Along the canal, the scenery was neatly beautiful. Large parks flanked both sides of the canal. Green trees, lawns and flower beds were everywhere. A paved trail ran through the whole bank area. Park benches were set up here and there. There were plenty of spaces by the canal for people to enjoy their leisure time.

Rideau Canal is about 200 kilometers long. The royal engineers had made sure that the canal was built to last. Today, the canal appears the same as it was built almost two centuries ago, perfectly functional. It has its original limestone locks, hand-operated cranks, wooden lockmaster houses and stone supply buildings. In winter, the canal is converted into the world's longest skating rink. The government employees skate to their offices and the university students skate to their classes. In summer, people bicycle to different locations through the trail by the canal, or enjoy canoeing or boating on the canal. During the season of Ottawa's famous Tulip Festival, the banks along the canal would be dressed colourfully by numerous tulips.

The guide introduced the canal in detail from past to present. When she talked about its construction in the old days, she said, "One out of five Irish workers had died from malaria in building this canal." Then she said, "Today, if you take a boat to go to Kingston through the canal, it will take you about twenty hours to get there." From this introduction alone, the tourists could see the changes of the place. It was simply impossible to imagine people dying from malaria in Ottawa today, and everybody knew that Kingston was only a couple of hours drive from Ottawa.

The guide's talk about the lost lives of Irish workers in building the canal had reminded Jim and Meilin of the lost lives of Chinese workers in the old days. Thousands of Chinese workers had died in building the trans-Canada railway in the late 19th century. It was said that one Chinese labourer had died for every two miles of the track. The totally different treatments the Irish workers and the Chinese workers received had happened after the constructions finished. The Irish workers had become the rightful citizens and quite many had risen to high social and political positions and some became the leaders of the country in later years. The Chinese workers however had been advised to go back China after the work was finished. After many dead Chinese workers, there were still about 17,000 survived. Some of them returned to China and some stayed in Canada. For those Chinese who had stayed, life had been much harder for them than for the Irish workers. Through the history of Canada, the Chinese had suffered serious discrimination and exclusion. They had been prohibited from higher education and professions, prohibited from public works and voting, and their property ownership had been limited. Those grave social injustices the Chinese had suffered here in Canada had lasted until the mid-20th century when things started turning better.

From the introduction of the guide, the couple could see that it was not easy to build the country and quite many people had suffered and even lost their lives in the construction process. Both the old established and the new Canadians should appreciate the struggles and sacrifices of those early people, no matter what nationalities they were originally of.

After Rideau Canal, the bus turned into a busy downtown street. Along this street, classy restaurants serving cuisine of different countries were closely lined up. A beloved candy store had a prominent spot in this street. Some accommodations for university students and favoured hang-outs of intellectuals had also squeezed in. Chinatown was in one of the branching-out streets. Meilin had a close at the Chinatown. Its red-coloured restaurants or stores were closely linked together and occupied a short part of that street. At this time of the day, the Chinatown looked not busy at all.

The busy street ended at the side of a broad street. At the opening spot, there was a farmers' market on the spacious sidewalk. Stands were set up under a large tent; people were selling local produces from their stands. Ottawa, though has no industries around, has a big experimental farm inside the city, probably to prevent the urban sprawl or to show the industrial country's will to stick to farming as well. The Central Experimental Farm is of 1,235 acres, not a small farm. The couple wondered whether some of the produces in the farmers' market here were from this city-center farm. Opposite to the farmers' market, there was an interesting food stand called Beavertail. The place was selling doughnuts of a different shape. There were no holes in those doughnuts. The thinly fried dough was shaped like a beavertail. Many delicious things were layered on the beavertails; they were chocolate fudge, cream, camomile, maple glaze, fruit spread or some other sweet goodies. Customers could choose any one of the toppings to be put on the beavertail. The guide said that when a President of the United States visited Ottawa, he came especially to this food stand to taste the beavertail. It looked that the beavertails were indeed very popular; people were lined up in front of the small food stand, waiting to get a bite on the beavertail. The couple liked this light-hearted humour and decided that they would not miss the chance of tasting this famous beavertail when they came to visit this street later on.

The busy street with its market place was only two blocks away from the Parliament Hill. The headquarters of the Canadian government looked so close to the common people's society and to ordinary people's daily lives. Were the government and the governing practices also close to the Canadian society and the lives of the ordinary Canadian people? Long time ago, a writer wrote that the Senate was a place for a bunch of lazy old boys to doze off their days. Was the situation changed today, how much had it changed or not changed at all?

The tour bus pulled into the bus stop of its starting point and stopped at the opposite side of the National War Memorial. There were plenty of museums, significant places and attractions in Ottawa. The tour bus only went through the route passing by some of those important spots. Even those spots glanced from the tour bus, Jim and Meilin felt that they could not cover them all in three days. However, after this bus tour, they had an idea what they would like to see in the limited time.

After the bus tour, it was still in the morning. The couple decided that their first tour destination would be the Parliament Buildings. It was not far to walk from the bus stop to the Parliament Hill. They soon reached the Parliament Buildings. Though the Parliament Buildings were by the main street, there were a large paved square and a lawn in front of the buildings. This large open space had set the Parliament Buildings some distance away from the street. There were no trees on the front square or lawn, so the frontal of the Parliament Buildings was in full view. Right now, there was a large stage set up on the square for the celebration of Canada Day which was the first day of July. A week or so was left before the big day.

The Parliament Buildings are formed by three large towered buildings. Even the two wing tower buildings are big. The buildings are of Gothic style with tall steeple towers covered by green copper roofs. The centre tower is called the Peace Tower, the tallest of the three, 302 feet high, which is dedicated to the Canadians killed in World War I. Each side of the top part of the square tower had a big clock. The Peace Tower is equipped with the famous 53-bell carillon that chimes at significant times. On top of the Peace Tower, the Canadian national flag is flying. The three Gothic-styled buildings were built 1859-66. The central block was destroyed by a fire in 1916, and rebuilt to the original design only without the wood interior panels. The library in this block had miraculously escaped the fire and remains entirely original.

Standing close to the Parliament Buildings, the couple could see the sharp steeples thrusting into the sky, generating a sense of power. The buildings were built with large greyish stones. Though Canada is a young country, the Gothic architecture and the greyish colour made the Parliament Buildings look rather ancient, as if they had gone through centuries. The complicated decorative carvings or moldings and huge pillars of the exteriors showed that tremendous efforts had been poured on to arouse awe from the beholders. Jim and Meilin were indeed impressed and overpowered. After admiring the magnificent exteriors of the Parliament Buildings, the couple turned their attention to look for the entrance to the buildings. The central entrance was closed. A long line of visitors were waiting at a side door to be let in. The couple lined up with them. The line was slowly approaching the door, as the visitors were filed up to pass a security gate. After everybody had been swept by the security device, the large group went in to wait in a hall, the visitor welcome centre. A guide would lead this group to see different halls that were open to the visitors.

The wait was not long; the visitors were soon led by the guide, a young woman, to tour parts of the interior. Jim and Meilin had visited some big provincial legislative buildings. They had to admit that the Parliament Buildings had crowned them all. Here, though only the centre block of the Parliament Buildings was open to the visitors, quite some important halls could be seen. The centre hall, if entering from the centre entrance, looked the grandest with very high ceiling and huge pillars. This hall was surrounded by walkways on two levels which led to different parts of the centre block. All the tall ceilings in different halls were intricately patterned with stained-glasses or some other styles of artistic designs. Huge sculpted tall columns curved on top to form vaults and to support large halls and walkways. Some mythic animals were sculpted on top of some columns and in corners of some ceilings. The guide pointed out that some sculptors had secretly left their signatures on those sculptures. Graceful white marble sculptures of religious significance were fitted to the walls of the centre hall. Marbled floors with artistic patterns were glimmering. Huge chandeliers were hanging down from tall ceilings in large halls and shining with gorgeous brilliance. There were huge valuable paintings hanging on the walls around; most of them were large portraits of kings and queens. A portrait of Queen Elizabeth on the second floor looked like that the Queen was standing on a balcony. The rich grandeurs and splendours of the architecture and displays reminded Jim and Meilin of some English palaces they had glimpsed over some TV shows. They felt lucky that they were seeing them now in person.

The more impressive place in the Parliament Buildings had to be the library, as no treasures could compare with the treasure of books. The library was a large round hall. All the original wood panels inside the library had been preserved and maintained well. The wood interior did not give any heavy feeling, as the ceiling of the hall was very high and the light-coloured wood panels with detailed carvings were shining with polish. In spite of being over one and half centuries old, the library looked new. Books filled the bookshelves which formed the circling walls. There was a second level of the bookshelves around the walls which could be reached from a long narrow circling veranda. On the second level, the bookshelves full of books reached to the tall ceiling. Some sliding wooden ladders had been fitted to the bookshelves around. To reach some books on top shelves, those sliding ladders must be used. On the red carpeted floor of the library, there were large and small cherry wood reading tables; most of them had light fixtures attached to them and maroon leather sofas around. One had to wonder how many busy politicians in the parliament had used this beautiful library. Right now, there were no readers, but visitors who were gawking, admiring and wondering what all these large quantities of books were about.

The two main halls in this block were of course the Hall of Parliament Assembly or the House of Commons and the Hall of Senate where the country's leaders, the members of the parliament and the senators would gather to discuss and debate the issues concerning the country's affairs and policies, and to present and pass bills that would become laws of the country. The Parliament Assembly Hall was bigger than the Senate Hall, but they were both grand oblong halls. The ceilings were exceptionally high with richly carved or painted patterns. The windows on both sides were in cathedral window style with engraved frames and stained-glasses colourfully patterned or pictured. The Parliament Assembly Hall had been lined with ascending layers of green leather seats on two sides. A red carpeted centre floor ran through the middle of the two sides of seats. A large long cherry wood table was on the centre floor and a large throne seat was sitting high in the centre head position of the hall. There was a second seating area set up the same way as the floor seating on two sides of large balconies. The Senate Hall was roughly the same style, but smaller with one level seating and red leather seats. The couple had seen the Parliament Assembly in session quite often over the TV news reports, but they had never felt such grandeur of the place than looking at it now in person. They were ordinary people who had no idea of the procedures of the Parliament Assembly. Still the hall had given them all the sense of dignity and significance of such an assembly.

The last place the visitors had been let to see was the Peace Tower. By a small elevator, the visitors had been gradually lifted up to the top of the tower. The inside of the tower was not very large and the ceiling was not high. The light fixture on the ceiling was made of many pieces of golden crystal glasses. The shining golden crystals covered the whole ceiling and gave the visitors a sensation of walking under myriads of glittering gold pieces.

There was an observation deck outside around the top of the tower. The visitors could walk on it and experience the panoramic view of the capital city and the surrounding area. The tower was tall; the visitors could see Ottawa City from different angles, the far-reaching Ottawa River and some distant mountains. The city, the river and the farther views of the mountains looked beautiful and peaceful. Looking down on the landscapes of this significant city, one could not help feeling the peace, the immensity and the beauty of this country. Though Canada has not experienced absolute peace, it has experienced relative peace since its birth. Generally speaking, Canada is a peaceful country; Canadians are quite fortunate to have lived a more peaceful and stable life than some other peoples in the world.

When standing on a higher point above the earth, quite some people would think not only the place they could see; their minds could easily expand to the whole country and even the world. While standing on a significant high point of the country – the top of the Parliament, how many Canadians had wished for a good future of the country and a peaceful world; that was unknown. There might be a few who had even felt the vulnerability and the loneliness of the planet earth in the infinitely vast universe. The minute speck of earth and its human world with enormous sufferings and fleeting joys would be only a brief moment in the seemingly infinite time and space. Nonetheless, the human mind which must be part of the unknowable God, the eternal mystery, conquers all. The human mind knows the sufferings, the joys, the love, the peace and the beauty which the infinite universe does not know.

The visit to the Parliament Buildings was an eye-opening or mind-opening experience to Jim and Meilin. Having seen the inside of the Parliament Buildings, the couple had a brief look at the outside ground. On one side of the ground, there were some sculptures on the green lawns under the shade of large mature trees. They were the statues of the first Canadian Prime Minister standing on a high stand, the Queen sitting in a chair and some other important statesmen of the country standing in different spots. They appeared all to be black-coloured marble or bronze statues. But a group of sculptures of women activists in women's movements was definitely bronze. The courageous women were having a tea party in a parlour, discussing women's rights. The visitors could sit with the ladies to have their pictures taken.

It was already afternoon when the couple left the Parliament Hill. They went back to the tour bus stop. There were quite some metal benches behind the National War Memorial for the public to sit down and have a rest. The couple had brought some food with them and could have their lunch there. When they had arrived at those benches, they smelt meat being barbecued from some food stands by the bus stop. The smell was very enticing; they went there to have a look. There were two large food stands on a big paved space between two large buildings. One food stand was serving barbecued pork ribs with special sauce and the other was serving hamburgers and poutine, French fries with cheese and special sauce on. The barbecued pork ribs smelt very delicious. There was a long line of people waiting to be served there. Jim and Meilin went to the food stand serving barbecued ribs. The ribs looked a bit fatty, but the stand also served pork stewed in the same special sauce. This dish was called pulled-pork and the meat looked lean.

The food stand the couple came to had a young black woman and a young white man serving the customers. They looked like the workers and not the owners for this food stand. During the three day tour of Ottawa City, Jim and Meilin had only seen three black people working in this city; they were this young black woman at the food stand, a decorative black guard around the War Memorial and another black security person in the Parliament Buildings. The couple had been in quite a few places of the capital city for the three days, they did not see a single Asian working in any of the places here.

The population of the Asian Canadians in Canada is not low and still growing. Canada is becoming a multi-coloured country. Ottawa is the capital city of the country, the best place to show to the whole country that the coloured people have a place in Canada. Contrary to the Toronto City, Ottawa seems bending on showing to the country or even to the world that Canada is very much a white man's country and the coloured people have no place here.

However, compared with the situation in Canada just half a century ago, the treatments to the coloured people here have improved considerably. Now the visible minorities can go to higher education if they are able to and a few of them have even gained good jobs and higher social status. But equality in all aspects of life between the whites and the coloured people is still far from being fully achieved. The government seems willing to give the coloured people a place in the country and to bring up their social status, but the society seems lagging behind. Quite some white people still regard the coloured people as second-class citizens or no citizens at all. The deeply rooted racial prejudice has resulted in less job opportunities and disadvantageous social environment for the coloured people here. To keep their votes from the majorities and their positions in the government, quite some politicians have to follow the will and whim of the white majorities. Those will and whim are often racially motivated to keep the coloured people out of all spheres of Canadian society. Some politicians can see that the unequal treatments to the coloured people are not good for the country, but their political practices demand that they keep up with and satisfy the discriminatory white majority in order to keep their own political positions.

Human beings, with their human minds - the spirit, and their human bodies - the material, are part divine and part beast. With this kind of imperfect combination, there has never been equality between man and man since the birth of human society, and will never have full equality in the future. To satisfy their selfish beastly desires, some stronger humans can always manage to take advantage of and to get on top of some other weaker humans. Equality is only the reveries of the extreme dreamers and idealists. However, because of the partial divinity in human nature, the dreamers and idealists have never stopped fighting for equality and a better human society. Because of their efforts and struggles, the human society is vastly different today than that in its primitive and feudal stages. The Canadian society is of no exception. The situation of racial discrimination in this country has improved through the times, but it is far from being exemplary in the world yet. It will be no surprise that more efforts and even fights to improve the conditions of the coloured people in this country will be one of the political scenes in the country's life now and then. Human beings have always had the drive to achieve perfection; even reasons tell them that perfection is impossible.

Jim and Meilin bought some pulled-pork to go with the food they had brought with them. The young black woman served them a big portion. They were a bit worried that the woman might get into trouble with her boss for this generosity, as everything the couple did or said now could be heard and seen by some people. The pulled-pork turned out to be very delicious. It was very tender, a bit sweet and quite spicy, like some Chinese dish.

After lunch, the couple rested a little while. Then they went to pay a visit and respect to the National War Memorial. The large and tall monument was sitting in the middle of a raised square. On top of the monument, there were the sculptures of an angel spreading wide wings over the soldiers. On the main part of the monument, an arched gate was formed and through the gate, a group of soldiers were pushing a horse and a cart through. The engraved years on the monument were 1814-1818, the years of the First World War. The black-coloured sculptures set on the whitish background made the monument look solemn and magnificent. On the ground in front of the monument, there was an unknown soldier's grave. This grave was quite symbolic and significant. As a matter of fact, almost all the soldiers who had sacrificed their lives for the country were nameless. How many Canadians could even name one of the dead soldiers in the recent Afghanistan War? Those soldiers died in service of the country and deserved the highest honor from the country. Yet, whether all the people could honour them and always remember their sacrifices were hard to tell. Obviously, the honors or respects were no longer the concerns of the dead, but the concerns of those who were alive today.

The National War Memorial in this central location of the capital city was established in 1939 to honor the soldiers who fought in the First World War. Later on, it was rededicated to all those who had served Canada in the time of war. Canada has been exemplary in keeping the Remembrance Day which is the eleventh day of the eleventh month every year. Large ceremonies will be held in every city, every province and especially at this spot in Ottawa where the National War Memorial is standing. The country's leaders, representatives of different organizations and large number of people will attend those ceremonies that will be dutifully televised by TV stations. People will wear red poppies to remember and to show respect and appreciation to the soldiers who had given their lives in the service of the country. This red-poppy-wearing tradition comes from the poem, "In Flanders Fields", written by Lieutenant Colonel John McCrae in WWI. In this poem, the poet has expressed the feelings and hopes of the soldiers who had given their lives in the war. Among rows of dead soldiers' graves, the red poppies were blossoming and the larks singing. The brave soldiers wished that they would be remembered and their sacrifices would not be in vain. Sure enough, a century later, the Canadians still wear red poppies at the time of Remembrance Day every year to show that they will not forget the sacrifices of the soldiers. On this day at the National War Memorial, the unnamed soldier's grave would be covered by the red poppies laid by the people who were attending the ceremony.

At the eleventh hour of the eleventh day of the eleventh month each year, the whole country will be silent for a minute. In this minute, people will remember the sacrifices those brave soldiers had made for the country. This special hour, day and month also has its traditional significance. At this same hour, day and month, the French front line in the First World War had declared truce; not a single shot was fired at this moment after a long bloody war. This special hour, day and month has thus signified peace. On the Remembrance Day, the Canadians are also reminded to remember that one of the noblest purposes of a war is peace. Canada has the tradition to send her soldiers to fight in a war, a battle or a mission for peace or some other obligations in the world. Those soldiers had served the country faithfully with their lives. On the Remembrance Day, nobody in Canada will hesitate to show their respect, appreciation and remembrance to the soldiers who had given their lives to the country, those who are still serving the country and the veterans who have had served the country.

However, ceremony is not every-day life. In recent years, there have been problems in the treatments to the country's soldiers and veterans. There seems a stinginess immerging in the consciousness of the country in looking after the welfare and well-beings of the soldiers and veterans. A writer once wrote that when the danger was approaching, people would admire God and respect the soldiers; when the danger was passed, God would be forgotten and soldiers would be slighted. For a very long period of time, Canada has not faced immediate dangers to the country proper. This might be the main reason that some people have started to grudge in taking care of the soldiers and the veterans. They cannot see that the army is still vitally important to the country's safety and well-being. The contributions of the soldiers and the veterans to the country should be, at all time, held in their gratitude and esteem. To slight the people who have given their lives to serve and protect the country is to disgrace the country.

After paying their respect to the National War Memorial, the couple went to have a look at a place with some sculptures. The place was not far from the War Memorial, which had a circle of sculpted bronze busts and statues on the ground level. Under this circle of sculptures, there was a level below the ground which might be the subway entrance. Those busts and statues were life-size and life-like. They were significant figures of the country; the famous Indian Chief, the highly esteemed army officer, the heroic woman nurse and so on. Jim and Meilin did not go to the lower level as they did not use the subway system. After the tour and picture-taking here and there, they were sufficiently tired. It was nearly five o'clock; they had to start walking towards the place where Frank's bus was parked.

When they reached the street where Frank's bus was, they saw that nobody was there yet. They had a little time to look around. The downtown area of Ottawa had plenty of grand buildings. They went into one at hand. It was a shop selling stamps. Even for a stamp shop, the size of it was impressive. The ceiling was exceptionally high which made them feel like walking into a museum. The collections of the stamps in the shop were so extensive, hard for them even to have a browse. Tired and thinking of catching the bus back to the campground, they left the shop after a brief look. On the other side of the street, there was a post office. The post office looked significant as there was a large emblem over the entrance door and some sculptures of lions sitting around. Jim asked Meilin to stand in front of the post office door to have a picture taken. While the couple were taking pictures, Frank came and put his friendly face in. Jim and Meilin thanked Frank for his valuable point in the bus tour. The three headed for the bus that would go back to the campground.

The other two old couples soon came and the bus started moving immediately. When the bus was on the highway, the chat started. Everybody liked to listen to Frank. When Jim got a chance, he recommended the pulled-pork from the food stand to the old folks, praising highly the taste. The old folks looked quite interested. The relaxed bus ride made the trip back short. They soon arrived at the campground.

When Jim and Meilin got to their trailer, they first had a little rest. Then they started cooking their supper. There was still enough pulled-pork for the night's meal and even for another meal tomorrow, so there was not much to cook. Surprisingly, the electric stove went off after a little while of their cooking. Jim checked the fuse box on the campsite and found out that the fuse was kicked off. He plugged the fuse back and they turned on the stove again. In no time, the stove went off again. They had not turned on the air-conditioner or anything else. It looked that there was not enough power for them to use even one electric burner. This was quite strange. Yesterday, they used the electricity for cooking and doing something else, and it did not give them any problem. In their present situation, it was possible that somebody had changed the fuse and made it unable to hold the electric current. But why? Then they realized that they had set up their trailer on the site that was numbered one. To escape the smokes from somebody's campfire, they had moved to this site and never intentionally chosen the number one lot. It looked that they were in trouble now because somebody did not like that they should be on this number one lot.

This was quite ridiculous. But the couple could do nothing but move. Tired out after the whole day's bus ride and sightseeing, they had now to pull up camp and move again. This time they chose deliberately the number nine site to settle down. After all the strenuous efforts of moving, setting up and stabilizing the trailer, they cooked a soup and had their supper. After supper, it was already late. They had no heart and strength to go out for a walk. After a shower they rested in the trailer and went to bed early. The night appeared problem free and they had a good sleep. Or they were just dog-tired; nothing bothered them even if there was something going on around. The number nine site caused no trouble for them. They had been left alone for the duration of their stay on this campground.

Next morning, they got up early. It would be another full day for them. Last night, Jim suggested that Meilin present her book to the Prime Minister since they were now in Ottawa. The first book Meilin wrote had been completed, which was mainly about her life in Canada. She wrote exactly what she had experienced here, first as a foreign student and then as a Chinese wife to a Canadian soldier. Jim knew well the problems they had gone through since they got married. He thought that if the Prime Minister knew what the ordinary people like him and his wife had to go through in life, he might do something to improve the situation. Meilin did not have much confidence that the Prime Minister would do anything, but she thought it was worth a try. So for the second day of Ottawa tour, the couple were not only to go sightseeing, but also to buy some computer diskettes and envelopes. Meilin had brought her laptop computer with her; she could download the whole book into a computer diskette. Modern technology did provide many conveniences.

When Jim and Meilin arrived at the place in front of the camp office in the morning, they saw that Frank had a different bus today. The top half of the bus had only a frame. Some canvases were rolled up on both sides. In a sunny day, this bus would provide a cool ride, but if it rained, it would not be comfortable with the canvases rolled down. Soon the bus riders came. Today, there were more people taking the bus; all were tourists. The newcomers were two middle-aged couples and a single old man. Frank announced his rules again before starting the bus. When the bus was rolling on the highway, the chatting started. Somehow, the topic today turned to the Quebec situation. In Canada, chatting concerning politics would often come to the Quebec situation.

"I cannot figure out why Quebec will want to separate from Canada. They will lose most of their trading partners and have to trade with the States only. It won't be good for the economy of their province," said Frank.

A middle-aged man with a French-looking wife immediately debated, "They have the Gulf of St. Lawrence connecting to the world; they won't be lack of trading partners."

"That will be quite difficult for them," Frank would not easily give up his point of view.

Soon the topic changed to some other things; Quebec situation was not an emergent problem for the driver and the tourists to argue about. The bus arrived at its destination with people still interested in chatting.

Jim and Meilin were going first to visit the Canadian War Museum today. It took them not long to arrive at the museum by the tour bus. The exterior of the War Museum was like a bunker, mostly camouflaged. The building was not tall and a large part of the roof was a piece of green grass land and there was one lookout tower in front. To the couple, the grass growing on top of the bunker roof symbolized regeneration and life going on after war. Destructive wars could wipe out human lives and what the human beings had built, but afterwards people would always find ways to continue and to rebuild. If a whole civilization had been wiped out, nature would then take over, life would go on and perchance that civilization might come back again in another form. Modern nuclear wars could bring the end of the human world and the world civilization, but it might take more to bring the end of the earth and to destroy any possible regeneration or rebirth on earth,

The inside of the museum was surprisingly large with quite some big halls. The exhibits of four large galleries showed the Canadian military history and how it affected the lives of the ordinary Canadians. Besides illustrations, there were physical displays showing the situations in actual combat, on home-front and in peace time. There was one gallery exceptionally big with high ceilings. A whole side of wall of this gallery was large glass windows stretching from the floor to the ceiling. In this gallery, there were military vehicles, artillery of cannons, tanks and even a fighter jet in display. The tanks were of different types from different countries; they had been used in different wars, from the First World War, the Second World War to the recent UN peace keeping duties. Jim was quite interested in the tank displays, as he had been a soldier in the Armoured Unit. He checked them carefully and asked a guide some questions. The guide was quite helpful; he even went in to check some detailed information in order to answer Jim's questions accurately. Then Jim pointed out to Meilin the type of tank from which he had gotten his head injury.

The fifth gallery was different; it stressed on the importance to remember the destructiveness of wars. In this gallery, large TV screens forming a half circle were occupying the top part of a hall. On the screens, different documentary films were showing the real happenings of the warfare of the Aboriginal Peoples, the South Africa, the First and Second

World Wars, the Cold War and the country's recent peacekeeping efforts. The actual war scenes with sounds and actions were presenting to the visitors the true devastating realities of wars.

Also in the fifth gallery, there was another special hall. It was a large square hall with nothing in it. The walls and the floor were made by grey stones. The ceiling was dark. Along the four sides of the hall, there was a narrow trough on the floor with water in it. The walls were bare with only one small piece of stone protruding near the door. The door was a narrow slot in the wall. The whole hall gave one a cold grim feeling. Was the artist trying to achieve the impression of a large concentration prison? It was hard to tell, as there was a large group of young people in the hall right now; their presence had very much deluded the effect. A man in his thirties, a guide or their teacher, was explaining something to the group. The young people all looked energetic and full of vitality. At this moment and in this hall, they remained silent and serious while listening to the teacher. The gloomy hall forbade any chatting or rowdiness.

In addition to the exhibits, the War Museum had 13,000 pieces of the Beaverbrook War Art Collections. Large paintings concerning war and war time life had not only artistic but also historical values. The displays of the War Museum were extensive. Everything seemed orderly exhibited. Still, wars presented in a museum were facts with limited physical evidences. Wars were the most destructive and cruel human activities in human life; a museum, no matter how big it was, could not show them all. Along the human history, most people who had participated or just happened to be in wars had gone through indescribable sufferings and horrors. Even after viewing the brief history of wars in a museum, any decent human beings would have the conviction that the greatest human efforts should be put on achieving world peace. After visiting the War Museum, Jim and Meilin had the strong wish that someday in the future the world would be eventually free from wars.

The couple had planned to go to two other places today. They practically ran through the whole War Museum and only spent a little more time in viewing the tanks. When they were leaving the museum, they saw people setting up large round tables in the front entrance hall. It looked that those people were preparing for some sort of celebration. Their work seemed to have just started. Many tables were still waiting to be set up in the large hall. Was there going to be a banquet in the War Museum? With Canada Day coming soon, somebody might have thought that the War Museum was a good place to celebrate. But a banquet in the War Museum looked odd to the couple.

To quite some people, a war is the last thing that deserves to be celebrated and even the winning of a war does not warrant a celebration, as so many people have died because of the war. After a war, the first thing for those people alive to do should be to honour those who have given their lives to bring peace; and most importantly, they should try to learn from the lessons provided by the tragic event and to prevent it happen again in the future. A War Museum is built for learning purposes and not for celebration which might lead to the wrong idea of glorifying wars. However, the couple felt that it was not for the short-time visitors like them to judge. The banquet might be a treat to the veterans on this special day and for them to remember the victory. Or it might just be that this front hall of the War Museum was a suitable large space to host a large function.

After the visit to the War Museum, Jim and Meilin got on the tour bus and headed for another big museum which was on the side of Gatineau. This museum was the Canadian Museum of Civilization. When the couple arrived at the museum, they were quite impressed by the look of the large building. The architecture of the building gave an impression of the soft sand waves, the indication of time. The colour of the building was sandy and its frontal was layers of soft gentle curves. The inside of the building was equally impressive with gigantic halls. This museum had two main themes, the history and arts of the First Nation Peoples and the history of Canada. There were illustrations and displays showing the country's history starting from the continent's pre-historical beginning through the migration, the native settlement, the exploration, the fur trading, the immigration to the modern era. There were life-size reconstruction of a native village and some other historical sites. In a huge hall with glass windows forming a whole side of wall to let sufficient light in, there was the largest collection of big pieces of native peoples' artworks, mainly the totem poles, wood carvings and sculptures. The history of the native peoples had been presented in the adjacent smaller halls. There were videos showing in a hall to give more information.

There was another huge hall showing the European settlement and the development of the country. The inside of this large hall had been turned into a sort of historical theme park with physical reconstructions to present history and development. They were started by showing crude farming, fishing, forestry and industry in the early stages and then coming to a small township with street and shops in the mid 19th century. Some museum staff in old-time costumes were walking around in this setting. A sky was made over the township. It was a large vault gently lit by a blue light. The sky looked almost real and put the visitors right in that town at that old time! All the interpretive presentations were so realistic in the museum; Jim and Meilin were quite impressed. Then there were modern-time records of developments and achievements of the country in another hall. The museum even included a Canadian Children's Museum and a Canadian Postal Museum. It was indeed a large museum.

Unfortunately, the couple could not spend too much time in this museum. But they were satisfied with what they had seen and felt that the museum had succeeded in presenting the country from the past to the present in a simple way. It was certainly a museum educational, entertaining and good for families. It must be quite hard for the museum to present the history and the development of a country without boring and burdening the visitors. The stunt this museum had pulled fulfilled its purpose of providing information and education.

Having run through two large museums, Jim and Meilin were famished again. It was already two o'clock in the afternoon. Though they had brought something for lunch, they decided to have something else from the restaurant which was in another large building not far from the museum. The couple walked by a large fountain, through a large garden and arrived at the building. The food court was in a large beautiful hall. Jim ordered a hamburger with French fries and Meilin had a chicken plate. The couple sat at one of the small tables in the garden to have their lunch. There were quite some small white-coloured metal tables and chairs in the garden. The whole area where the large museum and this building were located was by the Ottawa River. Besides the grand buildings, beautiful gardens were everywhere here. While having their lunch, the couple enjoyed the distant view of the Parliament Buildings, part of the Ottawa city and the Chaudière Falls on the other side of the river. In spite of all the troubles the couple were having lately, the bright sunshine, the beautiful scenery and a delightful lunch in the garden at this moment gave them a euphoric feeling that they were having a grand time of their life.

The couple finished their lunch quickly. They had to run to catch the tour bus for the last destination of their sightseeing today. They were going to visit the Rideau Hall, the governor general's home. Governor General is the representative of the British Crown in Canada. In formality, the British Queen is still the head of the Canadian state. In recent years, the position of the country's governor general had aroused quite some buzz. Instead of having the grey-haired white gentlemen as governor generals, which had been the traditional practice through history, the country bravely chose two ladies of Asian and Latin American origins to be the governor generals. A storm had swept the country after this courageous act. It was a pity that people were not ready for this kind of brave declaration of equality for women and coloured people in this country; they were quickly steered by the media to turn their backs to this forward move. Of course the media's action must be worked up by some group of racially orientated or traditionally minded power.

Not long after the lady of Asian origin was put on the governor general's seat, the scandals started flying around through the media. Attacks on her were mainly through the TV reports and newspapers. About her conduct, there was one thing particular for the media to shout about: the new governor general had spent too much money. After this, what had been kicked up around were mostly personal attacks. Every little dirty laundry of hers had been dug out and aired on. Her life, her children and even some squabbling she had with her neighbour became hot news. Of course, the media won. Before her term was over; she was off the big seat. After she was gone, a lady of Latin American origin was put on this honored seat. She did not file much better. Though the media seemed gentler towards her, she was dropped off after a short time. The public did not even know for what reason she had been taken off. Then everything went back to normal, back to the humdrum old way. A grey-haired white gentleman had been put on the big seat. The country went back to the quiet water of a small pond, no more big waves for this matter.

The two coloured ladies, in fact, looked the models of elegance and grace. They both spoke fluent English and French. No Canadian should have felt ashamed to have them as the representatives of the queen and to converse with the real queen. They both had grey-haired white gentlemen as their husbands. It seemed that all these could not appease some white Canadians. As for the two ladies, this honoured high position did not do them any good. They were not skilled or weathered politicians. Under the storm, they withered quickly and disappeared from the public scene without any ado.

The ancient Greek philosopher Plato had said, "No human affairs is worthy of great anxieties." Though the husbands of the two ladies were both philosophers, the ladies themselves seemed to have not much philosophical minds to deal with the treacherous situation in the big political arena. They were no match at all for the rogue media. The wears and tears soon showed up on their appearances. Even their sympathizers felt a relief for their sake when they were gone. In a short time, the country's attempt to raise the status of the coloured people on the highest level was defeated. Would there be enough courage left to try again in the near future? It did not look very likely. But the coloured people in this country might not give up hope easily.

One of the attacks on the governor general of the Asian origin was about a very expensive rug she had bought for the Rideau Hall. It was said that it had cost about ten or twenty thousand dollars. Jim and Meilin now had the chance to go to have a look at this notorious rug. After seeing the Parliament Buildings in Ottawa and the legislative buildings in some different provinces, the couple thought that the grandeur and extravagance of Rideau Hall must have topped them all and this expensive rug must be an unnecessary expenditure added to the extravagance.

The tour bus stopped at the gate of Rideau Hall. Jim and Meilin got off the bus. There was an iron-rod fence with a gate as the entrance to Rideau Hall and the ground. The couple passed the gate where a guard in full royal guard's uniform was standing on guard by a small pavilion. After entering the gate, there was a small building on one side, which was a reception office. There were a few displays in the office, introducing the Rideau Hall and the position of the governor general. The couple did not linger long in the office; they started walking towards the Rideau Hall. A long paved road was leading up to the top of the Rockcliffe Mountain where Rideau Hall was standing. Along both sides of the road, there were large mature trees on well manicured lawns. The slightly sloping mountain ground was large, beautiful and all shaded by large trees. There was only one small piece of native artwork – the stone Man, on the edge of the mountain facing the river. The road stretched long and it took quite some time for the couple to reach the top. When Rideau Hall was finally in view, the couple were surprised. The building was a simple plain old structure. Though there was a domed tower on the centre top, the building was not very large and had no ornamental sculptures, carvings or any kind of fancy architecture ornaments. The couple did not know what to make of it. They had an entirely different expectation for Rideau Hall, but now it appeared in an unexpected simple plain shape.

The official name of Rideau Hall is Government House. The residence has been the home and office of the country's Governor Generals since 1867 when Canada was born. The place was built in 1838 by Thomas MacKay, a Scottish stonemason who had also worked on the Rideau Canal. The important building is surrounded by 79 acres of park-like land.

The simple building of Rideau Hall stood on top of the mountain without any imposing air. It could never make the visitors think of the

Buckingham Palace in London, England. In front of the building, there was a small guard post or pavilion on one side. Right now, a small group of guards in red royal guard uniforms and tall black beaver fur hats were having the Changing of Guard ritual. Some tourists were standing around to watch the ceremony. Jim and Meilin joined the watchers. They admired the guards. The soldiers performed well the daily ritual. On the hot summer day and with the full uniforms and the fur hats, they were not even sweating. The fuller Changing of Guard ritual was carried out every day at a certain time in front of the Parliament Buildings, the same as the one being carried out in front of the Buckingham Palace in London, England. Jim and Meilin could not catch the one in front of the Parliament Buildings and had to be satisfied with this one in front of the Rideau Hall.

After watching the Changing of Guard, the couple went to the inside of Rideau Hall. The inside of Rideau Hall had surprised them again. There were only two large halls for the visitors to see. Both of them were partially blocked, so that the visitors could only stand on one side to view the halls. The halls were almost empty with very little to be seen. One large hall must have been used for banquets, but right now there was only the talked-about rug on the floor with nothing, no tables or chairs on it. In the head side of the hall, there was low platform acting as a stage. On the stage, there were some flags standing. The other hall was smaller and it must have been used for some casual receptions, which had some chairs and small side tables along the wall. One side of this smaller hall had windows facing a garden, but the visitors were not allowed to be on the window side to enter the garden. Rideau Hall was said to have the most beautiful gardens, but the visitors could have only a very limited glimpse of the garden through the windows of this hall. The whole inside of Rideau Hall looked a bit shabby even with the alleged expensive rug. The rug was beautiful and large; it had almost covered the whole floor of the large hall. The couple had doubts that the country had used those halls for some state receptions.

Walking on the long road again on their way back, the couple tried hard to figure out and to justify the inside and outside looks of Rideau Hall. Perhaps the way they looked was good for the country. Simple and modest appearance was normally the indication of honest character. Still the look of Rideau Hall did not do credit to the true condition of the country. After quite some thinking, the couple were still bewildered. Yet one thing was quite clear that the media's attack on the Governor General of Asian origin on this rug issue was unjustified. This had put the integrity and credibility of their other attacks in question. It was clear that the offence of the governor general might not only be because of her Asian origin, but also because that she had stepped out of the boundary of her duty. In trying to do something more, she had broken the traditional role of a governor general. She had tried to brush up a little bit of Rideau Hall, tour the whole country, meet and talk to people of different regions.

Even the ordinary people in this country knew that the position of Governor General was mainly ornamental without much actual power. The governor general would appear on some formal occasions of the state affairs such as some national ceremonies, courtesy shows towards foreign dignitaries, respectful chatting with the queen and so on. The governor general of Asian origin seemed to have done something more than her duties had called for. Her action and her appearance had offended or threatened some people, and thus caused her demise. In fact, what this governor general did was quite within the purpose of putting her on this position. The country wanted to show that the coloured people were equal with the white people; she appeared with her Asian face and her high position to all the people in different regions of the country. She not only brought this equality message to the people, but also showed government concerns and cares to all the regions.

It was quite beyond the couple's ability to figure out all the reasons of the attacks on the coloured governor generals and to push them off the big seat. Jim and Meilin gave up. Let the important and significant people worry about this kind of things. They were the smallest potatoes and were not supposed even to think of those things. Right now, because of their private thoughts being leaked out, they were in such a predicament, being chased, harassed and attacked at home and everywhere they went. However, to remain in the potatoes' state to keep themselves safe was hard to do. They were human beings no matter how small and insignificant they were. They would have their own thoughts as long as they lived and their thoughts would inevitably have something to do with the society they were in. At this moment though, they would leave those seemingly large thoughts behind and enjoy the sightseeing.

After leaving Rideau Hall, the couple caught the last tour bus to get to the centre tour bus stop where Frank's bus would be waiting. Before they got on Frank's bus, they went to some nearby stores and got some envelopes and computer disks. Under the urge of Jim, Meilin was going to download her first book to the computer disk and present it to the Prime Minister tomorrow.

The trip back on Frank's bus was as usual; there was cheerful chatting all the way. After the couple came back to their trailer, they needed a rest before attending to their supper. It had been another full busy day for them. Then, supper was simple and easy. After everything was done, Meilin downloaded the book and got prepared for tomorrow. They did not have a printer and could not write a covering letter, but her book had a "Forward" which was quite self-explanatory and it also had a "Cover" which gave her own name and address. The office of the prime minister only needed to open the CD and everything would be there. On the envelope, she was going to address it to the prime minister. The difficult part came at this point. She was not sure how to spell the prime minister's name correctly. Was it Steve or Stephen Harper? This was a serious matter. If she spelt the prime minister's name wrong, there would not be a minuscule chance that his office would open the CD, not even for security reason.

Meilin asked Jim and he was not sure either. Then she said, "Hon, could you go to ask other campers how to spell the prime minister's name? I have to be sure to address correctly."

Jim went out immediately with a pen and a notepad. He came back after a long time, with a bundle of newspapers.

To answer Meilin's puzzled look, Jim said immediately, "I had gone to several camp sites. Nobody could be sure. Finally, a woman gave me these newspapers. She said that the name might be spelt Stephan, as the prime minister might be of French origin, but she could not be sure. She said that the prime minister appeared almost every day on the newspaper and I could check it myself."

"That's a good idea," said Meilin, glad to see there was a sure solution to this problem.

The couple checked the newspapers. Sure enough, there was the news about the prime minister, of course with his picture and name. Meilin wrote down "the Right Honourable" in front of the prime minister's name, Stephen Harper, on the envelope. Years ago, when she was a student, under a professor's advice, she wrote a letter to former Prime Minister Brian Mulroney to ask for a job and a picture she happened to be in with the former prime minister. Now she remembered how to address properly and respectfully to the topmost leader of the country.

It is not so strange that people cannot be sure how to spell the prime minister's name. There had been other prime ministers in Canada with names even more difficult to spell; much less people would know how to spell their names. Another way to explain this is that the Canadians like most peoples in the world are not very much concerned about or interested in politics. Unless the country is in grave danger under some very corrupted government, people have normally paid little attentions to politics. To them, politics is the business of certain people and the politicians and some other important powerful people in the country have not much immediate bearings on their daily lives. Some people are simply resigned to the fact or thought that they cannot do anything to influence the policy making or how to run the country, so there is no reason that they should bother about politics.

Since the establishment of the country, Canada has a political system similar to that of Britain. There are the parliament, the multi-layered governing bodies of the federal, the provincial and the municipal, the multi-party system and the public elections to choose the leaders to form all levels of government. The political party that has most of their members elected to take the seats in the parliament will govern the country. The leader of that party will be the prime minister, the highest power position of the country. The duration of the government is four years. Then another election will be called and carried out in the country again.

Canada is a constitutional monarchy. Yet the political practice of the country is very much of democratic republic. After more than a hundred years, everything has gone status quo. Things are running smoothly and more and more under control. There are mainly three political parties in the country, the Progressive Conservative Party which is the heir of the Tory in the old time, the Liberal Party, the heir of the Whig and the New Democratic Party which is the heir of the Socialistic Party in the old days of this country. Through history, the Conservative Party and the Liberal Party have been mainly forming the federal government. The Conservative Party leans towards the right, working more for the people on the upper level of the society and the Liberal Party claims to work for all the people of the country, especially the people who are less privileged, but it mostly remains in the middle to keep themselves on the seat of the government, and sometimes they do very little because of this middle position. The New Democratic Party however leans more towards the left, working more for the people on the lower level of the society because of their socialistic policies through history.

Compared to most other countries, Canada is well-off. There are quite some rich people to form the high class in this country. With the progress of the country's economy, more and more people have been entering the middle class. Still, Canada is not a country that has no poor people at all. In recent years, the gap between the rich and the poor is growing bigger. Money means power. People with money control the power system. So, Canada has normally preferred the Conservative Party to govern the country. When there are some serious management problems, corruptions or scandals of the government, the country will settle for the Liberal Party to be on the governing seat as it normally remains in the middle. The New Democratic Party, the poor people's party, most of the time is the underdog, but occasionally it surges up to surprise the country. In recent years, the New Democratic Party seems undergoing some changes, tending to turning away from the most poor and pleasing more the middle class. This move might mainly aim at mounting on the governing seat of the country.

Through the years, the Conservative and the Liberal Parties, when on the governing seat, have both done some good things and made some mistakes. The country however has remained peaceful, developed marvellously and the Canadians have lived a better life than most peoples in the world. The multi-party system has kept the government in check from going wildly wrong. The Canadians have become more and more the complacent sit-back type. They either don't concern about politics or belong to a certain party to do everything that they are told to do. The elections, though costing more and more money, seem to be just the game-play by some small groups of powerful people and the going-through-procedures for the ordinary people. On the voting days, most people who don't belong to any party will not even bother to go to vote; those who belong to a party will vote according to the instruction of the party. Very small number of people will vote according to their own judgement and their few votes are easily cancelled out. So who will be governing the country, the provinces and the cities are decided by certain small groups of people. People normally do not know the people they will vote or have voted for. The elected leaders on the very top level seem to be known by the people a little better, as they are more in the public eyes.

As the country has developed well and the lives of the people are getting better, the Canadians are more and more resigned to the set situation. People are more enthusiastic about hockey games than elections. Government normally goes on for several terms under one certain party without change, which seems to provide more stability. Still, there are some draw-backs for this kind of situation of small groups of people controlling the whole thing. The political parties and some politicians are susceptible to the influences of some self-serving powers and even some foreign powers. In today's world, countries are getting more and more closely knit. In a way, this closeness is good for the development of global economy and the world peace. However, the relationship between countries is quite similar to the relationship between people. Closeness can cause some complications. Canada like other countries can be steered to work for the interests of God-knows whatever or whoever. Since people have formed the habit of following or turning a blind eye to political affairs, if the country has run into some trouble or danger, it cannot be found out until the after-effects set in.

Jim and Meilin were among the ordinary people who did not belong to any party and had no role in any political play. Jim had never paid attention to politics or whatsoever was going on in the political arena of the country. He had no knowledge of whatever concerning the political parties or the government and was easily influenced by other people's opinions and especially by TV reports. Meilin had grown up in China, known the seriousness of political dealings and arrangements and experienced their strong impact on ordinary people's lives. She had long formed an eye to watch political affairs. Having been adopted as a Canadian citizen and lived in the country that had more peaceful political on-goings, she had tried to turn a blind eye to the political affairs and to live a more peaceful life like Jim.

Things seemed to have changed for her after Jim and she had been singled out, totally lost their privacy and harassed and attacked all the time. She was angry. It seemed entirely unfair that she could not point out some wrong doings in some services and could not speak out and write about her mind at her own home. The present situation for Jim and herself had reminded her of the situation when she was growing up during the Culture Revolution in China when certain people had lost most of their basic rights; she and her family were among those unfortunate people. Out of anger, the couple started to talk whatever they liked to talk at their own home and Meilin wrote whatever she liked to write at her home computer. Then things got worse and more difficult for them to live a safe and peaceful life. As people around them were not politically tuned to see things clearly, they were easily led by some people with ill-intentions and joined the harassment and attacks on the couple. The drama was turning more and more ridiculous. Meilin could not understand why people were so blind that they could not see what they were doing was actually damaging their own rights and freedom.

However, for this night after a full day's sightseeing, the couple were tired out and had a good sleep. Right now they could not care less of all the troubles they were in, but enjoy a sound rest. Tomorrow would be another day for them to live the life they intended to live, no matter what other people would like to talk or think about them, or to do to them.

Next morning, the couple felt refreshed and were at the bus stop of the campground on time. Today, Frank had a brand new bus that was much bigger and had tinted-glass windows. Not long after the couple sat down in a front seat, other tourists came. Many more people got on the bus today. Besides some new middle-aged couples, there were two young couples joining the tour group. One of them was an interracial couple like Jim and Meilin; they were a young white man with a young Asian wife. They had a small boy of one or two years old with them. Now Frank's tour bus had two coloured passengers, two Asian women. Frank stated his rules just like he did every morning before he started the bus. The ride today was more comfortable. The new bus sat higher and moved more smoothly. The chatting initiated by Frank during the ride was as usual, interesting and enjoyable. The bus soon arrived at the city centre.

Today was the last day for Jim and Meilin to tour Ottawa. They did not lose any time in getting on the city tour bus to start the sightseeing. Their first destination today was the National Gallery of Canada. When they arrived at the site, they saw a giant glass building decorated by large colourful banners. They got off the bus and entered the building immediately. There was no time to lose when they knew how much there would be for them to see. They climbed a long sloped walkway inside the building to reach the gallery halls. The sensation of walking through the building could only be described as going through a big tall crystal palace. All along, there were gigantic glass windows or walls from floor to the high ceiling. The top reception hall was even more mesmerizing. Gigantic crystal lightings were hanging all over from the ceiling and everywhere crystal walls were in different artistic angles. The steel beams that were supporting the glass structure had been vanquished by the numerous crystal-glass fixtures, the place looked like a big crystal or ice palace.

On the second level of the National Gallery, which the walkway was leading to, there were quite some large gallery halls exhibiting paintings of some world renowned masters such as Van Gogh, Rembrandt, Picasso, Monet, Greco, Gainsborough, Degas, Chardin and Cezanne. The couple had visited the American National Art Gallery in Washington DC. They could not help making a comparison between the two large galleries. What had been shown in the Canadian National Art Gallery, though less quantity than that in the American one, were no less quality as those in the American one. As usual, the couple were awed by the collections of so many invaluable master pieces. On the main level of the Gallery, there were the displays of the works of the Canadian masters such as the Group of Seven, Emily Carr and so on. Besides the numerous paintings, the Gallery had a reconstruction of the historical Rideau Chapel with some collections of sacred art and silver pieces. Then there were halls exhibiting photographs, prints and sculptures, and places showing videos and films.

Visiting an art gallery, especially the high level one like a National Art Gallery, is a mental and aesthetic challenge to any intelligent person. The great artists simply have more sense and deeper feel in seeing the natural or human worlds. It is not easy for everybody to fully understand the meaning of every painting and artwork or to feel the heightened sense of passion or beauty imbedded in them. However, everybody can understand and feel a piece of artwork to his or her own capacity. The greatness of a painting or any kind of artwork lies in its multi-layered meanings or perspectives to generate different views, opinions or feelings. Though different people will see or feel differently from any piece of artwork, they cannot help all guessing what the artist, the creator, is driving at, what he or she is trying to express, to communicate or to indulge in.

For Jim and Meilin, the visitors with limited time and capacity, they had to be satisfied with browsing through all those treasures, hoping that in some way those great artworks would make an imprint and enrich their mental world. It had taken them hours just to run through the different halls. By the time when they came out of the Gallery, it had already passed noon. Before they found a place to have their lunch which they had brought with them, they checked a unique but strange piece of artwork standing on the large square outside the Gallery. It was a giant spider about the size of a large house. The spider was life-like, black and metal. It looked made of iron and painted with dark colour. While marvelling at such a bold creation of some artist, the couple were quite puzzled. Of course, they started guessing what the artist was trying to say. Was he or she trying to express or to state that the small creatures of the world were important and significant, or the small and insignificant were also beautiful? As the Notre-Dame Cathedral Basilica was standing across the street and facing the giant black spider, the couple naturally thought that the artist might be trying to express some feelings towards the church. It was quite common that some artists would use their artworks to speak politically or to express their ideology.

While the couple were admiring and wondering about this special artwork, a newlywed couple in their wedding dresses were coming out of the Basilica. A large group of attendants or guests was following them and seeing them to leave in a decorated limousine. Jim and Meilin turned their attention to the happy couple and the cheering party. While they were watching, their old bus acquaintances came along. Mr. Sherman had a paper plate in his hand. There were a piece of bread and a few pieces of salad on the plate. He might have save it to show Jim and Meilin that he would not eat pork. The other old folks must have finished their lunch in the restaurant. The couple greeted and talked to them, introducing enthusiastically the National Gallery to them. The old folks had visited the Royal Mint in the morning.

Then Mrs. Rayleigh said, "Such a beautiful couple, isn't it?" She meant the newlyweds in front of the Basilica.

"Oh, yes," Jim and Meilin agreed heartily.

"I've heard that the Basilica has been booked for two years by the people who want to have their wedding ceremonies here. The young couple must have waited long," said Mr. Sherman.

It was a wonder how fast some tourists could get some information about the local affairs. Jim and Meilin talked a little more with the old folks. Then they went and attended to their own meal in some private corner. During their lunch, they talked about the people wanting to have their wedding ceremonies in the Basilica.

"It seems that the giant black spider does not scare people from wanting to have their weddings in this beautiful cathedral," said Meilin.

"Just think, some people have to wait for two years to get married in this cathedral and then the first thing they see after their wedding ceremony is a giant spider," said Jim while eating.

"It is amazing that some young people today can wait that long. Perhaps some of them or their families would book the cathedral before they had even found a girlfriend or a boyfriend," commented Meilin.

The couple finished their lunch and gossiping. Afterwards, they walked to the Basilica. If the artist or architect wanted to express greatness and beauty through simplicity, he or she or they had succeeded through building the glass National Art Gallery. The Basilica, on the other hand, was an opposite example. The greatness and beauty had been expressed through complexity and intricacy. It was obvious that tremendous thoughts, efforts and labors had been lavished on building this Basilica, so that even the smallest detail would shine with beauty.

Such a cathedral was a good example that art had worshiped something else besides itself.

Notre-Dame Cathedral Basilica in Ottawa was built in 1839, but not finished until 1885. It is of neo-Gothic style. When Jim and Meilin walked into this big cathedral, all their minds and eyes were engaged in enjoying all that could touch them. There were many beautiful wood carvings, statues and so on. Many large stained-glass windows were showing splendid pictures of Bible stories. The carved ceiling of the Cathedral was so high which made the couple feel so small. There were only three or four other visitors besides the couple. The couple were sheepish and felt lost inside such a big cathedral with almost nobody around. The altar was large and the statue of Jesus was backed up by soft blue light. On both sides of the altar, there were quite some statues of other saints. Jim and Meilin were attracted particularly by the gilded statue of Madonna and Child. The holy mother was standing on a stand on one side of the altar close to the front walkway. She looked so beautifully peaceful and compassionate; the couple could not tear their eyes away from the statue for quite some time.

While the couple were admiring the statue, a middle-aged priest in black habit walked towards them. The couple turned their attention away from the statue to look at the approaching priest. When the priest came close, the couple found that he did not come to talk to them, but to attend to the donation box. There was a locked box for donations in front of the stand where the statue of Madonna and Child was on. The priest had a key to the box. He opened the lock on the box, but did not take any money from it. Then the black figure walked away from the donation box to linger on around the altar. This strange doing of the priest might not have aroused any suspicion or thought in Jim's mind, but it gave Meilin an ominous sting.

Meilin was an avid reader. Like many readers she had been deeply moved by the story of Victor Hugo's novel, Les Miserables. No reader of this novel could forget how a Christian priest had saved a man from falling further into a sinful life by his divine love and forgiveness. When the protagonist, a thief and fugitive, but actually a victim of social injustices, was caught by a police after stealing some silver utensils from the priest who had opened his home to him, the priest came not to help the police, but to save the thief by giving him two more silver candle holders in order to prove that he himself had given the thief those silver pieces. Thus the priest with Godly love and forgiveness had not only saved the thief from being thrown into the inhumane prison again by the distorted unjust law, but changed him into a new man highly moral and compassionate.

Was this priest in this beautiful Cathedral now trying to imitate the fictional priest in Victor Hugo's novel? If it were so, his action and intention were vastly different than that of the fictional priest. The difference was like the dark night to the bright day. This present actual priest was not showing two thieves his Godly love and forgiveness by opening the donation box to them, but viciously accusing two innocent tourists who were admiring the statue of Mary. The priest's intention or motive could be nothing else but self-gratification by carelessly and heartlessly trampling on two tourists. Of course this behaviour of the priest came from his racist frame of mind. An Asian woman with a white man standing long before the gilded statue and a donation box probably had given him enough evidence that they were thieves.

Religion or religions have done a lot of good things, but also a lot of bad things in human history. When religion has been involved with the high purpose of following the divine guidance in teaching the believers to have a moral and loving earthly existence, it has worked wonders in human life. When religion has been involved with worldly gains and especially political games for power, it has brought enormous disasters and miseries into human life. Still, religion has been a significant part in the civilization of human world. Today, with swift development of science and technology, more and more people have fallen away from the supernatural part of religion, and most of those who have stayed with religion are sticking more to its moral guidance. However, science and technology cannot be blamed entirely for today's unpopular position religion is in; the lack of faith and the corrupted or even criminal behaviours of some religious people including some of clergy have played a significant role in religion's decline.

After being the lead guidance for centuries, religion today is facing the crises of losing its influence and instructive capability in human life. Will it die out eventually? Not likely. No matter how religion is regarded, divine revelation, moral guidance, psychological comfort or opium, there will always be people wanting to believe that the world is something more than material manifestation only. Many people still have the personal experiences that lead them to aspire after something spiritual or even a spiritual existence after their material existence. For those people, religion will never die out. The problem is that the institutionalized religion is failing the people who are seeking spiritual development. This leads to the public realization that religion is desperately in need of reform. The ancient literature and dogma of religion can no longer work for modern man. If religion still wishes to have any influence and instructive value in human life, it has to be more open-minded, studying and understanding different beliefs and pliable with modern science and technology.

Jim and Meilin were Christians. Though ordinary, they both had some personal experiences to believe the possibility that the world was more than their eyes could see and hands could touch. However, the couple were Christians of a different type, more modern and open minded. They tried to keep an open mind towards other religious beliefs and were quite interested in Buddhism. They had gone to both Christian churches and Buddhist temples to attend to their services and to learn something that were being taught. After they had lost their privacy and suffered harassment and attacks, the couple could no longer go to a church or a temple. The Christian churches they went to would give them the same kind of harassment and attacks as they had suffered in the society, accusing them for being communists. The Buddhist temples would slight Meilin just like she had been slighted or discriminated by some white people. Meilin had criticized racism in her writing. Perhaps some people with power were trying to prove to her that she could be very well slighted or discriminated by the coloured people like herself. This kind of situation had led to the couple's further losing faith in the institutionalized religion which can be quite political and self-serving in some circumstances.

At this moment in the Basilica, though the priest's strange behaviour gave Meilin a bad feeling, she and her husband had long been used to this kind of behaviours from different religious, political or misled people. It was getting easier now for them to bear and to brush those trifling things off as some dirt and to go on with their life. Meilin nudged Jim and said, "It's enough. Let's go. We don't have much time left."

Jim agreed and the couple started walking towards the entrance door. While they were walking through the aisle between the numerous pews, a weighty middle-aged woman walked towards them. When they met, the woman started talking to them.

"Is this your first-time visit? A beautiful cathedral, isn't it?" she asked conversationally, but with authority. It looked that she was a long-time member or helper of the church.

"Oh, yes, it is a very beautiful cathedral," answered Jim eagerly. Meilin nodded her head to agree and presented a friendly smile.

The woman changed the topic swiftly. "Have you seen the big spider outside?" she asked.

"Oh, yes. A giant spider!" said Jim with an innocent smile.

"Have you noticed that the parliament buildings are under the big spider?" the woman asked again.

"Really? We haven't seen that," said Jim, a bit bewildered.

After this, the woman left the couple and walked away. It seemed that she came to the couple just to steer them to pay attention to the sight of the Parliament Buildings under the big spider.

When Jim and Meilin came out of the Cathedral, they looked at the giant spider from this side of the street. "Oh, my God! It was true," they thought. Through the pillar-like legs of the spider, the Parliament Buildings in some distance could be seen clearly. It looked like that the Parliament Buildings were between the claws of the giant spider! The couple started guessing the artist's mind again. Was he or she trying to show the significance and beauty of a small creature, to express some bad feelings towards the church or to say that the government was under the control of some dark power? It might be all of the above or none of the above. The giant black spider beside the crystal palace of National Art Gallery might just be an art ornament for esthetic purpose. One thing seemed clear to the couple that the church was aware that people might suspect that the spider meant something towards the church and wanted people to think differently. After a while of wondering, the couple were tired of the guessing game. Whatever the giant spider at this conspicuous spot meant would pass the on-lookers' minds. A moment later, the couple would, like many other visitors, no long bother about it.

After giving a last glance to the Cathedral, the Gallery and the giant spider, the couple mounted on the tour bus. They were sure that the spider would stand there for many more years, generating guesses and thoughts, just as the Gallery and the Cathedral would inspire and arouse awes. The tour bus moved on with the couple and some other tourists. It was already after three o'clock in the afternoon. The couple got off the bus at the farmers' market at the busy downtown street. They were going to taste the beavertail before finishing their Ottawa tour. The food stall that sold the beavertails was the busiest spot at the street corner. The summer day was hot. A lot of locals and tourists were gathering in front of the small food stand. Two lines of customers were waiting to be served. The place not only sold the sweet beavertails, but also ice creams. It looked that both the goodies were well loved. After some time waiting in the line, the couple bought a chocolate-fudge and a caramel-cream beavertails.

They were indeed very delicious. The beavertail-shaped doughnut was thin and fried crispy. With the quality topping, it tasted deliciously sweet with a delicate crunch. After tasting the beavertail, a cone of ice cream was a must in this hot summer day.

Jim and Meilin stood there by the food stall, enjoying the beavertails and ice creams with quite some other customers. People were standing in small groups on the spacious sidewalk at the street corner, eating and chatting. The scene gave the couple a sense of community. Ottawa seemed at this moment a city of leisure-seeking and pleasure-loving, instead of a serious central political arena of the country.

After the enjoyment of the snacks, there was still time for the couple to walk to the Parliament Hill which was about two blocks away. The last thing they had to do before leaving Ottawa was to deliver Meilin's book to the prime minister's office. The walk seemed long. After a day's tour, the couple were tired. Finally, they climbed up the hill and reached the Parliament Buildings. They found a guard at one of the entrance doors and asked him whether they could leave him the envelope with a computer disk for the prime minister.

"No, I cannot take it," said the guard politely. He then pointed the building opposite the Parliament Buildings on the other side of the street and said, "The prime minister's office is in that building. They have a window to receive mails for the prime minister."

Jim and Meilin thanked the guard and walked to that building. It was a large European style building with large thick wooden entrance door. The door was closed and impossible for them just to push the door open and walk into the building. The couple saw a microphone box with a button on the wall by one side of the door and knew that it was for visitors to communicate with somebody inside. Jim pushed the button and a voice came out from the box, asking what the visitor's business was.

"We come to give the prime minister a book," answered Jim.

"You have to go to the back of the building, sir. There is a window receiving the prime minister's mails there," the voice directed.

Jim gave his thanks and the couple walked to the back of the building. They found a small window with a slot under. The communication with the inside was also carried through by a microphone box. After Jim stated the purpose, the voice directed him to put the package into the slot. Jim did what he was told and then the couple had a glimpse that their envelope with the CD inside had been carried in by a moving belt. They knew that before it was picked up by the prime minister's office, it would go through a security check.

Now with this task done, the couple could go to catch Frank's bus. On their way, the couple started thinking whether the prime minister's office would look at Meilin's book. Jim had high expectation, while Meilin had almost none. She probably had more understanding of politics and knew that there would be near zero chance that the prime minister would give them any slight notice. In their present situation with so many people incited to dislike and even to hate them, no politician, let alone the prime minister, would dare to show openly any inclination towards them. If by a miracle, the prime minister showed some sign of acknowledgment to them, there would be no tell how many votes his party would lose for this action.

Things turned out to be like what Meilin had foreseen. The prime minister's office did not even send her a note to say that they had received her book. Jim was disappointed. Meilin, though could understand, could not help feeling a bit hurt. Many years ago when she was a Chinese student from China, she happened to meet the former Prime Minister Brian Mulroney who was giving a speech on an opening ceremony for a forestry centre. After the speech, the former prime minister walked down the platform to shake hand with the audience. Meilin had been pushed by the crowds to get close to the top leader of the country. The former prime minister had even talked to her for a brief moment. Afterwards, a picture was taken in which there were the former prime minister, Meilin, two other Chinese students and a background of other people. Later on, under the urge and encouragement of a professor, Meilin wrote a letter to the former prime minister, asking for a copy of the photo and recommending herself to work for the prime minister. She got an answer from the former prime minister's office with three copies of the photo. The reply to her job application was that the basic level of government had the priority to use her talent. Meilin had a laugh at herself on the bold and unsuccessful try.

Many years later, Meilin was now a Canadian citizen. She had given a book of her years' efforts to the present prime minister and the answer she got was no answer. She felt that when she was a foreign student here, she had some diplomatic value to a prime minister and when she was a Canadian citizen now, she seemed to have absolutely no value in the eyes of the prime minister and did not deserve even a nod. In the couple's present situation, there was no doubt that some coloured people might be paying attention to the couple's action and some might even have expected to see the prime minister giving a little sign of acknowledgement to this Chinese Canadian woman. To them, a tiny bit of acknowledgement might mean that the prime minister might personally do something to improve the conditions of the coloured people. Those people with such expectations might be disappointed from a no answer of the prime minister's office to Meilin.

However, there should not be too much disheartened feelings from the coloured people in this small case. Things have been improving concerning their conditions in Canada. Prime Minister Stephen Harper has already been exceptional in dealing with some issues concerning the coloured people, especially the Chinese Canadians who had suffered a lot of racial discriminations in Canada. During the late 19th and early 20th centuries, Canada had put a head tax of five hundred dollars to lower down Chinese immigration to Canada. Five hundred dollars was a large sum of money in the old days; not many people, especially not many Chinese people, could afford such a large sum at that time. From 1923 to 1947, Canada simply put on a Chinese Immigration Act to prohibit any Chinese immigrating to the country. This kind of extreme discriminatory policies put on by different levels of government through Canadian history had brought tremendous sufferings to the Chinese in Canada. Many Chinese workers who had settled in Canada could not bring their wives and children here and lived a lonely desolate life in this well-off country.

In 2006, Prime Minister Stephen Harper had finally apologized to the Chinese Canadians for the head tax and the exclusion policies, and a financial compensation had been made to those who had paid the head tax. By then, only 30 Chinese Canadians from the 80 thousand who had paid the head tax were alive to be benefited by the compensation. Years later, the premier of British Columbia followed suit and apologized to the Chinese Canadians for the discriminatory policies put on by the provincial government in the old time. The prime minister and the premier's apologies and the compensation, though as late as in the 21st century, is a significant progress in countering racial discrimination and achieving racial equality in Canada. In view of this, the reaction from the prime minister's office to Meilin's book should not be taken too much to heart by the coloured people, especially the Chinese Canadians and Meilin herself. People should know that every little action for the improvement of the conditions of the under-privileged or unfortunate people will leave a mark. The accumulation of those small marks will eventually make a large dent to bring large changes. Through history, there have been quite some white people who have fought courageously on behalf of the coloured people; their efforts and struggles have played a significant role in bringing the improved conditions of the coloured people in the country today.

Prime Minister Stephen Harper is a handsome intellectual in glasses. In his fifties, he is at a rather young age to be on this high position. But in today's world, many countries are on the trend of having younger leaders to lead their governments. To quite some Canadians, the prime minister looks like a person who can be stiff and head-strong, but not a person who will raise unexpected storms. His apology to the Chinese Canadians must have been a surprise to some white people. When the prime minister first came to this top position, there seemed a distance between himself and his family. After he has been on the head position, the country has gone through three elections in a short period of time and his government has advanced from a minority government to a majority one. In the meantime, his image has been gradually changing from being aloof and stiff to being kind and warm. The biggest change looks like to have happened in his family. He looks a much better husband and father. His wife and two children, a boy and a girl, have started showing love towards him and support to his political work. The first family has even staged a music show on TV for the nation to watch; he had played piano, his son played violin and his daughter some sort of drum. In public, smiles have come more easily on the prime minister's face and he has even shown attentiveness to his wife.

It is a common knowledge that most governments in the world today are no longer governments by individual rulers. They are governing bodies formed by groups of people, mostly the political leaders. Nonetheless, almost every country will still have a topmost leader, a president, a prime minister or other. It is definitely not easy for any person to hold this top position today. First of all, this topmost leader cannot act like a king or a queen in the old time, cannot set up his or her own rules or laws and do whatever he or she likes to do. For one thing, this person, once mounting on this modern throne, will be totally controlled by the demands of the country and especially the demands of his or her party. His or her personal and family lives will be under the eyes of the whole country. There is not much choice for him or her, but to live a life that is impeccable for the people who have put him or her on this pedestal.

Many years ago, somebody asked Abraham Lincoln how he liked being the president of the United States. His answer was, "You have heard the story, haven't you, about the man who was tarred and feathered and carried out of town on a rail? A man in the crowd asked him how he liked it. His reply was that if it was not for the honor of the thing, he would much walk."

Nobody in Canada has asked Stephen Harper how he liked being the prime minister, so no answer can be heard from him. Even if he had said that he liked his job, not many people would believe that it was his true feeling at all the time. One can be sure that he is not feeling all the glory all the time, as the job is not an easy one at all. If the prime minister's family life has been truly improved since he came to this top position, it will be indeed his personal gain from this honor.

Leaders, especially top leaders in today's world cannot have themselves fully to themselves. They have too much responsibilities and obligations to show their real selves to the public, as their true selves might not be the ones that the public have expected or wanted to see. They will certainly not try to offend or even attack certain groups of people, especially the majority, the rich and the powerful. Abraham Lincoln also said in one of his speeches, "These capitalists generally act harmoniously, and in concert, to fleece the people." No leaders will speak like this anymore, even if some of them know there is truth in the saying. The leaders today know their priorities, their responsibilities to their parties. To speak the truth sometimes, to offend the majority, the rich or the powerful will not get them anywhere and might even bring the downfall to themselves and to their parties. In view of this, Prime Minister Stephen Harper is indeed courageous to apologize and to pay a long overdue debt to the Chinese Canadians who are part of the minorities, the weaker part of the country.

For Jim and Meilin, the no answer from the prime minister's office to Meilin's book was quickly blown over in their minds. They knew well who they were and where their place was. They could try, but should not expect too much. Right now, after the delivery of Meilin's book, the couple walked towards the place where Frank's bus should be waiting. It took them only a few minutes to reach the street as it was nearby. When they had arrived, they saw that Frank's bus was there and some tourists were already waiting in the bus. Frank came soon. He and Jim stood outside the bus and talked for a while. The bus riders soon came one after another. When it was five o'clock, Frank counted the ones in the bus. Three were missing. It was easy to tell that the three missing ones were the young interracial couple and their small boy. The tourists and Frank waited for a while. The couple and their boy were nowhere to be seen. The day was hot. People then got off the bus and went to the Tim Hottens, the doughnut and coffee shop, to have something. Jim and Meilin also went to the shop which was just across the street. The inside of the coffee shop was comfortably cool. The couple ordered some cold juice.

Half an hour later, the tourists and Frank came back to the bus. The couple and their boy were still not there. People started losing patience. The single old man complained, "Everybody knows the rule. How could somebody be so inconsiderate?"

Somebody asked Frank whether the bus could start without the three. Frank answered, "Oh, no! The other day, I missed somebody; I was called back to get them when I was already home. We have to wait."

People waited and waited. First they stood outside the bus and then they got in to sit down, hoping that the couple and their boy would show up at any moment. A little more than an hour later, the couple and their small boy finally showed up. The late couple said nothing, no explanation or apology. There was no expression on their faces. They looked indifferent and being on some sort of mission or something in arriving over an hour later. Frank started the bus immediately after the couple and their boy settled down. This time, the ride back to the campground was silent. Nobody, not even Frank, had talked. Obviously, people were a bit mad about the inconsiderate young couple. Jim and Meilin might be the only ones who had some suspicion about this incident. Were some people displeased to see Jim and Meilin's seemingly popularity among some tourists and the bus driver? Were the young couple put on the bus just to do the damage control by making people dislike the interracial couple, which would naturally extend to Jim and Meilin? Having been through so many harassment tricks on their trip, Jim and Mailin could not exclude this possibility. The behaviour of this young interracial couple was way out of ordinary.

In Canada, interracial marriages are few and definitely not popular. The white people with the sense of white superiority dislike seeing this kind of marriages; they must think that interracial marriages contaminate the purity of their race. Though the country has been gradually seeing some important people having this kind of marriages, the general dislikes of it are not lessened. Most interracial couples are well aware of the situation and they normally keep a low profile. They are reserved, keep to themselves and try not to step on anybody's toes. These might be the only sensible ways to keep themselves out of troubles and to eke out a peaceful life in a not so friendly social environment.

Before the couple had totally lost their privacy, they had lived a solitary life. They had no friends and seldom went into any social activities. Though a lonely life, it was peaceful and they got used to and liked it. After they pointed out some wrong doings of some services, hell had broken loose. A peaceful life was a thing of the past and nowhere to be seen in the future for them. Quite some people considered that the couple should be blamed and hated for this happening. The couple had nothing to do with their own privacy being taken away and were of course infuriated by the situation. Their following attitudes were to talk and write whatever they liked at their home. In so doing, they had started stepping on almost everybody's toes at all time.

The incidence of the couple had caused quite some attention in the country. They got some supporters, but some people were scared that the couple might gain some popularity which might lead to some cause, and then some other people were sorely jealous that a lowly couple and especially a Chinese woman would cause so much attention. Everything the couple did or said started offending some people. The couple could no longer make a little charity donation without being suspected or attacked for trying to gain good publicity. In order to calm down the scared and jealous people, the couple cursed and used four-lettered words in their home conversations. They had tried hard to show that they had no desire or ambition for any political gain, as nobody would see or hear persons with political ambition doing what they were doing, especially when the ambitious persons were aware of being watched or listened into. Unfortunately, the couple's efforts were in vain. The scared people remained scared and jealous people remained jealous. The only change was that the couple's supporters were dwindling. The situation of dwindling support might not be caused by the couple's behaviour, but by the supporters' fear of being stampeded by the couple's adversaries. As for the couple, they had no longer cared whether they were being supported, liked, disliked or hated. They only wished that the whole thing would soon pass and they could return to their peaceful life again.

The couple were utterly tired of the farce. When the harassment was following them wherever they traveled, their patience was tested to the limit. No matter how infuriated, tired or impatient, the couple had no way to change the situation. Their rights and freedom had been grossly violated, but the whole thing seemed to be no concern of anybody, no concern to the involved power and no concern especially to the scared and the jealous. All these were because the couple were just ordinary people at the bottom of the society; they were counted less and deserved less. The Canadians would go to fight for democracy in some other countries, while some people in their own country would suffer injustices and lack of freedom. The situation the couple were in had forced them to think about those serious things which they had not been accustomed to.

The bus arrived at the campground. The tourists got off the bus. Almost everyone shook Frank's hand and thanked him. The old folks Jim and Meilin had got to know well for the three days did not even look towards their way. Even if the couple wanted to say goodbye to them, they did not have the chance. On their way walking towards their camping site, the couple saw a car drawing near to them from behind. The man and his French-looking wife were in the car. They slowed down their vehicle and asked Jim and Meilin if they needed a ride. Jim thanked them, but turned down their offer. It felt good to take a walk after the bus ride.

The three day Ottawa tour was finished, the few people the couple got to know during the tour would soon pass their life to become part of their memories which they might access from time to time. Life has been said to be a play, a game, a dream, so on and so forth. But it can sometimes be felt like a running river. What we have lived and experienced will become our memory, we cannot go back to live and experience the very same things again. Like the running river, they have passed. While we are drifting in this river of life, we will live with or meet different people of different characters and go through different events. Some people we have met will stay with us for a very short time like the debris floating away in the water; some will stay with us for longer time and some even long periods of our life. Short or long, good or bad, eventually we will part company. Some of the parting will be felt light or even a relief; some will cause excruciating pains. Good or bad events will also last short or long in our life. We all wish that happy events will last long and bad ones will be short or never happen. However, what kind of people and events we will meet in the river of life seem not fully under our control. All we can do is to fully enjoy and cherish the people and events we deem worthy of our time and emotions, bear the people and events that we loath and regret the time and emotions we have wasted on them, knowing that all will pass. After all, our time in the drifting river of life is short, pure happy moments seem rare and people we can whole-heartedly love or like are hard to come by.

The couple had a restful last night on this campground. Next day they found that they were still in high spirits. After breakfast, they packed up their things and pulled up their trailer. They were soon on their way to Quebec. Their driving out of the city was smooth. It was another bright sunny day. Ottawa City looked as beautiful as when they first came to it. Though there were a few unpleasant moments, the Ottawa tour was indeed memorable to the couple. They regretted that they did not stay longer. There were still many museums, attractions, parks and gardens they had not touched. They had no idea whether they could come again for another visit. While they were driving away, the Ottawa City in the morning sun looked so peaceful, clean and orderly; the couple could not help feeling proud of such a beautiful capital city for the country. Canada, though there are still grievances and injustices happening in people's lives now and then, is relatively peaceful, clean and orderly like its capital city. What had happened to Jim and Meilin might be quite exceptional, but definitely not the worst. Even when the couple sometimes felt like a despised son and an ill-treated adopted daughter, they still loved the country, simply because it was their home.

When the couple were passing through Ottawa again on their way back from their cross-country tour, they had noticed something strange. When they were leaving the city, they saw a huge electronic screen at the city gate with the large words: ABBOTSFORD MOVING. Abbotsford was the small city the couple were living in now. Was there a moving company called Abbotsford Moving in Ottawa? Was it such an important large company that could have such a large prominent advertisement at Ottawa city-gate? It looked more likely that the city was aware of the couple's passing through, displeased, yet glad that they were passing away. It was understandable that quite some Canadians might wish that the annoying incidence concerning this interracial couple would quickly pass. The couple would like to tell those folks that they were of the same mind, and might be even more eager for the annoying incidence quickly passing their life.

Then Jim joked, "If when we went home and found that Abbotsford had moved away, that would be something!"

Meilin laughed and chatted, "Abbotsford has tried, but cannot drive us away; it has decided to move itself instead. Let's just imagine that!"

The couple were aware that their rough criticizing words had hurt Abbotsford's or even the country's pride. They only wished that Abbotsford and the country could imagine and understand how its citizens felt when they could not talk freely even at their own homes. In the couple's minds, to wish the city and the country to be better for every citizen was not a crime. If their wish had caused some people to dislike or even to hate them, they were not the ones to blame. Their responsibility was not to return hatred with hatred. They knew action like that would only create more miseries in their own life. They had absolutely no responsibility or obligation to kowtow to some displeased people to ask for their forgiveness. Instead, they had every right to express their indignations and to denounce the racists for the wrongs they had done to them and for the gross violations to their rights and freedom.

CHAPTER EIGHT

QUEBEC

As Ottawa City seemed half on the province of Ontario and half on the province of Quebec, the couple were almost immediately driving on the side of Quebec. Not long, Ottawa and Gatineau were behind them. The trans-Canada highway in Quebec was mostly four lanes which was much more comfortable for the travellers. On both sides of the highway, there were some fields and dairy farms. The couple had driven through this highway quite a few times. Each time when they were passing through Quebec, they would notice two particular things. One was that, for a long section of the road, there was a strong farm smell. Whenever a farm smell is mentioned, people will immediately think of cow manures and haystacks. There was no mistake; the couple would smell those things for quite some distance. The farm houses and other farm production buildings were far away from the highway and dairy farms were not close by the road, still the stench would oppress them for quite some time. The smell might very well be the sulfur smells from some pulp and paper mills. Quebec is known to have a leading pulp and paper industry in the country; the mills might not be far from the highway. The second particular thing was that quite some travellers could be spotted camping at the resting places along the highway. This kind of free spirits was rare to be seen in other provinces. Quite a few times while passing Quebec, Jim and Meilin thought that they would try to join those travellers to camp at a resting spot, but they had never had the chance. It seemed that every time when they were passing those spots, it was in the morning, too early for them to settle for the night.

The province of Quebec is a sensitive spot of Canada. This province is mainly resided by French Canadians. For more than a century, it has a not so harmonious relationship with the English parts of the country. Quebec is a second most populated province in Canada and has almost one quarter of Canadian population. Because of the larger population, the two provinces, Ontario and Quebec have been the movers and shakers in the political affairs of the country.

Compared with other provinces, Quebec has the largest land. Most of its borders are connected with the ocean along the Hudson Bay, Ungava Bay and Gulf of St. Lawrence. Gulf of St. Lawrence narrows into St. Lawrence River which runs through the populated places of the province. The name of the province, Quebec, comes from Algonquian word meaning "where the river narrows". Quebec's history and life are closely connected with St. Lawrence River. The French came to this part of North America in the early sixteenth century, earlier than the English. Jacques Cartier, in trying to find gold for King Francois I by tracking a shortcut to the Orient, came to this area in 1534. In 1608, Samuel de Champlain arrived at the place near today's Quebec City to establish the first European settlement in North America. Following them, the French settlers came to the St. Lawrence River; they first traded furs with the aboriginal peoples and then developed their agriculture along the river in St. Lawrence Valley. In the early stage of French settlement, some of the settlers took native women to be their wives. They had thus created a different kind of people - the Métis. Métis mean half breeds in French, but toady Métis are generally the mixed blood of the white and the natives. Like the French, the Métis were strong adherents to the Catholic Church. That was why the Catholic clergy and the French Quebec had supported the Métis rebellion in 1885. Of course, the Métis had their legitimate grievances at that time.

In the early history, the French Canadians had been the pioneers in creating race equality in Canada. They had married into the native peoples, their host of this new land. Unfortunately, those early interracial marriages were coming out of sheer necessity and the close loving relationship had not developed. Having established a strong foothold on this land, the French Canadians had not treated the native peoples any better than their English cousins. The land disputes between them and the native peoples have been an ongoing issue. In recent time, their conflict with the Mohawks has shaken the country.

Whenever, the French Canadians or Quebec have been mentioned in conversations among the English Canadians, there will be some sense of dislike, a bit of annoyance and even some worry. It is probably known to the world that the French province of Canada has been fighting for its independence. It is true that the French Canadians have been fighting to preserve their culture and nationalism. But the firm separatists who want a total physical separation of Quebec from Canada are not a big portion of the province population; they are mainly some politicians. The ordinary French Canadians are normally regarding themselves as Canadians and content to stay within Canada.

The French Canadians' alienation or estrangement from the English parts of the country come from long standing grievances and injustices they have perceived through history. After the French and

Indian War and the British Major General James Wolfe's conquering the French colony in 1760, the Treaty of Paris ceded New France, today's Quebec, to Britain in 1763. After many years of war, the Quebec people could finally live a peaceful life. Following the conquest, the British Parliament passed the Quebec Act in 1774, guaranteeing the French Canadians their basic rights; the Roman Catholic Clergy was given official recognition; the French civil law was restored in Quebec; the Quebec government formed by a governor and a legislative council had the full power of internal legislation and taxation; the French language received official sanction and even the borders of Quebec were very much extended. The Quebec Act had gained the French Canadians' loyalty to British North America during the American Revolution.

However, after the British took control of Quebec, the Scottish and Irish settlers came to Quebec. They busied themselves with trade, railway and canal constructions to become the wealthy part of Quebec population, while the French Canadians engaged mainly in agriculture and remained poor. After the confederation of Canada, Ontario, their neighbouring province, had developed quickly, but Quebec lagged behind. For quite a period of time, the English, minority of the province, controlled the wealth and economy of the province, while the French, majority of the province, were poor and on the lower level of the society. The minority English owned almost all the large businesses and enterprises. They had their own churches and schools. They were the only minority group that could function well within their own community by using English only in a province where French was being used by the majority. Large stores used only English signs. The French Quebeckers must learn English to get jobs owned by English bosses and to raise their social status. The immigrants who went to Quebec would choose English schools for their children to assure a better future. The situation was gravely serious in the eyes of the French Canadians. Their culture, language and national identity were in danger of being erased and they were in danger of being assimilated by the English.

The French, we all know, are a people who will not take oppression meekly. The famous French Revolution had shaken the world, burned a lasting mark in people's memory and left a strong record in the world history. The French people in Quebec were true heirs of their revolutionary ancestors. Their fights to preserve their culture, their language and their identity had started ever since the establishment of the country. The first surge of their actions was triggered by the execution of Louis Riel, a political martyr in their eyes, who had fought for the French against oppression. In the peak of their fighting, there were even armed terrorist activities. Canada was forced to carry out the War Measure Act to send army to Quebec in 1970 in order to calm down the situation.

Through the years, the French Quebeckers had gradually organized in their fights. They had formed their political party, Parti Quebecois. The party had mobilized more and more people. When Parti Quebecois was in the governing seat of the province, they had passed their language law to change their school policy so that the French language would be taught to the Quebec children and the stores would use French signs. In 1980, they organized a referendum aiming at separating Quebec from Canada to a certain degree. With the play of some ambiguous political jargons, Parti Quebecois had got the dangerously high yes votes of forty per cent from the Quebecers. In a succession, Parti Quebecois had twice launched the referendum to ask the Quebecers' opinions, but twice the Quebecers turned down the idea of separation from Canada. After thinking it over carefully without being influenced by some hot-headed politicians, majority of ordinary Quebecers preferred to live a peaceful life as Canadians side by side with other fellow Canadians in the country.

The separatist fights of Quebec with the surges of referendum had literarily shaken the English parts of the country off their boots. Nobody would like Canada to be broken into two parts with a center part missing. People knew that it was high time that the country had listened and paid attention to the grievances and injustices that the French Canadians had suffered. The French Canadians demanded that their language being adopted as another official language in the country; the government complied. Now every government document and political articles are in both English and French, and every piece of merchandize of the country has both English and French labels. The French Canadians have demanded recognition and respect of their culture and language in every social and political aspect; now any politician who wishes to hold a significant government position must be able to speak both English and French. With the advantage of a large French population and aggressive political attitudes, more political leaders of French origins have entered the high level of federal government positions. Several prime ministers of Canada have been of French origins through the Canadian history.

Because of the political unrests in Quebec, the English there started moving away from that province. When the crises reached the level of armed conflicts, large number of wealthy English fled Quebec in 1970; some took away with them their businesses and national head offices of their businesses. The French Quebeckers have then filled up some high level positions vacated by the English and gained control of the province economy.

Though there have been years of heated political activities and movements in Quebec, the province has developed well socially, economically and industrially. Today, it has the second largest manufacturing industry of the country, next only to Ontario. Besides the pulp and paper milling, their textile, food and beverage processing, flour milling, sugar refining, petroleum refining, aluminum making and smelting, ship building and repairing, railway equipments and airplane crafts have been standing out to show prominences. The province mining industry stands at the fourth of the country, behind Alberta, Ontario and British Columbia. It is one of the largest non-metallic asbestos producers of the world. In agriculture, Quebec is also ranked the fourth in the country. It is famous for its butter and cheese. Its largest city Montreal can compare with the mega city Toronto in size, prosperity and living standards. Most of the province's manufacturing industries are concentrated in Montreal. The swift industrial development of Quebec largely depends on its well developed water power. Quebec today has the most extensive hydroelectric power and produces two fifths hydroelectricity of the country. All these have given the French Canadians more bargaining chips to talk to the federal government.

When the Meech Lake Accord, an attempt to reform the constitution in 1990, had failed, the French Canadians experienced again their disappointment in the government about changing their status. To them, asking the country to recognize that Quebec was a "distinct society" was a small request. However, the government has come to its senses to grant Quebec this request in a later time. Today, Quebec seems to have more and more people realizing that to remain in Canada is more beneficial for the province. There are so many stories from old time on to teach and warn those who are thinking of breaking away from their families or their communities. The ending for the runoff individuals has always been tragic. In the modern world, the danger is ever more prevalent in dividing a country. It will significantly weaken the country economically and defensively. As for the natives and the coloured people of this country, they definitely think that the French Canadians are not the only ones who have had grievances and suffered injustices. In their minds, if the French Canadians will compare their situations with the situations of the natives and the coloured people, they will become more tolerant and put the country first.

Jim and Meilin were driving towards Montreal. They had visited Quebec City, the capital of the province before. This time they decided to venture through Montreal, the largest city of Quebec. According to the map, their best choice for camping in Montreal would be the campground in Terrebonne, a place at the city skirt. So they were aiming at reaching Terrebonne. The couple came originally from Fredericton, a small city in the east. They were now living in Abbotsford, another small city in the west. They were used to small city living and were a bit leery of those big cities. The biggest scare for them of a large city was the complicated streets with heavy traffics. If it were not for the plan to visit a large city, they would simply stay on the highway, going through or bypassing that city.

The distance from Ottawa to Montreal was not too far. Towards noon, they were approaching Montreal. Very soon, the nice comfortable highway drive ended. They were running into the madness of heavy multilane traffics. Montreal is a large island city bordered by St Lawrence River, Riviere des Prairies, St. Mille Iles River and some lakes. At its west side, there is the confluence of Ottawa River and St. Lawrence River. The Riviere des Prairies goes through Montreal, cutting it into three islands, Montreal Island, Bizard Island and Jesus Island. There are mainly four bridges connecting the islands with the mainland. A mountain, the Mount Royal, rises up in the centre of Montreal. Terrebonne is a small town at the edge of Jesus Island.

When the couple were entering Montreal, they saw the streets going in all directions and every one of them was occupied by an endless line of vehicles. The couple were nervous, feeling every nerve tensed up and their four eyes seemed not enough to catch all the French signs. After some time running in the flow of the traffic, they were overjoyed to have suddenly spotted the sign – Terrebonne. Meilin shouted, "There! There! Turn there!" Jim manoeuvred the van and the trailer to turn to the side lane which would lead them to Terrebonne.

Soon after they left the heavy traffic flow, they were running on a small street, or more accurately, a suburban road. The traffic was much lighter on the small road. There were residential houses on both sides of the road. The couple heaved a long relief. They definitely liked better driving on the quiet road. The road ran parallel to a river which must be St. Mille Iles River. From Terrebonne, St. Mille Iles River runs into St. Lawrence River. The houses along the road were small, pretty and not closely connected. Everywhere the couple looked; there were trees and green lawns. The residential area along the river appeared peaceful and quaintly beautiful.

After driving quite some time on the road, the couple spotted a small convenience store. Meilin suggested that they should go to the store to check whether they were on the right track. The road was reaching far ahead. If they had made a mistake, it would be a long way for them to turn back. Jim stopped the van and went into the store. He soon came out of the store and informed Meilin, "We are on the right track, but nobody knows the campground."

According to the camping guide booklet, the campground was located on this small road. The couple decided to go on further. They drove again for a long time. The road seemed endlessly long and there was hardly anybody to be spotted on the road. The couple were a bit worried now. If they were on the wrong track, it would take them a long time to back out. Finally, they saw a young couple doing something with their vehicle on the side of the road. Jim found a spot to stop their van and trailer. They both got out of the van to ask the young couple for direction. The young French couple turned out to be unable to speak English. Jim showed them the map and pointed out where they wanted to go. From the young couple's gestures and a few familiar French words, Jim and Meilin were relieved to know that they were on the right track. The young French couple seemed trying to warn them that there was a broken-off part of this road that they should pay attention to. This was unexpected, because the map did not show the broken part.

Jim and Meilin thanked the French couple and went back driving again. After quite a while, they found out that the small road was indeed cut off. Before they reached the campground, the road came to an end. They were now driving into a place like a town centre. The road widened into a street. There were quite some vehicles in the street and some stores on both sides of the street. Some other streets were branching off from the street they were on. The couple were now totally lost, because they were on a street with a different name than that of the small road. How to get back to the former road on the other side of the town center; they had no idea. When they were going to stop and ask for direction again, the young French couple caught up with them in their car. They were gesturing from their car window, telling Jim and Meilin which way to turn. Jim and Meilin were quite happy and shouted loudly in English and French, "Thank you! Merci!" Merci, the French word for thanks, was among the few French words they could speak. They were glad that they could use it now for this occasion.

After this unexpected turn, the couple passed by a large bus terminal. The former road showed up on the other side of the bus terminal. It looked that the township centre and the large bus terminal had cut into the long river-side road. Both the town center and the bus terminal looked brand new. They were probably built after the map was made. Now the small road continued again. Not long after this broken-off part, Jim and Meilin spotted the campground sign by the road. They were very glad that their day's journey would finally end. It was already afternoon and they had not had their lunch yet.

The couple pulled into the campground. They got out of the vehicle to register in the office. The camp office was a residential house. The receptionist was a middle-aged woman. She and her husband looked like the caretakers or the managers for this campground. The office house was fair sized. The back part of it was used as the living quarter of the couple's family. The woman spoke passable English with strong French accent. Jim and Meilin soon got a camping lot and the direction to get there. When the couple drove into the campground, they saw that it was a big place and looked mainly for mobile homes. There were a large sports ground for adults and a smaller playground for children on the campground. Numerous motor homes and mobile homes were lined up along both sides of the driveway that could pass two vehicles. There were quite a few driveways going in different directions and they were all fully flanked by mobile homes. Though the motor homes and mobile homes were in decent shapes, they were so closely situated to each other. Jim and Meilin lived in a mobile home in a mobile home park when they were just got married in the east, and they had camped in quite some RV parks in different places of the west. This was the only place they had seen the mobile homes so closely linked together. There seemed hardly any space left between them. With a few feet apart, the dwellers must be able to hear everything that was going on in their neighbours' homes. The situation looked quite strange to the couple. They had just driven on a long road along which the houses were so far apart to each other. Those houses had plenty of land around. Suddenly, this mobile-home park was showing that there was hardly enough land to accommodate everybody and the mobile homes seemed piled on each other.

The couple drove through a driveway along the river where their assigned lot was located. The river must still be the St. Mille Iles River. They spotted the lot when the driveway was almost ended. The driveway ended at the foot of a hill. The lot they were going to park on was very narrow. On the left side of the driveway, there was the last line of trailers by the river. The lot they were going to park was on the right side of the driveway and on a slope higher than the left side. On the right hand side of their lot, there were only three trailers before the hill started. To back their small trailer up the slope and into the narrow lot looked difficult.

Jim and Meilin had a look at the surrounding. Though this line of sites was right along the river, not any mobile home or trailer had a view of the river. The place was fully blanketed by large broad-leaf trees and thick bushes. The sight of the river had been entirely blocked off by the thick green curtain. The day was hot and quite humid. It looked that even camping by the river; it would not be that comfortable. On their way driving towards this site, Jim and Meilin had spotted some higher area on the other side of the large sports ground. They saw some luxury motor homes parked there with quite some spaces between them. Now the couple were thinking that if they had a lot there, it might be more comfortable and easier to park their trailer on. Meilin suggested that they go back to check with the office to see if they could get a different lot there. Jim agreed promptly. The couple left their van and trailer on the driveway and walked back to the office.

The office woman told them that the lot they had been assigned to was the last vacant lot. Well, the couple had to be satisfied that they had even got this lot. To think of being turned away and having to find another place to camp had almost taken their breath away. They went back to their campsite. It took quite some doing for them to set their trailer up on that lot. After everything done, they were tired out and famished. To go to a restaurant to have a meal, they had to drive to the small town. They decided that it would be much easier to have something in their trailer. After a very late lunch, they rested. Before they could have a good rest, they had to have a shower to wash away the sweat and fatigue from the long drive. The next urgent thing for them was to find the bathroom to have a shower.

Guided by the campground map provided by the office, the couple soon found the bathroom without problem. The bathroom looked new and pretty. Behind the bathroom, there was another building for indoor recreation. The inside of the bathroom also looked new and pretty. It could be counted as the best bathroom the couple had seen in a RV park. Although there were a few small shower stalls with hardly enough elbow room, there was a large shower stall luxuriously beautiful. In front of this large shower stall, there was plenty of space leading to a wash-basin with a marbled counter and a large mirror. This type of bathroom facility could only be seen in a well-to-do residence. Everything in the bathroom was tastefully designed. The floor and walls were all beautifully tiled. The whole bathroom was clean and well taken care of.

The couple had a comfortable shower. The water pressure was good. The large shower stall might be for the disabled, but right now, nobody else was using the bathroom. After the shower, they felt refreshed and their spirits were picked up. Having done some simple laundry, they went out to have a look at the campground. They found a small lookout at the other end of the same driveway where their trailer was located. It was a spot where the trees and bushes had been cleaned away and the river could be seen. Judging by the width and the seemingly endlessness on both ends of the river, the couple thought that it must be soon running into St. Lawrence River. The river banks on both sides were high and the water was running quietly far down below. As there were no path to go down to the river and no beach could be spotted, the couple satisfied themselves by enjoying the river on this high spot. The wind at this opening spot was a bit cooler. Soon, the sun was tilting, but there would be quite some time yet before the summer sun finally set.

The couple went back to their trailer after seeing the river. There were not many other things for them to see, except numerous motor homes and trailers. As those homes were so close to the driveway, it would be impolite to stare at them. Most of the people staying on this campground looked like long term tenants and a few of them might be using their motor homes for recreation. But all of them seemed permanently attached to those narrow lots with their motor homes and trailers. Visitors like Jim and Meilin must be quite rare.

To rest in their own trailer was not easy. The couple had to turn on the air conditioner to battle the heat. In a small trailer, the loud noise issued by the air conditioner was quite unpleasant. As soon as the trailer was cooled down a bit, they would turn the air conditioner off. But very soon, they had to turn it on again. The day was indeed humidly hot. There was an additional thing that had bothered them. The trailer on their right side had a large fan which was giving out noise louder than their air conditioner. Even with all their trailer windows closed, they could hear the noise from their neighbour's fan, as it was only a few feet away from them. They prayed that the neighbour would turn the big fan off at night.

There was no such luck; the neighbour's fan kept on going and never stopped all night. The night turned out to be quite uncomfortable for Jim and Meilin. They could not sleep with their own air conditioner on because of the noise, and they could not open the windows because of the noise from the neighbour's fan. If they neglected both, they would be roasted in their small trailer. Finally, they settled on opening a bit of their left side window and trying to get some sleep. Maybe they were absolutely tired out; they did get some sleep in this hot and noisy condition.

Next day, the sightseeing was going to get on as planned. They had driven to the city centre of Toronto on their own, because from the map, things there looked simple and possible for them to handle. Here in Montreal, they did not dare to do the same. No matter how carefully they had checked the map. It looked impossible for them to manage the trip on their own. They decided to drive their van to the big bus terminal in the morning and to check out what they could do from there.

After breakfast, the couple drove to the bus terminal. The huge parking lot had almost been fully occupied by numerous vehicles. It looked that many people had taken the park-and-ride route. They came here from their homes, parked their vehicles here and took the public transits to go to work. Jim and Meilin found a spot and parked their van. The large bus terminal had a big office building which looked brand new. The office inside looked also new and clean. There were some metal seats for people to sit down to take a rest, a nice washroom, a ticket window for people to get their bus tickets and an information office with a long counter separating the office from the public section.

Jim and Meilin went to the counter first to ask for some information. A pretty woman in her early thirties received them. She spoke good English with a strong French accent. The young woman was quite thorough and she warmly introduced the whole transit system to the couple and told them how they could use it to get to downtown Montreal. When Jim and Meilin asked her for some tour guidance, she brought out different maps and tour brochures, trying her best to explain and help. The woman looked very much enjoying her work and the opportunity to use English. She kept Jim and Meilin for quite some time. When the couple left the information counter, they had a pile of maps, bus and subway train schedules and sightseeing brochures. They then went to the ticket window to get the bus tickets. They knew now that they had to take a certain bus to go to Laval and from there they could take the subway train to go to any place in Montreal.

Things went smoothly from then. They soon got on a bus. It took the bus about twenty minutes to get to Laval. For today's schedule, the couple had set their minds on the Olympic Park and the Botanic Garden which seemed on the track of the subway and close to each other. Jim and Meilin liked to visit gardens. Any place they went, they would normally go to check out the gardens and parks in that place. The Botanic Garden in

Montreal was one of the largest in the country; it had about 30 theme gardens and nearly 23,000 plant species. As for the Olympic Park, the couple had heard that it had cost Quebec a lot of money to build and the province had been paying the debts sustained from the project for years. In the couple's minds, this park must be something worth seeing.

Montreal's subway system, the metro, is massive. It is about twenty-four kilometers long and has twenty-six stations; each individually designed and brightly decorated. The subway station the couple entered in Laval was large and very crowded. The tracks for subway trains were on several levels. People and lots of people were going through the corridors and long conveyers up and down to take different trains. Jim and Meilin were carried along by the flow of people. They were slower than others, but had no problem to find the ticket booths and to get on the right train. The train was packed with people. From the numerous faces of the passengers, the couple could see that taking the subway train was part of their life and they had long been used to it; it had been the way they spent part of their life time and would be the way during their working life. They had no other better way, so they would endure and make the daily train ride as easy and comfortable as possible. When the train started moving, some people took out some materials to read, some looked indifferently at nothing, some seemed meditating with the rhythm of the train and some simply went to sleep. There were hardly any eye contacts between the passengers. The scene in the train illustrated a lonely large city life. Every individual stayed in his or her own shell. Though they were surrounded by a large crowd, activities and noises, each was essentially alone.

The distance between Laval and downtown Montreal seemed long. It took quite some time for the train to reach the spot where Jim and Meilin would get off. The subway station near the Olympic Park was large with tall ceilings; it was not crowded at all. Obviously, most people were using the subway system to go to work. Downtown area seemed not to be their destinations, where their work places were not located. A little while after the couple got off the train, they were walking in large spacious halls where only a few people could be spotted. It took quite some time for the couple to walk through those halls and find an office. They had to know from which side of the building they should exit to get to the Olympic Park, as there were quite some entrances and exits. The office people were friendly; the couple got the direction and plus they saw some people were walking towards the same direction they were going. Following those people, they left the station and reached the Olympic Park.

From early time on, Montreal has been hosting large international events. The Expo 67 is a well known early international trade fair Montreal had proudly held for the world in 1967. The year was also the centennial of Canadian confederation. Over seventy countries had come to Montreal to participate the exposition with the theme of “man and his world”. Today, Montreal has maintained quite some entertainment facilities from Expo 67 for locals and visitors to enjoy. The couple however had not the time or energy to find those facilities in such a large city. They had to be satisfied with what was convenient for them to reach. The Olympic Park seemed easy for them to find and walk to from the subway station.

The Olympic Park in Montreal had been built when Montreal was hosting 1976 Olympic Summer Games. Now when the couple entered the park, they saw two gigantic concrete buildings. One looked a large domed stadium with the roof shaped liked huge waves. The other was a huge higher building with a tall tower. The tower shot up like a gigantic surge from the waves. Though the buildings were massive grey concrete constructions, the gentle curves had given them a grace. However, to fully experience the effect of the huge waves and the surge, one must go to see them in a higher position of some distance away. At the close proximity, the couple felt overwhelmed by the massive concrete buildings. The tower was called Montreal Tower which could take visitors in a glass container through a cable to the top of the surge to view the city. The ascending and descending at the outside of the curved surge looked rather scary to the couple. The large building under the tower was the Olympic Stadium. The couple had a look at the massive inside of the facility. A huge swimming pool inside was open to the public and some swimmers looked lost in the huge pool. Even after seeing the huge facilities, the couple still thought that there must be some other buildings for the Olympic to put the province in debts. It looked impossible for only these two buildings, no matter how big they were, to make a rich province like Quebec lose so much money. Or maybe Jim and Meilin had heard it wrong. It was the Expo 67 that had actually done the deed, as quite many buildings and entertainment facilities were built for that big event. Anyhow, for years, Quebec had been in debts because one of those large events. The shortfall of Quebec from hosting such events has given a lesson to a nation, a province or even a city that extravagance should not be the way to pursue and there should always be ways to enjoy the honor of hosting big events without breaking the bank.

The two buildings and the surrounding grounds were so large that Jim and Meilin felt tired out by just walking around to view them. There were not many people around. When they finally saw a few passers-by, they asked them how they could get to the Botanic Garden which was supposed to be near here. Those people were also tourists and had no idea about the garden. When the couple were touring the outside of the Olympic Park, a drizzle started. It had explained why yesterday was so humidly hot. The drizzle now was turning into a rain. The couple saw quite some people walking into the domed building; they followed.

Inside the large domed building, there was a big function going on. The whole building had been turned into a zoo. There was a long line of people waiting to get into the zoo. Jim and Meilin changed their minds of going to the Botanic Garden. Since so many people were waiting to get into the zoo, there must be something worth seeing. They lined up with those people. It was also a way to avoid the rain outside; still they felt a great pity that they were unable to go to the Botanic Garden. Tomorrow there would be other things to see and they would not come back to this area again.

The large domed building was called Biodome. The exhibition in the Biodome tried to display four different ecosystems through recreating their natural habitats: a Tropical forest, a Laurentian forest, the St. Lawrence marine environment and the Arctic regions. Though the domed building was huge, it was not easy to accommodate the four ecosystems. Obviously, there was not enough space to show some representative animals, plants and sceneries of those strikingly different regions. The visitors could only be allowed in group by group. The long line of people waited for a long time and moved slowly to get through the entrance door. It was in the afternoon when Jim and Meilin had finally passed the entrance. The space inside was indeed limited. People lingered on long, and everywhere was crowded. There were some exotic tropical amphibians, reptiles, insects, birds and animals like the ring-tailed lemurs attracting children particularly; the kids stayed with the colourful birds and animals, refusing to move on. The Arctic hall had caught most adults' interest. The large hall had a realistic looking background of the Arctic. Quite some different sea birds were exhibited in this hall. The Laurentian forest was a man-made scene of a coniferous forest surrounding a beaver pond. St. Lawrence marine lives were presented in a huge saltwater tank with a rather severe background. For Jim and Meilin who had visited the large San Diego Sea World and Calgary Zoo, the live exhibition in a building, though educational, could not amaze them. Still, they admired the ingenuity and creativity of the Montrealers in putting all these together in one building.

After the zoo, the day was over. The couple had to spend time to get back to the trailer park. By the time they arrived at the trailer park, it was already in the evening. They were tired out like many other sightseeing days. But what they had to see in the trailer park was not going to give them peace of mind. All the trailers along the lane their small trailer had parked on had hung out small Quebec flags. The only trailers that did not have this show were their trailer and the three trailers on their right side. So the four trailers in the corner at the foot of the hill were the small no-show zone, English minority of course.

The couple had noticed earlier that all those closely linked trailers along this lane had the same kind of metal posts in front of the trailers and close to the driveway. The metal posts were all about two metres long and had a place to hang a flag on the top, which looked just made for this purpose. Now all those blue and white flags were hanging up with precision and uniformity along this lane. It was quite a view. Jim and Meilin were quite surprised to see this show of Quebec nationalism. They would not call it separatism. They knew that the ones really wanted Quebec to separate from Canada was only a small portion of French Quebeckers who were mostly politicians and well-to-do individuals. The people living in this part of the trailer park could only be counted as the people at the lower level of the society. They were the ones who had no problems to be Canadians.

Though Jim and Meilin had been in Quebec for very limited times, they could see and understand something about this province. To them, the show of Quebec nationalism was not a show of separatism, it was a card being played by some individuals for personal gains or power, a card played by some French Quebecers in pushing the government to improve the conditions for French Canadians and a card played to get more benefits and better bargains for the province. The ordinary Quebec people were normally quite friendly towards the English and other kinds of people. They looked happy to be Canadians. Jim and Meilin could not see any threat or possibility that Quebec would separate from the country. However, the wish to maintain and preserve their culture and language was the wish of most French Quebeckers; this was quite clear.

Some other things the couple could see in this province were entirely indebted to their present situation. All along their cross-country trip, they had noticed the police stopping some cars and pulling them to the roadsides. It seemed that there had never been so many such incidents before. The strange thing was that the cars the police had stopped had always been the colours of blue, grey or red and never a white one. Meilin's criticisms in her books had very much offended the police in Abbotsford. Since the harassment towards the couple had started, the Abbotsford police had put on quite some of those ridiculous shows of stopping certain coloured vehicles on the city streets. Now they were happening on the way of their cross-country trip. If this was a way of the coordinated police show of threats or harassments towards the couple, its effect on the couple was minimal. The couple only felt the thing rather strange and they laughed at all the white cars luckily escaping this kind of fate. Besides the incidents of police stopping certain coloured cars, the couple had also noticed quite some same coloured vehicles broken down along the way; again, never a white one. The couple had traveled across Canada for quite a few times. This was the first time that they had seen so many roadside incidents. Of course, they would suspect that this kind of ridiculous strange things might have something to do with the harassment presently going on in their life.

After quite a few years living in the situation of being harassed, attacked and threatened, Jim and Meilin had long been used to it. It had come to the point that they had neither fear nor worry about any of the threats anymore. The roadside incidents had only worked to break the monotony of the trip for them. However, they could see that they seemed now to be the object of official harassment or hostility. Being the small potatoes as they were in the country, they should feel honored by this kind of attention; that was if they could keep themselves alive long enough to enjoy it.

While the couple were traveling on the Quebec highway, they had noticed the same thing; the police were stopping certain coloured cars on the shoulders of the road. Some similar harassment had even happened in the trailer park where they were staying. At home in Abbotsford, they had some people laughing sinisterly for long times near their home. The laughter had no mirth and showed some dark intention. Here in this trailer park in Terrebonne, they heard the same kind of laughter near their trailer from a trailer nearby which was also flying the Quebec flag. Though the harassment to the couple by the police on their way and by some people in this trailer park was ill-guided, it showed that there were quite some people in Quebec who were loyal towards the country. They were well coordinated with the English parts of the country, even though some of them would put on a show of Quebec nationalism. This observation had further confirmed the couple's belief that there was no real danger that Quebec would separate from the country. The royalists were strong; they alone could keep the province stay put.

As soon as the couple entered their trailer, the flags flying outside had lost their significance. The second night in the trailer park was more comfortable. The rain had considerably lowered down the temperature. The neighbour's fan stopped towards mid-night. The couple had a restful sleep. Next morning they got up early and went to the bus terminal after a simple breakfast. Their schedule for today was to visit the old Montreal area where the Basilica of Notre Dame was located.

It took some time for the couple to arrive at the spot where they would start their tour. The subway station they got off was not far from the old area which was called the Place d'Armes. The area was large and along St. Lawrence River. The tourists who were not taking a professionally guided tour could cover very little of this area. Jim and Meilin were not ambitious. They wanted only a little taste of the old city area to have a feel of its history.

After leaving the large subway station, the couple soon walked through an old street. Like yesterday, a drizzle started again. They got the direction from a passerby of how to reach the Basilica of Notre Dame which was only about two or three blocks away. The old street they were walking on was sharply sloped. As the old city area was by the St. Lawrence River, the streets to reach the center of the area were on a descending slope. The street the couple were walking in looked not too old. Montreal's old area had been rehabilitated and rebuilt during the 1960's. The street was not wide and covered by stones or bricks. The red coloured stones were all cut into the same size, a little big than the bricks and laid well in order. The street looked clean and sturdy, no problem to last for a few more hundred years. The roadside buildings were two or three stories high and built by stones or bricks. Some of them were coffee shops or boutiques. They were linked together with no space between and lined up close to the sidewalk. With the rain and the grey sky, the street with the sober coloured stone buildings gave them the feeling of an aged European street.

Nowadays, it is easy to see different places in the world on TV. But to feel a certain place, one still has to go there. No matter how good the TV shows can be, they cannot give the feeling of the place. For that feeling, one must be physically in that place. While one is physically in a place, especially a different, strange or ancient place, the surrounding scenes with all their details will work on the person's mind and body receptors to force the person to feel, to think and to imagine the events and lives those places had experienced. While walking through the old Montreal street; the couple could not help but imagine what kind of things the street had gone through and what kind lives people or generations of people had lived in those old buildings. Were the things and lives totally different from the ones they knew or not quite that different? No one could tell what kind of feelings or thoughts a strange different place could trigger in one's mind.

The blocks were long; it took some walking for the couple to reach the Basilica of Notre Dame. When they had arrived, they could see that it was a big ancient-looking cathedral in Gothic style. There were two towers sticking up on both sides of the building's frontal to form a U shape. Before Jim and Meilin went in the cathedral, they were attracted by a group of sculptures on the street corner opposite the cathedral. The group of sculptures had formed a monument. The main statue in the centre top was a French man in a pioneer or explorer's apparel of the old time. He was raising a flag. At the foundation level there were four groups of sculptures facing four different directions. They were sculptures of ordinary people, women, men and children in different live-like postures and old European attires. The words carved on the monument were Maso Neuve 1642. The statues were well sculpted by some sculptor. The artist had long gone, but the works he had left were still showing excellence and being admired. The whole monument with all the sculpted figures looked ancient and the year carved on the monument was a bit faded; the 1642 looked a bit like 1842. Without a tour-guide to explain the significance of the monument, the couple felt confused. According to the history of Montreal, 1642 might be more likely to be the year.

In 1535, Jacques Cartier reached the head of St. Lawrence River and came to today's Montreal Island. He found a Huron Indian village called Hochelaga in the location. Then he climbed the mountain on the island which he called Mont Real and claimed the place for the king of France. Today that mountain has been called Mount Royal and the city's name - Montreal comes from the French words Mont Real. In 1603 when Samuel de Champlain came to this same spot, he found no trace of Indian village. In a few decades after the first recorded European came here, the Indian village disappeared. The first permanent European settlement in Montreal was established in 1642, the year matches the year on the monument. The settlement was based on a mission led by Paul de Chamedey, Sieur de Maisonneuve. The mission's prime purpose was to convert the Indians of New France to Christianity. Maisonneuve mission was under the protection of the evangelical society of Notre Dame

Montreal. In1663, the whole island of Montreal was granted as an estate to the religious order, the Gentlemen of St. Sulpice. Now all these fit the name and the year on the monument and the reason of this monument being built in front of the Basilica of Notre Dame. 1642 was the beginning of Montreal.

In 1759, the English led by General Wolfe took Quebec City. The capital of New France moved to Montreal. The following year, Montreal also fell to the British. After 1760, the Scots and Irish started coming to Montreal. They had pushed the commerce and especially the fur trade to the blooming stage. Before this time, the early history of Montreal had been heavily peppered by the French fighting the English and the natives for dominance. Montreal had become a city in 1792, but it did not receive the municipal charter until 1832. The substantial development of the city started after the birth of Canada in 1867, when the old city wall had been demolished for the city to span.

Today, Montreal is one of the largest cities in Canada and the largest French speaking city in the world, only after Paris. It is also one of the most industrialized cities in the country. Montreal shines today as the largest intellectual and culture centre of French Canada. Another important feature is the city being one of the largest ports in the world. After the opening of the St. Lawrence Seaway in 1959, Quebec's St. Lawrence ports have been connected with the Great Lakes and the inner ports of North America. Today, Quebec ports handle about one thirds of the country's national and international shipping. Montreal port was the largest in Quebec. It has about 23 kilometers of piers, berths and wharves, and 99 kilometers of terminal railroad. It has the show piece of modern harbour facilities with grain elevators, cold-storage warehouse and coal and oil docks.

Being a large and important city with a long history, Montreal provides loads of things and places for the visitors to see. Jim and Meilin, however, did not have the energy even to scratch the surface and they had to be satisfied with a little bit that were convenient for them to reach. Right now, they were going to concentrate on the Basilica of Notre Dame. When they entered the Basilica, they were amazed. It was not as large as the Basilica in Ottawa, but no less beautiful. The wood carvings everywhere were amazingly intricate and beautiful. Every detail had shown the artists' efforts and love. The wooden pews were gleaming through the polishing of numerous people sitting on them for centuries. On the large altar, there was a large statue of the crucifixion of Jesus Christ. Around this statue were a semi circle of statues of Saints that all looked enshrined. The whole altar was in a heavenly blue light which shone around and above. The walkway of the centre aisle through lines of pews was also light blue. Walking through this aisle towards the altar gave one the feeling of walking towards heaven. This feeling was also generated by the high ceiling. The Basilica gave the couple the feelings of serenity, purity and beauty. The stained-glass windows were mostly beautiful. They were big, each shining with colourful picture depicting some historical story of the city. The Basilica was built in 1820; in its place or nearby there was an even earlier chapel which dated 1656. Though almost two centuries old, the cathedral looked meticulously preserved and well taken care of. There was no doubt that it would last for more centuries to come.

Though there are quite some different religious beliefs existing in Canada, the country's main religion is Christianity. Most religious people belong to Christian churches. Nonetheless, there is no religious uniformity. Christianity alone has quite many sects. Like everywhere in the world, the two main sects of Christianity in Canada are the Catholic and the Protestant. In Montreal, 70 to 80 percent religious people are Catholic. As a matter of fact, most religious people in Quebec are Catholic. But in the English parts of Canada, most religious people are Protestant. There is no doubt that this kind of religious divisions has quite some influence in creating the rift between Quebec and other parts of the country. Along the history, the two main sects, Catholic and Protestant, had gone through many bickering, arguments and conflicts. Different ideas and views about this religion have been constantly debated and different practices have been carried out by different churches. The divisions and differences have very much hurt the relationship between the Christians and even affected their lives.

Today, with the general faith in religion declining, the arguments and conflicts between the two major sects of Christianity look ridiculous. If anything, it is high time for the two sects coming together to find ways to evolve and to better serve the spiritual needs of the Christians. Isn't the main Christian doctrine: love thy neighbour as thyself? If a Christian cannot love another Christian because he or she is in a different sect, how can a Christian love his neighbour with a different belief or worse, in a different race? Another major teaching of Christianity is forgiveness. The problem is that the Christians seem unable to forgive some other Christians in a different sect for some historical wrongs committed by them; how can they forgive other people who might have offended them by having different beliefs, looking different or not their same kind?

While visiting this beautiful Catholic Basilica, the couple could not help thinking about some of those problems concerning the religion of the country. However, they did not have much time to ponder. The morning service was going to start soon. The few early visitors were asked to vacate the place. Coming out of the Basilica, the couple turned left to walk along the street. The place was beautiful. In the centre of the street, there was a long green island of gardens with flowers, shrubs and small trees. In a place among the gardens, there was a small monument with a spearing top. The couple did not study the monument carefully, as Jim had to find and use a washroom. On one side of the street, there was a walled-in place which looked ancient. The couple walked there. A building of three storeys high was in front of that old wall. The couple decided to get into the building, thinking there must be a washroom in there. Unfortunately, the door of the building was locked. When they were just going to leave, a middle-aged woman came up and she had a key to the door. Jim and Meiling told the lady that they were trying to find a washroom. The lady smiled understandingly; she opened the door and said, "Follow me."

Jim and Meilin followed the lady and went into the building. Though the outside of the building was covered with bricks and looked rather modern, its inside was entirely wooden and looked old. Obviously, the building was old and had a face-lift in some later years. The couple followed the lady and walk through some long corridors which were all closed-in and with a few electric lights shining from the ceiling. The tunnel-like corridors were so narrow that if two people met midway, they had to walk sideway to pass each other. Nowadays, this kind of narrow corridors has no longer existed in modern buildings. The group then climbed a narrow wooden staircase to go to the second floor. Everywhere, the path was lit by electric bulbs hanging from the ceiling. It looked that only the rooms that flanked the corridors had windows to let the daylight in. Finally, the lady pointed to a door and said, "Here you are."

Jim and Meilin thanked the lady before she went away. After the washroom visit, the couple had a look at the place. The place looked genuinely ancient. Looking through a small window at the staircase landing, they could see what was inside that ancient wall. A square yard about the size of two hundred square feet was surrounded by ancient stone buildings on three sides. The centre of the yard was covered by crushed red rocks. The red square was laced by green lawns. The ground looked newly finished, but the buildings around the yard were indeed ancient. Two sides of the lawn had connected buildings of one storey high;

one side had a large building of two storeys plus an attic with a tall peaked roof; one side of the yard looked blocked by a small hill. All the buildings were built by large stones which had weathered into greenish grey. The windows of the buildings looked like some holes deeply set in the stone walls and the small attic windows were poking through the sharp slope of the roof. However, the window panes with white latticed wooden frames looked being put on in some later years.

The couple knew that not far from the Basilica, there should be the St. Sulpice Seminary which was dated 1685. Would this be that seminary? Obviously, the building they were let in was renovated and used as an office building now. But the yard and the stone buildings closely connected to it looked like an ancient seminary; they looked so solemn to show grimness and so solitary to show desolation. If it were the old seminary, many young men had spent their youth here in the old days, learning and aspiring to be priests to serve God with their lives; some turned out to be good priests, and some did not.

The missions supported and guided by the Catholic clergy had done some good things, but also some bad things in converting the native peoples to Christianity in the old days. While they had brought some diseases to the native communities, they supplied some medicine and taught some western culture and language to the native peoples. While they had instructed the western religion and values, they suppressed the native peoples' own beliefs, culture and languages. Quite some native children had been herded to live in some Catholic schools to be converted or assimilated, and some of them had ended up being physically or sexually abused by some priests. Today, the native peoples are holding the Church responsible for some crimes committed against their people.

The Catholic Church however had done a lot of good things for Montreal through the history. In the early times, the Church was the main force in social reforms, in fighting poverty and crimes, and in striving for equality. The Catholic Church was the fundamental force in setting up the education system and medical care in early Montreal. The Church had great authority and influence in people's lives then. Today, with more government facilities being put in place and different organizations rising up, the Church has lost quite some of its power and influence over the people. The Catholic schools are also no longer the dominant education system. Many public and private schools have flooded the system and very much diluted Catholicism in the learning world.

Coming out of the old building, the couple decided to walk towards the right side of the street. The street looked long and impossible for them to exhaust. They could only see part of it. Having walked some distance, they saw the street opening up. On one side, there were more shops lined up. The buildings all looked newly renovated; they were all in different bright colours and of old European styles with peaked roofs or small towers; most of them were two storeys high. On the other side of street, there was a large open space. Further away from the open space, there was a large modern building with colourful banners flying around in the wind. The couple looked at the far away building, wondering whether it was a gallery or a museum. To walk there, it would take all the energy they had left after the morning tour. It was almost noon now. They were thinking of going back to the subway station and to spend their afternoon exploring the underground city of Montreal.

The couple stood by the street and admired the large modern building far away. On the opening ground in front of the building, there were quite a lot of big red roosters. The roosters looked ornamental and might be lightings or water fountains. Everybody knows that rooster is the symbol for France, beautiful, feisty and protective. Those red roosters here had shown how boldly and tenaciously the French Quebeckers were sticking to their French root and culture. Through Canadian history, the French Canadians had felt being regarded and treated by their English countrymen as white niggers or second class citizens. This kind of feelings had often pushed them into a fighting spirit and actions to change their situations. In reality, the wires between the French and the English seemed to have been crossed. The French Canadians had not been much looked down upon than mostly regarded as conceited, hypersensitive and prone to act emotionally on the spur of the moment. As for Jim and Meilin who had not had much contact with the French Canadians, they found the French Canadians they had met gentle and elegant. It was hard for them to imagine that this kind of people could turn violent.

The drizzling that started in the morning had never stopped. The couple went back to the subway station after the excursion through part of the old city area. There was an entrance to Montreal's underground city in the subway station. The underground city of Montreal was quite famous; they wanted to have a look at it. The couple went to the entrance of the underground city as soon as they entered the large subway station. Though there were quite some stores and restaurants in the station, they felt that they did not have enough time for them. When they entered the underground tunnel, they were amazed. The tunnel stretched far and had different side branches and outlets to reach the important downtown streets above. The whole downtown area of Montreal could be accessed by walking through those underground streets. Each of them was about thirty feet wide and twenty feet high. It was brightly lit, well ventilated and with illuminated posters and advertisements on the walls. Though walking in the tunnel, Jim and Meilin felt quite comfortable. There were no vehicles running about and pedestrians were not many. They admired this kind system which had both lightened the pedestrian load aboveground and given people the comfort and incentive to walk around downtown Montreal to get to their destinations. This kind of underground streets might have very well lightened the motor vehicle traffic in downtown area too. If people walked more to get to the places they needed to go, they would use less their motor vehicles.

In the tunnels, there were plenty of signs directing to certain important streets and places above. Jim and Meilin followed the direction and walked towards McGill University. If they had time, they would like to have a look at that university. McGill University is the legacy of James McGill, a Glasgow fur trader. It is a large English university in Quebec and well-known for its medical faculty in the country. After quite some time of walking in the tunnel, the couple came to a large area where more lights were shinning and quite some shops showed up. No wonder people had called it the underground city. The place was not only to divert the pedestrian and motor vehicle traffics to the underground; it had offices, entertainment facilities, parking spaces and some different stores and businesses. Among the shops the couple came to, there was a large food court. Quite some restaurant stalls were here. The restaurant stalls formed a large circle to surround a large area where there were plenty of tables and chairs for customers to sit down and enjoy their meals.

Jim and Meilin bought some Asian food and picked up a table to have their lunch. It had already passed noon; the place was full of people having their lunches. Though the food court was large and brightly lit, the large amount of people eating and talking made it look very crowed and noisy. The restaurant foods were definitely not cheap. Being price sensitive, Jim and Meilin had a hard time to find the Asian food which was not too extravagant for them. In a noisy crowded place, to fully enjoy a meal was hard to achieve. All the people closely around seemed used to this kind of condition. Everybody talked loudly, which was the only way for people to hear each other. One table almost connected with Jim and Meilin's table was occupied by several intellectuals. A middle-aged man among them talked boomingly loud and constant to get the upper hand. The man had a large tray of variety Sushi rolls which must have cost a fortune. He skillfully managed the flow of his speech while eating the Sushi rolls one after another.

The restaurant stalls were run by different kinds of people and serving cuisines of different countries. Though Montreal's population is dominantly of French origin, it has long been a cosmopolitan city. According to the records, Montreal has quite some large different ethnic groups living and working here. Though Jim and Meilin did not see any coloured people working in the few places they happened to be in, they had seen some of them riding the subway trains and now some working in this underground food court. On their way to the subway station, they had seen street signs directing to the Chinatown here; they had a glimpse of a large building of traditional Chinese style. The Chinatown in Montreal looked not small. Still in the couple's minds, it must be more difficult for the coloured immigrants to find jobs in a French speaking city. The ordinary people the couple had met so far seemed friendly towards Meilin. Nonetheless, the couple could imagine that if Meilin started seeking a job here, the attitudes towards her might not be any different than those in the English speaking parts of the country and might even be worse because of the strong protective nature of some French Quebeckers. The couple's conjecture about the situation of the coloured people in Quebec might not be totally unfounded. Compared with the English speaking parts of the country; Quebec had hardly any coloured people showing up on TV screens on any of their social occasions or any records about the achievements of the coloured people and their participations in the political and economical lives of the province. There had hardly any prominent coloured people catching the eyes of the public in Quebec like the English speaking parts occasionally experiencing.

Jim and Meilin finished their late lunch quickly and left the noisy food court. They doubted that they could handle having meals in this kind of place very day. Though feeling neither refreshed nor rested by the lunch, they walked further in the underground street. When they saw a direction sign pointing to an outlet to the Queen's Square, Meilin suggested that they go up to have a look. Jim said that he was tired out and would just wait below for Meilin to have a peek. Meilin went up. The drizzle was still on and the temperature was not low. She could see a large church with spiked tower nearby and a tall statue which appeared to be some statesman, not the queen. The Queen's Square must still be some distance away. With Jim waiting down, she went back to the tunnel quickly.

The couple resumed their walk. Finally, they spotted the outlet for McGill University. They left the tunnel and went up. Downtown Montreal looked no different than downtown Toronto. Tall buildings were competing for style and grandeur. The shop display windows here seemed more tastefully designed. The couple saw streets going here and there and had to ask a passerby how to get to the university. It turned out that the campus of McGill University was still some distance away. The drizzle and fatigue drove the couple back to the tunnel. They gave up their plan to visit the university and decided to return to the campground.

Though having seen very little, the couple were impressed by the layers of streets in Montreal. Besides the numerous boulevards, streets and winding alleys, the six-lane St. Lawrence Boulevard on ground goes through the whole Montreal Island. Above ground, the elevated Metropolitan Boulevard also goes from the west to the east through the whole island. Then the massive subway system which the couple thought was the best in the country and the underground city added marvel and glory to the street structure of Montreal. However, being visitors, the couple could not see much of Montreal through riding the subway trains. As for walking through the tunnels to explore the whole downtown Montreal, they had to leave that to the young people. The couple had a little taste of this largest city in French Canada, touching a little bit here and a little bit there. They did not by any means have a whole view of the city and were already feeling overwhelmed by fatigues.

Through the tunnel, the couple reached a large train station. Montreal's underground city was connected with two large train stations including subway stations. They got on a subway train there. It took quite some time by the train and then the bus for them to get back to the campground. When they arrived at their trailer, the drizzle had stopped, but the air was now charged with humidity and heat again. After a little rest in their small trailer amidst the heat and the noise of the neighbour's big fan, they went to take a shower, hoping that after the shower, they would feel better. When they got to the bathroom, Meilin was shocked by the change in the bathroom. The beautiful large shower stall was full of urine stench. The whole walls of the shower had been pissed on. She tried hard to wash the walls with the water from the shower head, but was not successful in taking all the stench away. Who would do such a thing in soiling such a beautiful clean bathroom? With the harassment constantly following them on their trip; she could not help thinking that this was somebody trying to show hostility towards her. Were the French living here doing this? But this was their facility; they might have fewer motives to damage it. Jim and Meilin had paid for their short stay on this campground and did not bother anybody. More importantly, the French here seemed to have used the couple's stay to show their nationalism. It looked more likely that the loyalists had done this. They might not like the couple's stay here to give the French a chance for their nationalist show.

After the strenuous cleaning of the shower stall, Meilin had a very uncomfortable shower. Back to the trailer, she told Jim about the incident, stating her opinion, "To keep the country together is a noble cause; the loyalists have no need to resort to rascality! If it is the French racists' doing, it is not strange. The show of racist hostilities and hatred is the same everywhere, sinister, low and dirty!"

"All the way we have been harassed. It looks like that the same type of people are doing this kind of things," Jim put his thoughts in. To him, this was the continuation of the harassment they had been receiving along the trip.

Quebec's birth rate has been falling in recent times. Though a majority in Quebec, the French Canadians are a minority in Canada and a much smaller minority in North America. If the French Quebecers take up hostile attitudes towards the different immigrants coming to become Quebecers, the position of their French Island in the English Sea will be shakier.

The night turned out to be quite uncomfortable. The neighbour's fan screamed all night long; the couple did not have much sleep. If this kind of things happened in the English parts of the country, Jim might have gone to the other trailer to see if the owner could turn the fan off. Here in the French part of the country and with a show going on around, the couple thought that it might be better for them to keep quiet and to endure it. By quarreling with the neighbour here, a small thing might turn into a big thing. Next morning, they decided to leave the trailer park. They had paid for four nights, but had only spent three nights. After breakfast, they walked to the office to see if they could get some money back. The caretaker couple were both in the office. Jim and Meilin stated the reason of their leaving a bit earlier and asked for the refund for the night left. The French couple did not say anything, but quickly gave back the fee for one night. There was no expression on their faces to show that they were offended or angry. It seemed that they considered Jim and Meilin's earlier leave good for both sides.

Jim and Meilin pulled their trailer to the big bus terminal. They had to study the map to see how to get to the nearest proper highway. They both felt that the tour of Montreal was unsatisfactory and had no idea that they would ever come this way again. It was early in the morning. The couple sat in their trailer and discussed for a while. Finally they decided to venture into Montreal again and spend some of the day visiting another spot. Now they knew the route to get to the city and could leave their van and trailer in the parking lot here. They would get back early and carry on their journey after the last visit to Montreal. They were sure that they could find some place along the highway for the night. But what should be the last place they would see in Montreal? After some discussion, they settled on Saint Joseph's Oratory, an important religious and historical site in Montreal.

After the decision, the couple quickly left the bus terminal. The day turned out to be fine, though the temperature was still high. It took some time for the bus and then the subway train to get to the stop nearest to Saint Joseph's Oratory. From the subway station to the Oratory, there was still quite a distance. After leaving the subway station, the couple walked through a big street where tall buildings with large stores lined along. When they had arrived at the street where the Oratory was located, they saw some stylish residential buildings of five or six storeys high. Those buildings appeared to have stood here for quite some years, but were still in good condition. The street did not have heavy traffics; the residents along looked to have a comfortable life. The Oratory turned out to be a large cathedral. In front of the cathedral and a large ground around, there were a tall ion-rod fences and a grand gate with sculptured pillars in the center. On the opposite side of street, there was a Christian college with beautiful gardens.

After entering the gate, the couple were amazed by the large ground. There were large green lawns and orderly flower beds accompanying two wide paved paths leading up to the cathedral. In the center front, there was a large monument. The statue of Saint Joseph with baby Jesus in his arm was on top of the monument and four angels were on four sides of the foundation. There was the well-known carillon of 56 iron bells. The carillon had originally been made for the Eiffel Tower in Paris. It was a loan to the Oratory when it celebrated its Golden Jubilee. Later on, generous pilgrims bought the carillon to present it to the Oratory as a gift. Now it was a permanent fixture here. Carillon was a rare grand music instrument and understandably, not many musicians could play it. Casual visitors like Jim and Meilin would have no luck to hear its chimes.

Behind the monument and at the end of the flower-bed bordered paths, there was the hill. Saint Joseph's Oratory stood on top of the hill.

Wide and long cement staircases were leading up to the top of the hill to reach the Oratory. Then there were two sets of wide circling cement staircases on both sides as two arms holding up the foundation of the large cathedral. When an oratory was mentioned, people would think of a chapel for praying purpose. Jim and Meilin could see that Saint Joseph's Oratory was definitely not a chapel, but a gigantic cathedral. It was built by large grey granite stones and in Romanesque style. There were large tall stone columns in the centre frontal. A large greenish metal dome was on top of the several storeys high structure. From the guiding pamphlet, St. Joseph's Oratory is the tallest cathedral above the average sea level in the world, 856 feet high. It is taller than the Saint Paul's Cathedral in London, Notre Dame in Paris, Saint Patrick's Cathedral in New York and Saint Anne Cathedral in Beaupre. Locally, the dome top of Saint Joseph's Oratory rising on top of the hill is the highest structural point in Montreal.

This gigantic magnificent cathedral had been started by an ordinary Montrealer named Alfred Bessette. Alfred was born in poverty in August 9, 1845. His birth place was at the southeast of Montreal. He was the eighth child among twelve children of a poor couple. When he was eleven years old, he became an orphan. With little education he worked as a labourer, doing odd jobs here and there. In his late twenties, he joined the Congregation of Holy Cross and was named Brother Andre. He started his religious career as a porter for Notre Dame College in Cote-des-Neiges.

Brother Andre had personal confidence or preference in Saint Joseph, spouse of Saint Mary. He prayed to Saint Joseph particularly and constantly. When he was about thirty years old, Brother Andre became famous for his ability to heal sick people. He credited his ability entirely to his prayers to Saint Joseph. His fame spread quickly and people flocked to him from far and wide, seeking help. In 1904, with the help of his friends, he built a chapel to honor Saint Joseph. The crowds visited him each year while he lived. Today, though the chapel still stands on the hill, a giant cathedral has risen beside it. Brother Andre died in January 6, 1937 at the age of 91. A million people said good-bye to him at his funeral. On May 2, 1982, he was beatified by Pope Jean-Paul II.

Jim and Meilin climbed up those steps which were over two hundred of them. The climbing made their hearts pounding and their breathing difficult. They had to rest at every landing. After arriving at the front of the cathedral, they had to take a long rest before starting the tour. On the first level of the cathedral that was open to the public, there was a votive chapel. In this chapel, there was another Saint Joseph's statue on top of ascending layers of lit candles in glass containers. This statue of

Saint Joseph had his arms stretched towards everybody and a circular blue light was streaming down from the ceiling over him. Those candles were called vigil lights. In front and under the statue of Saint Joseph, there were normally 3,500 of those lights. In the whole chapel, there were about 10,000 of lit candle lights under the statues of different saints. The visitors and pilgrims could pay some money and light a candle to pay their respect or to present a prayer to the saints. The ceiling of the chapel was high. On one side of the walls numerous canes, crutches and some other aiding instruments were hanging. Obviously, people who had been benefited by the prayers to Saint Joseph and other saints were giving their testimonies by leaving their personal aids here for others to see.

Miracles and especially miraculous cures for diseases have been experienced and recorded everywhere throughout human history. Any intelligent person will not regard all of them as lies or shams made up by some charlatans. If they are all lies or schemes, how can so many people in every part of world be involved in them? Miracles and miraculous cures for diseases have not only been experienced by religious people. They have definitely not been claimed only by certain types of religion. They seem to be universal and exist always with human life. The difference of this phenomenon is that different people have credited those miraculous happenings to different powers or sources. People with religious beliefs will of course have the conviction that miracles are worked out by what they have believed in.

Christians, especially the Catholic have the strong belief that miracles are ordained by God and saints. Buddhists have the conviction that miracles are granted by their prayers to Bodhisattvas. The native peoples have put their trust in their shamans, medicine men or some other spiritual personage. Muslins have credited them to their belief system, and Hindus have praised their gods for those happenings. In the modern time, the scientifically minded people cannot entirely deny the existence of miracles, but they think that the human mind or psyche have something to do with their happening. After all, the whole matter is still a mystery in human life. No matter how strong some human beings' convictions and beliefs can be; the why and how some miracles happen have not had absolute definition or explanation. This issue is like quite some other things in the universe remaining unexplainable.

One thing is clear. For any miracle to happen; there must be a fertile ground or condition. Normally the ground or the condition is the human suffering or the strong human desire. Buddhism says that suffering is human existence or human life is suffering. Christianity states that God allows suffering for a purpose which is not fully known to humans. Sufferings, the normal condition for miracles, exist with human life and are a universal human condition. Human diseases are very much part of sufferings and therefore, miraculous cures happen throughout human history. The cures that have been considered as miracles are normally the cures for illnesses or diseases that have not been totally under the control of human capability. Of course, some of those illnesses and diseases have been controlled by medical science and technology later on. Still, new challenges have come up, which science and technology cannot fully handle. So miracles still have ground to happen. Besides, modern medical science has created a grey line to claim some achievements that might not be totally belong to it.

Some miracles and miraculous cures must have happened here in this spot of Montreal to have brought the construction of such a gigantic cathedral and over two million visitors and pilgrims still flocking here every year. It cannot be reasonably or scientifically decided whether the miracles have been rendered by God, Saint Joseph, Brother Andre or people's own minds. Religion, especially religion in the ancient times, has used miracles as the best tools to bring believers and converters to its fold. The Bible has recorded numerous miracles. For the miraculous cures of incurable diseases, Jesus Christ is the foremost healer. Later on, there is Saint Francis of Assisi who has been recorded to have psychic and healing ability. Here, in Montreal, Brother Andre might very likely have possessed this miraculous ability to heal people and to have attracted so many folks, both religious and non-religious.

Jim and Meilin were ordinary people. Like most ordinary people, they thought that it was not their place to judge or even to laugh at this kind of things which had mattered to so many people throughout human history. They lit two candles, one to Saint Joseph and one to Saint Mary, and said their prayers. If so many people had so strongly believed that some miraculous things had happened because of their prayers here, they would like to pay their respect and attention. Perchance, their prayers could be answered too; who could absolutely know or decide? Nonetheless, the couple were living in this modern time which had inevitably forced them to keep an open mind. They had also been equally impressed and moved by some beautiful magnificent temples erected by the believers with different beliefs. They would not deny themselves the chance to pay their respect to them by bowing down or lighting some incense too.

Whether this kind of behaviour like the couple's is coming from the modern man's dilemma in faith or good fortune in freedom cannot be easily discerned. People have found it more and more difficult to stick to the dogma of certain religion. This has caused some problems for them to observe some valuable moral teachings of the religion. They have found it more comfortable to think freely while being backed up by modern science and technology. Why should they be confined and squeezed to the corner by some ancient thinking formula? Who can stop them to be more flexible and to think by themselves?

After the tour of the votive chapel, the couple had a look at the crypt-church which was built in 1916. The statue on the altar was Saint Joseph holding baby Jesus in his arm. The statue was sculpted from marble and must be done by a good artist. Saint Joseph looked live-like and compassionate. The cathedral was indeed large. According to the guiding booklet, different layers of the cathedral had been built in different times. The top layer was the basilica for which the construction began in 1924 and finished in 1955. Jim and Meilin took the elevator and went to the top level after they visited the first level, skipping the middle. They were afraid that they would not be able to cover all the area of this giant cathedral within limited time.

When they entered the basilica, they were stunned by the height of the ceiling. It must be hundreds of feet high from the floor to the top of the interior dome. This was the only building that the couple had seen in their life to have such a high vertical space. Of course, they were not comparing a church building with a coliseum or some other public recreational buildings. They felt indeed lost and small in this basilica; even the numerous chairs in the hall looked lost in such a large space. The altar was also exceptionally tall and large. A large crucifix was on the altar, over which there was a vaulted mosaic art decoration and the background of the altar was a giant engraved art piece which made the altar look strangely a mixture of ancient and modern.

There were some pilgrims here sitting on or kneeing in front of the chairs. They were praying or meditating. Jim and Meilin sat down on the chairs, trying to take all these in, to rest and if possible, to meditate or say a prayer. Strangely enough, inside such a large spacious hall, they found it hard to concentrate. Their minds seemed to have spanned with the large space and could hardly focus on a point. After the vain attempt of meditation, the couple got up to look around. On the tall walls, there were some elongated black-coloured wooden sculptures which appeared to be some religious figures. They were modern arts, well done and quite fitting for the tall space. But more impressively were those large stained-glass windows. Those windows gave colourful pictures telling the stories of miracles brought about by people's collective prayers to God and Saint Joseph. Those miracles were of large scale and historical; they were the disappearing of a typhoid epidemic in Ottawa in 1847, avoiding a battle Quebec faced in 1711, the end of the hostilities from American troops in 1776, the founding of Ursuline Sisters of Quebec in 1633, the saving of a ship named Saint Joseph from ruin in 1639, the establishment of the Congregation of the Gentlemen of Montreal which brought the Christian elite together in 1694 and so on.

Another amazing thing in the basilica was the huge organ pipes. They were set up on the other side of the hall facing the altar. The instrument itself looked like a large piece of art work. According to the guiding booklet, the cathedral offered concerts periodically to the public. Jim and Meilin thought that the Montrealers were lucky to have the chance to attend to those concerts. With such a big organ, the music must sound grand. However, in such a big hall, how other music instruments would sound was hard to imagine.

After viewing all these, the couple could see this church's strong faith in Saint Joseph. There are seven functions which the Christian tradition has attributed to Saint Joseph: he is represented guardian of virgins, support of families, terror of demons, consolation of the afflicted, hope of the sick, patron of the dying and protector of the church.

Having seen the top level, Jim and Meilin had time to see the middle level of the cathedral. There was a large hall in the front section of this level which had large windows facing the outside. In the hall, there was a souvenir store with a long counter selling religious memorabilia. Many tourists were here trying to buy some souvenirs. Besides this souvenir store, the premises also had a cafeteria, a restaurant and resting place for pilgrims. This kind of service facilities provided by a cathedral was quite unusual. Whether the cathedral was still a sacred place for pilgrims or commercialized tourist attraction for common visitors could only be decided by individual visitors and pilgrims.

Jim and Meilin bought a little souvenir and then went outside to the large terrace which was behind the souvenir store windows and right in the front mid-section of the cathedral. On the terrace, they could have a whole view of the front ground of the cathedral and also a grand view of part of the Montreal City. Standing on the terrace and looking at the broad scene of Montreal, the couple felt that their visit to Saint Joseph's Oratory was worthwhile. Though from this angle, there were no skyscrapers to be seen, the vast sprawl of houses and buildings of the city was already impressive. The couple were convinced of the Montreal's status as the second largest city in Canada, next only to Toronto.

Leaving the terrace, the couple found the place to get some food. It was already afternoon. Though they had some snacks while sitting in the store area, they were quite ready for their lunch. After the lunch, they had to choose what to see for the little time left. There were still quite some places and things inside the cathedral they had not covered. Opposite the souvenir store, there was a museum exhibiting quite some religious arts, different Saint Joseph's statues and some other religious artifacts. Finally, the couple decided to go to the meditation gardens which they had a glimpse from on the terrace.

The meditation gardens had covered the whole hill side by the cathedral. The couple left the cathedral through the circling staircase and then walked on the meandering path through flower beds, shrubs and different trees. At different spots in the gardens, there were some stone sculptures. The theme of the gardens and the sculptures was the Way of the Cross, depicting Jesus' life, crucifixion and resurrection. The artist's efforts and accomplishment could be seen well. The sculptures, though looked crude, shone with an inner simplicity and purity. The couple were especially moved by the sculpture of Jesus' resurrection which was large and sculpted from white marble. This sculpture was on a tall stand situated on a higher ground and accessed by a wide cement staircase. Jesus' face looked so peaceful. Though marble, his robe looked floating in the air. The artist had successfully achieved the goal in creating the impression of Jesus ascending.

Lower down beside the sculpture of Jesus' resurrection, there was the fountain of redemption. A rectangular pool was flanked by two flower beds. At the head of the pool, there was a golden lamb on a stand. Under the lamb, there were seven streams of water flowing into the pool. All these were symbolizing the sacraments of the Church. The couple rested for a while by the pool. There were only a few tourists here. The place looked beautiful and peaceful. All the sculptures, the pool and the fountain were surrounded by flowers, shrubs and trees. The place was indeed ideal for visitors to wander, ponder or meditate. The gardens were the dream of Brother Andre. He wished that such a place would be conducive for pilgrims to think of the mystery of Jesus' passion.

It took quite some time for Jim and Meilin to tour the gardens and took some pictures. When they had finished, it was quite the time for them to leave. They had planned to go back to the bus terminal earlier today. It looked that when they reached the bus terminal, it would not be that early. The couple left Saint Joseph's Oratory with some regret that they did not have enough time to see everything. However, this day's sightseeing made them feel satisfied with their trip to Montreal; they had finally had a decent view of the city after being transported by the confined subway trains for the few days. The day's tour seemed fruitful because they had a better understanding of the people living here; most French Canadians were like everybody else, wishing to live a good life without sufferings.

The bus ride today was far from smooth. There was a serious traffic jam caused by an accident on the way back. The twenty minutes bus ride turned into an hour. The bus crawled inch by inch in a long line of vehicles. With the noise from the bus engine and the heat, Meilin felt very sick. Last night, the couple did not have much sleep. Sleeping deprivation could often trigger Meilin's motion sickness. Now her motion sickness had been worsened by a heat-stroke. Every minute in the bus now seemed a year of intolerable suffering for her. The whole surrounding including herself was being churned by a spindle; she was having a violent vertigo and could hardly breathe. Jim tried everything to help his wife, offering her the ginger, the pill and telling her to do deep breathing, but nothing worked. By sheer will, Meilin kept herself from passing out. When the bus finally arrived at the big bus terminal, she vomited out everything she ate for the day. Yet, she felt lucky and congratulated herself for being still alive. Once she lied down in the bed of their trailer, she was not going to be moved, hell or high waters.

Jim was worried and felt helpless. He opened all the windows of the trailer and tried everything he could think of to help. After quite some time of the treatment with cold water and fanning, Meilin seemed calmed down a bit. It was past seven o'clock in the evening now. Jim could see that they had to spend the night here on the parking lot. Once Meilin looked a bit better, he went to the office of the bus terminal. It would be better for him to ask for permission to stay here for the night. The bus terminal still had workers there. Jim stated the reason and asked for the permission to camp on the parking lot for the night. The ladies there showed sympathy and told him that it should be no problem for them to stay. Jim soon came back with the good news and a jug of water. Meilin felt a bit relieved that they did not have to move or go to beg the campground to take them back. Jim cooked a simple supper for himself. Meilin could not eat at all; she had some boiled water with sugar and salt in. The vomiting had caused quite some fluid loss. If she did not replenish the fluid, she would be seriously dehydrated and her condition would be further worsened. The night turned out to be much quieter than in the trailer park. At about eleven o'clock, the parking lot was almost fully deserted and traffic around slowed down to almost nothing. On such a clean and spacious parking lot with no other vehicles around, the air was much cooler. The couple had the best night of the few nights they had had in Terrebonne.

Next morning, Meilin felt better. The couple had a simple breakfast and started on their way before the parking lot was filled up again. They knew that there were quite many museums and art galleries in Montreal. They felt a pity that they did not visit any of them. Montreal was quite famous for its performing arts. The Place des Arts of the city housed the most modern concert hall that could seat 3000 audiences, Montreal's Symphony Orchestra and some other theatres. Quebec's world famous Cirque du Soleil was born in Montreal in 1984. Cirque du Soleil is "Circus of the Sun" in French. The Montrealers had turned the circus show into an artistic theatrical performance with wonderful music, dances, songs, gymnastic stunts and fantastic special effects. Cirque du Soleil never used animals in their performances. Jim and Meilin had enjoyed Cirque du Soleil performed by Quebec performers in Abbotsford. Still they regretted that they did not have a look at those grand facilities for performing arts in Montreal. The travelling to and from Montreal from Terrebonne turned out to be too strenuous for them.

Now they were leaving Montreal and soon they would leave Quebec. While Jim was driving, Meilin tried to rest and to recover from yesterday's ordeal. She might have motion sickness again riding in their van, but that was a much less possibility than in a bus. Trying to divert her mind to any physical sense that might trigger motion sickness, she watched the scenes along the highway. After some distance of driving, they were coming to the section where the highway was running side by side with St. Lawrence River. They were driving towards north which was the direction to the Gulf of St. Lawrence. The riverbed was getting wider and wider; the river was getting ready to enter the ocean. The scenes on the other side of the broad riverbed were becoming a dreamy silhouette. The land along the river became more and more flat. The fields along appeared to be cultivated farmland. In some places, the height of the river looked the same height as the land and the highway. From their vehicle, the couple could see the waves of the water tapping the thin line of the shore. Though covered mostly by the rocky Canadian Shield, Quebec has the St. Lawrence Lowlands which are flat and fertile. Most Quebec's agriculture productions are in this area.

A vast open space always has the miraculous power to change a person's feelings. The couple felt calmer and their minds seemed broadened by the wide scenery. To them, traveling across the country was most of all driving on the highway, feeling the vast land with all its beauty and power. The human society with all its hurried frantic activities, furies and noises could never compare with the beautiful peaceful nature. Though nature could churn up fierce storms and disastrous calamities, those natural calamities were never the same as the turmoil and storms caused by some intentional human hostilities and hatred.

Meilin felt her sickness totally gone and her spirits were high again. One of the facts in life is that people are often amused and comforted by medicines, but nature, people's mind or psych is the true factor to heal their ailments in most cases. The best physicians know the ineffectiveness of medicines for most ailments; they recognize the value of the art in improving patients' mental conditions.

The broad surrounding scenery had very much improved the couple's mental state; they started talking about different matters. They talked about the river water being so high and whether the land and the highway could be flooded sometimes. Then they rejected this thought. The river was at the verge of merging into the ocean; no matter how much water coming, the ocean could take it. When the couple talked about that they were soon going to be in New Brunswick, they were excited.

CHAPTER NINE

NEW BRUNSWICK

Near the border between Quebec and New Brunswick, the highway suddenly turned towards the east and the four-lane highway narrowed into two lanes. After the border crossing, the highway, though remained to be a two-lane highway, seemed to be wider with many three-lane sections. The shoulders on both sides of the highway were wide and driving on it was still quite comfortable.

Jim and Meilin had a long personal history with New Brunswick. Jim was born in Saint John, the largest city of this province. Meilin started her life in Canada in this province when she came to the University of New Brunswick to pursue further education. There were a lot of memories of their life in this province, which would remain with them for the rest of their life no matter where they would be in their later years. Though the couple had visited New Brunswick quite a few times after they had moved to the west of the country, each time of revisiting New Brunswick would still refresh those memories and bring excitement and anticipation to their minds at the start.

The scenery along the highway looked familiarly lovely. The trees and bushes on both sides of the road were profuse and vibrant. The land feature changed from flat of the eastern Quebec to gentle rolling hills. The traffic was very light. The couple felt that even the breeze seemed familiar. They knew that New Brunswick's scenery was most beautiful and glorious in autumn when the mountains, hills and valleys turned into the gorgeous colours of golden and deep red. Right now, in the middle of the summer, everything was green. Their vehicle was like a leaf floating on a green ocean, up and down with the large waves of the hills, free and joyous. In such a wonderful natural sphere, who would not forget all the troubles in the noisy cities and be intoxicated by the beautiful nature? The couple were totally immersed in the wonderfully green surroundings; their day-dreaming was only about their trip and the memorable former travels through this highway.

All along the highway, a wide section of land on both sides were mowed clean. At the edges of the thick woods, there were metal mesh fences. The couple found out that the fences on both sides had lasted the whole length of the highway across the province. In every certain distance, there was a gate on the fence. The gate was specially made, so that the wild animals that went astray to the highway could go back into the woods and could not come out again. Obviously, the fences were mainly for the protection of the numerous wild animals that lived in those thick wooded and bushed areas. Because of the abundant broad-leaf trees, different bushes and vegetations, various wild animals were numerous here. Without the fences, quite some of the animals could be the road-kills on the highway. Now with the fences and those gates, they were protected. Of course the fences had protected also the human travellers. Reports about some drivers being injured though their vehicles colliding with moose, deer or some other animals had been common in this province. Jim and Meilin were moved by this thoughtfulness and admired the tremendous efforts. New Brunswick was not among the wealthy provinces of the country, the expense in building such long fences on both sides of the highway must not be small.

New Brunswick is bordered on three sides with the ocean, surrounded by Bay of Fundy, Gulf of Saint Lawrence and Chaleur Bay. Its land belongs to the Appalachian Region and almost entirely covered by forests. Still under the influence of the glaciers, there are plenty of rivers and lakes in the province; the longest river is the 673 kilometers Saint John River that runs almost through the whole New Brunswick. With plenty of trees, bushes, vegetations and water, there are abundant wild animals, birds, migratory birds and fish. Some spots of the province are world famous for salmon fishing and hunting. However, flat fertile land for farming is scarce in this province. The economy of New Brunswick had mainly depended on exporting timber and fish in the old days.

New Brunswick is one of the four Atlantic provinces of Canada; the whole region is called the Maritimes. The other three provinces are Nova Scotia, Prince Edward Island and Newfoundland. The four eastern provinces are not among the rich provinces of the country and in fact have been thought as the have-not provinces. The main cause of the slower economical development of the four provinces has to be the long distance from the densely populated parts of the country, the strong competitions of the central and western Canada and the region's smaller population. The combined population of the four provinces has barely reached one tenths of the total Canadian population. The smaller population has put the four provinces not only in a disadvantageous situation economically, but also politically. They cannot send more political representatives to Ottawa to have their voice heard well, to have sufficient influence in the country's policy making and to bargain for their provinces. There had been suggestions made through the history that the four provinces should combine into one to increase their economical and political powers. But the four provinces had been widely divided and nothing came out from such suggestions.

Though the four provinces cannot compare with the rich provinces in wealth and developments, people in these provinces have enjoyed relatively the same living standards as people in the rich provinces, thanks to the federal government's equalization policy. Sufficient funds and subsidies have run into the four provinces to keep the schools, public facilities and benefits on the Canadian level and to help the provinces to develop.

Of course, the smaller population of the eastern provinces has its cause. Mainly, the investors and entrepreneurs find this area less profitable, because its natural and human resources are not as rich as in Ontario, Quebec or the western parts of the country. In today's world, the economical developments are very much globalized. Large corporations with their powerful capital are highly mobile and seek pure profits. Those powerful corporations with their money have great influences on the economy of a country, let alone that of a province or a city. While Canada's economical developments are largely directed by some large business headquarters in New York, quite some Canadian entrepreneurs have their investments and businesses set up in some other countries. With less investors and entrepreneurs putting their money and efforts in the Maritimes, the area's economical and industrial developments have been slowed down and cannot diversify well. Employment rate goes down in the depressed areas. Immigrants coming to Canada will choose the places where there are jobs; they will normally avoid Maritimes. Some Maritimers will migrate to the central and western places of the country where they can get jobs. Thus, the population growth has been kept low; this has inevitably affected the developments and growth of this region.

However, it is recognized by the country that New Brunswick is the best province in forestry conservation. It has done excellent work in the cultivation of forests and in keeping the forest fires and insects devastations low. The long fences along the highway probably also helps in all those conservation aspects. Besides this, the paper and pulp industry, the food processing and the fishery in this province have been carried out well in recent years. Anywhere people go in the country; they can pick up from grocery store shelves tins of delicious sardines and kippers packed by New Brunswick workers. Though difficult, farming here has been carried out in moderate scales. The hydroelectric industry has been developed to produce enough power to satisfy the needs of the province

Though there are some similarities between the four Atlantic Provinces, New Brunswick has some different characteristics. One difference is that one thirds of the population of New Brunswick is formed by French-speaking Acadians. For thousands of years, two native tribes, the Malicites and the Micmacs had resided in this region, living mainly on hunting. French settlers came to this land in the 17th and 18th centuries. They called this region Acadia and thus the French here were Acadians. The English settlers came in small number to this region before the American Revolution and they were soon strengthened by 14,000 Loyalists who fled American Revolution to settle in Canada. They were called Loyalists as they were loyal to and preferred to live under the reign of the British Monarch. Quite some of those Loyalists had been given land and financial support. Most of the Loyalists who came to New Brunswick had settled in Saint John. During the 19th century, the immigrants coming to this region were mostly from British Isles. After the World War II, a significant number of Europeans came to this province. The inflow of different immigrants had tipped the scale of the population formation from the early French majority to the later English majority. Like the French Canadians in Quebec, the Acadian Canadians had complained about discrimination and fought to preserve their culture and language. Their struggles have resulted in New Brunswick having had a premier of Acadian origin in the mid20th century and becoming the first province to adopt bilingualism.

Another different characteristic of the province is that the top rich has stood out so prominently that no rich people in other provinces can compare. Canada has about nine billionaires. K.C. Irvin in New Brunswick is one of them. Most ordinary Canadians cannot name those Canadian billionaires as they are normally not in the public eyes. The rich Irvin family is an exception. Everybody in New Brunswick knows the Irvin family and the power of the family. Mr. Irvin started with a one truck company, delivering fuels. Now the Irvin family is the most significant and major factor in the economy of the province. They own about three thousand gas stations in the east, paper and saw mills, large forest reserves, radio and TV stations, English newspapers, shipping, trucking and bus-lines. Many New Brunswickers work in the businesses owned by the Irvin family.

For Jim and Meilin at this moment, the economical or any other situation of the province was far from their minds. The beautiful and peaceful scenery had fully occupied their thoughts and feelings. They were driving towards Fredericton, the capital city of the province. Jim had lived in Fredericton for years, serving on the military base not far from the city. Meilin studied in the University of New Brunswick which was located in Fredericton. The couple had met and married in Fredericton and lived there for the first year of their married life. The gentle kindness of the people, the serene surroundings and the slow-paced peaceful life of the small city had lingered on in their memory long after they had left Fredericton.

When the couple were getting near Fredericton, they started thinking about their camping spot. From experience, they knew that the campground at the skirt of Fredericton must be full at this time of the year, especially the days near Canada Day. They also knew well now that no matter which campground they went, they would probably encounter harassment. After a little discussion, they decided that if they saw a Walmart or any other big store by the highway, they would camp on their parking lot, and next day they would arrive at Fredericton early in the morning.

Before the couple came across a camping opportunity by the highway, they saw a gas station, Irvin Gas Station of course. They pulled their van and trailer into the station and went to gas up. This Irvin Gas Station looked brand new, but it was not of the fancy modern style with large fully lit canopy over the gas bar and shining modern store attached. Later, they did see large new Irvin Gas Stations in the latest style. But this gas station had a store building of a simple residential house that had not been fully finished and the gas bar was of simple old style with a small canopy. There seemed only one middle-aged man working in this station. Jim filled up the gas tank. While paying the bill, he chatted with the service man, starting from asking about the distance from here to Fredericton. Coming from this area originally, Jim knew well the way or custom of communicating with the locals. The two men were soon on friendly base. Meilin of course was the listener as usual. From the two men's chat, it looked that the Irvin family were still spanning their businesses, especially the gas-station business.

Soon after leaving the gas station, the couple saw a large Walmart sign near the highway by a small town. They were happy. Jim slowed their van to get into the parking lot. The place was a little lower than the highway and surrounded by trees and bushes. It looked an ideal place to spend the night. They parked their van and trailer on the large parking lot. It was still afternoon, the couple were glad to see that there were a few other RVers who had the same idea and had already set up their rigs on the parking lot. Camping on a parking lot, the couple felt safer if there were a few other RVers camping together with them.

After the couple set up their trailer, they went to the Walmart. They could stretch their legs and pick up some food or other necessities in the store for the trip. They did some shopping and had their supper in the fast food restaurant of the Walmart. All these done, they got some water from the store and had a simple cleaning up. The walk around the outside area of the store in the evening was quite pleasant. The trees and bushes made the surrounding beautiful and peaceful. The air here was not as muggy as that in Quebec and they looked forward to having a good sleep on this parking lot. However, the time to go to bed on a parking lot had to be delayed. First, the summer day was much longer and total darkness would be around eleven o'clock. Secondly, the store would be open until eleven and the traffic around would be quiet down only after that time. Still, at about ten o'clock, the couple went to bed.

Nothing went smoothly on this trip. This night was the same. In the middle of the night, the couple were woken up by some loud noise. The noise came from a tractor trailer that had parked not far from them and the driver was letting the engine run without stop. This kind of things no longer surprised the couple. Even parking somewhere for a lunch break, they would encounter loud noises from some tractor trailers. One thing hard to understand was that in summer, those big trucks did not need idling to function well at starting time; why so many truck drivers would let their trucks running all the time when they were resting or sleeping? With the harassment following them all the way, Meilin thought that this was one of the harassment tricks pulled on them. It seemed that they had never experienced so many trucking noises in their trips before. As usual, Jim would try to exhaust all the "legitimate" reasons for those happenings until he had to give up and think the same way as Meilin. This time too, he tried to reason that this was still the truck driver getting used to the engine noises and unable to sleep without them.

Still, the couple wondered, with the wide public attention to environment pollutions, nobody seemed to have bothered about this kind of truck drivers' behaviours. Surely, the emissions from the constant idling of the large trucks could very well contribute to the air pollution. The idling of the large trucks the couple had encountered along the trip did not last ten or twenty minutes, but hours and even whole nights. This was in summer. Imagine in winter, with more truck drivers idling their rigs, the situation must be worse. For the sake of environment, the couple hoped that this was not a usual behaviour of the truckers, but a coerced act of a few truckers aiming at harassing them.

The couple, unlike the truck drivers, could not sleep in the continued booming noises. They got up, stabilized everything inside their trailer and moved. They had parked on a large parking lot and could move to another spot to minimize the noise impact from the powerful tractor trailer. After the efforts of moving, they managed to have a few more hours of sleep. Next morning, before the parking lot became busy again, they finished their breakfast and started driving to the highway.

In less than an hour, they reached Fredericton. They had a whole day to check things around. Once in the city, they dragged their trailer through the peaceful familiar downtown streets, feeling uncomfortable and out of place. The buildings, the stores and the church-like city hall along the streets, all looked the same. Everything was the same, clean, orderly and well taken care of. The trees along the streets had grown bigger; the green lawns around the red-brick government buildings still looked freshly green and well manicured. The couple pulled their trailer through the slow downtown traffic and headed for the city skirt on the other end. They decided to pay a visit to the trailer park where they had spent the first few months of their married life there.

Years ago when the couple visited Fredericton, they had visited the trailer park and knew there were great changes there. But for that visit, they had left hastily after going through one street. This time, they were going to have a careful look even if they had to drag their trailer around. They soon arrived at the trailer park. With a whole day at hand, they drove slowly through the streets of the large trailer park. When they had lived here, the park was much smaller. Now it seemed to have spanned so much with so many more streets and trailers added on. Though the streets here were mostly graveled, they were well leveled and rather smooth. There were no big puddle holes on the streets any more. The mobile homes all looked in good conditions. They had the latest house-style peaked roofs and sufficient spaces between them. The whole trailer park looked a comfortable residential area now.

"I cannot recognize my old place anymore! It is much better now," said Jim with amazement.

"Oh, yes. There are no holes on the ground and all the mobile homes look so good," Meilin added and then she suggested, "Let's see if our old neighbours still live here."

The mobile homes on the street where the couple had lived before had all changed. They looked like new and well taken care of. The couple were afraid to knock on any of the doors. Perhaps, different people were living in them now. They kept on driving to other streets. Then they saw a man outside a mobile home working on something. Jim stopped the van. The couple decided to ask the man for some information, though they did not have much confidence to get any result. The man was in his fifties and looked surprisingly like a white-collar worker. At the time when Jim and Meilin lived here, most people living in the trailer park were people on the lower level of the society and did not look so cultured. When Jim mentioned a few old neighbours' names, the man responded with a smile and provided information readily.

"Mrs. McDaniel had moved out of the park, but her son is still living here. I believe he is in the next street at 4622. Calvin Bowater is sick; he does not see anybody."

It looked that though the place were expanded and injected with new blood, the neighbours were still closely knit. The man living in a different street would know the couple's old neighbours living in another street. This kind of closeness of the neighbours was quite rare in a large city. Jim and Meilin thanked the man and went on driving to the next street. They found 4622 and parked their van in front. This mobile home was double-wide, which looked like a house. Jim and Meilin went to the door and rang the door bell. After a while, they heard somebody coming to open the door.

When the door opened, Jim was surprised and asked, "Nick?!"

The man who opened the door was in his late thirties or early forties, sitting in a wheelchair. He answered with equal bewilderment, "Yes?!"

Jim followed immediately, "I'm Jim Duihne. This is my wife Meilin."

After a short moment of puzzling, Nick's face broke into a realizing smile, "Oh, ya! With your beard, I can hardly recognize you. Where are you living now?"

"We are in British Columbia, taking a cross-country trip to have a look," Jim replied with a big smile. He was stunned that Nick, Mrs. McDaniel's son, a boy he had seen growing up, was this middle-aged man in a wheelchair.

"Well, come in then," said Nick and turned his battery-operated wheelchair around to lead the way.

The mobile home looked a one unit from outside, but inside it was still a single mobile home with a whole new side added on. The new side had mainly a long ramp gently ascending to the end of the trailer and then turning around onto a long level runway towards the front. The runway flanked the whole side of the single mobile home and went into a fair sized office in front. The single mobile home was almost all open on one side with only a piece of bedroom wall remaining. Everything, from the ramp, the runway to all kinds of beams was built by light-coloured wood. The whole place had adopted the modern interior design, open, spacious, comfortable and accommodating for a man in wheelchair.

Jim cried out with admiration while the couple followed Nick's wheelchair, "This is great wood work! Somebody must have put in a lot of efforts to make this for you."

"I did this myself," said Nick with quite some pride.

"Oh, really?! You have done an excellent job!" complimented Jim. Meilin too put in her praise. The couple were totally amazed. It was incredible that a man in a wheelchair could have done all these. But obviously, Nick was living here alone.

Nick had led the couple to his office where there were a large desk, the computer, some office equipments, three chairs and some decorative ornaments. The place was bright as it had the front large window facing the street.

After sitting down, Jim asked, "How come you are in a wheelchair, what have happened?"

"I had been stabbed on my back," Nick answered, but did not say anymore.

Jim did not pursue further and changed the question. "What are you doing now?"

"I'm doing some office work on the computer at home for some government agency," said Nick.

After this, Jim asked about his family. Mrs. McDaniel was a widow with three daughters and one son. When Jim moved his mobile home to this trailer park, Mrs. McDaniel took him under her wings and treated him as her son. Maggie, Mrs. McDaniel's eldest daughter was a single mother with two small children. After Maggie's mobile home being damaged, Mrs. McDaniel talked with Jim into taking the mother and her two kids in to become his boarders. The relationship between Jim and Mrs. McDaniel's family was rather close. When Jim and Meilin were getting married, Mrs. McDaniel lent her own wedding gown to Meilin. Now so many years later, the McDaniel family seemed to have gone quite some changes. Nick told the couple that his mother had moved away from the trailer park and was living in an apartment building now. He picked up the phone and called his mother.

"My mother would like to see you guys," said he, after putting down the phone.

The couple were glad to hear this and said that they would go to see her right now. Nick gave them the address and Jim and Meilin left Nick after more compliments about his work on his mobile home.

After leaving the trailer park, the couple pulled their small trailer through some of the city streets again. This time, they went through a plush area, driving along a beautiful street where aligned trees were large and mature, shrubs were vibrantly beautiful and different flowers in flowerbeds were blooming brilliantly. There were a lot of big modern houses in this street. They were of luxury styles and partially hidden by voluptuous shades of greens and various other colours of nature. Jim and Meilin knew Fredericton well. The most beautiful and luxurious area was even better than this. It was a street along the river. Big mansions with large beautiful front and back gardens were lined along that street facing the river. When Meilin was a student here, she had a picture taken with one of those mansions in order to keep the scene in her memory or dream. Then there were some mansions in the suburbs a little way from the city. Those mansions each had a large piece of land.

Inequality in human life is best shown by people's living conditions, especially their housing conditions. Fredericton is not different from any other cities in the country. Every city has its residential upper areas and lower areas. This residential classification is actually universal. Every country is the same. The only difference is that rich countries have more people living in middle and upper housing conditions and less in lower ones. Poor countries have more people living in lower housing conditions and even slums. The middle countries that are coming up towards a higher level have more people living in medium level housing conditions. Inequality has always been with human life; it had been so in the past, is so in the present and will be so in the future. However, tremendous efforts have been spent on improving the living conditions of all human beings through the history everywhere in the world. Today, the developed countries have more resources to improve the living conditions of the people on the lower social level, and therefore less excuses for not doing so. Jim and Meilin were glad to see the improvement of the trailer park in Fredericton. It did not matter whether the improvement was brought about by the government or some private company, it showed that the city of Fredericton was doing well and some nice things had been done for the less fortunate.

It did not take long for Jim and Meilin to find the apartment building where Mrs. McDaniel lived now. They were surprised to see this area. Having lived in Fredericton for years, they had never been in this area. There were quite some large apartment buildings here; they were four or five stories high and all built by red bricks. The streets through this area were paved and there were large paved parking lots around. The apartment buildings were well spaced out by nice green lawns, shrubs and trees around them. The whole place looked picturesquely orderly, comfortable and peaceful.

After several winding turns, Jim and Meilin got to the building where Mrs. McDaniel was in. Before they pulled their trailer into the parking lot in front of the building, they saw Mrs. McDaniel and Jenny, the second daughter, standing outside the building and waving to them. Having parked their vehicles and through the first warm greetings, the four walked into Mrs. McDaniel's apartment which was on the first floor. The apartment had one bedroom, a fair-sized sitting room, a bathroom and a kitchen. Mrs. McDaniel lived alone. Jenny just came from her place to meet Jim and Meilin after she got her mother's call. Jenny must be in her forties now. She had put on a bright red shirt, still looking young. Mrs. McDaniel was still a heavy smoker. The apartment was full of the stale smell of cigarette smoke. Her old mobile home used to have the same smell. The old lady had worked a janitorial job for many years and was now retired. It had not been an easy life for her, being a widow with four children.

The four sat down. Mrs. McDaniel chatted with her kind motherly tone. "I have often thought about you, wondering how you are doing. It must be quite some years now...."

The chat was carried out warmly. The four were like a family coming together after a long time separation. Jim talked things about their life after he and Meilin left Fredericton. Mrs. McDaniel and Jenny told the happenings of their family. Maggie had married a nice man and they were living in Nova Scotia. Her son was now a store manager in a western province. Jenny got divorced from Calvin who was now suffering from cancer. Jim and Meilin were glad that Maggie and her two children were doing well, but they wondered whether Jenny's divorce happened before or after Calvin got cancer. They did not ask. Jenny's son who was a tiny baby at the time when Jim and Meilin were leaving Fredericton was working now.

During the chat, there was the showing of pictures. Maggie and her whole family looked good. It was amazing how big her two small children had grown. Jenny only showed her boy's picture. It looked that her ex-husband and his son from his former marriage were totally out of her life. Jim and Meilin could not help wondering what had happened between them. Calvin was a nice guy. He acted as the photographer for Jim and Meilin's wedding. It looked that with the cancer, he was totally shutting himself off from other people. Was he fed-up with different pains, disillusioned or embittered?

The talk then changed to Jim and Meilin's trip. Of course, the couple praised the beautiful places they had seen and complained about the high cost of gas. Then Jenny asked, "Where were you planning to camp tonight?"

"The campground must be full now. We have to find some place to spend the night," said Jim.

"You can just park here on the parking lot, or you can park on your church parking lot," Jenny suggested; she did not forget that Jim and Meilin belonged to a church here.

"Good idea! We will try the church," said Jim gladly.

The chat did not last very long. Jim and Meilin said goodbye to Mrs. McDaniel and Jenny, and the four hugged with warm words, telling each other to take care. The mother and daughter came out to see the couple off with warm friendly waves. Jim and Meilin were glad that they had paid this visit to get to know what had happened to Mrs. McDaniel's family. When they left Mrs. McDaniel's place, they felt a bit guilty, thinking that they should have stayed a little longer. It seemed that the smell of the old lady's place had driven them out rather quickly. Long after they had left Mrs. McDaniel's apartment, the stale cigarette smell stayed on their clothes for a long time.

With plenty of public education, the number of Canadians who smoke has been decreasing. A big achievement coming out of the movement of a well-informed public about the danger of smoking is that Canada has had almost all the public facilities smoke-free. Still, the Canadian population is not totally smoke free yet. Human addictions to tobaccos, alcohols and all kinds of narcotic drugs are very hard battles to fight. Everywhere in Canada, smokers can still be seen and among them are quite some young people.

Jim and Meilin drove towards the church after they left Mrs. McDaniel's place. They talked on their way about the pleasant visit to Mrs. McDaniel. In a small familiar city, it was quite easy to reach any place they intended to go. They arrived at their old church in no time. Their church was a Mormon Church. The couple had never thought much of the difference of a Mormon Church from other churches. To Meilin especially, a Mormon Church's belief system had never occupied a large portion of her understanding of Christianity. This church had approached her when she was a student here. She could not forget the kindness of the church people who had opened their doors and hearts to her. Jim was the same mind. When some other churches had looked down upon him as a poor man, this church had taken him in and embraced him. The couple had never cared about which sect this church belonged to; they cared even less about some other people's prejudice against this church. To them, all the problems of a church were the problems of the church members, but all the churches were the same; they all had the same functions and taught basically the same doctrines of the Bible.

Their old church looked the same from outside, a sturdy brownish modern building. But the surrounding area seemed changed a bit. The parking lot was still paved and big, but one side of the neighbouring area looked different. There was a linked metal fence erected on this side. Over the fence, there was a large green lawn and a public swimming pool. They could not recall that the large lawn and the swimming pool were here before. The couple parked their vehicles on the side of the parking lot which was lined up by large trees and far away from the church building. In this way, their vehicles would be shaded by the trees and they would not cause any problem for the church members coming to park their vehicles.

After parking their vehicles, the couple walked up to the church. There were no other vehicles on the parking lot but one car. Today was not a weekend day. They were not sure whether there was anybody in the church. Still, they ran the door bell. Nobody answered. Then they pushed on the door; the door was locked. When they turned away to leave, the door opened. They were glad to see that there was somebody in the church after all. The man who opened the door was a large heavy set man in his forties. Jim and Meilin could not remember whether they had seen him before. After the greeting and introduction from Jim, the man smiled and said, "It's nice you come to pay us a visit. It must be a long drive from British Columbia. I'm Brother Anderson. Welcome."

"Thank you. Yes. We have been on the road for about a month now," said Jim.

The couple then told Brother Anderson that they had got married in this church and who was the bishop at that time. Brother Anderson told them that there were some changes in the church after they had left and a different bishop had been elected. In a Mormon Church, there are no professional priests; all the positions in the church are held by the elected church members. Brother Anderson then let the couple in to have a look at their former church. The church was not big and built by brownish bricks. Now the inside of the church seemed looking much smaller than the couple had remembered. This impression must be caused by the couple's visits to some huge cathedrals and basilicas in the country since they had left Fredericton. Compared with those big cathedrals, this church was quite small and simple. The congregation was in a big central hall which was surrounded by a corridor lined up by small rooms. The big hall could be separated by a screen into two parts, the front part was the congregation hall with the altar and the pews; the back part was used as a community hall. When there was a big conference, the screen would be pulled aside and the whole hall would be used. For Sunday services, only the front part was used. Jim and Meilin's wedding ceremony was held in a side meeting room and the wedding reception was carried out in the community hall.

So many years later, it was amazing how the place looked different from the couple's memory. In reality, the place had not changed; it had always been a small simple church. The couple, on the other hand, had changed. The small church still looked quite new; everything, from the floor covering to the wooden pews and light fixtures on the walls, looked clean and shiny. Brother Anderson talked to the couple while they checked the place, telling them different things; though the bishop was a different one, the former one was still acting as a council. One thing that had shocked Jim and Meilin was that Brother Needham had died of a tragic death.

"His wife left him; he committed suicide," said Brother Anderson sadly.

Though Jim and Meilin could not remember Brother Anderson, they could recall Brother Needham well. Brother Needham was in his late thirties when the couple were here. He looked handsome and intelligent. He was doing the janitorial and some odd works for the church and being paid. Brother Needham's wife was a pretty young woman. Jim and Meilin had noticed a few snobbish church members' attitudes towards Brother Needham. They also saw that Brother Needham had never shown that he felt lower than anybody in the church, but his young wife, though not angry with the snobbish people, looked uncomfortable with her husband and his position in the church. Jim and Meilin did not expect that she would eventually leave Brother Needham, because the woman was a good person, though a bit oversensitive. Besides, the marriages formed by

Mormon Church members were supposed to be for life. It looked that nowadays even in a Mormon Church there would be broken marriages and divorces. The couple thought that the broken marriage might be the main reason causing Brother Needham's suicide, knowing how much he had loved his wife.

Traditionally, marriage has been the sacred temple sheltering the sacred institution -family. In modern times, this sacred temple has been tittering and crumbling. The disintegration of marriages seems to have been more serious in the developed countries. More wealth and more freedom seem to have contributed to the breaking-downs of some moral codes, social order, convictions of certain beliefs built through thousands years of efforts. At present, the divorce rate in Canada has almost reached fifty per cent. The problems or breaking-downs of marriages have very much affected the stability of families. Unstable families have of course affected the stability of society. Many social problems have stemmed out from marriage breaking-downs, such as single mother with small children living in poverty, juvenile delinquencies, young students quitting schools, child poverty, to name a few. What have caused the failing of marriages and the disintegration of families are hard to be pinned down to one or two things. Many discussions and thinking have been concentrated on this issue and no single one can be accurate and problem solving. Many things can have worked to develop this situation, the change of social structure, the weakening of religious beliefs, new world outlooks, the shifting of customs and conventions and so on. Anyway, human life is no longer simple. The complexity of modern life has created more neurotic problems for human beings. Is human society evolving to a higher level or becoming more complicated with less order? Nobody can be sure.

While checking out their old church and being told some news about it by Brother Anderson, Jim asked for permission to camp on the church parking lot. Whatever had happened in their old church, the couple's priority was still solving personal problems at the present.

"No problem. Feel comfortable to stay and look around the city," said Brother Anderson warmly.

The couple came back to their van and trailer after the visit to their old church. They disconnected their van from the trailer and stabilized the trailer. They could take the van to drive around the city and leave the trailer on the church parking lot. While working on the van and trailer, all the couple thought and talked about was Brother Needham. When Jim and Meilin were in this church, Brother Needham had treated them sincerely and warmly. He had helped Jim to prepare their wedding reception from the start to the finish. The wedding gift he and his wife gave to Jim and Meilin was a soft all-cotton quilt which the couple were still using. On Jim's first birthday after the wedding, the couple had invited Brother Needham to be their guest. All the memories about Brother Needham were still fresh in their minds; they were indeed shocked by his tragic death.

While the couple were working on their trailer, Brother Anderson came out to talk to them again. He asked about their life in British Columbia. Luckily, he did not ask about the Mormon Church they were attending now and they did not have to answer such a question. In Edmonton, Jim and Meilin had encountered some racial discrimination in a Mormon Church; since then they had drifted away and wandered from church to church. In Abbotsford, with the happening of harassment, they no longer went to any church. For quite a few years now, the couple had stopped going to any church for Sunday Services. However, the couple's stop going to a church might not totally come from experiencing some racial discrimination or harassment; it might be partially from their changed or broadened views about religion as a whole.

Before Brother Anderson left Jim and Meilin to their work, he said, "If you want, you can come in the church to take a shower. I'll be here until seven o'clock. I cannot hear the ringing of the doorbell, but if you shake the door, I'll get the message and come to open the door for you."

Jim and Meilin thanked Brother Anderson for his kind thoughtful invitation. No hospitality could be any better than this offer. The couple very much needed a shower in this hot summer day. However, they were going to delay the shower until they had looked around the city. It was still morning. After Brother Anderson went back into the church, the couple drove away from the church ground and headed for the city streets. They decided to pay Mr. Sampson a visit.

Mr. Sampson was a friend of Professor Russell. When Meilin was a student in the university here, Professor Russell befriended her. The kind professor was a single mother whose four children had all left home, working or studying in other places. Professor Russell lived alone in a house in the old area of the city. She had invited Meilin to live with her. Mr. Sampson lived in a house next to Professor Russell's and he too befriended Meilin. The relationship between Meilin and Professor Russell was rather close for a period of time. Mr. Sampson was also a close neighbour and friend.

In no time, Jim and Meilin had arrived at Mr. Sampson's place. In Fredericton, there were some streets belonging to the old area. Here, most houses were built by wood and in Victoria style. The size of the houses was not as big as the modern ones, but they were comfortably sized and most had two stories. Some of old houses had front verandas, but most had no garages. The residents here were mixed; they could be professors, but they could also be workers or shop assistants. Some of those houses had been handed down for generations in the same families. The streets in this area were not wide, but there were sidewalks on both sides. The elm trees along the streets were mostly large and mature. Though a bit more crowded than those new streets with modern luxury houses, those old streets looked greener and were quite peaceful.

After parking their van on Mr. Sampson's driveway, the couple saw that the street seemed the same, but Mr. Sampson's house looked much better. It had a new coat of paint that was deep grass-green. The window frames were bright white. The house looked like new now. Mr. Sampson was a self-employed architect. Judging by the appearance of the house, Mr. Sampson's business must be going well. Mr. Sampson opened the door upon the couple's doorbell ringing. He was surprised, but glad to see Jim and Meilin. Mr. Sampson must be in his seventies now, yet he looked healthy and energetic. It looked that his house was still a favored place by his son's friends, the would-be musicians and the young love-birds who liked to perch here for some moments. When Jim and Meilin were invited to come into the house, a pair of young lovers was just leaving. The boy said goodbye to Mr. Sampson politely and the girl only smiled. Meilin was puzzled. Mr. Sampson's younger son must be in his forties now. Would he have friends so young? The young boy and girl had to be his grandson's friends.

The inside of Mr. Sampson's house did not have much change, still a bachelor's quarter, untidy with some convenience. Since the time when Meilin got to know Mr. Sampson, he had been a divorced man. It looked that he was still unhitched. The three sat down in the small sitting room. From Mr. Sampson's talk, Jim and Meilin got to know that he still had weekly gatherings with some of his old friends and was still into politics. Meilin knew that like Professor Russell, Mr. Sampson was a member of the New Democratic Party.

"I have been asked to be the local treasurer of the party. I was told that two treasurers before me had died not long after they had taken this position," said Mr. Sampson and followed up with his loud laughter.

It looked that Mr. Sampson was quite satisfied with his life and certainly not afraid that he might follow the footsteps of his predecessors in the political party very soon. The talk between the three was warm and casual. Of course, they had talked about Professor Russell who had moved to a Vancouver Island after retirement. Jim and Meilin had tried once to see her on that Island. They had found the place, but unfortunately, the professor was not home. Knowing Professor Russell, Meilin could imagine that she would still be busy with some kind of academic activities even in her retirement years.

Mr. Sampson had talked about the changes in Fredericton, which Jim and Meilin had not noticed yet. Knowing what Meilin would be interested, he informed that there was a new Chinese store in the city and a new superstore. Talking about stores, the prices of food would inevitably be included in the topic. Mr. Sampson did not feel that the prices for the basic food had increased much in Fredericton.

With the casual talk, there was also the showing of pictures. Mr. Sampson showed a photo of himself with his grandson. In this photo, his grandson was a baby. At the time when Meilin was living with Professor Russell, Mr. Sampson's elder son had married and produced a grandson for him. It was not clear whether the grandson in the photo was from his elder son or his younger son. While admiring the picture, Meilin joked, "You look as cute as your grandson!"

Mr. Sampson was quite happy to hear the compliment. After so many years apart from the old friend, Meilin felt that the closeness seemed still there. Then Jim and Meilin left Mr. Sampson's place after goodbye hugs. It was nice to see an old friend living a peaceful and satisfactory life in his later years and to chat with him, but the couple intended to get more things done and more places seen for this day. After coming out of Mr. Sampson's home, the couple decided to check out the new Chinese store and the new superstore mentioned by Mr. Sampson. On their way, Jim suddenly wanted to give his brother a call. Dexter, Jim's younger brother lived in St. John. The couple's next destination would be that city. Meilin agreed, feeling that it was better to know that Dexter was still living in the same place, so that they could go to visit him when they arrived at St. John.

The couple looked for a public phone booth while driving through the streets. After passing several streets, they did not see a single phone booth. They remembered that there were quite some public phone booths in the city before and wondered where those phone booths had gone.

Then they pulled their van into a gas station. They needed more gas and plus they could ask for some information about the phone booth.

After pulling up their van to the gas bar, Jim went to gas up the vehicle. Meilin also got out of the van to stretch her legs. She walked around and saw some teenage boys and girls sitting on the cement steps outside the store. The youngsters were all dressed in black; the boys had ear rings and the girls had nose rings. The young black figures had pale thin faces and were smoking cigarettes or some sort of cigarette-like things. Meilin was a bit shocked. She did not expect to see this type of teenagers smoking in the public place in Fredericton. When Jim and she were living here, this kind of scene had never appeared in the city. When Jim came out of the store, Meilin turned his attention to the youngsters. He too was quite surprised.

"Figure this type would be in Fredericton! They might be from other places," Jim tried to explain this away.

It was the season for travelling. Meilin could agree with his assumption. Then Jim told Meilin that the people in the gas station could not provide any information about the phone booth. When the couple were talking, a man in his forties was passing by and heard them. He was a local and provided the information the couple wanted.

"You are wondering about the phone booths? They had all been stolen!" said the man with indignation.

"Really, who would do such a thing?!" said Jim with astonishment.

"The hoodlums, of course! Probably for the metals," said the man. Then he suggested, "If you want to use the phone, you can try that big restaurant on the other side of the street. They might let you use theirs."

Jim thanked the man. The couple were thoroughly stunned now. The rebellious youngsters and the stolen phone booths could easily happen in a large city, but the couple could have never dreamt that they would happen here in Fredericton. It looked that their first impression about the city was wrong; the city had changed or was changing; it was no longer as peaceful as they had remembered. After some sighing, the couple pulled their van across the street and parked it at the big restaurant. Jim went in to borrow their phone. It was around noon. The restaurant would not be open for business until five o'clock in the afternoon. But Jim got in and told the clerk the reason of asking to use their phone.

"I'll pay fifteen dollars to make two long distance calls to St. John and Nova Scotia," said he.

Jim was allowed to use the phone. When he came out of the restaurant after a long while, he did not look well. "Both my brothers are in trouble. They are dying!" he said to Meilin with quite some emotions.

"What's wrong?" asked Meilin. She was alarmed, but thought that Jim might be exaggerating the situations.

"Doctors suspect Dexter has bone cancer. Mark is in hospital now for a big heart surgery," said Jim. His face was overcast with dark clouds.

"Don't worry! We'll soon be able to see them. There's no use to work yourself up into a frenzy. Everybody has to go some day. If it is their time, you can do nothing about it," said Meilin, trying to calm him down.

Jim was not close to his siblings or any of his relatives, but he was a sensitive man with a soft heart, and sometimes he could be overwhelmed by his own emotions. To divert his worried thoughts and sad feelings, Meilin suggested that they keep their former plan to check out the stores. The couple drove their van to the downtown area. They reached the superstore first. It was indeed a new store. In Fredericton, this new grocery store could be considered a large store, but compared to the superstores in the cities of central or western Canada, the store was not that big. However, it had a fair-sized parking lot and some shopping carts waiting on the lot. Right now, the parking lot was empty of vehicles, so the store was not open. The couple were puzzled. It was midday. How come the store was closed? The couple parked their van by the street and asked a passerby for information. They were told that today was Canada Day, so the store was closed.

Jim and Meilin almost jumped on this information. The traveling had totally thrown them off the track of time. Almost every one of their plans and thoughts was about where to go and what to see next. They had never even checked the date to know that today was the first day of July, Canada Day. The couple immediately drove their van towards the area where they knew the Canada Day Celebration would be held in Fredericton. It was good that they could attend the celebration to share some happiness of the city people. They did need some cheerfulness to change their gloomy minds caused by what they had just seen in the city and the bad news from the family.

The celebration for Canada Day would be held in the central downtown area by the St. John River. When the couple reached the place, they found the parking lots around were filled up by vehicles. It took them some time to find a spot to park their van. Upon their reaching the crowds, they were shocked. It seemed that this visit to Fredericton was an experience full of shocks. The couple had known the city well; the changes of the city they had gradually seen had very much surprised them. This time, the shock was coming from seeing the large number of people gathering here for the Canada Day Celebration. Jim had lived in Fredericton for many years and Meilin had also lived here for about four years. The couple had never seen so many people attending the Canada Day Celebration when they had lived here. The number of the party attendees must have over tripled from what they knew! This phenomenon meant one thing for sure: the population of the city had increased considerably.

Along the river bank, some restaurant stalls had been set up. This was a new thing which the Canada Day Celebration here did not have before. People were crowded around those stalls to get some food. The most popular stall was the one selling ice creams. A long line of people were waiting there to get some ice cream in cones. Jim and Meilin got some hamburgers first. Having satisfied their hunger, they lined up with the people to get those ice creams. The price of the ice creams was not high and the portions were generous. Hamburger and ice cream were all Jim's favorite food. He was happy for the lunch arrangement. Eating with the crowds and viewing the surrounding area of the city were indeed a treat.

The weather was very cooperative. The sun was shining brightly and everything looked cheerful and festival. Fredericton was straddling over the St. John River. The river bed in this area was wide; the river was flowing quietly with sun sparkles on the water. The southern part of the city seemed the same as before. But on this side, the northern part, changes were obvious. Fredericton's important facilities and buildings were concentrated on the northern part. Now further on from the temporary food stalls, there was a large paved area by the river. A large white lighthouse with red top had been erected on one end of the open ground. The actual function of the lighthouse might be for tourism, as a gift shop was inside the lighthouse. The whole area looked more open and attractive to the tourists who would like to have a good view of the river. All these were not here when Jim and Meilin were living in Fredericton.

Fredericton is one of the oldest cities in North America. For thousands of years, the Maliseet Natives had resided in this area. During the 17th century, some French fur traders came here to set up a settlement. They named the place, St. Anne. In 1760, the settlement was burnt down by the British in their struggles with the French for dominance on this continent. When the Loyalists fled American Revolution, some of them came to this area. They revived the settlement and named it Frederick's

Town after the son of King George III. When New Brunswick became a province in 1784, the town was chosen to be the capital city and the name changed to Fredericton. Today, Fredericton is well known for its beauty, heritage and culture. It is a city that intends to stick to traditional way of life. Quite some residents are interested in craftsmanship. The New Brunswick College of Craft and Design still produces pewter smith, quilters, potters and weavers. The city is known as the pewter capital of Canada. Then the culture here is manifested by people's love of literature, especially poetry. The Poets' Society is going on with readings by anyone who wants to share his or her work or tryout.

However, after twenty years absence from the city, Jim and Meilin found on this visit that Fredericton had changed. They could never have dreamt that they would be enjoying a meal with so many people on the river bank of the city, if they had not come to experience it in person. After lunch, the couple went to watch the concert. For Canada Day, every Canadian city will have a celebration party. There will be parades and concerts. Larger cities will have different food stalls set up for the party-goers and fireworks will be put on at night. Jim and Meilin had attended Canada Day Celebrations in Fredericton before. Meilin had once given a performance of Tie Chi with music for the Canada Day Concert here. The couple remembered that for the concert here before, there would be a small wooden platform erected in the centre of the green lawn and the crowds were a moderate number of people that filled hardly half of the green square. Today, the situation had totally changed. The stage was the large cement terrace in front of the museum, a stone building on one side of the green square, and the whole square was filled up by people.

Jim and Meilin had noticed that there were quite some coloured people in the crowds; they were mostly East Indians. At the time when Jim and Meilin lived here, the coloured people in Fredericton were hardly visible and they were mainly from a small Chinese community. Now when Jim and Meilin arrived at the concert, the performance had already started on the stage. On one side of this green square, there was a bronze statue of Lord Beaverbrook with the background of trees and river. A New Brunswicker, Lord Beaverbrook, when alive, was rich, powerful and mostly known in the country to be the merger king. He had merged many businesses into a few large corporations. The other prominent New Brunswicker that could match Lord Beaverbrook was Bonar Law. Born in New Brunswick, Bonar Law became the only Canadian or the only foreign-born Prime Minister of Britain in 1922. Right now in this Canada Day Celebration, nobody paid attention to the statue of Lord Beaverbrook or thought of Bonar Law, all the eyes were focused on the terrace stage. The performers were a group of Malaysian Canadians in colourful Malaysian costumes. They were performing a Malaysian traditional dance. The dancers brought a small hut and some poles made from bamboo to the front of the stage. They jumped over the bamboo poles and some wooden benches. The performance was crude, but cheerful and suitable for such an occasion. The other performances were mainly given by some solo singers accompanied by some musicians.

Jim and Meilin went to one side in front of the crowds. From this spot, they could see both the performance and the audience. They wanted to see if they could spot some familiar faces from the crowds. Though Meilin only lived in Fredericton for a few years, she had made quite a few friends here. After checking the audience carefully, the couple were disappointed. They could not spot a single familiar face. Meilin had known almost everyone in the Chinese community here before; she did not see a single face from that community. Two decades had passed; the faces might have changed or the former Chinese residents had left this city.

The crowds, the food and the concert had sufficiently cheered up Jim and Meilin. From the present formation of the city's population, the couple could understand a little better of some present happenings in the city. Obviously, the city was growing and the increase of the population would definitely be good for the development of the area. However, with the growth, the city would inevitably go through some growing pains. Some white people might jump out to claim that the different immigrants, especially the coloured ones had brought some problems to the city. But the reality might very much be different. Some established residents might not like the change of population formation; some shady characters might even be acting up to show their prejudices and resentments. Children were most susceptible to influences from the adults and their close environments. They were most easily misdirected or misled by some adults' behaviours or speeches to act up to show their tainted thoughts and feelings. The couple seemed to have found some explanation to the appearance of the rebellious youngsters and the stolen phone booths here.

After enjoying the concert for a while, Jim and Meilin walked towards the city streets. The two main downtown streets in Fredericton are the Queen and King Streets. All the important buildings are here. They are the library, the court house, the police department, the legislative building, the theater called the Play House, the City Hall, the Beaverbrook Art Gallery, the Anglican Cathedral of a replica of St. Mary's Church in

Snettisham, Norfolk England. The art gallery has some valuable art works of British and Canadian artists given by Lord Beaverbrook to the people here. The cathedral of Gothic architecture with a very tall steeple was consecrated in 1853. Quite some European-style buildings, ancient and modern, give the city a strong European accent. A long promenade of green lawns and mature trees is along the river. The statue of the famous Scottish Poet Robert Burns is standing on the lawn by the river. The whole place makes people think of a small city in England.

The couple knew all important places in Fredericton. But they had to ask somebody where the new Chinese store was. It turned out that it was only one or two blocks away from the central square. When they reached the store, they saw the store open. In the downtown area, the stores were in nice brick buildings. The Chinese store, though not big, looked good. The clerk of the store was a young Asian man. The couple were surprised to see that there were not many goods in the store. This was quite unusual for a Chinese store. A Chinese store was normally stocked full. Fredericton had a tiny Chinese store when Jim and Meilin lived here. In that old Chinese store, many things, from groceries, snacks, frozen food to some daily used materials, filled up every nook and cranny. This Chinese store looked brand new with shining glass display cabinets, but there were only a few goods. Perhaps the goods had not been fully shipped here yet.

After visiting the Chinese store, the couple went to get their vehicle. They were going to pay a visit to the University of New Brunswick. During the years when Meilin had been in Fredericton, her life was mainly on or around the campus. Those intense and interesting university days were still flashing in her memory now and then. On every one of the couple's visits to Fredericton, the university would be a must-see place in the list. The couple reached the university in no time.

University of New Brunswick is one of the oldest institutions of higher learning in Canada. It was first the provincial academy of arts and sciences in 1785 and received its charter as the College of New Brunswick in 1800. In 1828, it became King's College. In 1859, it ended its affiliation with the Anglican Church and became the University of New Brunswick. The university is well known for its well preserved old buildings and library of over 600,000 volumes. The beautiful campus is standing on a hill overlooking the St. John River and Fredericton.

The couple drove around the campus which looked empty. In the summer holiday, most students and staff had left the campus. On the Canada Day, the few stayed on campus must have gone downtown to attend the festival. When the couple came to the spot near the top of the hill, an area was blocked off for construction or maintenance. Everywhere else they went, the place looked the same. After driving up a sharp slope, the couple parked their van on a small central parking lot. The spot was graveled when Meilin was studying here. Two decades later, the spot remained graveled.

The couple got off their van and looked around. The red brick buildings stood quietly on the side of the green hill. The giant trees were still spreading large leafy branches to shade different spots. The greyish white Old Arts Building retained its dignified appearance on a lower ground. The historical buildings, Sir Howard Douglas Hall and Brydone Jack Observatory, still looked well. Sir Howard Douglas Hall was built in 1829, the oldest university building still in use in the country. The observatory was built in 1851.The large Harriet Irving Library stood on the higher ground, overlooking the campus. Meilin had her thesis written on the Stage Directions of Shakespeare's Romeo and Juliet with the help of some early editions of Shakespeare's plays right in this library. She was quite lucky that she did not have to go to England to do research; she could never afford the trip. Besides the early editions of Shakespeare's plays, the university library has preserved quite some rare manuscripts and books including the first editions of Charles Dickens, George Elliot and H.G. Wells. Right now, Meilin looked at the windows on the fourth floor of the library, thinking of those hard working days she had spent in one of those tiny thesis-writing rooms. She felt sorry that the hard work of herself and some professors did not come to any fruition in the targeted field in her later life. Still, she was grateful for being admitted and supported to study here and molded by the efforts of some outstanding professors. To a certain extent, the university and some professors were an important part in making her the person she was today.

While the couple stood on the parking lot, looking around, a security guard was standing outside the door of the Physics Department, watching them. The whole campus seemed having only the three people at this moment. After a while of viewing the empty campus under the stare of the security guard, the couple felt a bit eerie. They got in their van and drove away. It was late afternoon now. The couple were quite satisfied with the day's activities and decided to go back to their trailer on the church parking lot. In a small familiar city, they had accomplished a lot in one day. Tomorrow, they were going to go on to their next destination. Though there were still some other new things in Fredericton for them to see, the day's visit seemed enough for them. The only one important place they would like to visit was the military base in Gagetown, which was not far from Fredericton. The visit to the military base had been fulfilled on their way back from the trip further east.

Jim had served on the military base in Gagetown for many years. He had mostly good memories of this base. On their way back, the couple turned in to have a look on his old base. Of course, they could not barge in to nose around; they had only walked around the gate and checked out the store by the gate. The gate of the military base looked better and bigger than before. It had a spacious open ground in front and a few decorative tanks on both sides. There seemed no guards around the gate. The civilian tractor trailers were going in and out. The store was in the old position connected with the gate. The inside of the store looked bigger and had more goods. After the couple satisfied themselves with the gate and the store, they had a peek at the PMQ area, the living quarters of the military married personnel. The townhouses in the area looked the same, but there was a huge pile of filled garbage bags stacked in front of those buildings.

The visit to Fredericton and the military base had aroused some suspicions in the couple's minds. They had been harassed and attacked for quite a few years now. Meilin's writings seemed to have offended more and more people. No matter what the couple had said or what Meilin had written; everything of the couple or about the couple seemed to have got on the wrong side of some people. In order to protect themselves and to keep a peaceful mind, the couple tried to care less about what was happening to them. They knew that they could do nothing else but ignoring the harassment and attacks. In addition to the things happening to themselves, they had noticed that those people who had supported or sympathized with them seemed to have also been affected. During this trip to Fredericton and the military base, they had seen some signs which seemed to indicate that the university, the Chinese community, the church and the military base here might have all been affected by the situation, suffering some harassment and attacks as well. If the situation was like what the couple had suspected, they hoped that the good people here could see that they were not the ones to blame; racism, still circulating in the country and controlling some people's way of thinking, was responsible.

Jim and Meilin's situation has definitely shown that racial discrimination is still a problem in Canada. It does not matter that some coloured people will sometimes come forward to claim that everything is fine and everybody lives an equally happy life here, the reality speaks differently. Jim and Meilin's situation is a good example. If Meilin were a white woman, the situation might be totally different for the couple. There are still some white people in this country who cannot accept the coloured people being their equals. Those people are easily offended by criticisms coming from the coloured people. To them, those criticisms are not constructive and good for the country; they were attacks to and bad for the country. The same kind of criticisms coming from some white people will be received kindly. More seriously, those racially orientated whites cannot bear to see or feel any coloured people better than themselves; nothing can be more hurtful to their sense of white superiority than seeing or feeling this reality sometimes on some occasions.

Jim and Meilin's situation got worse, when their private conversations at home had been regarded as attacks to certain people or to the society. For this, the couple had received ample counter-attacks. Meilin's writing at home seemed to have hurt some white people's sense of superiority. To them, the fields of higher intelligence should be exclusively belonging to the whites; a Chinese woman who could write and even criticize had broken the social order and barged into the higher ground which she did not belong, and therefore she deserved to be punished, beaten or degraded. For years, the couple had suffered all kinds of attacks, abuses and even attempts on their lives. All these had only infuriated them more. Nothing now could stop them doing the things which were within their rights to do, speaking and writing their minds or simply being themselves. So the situation continued.

At this moment after touring Fredericton, the couple thought only about the visit and their rest in their trailer on the church parking lot for the night. When they had arrived at their trailer, they sat down and relaxed for a little while. Then they got their things and went to the church to take a shower. Brother Anderson came promptly to open the door for them as soon as they shook the door handle. The Mormon Church had two bathrooms; each had two small shower stalls. Those shower stalls were for people to take showers and change into and out of the white gowns before and after their baptism in the church indoor pool. The couple were baptised here. They knew that the indoor pool was the size about six by eight feet and the warm water was waist high. The shower stalls were quite small, but big enough to have a comfortable shower. So many years later, everything seemed to have been kept in the exact same condition, still new and clean. In no time, the couple had a nice shower and felt like new persons. After thanking Brother Anderson, they left the church and went back to their trailer. Now they could really take a good rest. For super, they prepared something in the trailer.

After supper, Meilin stayed in the trailer to clean up the dishes and Jim went outside to get something from the van. He came back after a while with a very worried face. Without waiting for Meilin to ask, he informed, "The woman is going to call police on us. She said that we could not park here..."

"What?! What woman? Why?" Meilin asked and was quite alarmed.

"The woman living on the back up," said Jim with some fear.

Meilin went out of the trailer immediately to see this woman. Jim followed. On the other side of the fence, the ground was over ten feet higher than the church parking lot. On top of the higher ground and above the tree line of the church ground, there was a residential house. Meilin saw a middle-aged woman standing on the higher ground close to the fence. When the woman saw the couple coming out of their trailer, she shouted, "You cannot park here! If you don't leave, I'll call the police!"

Meilin had seen some shrews in some large cities and especially in Edmonton when the couple were running a rental business, but she had never seen a shrew here in Fredericton when they lived here. The woman, though motherly looking, could fit the category of a shrew at this moment. Meilin was stunned. But before she could talk to the woman, Jim started mumbling, "We'll leave tomorrow morning. We are going to see my brothers, they are dying..." With these words, the tears were running out of his eyes.

The situation set Meilin on fire. She shouted at Jim, "Stop crying! You have no need to shed tears in front this person!" Then she screamed at the woman, "Is this your property!?"

The woman could not answer. Meilin continued her scream, "Go on! Go to call the police! This is the church's property; the church allows us to park here. Who gives you the right to drive us away!? Go, call the police now!"

Now the woman started mumbling, "It's just we have had troubles here before... If the church let you... you can stay..."

"This is not your property! It is not for you to allow us to stay!" Meilin shouted, and still could not quiet down her fury. Jim had dried his tears now and pulled Meilin away from the fence.

The couple went back to their trailer. For quite some time, Meilin could not calm down. To her, this incident was surely instigated by the harassers who did not want them to have a moment of peace all the way of their trip. Though she could not fully understand why there was so much hatred towards her and her husband, she could certainly vent her anger when she needed to. Meilin continued her ranting for a while in the trailer. After this encounter, the couple had no heart to go out for a walk. They took some books out to read in order to calm themselves down. At about nine o'clock when it was still bright outside, they went to bed. It took them sometime to fall asleep. In the middle of the night, they were awakened again by a loud explosion. They got up immediately and opened their trailer door to see what had happened. In the semi-darkness and with a streetlight nearby, they saw a middle-aged woman with two small children throwing firecrackers on the church parking lot not far from their trailer. Both Jim and Meilin knew quite well that this was not Canada Day celebration firecrackers the woman and the children were playing with; this was deliberate harassment towards them.

The couple had lived in Fredericton before and knew that this kind of bomb-like firecrackers had never been used here, not used in the residential area in the middle of the night and not used even on Canada Day. However, the bomb explosions of the firecrackers had been used in Abbotsford for quite a few years now since the harassment started towards the couple. On every Halloween night, some of those explosions would happen under the couple's windows and around the neighbourhood, not only in the middle of the night, but also in the wee hours of the morning. Those explosions would last for quite a few nights around the Halloween.

The name of Halloween is associated with Allhallow's Eve. The festival has its origin of the ancient Druids celebration of the day of Saman. On the night of every October 31, the Lord of Death would gather the souls of the wicked who had died during the past year. Then the harvest theme of Halloween comes from the old Roman festivals in honor of Pomona, Goddess of Fruit. This tradition was brought to Britain during the Roman occupation. Today in the western world, Halloween has very much become a children's festival. At the night of Halloween, children can play and visit other people's homes in the neighbourhood. Almost every visited home will hand out candies and snacks to the little visitors. The ancient legendary or mythic stories seem to have gone from the memories of the general public. But to make the night more attractive to children's imagination, the theme that in this night all the ghosts, goblins and monsters will come to visit the living world has been kept. The visiting children will deck themselves up in different costumes as monsters, angels, star-war warriors and so on. The traditional decorations and lightings concerning ghosts and harvest are still set up for this special night by quite some homes. However, the popping of fireworks and firecrackers has been a new thing for Halloween.

Fireworks and firecrackers have long been adopted all over the world for celebrations; they can greatly ram up the festival atmosphere. In Abbotsford, people seem to use them not only for public celebrations, but also for some private occasions. They will light up some fireworks or a few firecrackers in their backyards for some special family events. However, the bomb-like explosions of firecrackers in the middle of the night or the wee hours of morning is definitely the technique adopted by some shady people for the purpose of harassing and attacking others. Those people do not like the new custom of fireworks and firecrackers, regarding it the Asian way; for retaliation, they use those noise bombs in the middle of the nights to disturb peace, to create terror or to show their hostilities.

Since those firecracker explosions seemed a fixed feature of harassment in the couple's life now; there was no doubt in their minds that the harassers were behind this woman with two kids here in Fredericton to set up those explosions by their trailer in the middle of the night. Jim and Meilin were open target at this moment of time and the harassers would of course use the occasion to set those noise bombs on them. In Abbotsford, the couple had called the police numerous times on numerous nights to report those terrible attacks. Their reports and protests had met police shuffling and even offence. No police efforts had ever been made to put down or control the situation. Those "terrorists" in the darkness of the nights could play their noise bombs to their hearts' content and shook the neighbourhood to pieces.

It was sad for Jim and Meilin to see that the noise bomb attacks had been carried out even here in Fredericton. The couple stood at the door of their trailer and watched with indignation. Under their stares, the woman and her children let out two or three more explosions and then left the parking lot. The couple went back to their beds and tried to get some sleep, but to fall quickly asleep again seemed impossible. They talked and sighed about those bad things that had happened all along their trip. It seemed that many of those harassment attacks to them had been carried out by some ordinary people.

In Canada, most of the ordinary people are decent and capable of thinking and reasoning by themselves. There is a public awareness that racial discrimination is bad for the society and bad for the country. Still, sometimes and on some occasions, a few bad evil-purposed people can arouse the sentiment of racial prejudice in quite some people. The misled people in those racially orientated situations look very much like an aroused mob. In a mob, there are only a few bad characters with a certain evil goal and most people in a mob are just ordinary people who have been aroused and used for the occasion. Those ordinary people can only be compared to the mindless beasts in a stampede; they have gone totally blind, running with empty but heated minds under the whistle of a few bad characters. Of course, there are still a portion of people in a mob who are smart and have kept their minds clear. Those clear-minded people in the mob are just trying to protect themselves from being trampled by the stampede; they know that they have to go with the flow in order to avoid being run over by the mob. The beastly mindless rush under certain arousals or the human instinct of self-protection has thus created the condition for the occasions of mobs and riots in human societies. Canada, a developed and civilized country, cannot totally escape those occasional barbaric mobster situations.

After the explosions of the firecrackers stopped, Jim and Meilin got a little more sleep. In the morning, they pulled up their trailer after a simple breakfast and left the church parking lot. Though the couple had been stunned by a few things in the one day visit to Fredericton, they felt that they still loved this city. Those few unpleasant moments in one day could not erase so many good and beautiful memories of years of their life in this city.

The couple took Highway 102 to go to Saint John, which was a scenic route along the Saint John River. More importantly, the small village Wellsford was on this route. Jim's father was buried in the cemetery of Wellsford Village; the couple had planned to visit his grave at the start of this trip. Jacob Duihne, Jim's father, had been a poor man all his life. He had married twice and had three sons and a daughter. When he passed away, the welfare paid for a simple pine coffin for his burial. A funeral was held in a large church in Saint John and he was buried in this small village cemetery. When alive, Jacob had bought a burial lot for himself and a burial lot for his youngest son in this cemetery, because his first wife was buried here. There had not been a tombstone for Jacob's grave for many years after his burial until some years ago when Jim and Meilin were finally in a better financial condition and bought a tombstone for his grave. This had happened when the couple were living in the west. They came back to the east for a short visit when the military had given Jim a leave. The couple ordered a simple tombstone, but could not wait for it being done and put on the grave. They made the arrangement with a tombstone salesman. The money was paid and the cemetery location was given. The couple were told to put a mark on Jacob's grave and the tombstone company would put the tombstone on when it was finished. So many years later, Jim and Meilin were going to see for the first time whether the tombstone was there on Jacob's grave and how it looked.

The scenic route along Saint John River still looked as beautiful as the couple remembered. There were plenty of trees along the river and the houses along had ample spaces between them. Green lawns and beautiful gardens had been well looked after by those property owners. Saint John River runs through almost the whole province of New Brunswick. Many towns and villages are located along the river. Fredericton, the capital of the province, is at the mid-section of the river and Saint John, the largest city of the province, is at the end where the river runs into the Bay of Fundy. Besides the Saint John River, the populated areas of the province are along the Atlantic coast. New Brunswick is mostly bordered by the Atlantic Ocean. On the south, there is Bay of Fundy and on the east and north there are Gulf of St. Lawrence and Northumberland Strait.

It did not take long for Jim and Meilin to reach Wellsford Village which was located close to the highway. The Village had been totally hidden away by abundant trees and bushes. A gas station with a store by the highway was the landmark for the couple to know that they had reached the place. They pulled their trailer into the village. The place looked the same, green and peaceful. There were not many houses in the village and the few streets were short. The couple drove a short way to reach the cemetery. The cemetery looked changed a little; there were more tombstones on. The cemetery ground looked being well taken care of and the place was serenely beautiful. The couple had no problem to find Jacob's gravesite, as Jim had remembered that his father was buried in front of an apple tree. So many years later, the apple tree had grown into a large tree with big branches stretching around. Jacob's grave was well shaded by the apple tree.

The couple were happy to see that the tombstone had been set well on Jacob's grave and what's more, somebody had been taking care of the gravesite. The grass on the grave had been cleaned and there was even a small Canadian flag on the site. The couple knew that this could not be done by Jim's siblings who had never visited the cemetery after Jacob's funeral. Was this done by Jim's army buddies who lived around or some villagers who thought the grave belonged to a military veteran? No matter who did this, the couple were deeply grateful.

The tombstone the couple had bought was a small simple one of modern style. It sat flat on the grave with one side slightly tilting up. The black stone was polished. On the surface of the stone, the praying hands with two palms together were engraved. Beside the praying hands there were the words, "gone but not forgotten". Under those words there were Jacob's name and dates of his birth and death. The couple were satisfied with the tombstone. There were quite some large elaborate standing tombstones in the cemetery. Jacob's gravestone was simple, common and small, but it was here, just a small sign to show that a simple small ordinary man had existed here for a brief moment.

The couple were regretting that they did not bring some flowers. But most cemeteries did not allow fresh flowers. Jim had brought an apple to put on Jacob's grave. He said that apple was his dad's favorite fruit. The couple lingered on around Jacob's grave for a while, thinking about Jacob's life. Most probably they would be the last ones who would formally think of Jacob for this little while. Very soon, Jacob would be, like millions or billions of people who had left this world, gone to oblivion.

Jacob's first wife was a beautiful black woman who died while giving birth to her second son. The couple could not find her grave. Most probably, she did not have a gravestone. After the cemetery visit, the couple drove on to Saint John. On the way, they were comforted by the thought that they had accomplished having a gravestone put on Jacob's grave. The rest of drive to Saint John was not long. The couple soon arrived at the city. In Fredericton, Jim had talked with the wife of his elder brother Mark over the phone to get to know the conditions of his two brothers. Right now the couple had no idea of the whereabouts of Dexter, his younger brother, in Saint John. The only relative they could go to in this city was Judith, one of Jim's cousins. Among quite some Jim's relatives, only one of his uncles had shown some concerns to Jim and paid attention to his marriage and his life. For this uncle's kindness, Jim and Meilin had kept in touch with him and his family. A few years ago, this uncle had passed away and then his wife had gone shortly afterwards. This uncle and aunt had two children, a boy and a girl. Right now the girl, Judith, lived in the house left by her parents while the boy had long married and had his own homestead. Judith must be in her forties now and she had remained single.

Even with the address and several visits to the uncle's home, each time when the couple go to visit this uncle, they had to check the map and try to find the place. Compared with big cities in the central or western Canada, Saint John can only be considered as a medium-sized city. Still it is much bigger than Fredericton. There are some tall modern buildings in the downtown area of Saint John, but its old residential area is quite different than that in Fredericton. After about 14,000 Royalists settled in

Saint John during the American Revolution, Saint John became the first incorporated city in Canada in 1785. Saint John is an old city with a rather long history; the houses in the old area are in old European style. They are wood structures, mostly two or three stories high and closely connected to each other. Those old houses are lined along the sidewalks with only one or less than one foot spaces between each other. In the old area, it is hard to see a large piece of green lawn around. This kind of residential housing situation is subject to the danger of fires. If one old wooden house is on fire, it will be hard for the other close ones to escape the same fate. In fact, city of Saint John had suffered a big fire in 1877. Though the fire was not as big as the one in San Francisco America in the history, it was no less devastating; about 15,000 people had lost their homes. Today though those closely linked old houses are not many in the city, they still exist.

Most streets in the residential areas of Saint John were not wide. Jim and Meilin drove their van with the trailer up and down quite some slopes through the winding streets. Finally, they had reached the uncle's place. The late uncle's house was located on a high ground by the ocean. The area looked rather new. The uncle's house appeared in good condition and of comfortable size. Along the street, other residential houses were well spaced to each other. Green lawns and gardens were around them. Judith was home and quite surprised to see Jim and Meilin. She led the couple into the kitchen. Judith had put on more weight and seemed to have difficult moving around. Though in her forties, she had a face as smooth as the face of a baby. This might be the result of her overweight or suffering from diabetes. Jim and Meilin were glad to see that Judith had carried on her life as usual. The inside of the house had remained the same as when the uncle and aunt were alive; knickknacks accumulated by the parents through their life were everywhere.

After Jim told Judith the reason why they had come to see her, she started helping to check out the whereabouts of Dexter. She called a few relatives and even the welfare office. It took quite some time for her to have finally located Dexter. After this done, Judith said, "It is good that you have come here. Now, I can get the names of Meilin's parents."

Judith was doing the genealogy of the Duihne family and needed all the names. Meilin wrote done the Chinese names of her parents and handed to Judith. Then she asked to see what Judith had done for the family tree. Judith brought out two thick folders and Meilin started browsing through. She found out that Judith's genealogy had some important things missing which Jim had kept for many years, but listed quite some properties which did not belong to the Duihne family. Jim had a large coloured photo of their grandparents and also their will which had clearly stated the homestead of the Duihne family before the third generation of the Duihnes in Canada had branched into quite a few more different homesteads. The couple offered to send copies of the photo and the document to Judith. Then according to Judith's genealogy, the Duihne family was originated from Island and England. But Jim grew up with the knowledge from his father and grandfather, that the family was originated from Scotland. More importantly the family name was a Scottish clan name.

In Canada, quite some descendents of the early settlers from British Isles have vague ideas about the exact locations of their family origins. After several generations living in Canada, most of them have no concerns of this issue. Still some try to find out the exact location, the family tree and the family history. Jim and Meilin had to admire that Judith was taking the time and efforts to do the family genealogy.

It had taken quite some time for Judith to find Dexter's whereabouts and for the couple to look through the family genealogy. Then Judith started prepare her own lunch. She was working in a facility looking after some disabled people and had to go to work in the afternoon. As she had never offered even a cup of water to Jim and Meilin, the couple asked for some water and used her bathroom. Then they told her that they were going to park their trailer over the street opposite to her house. The street was quiet with very little traffic. They were not going to drag their trailer through those winding city streets again to locate Dexter.

Living in the same city, Judith obviously did not have any contact with her cousin Dexter, and her way of treating Jim and his wife after many years without seeing them was quite normal in Canada. The relationship between relatives in a developed country is getting more and more indifferent, and even to the extent of coldness. Judith had opened her door to Jim and Meilin and offered some help to locate Dexter. Some of other Jim's relatives might not even do this for him. Families have long been breaking up in the Industrial Age, as there are less or no needs for the family members to stick together. In the early Farming or Agricultural Age, family members had to stay together to work on the family farms. Family relationship was much closer then. Today, the era probably has to be considered as Electronic or Computer Age. The concept of family has been further diluted. Children have been driven out of homes as soon as they can be on their own. Less and less parents will take care of the college or university expenses for their offspring. Quite some students who graduate from colleges or universities have to start their lives with big students' loans to pay. One can often hear some young people complain that their friends have treated them better than their relatives. On the other hand, when parents get old, less and less children will look after them; very few old people live with their adult children today.

Jim and Meilin said goodbye to Judith and went to park their trailer on the other side of the street. The area looked like a residential area for the people of middle class. The houses around the area, though not the large luxury ones, were in good conditions. Green lawns, trees and gardens around those houses looked well. The location of the street was up on the mid section of a mountain and had a splendid view of the ocean. The residents did not have to worry about the danger of being swept into the ocean by the coastal storms, as they were situated quite high. The couple could not help making a comparison of this place with the western places along the Pacific Ocean. They knew that this kind of coastal location in Vancouver area was mainly occupied by the luxury mansions; each worth millions of dollars. The property taxes for those grand homes were higher than the annual incomes of lower class people. From Judith, Jim and Meilin got to know that property taxes for the home owners here at such a prime location were not high. Judith paid less property tax than Jim and Meilin paid theirs for a house in a small city in British Columbia.

While Jim and Meilin were getting to unhitch their trailer from the van, Judith came out and walked to them. She said, "You can park the trailer on my driveway. It is safer. I'm not sure whether they'll allow you to park it on the street."

Jim and Meilin thanked Judith and moved their trailer to her driveway. Though there was no garage with her house, the paved driveway could contain both the trailer and the van. Judith had already moved her car to a patch unevenly covered by gravel beside the driveway. When Jim and Meilin started to set up their trailer, Judith left with her car.

The couple were soon on their way with their van. It felt freer to drive the van around without the trailer. Once in the city centre, they attended to their lunch first. Then they went to a grocery store to buy some groceries for Dexter. In most of Dexter's life, he had been on welfare. When he was a child, he got polio and was crippled by the disease. When he was an adult, he was further crippled by a gambling fever. Whenever he got a little money, he would throw it into a gambling machine, fixated on the idea that those machines would eventually make him rich. Now approaching his old age, Dexter's crippled leg might be suffering from bone cancer and his chest suffering from lung cancer after life-long smoking. According to Mark's wife, Dexter was dying. Jim had no confidence that Dexter's gambling fever had got any better. The couple knew that Dexter's living condition would not be good and the best way to visit him in his present condition was to bring him some nutritious food.

The grocery store the couple went to was large and full of all kinds of food and other health and daily used products. Their prices were relatively the same as those in other parts of the country. The couple got about two hundred dollars of good food for short and long term uses. After this, it did not take them too long to find Dexter's place. Dexter lived on the third floor of a small apartment in the back of an old house. The house was located in the street of an old residential area where old wooden houses were closely cramped together. In the old days, those houses were owned by well-to-do people; they were quite big houses in Victoria style. Now the well-to-do families had moved to the suburbs where they had modern houses with green lawns and beautiful gardens. Those old houses had been left to the poor and lower-income families. Quite some of the old houses had been changed into rooming houses by the landlords. One big house could be divided into several apartments and rented out to several families or single tenants.

The couple went in an old house by the back door and then climbed up the narrow wooden stairs to reach Dexter's apartment. Dexter was home and happy to see Jim and Meilin. He looked much older with a bald head and more weight. The couple were dismayed to see that Dexter was still a heavy smoker. Every time when the couple visited Dexter, Jim would not say much about Dexter's smoking habit; he knew there was no use of harping on him. Meilin would still ask Dexter to quit smoking, telling him that it was not good for his health. Dexter would not promise that he would quit, only politely make excuses that he had tried to quit before, but failed.

Dexter had a small one bedroom apartment with a tiny kitchen and a small sitting room. Still, he had put a bed for himself in the dining area of the kitchen and sublet the bedroom to two single guys. In this way, he could earn a little money. However, once the welfare knew this arrangement, they cut more than thirty dollars off from his monthly benefit. Dexter had no complaint. All his life, he had taken whatever was given or not given to him. He knew there was no use to argue with the authorities and things might get worse if he did.

The air in Dexter's apartment was horrible. The landlord had ordered the tenant to paint the apartment walls green. Now the smell of the fresh paint mixed with the stale smell of cigarette smoke could choke a horse. As soon as Jim and Meilin walked into Dexter's apartment, Meilin went and opened the small screen door of the living room to let some fresh air in. Outside the screen door, there was a tiny balcony with wooden floor and metal rail. The balcony looked so shakily unstable; probably nobody had stepped on it for years. The couple did not see a bathroom in the apartment. They did not ask, supposing that Dexter and the other two guys had shared the bathroom with other renters in this rooming house.

Jim and Dexter chatted for quite a while. There was still love and closeness between the two brothers even after many years apart and with very little contact to each other. Dexter talked without much clarity about the bone cancer in his crippled leg. He informed that he was going to have MRI, Magnetic Resonance Imaging. Dexter looked quite relaxed about his medical condition and did not show much concern. Jim, on the other hand, was worried. Before the couple were going to leave, Dexter asked them to come tomorrow afternoon.

"Doc had prescribed some diabetic drinks for me. They are quite some cans. If you can help me to get them from the store and bring them home, it will save me some troubles," Dexter said with his casual manner.

Jim answered immediately, "No problem. We'll come tomorrow."

Dexter was also diabetic. He had no vehicle and depended on taxi for his grocery shopping, seeing the doctors and some other necessary errands. For a man on welfare, the expense on taxi was not a small amount. The couple left Dexter's apartment with their hearts heavy. Dexter's health and living conditions were not good and they could do nothing about them. Dexter had never asked for help. When they had given him some help, they would not hear thanks from him. For some Christmas, the couple sent some money to Dexter; they would not receive a letter from Dexter to say that he had received the money or that he was grateful. Dexter had been long used to his lot and the rules of life, everybody fending for himself and one taking whatever falling on one's head. He never expected his siblings or other relatives to help him. If he had received some occasional help from them, it was not a big deal to him. The money he had received from Jim and Meilin had mostly gone to the gambling machines and he seldom benefited from the help. Jim knew the situation clearly and had no heart to keep on the useless and wasteful kindness by giving Dexter money. To Jim and Meilin, it was a miracle that Dexter had not ended up homeless and begging for his daily food, and he was still on his feet, managing his own life. The couple felt a little relief after leaving Dexter's tiny smelly apartment. It looked that Dexter still had some time to live and was not going to die immediately.

After visiting Dexter, there was still time left for the afternoon. The couple drove to the Reversing Falls, the famous tourist attraction in the city. Jim had grown up in this city and Meilin had visited some tourist spots here before. Still, they thought that it was worthwhile to visit the Reversing Falls again. They soon arrived at the site. Reversing Falls are at the place where the rapids of Saint John River are rushing into the Bay of Fundy. When there are high tides, the ocean water will push the rapids and force them to run backwards. The couple stood on the view point high up on the cliff, looking down into the deep gorge. Though the tide was not that high at this moment, they could still see the currents fighting with each other and forming surges and whirlpools. A small motor boat was running in circles on this turbulent water, trying to ride the complicated currents and to conquer the whirlpools. At any dangerous natural spot in the world, there would be some daredevils to challenge and try to conquer the force of nature in order to get the adrenaline rush. There was no exception here at the Reversing Falls.

The couple watched the fierce flow of the waters deep down and admired the struggling boat. A middle-aged man who stood not far from them was doing the same. Jim started a conversation with him and asked about the fishing situation here these days.

The man happened to be a local and answered with a smile, "With the paper mill, the fish had long gone in this spot for years."

"Really! When I was growing up here quite some years ago, there were quite some fish around then," said Jim with a sigh. He felt sad but was glad that he had the chance to show that he had been a local here before.

Not far from the Reversing Falls stood a large pulp and paper mill with giant chimneys. New Brunswick's strong old industry, ship building, had long gone; as England and some European countries had stopped importing wooden ships. Now its main industry is some large pulp and paper mills, belonging to the Irving family of course. Saint John is the major industrial city of the province. Besides the mills, there are the oil refinery, food processing, metal smelting and some other smaller manufacturing factories here. Still the pulp and paper mills are the largest. Many people in this city work in the large pulp and paper mill right in the city. In the days when the wind is blowing the wrong way, the smoke and the stinking sulfa smell from the large mill will cover the whole city. The pollutants from the mill have very much affected the river and the living beings that depend on this water. However, with so many people's livelihood depend on the mill, people have to get by and live with some side effects brought by this industry.

From Judith, the couple got to know that an important issue was being hotly discussed in this city right now. There was the talk that another pulp and paper mill was going to be built in the city and quite some people were against it. With more awareness of environment pollutions caused by some heavy industries, every large industrial development will be under attacks and objections of quite some people. In fact, people or organizations have always been separated into two main parts, one part will have things done and the other part will prevent things to be done. As for the environmental protectionists nowadays, they have more legitimate reasons. Industrialization had started without any consideration of protecting the environment. After one or two centuries, the consequences of blind industrial developments to the planet have becoming more and more serious. If the human beings plan to survive on this planet for some more centuries, serious measures of protecting the environment have to be taken.

However, entirely stopping developments is not the absolute good solution. In Saint John, stopping development or going backwards means more people will have to live the life as Dexter and his roommates are living. The unemployment rate in New Brunswick is higher than that in the central and western Canada. Another mill will provide more jobs and improve more people's lives. So another option has to be considered and somehow people have to try to find ways that can accommodate both development and protection of the environment. Of course, it is easy to say this, but much more difficult to carry it out in practice. Hundreds of years of habitual traditional ways of development coming to this point cannot be changed overnight. However, human survival on the planet has never been easy. Still many innovations and inventions have moved human life to the present level. Will human beings stop walking at all because of some mistakes they had made at the time when they were learning to walk? People have to have confidence that some better ways will be found that can keep on the development of the world and the improvement of human life while protecting the environment. This attitude of confidence should at least be the first step in solving the problems the world is facing today. To go to extremes on one side's opinions and to care only for one side to win is not constructive and will not solve problems in the best possible way.

After seeing the Reversing Falls, the couple walked towards the other side of the street. There was a hill which looked like a new tourist attraction. They climbed up the hill and saw that it was indeed a newly created park for the locals and tourists. On top of the hill, there were some paths through the green lawn. By the paths, there were quite some wooden statues of historical or prominent figures important to this region. The wood carving looked not done by the professionals, but the efforts of the sculptors were admirable. Standing on top of the hill, the couple could see most part of Saint John. The city looked to have gone through some changes during all those years, but it was still familiar to Jim. He could point out some of the buildings he knew well. From the top, the city looked peaceful and not that cramped as from a close ground look.

Downtown area of Saint John has actually gone through quite some renovations. Modern skywalk and underground walk have connected the whole business area with the museum, conference centre, parks, historical sites and the waterfront recreational area. At the waterfront, one can see the whole Saint John harbour. Saint John is one of the most active ports in the east. The deep-water oil terminal receives some largest vessels of the world.

After the sightseeing, the couple went back to Judith's place at supper time. They told Judith that because of Dexter's need, they had to stay on her driveway for not only tonight, but also tomorrow night. Judith looked displeased, but uttered no objection. It was understandable that Dexter had never asked for help from the relatives; he knew that most probably the answer would be "no". At this moment, Jim and Meilin took Judith's silence for "yes". They had camped on Walmarts' or some other stores' parking lots, and would not mind camping on Judith's driveway for two nights. They would not ask her for anything else, perhaps a jar of water if they absolutely needed. The street was quiet with very little traffic. They expected to have two nights good sleep.

The couple had a simple supper in their trailer. After supper, they went to walk around the neighbourhood. On the other side of this coastal street, the mountain kept on rising. On the slope, there was an old cemetery looking down on Judith's and some other neighbours' houses. The couple walked to the cemetery to have a look. They knew that Saint John had a few tourist attractions that were related to the Loyalists who fled American Revolution to settle here. Those spots were the Loyalists' burial ground, their houses and their sea port. This cemetery, though looking ancient, had no sign showing that it was the Loyalists' burial ground. Jim and Meilin roamed among the weathered tombstones and found a few of them dated in the seventeenth century. They could see that Saint John was indeed a place that had been established for a few centuries.

Having passed through the cemetery, the couple climbed further up. The whole mountain had been developed into a residential area and there were streets reaching the top. On top of the mountain, there was an important national historical site. An ancient citadel was standing there on the peak with a tourist office and a small museum on the lower ground. The citadel was called the Carlton Martello Tower which was built in 1815. From the top of the citadel, one could see the whole Saint John City, the harbour and the Bay of Fundy. Besides the barracks, the citadel itself was a large tall round structure built by large stones. There were some gun-holes on the wall around. The ancient citadel had played a crucial role in the protection of Saint John and its harbour up to the Second World War. There was a wooden stair case huddling up on one side of the citadel, which looked like being built in later years for tourism purpose. The couple climbed up the stairs. Now they must be on the highest point of the city.

Standing on the high spot, the couple could see that Saint John, though not a very large city, had sprawled and covered quite a large area. This citadel, however, showed how big of a place Saint John was in the early years; it must be quite small that it could be protected by such a small fortress. It would be a joke to depend on this ancient citadel to protect the city today. However, on this high point of historical significance, the couple could imagine some of the happenings in the old time. On the side of the mountain which was facing the Saint John city, there must have been a settlement formed by some crude wooden cabins. The early settlers lived and worked in this area. The citadel had functioned as a strong fortress to fend off the dangers most probably coming from the ocean. Some of those settlers and soldiers could have been buried in the ancient cemetery Jim and Meilin had just visited.

Having enjoyed the historical site and the view of the city, the couple left the citadel. They then walked back to the street where Judith's house was located. There was still time, they continued their stroll along the street. The ocean view between the houses was magnificent. Further on, they encountered a branching street leading down to the beach. On the lower level and close to the shore, there was a cluster of residential houses. Those houses looked not as big and comfortable as the ones up here in this street and they were more closely connected to each other. Would those houses be at the mercy of the ocean or was the Atlantic

Ocean here on this spot gentler? The couple wondered. But those houses looked to have existed down there for quite many years and they might have belonged to the families of some fishermen.

As the side street was quite steep, the couple did not go down. They viewed the place from the top for a while. It had been a full day and they were tired. They walked back towards Judith's house. As soon as they came back to their trailer, they went to bed after a simple cleaning. The night's sleep turned out to be as they had expected, peaceful and restful.

Next morning, after the breakfast in the trailer, they left for sightseeing again. Dexter needed them for the afternoon; they had the whole morning to themselves. They had set their mind on visiting the Irving Natural Park which was a new thing to them. From the name of the park, it might be one piece of forest lands donated by the Irving family for public use. With the help of the map, the couple drove through a pretty residential area and arrived at the park. Irving Natural Park was a small peninsula. There was a road built from the main land to reach the place. The park had 600 acres of protected ecosystem formed by forest, tidal pools, salt marsh, mud flat, bog and a barrier beach. Every year, about 250 species of migratory birds would pass through here. The place was almost fully covered by large trees and thick bushes. Circling the deep green peninsula was a gravel road for visitors to enjoy their natural walk. Along this road, there were quite some lookout spots for people to see the ocean.

It was early morning. When Jim and Meilin arrived at the parking lot of the park, there was nobody else around. It was not a fine day. The sky was overcast by thick clouds. The forest area looked dark and forbidden. The couple sat in their van, enjoying the vast ocean view and waiting for more people to come. They would like to have some more visitors come to explore the park together in such a weather condition.

The ocean under the grey sky looked powerfully imposing. The waves were roaring loudly and beating the shore with mighty force. Further away from the shore, the ocean melted into the grey clouds and no horizon could be seen. One could be easily lost in such a vast misty grey world, feeling no personal existence. Nature was now in her overpowering gloomy mood; human presence or significance had been reduced to minimum. Mighty force of nature was everything everywhere, totally vanquishing the human sense of existence and importance with all the insignificant worldly worries and cares.

The couple had to pull their eyes away from the ocean to feel themselves again. They waited for quite some time. Finally a few men came and parked their vehicles. They then walked into the deep of the park. Three women came in one vehicle. They had a large dog looking like a Labrador. They too walked to the gravel road and disappeared into the forest. Obviously those people were the joggers who came to the park for their morning exercises. Jim and Meilin felt safe now. They got off their vehicle and started walking towards the forest. At the edge of the woods, they saw two outhouses. Of course, it would be better to use the outhouses before they started the walk. They had no idea how big the park was and how far the walk would be.

Coming out of the outhouses, the couple felt some drops of rain on their faces. The dark clouds had quickly brought the rain. The couple changed their mind and went back to their van; they decided to drive through the natural walk. They were not as young as the few people who had disappeared into the forest and it would be safer for them to drive. The gravel road allowed vehicles driving through. The couple were soon on the road. The woods along the shore were mostly smaller trees and bushes; the large tall trees were in the centre of the peninsula. Though the road was along the shore and close to the ocean, it went through the thick woods. From their vehicle, the couple had occasionally spotted some lookouts which gave a view of the grim grey ocean. If the day was fine, the ocean view must be spectacular. The couple felt it a pity that they came to this park in such a grey day. Midway, the road was turning to the other side of the park; they started driving back to the parking lot. The rain started pouring down heavily now. Large rain drops were beating down hard on their van, sounding like constant exploding of firecrackers. The rain soon formed a thick curtain; they could hardly see the road. The woods, the heavy rain and the whole universe seemed closing in on them. They were totally engulfed by the rainstorm. The rain with loud booming sounds was beating on their van. The thick rain curtain was blurring and blocking their view of the surroundings. Thunders were now rolling low over the peninsula with muffled dark threats. Lightening occasionally touched down, tearing the rain curtain and lighting up the ghostly woods.

Meilin was scared. She raised her voice to ask Jim, “If lightening struck our van, what would happen?”

“Don’t worry! The tires are rubber. Lightening won’t hurt us,” said Jim loudly, trying to assure Meilin and calming himself down as well.”“

Jim drove very slowly through the rainstorm. The visibility was only three or four feet. Even with the high beams on, they could not see much further. Luckily, there was not much wind; otherwise, they could very well be buried by the storm in this park. Not far after they turned on the curve of the road to go back, the couple spotted the three women with their dog standing a little way off the road. Jim drove on, passing them. Then Meilin said, "Let's pick up those ladies. Who knows how long the pouring rain is going to last."

Jim agreed. He backed the van and stopped at the spot where the women and their dog were standing. Then he went out in the heavy rain and opened the side door of the van, calling out to the women, "Coming on in! The rain might not stop for quite some time yet!"

One woman fumbled in the vegetations on the ground for a little while. Then the three women and the dog ran up and got into the van. All three started saying thanks, "Thank you guys very much. You have saved our lives. God bless you. We hope you'll be rewarded for this..."

Jim and Meilin had taken all the back seats out of the van to lessen the weight in order to tow the trailer. Now the women had to sit on the floor. The van was immediately filled up with the smell of the wet dog. Jim turned on the fan to the upmost scale to prevent the van being steamed up inside. The three women appeared in their thirties; they and their dog were drenched through and through. While Jim started driving slowly again through the heavy rain, the women were gradually relaxed and started talking with each other. From the way they carried their conversation, the couple guessed that the three were spinsters living in the same apartment building. The tall one talked anxiously and worried about how she was going to get into her apartment when she got home. In the rainstorm, in fear of being struck by the lightening, she threw away her keys. Though she tried frantically to find them in the rain, the keys had disappeared into the thick vegetations. There was no way that she could get them back. The couple now saw why she was fumbling on the ground before getting on the van.

The big wet dog stuck his head between Jim and Meilin. He was quite gentle and friendly. Meilin turned her head to pad the dog. Now the women noticed that Meilin was a Chinese. From this moment on, all their conversation or thanks to the couple were directed only to Jim; Meilin became a non-person to them. The women turned their dog towards themselves and played with him. The dog was pleased and wagged his tail. The big wet dog tail started beating on Meilin's face and she had to lean towards the side window to avoid it.

Further on in driving through the rainstorm, Jim saw a man sitting in a pavilion a little way off from the road. He stopped the van, rolled down the window and called out to him, "Come on in! We'll give you a ride. The rain looks not to stop soon."

The man sitting in the pavilion all darkened by the surrounding trees and the heavy rain thanked Jim but said that he could wait until the rain was over. The petit woman in the van complained, "There is no more space here in the van."

But Jim continued to invite the man to take the ride. The man then said, "Okay, thank you very much, sir."

The man came in and the three women huddled up to make a space for him. The man looked like a young university student, handsome and intelligent. The petit woman immediately started talking to him flirtatiously, trying to find out something about him. The young man was indeed from the university. But after a little pause, he said, "I'm delivering the mails there."

The women cooled down towards the man after getting the not so ideal information. When the drive was almost ended and the van was soon going to deliver the passengers to their vehicle locations, the young man asked Jim to stop the van. He said that his car was parked on the upper ground and he could walk up there. The rain seemed slowed down a bit, but it was still no less a pouring. Jim insisted driving him to his car. Under the young man's direction, they came to an upper parking lot and to the man's car. The young man gave his thanks and went to his car. Jim turned the van, heading for the lower parking lot. When the young man caught up, he honked his car to say thanks again. On the lower parking lot, Jim delivered the women and their dog to their vehicle. Again, the women's gratitude and goodbyes were only for Jim now. The women soon caught up and passed the couple to be on their way back to the city.

This coastal rainstorm was quite an experience for Jim and Meilin. On their way back from the park, they talked about the ferocity of the rainstorm and also the people they had picked up. They decided that the young man must be a university student and he was just using the delivery boy's position to turn off the women who were coming on to him.

The more eastwards the couple went in the country, the less coloured people they would see. Though the number of the coloured people in Fredericton seemed to have increased, the couple hardly see any coloured people in Saint John. They knew that in places where people were not well exposed to different coloured people, racial prejudice or discrimination were more serious. From the way Meilin had been treated by the three women, the couple could see how the coloured people were generally treated and what kind of social status the coloured people had here.

The morning was still young. Though the rain continued pouring down, the couple decided to pay a visit to the famous farmers market here. They drove to the downtown area and found the market. But they had to drive some way further to find a parking lot. When they had finally parked their van, the rain seemed to have increased power again. The couple sat in their van and waited for quite a while. When the rain seemed lessened a bit, they got off their van and walked to the farmers market, with umbrellas of course.

Saint John City Market, the city's farmers market, is in a large 1876 building shaped like an inverted ship's hull in honor of the city's shipbuilding heritage. It is believed that the market is Canada's oldest chartered market. The place is at the heart of the city. Jim knew the market well and even Meilin had visited it before. The size of the old market was impressive. The goods sold in the market were generally locally produced. They were mainly vegetables, different seafood and crafts made by the locals. The couple considered the specialty here to be the dulse, a sea alga which could be chewed as it was, very delicious and full of the taste and character of the ocean.

When Jim and Meilin walked into the City Market, they felt the market a bit different, smaller than they had remembered. Today was a week day, there were not many customers. The lined up produce stands had mainly vegetables. There were two major lanes in the center of the market, selling crafts made by the locals and imported. The seafood like lobsters, crabs and mussels which were plenty before could not be seen. In the corner of the market, there were a merchant selling different kinds of sausages and a merchant selling different kinds of cheese. Jim and Meilin were disappointed when they could not find the dulse. What had happened? One reason might be that it was not a weekend day and another reason might be that they themselves had changed. In over two decades, the couple had gone through many places and seen many big markets. Compared with some of the big markets they had seen, Saint John City Market seemed shrunk with fewer goods. The couple did not know what to think of this or what had caused this. Should they apologize to Jim's old birth place that they felt different about it now? Or should they just feel sorry that the city had not injected enough of the good new things, but lost some of the good old things?

The couple left the market without buying much of anything but a little vegetable. They went to a small restaurant and had their lunch. In the afternoon, they went to Dexter's place and picked him up to go to the grocery store. It was the same grocery store from which they had bought groceries for Dexter. There was a pharmacy in the store. The waiting for Dexter's prescription to be filled was long. While Dexter waited at the pharmacy, the couple went through the store and bought some more grocery for Dexter. Finally, Dexter's diabetic drinks were ready; they could load them and leave the store.

The couple delivered Dexter, his medication and grocery to his apartment. They said goodbye to him. However, this was not their last visit to Dexter. On their return trip, they came to Saint John again just to check on Dexter and to know the result of his MRI test. At the second visit to Saint John on this trip, the couple found the campground here, which was located closely at the city skirt on top of a hill. Besides the filled up lots for long term trailer and motor home owners, the campground had some lots for RVers and tenters. Though the site of the campground was much higher than the city proper, the campers could not totally escape the smell and noises of the pulp mill. Still, with the fully serviced lot and green trees around, Jim and Meilin were satisfied. The campground had a notice posted around; informing the campers that the water was not safe to drink as there was some sewer pipe reconstruction going on. But the couple saw that a large group of children had been brought here, who were camping not far from them, and some campers were drawing water from the taps. To be cautious, the couple went to a Walmart nearby and got some tap water from their gardening centre.

Behind the campground, there was a nice park which covered another hill and had a beautiful pond. The couple did not have much time and energy to walk through the park, so they had a drive through. In the evening, Jim chatted with their neighbour RVers who were a middle-aged French couple. The French couple had a nice motor home and were all set for a camping night. They had a bundle of well cut clean wood pieces for a campfire and two glasses of red wine set on the picnic table for a nice evening. Jim was carried away by the couple's polite manner. After a talk with them, he came back, got a large map of Montreal and went there again. He showed the map to the couple and asked them some questions about some sightseeing places in that city. Perhaps on their return trip, Meilin and he would check out some more spots there. The French couple looked interested and tried to locate the places on the map for him. After a long while, Meilin was afraid that Jim might bother the neighbours too much and went there to have a look. But she too was pulled into the discussion of some places in Montreal. The French couple were quite gentle and polite, but they seemed not that familiar with Montreal. For the whole evening, the four were bending on the map and talking about the places in Montreal. The French couple's campfire was neglected and their wine must have turned flat. All the time, Jim and Meilin had thought that the French couple were from Quebec. Only later on, they had realized that the nice couple might be Acadian Canadians living in New Brunswick.

In the British colonial period of this country, the Acadians were separated from the English-speaking majority. Until the mid-19th century, they were almost totally illiterate. Economically and politically, they were unaggressive, living mainly on credit from the English-speaking merchants. In 1713 when France ceded Acadia to Britain in the Treaty of Utrecht, the Acadians refused to pledge loyalty to the British Monarch. They were deported. Most of them fled to the interior of the region, but later on, they returned back to their hometown. In the mid-19th century, the situation started changing for the Acadian Canadians. In 1864, they founded St. Joseph's College, beginning what they called their renaissance which led to their cultural movement. Politically and commercially they strived to have wider share in the province. In 1960, they had the first Acadian premier elected in New Brunswick.

The French couple Jim and Meilin met in the Saint John campground must be Acadian Canadians here. They gave a strong impression to be well educated, and might be school or college teachers. Apparently they were living a good and peaceful life.

As for Dexter, when Jim and Meilin visited him again, he informed that he had not had his MRI test and did not know when he was going to have it. Dexter was never clear about his own medical condition or what the doctors were going to do for him. The couple, though worried, had no way to find out Dexter's exact condition. They were both irritated and relieved that Dexter's condition might not be that serious after all. Two years later, Jim and Meilin got the news that Dexter's cancer had developed; this time the cancer was of his mouth or throat. He had had a staged surgery. As usual, Jim had difficulties to get in touch with Dexter. When he finally got hold of him in the hospital, he found out that Dexter was indeed in serious condition. The surgery was a big one and Dexter could hardly talk. Jim tried to phone Dexter more often to know his condition, but he soon lost him again. It seemed that the hospital had released him before the staged surgery was finished and nobody knew his whereabouts. Then Jim got the news from his sister who was in Newfoundland that Dexter had missed his doctor's appointment and nobody knew where he was and what had happened to him.

Jim tried frantically to call Dexter, but his home and cell phones were all cut off. Jim had to call Judith and to ask her to check on Dexter.

Days later, Jim got in touch with Dexter again. Dexter had no money to put his phone on, so nobody could reach him. Now the welfare must have helped to have his phone put back; he was reachable again. It seemed that Dexter was still on his feet and still had not much idea about the medical procedures, though he was informed that he had cancer. He told Jim that some bones had been taken out of his mouth and he had to go to a dentist to have some sort of metal bridge put in for support. After several phone conversations, Jim and Meilin still could not have a clear picture of Dexter's medical and living conditions. Then Jim lost contact with Dexter again. There was no answer from Dexter to Jim's calls.

Quite a lot of things about and around Dexter's problems and his death a few years later had caused some suspicions in Jim and Meilin's minds. First, Dexter had never complained about mouth problem before; this cancer of mouth was very sudden. Secondly, a written notice about Dexter's cancer of mouth came at about Jim's birthday on a Valentine card. Thirdly, the couple got the information that some skin of Dexter's bum had to be grafted to his mouth after the first stage surgery. Then from Dexter, the couple got to know that the skin for grafting was from his inner leg.

With the harassment situation going on in their life, Dexter's cancer, surgery and death had triggered wild imaginations of Jim and Meilin. Would the harassers be so malicious as to abuse Dexter in order to give them the emotional attacks? Dexter was at the very bottom of the society and most vulnerable to be the victim of all sorts of vicious people. The couple knew how much some people had hated that they had a voice that was heard far and wide. In spite of the fact that they had nothing to do with this happening; they were still hated and regarded as the public enemy by some people. A lot of things had happened to them, which had made their life hell. One of them was that their dog had all his teeth pulled out when they had put him in the hands of some veterinarians for some teeth problem. It seemed that the harassers had instigated to have their dog abused or maltreated in order to render an emotional blow to them. The emotional strain and trauma the couple had to go through with their dog's subsequent sufferings and death had not fully healed; now it seemed to be Dexter's turn.

The couple tried very hard to explain away Dexter's situation. Dexter had been a life-long smoker and he could very well have got the cancer of mouth. Though he was at the bottom of the society and his life might not even be regarded as worth as that of a dog in some people's eyes, some doctors might still see Dexter as a human being, have his human rights to live a human life and to be treated humanely. The couple tried their best to think that Dexter had not been abused and killed for the purpose of attacking them; he had really got cancer and the medical procedures used on him were routine. This thought made them feel better. Who would be so evil as to abuse and kill a human being to render emotional attacks to other human beings? Then when they thought about the attempts on their own lives, suspicions came back thick and strong. Finally they decided that it would be better for them not to contact Dexter too much at that time and not to show that what had happened to Dexter would affect them deeply. They knew that they could not help Dexter. But if somebody was trying to get to them through Dexter, they still had the power not to give them that satisfaction. Perhaps this was the only way to help Dexter and to lessen the possibility of his being abused by some evil persons.

There was another incident in Jim's family in this part of the country that had aided the couple's suspicions in Dexter's case. Years ago, one of Jim's cousins of second line went to court with her mother to sue a rich man for sexual aggression or assault. For most sexual assault cases, it would be the girl's or the woman's words against the man's words. In this case, it must be Jim's cousin's words against the rich man's words. There was probably no witness or evidence. Jim's cousin probably had only talked to her mother about the happening or happenings. The court dismissed the case; the daughter and mother had lost. From then on, the daughter and mother were totally disgraced in the community. The news of Jim's ignominious relatives had even reached Jim and Meilin living thousands miles away. Of course, the public opinion was that the mother and daughter had tried to extort money from the rich man. If things had ended there with the mother and daughter living their disgraced life for the rest of their time, nobody would think more of this case. But not long after the case ended in court, the daughter died in a car accident and the mother too died conveniently of cancer. When Jim and Meilin got the news about the law suit, they felt a bit ashamed that Jim's relatives would stoop so low to extort money in this way. But when they got the news about the death of the daughter and mother, they had changed their minds. Who knows what had really happened between Jim's cousin and the rich man? And the death of the mother and daughter looked very suspicious. The whole thing made them think that the people living at the bottom of society were easier prey of violence and might have less chance of getting justice from the judicial system. In recent years, more aboriginal girls and women who had become murder victims in this country had shown this clearly.

Well, all the later events of Dexter had not reached the couple's minds yet at this moment in their first visit to Saint John. For the second night of camping on Judith's driveway, they had another good night's sleep. Next morning, they got up early and left Saint John while the traffic was still light. They were heading for Nova Scotia. The highway of New Brunswick soon put them in a good mood.

At home, the couple had planned to visit Fundy Park in this province. To them, Fundy Park was the most beautiful spot in New Brunswick. It was along the Atlantic coast at the Bay of Fundy. To reach it, they had to drive miles through the forest filled with large tall trees. As the park was quite some way off the highway and they had already been there before, they now decided to skip it. They had already been on the road for a little over a month and had the syndrome of pushing on to the final destination at this stage. Now in their minds, that final destination was Newfoundland, the most eastern province of the country.

On their way to Nova Scotia, the couple talked about the beautiful places in New Brunswick. They had mixed Hopewell Cape up with Fundy National Park. Hopewell Cape is a famous scenery spot in New Brunswick. The place is located at the narrower spot of the Bay of Fundy, where the tide is said to be the highest in the world. The couple had been there before. Though they did not see the high tide as it happened at three or four o'clock in the morning at that time, they would never forget the beautiful scenery of that spot. When they were in that spot, the ocean was at its lowest tide. They walked on the beach and were amazed by the rock formations on it. Those large sandstone rocks stood up on the sandy beach, several stories high. The tides had worked on those stones for eons to leave impressive natural artistic marks, but the tops of those rocks had remained untouched with green vegetations and even trees on. At low tide, those natural sculptures with their green tops on the sandy beach would leave their haunting images in the travellers' minds. At high tide, those green-toped rocks became small green islets floating on the swelling ocean. This scenic spot was definitely one of the unusual beauties of the natural world.

CHAPTER TEN

NOVA SCOTIA

Very soon the couple crossed the border between New Brunswick and Nova Scotia. The highway in Nova Scotia was relatively the same, mainly two lanes with plenty of three lane sections for the drivers who were in a hurry to get ahead. The shoulders of the highway were still quite wide and the traffic on the highway was light. Driving on the highway remained comfortable and enjoyable. However, as soon as the couple came to the territory of Nova Scotia, the fences on both sides of highway were gone. The landscape had slightly changed. The wavy rolling hills had increased their depth and were changing more and more to be mountains.

There are three provinces in Canada that are almost totally surrounded by the ocean. Nova Scotia is one of them. The other two are Prince Edward Island and Newfoundland. Nova Scotia is actually a peninsula. Except a narrow piece of land connecting this province with New Brunswick, it is entirely surrounded by the Atlantic Ocean. Nova Scotia is the second smallest province of Canada; next to Prince Edward Island. But it is the strongest province in industry, commerce and agriculture among the Maritime Provinces. Its wealth, though cannot compare with that of the central and western provinces, is well established by its mining industry of coal and some other minerals, manufacturing, fishery and agriculture. Nova Scotia is one of the largest gypsum producers in the world. Its fertile Annapolis Valley is one of the best apple-growing places in the country. Surrounded by the ocean, the province is the second largest fish producers in the country, next only to British Columbia. On top of these, Halifax, the capital of Nova Scotia, is one of the largest ports of the country, ice free year round. Halifax Harbour is one of the largest sheltered harbours in the world, stretching 22 kilometers long with an outer harbour of 10 kilometers. Its inner harbour is called Bedford Basin which is 26 square kilometers and able to accommodate world's largest vessels. Halifax harbour has always been an important military defence stronghold of the country through the history. All these have given the province the power and pride.

Micmac natives had resided in the Nova Scotia region long before the Europeans arrived. The first Europeans that touched or skirted the shores of Nova Scotia were the Norsemen, whose adventure happened about the 10th or 11th century. In 1497, explorer John Cabot came to this land and claimed Cape Breton Island for England. Then in 1534, Jacques Cartier came and claimed the region for France. However, the first permanent European settlement here was established by the French who founded Port Royal in the Annapolis Basin in 1605. This settlement was the first permanent European agriculture settlement in today's Canada. In 1621, King James I, the Scottish king, granted this land to Sir William Alexander and called it Nova Scotia, a Latin name for New Scotland. The name Nova Scotia has stuck and become the name of the province today.

In 1632, three hundred French sent by the Company of New France reinforced the small Port Royal Settlement and they were joined by another small group of Frenchmen later on. The early settlers of Port Royal became the ancestors of the Acadians in this region. During the following years, both the French and the British had made claims to this land. British and French monarchs issued charters to grant this region to their own people. Those charters were often overlapping the territories of this region. This had created the condition for conflicts. For the following century, Nova Scotia became the fierce battle ground in the fighting for continental dominance between Britain and France. The region of Nova Scotia had changed hands many times during this period of time. Even after the Utrecht Treaty in 1713 when France ceded Acadia including Nova Scotia to Britain, the fight between the British and the French continued in Nova Scotia. The French built the mighty fortress of Louisbourg on Cape Breton Island, determined to fight against the British control. In spite of the deportation, the French population increased. To offset the power of Louisbourg, the British established Halifax on the Atlantic coast of the peninsula in 1749 to be the trade and fishery centre. In the second half of the 18th century, the British finally captured Louisbourg. After this war, Britain gained the whole Canada in the peace treaty.

After the establishment of Halifax, the population of English-speaking settlers started increasing substantially. In order to effectively gain Nova Scotia, Britain encouraged the New Englanders to immigrate here. Beginning in 1760, about 8,000 New Englander came. During and after the American Revolution War, about 35,000 refugees, Loyalists, disbanded soldiers came and settled in Nova Scotia. They had doubled the population of this region then. The following years saw many more immigrants coming from British Isles and some other European countries. Some black people came to Nova Scotia with the New Englanders and the Loyalists. Some Jamaicans arrived here in 1796. Many of the blacks left by 1800, but some stayed. The large influx of English-speaking settlers and immigrants had offset the early French and English population ratio. Today, the Acadians barely reach ten per cent of the province population.

In the war that had lasted for many years, very few Nova Scotians took active part on either side. Among the Loyalists, there were many professionals and former office-holders. Because of their loyalty, they considered themselves entitled to the privileged positions in their new homeland. This had created the conflict between the old and the new settlers, which lasted a generation. Starting from 1810s, the Nova Scotians had their own leaders secretly to govern the province. In 1848, after a lot of struggles and noises without bloodshed, Nova Scotia was the first province to gain responsible government in the British Empire overseas. In 1867, it was one of the first four provinces to join the Canadian Confederation. Today, Nova Scotia is a rather well-off province among the Maritime Provinces. Its industry and economy are better diversified. With the support of some government and public funding and subsidies, some of the private manufacturing businesses such as Michelin Tire, Volvo and Litton Industries are well known in the country. However, there are also notable failures of large subsidized industries such as the Glace Bay Heavy Water Plant and the Sydney Steel Company.

Government or public funding and subsidizing to businesses are a common practice to promote industrial and economic developments of the country. This practice is not only used to help the development of the poor provinces, but also to support the industries of the rich provinces. Though there are quite some success stories coming out of this kind of arrangements, some failures are sometimes catching the eyes of the public. After the country's free trade agreement with the United States has been carried out, this practice has been under scrutiny. The problem however is that some businesses, especially the businesses in some poor provinces do need this kind of support to survive and to gradually grow. Even with quite some incentives, Nova Scotia has not attracted more large industries or businesses. Though the province's industry and economy have a lead position among the Maritime Provinces, it is still lagging behind the central and western provinces. In recent years, the finding of oil and gas off the coast of Atlantic Ocean has given hope to the province for further development.

The Nova Scotians are a proud people. Though the average income of the people here are only eighty percent of that of the people living in central or western areas of the country, they have managed to live a good life. Their capability and leading position in the east have provided the grounds for their pride. However, pride has often been the cause of both positive and negative effects. There is only a thin line between pride and arrogance. Sometimes, pride or arrogance can make people go too far on the wrong way to create bad outcome or even disaster for themselves. In the early days when Canada was a young new country, one of the premiers of this province had instigated to establish a Maritime Nation independent of Canada, because of the province failing to gain enough subsidies from the federal government. His suggestion had been quickly turned down by New Brunswick and Prince Edward Island. Nonetheless, this premier was largely supported and followed by the Nova Scotians. From early time on, the people in this province have had the hot-headed spirit of going it alone. Today, with the national and international situations becoming more complicated, Nova Scotians have probably become more clear-minded and cautious. In the social, economic, national defence or any other developments of today's world, even a country cannot entirely go it alone, let alone a province.

For Jim and Meilin, every one of their former trips to Nova Scotia had been confined to Halifax. Jim's elder brother Mark had lived almost his entire life in that city. Jim, when young, had gone to Halifax a few times with his father and Dexter to visit Mark. After he got married, he had taken his wife Meilin to Halifax twice to visit Mark and his family and to attend Mark's wedding of his second marriage. Halifax was thus another familiar city to the couple in the east of the country.

Halifax is the largest city not only in Nova Scotia but also of all the Maritime Provinces. Of course, compared with the largest cities in Canada, Halifax can only be considered as a large city on the second level. The largest cities in Canada are Toronto, Montreal and Vancouver. With the development of petroleum industry, Calgary today is quickly catching up and gaining the largest city status. However, the country's power is concentrated in the power triangle of Toronto, Ottawa and Montreal. Besides being the largest eastern city, Halifax is also an important industrial city and seaport. Canada has three major important seaports; Montreal Port is the central one dealing with the central national and international waterway transportations, Vancouver Port is the western one dealing with the national western and Pacific waterway transportations, and Halifax Port is the eastern one dealing with the national eastern and Atlantic waterway transportations. Halifax's ice-free seaport is also an important supportive route for the central vein. Of course, there are more seaports of the country which have also carried out some of the waterway transportations. Ontario's ports and the Great Lake waterway transportations have been important business portals between Canada and the United States.

A coastal city, especially a city with a large seaport, will inevitably be involved with some big marine events. In 1912 when the famous Titanic sunk in the Atlantic Ocean nearby, Halifax became the last resting place for some of the people who had lost their lives in that disaster. The ill-fated Titanic has aroused so many people's imaginations through history; numerous books and films have been born from this shipwreck. However, the most striking and moving record of Titanic's demise is that seventy percent of women and children had survived this nautical disaster while only twenty percent of the able-bodied men escaped the doom. This statistic has given a very significant evidence of the chivalry and nobility of human nature. In a life and death crisis, human beings had saved the weak. This disastrous accident had happened a hundred years ago. At that time, were human beings simpler, having more virtuous and noble qualities? Today, human beings seem to be smarter, but more neurotic and selfish. One can only hope, but not be sure, that if a disaster of the same scale as that of the Titanic happens today, the same kind of human self-sacrificing noble spirit will still shine through.

Besides the Titanic, Halifax had seen another big disaster which was also related to the nautical activities. In 1917, Halifax had lost about 2,000 of their residents from a large explosion in their harbour. A French WWI ammunition ship collided with a steamer, causing a fire and then the ammunition ship was blown to pieces, heaving the steamer to the shore and leveling the whole north end of Halifax. It is quite lucky that the city has still some historical sites and buildings preserved after such a powerful explosion.

Halifax, above all, is known for its military significance. It has been an important naval base through history. After the British gained supremacy in Canada in 1763, Halifax served as the Atlantic Headquarters of the Royal Army and Navy. During the World War I and World War II, Halifax became a life-line to the war-torn Europe. Canada, though a country with a small population, had contributed largely to different wars in the world against aggressions and for peace. During World War I, Canada had sent 625,000 men and women to the war. More than 60,000 of them died in this war and many others were permanently disabled. At this period of time, Canada had a population of only eight million. During the World War II, Canada had about one million men and women in the military services national and overseas. About 40,000 were killed in this war. At this period of time, Canada's population was 11.5 million. Besides the lives of men and women, Canada had contributed large quantities of supplies of all sorts during the two World Wars. During the World War II, a massive Allied Convoy had formed in the Bedford Basin Harbour. From this harbour, the Royal Canadian Navy escorted thousands of cargo ships full of munitions, food and other vital war materials to Britain.

War is the most cruel and destructive measure used by human beings to kill and destroy each other. Through human history, wars have been the everlasting nightmares accompanying human life. After the First World War, the world heaved a relieving breath, thinking that the human race had finally ended wars and from then on the world would be bathing in peace. But not long, the Second World War started in an even larger scale. When this war was finished, people rejoiced again, thinking that this must be the last war and peace would surely dwell in the world from then on. No such luck. After the Second World War, different types of wars in the world had never stopped.

From this kind of historical experiences, human beings no longer dare to dream about world peace again. Almost every country has been in constant alert, preparing for wars. Today, the modern science and technology have pushed the arms and weaponry to such a height that they can destroy and wipe out the whole world civilization in a very short time. Now when people anticipate or think of the inevitable Third World War involving nuclear weapons, they will worry about the survival of the whole human race. Where or what is the human race heading to? Nobody can see clearly. Many have racked their brains to think of ways to prevent wars. But with numerous causes that can lead to wars, prevention will never be easy. One thing however is sure that the main root of all evils is greed, greed for possessions, wealth, power, control and satisfying all kinds of human desires. The worst characteristic of greed is that its appetite can be insatiable. It looks that as long as some people can gain and profit from wars, the bloody wars will continue; they will happen and continue until the whole human race is wiped out from the face of the earth or the whole earth is destroyed and impossible for human habitation. If greed can be rooted out of human nature, world peace can probably be achieved. Yet, greed is part of human nature. Rooting out of greed from human nature will probably be even harder than preventing wars. The human race has thus struggled in this miserable dilemma for millenniums.

For Jim and Meilin, the ordinary people, who had mostly concerned about their ordinary daily life, the important military features of Halifax did not have much weight on their minds. Still, they had been quite attracted by the Halifax Citadel, a historical military site in this city. Halifax Citadel had been built and rebuilt quite a few times through history and it was fully finished in 1856 to protect the city and the harbour.

Citadels are important military defensive structures in the old days. Halifax Citadel is a large fortress. Nova Scotia has quite some historical sites, but Halifax Citadel is the most favoured spot of the visitors. It is a large star-shaped fortress built on top of a hill. The whole structure is sunk into the earth, and therefore it is hidden from the view. From any angle of the city, it can only be seen as just a hill standing off the coast and looking over the city. The citadel has one gate. The inside walls are built by large timbers and mortar. All along the walls, there are well-built wooden rooms. Among the rooms, there is a large wooden building which had been used as the headquarters of the fortress. The whole structure looks very strong; the large timbered walls and buildings seem to be able to last forever. The outside walls are the thick earth. Essentially, the whole hill top is the citadel. With all those buildings inside, there is still sufficient land in the centre. One can imagine, during the war in the old days, people and even their livestock might have come in here for protection. There were storage of food and a well for water. The soldiers could go up to the wall where there was an earth path all around, shooting the enemies trying to get up to the hill. The cannons of the citadel could reach and protect the harbour.

Today, the citadel's gate is open daily to visitors in warm seasons. The large building inside has been turned into a museum. There is daily noon gun shooting and other costumed enactment to entertain the visitors. Jim and Meilin had visited this fortress twice. Each time, after going through the inside, they would mount on the earth path on the wall to have a view of the city. Halifax, being the capital city of Nova Scotia, had quite some tall buildings in the downtown area by the coast. From Citadel Hill, they could see not only the business and office towers, but also the harbour and the different sides of the city. Halifax's landmark building was also on the hill but a little lower than the citadel. It was the Tower Clock. The tower was commissioned by Prince Edward of Kent, Halifax's commander in chief during 1794-1800. It was built by red bricks and square-shaped with large clocks on four sides. The steeple top had shown its traditional European style. From all directions, the city people could see the hours on the clocks. The Tower Clock was built for the purpose that people would not tarry and would set about diligently their daily business in their endeavours. Halifax was indeed larger than Saint

John, New Brunswick. Being a manufacturing center of Nova Scotia, it had its oil refineries, ship-building yards, rope factories, textile plants, steel and metal works and so on. Its harbour was a working harbour, busy with exporting trade of fish, fish products, lumbers and apples.

Besides the Halifax Citadel, Nova Scotia has more than a hundred historical sites. The most important one is the Port Royal National Historical Site. The original settlement of Port Royal had been destroyed. The present Port Royal is rebuilt to its original state. The early settlement of Port Royal had started quite a few firsts. It had grown the first crop of cereal in Canada and built the first water-powered mill in North America. It had established the first North America recorded social club called "Order of the Good Cheer". It produced Canada's first European play. The wood structures of the settlement were built by interlocking wood beams without a single nail, the early 17th century French architecture. The place was protected by a palisade and a cannon platform.

Then there are the Louisbourg ruins which are also important marks left by history. Nova Scotia is a province full of history and worthy of visitors' time and efforts. Halifax also has its historical sites, buildings, nice museums and galleries. But on this trip, Jim and Meilin were going to skip Halifax and other places in Nova Scotia. Mark, after his first wife passed away, had moved away from Halifax with his second wife. They were now residing in Walton, a small coastal place in Nova Scotia. After Jim got the information about his two brothers' health conditions, the couple had set their minds on visiting them. They had seen Dexter and felt that he was not going to die immediately. Now they were going to see Mark, hoping that his condition would also not be too serious.

Mark was Jacob's first-born with his first wife. At about six or seven years old, Mark's mother died. The death of a mother was very traumatic to a small child. Mark resented his father for his mother's death; he became sulky and moody, estranged psychologically from his father. Mark was a beautiful child with a head of curly hair and light chocolate skin. But being half coloured meant that he was going to have a very difficult life in the first half of the 20th century. From the start, he was never accepted by other children or adults in the neighbourhood. He attended school for a few days and was called by other child white-nigger, beaten and kicked around. He quit school immediately and never went back again. When Jacob got married again and had more children with his second wife, Mark was being neglected. The first child felt deeply hurt, being abandoned by his father and disliked or hated by all other people around him. Born with a strong character, his resentment to his father and his step siblings increased and his anger towards other children and people around him heated up. To fight back, the only way he knew was to act up and to make troubles. People were cruel to him; he returned cruelty to them. When the neighbours came to complain about Mark and the police took the mischievous boy to the door, Jacob's only way to punish and teach Mark was to give him good beatings. The beatings had only turned Mark's resentment into hatred towards his father.

When Jim and Dexter were growing up, they worshiped their big brother, the trouble-maker. No matter how hard Mark pushed them away, they followed him like two puppy dogs and would do anything he told them to do. Things got worse with Mark when he was a teenager. While the society repelled the mongrel, the bad crowd took him in. From then on, Mark with his cohort went into more serious troubles. The police could no longer handle him. Knowing that his father was no help, the police gave Mark the ultimatum, "Leave New Brunswick and never come back!"

Mark fled to Nova Scotia and went to Halifax. It was a scary situation, being a teenager in a strange city alone and homeless. Mark survived. What did not kill him had made him stronger. With the progressing of his age, the dark pigmentation on his skin faded and he looked more and more like full white. In Halifax, nobody knew his history, family background or racial origin. Mark left his past behind and started a new life. Without any education, he could only find some odd labouring jobs. He made a minimum living for himself. The white labouring class in Halifax accepted him as one of them. From then on, Mark identified himself with the white, renouncing or forgetting his half-coloured origin. His life became less troublesome. Though illiterate, he learnt things by doing them and went through many types of low-level jobs. Born smart and with a strong character, he soon learnt quite some surviving tricks. By listening to people, he got to know the affairs of the city and the country. He learnt to talk eloquently about some politics, things people concerned and most of all about different vehicles. He could sweet talk to people to endear himself to them. There was an inner strength in him that compelled people to respect him. Deep down at heart, he kept a distance from the people around him to prevent himself from being hurt. Life became cold calculations of how to manipulate and use others to serve his needs. People are normally attracted by strong persons. They like to stick around the strong, try to please them and willingly to be manipulated or used by them. Mark thrived in making friends.

When Mark was nearly thirty years old, he met Ethel, a widow much older than him. Ethel had three children. Her elder boy and girl were older enough to leave home and start on their own. She lived with her youngest daughter Carol, still a small girl. They had a tiny house. Ethel and her small girl took Mark in and gave him a home and an instant family. In the beginning, it was all a cold calculation of Mark to have a free home with everything taken care of. With time passing, Ethel and Carol's love softened him. He forgot his original plan and started being a true husband to Ethel and a loving father to Carol. It was a very moderate home and family, but Mark was satisfied. He became a good family man.

Deep down in Mark's heart, there were still feelings for his father and the want of his father's approval. After he was totally settled with Ethel and Carol, he contacted his father and told him that he had formed a family in Halifax. He wanted to show to his father that he had come out alright and was doing better than his two stepbrothers. Jacob was overjoyed. So many years without hearing anything from Mark, he had finally had his prodigal son back to him. As Mark would not go back to New Brunswick to visit the family, he took Jim and Dexter to visit Mark and his family in Halifax. Mark only wanted to let his father know that he came out better than his brothers and had no heart to treat his father and brothers in his tiny home. But Ethel was a very hospitable woman. She treated the father-in-law and brothers-in-law with the best she could afford. Jacob loved the beautiful small granddaughter from the first sight and his heart was melted by her sweetly calling him grandpa. Mark's father and brothers all thought that he was married and Carol was his daughter. From then on, when Jacob missed his granddaughter, he would take Jim or Dexter to visit Mark and his family. He knew his son well and would joke, "Let's go to Halifax to agitate Mark."

When Jim and Meilin were going to be married, they invited Jim's siblings and some other relatives to their wedding. Dexter came and was Jim's best man. Judith and her mother came to attend the wedding. Jim's sister sent a gift. Mark did not even send a card. Meilin ignored Mark's cold attitude towards the marriage. Jim was not offended; he was habitually loyal to his elder brother no matter what he did to him. After the wedding, the couple soon went to live and work in the west. When they came to the east for a visit, they went to Halifax to see Mark. That was the first time that Meilin had seen Mark and his family. As usual, Mark received his stepbrother with displeasure. Ethel however cooked some simple but delicious meals for the brother-in-law and his wife. Meilin was quite struck by Mark. He had a tall and strong figure and a handsome and almost dignified face. From Mark's appearance and talks, nobody would think that he was illiterate. Though Mark talked sweetly to Meilin, she could sense that there was a cold hard core in him that was hostile and discriminatory towards her. Sure enough, when Meilin turned her back, Mark talked to his brother, telling him that if their father were alive, it would not be so easy for him to marry a Chinese woman. Mark's transformation to a full white man was thorough; he even took some white racist traits of prejudice against the coloured people. After the first visit, Mark did more things, trying to do harm to his brother's marriage. Meilin was a sharp woman. She could see that Mark's hostility towards the marriage of Jim and her was not only out of racial prejudice, but also out of jealousy. He had heard that the Chinese woman his brother had married was well educated, the marriage was going well and his brother was living a good life. He was quite jealous that his stepbrother was doing better than him after all.

On the couple's first visit, Jim and Meilin stayed with Mark and his family for two days. In the two days, Meilin got to know that Mark was a strong and very complicated character with a messed-up and distorted psyche. Obviously, he had the magnetic power to attract the people around him. His tiny home was constantly visited by some friends. He talked eloquently with them. There was not much emotion in his talks. He talked evenly and calmly, having no intention to interest others or to show off himself. Yet the calm evenness made his talks convincing and even authoritative. It was indeed amazing to see a man without any education having such great ability to control and power over others.

In the second half of the 20th century, the situation of racial discrimination was changing to the better. The social status of coloured people, especially the black people, had risen. Mark skillfully rode the wind of time and was benefited by the changes. He could finally put his black mother's picture in his tiny living room and tell people that his mother, when alive, was a nurse. Now, instead of being discriminated, he received respect and admiration.

When Mark was nearly sixty, fate struck again; he had to face a crisis that seemed worse than the ones he had faced when he was growing up. Ethel was approaching seventy with a very serious heart condition. Mark had to consider his own future. He got close to Danna, Ethel's closest old friend. Danna was a long time widow, a little younger than Ethel and in better health condition. Danna had a widow's pension, a little Canada pension and an old age pension. She was financially secure. There was no love at lease on Mark's part. It was all out of his cold calculation. If

Mark had any true feelings for others, they were mainly for Ethel and Carol. When Ethel found out the closeness between Mark and Danna, she felt deeply hurt. She had a small pension and Mark had a small unstable annual income. For thirty years, she lived a very thrift life, saving every penny and even Christmas wrapping paper to make the home a safe and comfortable haven for Mark. Now Mark betrayed her. The pains she felt were simply unbearable. Mark tried to explain that there was nothing going on between him and Danna, but Ethel would not listen. After thirty years, she got to know Mark well and would not believe him. There was a brawl and Ethel threatened to throw Mark out. The fight brought back the miserable memories of Mark's childhood. He deeply regretted that he had let Ethel and Carol get close to his heart and now he had to suffer the hurts again. He was getting old; homeless no longer meant adventure but doom to him. The old fury and hatred came back to his heart. This time they were directed to Ethel and Carol.

Ethel could not stand the fierce fight and died suddenly from her heart condition. Mark manipulated Carol to stand on his side and help him to fend people's suspicion that he had caused Ethel's death. Carol loved and listened to Mark even better than she did to her own husband. Of course, she did everything to protect Mark. After things settled down and Mark got the tiny property and the little savings, he cut Carol out of his life completely. Carol wanted only the old clock of her mother's; he would not even give her that. The complete severing of the tie with Mark was quite painful for Carol, but she had finally got to know Mark.

Jim occasionally called his brothers to check how they were doing. Through the phone call in 1999, the couple were shocked to know that Ethel died about six months ago and Mark was going to marry Danna. In the phone conversation Mark told Jim the date of his wedding and hinted that he would like his brothers to attend his wedding. Jim and Meilin were living in the west of the country. They had to run thousands miles to go to Halifax. Meilin was against the trip. She suggested that they could send a card which was already better than how Mark had treated their wedding. Jim however habitually wanted to please his elder brother and wanted to take the trip. To satisfy Jim's wish, Meilin compromised. The couple took the occasion to travel through the United States. After touring a few American cities, they went to New Brunswick and picked up Dexter to go to Halifax. The three arrived two days before Mark's wedding. When they came to the door of Mark's home, Mark would not open the door to them. After a long time knocking, Danna came and opened the door. Mark's cold reception to his brothers and sister-in-law was shocking. The following day and the wedding day were equally unpleasant for Jim and Meilin. Mark would not treat his brothers and sister-in-law with a cup of water. On his wedding ceremony he openly showed that his family were nothing to him. He was sitting with his friends and some important church persons on the honored seats on a stage; his family were with the audience quite some distance away. Most of those on the stage looked indifferent to the honored seats. Meilin was shocked and did not know what to think of Mark's behaviour. Jim must have made a mistake that Mark wished him to attend his wedding.

The wedding was held in a church. There were quite some church people attending, but not a single wedding gift was given. As usual, Mark's family went along and tried their best to please him and to show that his family were supportive of this marriage. If Mark did wish his brothers to attend his wedding, he probably only wanted them to appear in front of the church people for this brief moment to show their support. To his friends, he had always shown that his family had mistreated him and were nothing to him. Meilin did not know the full story of the family, but she herself had immediately being discriminated and mistreated by Mark just because she had married Jim. She had not been in Mark's life at all, but received Mark's hostility. She wondered how Mark would tell his friends that his Chinese sister-in-law had mistreated him. After Jim's father died, Jim seldom saw Mark. In their 25 years marriage, Jim and Meilin visited Mark three times. They had met such vile attitudes from Mark each time they went to see him.

From Mark's talks and behaviours during the wedding days, Jim and Meilin could see that Mark was holding tremendous hostilities and animosities towards Ethel, his wife for thirty years. It was the first time that he had told that he and Ethel were never married and Carol was not his daughter. Jim and Meilin could hardly believe what they had heard. However Mark could not list anything to show how bad Ethel had treated him. Half-veiled, Mark expressed that Ethel had greatly offended him by disobeying him to treat his father and his stepbrothers too well.

Mark was quite affectionate to Danna, claiming that after Ethel's death, he wanted to commit suicide; it was Danna who had saved him. His words showed no feelings for Ethel, impossible for Jim and Meilin to believe that he would kill himself because of Ethel's death. They could see that Mark's sweet words were only to please Danna. However, the couple soon saw that his affection for Danna was all a surface show. Mark had long habitually trusted the loyalty of his brothers. He knew that no matter how badly he treated them, they would be faithful to him, love him and try to please him, and therefore, he normally showed his true self to his brothers. When Danna turned her back, he told Jim that Danna was eight years older than himself, hinting that she would surely die before him. Again Jim and Meilin were shocked to see that his new marriage was totally out of cold calculation and there was no love on his part at all.

After Mark's wedding, Meilin told Jim that she would never go to visit Mark again. Jim agreed that they would never see Mark again. Right now, knowing that Mark was dying, Jim's love for his brother took over; he forgave all the hurts and harms Mark had hurled on him, wanting to see how he was doing. Meilin felt that she could not refuse Jim's wish; they were still brothers after all. Even after all the shocks at Mark's insane behaviours, his cold vile manipulative person and his outrageous hostile treatments to his family, she could still understand that Mark's traumatic childhood, his up-bringing, the social environment and social condition had made him the person he was. She agreed that they were going to see Mark the last time.

The couple were now driving in Nova Scotia to see Mark and Danna. The comfortable highway drive was going to end soon when the couple had to turn onto a side road to reach Walton where Mark and his wife were living now. From the map, Walton looked sitting at the shore of Cobequid Bay. When they reached the turnoff to the side road, the couple saw a red truck sitting on the shoulder of the turning point. This kind of scenes was now looking ridiculous and laughable. They knew that they had been followed by the harassers along the way, and they also knew that their destination was known and some preparations had been made by the harassers and waiting for them ahead. This red truck looked very likely to be one of those preparations. However, instead of feeling that they had been called red or broken-down, they felt that the red truck served as a direction mark for them to turn to the correct road to reach Walton.

Soon the couple were on a small country road leading to Walton. Their driving nightmare started very soon after they were on this road. The road was narrow, but passable by two vehicles. Though paved, the surface of the road was full of potholes, large and small, deep and shallow. Driving on this road was like performing an acrobatic stunt, twisting and turning at every second to avoid the holes. Even with years' military driving experience, Jim could not handle this road well. The couple were now like sitting on a shaky rollercoaster and their old bones were on the verge of being shaken apart. Having driven through numerous small roads and even some gravel roads, the couple felt that this was the worst they had seen.

It was very strenuous to drive on the pothole-ridden road. Soon Jim was tired out, still the road looked endless. Sparsely, there were some houses along the road. Trees and bushes were small; they must have been affected by the coastal weather. The fields looked wild with weeds and grass only. At home, when the couple got to know that Mark and his new wife had moved to Walton, they had imagined that Walton must be a beautiful place by the ocean. Their imagination might be triggered by the book, Walden, written by Thoreau. The writer had built a hermitage in a country place called Walden and lived there for over two years. The idealistic solitude life and the beautiful country scenes described by Thoreau had the name Walden permanently connected to natural beauty, peace and simple life. The name Walton was so close to the name of Walden. The couple could not help thinking that it must be a place as beautiful as or even more so than Walden, as it was by the Atlantic coast.

Mark had lived almost all his life in Halifax. He and Ethel had that tiny house there. The house had no back or front yard, only a small piece of paved driveway. Jim and Meilin felt glad that Mark had finally realized his dream to live a worry-free peaceful life in the country. From Mark's description over the phone, the couple knew that he now had a house on a piece of land. The couple thought that his acreage at the coastal area must be an ideal place for him to spend the rest of his life. They were curious, hoping to see how the place looked like. After knowing that Mark's present medical condition, the couple had mixed feelings. It looked that Mark had finally achieved his goal, but his time left was limited. The information about Mark's present condition had caused their decision to visit Mark and his wife. Now they ended up on this terrible road. They wondered how Mark with his heart condition could handle this road.

Living in the country, people will have fresh air, beautiful and spacious surroundings and a more peaceful life, but they normally will not have the convenience of getting their groceries, having timely medical attentions and enjoying more social and recreational activities. Mark was in his sixties and his wife was in her seventies. They could do without the social activities, but they definitely needed their groceries and medical cares.

After a long while driving on the terrible road, Meilin felt that her heart could not stand the bouncing and jerking much longer. She cried out, "How long is this darn road going to last? My heart is going to give out and our trailer is going to be shattered to pieces!"

"It shouldn't be very far now. From the map, the distance is not far," said Jim, trying to comfort Meilin, but he looked to have also come to the end of his endurance limit.

Finally, the couple came to an area where there were some large trees by the roadside. And they also saw some street or road signs. They felt a great relief. During this long distant difficult drive, they had only come across two other travellers. They could not stop others to ask for direction. Now when they saw a house appearing by the road side, they stopped their van and trailer. A rest was very much needed, and they could ask the property owner for some information.

The couple got out of their van and stretched their legs first. They walked a little bit around to relax their muscles and nerves. While they were resting, a middle–aged man came out from the house and walked towards them. In a country place where there were not many strangers around, a couple with a van and a trailer stopping by the road were bound to arouse some curiosity. Seeing the man walking up, Jim went to meet him. He asked the man whether the place was called Walton and where he could locate Mark Duhine.

The man smiled and said, "Well, you are in the right place. Mark's house is the third one ahead by the left side of the road."

Jim and Meilin were overjoyed in hearing this. They thanked the man and went back to their vehicles. They started driving immediately, thinking that Mark's house was just a short distance ahead. But it turned out to be quite a way to reach the third house. Walton looked like a small residential community. There was no store around and the houses had each quite some land and were quite some distance apart from each other. When Jim and Meilin came to the third house, they stopped on the road. It was safer to make sure that Mark lived in this house before they started to pull their vehicles in.

Jim got out of the van to go to the house to check. Half way on the gravel road towards the house, Mark came out of the house. Like the other homeowner, Mark watched and saw that his property was being approached; he came out to check. Jim and Meilin were both surprised and glad to see that Mark was home. They were worried that he might still be in the hospital, and they had planned to go to the hospital afterwards. Mark was unhappy to see Jim and Meilin, but he directed Jim to pull their vehicles in and park them at the back of his house.

After the vehicles had been parked, the greetings began. The couple were stunned to see that Mark was now a totally changed man. He was like a coat-hanger with clothes hanging on and could be blown away by the wind at any moment. He looked very gaunt and weak, and his hair had turned snow white. He wore a black eye-pouch over one of his eyes. There might be some pirate's character in him; the black eye-pouch suited him and gave him a little spirit, otherwise he would look like a very weak sick old man.

Jim and Meilin were sad to see Mark in such a poor physical condition. Mark had always been a strong man. His built had come from his life-long labouring work. The best and the last of his jobs was working in a used auto-parts place, a junkyard where all kinds of used vehicles were packed in and people could go there to pick some parts which were still usable. Mark got injured by moving the heavy auto-parts around when he was near his retirement year. After quite some efforts, he got a disability pension from Canada Pension Plan. Now he must also have the old age pension. His financial situation was finally safe and secure, but it looked that his health was failing fast.

Though looking very displeased, Mark shakily arranged to have the newly arrivers to have their trailer connected to the house electric power. In order not to bother Mark too much, the couple did not do anything else, but went into the house, so Mark could go in to sit down. Danna looked in better condition, though she had also been in the hospital not long ago and had a large kidney stone removed. Mark had just been released from hospital and he had not had a heart surgery. The doctors said that his coronary arteries had been blocked too massively and they could do nothing for him. He was sent home with medications to live as long as he could. As for his eye-pouch, one of his eyes was very sensitive and he felt more comfortable by putting the eye-pouch on. His eye problem might be caused by the blockage or burst of some blood vessels in his eye. After several heart attacks, there were not many whole parts left in his body.

The house Mark and Danna had now was a comfortable bungalow. There were two bedrooms, a bathroom and a large kitchen with a dining area and a large sitting room all on the main floor. The basement was smaller, as part of the main floor was added on. Mark proudly announced that he had people add the whole dining and sitting room area after they had bought the property. With the kitchen, dining room and sitting room all in one, the inside was of a modern open design which looked spacious and comfortable.

The chat between the four was not long as it was already passed noon and Jim and Meilin had not had their lunch yet. Mark invited his brother and sister-in-law to use their water and the bathroom, but did not offer a cup of drinking water. The couple went out to stabilize their trailer and cook up their lunch in the trailer. After lunch and some rest, Jim and Meilin took their towels and clean clothes and went back to the house to have a shower. While they were having their showers by turn, Mark and Danna were having their nap. After the shower, the couple went out to have a look at the acreage.

The place was not situated by the ocean at all. There was no view of the ocean. For a little over two acres, Mark seemed to have cleaned more land than he owned. His house was sitting in the center of a large piece of cleanly mowed land. There was one big elm tree in front and on one side of the house. The house had a big deck in front and an extended walkway hugging a whole side of the house to reach the back door. The deck looked new. It must also be built after Mark had bought the property. Besides the house, there was a double garage sitting a distance away from the house and two vehicles parked outside of the garage. From the house, the public road could be seen and the neighbour's house across the road was also in view. On three other sides over the property, there were thick woods. The trees were not big and there were plenty of bushes. The neighbours on two sides had been blocked off by the trees and bushes, but the neighbour at the back had put a small trailer at the edge of the woods, taking advantage of the open space of Mark's property. The whole place looked green and peaceful; it would be ideal for Mark and Danna to live a peaceful life, if they were young or in their middle ages. Jim and Meilin knew how dear and precious this acreage must be to Mark after all the struggles he had gone through. They could understand how Mark would feel when looking at this piece of spacious land and his comfortable home all owned by him now.

Having checked Mark's property, the couple went back to their trailer to have a little nap. The bad road had taken up all their energy and strength; they needed badly to lie down for a while. The questions of how Mark and his wife were handling the road and other necessities for living here had to wait until all were rested.

While the couple were having their nap in their trailer beds, a very strange thing happened. Jim soon went to sleep and started snoring. Meilin too went to sleep or was in a half sleep mode. She was suddenly wide awake by a strong feeling. Clearly she felt a presence in their trailer. She immediately and instinctively pinpointed that the presence was the soul or the spirit of Mark. It was a dark force with strength and a push, totally different from the sick weak old physical Mark. Meilin was very much startled and puzzled. She could not understand why she had immediately thought that Mark's soul was here. Looking at Jim, she saw that he was fast asleep and snoring away. Obviously he did not feel a thing.

While the sleepiness had totally gone from Meilin, the feeling of the strange dark presence had also gone without a trace. Meilin lay there with her mind full of thoughts, trying to solve the puzzle. She was certain that she was not dreaming about it; some strange thing had indeed happened here a moment ago. She was also certain that she was not imagining this thing. Meilin was not a superstitious person and, to a large degree, she was on the modern science bandwagon. Many people would swear that they had seen ghosts and quite some psychics had claimed that they could not only see the dead people, but also communicate with them. Meilin had never seen a ghost or a spirit before and certainly had no power or ability to communicate with any of them. However, a personal experience at her early age had made her keep the possibility of the existence of souls or spirits in her mind or thinking. In that experience, she felt distinctively that her own soul had left her body for a brief period of twenty minutes or so. The pure soul experience was so profoundly calm and peaceful that she would never forget it. Unfortunately, she had never had the same experience again in her later life.

Whether there are souls or spirits has been a question thought and discussed about ever since human beings could think. In fact, this question is only a branch from the large question of whether the world is fundamentally spiritual or material. People have argued, debated and even fought with each other for their views and beliefs on this matter. In ancient times when the majority people were tending towards the spiritual side, the religious people had beaten down and even persecuted the minorities who had held the views of materialism. Today majority people have turned towards the material side. The new breed of people has prided themselves to be advanced and scientific, and they look down upon, sneer at and despise the people with spiritual views. Things have always been like what Voltaire said, "Our wretched species is so made that those who walk on the beaten path always throw stones at those who teach a new path." The only difference is that the beaten path changes with the changes of time.

However, there is one thing that all people seem to agree. It is that the world consists of the seen part and the unseen part. With the development of science and technology, many discoveries have been made in both the seen and the unseen parts. In the year of 2012, the scientists are pretty sure that they have made a very significant discovery in the unseen part of the world; they have discovered a subatomic particle which is a decisive part in the making of the galaxies, planets and the living beings. This discovery is indeed a profound one which will shake the world outlook of many people and especially the religious people or people who held spiritual views of the world. However, whether this discovery will be the last fatal blow to religion or it will actually bring religion close to science and provide the much needed scientific explanations for religious beliefs, people have to wait and see.

This significant discovery has caused worldwide attentions. Almost every country has made it the important news to broadcast over their TV screens and other media methods. As this subatomic particle is considered as the decisive part in creation, people have called it "God Particle". Scientists however have called it antimatter or Higgs boson. The name Higgs boson comes from the fact that the existence of this particle was suggested by a British scientist named Peter Higgs in 1960. Higgs, the physicist, had a theory: the universe is bathed in an invisible field like a magnetic field; every particle feels this field, but the effect and result of different particles get is different; if a particle can move through the field with little or no interaction, there will be no drag and the particle will have little or no mass; but if a particle interacts with the field, it will have a higher mass. This theoretic field is now called Higgs field. Higgs field is understood as a medium which exit everywhere and it is made up of unseen particles called bosons. This is how the name Higgs boson comes into being. The heavy particles gain mass by interacting with Higgs bosons.

Now the scientists claim that they have found Higgs boson. This means that they have found the source of how the universe comes into being. If this discovery is absolutely true, human beings have almost got it all on the knowledge of both seen and unseen parts of the universe. Nonetheless, even with this significant discovery, we still have to put the big question aside for a while, as it is too big to resolve and to get a definite answer that everybody will agree. Let's come to the old question whether there are souls and spirits. Since so many people through the human history have felt or even seen something concerning this matter, we cannot simply dismiss it entirely. We cannot say that all these numerous people are lying or hallucinating. Anyway, we can imagine and innovatively conjecture just like the scientists. Suppose we do have souls or spirits which are composed of the finest particles. Those particles move through Higgs field without gaining mass until they have come across suitable conditions. Under those suitable conditions, they merge with heavier particles to gain mass; this means the soul particles combined with particles of biomaterial nature to form embryos, and thus human beings come into existence with spirits and bodies. At the death of the human beings, the souls or the spirits, being the lightest particles, will separate from the material bodies and enter the Higgs field to meet another suitable condition again.

Some souls may have gone too deeply with their material bodies into lives. Those lives have left strong imprints on them. Even after the bodies have perished, those souls have carried the imprints or identities of those lives. This type of souls can become the stuff formed by slightly heavier particles than those of normal souls. They can remain in places familiar to them even after their material bodies have gone. If some souls have gained enough strength by life's imprints to gain their own identities, they may even be able to take some actions of their own, independent of their live bodies. A few human beings with a deeper inner sight may indeed be able to feel and see this kind of souls or spirits.

Of course, these are pure imaginations or conjectures. But to think of it, almost all discoveries through human history have been started first by imaginations and conjectures. Scientists' imaginations and conjectures are mainly based on reasons and scientific theories. Ordinary people's imaginations and conjectures are mainly based on feelings and wishes. Nonetheless, all imaginations and conjectures have the potential or possibility to be proved as fallacy or truth. What's more important is that people who have open and flexible minds and who can courageously imagine and conjecture will live a much richer life. The progress of the world, the civilization, the human society and human life normally benefit from those people with open flexible minds, who are able to imagine and conjecture. On the other hand, people who have closed and inflexible minds and who strictly walk on the beaten path normally live a dull life. The actions of this type of people can sometimes interfere or even delay different progresses.

Imaginations and conjectures have always been needed to improve the world and human life. They are the indispensible force in the developments of all aspects of human world in different times. But even with continued important and significant findings, there are still many things in the world and the universe, which are unknown and unexplained by human beings. It is far too early yet for human beings to claim that they have known it all, if there is even a time or possibility for them to make such a claim.

Right now in this ordinary couple's small trailer, when Jim was awake from his nap, Meilin told what she had just felt or experienced a moment ago.

"We should invite Mark to our trailer to have a look when he got up," said Meilin at the end of her talk.

Jim was an open minded man. He had no doubt that Meilin had experienced some strange phenomenon which involved Mark's soul; he readily agreed with Meilin's suggestion. The couple then went to the house. Mark and Danna were both in the sitting room. The four continued their chat first. From Mark's appearance, Jim and Meilin felt that his physical condition was very poor. He was like an oil lamp with the oil almost all dried up and the flame was going to be extinguished very soon. But from Mark's talk, they felt that there was still some life left in him. He could still talk eloquently, though weakly. Meilin could see that if Mark had some education and some wealth backing him up, he would have made some sort of a leader, good or bad, he could go either way.

During the chat, Mark asked Jim and Meilin, "How are you doing in the west?"

Before the couple could answer, Mark remarked, "From Quebec on, the places are not so good. The west is the worst, gone to the devils. If you leave your vehicles outside, next morning the four wheels will be gone."

Jim and Meilin were surprised by Mark's comment. They looked at Mark and saw that he was not joking. He looked serious and spoke with authority. The couple smiled at each other and wondered what other horror stories the Nova Scotians were telling each other about other parts of the country. However, they could understand why the Nova Scotians did this; they were trying to do what they could to keep their people in their province, even if they had to resort to making up some stories about those rich brats of the central and western provinces.

"It's not that bad in the west. We are doing okay," said Jim.

Mark then talked about how the good premier of Nova Scotia was working on creating jobs for the people here. His voice was weak, but he kept his talk with a calm tone. Then, for some reason, the conversation went to some strange things of the world.

Mark said, "You would not believe if I told you what I had seen..."

He was going to elaborate, but then he checked himself and only talked about his seeing Jesus. He raised his right arm with its palm forward and said, "Jesus looked at me with this gesture."

Obviously, the gesture was a warning sign meaning "no" or "forbidden".

Jim and Meilin were puzzled. They wondered if Mark had really seen some images; his vision of Jesus seemed very much related to his Christian belief. The suspicion came back to Meilin that Mark's soul might be able to act independently of his body and his spirit might be able to see more than his physical eyes. When the chat came to the end, Jim invited both Mark and Danna to have a look at their trailer which was new and in newest style. Danna turned down the invitation and Mark came out to have a look. In the trailer, Mark gave some praising words about the design of the trailer, but did not show much interest. Could it be that Mark had already seen the inside of the trailer?

When the four resumed their chat in the sitting room again, Mark got visitors. Jim and Meilin were quite surprised. They had been worried that at their age, Mark and Danna would be lonely and have more difficulties living in the country. Now it was just like in the city where Mark had never lacked visitors. The couple did not expect that in such a remote place, Mark would still have visitors. The newcomers were a man and a woman in their late thirties or early forties. They were husband and wife. It turned out that the man was Mark's so called adopted son, Eddy. In fact, Mark had never raised Eddy. In Halifax, Mark's tiny home was Eddy's refuge. Whenever Eddy fought with his wife or his wife drove him out of their home, he would come to Mark and Ethel to pour out his pains and sufferings. As the fights between Eddy and his wife were often and Eddy's presence in Mark's home was frequent, Mark and Ethel jokingly called him their son. Now Eddy and his wife were living not far from Mark in this country place. Jim and Meilin did not ask whether it was Mark first moved here or Eddy came first. Anyway, this must be a great help to Mark and his wife. Eddy could come to check on Mark and Danna, chat with them and offer some help. Jim and Meilin were glad to see this arrangement, and especially when they got to know that Mark had totally falling off with Carol.

Eddy's wife looked a sharp woman, but it looked that their relationship was okay now. As soon as Eddy and his wife came, Mark took Eddy outside to see the new tractor mower. Jim and Meilin followed. The new mover was still in the wooden crates on the deck, waiting for Eddy to open it. Mark, though without education, had a laptop computer and could order things on line. He had bought the tractor mower on line and had it delivered to his country home. Mark could no longer mow the lawn. He paid for others and especially Eddy to do this job for him. As for grocery shopping and visiting doctors, he and Danna had to depend on others as well. There was a woman in the neighbourhood, who charged a small fee in driving people to and from the nearest small city, Windsor, which was about forty kilometers away from Walton. Mark said that the road to Windsor was not as bad as the road Jim and Meilin took to come in. Truro was another city which was about sixty kilometers away from Walton. It was located by the highway. From the skirt of Truro, Jim and Meilin turned into the small road to reach Walton. It looked that they had driven on that horrible small road for about sixty kilometers to come here. Mark and Danna normally went to Windsor for shopping and visiting doctors. After Eddy and his wife left, Mark started complaining that it was hard to get help from Eddy now; for days he would not come to see and take the crates off the new tractor mower.

Next day, Jim and Meilin booked the ferry tickets by phone to go to Newfoundland. They had to use Mark's credit-card and pay him the money. The couple did not have a credit-card. Years ago, they did have one of those cards. Before they started to use the card, somebody else had used it ahead of them in another province. They got a bill from mail for the charge to their card. Furious, they cancelled the credit-card and never got another one again. Now when traveling for long distance, a credit-card seemed a necessity sometimes. They could not book a ferry ticket over the phone without it and they were told that they could not buy tickets at the ferry office.

The ferry would take off two days later. It would start from North Sydney Port, Nova Scotia and arrive at Port aux Basques, Newfoundland. It would take about six hours to cross the Gulf of St Lawrence to reach Newfoundland. For the return navigation, the couple chose to take off from Port Argentia which was near Saint John's, the capital city of Newfoundland. For the return journey, the ferry would be ploughing the Atlantic Ocean for fourteen hours. The fees for such a long distance ocean ferry were surprisingly low. With the return ticket, it was over three hundred dollars for each person and their vehicles.

The second day after they arrived at Walton, the couple stayed with Mark and Danna, watching Mark taking lit cigarettes from Danna to have a few puffs. He claimed that he did not inhale; only played with it. Mark, a life-long smoker, had quit smoking because of his serious heart condition. It looked that the quitting was not that absolute. Then Eddy came again to chat. After Mark's complaint about Eddy, Jim and Meilin were suspicious that Eddy might come to keep an eye on Mark's guests. The second day of the couple's stay was not peaceful. The neighbour across the road had started his bulldozer in the morning. He moved earth around his property near the public road all day long. The loud roaring of the iron beast shattered the peaceful surroundings, turning the serene country place into an industrial site. Jim and Meilin knew that this might be the harassment prepared here especially for them. For all the noise attacks they had received along the way, they had anticipated this kind of happenings; it was not a surprise to them. But the disturbance had very much agitated them.

It might be that the noise had driven the three men out of the house. They went to the back of the acreage to check the vehicles and the garage. To many ordinary Canadian men, the most interesting things to talk or discuss about were their vehicles. Mark had two old vehicles; one was a van and the other was an eight cylinder old car in mint condition. Mark talked proudly of the old car, "It rides smoothly like the Rolls-Royce. You won't feel a thing!"

Also to escape the noise, Meilin went to their trailer where the impact of the noise from the powerful machine was smaller. She watched the three men from the trailer. Mark was all hunched up and looked going to collapse at any moment. It was a marvel that he would be out of bed and around the cars, talking with interest.

In the evening when the neighbour's bulldozer had finally stopped, the chat started in the living room again. Mark brought out two small gulf balls in a fancy box which looked brand new. He took out the gulf balls to show Jim and Meilin how big the kidney stones taken out of Danna were. Mark was not a gulf player. The couple wondered why Mark would especially buy those gulf balls; to show others the size of his wife's kidney stones or to celebrate that his wife would go before him. Danna was not Ethel. She would not cook for Mark, let alone cooking for any guests. Over the phone, she told Jim that his two brothers were dying. Probably she believed or wanted to believe that Mark was surely going to die before her. Right now Mark and Danna, both of strong characters, were like two sick old birds, each waiting to see the other drop first.

Then when Meilin went to the bathroom, Mark shoveled the gulf balls to Jim, saying, "Here, you keep them."

Mark would not treat his brother with a cup of water after many years without seeing him, but he would like to show that he was looking after Jim's interest, wishing that his wife would get some diseases and croak before him. Jim knew what his brother meant, but he pretended not knowing and refused the offer, "I don't play gulf. I have no need of them."

Mark would not listen and pushed the balls to him. Not wanting to offend Mark, Jim took the balls.

Two years later, Mark won; his second wife died, and he kept on living. When Jim and Meilin got the news, they were utterly stunned. On this last visit, they thought that the days left for Mark were very limited and they even doubted that he could see next year. Miraculously, Mark had stayed on. He had beaten two wives in the race of living, lasting longer and covering more distance. This might be mainly the result of his strong will to live. The oil had already dried up, but the flame had been kept on burning by sheer will-power.

Is there a scientific explanation for will or will-power? This invisible force belongs to spiritual sphere and has been used freely by humans since they existed. Christianity says that God allow humans to have free will; Buddhism advises people not to use their will as it will make them cling to or exert their self or their ego, which should be dismissed as an illusion. Anyhow, the humans have used this force freely and it has helped them to create numerous miracles. With their strong will-power, they have conquered not only some incurable diseases, but also some insurmountable difficulties in different battles. However, any good thing will have its negative side. Using will or will-power is of no exception. From the beginning of human history, the stronger human beings have forced and exerted their will over the weak to gain advantages for themselves and to do harms to others. On the other hand, the weak, when sticking to their will-power, have sometimes conquered the strong. When it comes to this invisible spiritual force, there is no telling what amazing result it can bring.

After Danna died, Jim kept on calling Mark to check how he was doing. Mark kept on giving positive information about his health. He had gained weight, and from the computer he could get any Asian woman in some Asian country to come to live with him and take care of him. Mark was now being taken care of by Danna's niece, a woman in her fifties. Jim stopped calling Mark afterwards. He had finally fed up with Mark's slighting his wife and trying to drive a wedge between them. In spite of his habitual loyalty to his brother, Jim would not change his love for and loyalty to his wife. He knew well that Mark was really trying to do harm to him. Besides, he could well sense that Mark was paranoid to mistake his concerns for him as his wanting something from him.

Three years later after Danna's death; the couple got the calls from Jim's sister and Dexter that Mark had died suddenly. Mark's funeral was held in a church in Cape Breton where Danna was born and he was buried beside Danna in a cemetery there. The couple had arranged to send a wreath to Mark's funeral. Mark's sister and younger attended the funeral. The noisy neighbour with the bulldozer claimed that he was the executor of Mark's will; he hired a lawyer for himself and would not open Mark's will to his siblings or anybody else. Mark's belongings of any value and his credit card all disappeared after his death. There was an autopsy made on Mark's body. But his family had received neither the autopsy result nor the copy of his will. Mark's death remained a mystery to his family and his property seemed vanished into thin air.

After Danna's death, Mark had first celebrated his winning, but not long he realized that his own death was approaching. He had struggled hard to gain what he had, but when he had finally gained it all, he could no longer enjoy any of his gains. He tried to spend it all in the last few years, but he could hardly eat. He bought a new four-wheel-drive vehicle, but he could no longer drive. He had spent his life, a hard and difficult life, in building his castle, but now he could see that his castle was a sandcastle built on the beach, the cruel relentless tide of time was going to lick his castle and himself away and the water had already come to the base of the foundation.

Looking back at his own life honestly, he had finally realized that he had been mean towards his family. He worried about how he was going to face God's judgement and how to face his father. He had promised his father on his deathbed that he would look after Dexter. He never did anything to help Dexter, but kept on his resentment and hostilities towards his siblings. Perhaps there was still time to redeem himself. He decided to make some amends. He packed up some of his clothes and other things in his vehicle. He was going to give them to Dexter. The niece would drive him to Saint John, New Brunswick. It would be the first time for him to go back to New Brunswick after so many years of being exiled from that province. After this decision and preparation, Mark died suddenly the next morning. He never made it back to New Brunswick or to make some amends to his siblings.

Mark's small property might be highly valued in the eyes of Mark and his Walton neighbours, but it was pitiful in the eyes of Jim and Meilin. Even if Mark had built a castle there, the couple would not think it twice because of the horrible road to reach it. But the strange behaviours of the self-claimed executor had very much agitated them and aroused quite some suspicions in their minds about the circumstances around Mark's death. However, the agitations and suspicions were soon blown over in their minds and they went back to their own life. Mark was dead. All the bad unpleasant things they had experienced from him were forgiven and soon to be forgotten. The thoughts about Mark and his life would also leave their minds soon. They could see that, after all, Mark was mainly a victim of racism and victims of racism were many.

But right now, the couple were finishing their last visit to Mark when he was still alive. Early next morning, Jim and Meilin said goodbye to Mark and Danna. Mark was glad to see them leave. The couple were aware that though they had stayed in their own trailer, to some extent, they had still bothered Mark and Danna. For one thing, the loud noises from the neighbour's bulldozer might be caused by their arrival. With the serious heart problem, if Mark's hearing was not bad, the noises could have been too much for him to bear.

The couple pulled their trailer out of the acreage. There was only one public road around. To go further on, they would reach Windsor. But they had to take the road they came in to go to Truro, as they had to go back to the highway to reach North Sydney and another scenic place they had planned to go. Cape Breton Highland is a national park and the largest park in Nova Scotia. The Cabot Trail around that park is famous, claimed to be one of the best scenic places in North America. The trail goes along on the side of the mountain range. On one side of the trail, there is the ocean. The breathtaking views along the trail have long been favored by the travellers. Many people have said that the scenery would remind them of the beautiful Scotland; that is if they have seen Scotland. Jim and Meilin had planned at home that they were going to go through the Cabot Trail to see the beautiful scenery. Now they had a day and a night to do so. They would drive through the trail and camp in the Cape Breton Highland National Park for the night. Next day they would go to North Sydney to catch the ferry. The ship would start off at about 9:00 PM. They would have plenty of time for everything.

At this moment, they had first to drive through this terrible road again to reach the highway. The return drive through this small road proved to be even more difficult. Besides the potholes, the road had been littered with dead porcupines. When they drove in the day before yesterday, they did not see any dead porcupines on the road. Now there were so many dead porcupines on the road. Suspicions naturally popped up in the couple's minds.

"How come so many dead porcupines on the road suddenly!?" said Meilin, feeling very much alarmed and irritated.

"Probably, this is their mating season," said Jim, As usual, he tried to explain things off.

"How come their mating season in the middle of the summer!?" Meilin did not believe and continued angrily, "It will take an army to go through this road in one day to kill so many porcupines, but we have hardly seen any other vehicles on this road. This must be the doings of the harassers again. Now they are saying that we are the porcupines and will be killed. If they ask me, I'll tell them that they are the jackasses doing the biddings of the jackals! They don't think that if the porcupines and all the small creatures are gone, the jackals will eventually swallow up the jackasses!"

It was one thing when the harassment, the attacks and the abuses were done to the couple. But when the misled people started to abuse and even kill small animals in order to put up stupid malicious shows to threaten the couple, it was quite a different matter. This kind of behaviours was even harder for the couple to ignore and forgive. Those small animals had never bothered them and they did not deserve to die just for those jackasses and jackals to vent their hostilities and hatred towards the couple. The situation of the couple had best shown the strong forcing their will over the weak. Some people with power considered the people living in the lower level of the society and especially the coloured people were lesser human beings who did not deserve a good life as they did and had no rights to think and express themselves. With their power, they thought that they had all the freedom and rights to harass, oppress, abuse and persecute some of those weak and less fortunate people.

It took a lot of efforts for Jim to maneuver the van on the road. He tried hard to avoid running over those poor dead porcupines. In so doing, their van and trailer had to go more through the holes. The bouncing and jerking became violent. Meilin thought that not only their trailer, but their van was also going to be shattered. Perhaps the couple had been protected all along their way. This time too, they had miraculously survived this horrible road. They had been worried that if their vehicles broken down on this road, they might be unable to get out easily. All the time while they were struggling on this road, they did not meet any other traveller. Finally they came out. When they spotted the end of the small road, they broke out a long sigh followed by a laugh, feeling that they had conquered a monster.

After the couple got out of the small road, they were utterly exhausted. They pulled their vehicles to the first gas station they saw by the highway. They needed a rest and their van needed gas. Jim parked their vehicles in the gas station without going to the gas bar. The couple got out of their van. They had to walk around to relax their nerves and muscles first. While they walked around the small gas station, they noticed that the wheel on the driver's side of their van looked low in air.

Jim said, "I did not run over any porcupine. The tire should not be punctured."

The couple rested for a while. Then they gassed up their van and pumped air into all the tires. After everything done, they were on their way again. Driving on the smooth highway was indeed a joy after coming out of the nightmarish drive on that small road. Nova Scotia's highway was in good condition, better than some parts of the highway in Ontario. The traffic was light. When the vehicle was running down a rather high mountain, they had the soaring feeling, absolutely relaxed and free. On this sunny day and out of the nerve-racking small road, Jim and Meilin felt like in heaven now. When they were on the higher parts of the highway, the views were spectacular. Though the mountains here could not compare with the Rocky Mountains for magnificence, they were picturesque as water-colour paintings. The different heights and sizes of the mountains showed different shades of greens and blues because of their different distances from the highway.

The couple's enjoyment on the highway did not last long. Jim felt there was something wrong with the van. He pulled the vehicles to the shoulder of the highway. The couple went down to check. They found the wheel on the driver's side was much lower now. There was no doubt that this tire was punctured. They had two ways to fix this problem. One was to change it with the emergency tire which was smaller than the normal tires. The other was to pump it up with air and drive until they came across an auto shop. They took the second option and pumped up the tire with their hand-pump and continued to drive. The couple had to repeat this air-pumping operation three times before they came to the skirt of a small city.

The place must be a city, as there was a Canadian Tire by the highway. Canadian Tire is a large retail corporation with many branches in Canada. Its first store was established in Hamilton, Ontario in 1922. Today, it has 479 stores across Canada and employs more than 58,000 Canadians. Canadian Tire stores sell largely automotive parts, accessories and services. In addition to these, they also sell home, sports and leisure products. Every Canadian Tire store has an auto parts and repair shop. The prices for repairing works on vehicles of Canadian Tires are normally fair. Jim and Meilin usually went to Canadian Tire for the maintenance and repairs of their vehicles. Now when they saw a Canadian Tire by the highway, they felt that they were saved and their problem was already solved. They pulled their vehicles to the parking lot of the store. The parking lot was empty, which was a bit strange. When they got out of their van to check the store, they saw the door closed. Then it hit them that the day must be Sunday and most of the businesses were closed on Sundays in Nova Scotia.

There was no way that the couple could drive further without the tire being repaired. They had to wait here until tomorrow. Their plan to drive through the beautiful Cabot Trail was blown. In a long distance travel, unexpected situations could happen and they would not bother the travellers too much when they had convenient access to have the problems solved. The couple soon settled down to wait until the punctured tire was repaired. This Canadian Tire store was located on a higher ground. They would have a broad view of this part of Nova Scotia. Only the city proper seemed a little distance away from the highway. They could not drag the trailer with a busted tire to explore it.

When the couple saw some serviceman around the store, they went up to ask for permission to camp on their parking lot for the night. They explained the situation and got the answer that there was no problem for them to stay overnight. After this settled, they even went into the store and got some water. The rest of the day and night were peaceful and relaxing. The tire seemed getting worse. They found the hole and put some chewed-gum on it, trying to stop the air leaking, but it was no use. Then they jacked up the van and kept the pressure away from the flat tire. The couple had a nice sleep on the parking lot this night. The air was cool and fresh. The traffic on the highway was light and almost stopped at about nine.

Next morning, as soon as the door of the store was open, the couple got in. They were the first to be served. While the technician was repairing their tire, they watched not far away. Soon the technician got to the bottom of the problem. He pulled out a nail of four inches long from the tire and was puzzled. Normally, when a vehicle ran over a long nail, the nail would not go all straight in; a part might be bent. Besides, a four inch long nail would not lie on the road with its point sticking straight up. The couple saw what was going on. They were not puzzled, but suspicious. It was less likely that they had run over this nail, but more likely that the nail had been punched into the tire by somebody. It gave them a chill to think that they had driven through that small road full of holes and dead porcupines with a nail in their tire. They could have very well been marooned in that wild countryside. They felt very lucky. As the nail was straight in, it had stopped the air leaking out too swiftly. Nothing more serious had happened. They were safe and sound, waiting for the incident to be a past ordeal.

The repair work on their tire was done in a short time. When the couple went to pay the fee, they were told that there was no charge for tire repairs in Nova Scotia. This was totally unexpected. Nova Scotia was the only province that showed this kind generosity towards the drivers and travellers. The couple were quite grateful. They thanked the store people not only for the tire repair but also for letting them to stay on their parking lot overnight. When the couple were driving away, their feelings were mixed. For such a good deed of the province, it took a hard way for them to find out.

All the way on their trip, they had met numerous Canadians who were kind and helpful to strange travellers. But all the way, the couple had also received harassment, attacks and even attempts on their lives. They knew that those harassment and attacks had been instigated or organized by some bad people who had some power; otherwise it would be impossible for the harassment and attacks to follow them all through the country and for so many people to carry out those bad things. At the start of their trip, the fleet of yellow school buses with the words "lynch" had already warned, threatened or foretold what would be waiting for them on their way. Some people might wonder why this kind of things would happen to an ordinary couple in a peaceful country like Canada.

The couple had offended some powerful people who wanted them either being killed or living a life in hell. They had no way and no power to stop the persecution on them. The couple's offence was simple; they had pointed out some bad services to the military veterans. In so doing, they had interfered or interrupted some large companies or corporations from gaining profits by providing those services. The couple had never had any wish or ambition to fight with some companies or corporations. They knew the Goliath's power and they were no David. They had only tried to protect themselves from being run over, as Jim's pension, their livelihood, was at stake. However, their fight for themselves seemed to have done some damages to or offended some large companies or persons with power. The government had allotted funds to take care of the disabled veterans. Private companies could bid for the contracts to provide those services. Jim and Meilin's pointing out some of the bad services might have contributed to causing some companies either to lose the opportunities of obtaining those contracts or to lose the contracts they had already had. Or the couple might have accidentally interfered some large power struggles between some forces unknown to them.

When money is involved, there will be war. First, the couple, the big mouth piece, had to be stopped and put down. The process started with some local people in Abbotsford being used to frame the couple. It seemed to them that the best way to beat the couple down was to find something to accuse the man as a sex-offender; then anything the couple had said would be discredited. What had happened to the couple when the framing or persecution process started was hellish. They could not take a walk around their neighbourhood without some people setting some children onto them and hiding in some vehicles with cameras ready to take pictures if they had even talked to those children. When this trick failed, the small children were sent to the couple's door. The persecutors used any chance they could find. When Jim was alone in their trailer to sort out something, children would be sent to lurk around. Of course, nothing worked for the persecutors. The couple were upright law-abiding citizens and crimes had no opportunity to stick to them. Other extreme measures had also been used. The couple's garbage bins had been searched. Probably, Jim's hair had been collected from the garbage bin for the use of framing him for sex-offence or even murder. Their home had been broken into and searched numerous times while they were not home.

After the framing work set up by the persecutors had failed, the rumours and slanders about the couple started. By this time, the couple had totally lost their privacy. Whatever they had talked about and done at their own home were open to the public. This seemed to have worked to the couple's advantage. Now everybody could see by themselves what kind persons the couple were. Meilin started to write about what had happened to them, hoping that when the public knew the truth, all those travesties and injustices to them would cease. No such luck for the couple. They were ordinary folks at the bottom of the society and had no power to influence the public. The harassment and persecution to the couple lasted for years. Even after the government had changed the policy and no companies could monopolize those profitable contracts anymore, the hatred towards the small couple did not go away, but increased.

Meilin's writings were not refrained from criticisms and especially criticisms on the problems of racial discrimination. This had offended more people. To quite some white people, a Chinese woman's criticism on racism was an alien's outrageous attacks to the country. The couple then had totally lost peace and safety in their life. Wherever they went and whatever they did they would encounter harassment and attacks. Walking into a shopping store, they would get noise attacks or the shrieks in the microphones hinting that they were going to go down. Going to the doctor's office, they would receive different treatment or sinister shows put on by some people. Different arrangements or tricks had been pulled to make the doctors do harmful things to them. Their family doctor had refused to see them, when they refused to accept his push towards the wrong diagnose of some cancer. They had to go to different doctors. Any doctor they saw regularly afterwards would eventually be corrupted by the persecutors and turn foul towards the couple. Any medical facility they went, they would meet some hostile medical workers who would openly do something to endanger their health. They ran ever greater danger of being abused or even killed by going to the hospital emergency room. Their auto care went haywire. Bad things happened to their vehicle even under the care of some trusted auto shop. If they parked their vehicle in a quiet public place, it would be vandalized. The costs for the damages done to their vehicle by either the mechanics or the vandals were soon mounted up. The bank, the post office and all other companies had started giving them altered or down-graded services. On the whole, the couple had lost their quality life, quality health care and quality auto care; they had simply lost safety and security.

In the later period of the war against the couple, the cause had been shifted to the hatred partially out of jealousy. Meilin's writings became popular and quite some people read them over the computer. She worked at home and had no wish to publicize her writing before they were finished, but people got into her computer and read ahead. The publicity of her writing had greatly offended some people who had power, wealth, popularity and any other good things the society could provide. To them, a Chinese woman gaining popularity should not be allowed and especially when she was criticizing the society. The indignations and hatred towards the Chinese woman turned quite some people crazy. They tried to use any possible way to beat her down. Of course, in order to beat her down, they had to beat her husband down as well. With power, those people aroused hostilities and hatred from ordinary people towards the couple. Of course they had also to use the weapon of patriotism. The couple had exposed the bad side of the society and this seemed to have caused the country to lose face. They turned the war against the small couple as the war to protect the country from the couple. In fact, their true motives were to protect their own personal power and positions above the lower ordinary people, especially the coloured people. No matter in what sphere, intelligence or otherwise, those lower people should not be allowed to get on top of them, as that would damage their images of authority, prestige, respectability and any other socially considered higher qualities.

Of all kinds of tricks being pulled on the couple, the most effective one was still racism. Once the white folks were misled to believe that this Chinese woman was trying to put down the white race, quite some white people, upper or lower classes and even the white beggars, jumped in to join the attacks. Of course, this kind of public awareness of the situation could not be possible without the distorted and ill-purposed information fed or hinted by the powerful modern communication tool – the television. Ever since the problem started and the couple lost their privacy, some side shows on TV stations were in combat position to destroy the couple. All kinds of insinuations and masquerading shows had been put on to slander, to degrade and to smash the couple to pieces.

It made one wonder why a knife for butchering the ox would be used to kill the chicken. The couple were small and ordinary. Why would so many efforts have been put on to destroy them? To think it carefully, the problem could be pinpointed to racism again. The Chinese woman daring to criticize the white and the society was like a declaration of war against the white race. In such a frame of mind, some people were determined that no efforts should be spared in putting her down; otherwise the yellow race would jump on top of the white race. Very easily, the attacks to the Chinese woman turned to the attacks to the yellow race and the red communist. Meilin came from China. With her criticisms, she was surely a red communist in quite some people's eyes. All kinds masquerading shows on TV started promoting delicious ways to kill and eat up the yellow red.

Every little hint of the attacks on the couple or on the yellow race by the masquerading shows on TV had been duly noticed and absorbed by the public. By putting on those racist shows, the TV had achieved what the Ku Klux Klan could not dream of. Consequently, the couple were encountering more and more people in their daily life, who would put on some racist shows full of hostilities and hatred to attack them. What had made their hearts ache more was to see quite some children following the adults to be some little bigots.

However, the basest trick in this case had yet to be the one that used the coloured people to harass and attack the couple. In this way, no complaint of racism would be believed. One would not see the coloured people in this country sticking to some sense of superiority of their coloured race and rising up to protect this fantasy. To them, the priority of their life in this white predominated country was to survive. If some people with power told them to harass or attack this interracial couple, of course they would obey and do it for their own survival or even some benefits.

The living and working conditions of the coloured people in Canada today is much better than that in the first half of the 20th century. The coloured people have much more opportunities to participate as members of the society. Obviously the situation of racial discrimination has improved considerably. Still, the equality between the whites and the coloured are far from fully achieved. If one asks the white people, most of them will say that Canada has no more racial discrimination problem. If one asks the coloured people, most of them will say that racial discrimination is still a problem of this country. Most white people have not fully accepted the general population of coloured people as equal citizens and most of them will not even admit this fact. As for Meilin, a Chinese woman from China, her view about this issue was clearly on the side of most coloured people. This view was entirely from her life experiences. Having lived in Canada for twenty-six years, she knew the lives of the coloured people here better than a white; she herself had never felt being fully accepted as a citizen, let alone an equal citizen. Jim, her white husband, would also have the same view as that of most coloured people. His marriage to a Chinese woman had rendered sufficient life experiences for him to say that racism was still a problem in Canada.

Many years ago, Mark Twain said, "There are laws to protect the freedom of the press's speech, but none that are worth anything to protect the people from the press." Things did not change much in the present. The law fully protects the TV's freedom of speech, but there was nothing worth much to protect the people like Jim and Meilin from the TV. The TV stations had a few coloured staff. They considered that they had shown sufficient race equality among their own employees and enough to cover some racist side shows on TV. Those people with racist views or orientations had used this advantage to beat down the couple and the yellow race that were trying to raise their heads. In their eyes, the white race's supremacy and upper position in the society had to be protected by any means. The whole situation and what direction it was heading to had stunned the couple.

Ignorance breeds prejudice, prejudice breeds fanaticism and fanaticism breeds dangerous insane actions. The white race is indeed a peculiar race. For some illusory sense of superiority, many will act foolishly, ridiculously and even insanely. No wonder Lyndon B. Johnson, a former president of the United States once said, "If you can convince the lowest white man he's better than the best coloured man, he won't notice you're picking his pocket. Hell, give him somebody to look down on, and he'll empty his pockets for you."

Seeing that all their efforts to complain or explain about what had happened to them would not make any difference, the couple gave up. They were not the type that would martyr themselves for some illusory truth, justice or righting the wrongs. In spite of the circumstances, they tried to live and enjoy their life. If they could not save people from the sufferings of their hatred and jealousy, they could at least ignore them and save their own peace of mind. They would handle the problems when the problems coming pounding on their door. In the meantime, they would live their own life as they pleased, speaking and writing what they liked to speak and write.

Right now after the ordeal of the bad road and the punctured tire, the couple concentrated on their trip ahead. They decided to drive to the ferry in North Sydney right away. Though they still had a full day, they thought it was better to take time to drive there and get rested before they boarded the ferry.

Nova Scotia does not have a large territory, but the landscapes of the province are very much varied. Soon after the mountainous area, there is the lake area of Cape Breton Island which is entirely separated from the rest of the province by the narrow Strait of Canso. At the narrowest part, the strait is only 1.2 kilometers. The higher part of the island is the Cape Breton Highland where the national park is located. The lower part of Cape Breton has plenty of lakes and islands. The scenery appears also beautiful on Cape Breton Island. The Nova Scotians have used well their geographical variations to develop their recreational tourism. In winter, there are ski spots and in summer, there are camping, boating, hiking, fishing spots for visitors and locals.

In recent time, there is a significant feature coming into Nova Scotia's tourism. Bluenose, the famous large wooden sail-ship has been brought back from history to join the tourist services. Almost every Canadian knows the story of Bluenose which is a piece of important history of the country, one of the national symbols and proud heritage of the Maritimes, especially Nova Scotia.

Sailing is the oldest method used by human beings for waterway transportation. It can be traced to prehistoric time. For the recent few centuries up to the World War II, the industry of sailboat and sail-ship building had soared. For nautical navigation, sailboats had been developed into large sail-ships. People had used large wooden sail-ships for global trade, for fighting in battles and for fishing on the sea.

During the 19th and the first half of the 20th century, the Canadian wooden shipbuilding industry had developed fast in Maritimes and especially in Nova Scotia. In the early 20th century, Nova Scotians used oak, fir and pine to built large sail-ships called schooners. Each of the schooners could be one hundred feet long with huge sails. Normally, a schooner would have three masts which stood as high as a ten story building. For larger cargo schooners, there would even be six or seven masts. With the large sails, the schooners could navigate with high speed and because of their large size; the schooners were trustworthy in bad weathers on the ocean. The hulls of schooners were very large and could hold tons of fish or other goods. When the schooners sailed on the ocean, they looked elegantly beautiful and graceful. When they were anchored in the harbour, the Nova Scotians lovingly called them their grand bank ladies. Nova Scotians used the schooners mainly for fishing. The North Atlantic Ocean was quite turbulent. Even with large schooners, many fishermen had lost their lives in ocean storms.

In 1920, a US senator proposed and established an annual international schooner race to promote shipbuilding industry and fishery. Canada joined the race. In the first race, Canada lost to the US. Then Lunenburg, Nova Scotia built a schooner aiming at winning the race. They christened the schooner, Bluenose. For the next three years, Bluenose came out the first to win the race. The whole Canada went into a fever of pride brought by Bluenose. No higher praises could be expressed by the Canadians for their beloved Bluenose. Nova Scotia was the province that had the first post office of Canada in 1754. After the winnings, the post office had put the image of Bluenose on the early Canadian stamp. Then the Royal Canadian Mint had also used the image of Bluenose on the ten cents coin and 50 cents bill in those early years.

The other important thing of Bluenose's winning was that the Canadian nautical success was being recognized by the world. The reputation of the Canadian built schooner with high quality and high speed had quickly spread to Europe. The demand for Canadian built wooden ships came in from Britain and other European countries. This had pushed the wooden shipbuilding industry to a height the Maritimes had ever seen. The shipbuilding and exporting businesses had brought considerable wealth and prosperity to Nova Scotia. The province had experienced its golden time in this period of history.

Nothing remains the same forever. Towards the Second World War, the motor boats, the metal boats and the U boats had gradually made their debut. People's attentions had shifted to new gadgets. Bluenose's last win was in 1945. The atmosphere for this winning was greatly changed. Hardly any enthusiasm or attention was shown by the Canadians to Bluenose's last trophy. People's minds were entirely occupied by the war. With the time passing, Bluenose and other few famous schooners all could not escape the fate of being broken or swallowed up by the fierce ocean storms.

However, Bluenose has been immortalized in Canadian history and Canadian spirit. Its immortal status is not only coming from its images being stamped, coined and billed, but also from its having lived well in people's memories. Today, the Nova Scotians are nostalgic for the past glory; they have spent millions of dollars to rebuilt Bluenose which they have christened Bluenose II. Now Bluenose is reborn to serve the visitors, to refresh their memories and to pass a piece of history and heritage to later generations. People can have a look at the beautiful schooner to admire the excellent craftsmanship of wooden shipbuilding, to watch the grand bank lady with her beauty and glory, or even to sail on her to feel her quietly and gracefully gliding on the ocean. The past has long gone, but people still have ways to experience the past and to appreciate the efforts, the struggles, the sacrifices and the achievements the foregone people had gone through.

When Jim and Meilin were traveling through Nova Scotia, they did not have the information that Bluenose was being rebuilt and going to be in service for tourism. The idea of going to Lunenburg to pay a visit to Bluenose had never entered their minds. At this moment, their thoughts and attention had started shifting to Newfoundland. The drive to North Sydney turned out to be quite slow. The distance was not that far, but they had to wait for long intervals on the highway because of some road reconstruction. At the start of traveling through Cape Breton Island, there was a nice tourist centre just after they crossed the small bridge over the narrow Strait of Canso. The couple had taken a break there and got some information. A clerk in the centre told them that if they took the scenic route they could avoid delays by highway repair works. Probably the clerk had been mistaken or misinformed, as the couple's vehicles with a long line of other travellers' vehicles had waited for two or three hours on the scenic route for the highway reconstruction crews to clear the way. Luckily the couple had allotted plenty of time to catch their ferry. The delay did not make them sweat.

The couple reached North Sydney at noon. First, they had to gas up again and ask some information about the location of the ferry. While they were doing this, another customer, a middle-aged man, approached them and said, "You are going to the ferry? Follow me. I'm going there too."

Jim and Meilin thanked him. After the gassing-up was done, they followed the man's truck. The distance to the ferry was very short from the gas station; only two or three intersections along the way, but the intersections were connected with the highway, which made the route complicated. When they were near the ferry, the man stopped his truck. Jim stopped their van too. The man came out and talked to them. He said, "If your ship takes off later, you'd better go to wait at India Beach. There is not much parking space at the ferry for vehicles that have to wait for a long time."

It would be hours before Jim and Meilin would get on their ship. They thanked the man for the information, asked the direction to Indian Beach and headed there. The distance to Indian Beach was also short. The couple were glad to have come to this spot which was a historic site. The beach was large with partially sandy and partially green grassed areas. There were a building with a small restaurant and a covered platform on the beach. On the back wall of the platform, there were some round cabin windows. A wooden bulletin-board stood before the two structures, introducing briefly the history of Indian Beach and North Sydney. On the side of the beach that was connected to the mainland, there was a large sports ground on the green lawn.

The couple parked their vehicles on the side of the beach facing the ocean. After lunch, they checked around the place. The large beach reached into the harbour. On the left side of the beach, there was the ocean stretching to the horizon and on the right side and across the water, there was a long pier also reaching into the harbour. According to the illustration on the bulletin-board, Indian Beach in the ancient time was the summer fishing ground of the aboriginals. That was probably why it was called Indian Beach. In summer, the natives fished here with their tepees set up on the beach. In winter, they went to the mountain valley where their tepees were protected from cold wind. The construction of the pier was started in 1832 for shipping coals from this area. With the existence of the shipping pier, the European settlement started thriving around this area. By 1834, a railway about three miles long was built here to connect the pier with Sydney Mines. This three mile railway was the first railway in North America that had all iron rails.

The pier had gone through up and down times with the up and down industrial developments of the area. In 1902 when the Nova Scotia Steel and Coal Company was doing well, the 600 feet long pier could handle all sizes of vessels. Later on, the coals were no longer shipped from here and the long pier was dismantled. A large pier for shipping iron ore from Newfoundland was built somewhere else. When the steel plant was closed after the First World War, that pier was also dismantled afterwards. However, the European settlement stayed and developed into today's Sydney, a coastal city in Nova Scotia. The long pier stands in the harbour today is mainly for the ferry ships carrying people, vehicles and goods to and from Newfoundland.

Indian Beach had not been used by the natives as fishing ground for generations. For the recent few hundred years, the beach had seen great changes brought about by industrial development. First the long pier and railway had been built at the harbour. Large cargo ships carrying coals came and went day and night. After the coal shipping stopped here, the beach had been used by different military units. During the First World War, the US Navy used it as a seaplane base. In the Second World War, Indian Beach was known as the Boom Defence. Together with the Halifax Harbour, it was the assembling point for the convoys that protected the supporting shipments to Europe.

The couple walked around the large open beach. They could well imagine what this beach had gone through. For thousands of years, every summer, some natives would set up their tepees on the beach. Along the seashore, their boats made from tree barks, animal skins or hollowed-out tree trunks would be lined up. The racks made by tree branches for drying up the fish would not be far from the shore. Children would run around, laughing and shouting. Women would be busy cleaning up the fish caught by the men and hanging them up on the racks to dry. On the back of the beach, the hill was fully covered by large trees. Far away on the horizon of the ocean, nothing large had ever appeared. The dominant sounds around them were the wind, the pounding waves and the cheerful shrieking of the sea galls.

Then in the recent two hundred years or so, the beach had seen a totally different scene. The industrial hustle and bustle came. Large cargo ships with coals coming and going in the harbour. Temporary military accommodations had been set up on the beach. Wooden runways were built for the small planes. Large heavy military vehicles, equipment and supplies came and went constantly. The noises made by man and machines had over-powered the roar of the ocean. In weekends and holidays, men in uniforms would entertain themselves with some simple sports or games on the beach. In the evenings, the lights from the residential houses on the hill at the back of the beach would make the soldiers homesick.

Now, the old days were long gone. The beach seemed peaceful again, with only two small structures on and occasional ferry ships coming and going in the harbour. The sounds of nature dominated most of the time again. The main marks left by the long-gone past were on the beach ground. Being pounded and compacted by heavy military vehicles and equipments, the sand mixed with earth had formed a very hard surface. Large and small holes were everywhere on the ground. The only soft sandy part of the beach was along the shore. It took some efforts for Jim and Meilin to find a piece of relatively level ground to park their van and trailer.

The couple walked along the shore. Some transparent green pebbles caught their attention. Were they emeralds? How could it be? The gems would not be at the seashore. They started picking some of them up. When a few locals showed up by the shore, the couple asked them what the green pebbles were. The locals laughed and said that they were pieces from beer bottles. Some beer bottles had been smashed by some old military residents or locals here along the shore. Years later, the ocean waves had polished them into jewels.

After supper in the evening, the beach came to live. Many vehicles came. Some people started having a football game on the sports ground. Then the simple stage was occupied by the local musicians who were performing some folksongs accompanied by music. The audience, some staying in their vehicles and some sitting on their lawn chairs, enjoyed the performance. The beach and the ocean were matching up well with the peaceful and cheerful scene created by the humans. Would Indian Beach have this kind of human activities for many years to come? Or would it have to see the military men and equipments again soon? Who could tell? No prediction would be possible; people could only hope for peace.

Jim and Meilin enjoyed the music with other people. In the meantime, they saw a large ferry ship came into the harbour and pulled up to the pier. They knew that it must be their ferry. They left Indian Beach while all the activities were still going on. They had a ship to catch and could not be late for that.

When the couple arrived at the port, a line of vehicles had already formed, waiting to go to Newfoundland. The couple had to go to the ticket office first to get their tickets. When booking the tickets over the phone, they had only got a confirmation number. The port had a fair-sized building with a waiting area, washing rooms, an information booth and a food court. The ticket windows were two. When the couple got to the ticket window and presented their number, they were told that there was some mistake made and they had to pay over ninety dollars more for each ticket. Over the phone, Jim was asked whether he was a military veteran. With his affirmative answer, he got a discount price for the tickets. Was the discount off when it was known who the couple were? Though suspicious, the couple paid the additional charge. They still felt that the fees were not high, considering how long the ocean voyage would be.

The waiting to board the ship turned out to be long. The loading did not start at the scheduled time of 9:00 PM. People went to the waiting area when being informed the delay. It was more comfortable there; they could move around and read some sightseeing brochures. When the daylight had totally gone, a drizzle started. Many people came back to their vehicles in case the rain turned heavy. While they were waiting in their vehicles, the rain did turn heavy. The temperature dropped considerably. Between 10:00 to 11:00 PM, the loading finally began and the line of vehicles started moving.

CHAPTER ELEVEN

NEWFOUNDLAND AND LABRADOR

The ferry was as big as or bigger than a large cruise ship. On the main level, the large cargo hull would hold many motor vehicles ranged from small cars, trucks, RVs to large tractor- trailers. The ferry had two large gangways, one in front and another at the back of the ship. Now the back gangway was open and all the waiting vehicles started driving through to enter the hull. There were quite some lanes marked on the floor of the hull for the vehicles to be parked in lines. The main reason for Jim and Meilin to consider the ferry fees not high was that not only they themselves, but also their van and trailer would be shipped over the ocean.

The long line of the vehicles moved orderly into the large hull of the ship. Jim and Meilin noticed that some vehicles like their own came from other parts of the country; they had the license plates of British Columbia, Alberta, Ontario and so on. It looked that Newfoundland had attracted visitors from all over the country. The couple had also noticed that the large ferry was named after the first premier of Newfoundland - Joseph Joey Smallwood. It was quite appropriate that the ship connecting mainland Canada and Newfoundland Island should be named after Mr. Smallwood.

Newfoundland is the youngest province of the country; it joined Canada in 1949. For a long period of time before joining Canada, the main politics of this province was people's fighting or debating over the issue whether they should join Canada. Mr. Smallwood was the prominent politician in Newfoundland after World War II, who worked tirelessly to bring Newfoundland into the large Canadian family. He had used an old seaplane and a loudspeaker to talk to the Newfoundlanders who lived along the coast of the province. After Newfoundland became part of Canada, Mr. Smallwood was elected the premier of the province and he had remained in this position for over two decades.

Now all the passengers and their vehicles were going to be carried over the ocean to Newfoundland by Joseph Joey Smallwood. Quickly, all the vehicles had been parked orderly in lines in the large hull. People turned off their engines, got out of their vehicles and started going to their sleeper cabins or the large lounge. As the voyage was only six hours, Jim and Meilin had bought the tickets for the lounge which was on the top level of the ship. After leaving their van, they climbed long flights of stairs to reach the area. They were much slower climbers. When they had arrived at the lounge, other people had already been there and occupied the seats by the large windows. The ship looked brand new. The sitting area was beautifully designed and it looked like the large lounge of a cruise ship. The seats were mainly long sofas. People rolled up their jackets to make pillows and some had already stretched out on the sofas for a nice sleep.

There were plenty of sofas left in the centre area around some pillars. Jim and Meilin picked one around a pillar and made a pillow with their carry-on bag. They too were ready for some sleep. Before settling down, Jim went to other areas of the top level to have a look. The whole top level was indeed designed as that in a cruise ship. There were the souvenir shops in one area and a large food court in another. Everything looked brand new. After Jim came back to the lounge, the ship had already started sailing. There was no use to peek at the ocean or the sky. It was reaching midnight; from the large windows of the lounge, only darkness could be seen. Inside the lounge, the lights had been dimmed for the passengers to have a good sleep. Jim soon went to sleep on the sofa. Meilin however was soon in trouble.

Not long after the ship started sailing, Meilin started to feel the turbulence of the ocean. Though the ship was large, it was rocking up and down and every other way in a nauseating slow motion. It looked that the ship was sailing against the current or the ocean was not calm at all. She tried to endure it as best as she could at first. Then every minute turned out to be an unbearable torture. The whole lounge started spinning and her head and stomach went with it. She staggered to the washroom to throw up. The washroom was new and stylish, not a bad place for her to remain there for a long time.

Some years ago, the couple had taken a cruise ship to Mexico. On the return voyage, the ocean was quite violent. Meilin had suffered severe seasickness on that trip. She swore at that time that she would never be caught on an ocean-bound ship again. Now again she was on a ship over the ocean! Never say never. Very easily people can forget the past experiences or sufferings and do the same thing or go on the same road which can be perilous to them. In Meilin's case, it was a tiny personal thing which would not affect anybody else but herself. On the other hand, the whole human history with all kinds of human affairs is a very large matter. The absurdity is that the human beings have also gone the same circular ways. No matter what kind of miseries, disasters and destructions the human beings have experienced, nothing seems to be able to prevent them from doing some of the same things which will lead them to the same troubles, sufferings and misfortunes. History indeed repeats itself. Do people ever learn from history? They hardly do; they are quite forgetful. Time erodes their memories. Different generations have different experiences. The past experiences are easily ignored by the new generations that have not experienced them. What seems more significant or amazing is that human nature seems unchangeable. There will always be some human beings who are warlike trouble-makers; peace is not in their blood. For some immediate profits or gains, those people will push the world onto the same old road that the human beings seem to have always been travelling on. The human world seems never able to move forward but pendulum moves in the sphere of war and peace.

Staying in the washroom and vomiting had effectively concentrated Meilin's mind on her spinning head and uprising stomach. If there were some side-track thoughts, they were only about her forgetfulness of the bad past experiences and how she was going to survive the terrible ordeal now. There were definitely no thoughts about the world situation or human history in her mind at this moment. Sickness normally makes people concentrate their minds on their physical pains and sufferings. People will be amazed to find out how fast and well their minds can be narrowed down and focused, when they know that they have only a short time left to live.

Meilin struggled to calm down and to balance her head and other physical discomforts. After a long while, she felt a little better. When she staggered back to the lounge to try a little rest, she saw that Jim and almost all other passengers were fast asleep. She envied them who seemed not affected at all by the rocking, waddling and swaying of the ship. Meilin had to visit the washroom a few more times before the ship was finally approaching Port aux Basque in the morning. Jim woke up just before the ship was going to enter the port. Meilin felt a little relief that her ordeal would soon end. Jim and other passengers went to the food court to have breakfast. It was impossible for Meilin to do the same. Jim was worried about his wife, but he could do nothing more for her; she had already had the gingers and the pills for motion sickness.

Before the ship was fully docked, all the passengers had already been waiting in their vehicles, ready to leave. When the ship was firmly stabilized, the front gangway was open and people started driving out in an orderly fashion. It was indeed a great relief and joy for Meilin to finally sit in their van which was now moving smoothly away from the ship. She still felt weak and was not fully out of the seasickness. On their way out of the port, the couple saw an ambulance coming in. It looked that there was somebody who had suffered even worse than Meilin on this voyage.

When the port was behind them, Meilin told Jim that they had to find a spot to stop; she needed badly a rest on the firm ground to recover from her seasickness. Luckily, not far from the port, there was an information centre. Jim pulled the van and trailer into the parking lot of the centre. The couple rested in their van for a long time, Meilin had finally felt her head and stomach relatively settled down. It was early in the morning. The air was cool and very fresh. The couple looked around. Close to the harbour, there were some dark-coloured rocky mountains which gave a different sensation to the couple who had seen this island the first time.

After Meilin had finally had some food, the couple went into the information centre. The centre was a stylish modern building inside and out. The couple were quite surprised to see such a visitor centre in Newfoundland. All the information they had gotten so far about Newfoundland had preconditioned them to think that Newfoundland was a poor province and the man-made structures here would not be as good as those in the mainland Canada. Now the first building on the road they had seen was not only as good as but also surpassed some of the information centres in the mainland of the country.

Newfoundland is formed by two parts, Newfoundland Island and Labrador. Labrador is entirely separated from Newfoundland Island by the ocean and connected with the northern part of Quebec. In 1927, Labrador's border was defined and the territory was granted to Newfoundland. In 2001, this tenth province of the country was renamed as Newfoundland and Labrador. The recorded first white man who had found Newfoundland was John Cabot. He sailed to Newfoundland in 1497 and his voyage was commissioned by Henry VII of England. There is an entry in the Privy Purse of England dated August 10, 1497, which says, "to hym that found the new isle, 10 pounds." It looked that John Cabot had gained 10 pounds for his discovery of the island and the place had thus gotten its name, Newfoundland, newly found land. However, both Labrador and Newfoundland had been set foot on by some other Europeans much earlier than John Cabot. In the year 1000, the Vikings had come to Labrador and then Newfoundland from Greenland and Iceland. Because of the very harsh nature conditions, the Vikings stayed for a few years and then left, but they had left some markings of their life here in that early time.

John Cabot claimed Newfoundland for England. After exploring this area, he reported the good fishing grounds in this part of the Atlantic Ocean. His reports had brought European fishermen to Newfoundland. However, fishing was seasonal and permanent settlement seemed unnecessary in this early time. The English merchants also prohibited the fishermen to settle down on this island, because they were afraid that the population would cause the establishment of a local government which would interfere with their operation. In the mid 17th century, England was even persuaded to pass a law to prohibit settlement along the Newfoundland shore. Nonetheless, in the late 17th century, European settlement started in Newfoundland. The early-comers were employees of wealthy fish merchants from western England and southern Ireland. Not long, good fishing in this area had attracted some French fishermen who settled down on the Islands of St. Pierre and Miquelon. Later on, the French shore was set up for the French. Then some American fishermen came also and gained some landing rights here.

Of course, like other parts of Canada, Newfoundland had been inhabited by the aboriginals long before the European settlement. The early native residents here were Beothuks and Micmacs. Later on, the Beothuks had been forced into the interior of the land by the white settlers and the Micmacs. In the early 19th century, the Beothuks had been entirely wiped out.

In the early times, the only industry here in Newfoundland was fishing and sealing. The fish and seals were abundant which had brought prosperity and more immigrants. However, all other necessities for people to live on this island had to be imported from England, Canada and the United States. What the island exported was mainly salt cod which had gone to the Mediterranean countries, South America and the West Indies. Importing with high prices from rich countries and exporting with low prices to poor countries had kept the living standards of Newfoundland quite low.

The government of Newfoundland developed slowly. In the 18th century, Naval officers acted as governors and self-appointed fishing admirals. In the 19th century, Newfoundland established representative government formed by a bicameral legislature. Before Newfoundland joined Canada, the Island was a British colony with an elected legislature and a responsible cabinet. But during the Great Depression, England suspended Newfoundland's constitution and the colony was governed by a commission headed by a British governor. When Newfoundland joined Canada in 1949, the responsible government was restored.

In the 20th century, the fishing industry in Newfoundland had gone down because of overfishing and dropping prices of fish. The large Spanish and Portuguese trawlers ignored the quotas and had contributed further to the depletion of fish stocks. The situation had forced Newfoundland to diversify their economy. Today, Newfoundland is no longer a province that will be strangled by the single fishing industry. Large iron ore mines have been developed in Labrador. Copper, zinc and some other minerals have also been produced. Pulp and paper industry has been developed. There is a large potential for hydroelectricity industry in this province and it has been partially developed in Labrador. Newsprints and paper have worked for gains. Even sand and gravel have brought some profits. Newfoundland has now some manufacture industry for its living necessities. Still, the province has quite some way to go to catch up to the same level of prosperity of the central and western parts of the country. Like Nova Scotia, the province seems also putting some hope for the future on the off-shore oil development.

What have attracted the modern ordinary visitors to Newfoundland are mainly its unique sceneries including the drifting arctic icebergs, the whales and the tremendous number of seabirds. The geologists come here to study the geologic history of the land and the biologists come here to check the habitation of the seabirds. Jim and Meilin belonged to the ordinary visitors who came mainly for the sake of visiting this remote Canadian province and enjoying all that nature could offer for the ordinary people to enjoy.

The couple got some information from the tourist centre. They then walked around and picked up some tour brochures. Meilin needed time to feel the firm ground and they stayed around the centre for about three hours. Finally Meilin said that she was okay to move on.

When the couple were driving out of the information centre, it was already late morning. The sun had come out. On their way, the scenes along the highway looked fresh and exceptionally bright. The whole Newfoundland Island is a plateau tilting towards the east. The vast open land surrounded by the ocean looked extremely airy and spacious. The highway was in good condition and the traffic was quite light. The couple felt that they had entered a new and clean world. Along the highway, the land was mainly even and occasionally there were some individual mountains shooting up from the rather flat land. There were large bodies of water here and there. The signs by the highway marked those waters as ponds with different names. To the couple, those ponds were as big as small lakes.

"The Newfoundlanders are living close to the ocean. They see daily the huge body of water in the world. Those inland lakes to them are only ponds," remarked Meilin.

"Yes, but to us, they are lakes," Jim joined in to agree with his wife.

The couple were now fully relaxed and their minds were on the scenery along the road. There were not many trees around, but the flat spacious land and the sudden shooting-up mountains were brightly green; the ponds or lakes were clearly blue. What had mostly struck Jim and Meilin, the new travellers on this land, was the very fresh clean air. The couple had never smelt the air so pure anywhere else. They breathed deeply and filled up their lungs with the absolutely pure air which almost felt and tasted sweet.

Newfoundland started as an island for the fishermen. When the fishermen came, they all settled down along the coast. Up to the modern time, Newfoundland's villages, towns and cities are all located along the coastal areas. Every small village or town is called an outport by the Newfoundlanders, as they are all started as seaports. Each of the village or town has a harbour with a group of fishing vessels anchored in. Old Newfoundland village or town had its typical scenery: a few weathered wooden houses supported by wooden poles were perching on the rocks near a harbour; some wooden boats were anchored in the harbour and the background was the vast grey ocean. This kind of scene must have aroused numerous imaginations of poets and artists; the haunting solitude or isolation, the closeness to the powerful ocean and the indication of a simple honest hard life must have been the brain food for the sensitive or sentimental minds.

Up till today, the interior of Newfoundland and Labrador are hardly inhabited by the humans. The large areas of inland have remained pristine and so also is the air. All along the highway, the couple did not see any farm, any residential place or any kind of man-made structure. Newfoundland's land is mostly not arable and agriculture is a small portion of its economy serving only the locals. However, the unpopulated inland was now very much enjoyed by the travellers like Jim and Meilin who had always lived in a city where noises and polluted air were norm. The couple felt that they were fortunate to have come here, otherwise all their life they would have never known what the absolutely pure air smelt like.

After driving for a while, the couple came to an area where the vast ocean showed up on the left side of the highway. The ocean accompanied the highway for a long distance. When the couple were thinking of stopping their vehicles to enjoy the ocean, a lookout spot appeared on the right side of the road. All across Canada, the highways travelled by the couple had lookouts in different spots for the travellers to enjoy the beautiful scenes along the way. Those lookouts also served as resting places for the road-runners and they were sometimes equipped with picnic areas and washrooms. Some provinces had more of those lookouts by the highway and some had less. The couple were glad to see a lookout spot here in Newfoundland with such a grand ocean view.

They pulled their van and trailer into the large paved parking lot and made sure that the front window of their van was facing the ocean. They got out of the van and were immediately engulfed by the powerful ocean view and the strong wind. The highway, the lookout and the ocean appeared on the same level, and there was no beach along the shoreline. This had made the ocean look so close to the lookout and the myriad of ocean waves seemed filling up all the space around them. The sun shone brightly, but the ocean looked deep blue as if fathomless. The billowing waves had turned the enormous ocean into a gigantic liquid body, alive and moving. The horizon could be seen; the ocean looked rising up to meet the sky at the very end of the earth. The couple had seen ocean in quite some different places, but never had they seen it showing such powerful magnificent beauty. The effect might have partially come from the fact that there were no human structures or activities around. To be just with the ocean and surrounded by the ocean, one could more deeply feel the mystic beauty of the indifferent ocean. In such a pure natural environment, one felt that ocean was all there was, larger than everything, merciless without judgement or justice, powerful and immense without any intention to conquer or control; its power and indifference made its beauty and magnificence beyond human comprehension and description.

Though the couple had been enchanted and overpowered by the majestic ocean, they were quickly forced into their van by the strong wind. It was a midsummer day, but the powerful ocean wind carried a chill. Still, the mesmerizing ocean had kept the couple lingering on at this spot for a long while. They sat in their van quietly. There were no words that could express their lost feelings. Facing such a powerful view of nature, they felt the smallness and insignificance of their own existence and probably even the existence of the whole mankind. To gain their composure and balance, they finally pulled their van and trailer out of the lookout. They were not entirely lost yet and knew that they had a trip ahead of them. After a while of driving, they had finally passed this area where the ocean was almost connected or merged with the highway. They knew that the memory of this powerful ocean view would remain with them for the rest of their life.

A little while past the noon, the couple spotted another resting place by the highway. This lookout was on a higher ground by a river. The green mountains in this area were connected with each other and large trees had covered the mountains. The river was flowing deep down and mostly hidden away by the thick woods and vegetation. The resting ground was also well shaded by trees and bushes. A washroom was at the end of the ground. The couple stopped here to take another rest and to have their lunch. The place looked beautifully green. With the clean pure air and the rather cool temperature, the serenity of the place was penetrating their mind and soul. They very much enjoyed the stay at this spot. After using the washroom, they had their simple lunch. While they walked around the place, trying to relax more, another vehicle pulled into the place. A middle-aged couple got out of their truck. They too used the washroom and then started to walk around. The couple were stout ordinary type folk. Jim soon struck a conversation with them.

The later arrivers turned out to be Newfoundlanders who had indeed the simplicity and honesty of the ordinary folk. They were friendly and happy to provide information for Jim and Meilin, the strange travellers, who had landed on their island the first time.

"If you want to see the puffins, you should go to Bonavista," suggested the woman good- naturedly.

"The road to turn to Bonavista is ahead." The man also warmly offered information.

The four chatted for a while. Jim and Meilin thanked the couple for the information and showed great interest in what the local couple had to say and offer. Then the conversation turned to the traffic on the highway.

"It is a pleasure to drive on the highway here. Compared with some highways we had gone through across the country, the traffic here is very light." Jim chatted. He was always happy to talk to people who were in good spirit and easy to talk to.

"Still, accident can happen here," said the man.

"Really!? It looks impossible to have an accident on your highway," Jim said with surprise.

"The road can be treacherous in winter," said the woman and then continued with a grave manner, "Years ago, three brothers were killed on this very spot, three brothers from the same family..."

Jim and Meilin were quite moved by this information. Not only because that three brothers had died here in an accident at this very spot years ago, but also because that this local couple, probably from Bonavista, could remember this accident and tell the strange travellers with sorrowful expressions on their faces. Jim and Meilin had lived in cities where TV reports about vehicle accidents or some bad crimes were almost daily. Even for some horrendous accidents or crimes, the news probably would not stay in people's minds for long and then they would be replaced by some other news of bad accidents or crimes. To Jim and Meilin, this local couple's information showed that big accidents or bad things were probably not happening so frequently here as in some large busy cities in other parts of the world, and therefore, people here had kept the memories of those things and been affected by them for a much longer time.

In today's world, people are constantly bombarded by bad news over TV. Wars seem a daily happening in some parts of world. Killings and horrendous sufferings of innocent people from wars, diseases or poverties have become news that can no longer deeply touch people. Though the access to information becomes easy and fast, the horrible events still seems a remote happening that can hardly touch people's daily life. Because of the high frequency of their happenings, those events gradually become "normal". It seems that they are bound to happen and nothing can stop or prevent them from happening. Those large scaled disasters and miseries seem to have never a chance to get to where they live or to touch their own life. Too many and too frequent terrible happenings in somewhere else of the world have turned people indifferent or numb towards them. Their humanity seems to have been gradually drained by the same type of terrible news again and again. A wall has been built in their hearts to prevent them from feeling the same pains and sufferings those people in remote places are experiencing. They feel that if they cannot prevent or stop those happenings, there is no use for them to go through those horrible emotions. If the whole world is turning cold, hard and indifferent to the cruel realities some places in the world are facing daily, people seem to be able to put the blames on the fact that the same cruel realities happen too frequently or too constantly. People can get used to anything if it repeats enough times. Apathy seems always rule in the end.

However, this apathy or indifference towards tragic world events has more or less influenced or affected people's immediate daily life no matter where they live. Nobody can fully deny that people's forgetfulness or indifference to their bad local accidents or crimes has been influenced to a certain degree by their apathy towards the bad happenings in the world. For Jim and Meilin, meeting this Newfoundland couple who remembered and sympathized an accident happened here years ago made them feel a breath of fresh air in humanity. It seemed that in this remote area, the simple people had still kept their hearts warm for their neighbours. In quite some places of the world however, people's humanity was in danger of being engulfed by apathy, by fear of or hatred towards their neighbours.

The chatting lasted for a while. Then the local couple left; they probably had the impression that the two travellers were going to Bonavista to see the puffins. Jim and Meilin were indeed interested in seeing those colourful Atlantic seabirds, Newfoundland's provincial birds. They had seen the lovely puffins with big colourful bills on pictures and TV shows, but they had never seen any live ones in their natural habitation. According to the local couple, the puffins were gathering in large quantities at certain spots along the coast, but they were not large birds at all. The pictures and TV shows must have exaggerated their size, as Jim and Meilin had never thought that puffins were small birds.

Jim and Meilin discussed whether they should go to see the puffins in Bonavista. Reluctantly, they gave up the idea. Though they had travelled across the country, they were not extensive travellers at all. They sampled different places and things along the way, but never ventured too far away from the main highways. They had camped at certain spots along the highways and then wandered into large cities or some other places nearby. Bonavista seemed some distance away from the main highway. The couple worried that they might not have enough time for long excursions. At home, they had planned to visit Gros Morne, a beautiful national park in Newfoundland. Afraid of having not enough time, they had even given that up. Their return ferry was scheduled to take them back to the mainland in a little less than a week. They would only have enough time to go through the main highway to reach Saint John's, the capital city of Newfoundland. After touring that city, they would go to the seaport at Argentia where the returning ferry would take off. Before they would board the ferry, they would have enough time to find a campsite at Argentia to stay there for a little while. Near Argentia, there was Cape St. Mary's Ecological Reserve where thousands of seabirds were gathering. The couple had set their minds on visiting that reserve.

Visiting Saint John's was a settled plan in the couple's minds. Not only because it was the capital city of this province, but also because Jim's sister and her husband lived there. In their childhood, Jim's sister had been separated from the family. After Jim's mother walked out on the family, His sister was adopted by an uncle who was doing better than Jim's father. The uncle owned a retail store in a small place in New Brunswick. Jim's sister had grown up in a better-off environment and had a rather different life than her father and brothers. Even when they were adults, the brothers and sister had not had much contact with each other. Still, to Jim, Esther was his sister. Since he knew where she lived, he would like to see her and to know how her life was.

Canada is a large country, territory wise. To travel across the country was already a huge endeavour for the couple. It was impossible for them to visit every interesting place and to see everything worth seeing. Doing that would probably take them a year or more. They did not have that kind of ambition and energy. What they could do was to keep on to the main track and to visit some important places and sample some interesting things along the main track. To visit some relatives in the east where Jim was born and grown up was in the couple's agenda, as this might be the last time for the couple to come to the east. No matter how Jim's folk would receive him and his wife, the couple would like to see them the last time.

After their lunch and a good rest in this beautiful and peaceful resting place, the couple started driving again. Port aux Basques was located at the west end of the island and city of Saint John's was at the east end of the island. The drive from the west end to the east end would take the couple a whole day. Jim was surprised to see how big Newfoundland Island was. He had always had the impression that Newfoundland was small just like the other Maritime Provinces. On their long drive from the west end to the east end of the island, the couple decided not to push it, because Meilin had not totally recovered from her seasickness. During the drive in the afternoon, they had paid attention to signs of campgrounds along the highway. It took some time for them to spot one.

The campground that had caught their attention was a little way off the highway. The couple had to turn to a side road to reach it. Still they decided to go to this campground, as they were afraid that they would not see another campground along the highway again. After a while of driving on the side road, the couple arrived at the campground. The place must be near the ocean. There was another road in front of the campground, which must be leading to an outport. The campground here was no different than the campgrounds in the mainland. In fact, the ground here was more open and spacious. At the border area of the campground, the long-term tenants had set up their trailers and motor homes in the shades of some large tall trees. The couple got a lot in the center open area which was for the passing travellers. The lot had full service for RV. After they set up their trailer, they had enjoyed a good shower. The bathroom of the campground was clean and looked like newly built.

The afternoon was still young. After the shower, the couple walked around the campground. The camp office was in a small house which looked like a pavilion. Jim chatted with the office clerk to get some information about the distance from here to Saint John's. He was told there was still a couple of hour drive to reach the capital city. On the opposite side of the campground, there was a large barn-shaped building with a sign - Insectarium. It must be a nature museum exhibiting different insects. However, the place looked not open as there was no vehicle parked around. The couple did not venture there. They walked around the campground and took some pictures. A giant ornamental strawberry was not far from the camp office, which made the place look more country. The walk was relaxing. Even in the afternoon of the midsummer, the temperature was not high and the air remained cool and refreshing. After the walk and picture-taken, the couple came back to their trailer. They prepared their supper in their trailer. The whole afternoon and evening on the campground turned out to be pleasant. Maybe, it was because of the fresh clean air and the cool sunny weather, the couple had the impression that life here must be pleasant. They talked about moving to Newfoundland. Then they checked off the idea, thinking it might be too difficult to get to somewhere else from the island.

Next morning, the couple took their time to get started. After so many days on the road, morning start became routine. But today on Newfoundland Island, it seemed more pleasant and not rushed. When they were on the road again, they felt thoroughly rested and energetic. The morning sun shone brightly. The air was deliciously cool and fresh. The drive ahead was anticipated not too hard. With the light traffic on the highway, they had the leisure to enjoy the beautiful bright natural scenes. They counted this morning one of the highlights of their trip. Right now, the intense nerve-racking drive in the heavy traffics of a large city or a long tiresome drive on a road to reach a certain place was the thing of the past. They could fully enjoy this pleasant moment without worries or concerns. To the couple, one of the most enjoyable and memorable times of their trip was just driving on the highway, especially driving on the peaceful highway with the beautiful natural scenery along the way. The drive from the campsite to Saint John's was indeed memorable. When the drive was pleasant, the distance seemed shorter. At the time when the couple reached Saint John's, the morning was not over yet.

Saint John's is one of the oldest cities in North America. From the sixteenth century on, its perfectly sheltered harbour has attracted European explorers and fishermen. The name Saint John's comes from the feast day of Saint John, the Baptist, which is said to be the same day when John Cabot found Newfoundland in 1497. From early time on, Saint John's has been the principal port and political and commercial centre of Newfoundland. Geographically, the city is the nearest spot in North America to Europe. From here, Guglielmo Marconi received the first trans-Atlantic wireless message in 1901. Also from here, Captain John Alcock and Lieutenant Arthur Brown successfully completed the first non-stop trans-Atlantic flight to reach Ireland in 1919. The flight took them sixteen hours. Like some other old cities in North America, Saint John's had also suffered a disastrous fire in 1892, which had left 11,000 people homeless at that time.

While approaching the city skirt of Saint John's, the couple did not see any skyscrapers looming ahead. The city caught them by surprise when they were still enjoying their highway drive. As usual, the couple pulled into the first gas station they came across. They could gas up their van and ask for some information at the same time. Jim wanted to know how to get to Smith Street where his sister lived. Coming to a strange city, the couple thought it would be better to go to the relatives first. If they could find a parking space there, it would be great. If they could not park there, Esther could provide some information about the city and how to get to some nearby campground. After gassing up their van and getting some information, the couple were ready to drive away from the gas station. At this moment, a woman in her thirties or forties came up to them.

"I heard that you were asking about how to get to Smith Street. I am going that way too. You can follow me," said the lady with a smile.

While the couple were gassing up their van, the lady was also gassing up her car. The couple were grateful for her offer. Although the city did not look very big, it was an entirely strange city to them. The lady's kind offer would save them a lot of trouble to get to where they wanted to go. The couple thanked her sincerely and followed her car into the city streets. They went through some wide streets. There was a centre isle running in the middle of the six-lane streets. On this centre isle, there were trees lined up. The sidewalks were wide on both sides of the streets and the buildings and residential houses were way back. There were no high buildings around; the city looked spacious and clean. This area with the broad streets looked new and built in modern time. With sufficient lighting and orderly lined-up trees; the place showed the quality and style of a large city.

The drive on the wide streets was not long. Then the couple saw the lady stretching her arm out of her car window to point to a side street on the right. They knew that she was telling them to turn that way. They also saw that her left signal light was turned on and knew that she was going to the different direction. Jim sounded the van horn to say thanks to her and then turned their van into the right lane. Then the couple looked at the street sign and saw that they were already on Smith Street.

Jim and Meilin were indeed thankful that they were so easily landed on the right street. Though the streets here appeared not complicated, it would still take some efforts for them to get to the right place on their own, as they did not have a Saint John's city map. When they were driving on Smith Street, they were very much surprised to see that it looked like an upper area of the city. The houses on both sides were the comfortable modern affluent type, and each of them had a large front garden. In this prime summer time, all the gardens were thriving with shrubs and flowers. There were plenty of large trees along the street and around each house and garden. Jim and Meilin had doubts whether they had got the correct address for Esther's home. For as long as they could remember; Esther and her husband had never been that well-off. How did they land in the upper area of Saint John's?

The street was not long. The couple soon found the house they were looking for. It was a fair-sized house with an attached garage in front. Obviously, the house had a livable basement, as the front entrance door to the main level was to be reached by climbing up quite a few cement steps. The living room window in the front was quite big. The outside look of the house gave the couple the impression that the property owners lived a good comfortable life. As the house was located at the corner of an intersection, the couple parked their van and trailer at the side of the house. Right or wrong, they were going to knock at the door and to see whether Esther was living here.

Upon their knocking, the couple were both happy and surprised to see that it was indeed Esther who opened the door. Esther was quite happy to see her brother and sister-in-law. Before Jim and Meilin were let into the living room, quite some questions had already been asked. Esther had answered them in her unrushed manner. Of the three brothers and one sister, Jim and Esther had rather similar characters, open and good natured with a soft heart.

Esther, her husband and their children had lived with Esther's adoptive parents in New Brunswick for quite many years. After her adoptive parents passed away, Esther and her family moved to Saint John's where the parents of Dalton, Esther's husband, lived. At the time Dalton took his family to live with his family, his mother had already passed away and his father was seriously ill. Not long, his father passed away as well. Dalton's parents had been doing well in their life and left this house in the upper area of the city to Dalton and his family. From this trip, Jim and Meilin got to know that Dalton's parents were his adoptive parents. Dalton was of native origin; he and his sister were both adopted by Mr. and Mrs. McConnell, a well-to-do white couple.

Esther led Jim and Meilin into their living room. All the time, the chat between them had not stopped. The living room was fair-sized and well decorated. The main tone of the room was pink. The large living room window had let in plenty of light which made the pink room warmly bright.

"Did you decorate the place yourself?" asked Meilin admiringly.

"Yes," Esther answered. Then she pointed to the pictures on the walls and said proudly, "Those are painted by me as well. I have taken some painting lessons."

The pictures were water-coloured landscapes. They showed the rather careful efforts of a learner. The picture of a sunflower however had a flow of skill and talent. Jim and Meilin were amazed. They poured out their praises and admiration. After viewing the pictures and the living room, Jim and Meilin had also had a peek of some other rooms on the main floor. The kitchen was quite big. There was a large counter with draws in the centre of the room, which was typical modern kitchen style. The appliances with other counters and cupboards were all along the walls. The dining room was half the size of the kitchen. It had contained a large oval dining table with chairs and a big glass-door china cabinet. A nice china set was neatly lined up in the cabinet. The whole set of dining room furniture was of red cherry-wood. A large screen door opening to a wooden deck outside was at the back of the dining room, giving a view of the backyard garden. The backyard had a green lawn surrounded by different shrubs and flowering plants. There was no doubt that the whole set of the dining room furniture and the landscaped backyard garden with deck were the original inheritance from the late parents. There might be three bedrooms on the main floor. Jim and Meilin were not going to check them. While they were checking the small computer room, a man in his late thirties or early forties came out from one of the bedrooms. Esther introduced, "This is Nathan, Kathy's husband. Jim, you should know Kathy."

"Of course I know Kathy. How are you doing?" Jim greeted Nathan with a big smile and stretching out to shake Nathan's hand while Esther introduced him and Meilin to Nathan.

Kathy was Esther's other sister, the birth-daughter of Esther's adoptive parents. Both Kathy and Nathan had been serving in the military for years. Now they were both released from the army. Nathan came to Newfoundland to find a job. He stayed with Esther and Dalton while going on job hunting.

"Our computer expert had a job interview yesterday. He said it was very promising," said Esther, looking at her brother-in-law fondly.

Nathan, specialising in computer technology, was trying to find a job related with computers after his release from the army. He looked a rather intense person, reserved silent type. However, Esther's out-reaching character and manner seemed to have easily drawn him out. Soon Jim and Nathan chatted along about the military.

Near noon, Dalton came home. Jim knew Dalton. For Meilin, this was the first time that she had met all these Jim's relatives. Dalton had worked as a school-bus driver for some time. Now the bus company was also running a chartered tour-bus business. Dalton was both the manager and the driver for this new business. Dalton did not look a native man at all. If Jim and Meilin did not have the information, they would never have guessed. The only thing that had caught their attention about Dalton's appearance was that when he talked, his eyes were bulging. Esther and Dalton were both in their fifties and a bit dangerously overweight. Dalton was glad to see his wife's relatives. After some chat, Jim asked if he could park their van and trailer somewhere around.

"No problem. You can park them behind the backyard garden where I parked my school-bus. I will move the school-bus back a bit. There is plenty of space for your van and trailer," said Dalton without any hesitation. Then he asked warmly, "Do you want to park the trailer now? I'll go to move the bus."

"Okay, let's do it now," said Jim happily. It was a relief for him to have the parking problem solved so quickly.

Both Jim and Meilin followed Dalton out. The back lane of this line of residential houses was a small street. On the other side of the street, there was a large sports ground of a high school. The whole place looked very open and spacious. Dalton had parked his school-bus behind the backyard garden. He moved the bus towards the neighbour's back section and assured Jim and Meilin that the neighbours would not have any problem. Jim moved the van and trailer to where Dalton had parked before. Esther came out from the screen door with an electric cable and a water hose. Soon, the couple's trailer was equipped with electricity and water.

Jim and Meilin thanked Esther and Dalton from the bottom of their hearts. They had not expected this kind of warm welcome, so everything was doubly appreciated by them. The couple were surprised by the different attitudes of their relatives here. They came to the conclusion that Esther and Dalton must be well influenced by the social environment and local customs here. They had heard about the warm hospitality of the Newfoundlanders towards visitors and strangers who were in need of their help. Now they had personally experienced it from the treatment they had received from their relatives.

After everything was settled, Jim and Meilin decided not to bother their host and hostess any further. They told Ether and Dalton that they could manage the rest of things by themselves. The only immediate information they needed was how to get to the nearest bank. They needed to withdraw some money.

"After you rested and had your lunch, Dalton can take you to the bank. Any time you feel like it, you can come in the house to take a shower. As for me, I have to go to work now," said Esther with her relaxed manner.

From the chat, Jim and Meilin had already known that Esther was working as a housekeeper for the old former mayor who lived just a few houses away and she could walk there to work. Esther did not have much education. The jobs she could find were mainly housekeeping. Her former housekeeping job was not that good. Now this one working for the former mayor and his wife was quite ideal for her.

The whole afternoon turned out to be nice and relaxing for Jim and Meilin. They got settled down and had their lunch. After that, Dalton insisted to take them to the nearest bank with his car. On their way to the bank, Dalton pointed out a school to them and said, "I went to this school when I was growing up. It is a private school."

Jim and Meilin had noticed the proud tone of Dalton's voice when he talked about his school. Dalton was the first native man Meilin had such a close contact with since she came to Canada. In the Canadian cities she had lived, she saw and met some native people on some rare occasions. When Jim and she were running a rental business in Edmonton, they had some contact with some native people who happened to be their tenants. Those native tenants were all jobless and on welfare. She had never personally met a native man with a good job and had attended a private school; Dalton was the first. She was both glad and amazed to see that there was not any sense of inferiority or resentment in Dalton's manner or attitude. It was clear that he had never felt or sensed that he was any different than the white people around him. She had also seen that Esther, his wife, loved him and Nathan, his brother-in-law, also loved and respected him. From a very short time interacting with this family of their relatives, Jim and Meilin could see that Dalton was quite intelligent and could hold himself up well; his generous and open characters had earned the love and respect of his family and probably the love and respect of the people in his work place as well. This new experience had confirmed Meilin's belief that natives or any other coloured people, if given a chance, could blend well into the white society and become loving, loved and contributing members of the society.

After the bank trip, Jim and Meilin went to their trailer to rest. Later in the afternoon, they went into the house and had a shower. After supper, when they figured that everybody would be retired for the evening, they went to the house to chat with the relatives again. This time the five of them sat in the sitting room; the chat went on with the TV on. The atmosphere was genuinely warm just like a family gathering together; everybody was relaxed and the talk was casual. Dalton talked about finding his birth mother in recent time and it was a special experience for him. He then talked about his wanting to regain his native status.

"You have to think carefully about that," Jim said with quite some concern. Then he added, "There are still quite some prejudices towards the natives in the society."

Nathan nodded his head to agree with Jim, but Dalton waved off their worries and said, "Not here. I'm a native by birth. I think I should have the native status. Besides, with the native status, all my medical care will be covered."

Meilin was amazed to see Dalton's perfect poise about his native status, but she was of the same mind as that of Jim and Nathan. It was understandable that Dalton would like to connect with his native root, but what the native status would do for him was questionable; it might cause discrimination towards him or make his life more difficult in a white predominant society. Dalton was continuingly surprising Meilin by showing his full confidence and assurance as an equal person in every way in the society. Of course, Dalton had his practical concern in this matter of gaining his native status. Perhaps, he had the foresight or instinct that the full medical care coverage would be important for him in the future. Native peoples enjoy some special benefits in the country, but there seem also some restrictions on them. A couple of years later, Jim and Meilin got the news that Dalton did gain his native status, but he had lost his job because of the problem with his eyes; he had found another job, but the new job paid less and then he could not work any longer because of his health problems.

At this moment, Esther was the one who completely supported Dalton's wish to gain his native status and she even talked about that she herself was going to check into the Duhine family history to see if there was any native connection. "Perhaps, I can gain the native status too," she said wishfully.

Meilin loved Esther for this. All the time, there was never a hint of Esther's thinking her husband different because of his native birth. If possible, Esther probably would like to become a native as well. Love is indeed powerful, which can push away the barriers between different races like they were paper-walls. This kind of love is so special in Canadian society, because the racial barriers in quite some people's minds are still as thick as impenetrable.

The chat went on to other things. Knowing that Meilin would be interested, Esther offered the information about some local Chinese Newfoundlanders. She said with a smile to Meilin "I have seen them having their community meeting or activity in a school."

Meilin was indeed interested. She had not expected that there would be Chinese or any other Asian Canadians in Newfoundland. It was such a remote province with a noted high unemployment rate; the job opportunities for the Asians might be quite slim here. She was quite surprised that there was even a Chinese community here in Saint John's.

The chat continued; everyone seemed enjoying it. Both Dalton and Esther looked happy to have their relatives with them. Esther and Dalton had two sons. Their younger son died of leukemia. Jim and Meilin had seen the photo of this son, a lovely boy, in their small computer room. Their elder son was now an adult who was working, married and living in New Brunswick. When there were no visitors, Dalton and Esther were living in this house by themselves. They looked like a couple who would enjoy more with family and friends around.

What is happiness to most of the ordinary people? It must simply be having jobs they like or can get to like, and having no worries about their food and shelters. On top of the basic criteria for happiness, for some of them, being surrounded by families and friends will make their happiness complete. It is actually a blessing for people whose needs are the basic ones; it is easy for them to reach happiness. Dalton and Esther seemed belonging to those ordinary people who had gained the basic necessities to feel satisfied and happy. If they had some ambition of gaining some more money or being well taken care of when they were old, the moderate ambition would not land them in big troubles. It was nice for Jim and Meilin to see that Esther and Dalton looked satisfied and enjoying their life. In today's world, quite some people seemed crazy, craving for this and that, running after or fighting like hell for things which they did not even know clearly what they were, and they were not easily feeling satisfied and happy with what they had.

Then Jim talked about the plan for their sightseeing tomorrow and asked for some information about the city.

"I'll check with the office. I may be able to take you and show you around," Dalton said generously.

"Oh, no. We cannot trouble you like that. We have travelled across the country. We can manage it here by ourselves," said Jim and then added gratefully, "But thank you very much for the offer and everything you have already done for us."

"Let Dalton take you around if he can. He knows where to go and what to see. He takes the tourists around often. It will save you a lot of trouble," said Esther with her motherly or sisterly manner.

The evening went quite pleasantly. When Jim and Meilin came back to their trailer, it was past nine o'clock. The couple went to bed immediately. Tomorrow would be a full day for them. However, falling asleep was not easy. There were some vehicles zooming through the back street and the high school kids stayed on the sports ground quite late. Finally, all quieted down and the couple had a good sleep.

Next morning, the couple got up early and were ready to start their tour of the city. Dalton also got up early and came to tell them that he could take them around for sightseeing. Jim and Meilin were grateful for this offer; it would indeed save them a lot of trouble. They asked Dalton to drive their van which was already disconnected from their trailer, but Dalton insisted on taking them in his own car. By now, the couple knew that there was no use to argue with their host. They were feeling overwhelmed by the hospitality.

Dalton's car rode smoothly. After some turns, they were going through the old downtown area. The old downtown area of Saint John's was typical old European style. There were no tall buildings. The shops, stores and restaurants were in some wooden or brick buildings which were one or two stories high, in different colours and connected to each other. The street however was rather wide, which must be the improvement in modern time. The place very much reminded them of the traditional European city or town in the old time. Quite a few pubs were along the street. One of them was named Fat Cat Blue Bar.

Jim said, "I've heard of this bar; it is quite famous."

It was not important whether the bar was famous or not. This bar and the other pubs must be places used by many fishermen coming from different European countries when they were home from their fishing trips. Some drinks with music must have been the joy of life for generations. The drive then went through some turns. They had spotted the statue of Gaspar Corte-Real, an important Portuguese explorer in the early time. However, the city's more important history was recorded by the Sir Humphrey Gilbert Plaque on Water Street. Sir Humphrey Gilbert had established the royal standard of Elizabeth I here in 1583, paving the way for British reign on this land.

Dalton turned the car into a narrow street ending at an old restaurant and pub by the water. The place looked like a small closed-in harbour. At the back of the restaurant, there was a wooden wharf flanking the whole side of the restaurant. On the other side of the narrow harbour, there was a rocky bank. The bank rose straight up, looking like a rock cliff. The harbour had a bend; the rock cliff had totally blocked the view of the ocean, leaving a narrow path as an entrance to the harbour. The rock cliff had fully sheltered the small body of water from the ocean storms. On the left side of the small harbour, the sloped bank was covered by a green lawn. On the green land, there were a few bungalows; they were the modern type bungalows without the tall wooden stilts to raise them above the ground, but sitting on the lawn with foundations. This small corner harbour must be favored by the old fishermen with small wooden boats. They would come in and hitch their boats to the wharf, enjoying a drink and a meal in the restaurant. There was no way that large ships could get into this small harbour, as the outlet to the ocean was so narrow. There was no way the small harbour could even be spotted from the ocean. The place looked secretively mysterious. It looked that this old spot was left partially intact in Saint John's for the old time sake. Some artists were here, painting the darkish rock cliff, the old restaurant with its wooden wharf and the yonder sloped green lawn with the bungalows in different colours.

Dalton left Jim and Meilin on this spot to enjoy the scene for a little while. There was no parking spot here; obviously, the restaurant mainly served the fishermen coming by boats. Dalton came back soon to get the couple. The tour continued after this. Dalton did not explain about this old corner harbour, but the couple had got the hint of a heritage place left from the old days. It was not entirely as they had imagined that an old small Newfoundland harbour should be. To experience that, one probably had to go to a small outport.

Dalton drove by the big harbour afterwards. The harbour was indeed fully sheltered. Tall cliffs had surrounded a large body of water, leaving a not-too-wide pathway to the open ocean. On this body of water, anchored quite many ships, large or small and in different colours and styles. On the rocky cliffs, some modern houses were perched. The houses were not very big, but ordinary sizes. Those houses would have both views of the harbour and the ocean. Jim and Meilin had been used to seeing large luxury houses occupying some spots with ocean or other kinds of water views in other parts of the country. They were surprised to see the ordinary small houses here with the grand ocean view.

Dalton might have noticed the puzzled looks of Jim and Meilin; he said, "The well-to-do people here have their homes inland."

"It must be the strong ocean wind on the cliffs that has turned away the rich. Besides, living on the island surrounded by the ocean, the ocean view must have become ordinary," Meilin commented.

The car then started climbing a mountain. When it reached a rather high level, Dalton stopped the car at a lookout. It was a spot that had a good view of Saint John's. Looking down at the city from this angle, the couple saw houses sprawling over a large area and they were not high buildings. There were only some church steeples and one tall tower building sticking up among the lower buildings. From this high point, the city looked slumbering peacefully. The couple could not help thinking of the city's seniority and geographical position on this island fully surrounded by the Atlantic Ocean. They were affected by the tranquil scene. This tranquil feeling must have been aided by the fresh pure ocean air which seemed to have a peaceful intoxicating effect on them.

Finally, Jim broke the silence by asking, "What is that tall building?"

"That's the government office tower," said Dalton and then he added, "My sister works there."

Again, Jim and Meilin sensed the pride in Dalton's voice. The information had added amazement to what Jim and Meilin had already felt about Dalton. Newfoundland has been putting efforts on diversifying its economy, but fishery is still its main industry. The fishing industry has been depressed for quite many years. Newfoundland's unemployment rate has been ranked high in the country. Here, in this place where jobs were supposed to be scarce, Jim and Meilin had met their relatives with satisfying jobs. What amazed them most was that Dalton and his sister of native origin had good jobs. In their life experiences, this was definitely one special encountering. For this, they had affection and respect for this place. Not only the island and the ocean, but also the society here seemed to have given them a fresh clean breath of air and a harmonious feeling. They hoped that more coloured people here and in the whole country could enjoy the same equal treatment as Dalton and his sister had enjoyed. They could see that the equal treatment had given Dalton and his sister a quality life.

"Wow! We heard that it was very difficult to find jobs here in Newfoundland. We are definitely surprised and happy that you, your sister and Esther all have good jobs," said Jim sincerely.

"Oh, yes. It is amazing! If Newfoundland can achieve this; I don't see why the whole country cannot," said Meilin with a sigh. From her personal experiences, she certainly wished that everywhere in Canada, the things that happened to Dalton and his sister here could happen to many more natives and coloured Canadians.

Then unexpectedly, Meilin asked Dalton, "Is Esther's employer treating her well?"

"Oh, yes. They treat her like family," answered Dalton with assurance.

After leaving the lookout, the car went further up to the top of the mountain. There was a large flat area on the mountain top. Dalton drove for a while on the flat mountain top and then parked the car in a parking lot. The three got out of the car. Dalton led the couple; they walked through a path and reached the very edge of the mountain. Now they were standing on top of a cliff which shaped like a spearhead pointing to the ocean. Dalton introduced the place as Cape Spear. There were rails shaped like an arrow on this sharp cliff point. At the head of the arrow-shaped ground there was a small simple wooden cross, well-weathered and rugged. On one side of the rail there was a sign stating the name and simple fact of the place.

"This point is the most eastern point of the North America Continent," said Dalton, acting like a tourist guide.

This sharp cliff point now had quite some significance to Jim and Meilin. To think that they were now standing on the most eastern point of a continent made them feel excited. They asked Dalton to take a picture for them, so that they would have a memorabilia to show and remember that they were here on this most eastern point of North America. After the picture taking, the couple looked around. From the top of the spear head, they looked way down on the ocean. The jutting point was bracing the powerful beatings of ocean waves. The waves were pounding at the black rocks with such a force and giving out loud rumbling roars like the rolling thunders. Thick white foams were formed by those constant pounding rushes. The rocks at the bottom of the cliff were permanently embedded in the white foams that looked like swirling snow. Further away, the immense ocean looked peacefully serene, as if it had nothing to do with the fierce poundings at the rocky cliff shore here.

The wind was very strong at the cliff top. After enjoying the ocean and the foamy surging waves for a while, the couple turned their heads towards the land. At the back of the spearhead point, there was a citadel. Most part of the citadel was buried in the ground with only the top showing. In front of the citadel, there was a space sunken into the ground like a quarry. A rusty cannon about eight to ten meters long was in the quarry. It would be impossible to see the citadel and its large cannon from the ocean. This was the first time that Jim and Meilin had seen an old-time cannon so big. The citadel and its big cannon had aroused quite some imaginations in the couple's minds. What kind of battles had been fought here at such a dangerous spot? Who would have braved the turbulent violent ocean to approach the island at this point? Then they figured that with the big long cannon and the high position, the fire range of the cannon must have been able to reach and protect the harbour from here.

After viewing Cape Spear, the three walked back through the same path. Not far from the spearhead point, the rocky cliff ridge rose even higher. On top of the ridge, there was a lighthouse. Jim and Meilin could see that a lighthouse was indeed necessary at this location to warn the ships; the powerful waves could easily push the unknowing ships to this point to be smashed to pieces. They got to know that this lighthouse was built in 1835, which was one of the oldest surviving lighthouses in Newfoundland and served as an important approaching light to Saint John's for more than a century. At the foot of the cliff ridge there was a small gift shop. Jim and Meilin did not climb the cliff ridge to reach the lighthouse like some other tourists were doing, but had a look at the gift shop.

Dalton was with them all this time. He must have been in this place many times. The couple did not want to let him wait too long. The three were soon on the way again. After driving a little while, Dalton stopped the car at the entrance of a small village which was located on one side of the mountain top. The village was small and had only a few houses. Dalton had no intention to get out of the car, so Jim and Meilin remained in their seats too.

Then Dalton started talking, "When I was driving the school bus, every morning I parked the bus here, waiting for the kids to come on board. The sea sometimes was totally wrapped up by the mist. Sometimes I could see the sun coming up. I sat here, drinking my coffee, waiting and watching..."

The spot where Dalton parked the car was a little higher than the village. From here, the ocean could be spotted over the trees and the village houses. From Dalton's tone and expression, the couple could see that he had deeply felt the beauty and power of the ocean. Did he also have the same sensation or feeling as his ancestors who had felt that the ocean had embodied a mighty powerful spirit just like the bear, the eagle and the buffalo?

The place was called Black Head. From the ocean, this place with trees high on the rocky mountain might look like a black head. The small village or community looked to have only one street. Dalton's bus had to stop here as there was no way for him to turn his bus around inside the village. Anyway, the couple at this moment imagined the quiet time and the beautiful ocean views Dalton had enjoyed at this spot many mornings. They appreciated that he had shared this experience with them.

The car moved on after this interval. It moved to another mountain top. Jim and Meilin could see a tower on top of this mountain and there were quite some tourists around there. After parking the car, Dalton said, "This is Signal Hill, a national historical site. Go ahead and have a look. I'll wait here."

Jim and Meilin got out of the car and walked towards the tower. There was a stone wall about two feet high along the mountain ridge and a walk path parallel with the wall was leading to the tower. Some of the tourists were walking on the path and some were standing behind the wall and looking at the ocean. At this spot, they could see the ocean accompanied by some mountains along the shore. Under the bright sun, the view was charmingly beautiful. The place was called Signal Hill, but it was actually a mountain. From this mountain top, the couple could see Cape Spear not far and much lower than the spot they were standing on now. This mountain did not have cliffs at the edge; instead, the sloped mountain sides were covered by green grass and other low wild plants. There were no trees around. Obviously, under the green surface layer, there was the solid rock, impossible for trees to grow. The couple saw more tourists around the tower and some of them were getting into the tower. The tower was built by large stones. It was a two-story old style building with a tower a bit taller than the building. Both the building and the tower were not large and hexagon shaped.

Approaching the tower, the couple saw a large metal plaque on one side of the building's foundation. They went close and saw the following statement engraved on the plaque:

BATTLE OF SIGNAL HILL

> The hill was the site of the decisive assault by British troops on the French Lines, September 15, 1762, in the last phase of the battle in North America between the forces of Great Britain and France. The victorious attack, led by Captain Charles MacDonell, compelled the French to surrender St. John's to the British army under the command of Colonel William Amherst and confirmed British possession of the Island of Newfoundland.

Of course there was also the French version on this monumental plaque. Now Jim and Meilin saw the significance of this hill. During a period of time in the history of North America, roughly from the seventeenth century to the eighteenth century, there were quite some battles fought between the British and the French armies for the dominance of this continent. In Canada, those battles were mainly in the east of the country. While travelling through the Maritimes, Jim and Meilin had seen quite some sites left by those battles. Newfoundland was of no exception. There were quite some battles fought between the British and the French for the control of Newfoundland and Labrador and its fishery until the Paris Treaty in 1763 when France ceded Canada to Britain. Here on the Signal Hill, the British won the last battle and finished the war.

Standing in front of this monumental plaque, the couple could appreciate the peaceful co-inhabitation of the people of English origin and the people of French origin on this land for more than two centuries. If there is still some squabbling now and then between these two peoples in recent times, it is quite understandable. Anyhow, these two peoples are the lead Canadians now; most of them are trying to create more harmony and lessen differences between themselves.

The tower on the Signal Hill however had a different significance. It was called Cabot Tower. Its cornerstone was laid in 1897 to mark the 400th anniversary of John Cabot's coming to North America and the 60th anniversary of Queen Victoria's reign. The tower was fully completed in 1900. In the beginning, the tower had functioned as a signal station. Today there was a small museum inside, exhibiting some history of communication and signaling. Jim and Meilin walked around the tower, admiring its endurance. After more than a hundred years, the tower looked perfectly strong and stable; no doubt, it would stand on this hill for many more years to come. In Jim and Meilin's minds, Signal Hill with Cabot Tower was definitely the landmark of Saint John's. It showed the history, hardships and fortitude of the people had gone through here.

Not far from Cabot Tower, there was a signpost with quite a few sign plates on. Each sign was marked with a place name such as Ottawa or London; the arrow of the sign plate was pointing to a certain direction to indicate the direction of that place and the mileage to show the distance between the mentioned place and Signal Hill. One of the sign plates was for the famous Titanic. According to the sign, Titanic met its demise on the north side three hundred eighty-five miles from Signal Hill. It was well known that the mighty unsinkable Titanic had been sunken by a mightier under-water iceberg near the coast of Newfoundland. The couple looked at the sign, thinking that there was really nothing in this world that could be absolutely sure of its safety or endurance. Human complacency sometimes looked quite ridiculous.

Jim and Meilin did not linger too long around, as Dalton was waiting. Soon the three were in the car on their way again. The next place Dalton took Jim and Meilin to see was Johnson Geo Centre which was not far from Signal Hill. The centre was a geologic museum in a modern glass building that looked tilting halfway down. The architect must have had some humorous inkling in designing a glass building almost falling down on the side of the rock-mountain. Dalton let the couple go in to check out the centre and he again waited outside. To the couple, the centre was the first of this type of museum they had seen. It displayed the geologic history and rock formations of this area. On the lower level, the center was built underground and one side of its wall was the rocky side of the Signal Hill. There were layers of rocks which the scientists had studied and identified the exact formation times. Those rock layers ranged from hundreds years old to thousands years or even millions years old. The oldest rock formation here had ranked among the oldest in the world.

The couple were fascinated by the exhibits. Compared with the lives of the inorganic materials, human life was so short. However, the human curiosity had made them to see and to study the exact material world millions years before, and the human mind and imagination had taken them wandering as far as they liked into the far future. There were some other exhibits concerning natural science in this centre, but those exhibits were the same as that in the similar science centers in other cities. However, this centre had another special thing; the whole center was heated by six geothermal wells five hundred feet deep. This kind of facility could certainly arouse sufficient awareness of how infernally hot was the core of our globe, and what kind of fierce boiling force was under our very feet, waiting for the chance to burst up. On the other hand, it showed that there were opportunities for human beings to harness and control this and other natural forces and turn them into energy to serve the human needs.

It did not take long for Jim and Meilin to go over the specialties in this center. They were glad that Dalton had brought them here. What they had seen here had somewhat helped to open their eyes and minds to the planet they were residing on; it had also made them to see how minuscule they were and how short their time of staying on the surface of this hot and fast moving globe was. They could imagine that the geologists or students of geology would be much more interested in the exhibits here than them.

When they came out from the exhibition halls, Dalton was waiting for them in the reception hall. The three were soon on their way again. It was past noon, high time for them to have lunch. Jim and Meilin wanted to treat Dalton to some Chinese food in a Chinese restaurant here. Jim asked whether Dalton knew a Chinese restaurant around.

"No, I don't think there is a Chinese restaurant around this area," said Dalton.

"Then, is there a Wendy's around? Meilin and I liked Wendy's food. They have some healthy food," said Jim.

"Yes, there is a Wendy's near here," said Dalton.

"Let's go there have our lunch then," said Jim and was glad to have the lunch place settled.

Jim and Meilin lived a simple life. Their restaurant visits were normally confined to a few Chinese restaurants or fast food restaurants. Though they very much wanted to treat Dalton to a good restaurant lunch, they did not know much about expensive restaurants and had no heart to try them. Soon the car left the mountain area and was going through the city streets again. Not long, Dalton pulled into a Wendy's parking lot. The menu and price of the Wendy's here appeared no different than those of other Wendy's restaurants in the mainland. The two men had their beef burgers and French fries and Meilin had her chicken burger and a big baked potato. Dalton got the impression that Meilin was quite health-food minded.

The afternoon's sightseeing started soon after the lunch. Dalton took the couple to the Basilica Cathedral of Saint John the Baptist. Jim and Meilin were amazed to see a big cathedral here in Saint John's. The cathedral was not far from the harbour. In front of the cathedral, there was a large green lawn with paved paths. At the forefront of the ground there was a large Romanesque gate with three vaulted entrances. A statue of Saint John was on top of this gate. Obviously, the gate was symbolic. It was a stone structure, standing alone without walls connected to it. But the gate looked grand and reminded them of some ancient European palace or sacred temple. In the center of the ground, a paved path circled around a large statue of the Holy Mother Mary with Her arms folding over Her heart. Having gone to quite a few basilica cathedrals through the country, this was the first time that the couple saw a large statue of Mary in such a prominent position. The Holy Mother stood on a stand about twenty feet high and looked very graceful and compassionate. The couple could fully understand Her position in the fishermen's hearts.

In the old time, there were not many people like the fishermen that had to face so many dangers in making a living by fishing on the sea. North Atlantic is the most dangerous ocean in the world. Storm can come from nowhere and the ocean can turn violent at any moment. From old time on until even recent time, many Newfoundland fishermen have lost their lives on the ocean. The fishermen's lives are at the mercy of the indifferent unpredictable ocean and weather. From the start when they have launched their fishing vessels, many perils will be waiting for them on the open sea. In a fierce storm in the old time, when their lives were hanging on a thin threat, many would feel that they had absolutely no control over their own fate. In those perilous moments, they hoped and trusted the divine to intervene and to see them through. Facing the tremendous fierce force of nature, human strength could fade away into nothing. Yet hope never died even in the most hopeless situations. For the fishermen, their hope for the protection from some powerful and compassionate divine force was their savior for their mental stability in the gravely dangerous time. Only the divine could be mightier than the powerful capricious nature. The Holy Mother after all was the most compassionate and would in any circumstance help even the fishermen out of the hopeless situations. Naturally, many fishermen had put their hope and trust in the Holy Mother. After some of them had survived those most dangerous storms or other grave situations, their faith in the divine force was reinforced.

In the ancient time when the humans were not strengthened by the knowledge of modern science and technology, human beings had depended on their intuitive senses to survive all kinds of dangerous situations. In the beginning, human beings had to develop their instincts and intuitions in order to survive in a hostile world. Their spiritual sense had thus developed first. They might be able to connect to a different level of reality. Their visions and insights might be much different or sharper than the modern man. They trusted and depended more on the spiritual side of themselves and the world. Even with today's advanced science and technology, no scientist or scientific equipment can prove that some strange phenomena are purely material and be absolutely sure that there is no intervening force in some situations and on some occasions.

Today, many modern men with their developed intelligence and degenerated intuitive abilities will find those spiritual intuitions or visions as nonsense. With the powerful modern vessels, the fishermen today are indeed safer in navigating and making a living on the sea. Just like in every other aspect of human life, the fishermen today have trusted more human strength, protection and control over their lives. Human beings are becoming stronger and more material minded; they are gradually losing their spiritual and intuitive senses. In such a modern situation, religion is losing its grip on people's faith and trust. If there are some different levels of reality, the humans are definitely sailing away from them.

Looking at this beautiful cathedral in Saint John's, the couple wondered whether it too was losing attendants. They knew quite well that many church-goers today were mainly staying for the moral teachings. Some of the church-goers and even some priests could be more secular than the lay people or atheists. Still, deep down in their hearts, quite many people in the western world wanted to believe in God. Faith and belief in religion had given them a moral centre to hold on to and provided purpose and meaning for their life. Moreover, they wanted to have a celestial power over the powerful earthly leaders and authorities they could not fully trust and have faith in. On the other hand, those earthly powers were just glad to put God on the topmost position, as this front could empower and moralise them in their ruling or governing. Still, for quite many ordinary people today, to believe in God was simply to believe in the continuation of life. They wanted to believe that there was life after death, no matter that life was in spiritual form, on a different level of reality or any other formation. However, even with quite many people still believed or wanted to believe that there was God, or some divine energy or force, the institutionalized religion however was losing its power and authority over the modern human beings. People could no longer be easily controlled by some dogmatic religious rites and rituals; they were more open-minded and wanted to think and figure things out by themselves.

The couple walked around the grounds, admiring the statues of Mary, Saint John and two other saints on the front wall of the Cathedral. Standing on the ground here, they could have a narrow view of the harbour. The weather was amazingly good. The sun shone brightly and the air was nicely fresh and cool. The cornerstone of this cathedral was laid in 1841 and the building was fully completed in 1855. At the time when Jim and Meilin were looking at it, it was one and half centuries old, but the greyish white stone cathedral looked young and energetic. When the couple walked into the cathedral, they could not help feeling the beauty of its design. Though there were not as many elaborate decorative ornaments, woodcarvings and statues as the basilica cathedrals in other large cities, its stained-glass picture windows were no less beautiful. The couple were quite attracted by the tall ceiling that was patterned and painted in gorgeous colours. The congregation hall was large and the pews were separated by some large pillars and lanes into three sections. The set-up of the altar was the same as that of other basilica cathedrals, but there was a glass case in front of the altar. Inside the glass case, there was a white marble statue of Jesus Christ lying down. In the couple's eyes, this cathedral showed a beautiful simplicity.

Worried that they would make Dalton wait too long, the couple came out of the Cathedral soon. They praised the cathedral when the three were in the car again and said that they did not expect there would be such a large and beautiful cathedral in Saint John's. Dalton looked pleased. Dalton and Esther were Christians and they kept on going to church on Sundays. From the short time with their relatives, Jim and Meilin could see that Dalton and Esther loved this city and their life here.

The next place and also the last place Dalton took the couple to see was The Rooms, the Museum, Art gallery and Archives of Newfoundland and Labrador. Dalton dropped the couple in front of the large museum and told them that he would come back to pick them up later. While watching Dalton driving away, the couple surveyed the large ground in front of the museum. The open ground was covered by a large green lawn with a circling walkway. It was the size of at least two football courts. The building of the museum matched up well with the size of the large front ground. There were some wide stone steps leading up to the museum. The front structure of museum was quite different than the couple used to see of a museum building. One side of it was fully modern with glass and steel frames; the other side was quite simple, a blank wall with a peaked top. Was the architect trying to combine the old and new styles in the design of this building or were the two large buildings built in two different times? The couple could not figure out. Anyhow, the outside look of the museum and its huge ground had already given them the impression that it was a large city's culture facility. The yardstick in judging a city is not only to measure how big and how many skyscrapers the city has but also the quality and quantity of its culture facilities. The geo centre, the cathedral and the museum had given Jim and Meilin the impression that Saint John's was a large city, even though the size of the city was not that big and there were not many large tall buildings around here.

The inside of the museum was very modern. The floor of the foyer, the pillars and the wide swirling staircase leading to the second and third floors were all made of gleaming black marble. In modern time, black colour is quite often used in interior designs to show class, luxury or wealth. The couple were no experts in architecture or interior designs. Still, the contour and the shining black marble made them feel the class and expensiveness.

The couple started their tour of the museum by going to the gallery first. There were plenty of local artists' works, mainly the paintings of Newfoundland landscapes. One small sculpture had caught their attention. It was a man being crucified on a fish. Though the sculpture was small, it was extremely well sculpted. The couple could imagine that this sculpture was very meaningful to the Newfoundlanders. For generations, Newfoundlanders had depended on fishery for their livelihood. When the fish crops were depleted because of overfishing and the whole fishing industry was depressed, they had inevitably felt being strangled or crucified by the single fishing industry. It was clear that Newfoundlanders had long seen that one industry for their livelihood would be disastrous and diversifying their economy was of paramount importance in developing their province. For years, they had put their efforts in this endeavour. However, their resources and their isolated geographic position had been the hindrance for them to march quickly to catch up with other well-to-do provinces.

Nonetheless, on this trip, Jim and Meilin were quite surprised to see that Newfoundland was in a much better condition than they had imagined. The information they had got about this province had never been that good before. They had always thought that Newfoundland was the poorest province in Canada where unemployment rate was high and quite some people had to depend on government help. Now they saw that people here actually lived a life relatively the same as people lived in the mainland. Their own relatives here had jobs and lived a life they were satisfied with. This showed them the truth of an old saying – seeing is believing; one should never fully trust what one has heard.

The museum had quite a few halls for arts displays. One hall had exhibits that were a quite different type of artwork. They were sculptures made by some soft thin tree or bush branches. The branches were very supple; they had been bended and curved so well to make different human figures. The tree-branch human sculptures looked vividly alive. A couple of branch figures were ladies bent over in doubles and dressed in gauzy thin gowns. It was amazing what marvelous work the artist had created by using tree branches. Through the creation of those human figures, the artist had brought nature into the very fabric of the artwork, showing the beauty of human body. Of course, the artist might want to show something else concerning the humans and nature. Human body is part of nature and naturally beautiful, but what kind of beauty the humans seek to decorate their bodies sometimes can be far away from naturally beautiful. Whatever else the artist wanted to say, Jim and Meilin did not want to guess. They liked this creation and thought them natural and beautiful; that was enough for them.

The museum stood quite tall. It was also near the harbour and the downtown area. From the large windows of the upstairs hallway, the couple could see the harbour and some large downtown buildings. They had gone through the old downtown area of the city. Now from this angle, they could see the city centre. Saint John's city centre looked not old and the city did have quite some large buildings to show that it was up to modern date.

A whole section of the museum with the old style front was dedicated to the history of the province. It had in one area displayed the early scenes of human and animal inhabitants and in another area displayed Fort Townsend, an eighteenth century British fort that had existed at the very site of the museum. The exhibits did not neglect the early security or police force of this island which had existed since 1870. Whether it was because of the museum being built on the site of the old fort, or because of the fishermen's habit of keeping things simple, the large modern museum was called The Rooms. To Jim and Meilin, the simple name of the museum, the two different architecture styles and the all sorts of exhibits and records showed a quite unique museum. The couple flew through the numerous exhibits. They did not spent much time to exam them carefully. They were afraid that if they finished too late, Dalton would wait outside too long for them. Anyhow, they were the samplers of all the things they had gone through in this cross-country journey. They were satisfied with the quick peek on what Saint John's or Newfoundland had to offer.

The couple actually came out of the museum earlier than they were expected to. They had waited a little while before Dalton came to pick them up. On the drive back home, they thanked Dalton from the bottom of their heart for the tour of the city. In a strange city, it would normally take them a long time just to find the places that they wanted to see. Because of the difficulties of finding and getting to those places, they would normally see very little. Today, Dalton had taken them to so many important places of Saint John's; they felt the tour a windfall in their sightseeing here. However, it was a rush through and the couple had missed quite many things. They did not check the museum in the basilica cathedral and did not go carefully through the historical part of The Rooms. Yet, the couple were tired out after the whole day sightseeing. Though there were still quite some places of interest and historical significance in the city, they stayed close around the house and in their trailer next day. They were going to leave for Argentia tomorrow and needed to be rested for that. Esther had told them to be sure to come to the house to have supper with them and they were going to have a barbecue.

In the afternoon, the couple went to a superstore to pick up some things for their trip and for the barbecue. The superstore here looked no different than the superstores in the mainland; it was large, bright and full of different goods. They found the prices of quite some different items here were relatively the same as those they had paid for their daily living in the west. They bought a cake and a large bowl of salad to contribute to the barbecue party. They thought that their contribution might save Esther some work.

In summer, a barbecue is a favoured meal arrangement on occasions for some families to enjoy some festival atmosphere; it is also a casual but warm way to invite and treat some friends or relatives. People love to eat meat, fish or other different food barbecued in the ancient way on an open fire. With a barbecue, everybody can join in to make the meal, and there will be plenty of chatting and interaction during and after the barbecue. Having the family and friends around a barbecue in the backyard of their homes is the next best thing to having the same party around a bonfire in a natural setting. Even with the modern equipment for barbecuing and the homes around, it can still remind people of those meal times full of closeness and joy around a bonfire in the wildness. It makes them think of nature, the forest, the riverbank, the starry sky, the story telling, the heart-felt singing and laughing. Perhaps, in their heart of hearts and bone of bones, people still have a nostalgic feeling for the ancient time when they had lived in the wilderness and ate their food around the open fire. Meat or fish barbecued by the open flames still possess the utmost lure for their taste buds.

Jim and Meilin came to the barbecue party in time. Dalton, Esther and Nathan had just started preparing things for the barbecue. Dalton told his wife that Meilin was a health food buff, so the chicken breasts would be used for barbecuing. Both Esther and Dalton were pleased with and appreciated Jim and Meilin's contribution. The preparation for the meal was now only to barbecue the chicken breasts and bake the potatoes. The three men went to the front porch to do the barbecuing; Esther and Meilin remained in the kitchen to do the rest. The potatoes would be baked in the microwave oven, so that they would be ready in no time.

In the large kitchen, Esther was busy with the preparation. She would not let Meilin help.

"Just sit down and talk with me. There is not much to do. I can handle it," said Esther.

Meilin still tried to do something, but was turned down. She knew there was no use to fight with Esther, so she sat down to watch and talk. Esther was of sunny characters, very open. There was no trace of affectedness in her manner. Everything she had felt or thought was open in her talk and on her expressions. She was so plump, shaped like a rugby ball, moving around and doing things nimbly energetic. Meilin could not help liking her. It seemed that this was not the first time that she had seen and talked to this sister-in-law of hers. Esther talked mainly about Dalton. Obviously, she loved him tenderly and well. While they were waiting for the potatoes to be baked, Esther showed Meilin the gun-case she had bought for Dalton as a birthday gift. It was a long wooden case with a glass door. Dalton had a few hunting rifles standing inside the case. He was, after all, of native origin and still a good hunter. In their deep freezer, there were always meat of wild games Dalton had got from his hunting trips.

"A friend of ours has made some sausages from the moose Dalton had shot last time. Perhaps you would like to take some with you when you leave?" Esther chatted along happily.

When Esther started setting the dining table, Meilin questioned, "Are we going to eat in the dining room?"

"Yes, you are still the first time guests. We can't be too casual, can we?" Esther answered.

"Of course, we can. Jim and I prefer that you don't treat us like guests," Meilin protested.

"Still, we don't know whether you'll ever come again. Let's eat here at the dining table and you are going to sit at the head seat," said Esther decisively.

"No, I definitely should not take this seat." Meilin argued against this arrangement, but Esther dismissed her disagreement.

"I would like to sit with Jim. We have never been sitting together to have a meal since we were separated when we were kids. Besides, sitting by the kitchen door makes it easier for me to attend to things. You should not mind of those dining table rituals, we have never cared about them. We are not those rich people, you know," she said frankly.

The two women chatted on in the kitchen about the small things while the three men were with the barbecue outside. Nathan was in charge of the barbecuing. He was very patient, making sure that the chicken breasts were well cooked and not burnt. Nathan was still very much a well-trained military man, doing everything precisely well. Because of the strict military regulations, he remained slim, no belly showing yet. After Jim and Meilin returned home from the cross-country trip, they got the news from Esther: Nathan had got that computer job in Saint John's; he had brought his wife and two kids there, and the family had bought a house in that city. Jim and Meilin were glad that Nathan and his family had settled down in Saint John's to become Newfoundlanders; Esther and Dalton would have some relatives around them.

For the barbecue right now, when everything was ready, the whole group sat around the dining table. Esther and Jim sat on the side near the kitchen door and the rest three each had a whole side of the table.

Jim was given the honor to say the grace before the dinner started. He gave thanks to the Lord, the host and the good companies for the supper. The dinner turned out to be a delight. Everybody was relaxed and enjoyed the meal. The chicken breasts were highly praised. The fresh chicken meat was well barbecued and not burnt; it tasted naturally sweet.

After supper, the men helped to take the dishes to the kitchen and then they disappeared into the living room. The women stayed in the kitchen to wash the dishes. Esther still did not allow Meilin to help. She put the dirty dishes into the dishwasher and cleaned up everything else. Having worked as a housekeeper, Esther probably formed the habit of taking control of the house works. Meilin sat at the center counter and chatted with Esther until everything was finished. Then they joined the men in the living room.

The chat tonight was focused on the trip Jim and Meilin were going to take tomorrow. Dalton told them to take a short cut to reach Argentia and even pointed out the way on the map. When they got to know that Jim and Meilin had travelled across the country without a cellular phone, they were all stunned. Nowadays, almost everybody had a cellular phone and many started having iphones. Travelling long distance without a cell-phone was unthinkable to most people. A cell-phone was a definite must in any kind of situations, especially for safety or other emergency situations.

"What can you do without a cell-phone if you broke down on the way or lost in some remote area?" asked Esther with a worried look.

"There will be plenty of other drivers on the main track; we can ask for help. In the remote areas, there will be no reception signals for the cell-phone to work anyway," Jim answered. He and Meilin had not felt great inconvenience of travelling without a cell-phone.

Still, Dalton and Esther would not have Jim and Meilin continue to travel without a cell-phone. They had several cell-phones. Dalton went to another room and dug out a spare one right away.

"Use this one please. There is still enough time and power left in it," Dalton handed the phone to Jim.

Jim tried to turn it down, saying that it seemed quite unnecessary to have a cellular phone, otherwise they would have had one, and they now definitely would not want to give him and Esther the trouble of using their phone.

"It's no trouble at all. We have a few. If you like, you can mail it back to us when you are home."

Dalton would not listen to Jim's refusal and pushed the phone into his hand. To make Dalton and Esther feel better, Jim accepted the phone, but said, "We probably will never have to use it."

"We hope that will be the case, but have the phone with you will be much safer," said Esther, looking relieved.

Only a few hundred years ago, most human beings had to walk anywhere they traveled. Men went out to hunt, leaving their families or communities for long periods of time. Some of them would never return home, being eaten by other animals or having lost their lives in other ways. Those people with more adventurous spirits and liked to explore; their families or communities would never have much expectation for their return. Nowadays, people travel with the convenience and comfort of different modern equipment, carried by fast moving motor devices on the roads, over the water or in the sky. On top of this, they will carry their computers, cell-phones or ipads with them, and be able to keep in touch with their families and any other kind of associates or protective offices at any time. Thanks to the development of science and technology, human life has been very much improved. Unfortunately, human nature has not been improved in an equal scale. The humans are still constantly fighting and killing each other. Wars are still breaking out here and there. More deadly arsenals have been created and they can cause massive destruction and death. Luckily, the humans have multiplied in astronomic numbers and have plenty to spare. What's more, in their hurry to improve their lives and to get on top of everything and everyone, the humans are destroying their home planet in a deadly speed. It looks that very soon, luck will run out on everyone.

Jim and Meilin had a last peaceful night in Saint John's. Next morning, they got up early and went to the house to say goodbye. Dalton and Esther must have anticipated this. They were already up and waiting for them. There were hugs and kisses with the parting words. Jim and Meilin invited Dalton and Esther to come to the west to visit them, telling them that they had space in their home for them to stay during their visit. It seemed that this newly formed close relationship between them was going to last for years to come. Unfortunately, with the present life situation of Jim and Meilin, how this relationship was going to develop was entirely out of their control. Not long after they had returned home and mailed the cellular phone back to Dalton and Esther, they heard nothing more from them. They had not received returns from their relatives in Saint John's even for the Christmas card they had sent to them. There was only one explanation for this out-of-character behaviour of Dalton and Esther: they had been affected or controlled by the harassers not long after the couple had left Saint John's. The couple had quite anticipated this happening which was not different than all the things that had happened in their life since the harassment and attacks started on them, and they could understand the difficult situation Dalton and Esther were in.

Ever since the couple's total loss of privacy, their conversations and Meilin's writing at home were causing more and more troubles for them. It seemed that whatever they had said or written at their home had greatly offended some people. In the minds of those offended people, ordinary people like Jim and Meilin should be kept in a mute condition for the country to be easily governed or controlled and the present social order to be maintained. The sudden publicity of the voice of Jim and Meilin was probably unprecedented and hurting quite some people for different reasons. Like most people at their own homes, this couple would not talk prettily all the time and would quite often complain and criticise about something. In their situation and with their life experiences, Jim and Meilin's conversations inevitably carried some harsh criticisms on injustices or racial discriminations and even curses sometimes as well. Of course, there would also be some praises if they had encountered something worthy of their praise. Unfortunately, in their present situation, whatever the couple had said would turn out to be offensive to somebody and bring hostilities and hatred towards them. However, in the couple's minds as in most people's minds, they believed that they had the utmost freedom to speak their minds at their own home, and whatever peril the situation would bring could not force them to give up this basic human rights and freedom.

What a painful disillusionment the couple had to go through during this period of their life! Because of their truthful expressions at their own home, the couple had become the public enemy. Of course, not all the Canadians would see the couple in this way. But for some people, this couple's behaviours at their private home were definitely not good for the social order. They felt being threatened by the couple's criticisms. In their own private homes, those people might very well have cursed up a storm about this couple's sharp criticising rebellious talks becoming publicised. They probably worried that the couple might set up a bad example and influence other ordinary people and especially the coloured people. They might also be afraid that the more this ordinary couple had been raised up in the eyes of the public, the more the powerful, the rich and the upper level people might lose their importance and respectability.

In their eyes, this king of breaking of social order should never be allowed and things definitely had to be done to control the situation.

The actions taken to control the situation had been duly felt by Jim and Meilin. They had not only lost their privacy, but also their peace and security of life. A campaign had been launched to turn them into the bad guys. This campaign of course had to be led by the powerful media. Thus, the attacks, hostilities and hatred had been hurled onto the couple in open or hidden ways through the TV media. The couple had been effectively isolated from the society; even their neighbours and their relatives had turned their backs to them. It was probably thought that in this way, whatever the couple had said or written would be rendered ineffective and none-influential in the society.

Jim and Meilin had felt this vicious campaign against them outrageous. In their close life circle, they had met the hostilities and hatred towards them from their neighbours and the local people whom they would have some contact with in their daily life. Their relatives were very few and living far away from them. Still they had gradually felt the estrangement and even instigated attacks and hostilities through them. The ordinary people and especially the couple's relatives were of course being used in the attacks; they would not act out in those ways on their own, as the couple had hardly offended them in any way.

No matter how hard the couple had tried to think the whole thing through, they could not, for their lives, figure out why so much hostilities and hatred had been poured onto them. What they had talked and criticised at their home were just ordinary complaints and criticisms that almost all other people had done in public or at their own homes. The severity of the couple's criticisms had never reached the level that some other published books and produced films had already done. When the open threats and actual attempts had been made on their lives; the couple were pushed to the limit of their tolerance. Though they were Christians, they were far from the exact Jesus type meek Christians. If being slapped on one side of their cheeks, they would slap the attackers on the other side of their cheeks. When suffering from all kinds of insults, vicious name-callings and death threats, they used whatever name-callings they could find to fight back. However, in any case, the couple were much more civilized than some of those high-up privileged people who had the power to use all kinds of tools for the malicious attacks. They could use the public servants, the store service people and the medical workers to make the couple's life hell and to endanger their lives. They could use the media that was the most effective communication tool with large social influences to turn the couple into the public enemy and to bring more hostilities and hatred onto the couple and even onto the whole yellow race. If the couple's criticisms on racism had hurt some people, the racist counter-attacks launched by the powerful through the media had hurt the society and the country much more. The little whitewash that had been put on to cover those open racist malicious attacks was of no remedy for the injuries suffered by the couple and the society. As for the couple, with all those abuses and persecutions they had suffered for years, they had never gone out of their private space to call some people names, to harass or abuse others in order to vent their hurts. They had never thought of harming or putting death threat on anybody.

The most absurd or ridiculous thing in this event was the calling or roaring for the couple's downfall. The couple were very ordinary people at the bottom of the society. Jim was a disabled military veteran and Meilin, his wife, had no job and was sitting at home and doing a little writing. In their life, the couple had never been in any social or political position and had never had any desire to climb any social ladder. Many worldly things that were extremely important to some people were unimportant or worthless to the couple. In the later period of their time, what they had wished for was only a secure and peaceful life. Now peace and security were taken away from them for some unclear reason. The couple were sitting at the very ground level of society. It was hard for them to figure out where those hostile people wanted them to fall. The only place they could fall to from their present position was death. It looked that some people wanted to punish them by death, all because of their home conversations and writing. They could see that this wish had already been carried out by quite some attempts made on their lives. The hate campaign launched on the couple had achieved some success. The whole situation was viciously absurd beyond the couple's comprehension. Many sharper criticisms had been published, broadcast and played out even by the media themselves. Why should the couple not be allowed to talk and write at their home? Why, for this, they had to be punished by death? Some people must have gone insane or totally lost their minds. Meilin could write and express herself well. But so far, she had never forced her writing on anybody; instead, her writing had been read by people without her permission. Still, her skill in writing and her criticisms must have hurt some people's sense of superiority. Jealousy must have fanned up the racist flames and burnt all rational senses out of those people.

However, what had happened to Meilin was not singular. The general situation in the country was that the talks, speeches or statements of antiracism out of the mouth of coloured people would often meet attacks, hostilities and hatred, while the same talks, speeches or statement out of the mouth of white people would gain credits or praises. It seemed that the coloured people could only receive racial discriminations and could not express their indignation against them. White people however, some the renders of racism, could be the fighters or heroes against racism.

The situation had very much infuriated the couple. As human beings, they had every right to say what they wanted to say and to write what they wanted to write at least in their home. Was Canada still a democratic country? Was the country so scared that it must deprive its citizens of the equal rights and freedom to feel secure and safe? Were the couple's home talks threatening the country's security and safety, or was some people's wanton use of power to abuse and persecute ordinary people truly harming the country? The callings for the couple's death could not force them to give up their basic human rights and freedom, but made them stick firmer to protecting them. If they were going to be killed sooner or later, that would be more reason for them to do whatever they wanted to do for the time left to them.

The tricks of trying to isolate the couple from others were a joke to the couple. Being an interracial couple, Jim and Meilin had never felt that their marriage had been fully accepted by the society. Ever since they got married, they had lived an isolated and friendless life. It was a lonely life, but they had learnt to love it and enjoyed the solitude. What damages the isolation attempts could do to a couple who had preferred and enjoyed a solitude life? None. The pity was that the isolation tricks tried on the couple did not include stopping the harassment, attacks and threats to them. They were not being left alone. Some people under the control of the evil persecutors were rudely trudging into the couple's life to make sure there was no peace for them at home or anywhere they travelled.

Well, at this moment when Jim and Meilin were driving away from Saint John's and heading for Argentia, their minds were like the sunny sky, clear of any dark clouds of their troublesome life; they were focused on enjoying this precious present moment that was free of any bad things. After some time driving on the main highway, they turned into a side road, the shortcut to reach Argentia. Very soon troubles started. On this side road, there was quite some road construction work going on. The workers were working on widening the road. Long stretches of the road were covered by coarse gravels; driving on the road became difficult. The couple were worried that they would get another flat tire, and it would be more difficult to get repair work done in this remote area where no residential or any other human structures were around. Luckily, their tires had held out and no mishap occurred. However, the drive had to be kept in a very slow pace on the rough road and quite often they had to stop and wait for the construction crews to work on certain spots. It took them quite some time to cover this not so long distance; they wondered whether it would have been better if they had not taken the shortcut.

In the afternoon, the couple had finally got near Argentia. They had turned onto a better road and felt a relief. Argentia seemed not a big place. The ferry was actually a little distance away from the town. A campground or RV Park was near the ferry. The couple did not go into the town, but headed for the campground. The first thing for them to do now was to find the RV Park, settle down and have their lunch.

It was not hard to find the campground. In a small place where there were not many roads or streets; finding certain places had always been easy. Besides, the campground signs had been considerately posted in different spots to lead those who were looking for it. Soon the couple arrived at the correct site. The RV Park was located on the flat top of a small mountain. It looked a newly built large campground. The whole site was covered with fine new gravels. There were quite many fully serviced sites for RVs and subserviced sites for tents. Not far from the campground, there was the ocean. From the high-up campground, the view of the blue ocean and the green area surrounding the campground was breathtakingly beautiful.

The couple pulled their van and trailer to the front of the campground office which was a large new residential house. The building not only housed the office, but also the bathroom and laundry facilities. The couple went into the office and had the registration done for two nights. Then they parked their van and trailer on the lot they had chosen. It was a very spacious campground. There were a few other RVers who had parked their trailers or motor homes a little distance away from each other. The whole place was open and there was nothing to block the view of the ocean. Jim and Meilin felt that they had finally made it; they could now live in a place that had a broad view of the magnificent ocean. The charge for this accommodation on such a great location was twenty-five dollars per night, quite low, compared to the RV park charges in the mainland which had most past thirty dollars and some even reached forty or fifty dollars per night. Moreover, no RV parks in the mainland had such a splendid view of the ocean. The pity was that the couple could not stay long to enjoy all these; their ferry would leave Argentia in the evening the day after tomorrow. They regretted that they did not book the return ferry at least one more week later. It took them so much efforts to come to Newfoundland. They had hurried through the few days, did not fully enjoy the place and then had to hurry back to the mainland.

After everything settled and their trailer stabilized, the couple had their lunch. For the rest of that day, they rested, walked around and enjoyed the view. From the high ground, the ocean looked deep blue and very calm. Under the sunny sky and aided by the absolutely pure air, everything around looked surreally clear and bright. A few ships glided on the quiet blue ocean. They were very small because of the far away distance and looked like painted ships on blue glass ocean. Everything looked dreamily beautiful and peaceful.

There were no other buildings around the campground. Backed by other treed green mountains, the campground was serenely secluded. The gentle cool summer wind breathed through. With the ocean close-by, the wind seemed to have carried the smell or essence of the ocean. Down under the mountain and a little distance away, there were some greyish concrete buildings in an open flat area by the ocean. No human activities were around those buildings; they looked like some abandoned military facilities, perhaps hangers for aeroplanes. During the Second World War, Newfoundland and Labrador was a strategic defence line; both Canada and the United States had military bases on them. Those abandoned buildings might have belonged to the Air Force of the United States which had set an air base around here in that war. Now everything was quiet, no activities of any kind were around and the place was returned back to peaceful nature. The ocean, the sky, the mountains and the wind were taking control. People could enjoy nature again without the threat of dark war clouds hanging over their heads.

The night on this mountain top by the ocean was the most peaceful camping night the couple had enjoyed in their trip across the country. Next morning, they got up early and had their simple breakfast. They had a full sightseeing day ahead of them. Today, their tour would be fully focused on nature. They were going to visit Cape St. Mary's Ecological Reserve in a coastal place called St. Bride's.

The drive to reach this natural reserve turned out to be a rare joy. They had left their trailer on the campground. Driving the van only made them feel freer. Though the road was not wide, it was paved and the traffic was very light. The small road was winding and had quite some ups and downs from the start. At some spots, they were like driving straight into the broad ocean and then the road suddenly turned back towards the land. A few small valleys were along the way and there were some cultivated farm land with a few farm houses in those valleys. These were the only farm land and farmhouses the couple had seen on their trip through Newfoundland Island.

The nearer the couple were getting to the nature reserve, the more even the land became. The road had become a long straight stretch, and the landscape had turned into large open flat terrain on both sides of the road. The scene here looked otherworldly isolated or even desolated. The land was obviously not arable. There were only stubby low bushes growing here and there. The vegetations were unfamiliar strange ones to the couple; they were growing close to the ground and looked tolerant to salty and sulphuric conditions. The couple could not help admiring those bushes and plants. They could imagine what kind of harsh conditions they had to endure. The soil looked full of salt or other kinds of minerals. The place looked a salt marsh area. The coastal wind must be ferociously strong most of the time. In winter, the temperature in the stormy weather must be terribly low for any live to survive. Yet those bushes and plants thrived here. They did not look lushly green, but greyish or silvery. They gave the couple the impression of their hardiness or utmost toughness.

It was still morning when the couple reached the nature reserve. There was a large red-roofed modern building on site. It was an interpretive centre called Dr. Leslie M. Tuck Centre. The couple parked their van and got out to stretch and relax first. The whole place was a large open area, a highland plateau thrusting into the ocean. In addition to the red-roofed centre building, there were two other houses nearby, which must be the residences of the people who were working in or maintaining the place. A few large woolly sheep were roaming close to the houses. At the edge of this highland, there was a lighthouse. Now here was the typical Newfoundland scenery, the wide open sky, the broad ocean, the green mountains of flat or round tops and no trees around.

The couple had a moment to enjoy the deep blue ocean way down under the cape highland. Then they walked on a long boardwalk to reach the centre. They needed information before venturing into the wilderness. The centre had a large reception hall. Quite a few other tourists were already there. There was not much for the couple to bother the clerks behind the long information counter. The literature or information about the place and its wildlife residents, the different kinds of seabirds, had already been posted on the whole side of the large walls.

Jim and Meilin did not linger long in the centre. They were eager to see the seabirds. After using the centre's washroom, they followed the other tourists and headed to the place where the birds congregated. They walked on a small path that meandered on the highland plateau along the coast. The weather was exceptionally good. Though the wind was strong, it was pleasantly cool. The soil here seemed not too harsh. There were green grass and bushes to be seen. The couple were soon attracted by the flowers everywhere on this highland. They were mainly blue irises and yellow buttercups clustering in large patches. The couple were astonished to see so many such flowers here. In their minds, irises were the softest flowers and their beauty mainly lying in the gentle flow of their large pedals. Here, these gentle flowers survived in the severe natural conditions and were thriving on the highland along the ocean coast. Though the blue flowers appeared smaller and their flower stems were not shooting high above their bayonet leaves, they looked robustly healthy.

The couple were not too surprised to see the yellow buttercups. They were tough wild flowers and could survive almost anywhere. Here under the bright sun, the shining pedals of the small yellow flowers were like twinkling stars among the blue irises and the deep green leaves. The colours of green, blue and shining fresh yellow formed elegant vibrant pictures in this broad wilderness. Jim and Meilin lingered over those colourful patches and tried to find the best spots to take some pictures. Soon the couple were far behind the other tourists. They were not worried, as it seemed there was only one path through this coastal highland.

After about twenty minutes of walking and checking around the flowers and scenery, the couple reached a place that looked like a small bay. A concave had formed at the high bank of the shore. This kind of shoreline was something that the couple had never seen before. The small bay was surrounded by cliffs that were shooting straight up from the ocean hundreds meters high. The rock cliffs were so steep that they looked like rock walls with lines of narrow ridges on them. Tens of thousands seabirds were here, some resting on the ridges of the cliff walls, some flying in the sky and others were diving into the ocean to get something to eat. Never in their dreams, could the couple imagine a scene like this. Though they had seen some similar scenes in some documentary films, those scenes on screens could not compare with the actual scene they were viewing now; they themselves were right in this majestic nature scene. The couple sat on the rock on top of a cliff, watching and trying to take everything in. Their eyes followed the flying birds, seeing them diving straight down into the deep blue ocean or flying around the cliffs and in the sky. They turned their eyes to the rock cliffs sometimes, trying to watch the resting birds on the ridges. Intermittently, they viewed the whole magnificent scene with all the numerous birds, vivid, awesome and full of live.

The scene was so overwhelmingly powerful that the couple had lost themselves in it for quite some time. Then they realized that other tourists were not here with them. There must be another spot that might be even more awesome. The couple got up from their rock seat and decided to explore further. They walked back from the path they came in and came to the point to see that the path was leading further on to another coastal area. They had missed this path because it went down at a deep of the land. After walking on the new path for a little while, the couple spotted the tourist group at the edge of another shoreline. Even from a distance, they had already heard the loud tumultuous sounds coming from countless birds.

Jim and Meilin joined the other tourists. They saw another bay here secluded by surrounding rock cliffs. There were much more seabirds here. On one side of cliff bank, there was a large sandstone rock or a hill shooting up from the ocean to reach the same height as the highland. The peak of this special rock or hill was separated from the cliff bank for about ten feet. All the attention of the tourists standing on the bank was focused on this large sandstone rock which was fully covered by seabirds and their nests. From the information provided by the interpretive centre, the couple could see that almost all the birds gathered on this rock were northern gannets. They were rather large white seabirds with yellowish heads. Their faces and long beaks had straight black lines that looked like being painted on and their wind tips were black. The gannets were built or shaped in the way that they could dive into the ocean like the shooting of the arrows and swim in the ocean water with high speed to catch their prey.

It was the first time in Jim and Meilin's life that they had encountered so many seabirds in such a close range. They felt that they had walked into a birds' colony or a birds' kingdom. The beautiful birds had no fear of and paid no attention to the humans who were so close to them and watching them. They were busy with their own businesses. The numerous adult birds and many of their chicks had almost occupied every inch of the large rock. There were constant activities in the birds' kingdom and the noises they had issued out could only be compared to the noises coming from a large human audience of a concert, screaming, shouting, cheering and laughing all at the same time. Gannets are faithful birds. Each summer they come back with the same mates and to the same nests. On this nature reserve, there are over 53,000 gannet nests. It was definitely not an exaggeration for the couple to see the place as the birds' kingdom.

The seabirds had not only fully occupied this large rock; some were flying in large flocks around this area. Many other types of seabirds could also be spotted flying or resting on the ridges of the cliffs around. Besides the gannets, the seabirds here were mainly common murres, thick-billed guillemots, black-legged kittiwakes, razorbills and black guillemots. As this cliff-walled bay was so big, Jim and Meilin could not easily make out what type of other seabirds were flying or resting far away on the opposite side of the cliffs. Still, to them, the northern gannets were for sure the majority here. The next large number belonged to the type of smaller black and white birds. The couple decided that they must be the common murres.

All the tourists looked stunned but extremely attracted by the scene of the birds' kingdom. Like Jim and Meilin, they all took out their cameras and camcorders and started taking pictures or video-taping the amazing scene. It looked that the cliff shoreline here had provided the best shelter for the countless seabirds; it had effectively blocked the strong ocean wind and storms. The quiet water inside the small bays must have harboured plenty of fish and other marine lives to support such large numbers of seabirds. No wonder the Newfoundlanders had called the place, Cape of Saint Mary's. The place looked like the compassionate Holy Mother stretching out Her arms, embracing, caring, loving and protecting all the countless birds.

People lingered on at this spot for quite a long time, reluctant to leave the birds' kingdom. The bay was full of lives with busy activities and loud noises. Further on, the deep blue ocean looked unusually serene. In nowhere else did the couple have so deeply felt the immensity of the sky, the ocean and the beautiful earth teeming with all kinds of lives. On their way back and when all the sounds of birds were out of their hearing range, the couple were once again surrounded by the quiet highland with only the wind sweeping through. Without the hustling and bustling activities of the birds, there were only the light blue sky, the deep blue ocean, the darkish rock cliff shoreline and the green flat top of the highland plateau. The red roof of the interpretive centre gave a needed touch to vivify the nature scene, so that the visitors would not feel totally lost in this vast wilderness.

When the couple came back to their van, it was already afternoon. They were famished and quickly garbled down some food they had brought with them in the van. After resting for a while, they reluctantly left the nature reserve. The drive back to the campground seemed faster. On the way, the couple talked only about the birds' kingdom at Cape Saint Mary's and felt that the visit had made their cross-country trip worthwhile. The experience of being in the birds' kingdom was indeed worth all their efforts and troubles to travel the thousands of miles from the west of the country to the east end of the continent, even if they had only visited this beautiful cape with all those numerous seabirds.

To end this day's sightseeing, the couple stopped at Argentia on their way. The town seemed not that small. There were a large church and a large grocery store. The residential houses here looked no different than those in the mainland. Most impressively, there was a long stretch of boardwalk along the seashore at the skirt of the town. Like other places on the Newfoundland Island, the town was located at the coast. The couple decided to have a walk on the boardwalk. They stopped their van in front of a nice funeral home that was by the boardwalk and facing the ocean. The funeral home looked new and its size and appearance showed that Argentia must have all kinds of facilities and services. Abbotsford, a small city that was swelling bigger by day and had a large hospital built recently, had only one funeral home.

Birth and death are two largest events in human life. These two major events have always been regarded and treated differently. Traditionally, birth is regarded as good and worth celebrating and death bad, a tragedy. For most ordinary people, death will be tucked away as quickly as possible. Babies are born into this world in large hospitals in the modern time and ordinary people die to leave this world normally in a funeral home, a small place. From ancient time on, death like life is highly ranked and unequal affairs in human life. In the old days, the poor and insignificant might die miserably and be buried in most undignified and even horrible conditions. The kings and queens and important, powerful or rich people might die also miserably, but surrounded by comfort, luxury and all the concerned people. Their burials would be extravagantly rich with all kinds of rituals. Their tombs would be filled with treasures to ensure an equally good life in the next world. In the modern time, the funerals and burials as those for the ancient royalties and aristocrats are banished. Still when the important, powerful or rich people die, there will still be grand funerals held in large cathedrals or state funerals held in significant halls. There will be plenty of high praise eulogies, beautiful music, blessings and prayers by large group of priests, relatives and many other people. However, no matter how significant the dead are, there will be no more treasures buried with them. Obviously, people no longer believe that the dead will need the material wealth even if there might be another life waiting for them in another world or another reality. For the modern ordinary people, their death will be simpler affairs. According to how well the dead had done when alive and their family financial conditions or social status, most will have a funeral. There will be some eulogies to remember the life of the dead and some rituals performed by priests or funeral-home conductors. The burials will be simple and most might be cremation. For people who have no families or friends, their death affairs will be even simpler. There will be no funeral and the dead will mostly be cremated. However, there is no need for the poor, the insignificant or the lonely to fear death, the ultimate equalizer; it comes to all. There is no need for people to lament how vastly different fate has dealt them in life and death. Time erase and iron out all the inequalities. After a few centuries, who remembers who had been who? The bones dug out from the pyramids will not be any different than the bones found from the pit that had buried numerous victims of massacres. Some great names and deeds will be remembered, so also will be the crimes of the notorious evil ones.

However, funerals are changing in the modern time. Large or small, funerals have started focusing on the contributions the dead had made in their lives to the world, the country, the society, the communities or the families. They will often turn out to be the celebrations for the lives of the dead and the inspirations to the living. They can be beautiful and full of positive atmosphere. The dreary heavy funerals are phasing out of the modern society. Perhaps, people's view of death is also changing. Still, human beings are born with the fear of death. They might not fear of being dead, but fear the stroke of death. The fear of death is both a blessing and a curse in human life. On the one hand, this fear has preserved their lives and kept them from venturing into life-threatening situations. On the other hand, life lived in any fear is not a free life. Fear of death is very much part of the bondage in human conditions. In any case, birth and death should be equal events in human life. Many things have been said about death by different kinds of writers and thinkers. A religious sage even thinks that birth brings the human beings into a nightmare and death leads them to the wakening from the nightmare. How much truth this kind of thinking bears cannot be decided by anyone, as nobody has ever told us his or her experiences from this kind of wakening.

The majority of people can never be freed from the fear of death no matter what sayings or thinking about death have been floating around them. All kinds of worst thoughts and imaginations have been associated with death or life after death, the ultimate unknown and unknowable. The tragedy is that death is the definite end for every living being, no matter how they dread this ending or the moment of death. To lighten this fear or dread, many more thoughts or imaginations have been created by human beings about life after death; some of those imaginations and suppositions seem to carry some creditable facts and proves. There is definitely no harm to those who have the belief or conviction that life continues after death. With a relatively calmer mental state, those people are normally the ones who can deal much better with death, the dark scary monster. Nonetheless, science so far has not backed this kind of belief. This fact seems not significant to the believers. To them, science has not solved many problems concerning spiritual matters and it is only a matter of time that scientists with their material equipment will see the truth, the truth they have long sensed or felt with their sixth sense.

Even though Jim and Meilin had kept an open mind towards death, like most ordinary people, they could not get rid of certain prejudice against death. They too could not treat birth and death equally. Death still brought grim, bleak and depressed feelings to them. They had attended a few funerals carried out in churches, but never in a funeral home. Now even with some curiosity about how the inside of a funeral home would look like, they would not visit the one at hand without any proper cause.

After parking their car, the couple went straight to the boardwalk. The sun was now tilting down towards the west, spraying the ocean with myriad of golden sparkles which were hard for them to lay eyes on. It was a normal bay here. The mountains far away on both sides appeared shadowy. The couple would not leave such a beautiful ocean scene without taking some pictures. Then they walked on the boardwalk along the shore. The wooden boards of the boardwalk had been washed and weathered so clean by the coastal rains and storms; they turned white. The couple felt comfortable and relaxed walking on the white boardwalk and enjoying the beautiful ocean scene. Like any other coastal areas, the wind here was also very strong. The couple soon finished the walk and went back to their van. It was not far for them to drive back to the campground from the town. After a whole sightseeing day, they were tired out and needed a good rest.

When they got to the campground, it was already past their normal supper time. Still they took a rest first. The evening on the campground came with some disturbance. After supper when they were getting ready to go to the office building to take a shower, the manager of the campground, a middle-aged stout man, came to their trailer door. He informed the couple with a grim or accusing manner, "There will be no water for two hours."

"No problem," Jim said to the manager and then he thanked the manager for coming to inform them about this.

From the manager's tone and manner, the couple sensed that the manager might be blaming them for bringing this trouble to the campground. The couple knew that the manager might very well have some ground for blaming them. They were aware that the harassment and attacks to them had followed them to Newfoundland as well. Only in Newfoundland, the harassment to them had never been carried out too far. The Newfoundlanders seemed sticking to their hospitable nature and could not or would not do things too drastic towards their guests, even if their guests were an interracial couple and hated by quite some mainland people. Living with the ocean, the Newfoundlanders seemed to be more broad-minded; the sense of racial discrimination did not go too deep into their minds and hearts. Unlike some of their countrymen in the mainland, they did not have the heated or distorted spirit to fight for their turf and did not seem to have the fear that their turf was being invaded by other kinds of people. So far, Jim and Meilin had met some stares from a few people here that looked under some influence. Considering what the couple had gone through, the stares here were so mild that they were hardly noticeable. This water stoppage on the campground was a surprise, but not a big surprise; they had experienced much worse in the mainland.

About twenty minutes later, some camping neighbour announced that the water had come back. The couple were glad. If this water stoppage was brought upon the campground by the couple's presence, it looked that the harassment was not carried out to the end. This proved that the Newfoundlanders were not that easy to be corrupted and more people would do the right thing.

After the water crisis was over, the couple went to have their showers. The shower facility was clean and the water pressure was good, considering the place was high up on the mountain. The nice showers had relieved the couple's fatigue from the day's sightseeing. They had another best night's sleep. Next morning, they decided to walk around and check things out close-by. They had spotted a tourist centre by the highway just before turning to the small road to come to the campground. They decided to go there to have a look. They were going to leave the island today, but they had almost a day to look around. The ferry that would take them back to the mainland would start off in the evening at about five. Going to visit the tourist centre would give them a destination to walk and enjoy the quiet road. After the tourist centre, they were going to check out another building which was in the valley and not far from the campground; it looked like a museum.

The walk turned out to be very pleasant. Since they came to the Newfoundland Island, the weather was very co-operative. Today was the same. The sun was shining brightly and bathing everything in its glory. The air was cool and fresh. There was hardly any traffic on the road. The road was bordered by abundant trees, bushes and different plants. All the green leaves were shinning in the sun, vibrating and emitting energy. The walk turned out to be like a walk through a park in a very fresh morning. When driving by the tourist centre, the place seemed a short distance to the campground. Now they found out that it was quite a long distance to reach by walking. When they arrived at the centre, they were tired out. The centre was a nice modern building. The reception hall was large, bright and had high ceilings. The couple rested first and then checked the information and brochures concerning the tours and sightseeing for the whole Newfoundland and Labrador. Only they were thinking that it was a pity that they might never come to visit Newfoundland again. After the looking around and resting, it was the long walk back to the campground.

When they reached the campground, it was already noon, high time for them to have lunch. After the lunch, they rested for a while and then decided to vacate the campground. They felt sorry that they did not visit the museum. It might not be feasible to spend the afternoon in visiting the museum, as they had no idea about the ferry situation here. They felt safer to get to the ferry earlier. After the rest and a last look at the beautiful ocean and the scene surrounding the campground, the couple packed up their trailer and left the campground. On the whole, they felt the trip to Newfoundland Island one of the most satisfactory and memorable. They were sorry that they had to leave after such a short time visit.

It was a short distance drive to the ferry. They were the first to have arrived for the scheduled ferry. Having parked their vehicles at the lane assigned to the passengers for the numbered ferry, they had a look at Port Argentia. It was a large port and had a large paved parking lot for the vehicles waiting to aboard the ships. The modern terminal building of the port looked new and designed as a large ship. Inside the building, there were large waiting areas with metal chairs on the first and second floors. The ticket office with a long counter was on the first floor and beside it; there was the area for the restaurant and a small store. Port Argentia looked more modern, much bigger, and better equipped than Port North Sydney. As a matter of fact, all the public facilities the couple had seen on the Newfoundland Island looked modern, spacious, clean and well managed.

The couple rested in the large waiting room on the second floor. They could see the harbour through the large windows here. The harbour looked quiet and there were not many activities around. Leaving the harbour quietly resting under the bright sun, the couple turned their attention to the waiting room. There was a large TV set in front of the sitting area. They settled into the chairs and watched TV to kill time. Not very long, a clerk came and called them to take their vehicles to an auto-bay to have them washed clean. This was a new thing to them. The couple went out and pulled their van and trailer to a large hangar; some other passengers had also arrived and they followed behind the couple with their vehicles. Soon the door of the hangar opened. They drove their vehicles in and went through the procedure like a car-washing. But the powerful water jets on the floor washed only the bottoms of their vehicles. After this done, the tires and the whole bottoms of their vehicles were thoroughly cleaned. The couple realized that this washing was to prevent the travelers carrying anything from Newfoundland Island to the mainland. The couple were quite puzzled. To them, the island was much cleaner than the mainland. The air, the large uninhabited interior land and the ocean here were all so clean. It seemed that the travellers' vehicles from mainland should be washed clean before they came onto Newfoundland to prevent them from contaminating this pure clean island. Oh, well, what could the ordinary people like Jim and Meilin know about the purpose of this kind of regulations or restrictions? They might be necessary to protect the ecosystem. The plants and vegetation on the island might be much tougher; once landing on the mainland, they might take over and squeeze out the weaker mainland plants and vegetation.

The waiting was long. At about eight or nine o'clock at night, the ferry ship started loading the passengers and vehicles. The ship was again large and named Joseph Joey Smallwood. This time, Jim and Meilin would be in the sleeper cabin. They found out that the sleeper cabin was at the bottom of the ship. Each long cabin was like a sleeper car in a train. The cabin car contained a line of sleeper sections or booths on one side.

There were four bunk-beds in each booth and no door for any booth. A long narrow walkway was on the other side along the cabin booths, a passing way used by all the sleeper passengers.

Jim and Meilin soon found their beds. Before the ship started sailing, Jim insisted taking Meilin to see the ship's doctor. He was not going to take the risk of letting his wife go through the serious seasickness again. In any case, the doctor should be informed about the danger she might face. He wanted to see what remedy or precaution the doctor could provide for his wife's condition. The couple found the ship's small medical office on the top level of the ship. A nurse received them. Jim told the nurse about his wife's seasickness problem and her heart condition. The nurse provided them with some paper bags in case of her vomiting and some pills for her motion sickness. The couple accepted the paper bags, but refused the pills. They had not only motion sickness pills, but also sleeping pills. This time they were fully prepared.

The return voyage turned out to be much more comfortable for Meilin. The four beds booth had only Jim and Meilin. The couple found the booth private. Meilin had taken a sleeping pill and did not have to vomit. Partially because of the sleeping pill and partially because of the sleeper cabin locating at the ship's bottom level, Meilin spent the fourteen hours sailing in a stable condition. All the time she was in a half sleep mode and had noticed that the nurse had come down near their cabin to check on her. Towards morning, Meilin went to the washroom. Now she saw that the ship was much older than the one they had boarded to go to Newfoundland. The toilet stalls in the washroom here were made of wooden boards painted white. The place was clean, but it creaked and groaned while the ship was sailing on the ocean.

Boarding on a ship to sail over the ocean, no matter how big the ship is, you are in a confined area and in danger of being drowned. During the sailings to and from Newfoundland, the couple had never at any moment thought or felt that their lives were in danger. They probably knew instinctively that the ships were safe and the sailings would be safe. Sure enough, next day towards noon, the ship reached Port North Sydney. They were safe and well through the voyage over the dangerous Atlantic Ocean. Leaving the ferry, the couple were immediately under the heavily overcast sky in North Sydney. The chilling drizzle had already started. The gloomy weather here made the couple miss the sunny bright Newfoundla-nd immediately.

CHAPTER TWELVE

PRINCE EDWARD ISLAND AND COMING BACK HOME

Having left the port, the couple pulled their trailer to the parking lot of a Canadian Tire store which was near the port. By now they had already driven more than eight thousand kilometers. Before they could travel further, they had to change the oil of their van and check if some other things needed to have maintenance done. The day happened to be Sunday again; the store was closed. Jim and Meilin decided to spend the night on the parking lot and next morning they would be the first to be served. Jim again asked the permission from somebody of the store to stay on their parking lot and he was given the permission.

At night, it took some time to have quietness on the parking lot; the traffic on the streets around was rather heavy until after ten, but the couple had managed to have some sleep. Next morning, the rain stopped, but the sky was still overcast. The mechanic of the store did look at their van first, while the couple had their breakfast. Then the engine oil had been changed, the parts that needed to be lubricated had been oiled and a burnt-out taillight had been replaced. After all these done and their van being returned to them, it was still early in the morning. The couple hitched their trailer up and were on the road again. Not long after they were on the highway, their van started giving out some loud noise. The couple were alarmed and stopped their vehicles by the roadside. Jim checked carefully and could not find anything wrong with the van. They decided to keep on going to see if anything else would come up.

The noise came up a few times more, but it seemed dying done, so the couple kept on driving. They did not want to go back to North Sydney. If there was really something serious, they could have it looked at by some auto shop on the way ahead. Soon, the couple came to the hilly area of Cape Breton. Here, abundant green trees and thick bushes covered the hills and valleys. But right now a thick fog had covered this area; they could hardly see anything much further. Jim slowed down the van. There were other vehicles on the road and every driver had slowed down. When the visibility was so poor, the utmost caution had to be taken. Now all the vehicles on the highway were moving slowly in this pea soup; their muffled headlights were showing faintly. The whole foggy surrounding and the dim lights moving around were like some scene in a muddled dream. Luckily, they soon passed the foggy area. Further on, the fog had turned into mists which were floating and drifting in different spots. The couple felt now driving through a beautiful fairyland. The mists veiled some parts of the green hills and valleys and revealed some other parts, giving the land a mysterious beauty. The couple very much enjoyed the rare beautiful scene; meanwhile they were feeling a bit relieved about their van. The noise occurred in longer intermittence and sounded less threatening now.

When the couple came to the lake area, the mists had totally gone. Though the sun was not out yet, they could see farther away. In this early morning, the straight highway in this area was already crowded with traffics. Still, the couple noticed the turn-off road to the port where people could take the ferry to go to Prince Edward Island. They also knew that a bridge had been built, which connected New Brunswick with Prince Edward Island. The bridge was finished in 1997 and named Confederation Bridge. It was an amazing bridge-building stunt. The bridge crossed the Northumberland Strait of Gulf of St. Lawrence, stretching about fifteen kilometres long to link Prince Edward Island to the mainland. Many large pillars of fifty-five meters high supported the bridge and ensured its endurance over the ocean.

Prince Edward Island was a familiar province to Jim and Meilin. When Jim was a young man under twenty, he had worked on this island as a farmhand. He knew the island well. Meilin had traveled through this island when she was a student in the University of New Brunswick. At that time, she was new to Canada and heard about the beautiful island. Besides New Brunswick, Prince Edward Island was the first place in Canada she had ventured to have a tour. After the couple got married and moved to the west, in their first trip back to the east for a visit, they especially went to Prince Edward Island just to drive across the newly built Confederation Bridge. The driving across the long ocean-crossing bridge had left them a lasting memory. It took them almost half an hour to cross; the speed was limited low and the ocean wind was strong. When moving on the bridge, they were surrounded by the ocean. The bridge stretched ahead so far; it seemed not connected to the land on the other end, but reaching to the sky. The experience of driving on such a long bridge over the ocean was indeed unforgettable.

Prince Edward Island is the smallest, but not the least significant province of the country. When this province is mentioned, three things will normally pop up in people's minds. First, the island is the birthplace of Canada. Second, it is the place that produces the world's best potatoes. Third, its pastoral beauty and peaceful country life are well known in the world because of the novel, Anne of Green Gables, written by Lucy Maud Montgomery.

The recorded first white man came to Prince Edward Island is French explorer Jacques Cartier. He found this island in 1534 on his way up to the St. Lawrence River and claimed it for France. In 1603, Sammuel de Shamplain mapped the island and named it Ile St. Jean. In 1745, the British took control of this island, but three years later returned it to the French. Then three years later again the island was reverted to the British. In 1763, the Treaty of Paris had made this island permanently British. Of course, this island too was resided by the natives before the white people came. The Micmac natives had lived on the island during the summer months for thousands of years. In 1799, the island had its present name, Prince Edward Island, named after the Duke of Kent, father of Queen Victoria. Before the name was settled, the British had already divided the land into 67 lots; each lot was about 20,000 acres. The Crown of England gave those lots to its creditors in a lottery, hoping that they would see about developing this island. Unfortunately, those landlords were not interested in developing this land and they had remained absent landlords. After the French had fled or deported from the island, for a long time, the population on the island remained very low, only a few hundred. During this period of time, the Europeans could get free land in other parts of North America; few would choose to come to Prince Edward Island to lease land from the landlords.

In the beginning, Prince Edward Island was administrated by Nova Scotia. After the land was distributed to the British landlords, they had managed to have a constitution and government of the island's own. In spite of the system of absentee landlords, the population of the island gradually grew. In the late 18th century, several hundred of Roman Catholic Scots came. Then about two hundred American Loyalists fled here from the American Revolution. In 1803, Thomas Douglas, the Earl of Selkirk brought about eight hundred Scottish peasants here. However, there were constant conflicts between the tenants and the landlords. The peasants who had leased the land from the landlords had no hope to buy the land from them, and therefore they had no incentives to develop the land. Besides, the local political changes had brought a modern system of cabinet government on the island and domestic policy was entirely decided by the locally chosen premier and his cabinet. The lieutenant governor appointed by the British only dealt with external affairs. The local government had often clashed with the mother British government in fighting for the local rights and interests.

During the 1860's, as the system of absentee landlords and the peasants' hopeless situation of owning the land had very much hindered the development of the island, the talks had started about a union of all British North American Colonies. The sparks of independence that started on this island and some other parts of the country were soon inflamed. In 1864, the founding fathers of Canada had the first Confederation Conference in Charlottetown, today's capital city of Prince Edward Island. The negotiations soon started, which had eventually resulted in the founding of Canada in 1867. However, Prince Edward Island was not among the first provinces that had joined the union to form the Canadian nation. The delegates from the early joined provinces did not allow the newly formed federal government to provide the island with the needed funds to buy the land from the absentee landlords. A few years later, in 1873, the island joined the Canadian union as it was threatened by bankruptcy in building the railways. The Canadian federal government assumed the island's debt and provided a loan for the island to purchase the land from the British landlords.

By the mid 19th century, Prince Edward Island had started experiencing an economic boom in fishing, lumbering, ship-building and agriculture. It had not only sold its produces all over the world, but also sold those wooden ships that had carried those produces. At the time when the furs were in fashion, the island raised silver foxes and had the world's first fox ranch. The furs of the black fox had a silver sheen, which was highly demanded and highly priced in the market at that time. The island was doing a hot business with the fur industry. Some breeders had paid up to thirty thousand dollars for a pair of live foxes, which was a fortune in those old days. When the fox fur was a bit out of fashion, the island raised minks to follow the trend. Then in 1930, the bottom of fur market fell out, which had finished the fur industry of the island.

The small island had no forest or large woods. In building the wooden ships, the islanders had depleted the trees on the island. After the demands for furs and wooden ships went down and fishing industry became depressed, the islanders turned their efforts to agriculture. With the trees gone, the islanders found that most of the island red soil was arable and rich for growing all kinds of things, but they had concentrated mainly on growing potatoes. Prince Edward Island today is one of the important potato growers in the world. The potatoes produced here are the best. The island has sold potatoes and especially seed potatoes all over the world.

Jim knew all the things about growing potatoes on the island. He had worked hard on the farmland here when he was a youngster. He had enjoyed the peaceful country scene while working in the fields. The sandstones of the island had been weathered into a loam rich in minerals. After being leveled and turned into farmland, the potatoes and other farm produces thrived in the red soil year after year. When the crops were growing in the fields, the green fields bordered by straight lines of red paths formed beautiful pictures. After so many years away from Prince Edward Island, Jim could not forget the time when he had worked on this land. When he had the chance and time, he brought Meilin to the island for a visit.

At the time when the couple had visited the island, things had changed for the farmers here. There were not many small farms left. The small potato farms had been taken over by large corporations and potato growing had become a mass production industry. Still Jim had no problem to find the house of a couple he knew well here. When they knocked at the door, the person came out and told Jim that the old couple who used to live there had moved. Following the direction given by the new owner of the house, the couple found Jim's old friends in a double-sized mobile home. It was not a surprise. In Canada and especially in the rural areas, old people liked to move to smaller living quarters when they were old. This might be that the children were all left home and it was easier to maintain and take care of a small place than a big house, and then it might also be that their incomes had shrunk and they needed the money from selling their houses to maintain a quality life.

The old couple received Jim and Meilin with warm hospitality. It took some time for them to recognize Jim. With his beard and other features that came with age, Jim must look quite different than the youngster the old couple had known many years ago. Once they fully recognized Jim and remembered who he was, the old folks treated him as if he were still a poor farmhand, the cocky youngster. They brought out some sweet pastry for their guests and talked about the old days. Jim asked about some people he knew here and got to know that some young ones had left and some others had changed farming career to something else, but Jim's old boss was still living in the same house with the same farmland.

Meilin was interested in the chit-chat, but felt a bit uncomfortable about how the old couple treated Jim. For so many years, Jim had worked different jobs and served in the military for almost two decades. After he got married, he and Meilin lived in different cities and visited some different countries. On the whole, he had experienced many more things in life. Still, once a farmhand was always a farmhand to this old island couple. Jim to them was still the same poor farmhand who had been joked or mocked around and condescendingly treated by the local folks. Perhaps if Jim had become a rich man or a high-positioned politician, the old folks might change their minds about him, providing that they had seen him on TV. Jim found nothing wrong with the way the old couple treated him now. He was happy that they had recognized him and even remembered the nickname they had given to him.

After leaving the old folk's place, the couple headed for the home of Jim's old boss. They soon approached a fully stuccoed two-story house on a farmland. The couple parked their vehicle near the road leading up to the property and then walked towards the house. Before they reached the house, a middle-aged woman came out from the house and asked them what their business was in approaching their property. Jim stated the reason for the visit. The woman answered with a long face, telling him that the person he looked for was not home. It looked that the old folks Jim and Meilin had just visited had phoned Jim's old boss, telling him that his old farmhand so and so had come for a visit, with his Chinese wife! Meilin knew that this old farm boss of Jim's had ill-treated Jim when he worked here; when he laid Jim off, he had even taken the first car Jim had bought and paid for quite some months. To her, the way this woman's reaction to their approaching showed that Jim's old boss had neither forgotten the past nor forgiven Jim. As for Jim, though he remembered the past, he had long forgiven his old boss for the maltreatment he had received from him. The fact that he had brought his wife to visit his old boss showed that he no long harboured any bad feelings towards him.

In life, it is normally harder for people to forgive those people whom they have wronged or mistreated, because those people have become the reminders of their wrong doings. This goes the same with the situation of prejudices or discriminations. It is harder for people to forgive those who have suffered prejudices or discriminations, because of the very fact that the victims are the constant reminders of their wrong doings. As for those who have suffered from racism or any other prejudices, if given them time or any sign of improvements or changes of the wrong-doers, it is easier for them to forgive, forget and move on.

The shutting-the-door reception from Jim's old boss did not dampen his spirit at all. He drove his wife to see the old spots he had frequented in the old days. The old corner store was still there. The old gas station had been replaced by a new one, but it was still in the old spot. The country roads were still beautiful and peaceful. There were quite many beautiful places on this island Jim wanted to show to his wife. To Meilin, the island looked to have had quite some changes from the time she had first visited here; that was about two decades ago.

Prince Edward Island has quite a few nicknames. It has been called the Cradle of Confederation, because of being the birthplace of Canada, Spud Island, because of its agriculture resources, Canada's Garden Province, Garden of the Gulf and Million Acre Farm. The natives have called it Abegweit, meaning "cradled in the waves". The island is indeed a beautiful garden cradled in the waves of Atlantic Ocean. It has no high mountains, but there are some rugged red cliffs along the southern shore. The land is lying rather even with occasional gentle rolling. Everywhere, there are farm fields with crops, green pastures with cattle and many parks. The roads on the island are many, most not wide, but all paved. There is only one city, Charlottetown, but there are quite some small towns and villages on the island. Each place is not far from the ocean.

When Meilin visited here the first time, she drove the first car she had bought and carried three other Chinese students with her to enjoy this famous Canadian island. She and the other students were enchanted by the beautiful and peaceful pastoral scenes. The small roads winded through the fields with thriving crops, the green meadows were here and there, large leafy trees were clustering in different spots, the land was gently rolling, the clear ponds and occasional lakes showed up in different places, and all looked picturesque. They admired the beautiful farmhouses dotting here and there, and the black and white cows and cattle grazing peacefully on the green pastures. They imagined that life here must be very peaceful and in a slow pace. Everything looked so sweetly charming as described by Lucy Maud Montgomery in her novel. It seemed that all the things on the island were preserved just to stay in this most ideal condition and in this most ideal moment of time.

They visited the Green Gable, a green roofed white house, which was the home of the adopted orphan girl Anne, the protagonist in Montgomery's novel, and the actual childhood home of the author. They saw that not only this green gable with its beautiful natural surroundings, but also the whole island had done credit to Montgomery's beautiful book. The four students spent more time in Charlottetown. They were amazed by the large modern Confederation Centre which had several theatres, a large art gallery, a public library and an outdoor amphitheater. The centre to them was not only the national memorial to the founding fathers of this country, but also the embodiment of cultural wealth of Canada. They got to know that every year there were many music performances and heritage shows in those large theatres; the art gallery had over 15,000 works of Canadian historical and contemporary art; and the different exhibits included the original manuscript of Montgomery's Anne of Green Gable. There were quite some other historical sites in this city that had aroused their curiosity and interests. The Founders' Hall where the Fathers of Confederation met to have their first meeting was the most important one. Through the life-like statues of the founding fathers, the exhibits and different devices in this site, the students learnt the beginning and the evolution of Canada. The whole Charlottetown gave them the impression of a well built and well preserved European city. Its beauty and tranquil atmosphere were quite similar to that of Fredericton; only its cultural facilities were much grander.

With a few dollars in their pockets, the students went to a seafood restaurant in Charlottetown for lunch. The Malpeque oyster of this island was famous and they wanted to have a taste. When you were young and especially when you were studying in a university, the world seemed waiting to serve you a good future; there were no worries about tomorrow's meals even for the poor Chinese students. Fishery has remained an important industry in Prince Edward Island. The catches are not large quantities, but the qualities are high. The lobsters and Malpeque Bay oysters here are world famous. Meilin had never tasted lobster or oyster in her life. The two male students seemed to have more knowledge of world famous food; the two female students had to take their words for the good taste of the oysters here.

The seafood restaurant was full. There were no empty seats; still some more people were waiting at the doorway to get in. It was obvious that the island did not lack national and international visitors; the restaurant guests were not only local or national but also international. The students found out that the restaurant did not serve oysters that day but had red lobsters. They ordered a red lobster to go. In this way, they did not have to wait long for a table in the restaurant and the cost was lower than if they were dining in with some other things. For Meilin, it was the first time in her life that she had tasted red lobster. The fresh sweet taste of this special seafood had left a very favorable memory in her mind.

Another special memory from the first trip to this island had also stayed with her. Being occupied with the interesting things around, she had left her purse in a tourist centre. She did not realize this loss until the group had reached another sightseeing spot. This happening had caused quite some worries for her. Though there were not much money in her purse, losing her identifications meant a lot of troubles for her. The whole group went back to the tourist centre to look for her purse. On the way, Meilin thought that there was not much hope to find her purse in the centre with many different tourists, and the whole trip was suddenly darkened by the loss. When the group came back to the centre and she inquired about her purse at the information counter, the clerk immediately presented her with her purse. She was overjoyed with the regaining of her purse; her relief and gratitude must have been well felt by the clerk and the other three students from her verbal and facial expressions.

In today's world, people in large cities have felt less secure and safe in their homes or walking through the streets. Incidences of people being robbed at the point of a knife or a gun are not uncommon, and sometimes surrendering a purse or a wallet may or may not save their lives. Here on this island, a lost purse will be so surely returned to the owner. This shows that small places are still relatively clean of quite some bad things or crimes that are preying large places; people in small places are still relatively more honest, which makes those places relatively safer and more peaceful.

Many years later when Meilin came with her husband to visit Prince Edward Island again, many things looked changed. They had noticed quite some first-class golf courses. The island had quite a few large beaches with fine white or red sands for locals and visitors to enjoy. Now the holiday idlers seemed to have increased considerably on those beaches. What had caught their attention especially were those large new high-rank hotels, shopping centres and public facilities. The couple were very much intimidated by those modern luxury hotels. There was no need for them to enquire; they knew that the charges for those accommodations must be quite high and out of their league. Knowing the ambitious Prince Edward Islanders, the couple could see that they were very much bending on turning the island to a first class vacation destination especially for those who could afford the high life, possibly Canada's Hawaii, for summer only of course.

Though scared by those expensive new facilities on the island, the couple were very much attracted by the new Confederation Bridge. Once landed on the island, they tried to take a picture of the bridge with themselves in. Along the shore facing the bridge, a street and a lot of new houses were built. Though the island was mainly of peaceful pastoral scenes, Prince Edward Island was the most densely populated province in the country. It looked that its population was still increasing. The couple could not find an ideal spot to take the picture; the houses had blocked the view. While they were walking up and down in the street, camera in hand; a middle-aged man came out from his house and approached them.

"Hi, are you looking for a place to take a picture of the bridge?" the man asked the couple with a warm smile.

"Oh, yes. It's hard to find a good spot," answered Jim.

"Come to my backyard. You can take a good picture there," the man invited.

"Thank you very much. It's very kind of you to offer this," said Jim gratefully.

The couple followed the man and went into his backyard. The man even took some pictures for Jim and Meilin, so that the bridge and they both would be in the pictures. The bridge was so long; it was impossible for the picture to contain it whole. The couple had to be satisfied with what the picture could cover. They thanked the man sincerely for his kindness and left with grateful feelings. This experience had given Meilin the impression that the islanders had not changed, though the place had changed quite some. If she had lost her purse here today, it would still be returned to her promptly.

Perhaps it was because the couple had known Prince Edward Island too well or because they were somewhat tired from the long distance travelling, they decided to skip the island this time. By reaching and touring some of Newfoundland, the couple felt that they had fulfilled their goal for this cross-country trip. They had been on the road and visiting different places for almost two months now; it seemed that it was high time for them to go home. However, thinking of home was easy, but getting to it would still take them many days of travelling. The couple passed by the turn-off road to go to Prince Edward Island and kept on driving.

On their home-bound journey, the couple had stopped only in a few spots to have some quick visits. This had made the return trip much faster. In a little over a week, they were approaching Edmonton, Alberta, the neighbouring province of British Columbia where their home was waiting. Before reaching home, they decided to stop in Edmonton to have their van repaired. The front windshield of their van had been broken near Winnipeg; they decided to have it replaced in Edmonton. Alberta did not have provincial sales tax; the cost for the windshield replacement would be lower. Since they were going to pass through Edmonton, they thought that they should take this advantage.

The couple camped in the same RV Park at the city skirt. Next day early in the morning, they pulled their trailer out and drove to an auto-glass repair shop in Edmonton. Having lived in Edmonton for ten years, they knew where to go to get things done. When they arrived at the auto-glass shop, the door of the shop was just opening. They were the first customers for service. The couple disconnected their van from the trailer and the shop technician soon took their van into the workshop. The couple thought that the replacement of a windshield would not take long and they could drive to British Columbia immediately afterwards. They had dragged their trailer into the city and parked it on the shop's parking lot for the take-off after the repair job was done.

It turned out that the couple had to wait from early morning until five or six o'clock in the evening to have the windshield replaced. The shop technician pulled their van out from their workshop just before the shop was closing; the receptionist walked them to the parking lot after she knocked the office door. The couple were the first customers to come and the last to leave. The auto-glass shop was a rather large one; during the whole day there were only a few customers. It looked that things had been deliberately delayed, so that the couple were the last to be served in the last hour. The couple had asked the reason of the long time waiting and got the excuse that the shop had to wait for the ordered windshield to be delivered to the shop. The auto-glass shop was a large one only working on auto glass. It was hard for the couple to believe that it did not have windshield in store for a popular North American van. Besides, while waiting in the reception room, they did not see any delivering truck coming.

Since the harassment and attacks started, Jim and Meilin had encountered the treatment of being served the last or the worst quite many times; they faced and endured patiently the situation this time as well. They suspected that the hate campaigners were behind this kind of tricks, but could do nothing about them. There was no use to accuse or push the auto-glass shop; people had to do what they had been told or ordered to do in some circumstances. Directly or personally, the workers might have nothing particular against the couple at all.

Jim and Meilin knew quite well for what purpose or reason this kind of treatment or abuses had been hurled onto them. Since they had lost their privacy and their home talks and writing had been open to the public, some people of power must have thought that the couple had to be put in their place. To them, this couple were out of their place by imposing their opinions and criticisms on the public, which were strictly the domains of the important and powerful people. However there was not much they could do to put the couple in their place, as the couple were not the ones to put their home talks in the public and they had every right to talk whatever they liked at their own home. So those people offended or hurt by the couple's private talks could only pull up some tricks to have the different service people to serve them the last or serve them with some abusive manners. The couple were at the bottom of the society; they could do nothing to stop those abuses. Having not faced any obstacle, the abusers went further to have people in some critical positions to do more harm to and even to kill the couple. They might have realized that the only way to stop the couple to talk in their home was to shut them up permanently. The couple were not in any social position from which they could be pulled done, or having nice jobs to be laid off; the only ways to vent their angers and hatred and to satisfy their vengeance were to use different people to pull tricks, to do harms or even to permanently silence the couple if that could be managed.

As for the couple, they had never felt that they were out of their place or had done anything wrong to deserve punishment or even death. They knew well that they were at the bottom of the society and had never even aspired to change this position for a higher one. In their condition and situation, they knew that there was no use for them to dream that sort of things. If even their lives were being threatened, how could they dream that anything good would be allowed to happen to them? However, like everybody else, they had their inner world or their inner being, a place innate with their birth. In this inner place they had absolute freedom to think and express themselves. Their home, their private space, was the most important and the last refuge for their inner being. If people thought that the couple were out of their place because they had used their birth rights to dwell in this inner place to freely think and express themselves, they were certainly the ones that were out of their true places and out of their pure natural minds to become evil and the enemies of human rights and freedom.

People living in all kinds of societies of this world all have certain places assigned to them by the society. They are in different social levels or ranks. After long, people have often been identified only by the social places or circles they belong to; their ranks or positions have been mistaken for their persons and their social status mistaken for their personal qualities and values. As a matter of fact, all those ranks, positions and status are but exterior decorations that cannot decide or change what kind of human beings they truly are. No ranks or positions can change the inner world or inner beings of any people. No matter how high or how low the place people belong to in a society, their inner world or inner beings which come with their birth hardly go with the exterior decorations. The inner world is, after all, people's true place and their true selves. In this place, they are the most honest and most true to themselves, even though some people may not be honest or true in this inner world of theirs. The concept of freedom of speech comes from the recognition of this innate place of every human being; the place is the birth right of every human being; it represents the true human being, and therefore people have the right to be themselves and to speak and express truly what they have thought or felt. Prohibiting the human beings to have their birth rights as humans to access and express their inner beings is against the law of nature and an inhuman act against the human race. All civilized people and societies recognize this truth.

Most people do not like to show their inner selves to the public; they feel uncomfortable to show others what they really are. However, people's speeches and actions in their daily lives often betray their wishes to hide themselves and give a true picture of their inner world. In fact, people normally win true admirations, respects or love by showing their true selves if their inner beings are truly great, compassionate, loving, virtuous or decent. Nobody will expect to see a perfect human being with a perfect inner world, but people generally like to see others and especially those important and powerful people with a bright and good inner world, and dislike to see some people revealing a dark or evil inner world through their speeches or actions. Nobody can truly change other people's inner world for the one they deem proper. Those people have to dislike their own inner world and want to change it for a better one by themselves.

For Jim and Meilin, their home was the place they could be more themselves, thinking and talking freely. In no way, they would give up their home as the refuge of their inner being to become some mute robots simply because some people disliked their talks and writings at home. Giving up this last refuge meant giving up the very basic right to be human, which was equivalent to giving up their lives. By now they knew well that they could not change others. Their complaints about the harassment, abuses, death threats or attempts on their lives would only bring more of those things. What they could do was to go on with their life as best as they could in spite of the situation and to face and deal with whatever was coming at them with fortitude.

The couple stayed in their trailer first to wait for the repair on their van to be done. The temperature rose quickly with the day progressing and the sun climbing up, the inside of the trailer became too hot. Though Edmonton was a city located rather north, it could get very hot in summer. The couple left their trailer and went into the reception room where there was a space with chairs for the waiting customers. The shop was air-conditioned, cool and comfortable. For the whole day, the couple stayed in the office and went to the trailer to get some lunch only. Without the van, they would not walk some distance under the hot sun to go to a restaurant for their lunch. All day long, the couple checked and read the magazines in the waiting area. An event had just happened in the United States at this time; the star singer or pop king, Michael Jackson, had died. The magazines were full of articles and pictures of this event.

Canada has only the world's superpower United States as its close neighbouring country and is greatly influenced or affected by this Giant politically, economically and culturally. If the United States has a sneeze, Canada is bound to feel the vibration or even to catch the cold. In the cultural sphere, Canada is simply being overwhelmed or overrun by the United States. The film industry of this country has been totally dwarfed by the giant film industry of the United States. The Canadians know well almost every important American movie, but very little about any Canadian movie. The quantity of Canadian movies is so small compared to the large quantity of the American ones. Asking any Canadian, he or she will name quite some American movie stars for you, but probably cannot tell a single name of Canadian actors or actresses.

Nevertheless, some Canadians have made it in the United States and become film stars there. Canada is not lack of talented people, but it seems that those talents can make it in the United States easier than in Canada. One cannot help wondering why things will go on like this. One possibility is that the mediocre have occupied some important positions here in Canada to make sure that most talents will not get up on top of them. So the pebbles get polished and diamonds get dimmed. Another possibility is that the Canadian success is more reserved for the whites and the coloured are rarely included. Canada has already a lower population and therefore not many people succeed. The same situation seems also true in the book world of these two countries. The United States has been constantly generating best sellers, Canada has only a few and quite some of the few are the old ones that have been kept on going in the market. Canada is for sure not lack of talented people who can write or perform; why is the cultural sphere depressed? Is it being intimidated by the Giant United States or the Canadian talents being suppressed by some powerful mediocre in their own country? The Canadian government seems trying to promote the culture of Canada's own at all times, but nobody is sure why the result has remained minimal.

Ordinary people don't care much about those things concerning the history or development of the country's culture; they seek only what can entertain them more effectively and what can satisfy their mental or spiritual needs. They treat and treasure the American stars as their own and appreciate the good American writers as their own. People can only wish that the Americans will treat the Canadian talents in Canada the same way to make their life and development a bit easier.

Right at this moment, the Canadians obviously treated the death of Michael Jackson, the American pop king, as a serious event. Numerous articles about him and his death were filled the magazines; quite of those magazines were American of course. Jim and Meilin had paid full attention to the numerous pictures of Michael Jackson, the pictures of the star's face from his childhood to his adulthood and before his death. Those face pictures had well illustrated the changes of this star and told a lot about his person and his life. The impression those pictures gave to the couple was that another American star singer was destroyed by fame and fortune. The changes of Michael Jackson's face seemed to have clearly shown the turmoil and sufferings the star had gone through in his short life. The first American pop king, Elves Presley, also died young. To the couple, the well loved star was also destroyed by fame and fortune.

Life can be tragic to some people who cannot get what they wish for, but it can also be tragic to some people who get what they wish for. Power, fame and fortune can indeed corrupt and destroy some people. Jim and Meilin could see this more clearly now. They were far away from power, fame and fortune, but their present situation had pushed them into the limelight. Simply because of their voice being heard and Meilin's writings being read by some people, they had to face attentions, hostilities and hatred. They could imagine what more those people who had actually gained power, fame and fortune had to face in their lives; there could not be all admiration, respect, love or happiness for them.

Power, fame and fortune are serious trials for people who have them. The trials come not only from the corruptive nature of power, fame and fortune, but also the public's reactions towards the people who have them. Different reactions from the public towards the "lucky" ones can distort and change their perceptions about themselves and the world. Some people cannot stand those trials and become the victims of the circumstances, whereas some can stand the trials, come out unscathed and benefit not only themselves, but also the country, the society or their communities with what have fallen onto them.

The very same situation is true with countries. Power, fame and fortune can very well corrupt and ruin a country; there can be even more serious trials for countries to go through. It is well known that a group, a people, a nation or a country are more susceptible to madness than the individuals. The world history has had ample examples of those large victims of power, fame and fortune. However, the countries that can stand those trials can benefit large number of people, not only the people of their own countries but also peoples of the world.

The couple spent the whole day reading magazines; the day thus passed without much of their notice. After everything done and their trailer being hitched to the van, they drove to a restaurant at the city skirt. It was already past their normal supper time and they needed to attend to their stomachs first before they could decide what to do next. After supper in a fast food restaurant, they felt that they had the energy to drive for some distance. There would be still a few hours of daylight. If they cover some distance this evening, tomorrow's drive would be easier. It would take them about twelve hours to drive from Edmonton to Abbotsford.

Encouraged by the thought of an easy drive for tomorrow, the couple drove to Hinton and camped there for the night. They had to stop at Hinton anyway to get Vixy's ashes. After so many days travelling through the country, their sadness for losing Vixy had dissipated quite some. Every living being had to leave this world or this life sooner or later; maybe it was better for Vixy to leave his sufferings here. Who knows? Vixy might enjoy a better existence somewhere else in a different form now.

Next day, the couple did have an easy drive. They reached home in the afternoon. Their house, yard and everything seemed in order. They were pleased that they could take a good rest now to relief the fatigue from the long trip. During the following days at home, they were in a celebrating mood. With all the ominous threatening hints or signs they had received at the start of the journey and what had happened to them on the road, they came back safe and sound. This showed that Canada was largely a safe and friendly country. In their situation, they had received different kinds of harassment, attacks and even some attempts to endanger their lives, but they came out unharmed. They started the trip, trying to escape the harassment at their home city, but found out that the harassment and attacks had followed them wherever they went. This had taught them that it would be better to stand on their ground to face and deal with the problems at home than try to escape them. By now they had totally given up the thought or idea of moving away from Abbotsford; it looked that wherever they moved to, they could not move away from the same situation.

Though there were some unpleasant moments and serious encounters on their journey, the couple had met quite some good and kind people throughout the country. They believed that those good people would stay in their memories much longer. The worthiest thing for them to celebrate was that they had had a closer look at Canada. The beautiful vast natural country had made them feel proud to call it their home, though they would not dare or be allowed to feel the same with the society. The beautiful land would not be offended by their affection and calling it home; it would embrace everyone equally and everyone equally belonged to it. It was a great feeling to think of this vast beautiful country being their home, just as their feelings about their small home in the small city. There would be problems and difficulties in their life and their small home would be infested by disturbances, but there was no place better than their own home.

Abbotsford seemed not changed; it was the same as they left it two months ago. A week later after they were home, there was a function going on in the city; the multicultural festival was being held in the Exhibition Park. Feeling rested, Jim and Mcilin went to enjoy the festival. Multicultural festival had become an annual event of the city in the recent years. The couple would attend it every year, if they knew when it would be on. The Exhibition Park had two large hangar-like buildings which the city used for fairs and functions.

The couple went to the festival at about noon. They parked their van in the large parking lot and went up the hill to the exhibition buildings. The two large buildings were of metal structures and each had four big doors, two in the front and two at the back. The main activities would normally be held in the larger building and some side activities would be in the smaller one. Now the two buildings were being used for the festival. The couple went to the large building first. The three big doors of the building were locked; only one door was open and this one open door was half blocked by a police car. The situation made the couple feel uncomfortable. This was a festival. They could not understand why the city would treat it with such a high alert. Were the police here in such a stance to protect the coloured people or to show force in order that there was a riot breaking out from the festival? But if there were some unexpected incidence happening during the festival, this blocked-door situation would very much endanger many people's lives. It seemed an unspoken knowledge or agreement in the city that the multicultural festival was the festival of the immigrants and especially the coloured immigrants. Most coloured people in the city would come to the festival, and only a few whites would join in.

With the change of immigration policy starting in the 1960s, the population of the coloured people in Canada have been gradually increasing. After half a century, the population of the coloured people has reached about thirteen percent of the country's population; some provinces have more coloured people and some have less. Statistics Canada has predicted that by 2017, one of five Canadians will be visible minority and fifty percent citizens in Toronto and Vancouver will be formed by visible minorities. The importance of different people understanding and getting along with each other is getting more obvious in Canadian society. The Canadian government has set up multicultural programs to ease the newcomers' entering the Canadian society for both the established Canadians and the new ones. Compared with the assimilation policy over the native peoples during the late 19th century and early 20th century, this multiculturism policy is gentler and more considerate. It has encouraged the newcomers to keep the heritages and cultures of their origin countries, hoping that different cultures the newcomers have brought from all over the world will enrich the culture of Canada and in the meantime the newcomers will feel more at home in their newly acquired country.

In dealing with the changes in the growing Canadian population, multiculturism is indeed a well-thought and considerate policy, if it has worked. But more and more people seem to have started thinking that it is a failed attempt. It is hard for any program or plan to achieve one hundred percent success of what is targeted. To Jim and Meilin, if the multiculturism program has not had the full projected result, the attacks and rejections to the program are too hasty to call it a total failure, and those opponents of multiculturism might very well have something to do with its not so ideal result. They could see that the problems came mainly from the lack of support of the old established white people. Quite some white people considered what the newcomers had brought from their origin countries were beneath them and beneath Canadian or European culture. The white people normally would have nothing to do with the activities initiated by the multicultural programs; the most some of them would do was to have a peek at some newcomers' performances on some occasions.

With the large injection of the coloured population into Canada, the hope of injecting some different cultures or ideas into Canadian culture and society is very low. The blocks and barriers put up by the established Canadians are strong. Quite some people will not accept the newcomers, especially the coloured ones, as equal citizens, let alone the cultures they have brought from their origin countries. The general coloured newcomers cannot enjoy equal opportunities in the job market and their social status has remained low. With lower social status, the different cultures they have brought into this country have been naturally looked down upon. The functions like the multicultural festival are meant to bring together the different people, the old and the new, so that they can learn from each other, understand each other and eventually become one. If most whites will have nothing to do with those multicultural functions or programs, no matter how eager the newcomers want to contribute to the society what they have brought here and want to understand and be understood by the established Canadians, the good idea of multiculturism will not work. Even though some established Canadians will watch a few newcomers' colourful shows, they will neither learn much from different cultures, nor truly understand the different newcomers.

The coloured newcomers are largely blocked from the white society. The white people have their churches, their entertainments and functions that very little coloured people will be in. The coloured people huddle in their own communities, having their own temples and churches and amusing themselves with their own activities. The white people will not even step into their small stores, let alone their small gatherings or functions. Under such circumstances, it has been a miracle that those multicultural programs and functions have been going on for such a long time. This little success has mainly resulted from the support, efforts and attendance of the coloured newcomers. Now more and more complaints have been heard about those programs; more of the complaints are about the cost of those programs and some about the multicultural programs being the cause of the coloured people keeping to themselves and not merging into the Canadian society. It looks that people are not even willing to see the real cause why those programs have not worked well and whether they can be improved. People like to go their old ways and they have no intention to dismantle those racial barriers they have put up against the coloured people. The social ranks or classes have to be protected and the coloured people have to be kept in their place and their level. An equal togetherness of all different people will threaten the established social order. Now the multicultural programs are being used as the scapegoat for the barriers put up by the established white people to prevent the coloured people from fully entering the Canadian society.

Jim and Meilin were now concentrated on enjoying the multicultural festival. Inside the large exhibition hall, a large stage was being set up on one side. In front of the stage there were quite some metal chairs for the audience. The stage and the sitting area had occupied half of the hall. The other half had quite some stands set up by different groups in the city; they were different religious groups, culture groups, government offices and the police department to present themselves and to show what they were about. Some merchants had also set up their stands, selling some goods related to their cultures or origin countries.

The performances were indeed multicultural coloured. The East Indian children in the traditional East Indian costumes danced with their traditional music, which was full of festival atmosphere. The Irish children in Irish traditional dresses danced energetically with the fast beats of fiddles. A Chinese gentleman offered an excellent Tai Chi performance with traditional Chinese music. Some white ladies and gentlemen in their fifties and in both modern and traditional Scottish costumes danced elegantly with Celtic music. The Ukrainian dancers in their colourful traditional costumes also performed wonderful dance. Some Eastern European ladies and gentlemen sang some sweet songs of their tradition. The Japanese ladies gave a fashion show of their traditional costume and they even dressed up a small white boy with the Japanese traditional clothes, who looked so cute. The international students from the college offered a fashion show too; the young students in different colours dressed up in different traditional costumes of their countries walked through the stage. A youth group put on a short play created by themselves. Some Abbotsford white ladies in some exotic dresses performed a belly dance of exotic oriental tradition, which was well done and showed how much efforts they had put in to learn this kind of dance. The large microphones were blowing out so loudly the different kinds of music from different parts of the world; the roof of the building seemed in danger of being raised. Jim and Meilin were very much impressed by all these performances and thought that the snobbish people who would not come to the festival did not know what they had missed.

However, no matter how much they had enjoyed the shows, the couple felt a bit uncomfortable about the white ladies' belly dance. Knowing the attitudes of some white people towards the multicultural festival or multiculturism here, they suspected that this show might be put on to mock the festival or multiculturism. To the couple, the multicultural festival was meant to be an occasion for different people to express themselves through their heritages and cultures of their origin countries; the festival should promote understanding and respect between different people. The white ladies' exotic oriental belly dance looked more of a party crasher than a contributor. If the belly dance was not meant to ridicule or degrade the multicultural festival, the couple still wished that the belly dance would not be the only thing the white people here were willing to learn from other cultures.

The festival gave the couple the impression that the organizers had spent tremendous efforts in putting all these together and including everything and everyone. It was a pity that the audience was mainly the coloured people; a few white people came, and some left quickly as if they were afraid to catch something from the noisy gathering. The mayor of Abbotsford had never shown up in any one of these festivals. He must know well that as long as he pleased the white majority, he would be problem free; coming to the multicultural festival might very well bring problems for him from the majority. One year, a nearby native tribe came to the multicultural festival and offered a performance. They danced in their traditional native costumes a dance of boating; the tribe leaders had even joined the dance. It was hard to see the natives around and even harder to see them joining such functions in the city. Jim and Meilin thought that the mayor of the city should have offered some kind of show to match up with the natives and their leaders' generous and friendly efforts. As a matter of fact, if the mayor were a well-versed politician, this festival should be the best occasion for him to show his fair and kind leadership towards all different citizens and nearby native peoples.

People normally follow the political leaders in their political views and social behaviours. If more political leaders treat all different citizens equally, strive for their equal opportunities in the job market and bring up their social status, the racial discriminations and tensions in the society will surely go down. Unfortunately, it seems that more political leaders have put their priority in gaining or preserving votes. To achieve the goal of gaining the maximum votes, they are often following and pleasing the sentiments and whims of the majority whites, instead of leading them to do the right things for the society and the country.

Next year when the multicultural festival came again, the police car blocking the only opened door situation was gone. The city must have realized how ridiculously they had treated the multicultural festival. To Jim and Meilin, the blocking-door situation signaled the fear of the city or the police towards the coloured newcomers. The fear came from not only their lack of understanding of the different people, but also knowing that they had not treated those coloured new citizens well and equally. If they had gotten to know those newcomers and treated them as equal citizens, this fear would not exist at all.

In the whole country, the coloured Canadians are among the most peaceful and law-abiding citizens; there have never been any large incidence of large group of coloured people disturbing peace and order of the society. This small change made by the city or the police concerning the multicultural festival had raised the couple's hope; perhaps someday in the near future, the barriers put up by some white established people to prevent the coloured people fully entering the society as their equals would be gone. But they knew that they could not be too optimistic for this to happen soon. The changes would come, but they would come slowly and gradually, and perhaps never thoroughly. Nothing would be more difficult than to change people.

The functions like the multicultural festival are normally accompanied with different kinds of food being served; they are different cuisines prepared by different people according to different countries' traditional ways of cooking. Abbotsford is of no exception in this category. People recognize that in getting to know different cultures of different countries, being familiar with their different culinary arts are an important part.

In Abbotsford, a large tent would be set up by the exhibition building for each multicultural festival. In the tent, some food stands would serve food of African style, Asian style, Italian style and Canadian style. However, Abbotsford was not a large city; the food stands here for the festival were only a few. They normally make Jim and Meilin miss the same type of festival that was held in Edmonton each year. The Edmontonians called it Heritage Days; the festival would last for three days. Many large red tent pavilions would be set up in a large park in the city. Each different group of people would have a pavilion. In addition to the pavilions there would be a stage set up by each pavilion. People would show and sell their goods related to the cultures of their origin countries in their pavilions, cook their special traditional cuisines to serve the visitors in front of the pavilions and offer their traditional performances on the stages. This annual large scaled festival with all kinds of delicious food of different styles and all kinds of wonderful performances of different cultures had left a warm and lasting memory in the couple's minds. They were especially impressed by the large number of white attendants to the festival. Of course, they had also heard complaints and mockeries from some white people there about the multicultural festival.

In spite of the dislikes and complaints of some white people, Canada is becoming a wonderfully diversified and multi-coloured country. Still, the country is primarily of white population and people are strongly attached to certain habits and traditions. During the Canadian National Day or the New Year Eve's Celebration, some concerts will be put on in different provinces. Those concerts will be the shows mainly by the white solo singers. To Jim and Meilin, those concerts were rather plain and could not fully represent the true colour of the country. They hoped to see in the near future that those important national festivals would add some wonderful and colourful performances by different types of Canadians. They were sure that the inclusive style of festival celebrations would make all different people feel included as equal and full citizens.

Unfortunately in Abbotsford, multiculturism seemed stalled. Even the multicultural festival went downhill in recent few years. Only one group of performers would be singing on the stage. The stands of the organizations, governments and sellers were reduced. Now not only few whites attended the festival, but also few coloured people came as well. It looked that the opponents of multiculturism had won. The couple hoped that the Heritage Days in Edmonton was still going on well every year.

CHAPTER THIRTEEN

YUKON

Jim and Meilin rested and waited a year before they took another long trip to visit the north of Canada. In this vast country, Canada is mostly populated along the south of the land. Most provinces have their large cities, towns, villages close to the long south border connected with the United States. The populated areas have all kinds of industrial, agricultural and commercial developments. The northern part of the country has a much lower population with less developments; this part has been more resided by the aboriginal peoples. Canada is a country near the North Pole; its vast northern part includes the Arctic areas. The country is well known for its extreme winter cold temperatures. It is quite natural that people will choose the southern part of the country for living and producing. As for some native peoples, they have settled in the northern part and the Arctic areas for thousands of years after they came to this continent; those who have stayed in these areas have gotten used to the climate and conditions. For thousands of years after they landed on North America, many natives have migrated to other parts of the continent; those remained in the northern part now are not a large number of the total native peoples in the whole continent. But in view of the total number of the native peoples in Canada, a considerable number of Canadian native peoples are still residing in the northern part of the country.

The whole vast northern region of Canada has been divided into three parts: Yukon Territory, Northwest Territories and Nunavut. The Canadian aboriginal peoples consist mainly of the natives, the Inuit and the Métis. Yukon Territory, now officially Yukon, has a population of a larger half of white people and a smaller half of native peoples and the Métis. The Inuit consists of both Inuit and Inuvialuit; they are also known as the Eskimos. Today, the Inuit mainly reside in Nunavut; the natives, the Inuvialuit and the Métis mainly reside in Northwest Territories. The northern natives call themselves “de-ne” or “de-nay” meaning “the people” and Northwest Territory “Denendeh”. In the native languages, Nunavut means “our land” and Denendeh means “land of the people”.

As late as 1930s, the European settlers had thought that the aboriginal peoples on this land would gradually die out. Some famous anthropologist had predicted that the native tribes would eventually disappear. Against their views of the future for the aboriginal peoples, the natives have survived and their numbers have even greatly increased in recent years. The native peoples have increased to more than half a million, the Inuit have reached over thirty thousand and the Métis who have never been registered as the natives have also reached about half a million. Today, the Inuit, the natives and the Métis are the main population of the Northwest Territory and Nunavut. In Yukon, the natives and the Métis are a considerable number, about one fifths of Yukon's population.

In the recent years, the views about and the treatment to the native peoples by the Canadian government and the non-native Canadians have changed considerably. In the old days, the white settlers considered the natives good for nothing and would disappear. Now nobody seems holding up those views any more. Through history, the natives had received plenty of maltreatments from the whites. With the language and culture barriers, they had signed quite some unfair treaties with the white people and then even some of their treaty land had been sold by the government to some white settlers for farming. Today, the natives are well equipped to fight for their own rights. Since 1980s, the Canadian government has recognized that Canada is a multicultural country; many native issues and rights have started to be looked at with fairness and justice. The native peoples have won quite some battles in different issues. In 1993, The Nunavut Land Claim had been passed, under which the Inuit had given up any future aboriginal rights to their traditional land in return for the power to govern their own territory. Northwest Territories has also set up some native self-government. Yukon in recent years has recognized some native tribe's self-government. The natives in the north of Canada have shown that they are fully capable of the governing task. The southern natives' dream of self-government has been partially realized by the northern natives.

Of course, there are still many problems exiting with the native issues. The native people's living standards have to be further raised, the native reserves need further developments, and the relationship between the natives and the non-natives needs further improvement and so on. However, compared with the natives' conditions a few decades ago, improvements have happened, which have given much hope for a better future. With the increasing population of the native peoples, the country has the opportunity to develop the potentials of the first nations to strengthen their economical and other forces.

Jim and Meilin had set their minds on visiting Yukon for this northern trip. They packed up their trailer and drove for a few days to reach Whitehorse, the capital city of Yukon. When arriving at Whitehorse, they found a campground at the city skirt. The campground had fully serviced sites for RVs. The couple got a site and set up their trailer. They would stay in Whitehorse for a few days to tour around the city. The campground was well equipped; there were a large office, a souvenir store, nice bathrooms with quite many shower stalls, laundry room and even a computer room. The campground was in a wooded area; all the lots were among the trees and close together. Quite many RVers had already set up their rigs; the big motor homes were on the larger lots along the border area and the smaller RVs were in the centre woods. The place looked rather crowded with numerous RVs. It was in July. People were all thinking that this was the best time to come to visit Yukon. Then, there were quite some other RVers just passing here to go to Alaska of the United States.

Yukon attracts tourists mainly for its legendary glory of Gold Rush in the old days and its wild natural beauty of magnificent northern mountains, ice fields, glaciers and turbulent rivers. On their way to come to Yukon, the couple had seen an old sign near the border between Yukon and British Columbia. The old green sign had those words on it:

TO THE GOLD FIELDS!

In the 1860's the fabulous Cariboo goldfields were a lure to thousands, miners, traders, and adventurers, many afoot, some with wheelbarrows, shared the pioneer route with mule trains, plodding oxen, freight wagons, and swaying stage-coaches.

Havens for man and beast were the road-houses and stables every 12-14 miles along the way.

This sign had vividly illustrated the gold rush in an earlier time, but the greater gold strike had happened in 1896. Large quantity of gold had been discovered on the surface level of Bonanza Creek near Dawson City in Yukon. George Washington Carmack with two natives who made the god strike had spread the news in the United States, which started a stampede of gold diggers rushing to this area. In about five years, about 100 thousand people had come into Yukon, dreaming to strike it rich. Some did make a fortune, but many had lost their lives in trying to get to the gold fields through the very harsh terrains of Yukon and in battling the severe winter climate of the northern region.

In the old days, there were hardly any road in Yukon, let alone the roads to reach the area where the gold fields were. The only paths were some trails. The best transportation means then to get to Yukon and to the gold fields were by boats. Most people took the boats or ships to get to Skagway of Alaska through the ocean route. From there they soon got into Yukon Territory. After entering Yukon, they had first to go through the mountainous passes by climbing over quite some high mountains. The Royal Canadian Mounted Police stationed in the area then had made sure that the prospectors would each take a year supplies to enter the wilderness. The prospectors had often to carry the personal supplies to the top of the snow covered mountains, come back down to take some more and then climb again. The hardships those people had to go through was hard to imagine.

After the mountain passes, they had to get to the head of the Yukon River. The Yukon River could lead them to Dawson City where the gold fields were. Besides the snow-covered mountains, the rapids, the currents and the rocks of the perilous Yukon River had taken many more lives of the gold-diggers who had constructed anything that were floatable to navigate the turbulent waters. The most dangerous were the swift currents and rocks in the Whitehorse Rapids called the Thirty Miles and Five Fingers rapids. When the prospectors reached Whitehorse, they would take a rest. In those old days, it would be lucky if there were some road-houses and stables along the way; Whitehorse was of no exception. Many had to pitch tents here to rest for a little while before pushing on further. After Whitehorse there were still over 900 kilometers of dangerous waters to battle before they could finally reach Dawson City.

The first gold strike in this great Gold Rush was made in Bonanza Creek, a tributary of Klondike River; this event has been remembered as the Klondike Gold Rush. From 1896 to 1904, the Klondike creeks had yielded about $100 million in gold. In the old days; this was not a small number. The Gold Rush soon brought the railroad building through the region. First, the rail went from Skagway to Whitehorse and then from Whitehorse to Dawson city.

Dawson settlement was at the confluence of Yukon and Klondike Rivers. Being flooded by large number of prospectors and other kinds of people providing services, it instantly became a city. By 1898, there were over thirty thousand people residing in Dawson City, making it the largest city in the northwest of the continent at that time. The famous American writer, Jack London, was among the then residents of the city. His novel had depicted his life experiences in this time and at this place. In Dawson City, London had his dog, Buck, a St. Bernard and German Shepherd cross. Later, he based his main dog character on Buck for his novel, Call of the Wild. Besides Jack London, there were quite a few other writers and poets who had written some colourful tails based on their life experiences at this place in this time.

Today, there is the Klondike Highway connecting Whitehorse and Dawson City and reaching to Alaska. Mining here produces not only gold, but also silver, zinc, lead and copper. The diggings have gone deeper by large machines. Panning for gold has been left to the tourists to taste and enjoy the old way of getting a little gold.

Whitehorse was also born in this period of time with the large influx of people; some of the gold diggers left after the surface gold were exhausted, but some stayed. The population of the place fluctuated greatly with the high and low periods of the Gold Rush. During the World War II, the personnel of the US Army who were building the Alaska Highway had moved to Whitehorse. Different services and construction supportive crews came with them. This had boosted and confirmed the city status of Whitehorse. In 1953, the capital of Yukon Territory moved from Dawson City to Whitehorse. Today, Whitehorse is the center of communication, transportation and distribution of Yukon. Federal and Yukon government offices are here. The territorial headquarters of the Royal Canadian Mounted Police is also here.

Having rested on the campground, Jim and Meilin went into the city of Whitehorse next morning. They were surprised to see a well-built clean modern city. Whitehorse was not a large city and there were no skyscrapers here, but it had all the facilities and services that a modern large city had. There were the Superstore, the Walmart, the Home-Hardware and all kinds of other stores and restaurants. The main streets were lined up by beautiful stores and restaurants with the standards or status favoured by modern tourists. Tourism looked well developed here. Quite some attractions and historical sites were well built and preserved. Among the modern buildings, there were a few old log houses preserved in a street; one of them was big, three stories high. The couple were amazed to see such a big log house. It must have been used by a large group of people in the old days and now it was still functioning as an apartment building. The couple wondered whether it was built by the army in the 1940s or built even earlier in the Gold Rush time. The big log building was still strong and stable, occupied by quite some residents.

The couple drove around the city for a while and then stopped first at the tourist centre. The centre was a large modern building of traditional wood structure by the river. Inside the centre, there were all kinds of travelling information and tour brochures. The large bright hall had some sofa seats for the tourists to sit down and to watch a video. The video gave some information about what the tourists had to pay attention to when venturing into the wildness of Yukon and especially how to deal with the situation of encountering bears. The centre had also displayed gold and some other minerals of Yukon. When the couple went to the long information counter, the clerk presented them with two explorers' passports. The passport was the same size as the real passport and had quite a few pages. It had a large golden seal of Yukon Gold on the deep blue cover. The clerk told them that for each tourist attraction they had visited in Yukon, a page of their passports would be stamped by the visitor office on that site. When they had collected enough stamped pages, they would win some Yukon souvenirs or even certain amount of Yukon gold. The couple were quite impressed by the innovative way Yukon had created for tourism. They would of course try to win the Yukon gold.

Outside the tourist centre, the treed and gardened ground was beautifully decorated by some artworks. A large wooden platform with benches had provided the locals and visitors a place to sit down and view the Yukon River. The riverbed in this area was wide; the water flew swiftly and quietly. The peaceful scenery could not arouse any imagination in the couple's minds of the chaotic days here in the old Gold Rush time. The sun shone brightly; everything looked beautiful as if they had always been looking like this. A small train stopped by the wooden platform; it would carry the visitors to see some parts of the city. The colourful train looked like a toy train for children. The couple decided to drive their van and to walk around the city. Having visited some mega-cities, they felt that they could comfortably handle Whitehorse on their own.

After the visitor centre and a rest on the wooden platform, the couple went to the museum nearby. The museum was a large steamship anchored at the bank of the river. At the time when they were coming into the city, they had already spotted the large wooden ship. From the visitor centre, they got to know that it was a museum and the tourists could have a guided tour on the ship. The ship was called SS Klondike II. The steamship museum was a designated national historic site. Before the railroad had been built to connect Dawson City with Whitehorse in the old days, the steamship called stern-wheeler had provided services to carry people and goods to and from the two places. Quite some other steamboats also navigated the Yukon River then. The original Klondike was the largest stern-wheeler then. There were quite some casualties of the steamboats during that time; the first Klondike struck a reef in 1936. The same year, SS Klondike II was built to take over the services. Now SS Klondike II was serving as a museum.

As soon as the couple and some other tourists were aboard the big stern-wheeler, the guided tour started. The tour guide was a middle-aged woman; her guiding talk was fluent, loud and clear. The ship was indeed big, more than a hundred feet long. Though an old ship, she was superbly preserved and in mint condition. The tourists were first led through the bottom level of the ship. The large hull had been separated into several compartments. In the storage area there was a large metal chamber, the boiler or furnace to generate steam. The chamber was as big as a room with a large gaping door. Big pieces of wood would be fed into this chamber; the burning of the wood would generate energy to power the steam engine. Large piles of tree trunks, each about a meter high and two meters long, were on one side of this metal chamber. Each pile of wood was a cord and a cord of wood must be weighing a ton. In the old days, the ship had to buy many cords of wood along the way. At each place the ship had docked, there were people with cords of wood waiting. The wood suppliers would wheel the wood to the ship. There would be a single wooden plank laid to the ship from the shore. Each worker would put a cord of wood on a one-wheeler cart with two handles and then he would wheel the cord of wood through the single wooden plank to the ship. Along the way, the ship had to stop quite a few times to buy wood in order to keep the steam engine going and the ship sailing. It would take two and half days for the ship to reach Dawson City from Whitehorse. The return trip was against the current and more difficult, and it would take five days to accomplish the voyage. The couple were amazed to see the tremendous labors involved in the old-time navigation. They believed that today there would be very few workers who could even handle those cords of wood with a single-wheel carrier. Heavy labour-demanding work has all been done by machines nowadays.

On the other side of the metal chamber, there were different goods piled up; they were all in their original packages, wooden crates, sacks and boxes. The canned goods were with original labels of that period of time. It was amazing that people had kept all those antique wrappings. Yukon, especially Yukon in the old time, did not have any agriculture activities. With a sudden increase of population and all having to be fed, clothed and equipped, shipping food and all kinds of necessities was a huge task. Quite a lot of efforts and labours were involved in transportation and providing services.

The tourists then viewed the engine room and the dining room for the crews. Even with the antique type of engine, there were plenty of gadgets to amaze the visitors. After the tour of the bottom part of the ship, the tourists were then led to the top level where there were cabins and dinning lunge for the passengers. The cabins were ranked in different classes, but even the first class cabin was only a tiny room with a narrow bed. The dining room for the passengers was rather large and decorated in a decent good-life style of the old time. The dining room also served as the lunge; the passengers could comfortably rest in the soft chairs and play cards on the dining tables. A large kitchen was behind and connected with the dining room. The passengers could peek at what was cooking. The last place the tourists visited was on the topmost level of the ship. There was the helm's room on this level. The helm's room was not big, but it could comfortably accommodate three people working there.

The large wooden ship museum was indeed well preserved. The deck was gleaming with coating and polishing. Everything was kept in its best original state. Jim and Meilin had enjoyed the tour and felt that they had learnt something which was part of the history here. Canada has quite some historical sites throughout the country. They help the later generations to appreciate what efforts, hardships and labours the former generations had gone through in building up the country and to see the human spirits, perseverance and fortitude in trying to make life better.

Histories are made not only by the deeds of kings, queens and great important powerful peoples in different places and different times, they are also made by the bloodshed and lives lost in different battles and wars by many ordinary soldiers, and made by many ordinary people's hard works, their tremendous amount of sweat shed and lives spent in building up communities and countries and in improving lives through hundreds and thousands of years. As a matter of fact, the histories of the struggles between the powers and the powers changing hands or the systems alternating are normally told by the winners; their objectiveness cannot be one hundred percent. The histories of what the ordinary people and soldiers have made in protecting, building up communities and countries and improving lives are written on the very existence of those communities and countries and on the improved lives that everyone can see. The histories of the later are more objective and have more evidence to prove their truth. They have left more physical records of the past events and experiences. Those records are not only being preserved by books, pictures, stories, plays and films, but also by some physical objects or sites. After many generations have gone by, many past events can still be presented by those physical records or sites to make people see and feel what the former generations had gone through.

History is knowledge; through its records, people can learn and remember the past. The lessons learnt from history can prevent the past mistakes repeating and reveal the best ways for people's present and future pursuits. The saddest thing is that history has often shown that people don't learn from history and some past tragic and disastrous mistakes do repeat themselves. Whether people will learn the lessons from history totally depends on themselves, still the records and knowledge are there; hopefully they will be there for a very long time, so that the future generations will still have the chance to learn and be benefited by the knowledge.

After the visit to the SS Klondike II, it was already noon. The couple went downtown, trying to get some food from some restaurant, but some loud music and a crowd in a spot by a main street caught their attention. At this spot, there was an amphitheatre formed by a round cement stage surrounded by a lawn and a set of ascending wooden bench seats on one side. A concert was going on. A singer was singing on the stage and some musicians were playing music to accompany him. The audience not only occupied the wooden seats, but also sat on the lawn and at the picnic tables. The singer sang some lively folk songs and told jokes between his songs. Both his singing and joke cracking amused the audience greatly. Jim and Meilin would not miss the chance of enjoying the performance. They got some food they had brought in their van, sat at a picnic table with others and watched the show while having their lunch. The performance, the audience's loud laughter and applause had set the place on festive fire. Jim and Meilin enthusiastically enjoyed the show like all the people around them. They were very much impressed by Whitehorse's efforts not only to make the place attractive for the tourists, but also a happy and cheerful place for the people living here. From a small information booth by the street, the couple got to know that this kind of shows was going on in the city almost daily during the summer months.

In the afternoon, the couple visited the Old Log Church Museum. The old church was built in 1900. It was now a museum, presenting the history of Anglican Church's missionary work in Yukon. The couple had visited quite some large basilica cathedrals through the country. Still, they were quite impressed by this church built by large logs. It was well built, sturdy and fair-sized. The large congregation hall was now hosting quite some exhibits which were not only about the history of the Anglican Church here, but also about the natives and the Inuit.

The first white people who came to the Arctic areas were the whalers and sealers from Europe; they came in the 16th century, seeking whales and seals. Both the Roman Catholic and Anglican missionaries were the next; they came in the mid-18th century. Then in the late 18th century came the fur traders of the North West Company and the Hudson's Bay Company. In their first encounter with the white people, the Inuit did business with the whalers; they provided the whalers with meats and labours in exchange for their advanced tools, guns and whaling boats. The first dealings with the white people had brought the aboriginals grave sufferings and death. Having never encountered European diseases before, the Inuit had no natural immunity towards them. They were soon infected by Measles, Small Pox and Tuberculosis. Nine out of ten Inuit died of those diseases then.

The Roman Catholic and Anglican missionaries had brought some education and medical care to the northern aboriginals. The Catholic Church had more influence at first, as they had the help of more priests, lay brothers of Oblate order and the nuns, especially the Sisters of Charity or the Grey Nuns which was a Canadian order. The Anglican Church had the support of the Hudson's Bay Company. Not long, the Anglican Church dominated Yukon including the Oblates along the Mackenzie and Liard rivers and around the Slave Lake. The Anglican Church missionaries soon went farther north and the Catholic Church missionaries followed. There had been some competitions between the two Churches in this region throughout history.

The relationship between the northern aboriginals with the European whalers, the fur traders and some later settlers' constructions had brought more sufferings than benefits to the aboriginals. When the white people needed the aboriginals' business and help, they had kept them around, and when they no longer needed the aboriginals, they dropped them and pushed them back to their former settlements and their old ways of existence. But under the influence of the white people's ways of doing things and their advanced tools and technology, the aboriginals had gradually lost their own traditional ways of working and living. The disappearing of their simple and clean ways of life formed by thousands of years residing in the extreme north and the hastily acquired new European ways had brought poverties and many sufferings to the aboriginals.

For about two centuries, some help and care the aboriginal people had received from the white newcomers were mainly from the church missionaries. Although there were some individual cases of abuses rendered by the missionaries to the aboriginals, most of the missionaries had worked sincerely, trying not only to convert the aboriginals, but also to improve their living conditions. Up to the mid-20th century, the two Churches provided moderate education and medical care to the people of the northern regions.

In the old days, the working and living conditions for the missionaries in the extreme North were very hash. In this log church museum, Jim and Meilin had seen some exhibits which showed the situations at that time. Some missionaries had died in those missions. A bishop had almost starved to death, surviving by eating his own leather boots. The couple believed that this was the real historical record, not some imitation of Charley Chaplin's movie. They could imagine what hardships those missionaries had to go through on this extreme northern land in those old days.

After the visit to the church museum, the couple had some time to do some shopping. The Superstore in Whitehorse appeared to be no different than the Superstores in other provinces. The large bright grocery store sold not only different food items but also other goods for daily living. The prices for the groceries and other goods here were relatively the same as in other provinces. Having bought some groceries from the Superstore, the couple then went to the Walmart. Their camera was giving them some problems; they decided to buy a camera here. Yukon, like Alberta, had no local sales tax. Buying a camera here could save them a little money. After quite some running around, checking and rechecking, the couple finally bought a camera of the latest model.

At the end of the day's tour and checking around, Jim and Meilin decided that they liked this city. They had expected to see a lot of natives here, but they had seen mostly white people around. Still they had noticed that compared with other cities, the natives were visible here. Most importantly, they had seen some natives working in some stores; this was a thing that could hardly be seen in any other Canadian cities.

The night on the campground was relatively peaceful. After a nice shower in the good clean bathroom, the couple felt refreshed and sleep came naturally. Next day, the couple's agenda was to visit Yukon Arts Centre. They knew that Yukon's Archives and Yukon University were also by the arts centre. They were glad that they could visit them all. The three important institutes of Yukon were located on top of a hill at the skirt of

Whitehorse. The distance was not far from the campground. The couple soon arrived at the location. After parking their van in the spacious paved parking lot, they looked around. The place looked beautiful. The arts centre, the archives and the university were almost connected with each other. They were all moderately sized. The arts centre was a two story modern building with a glass front. The archives were housed by a one-story brownish brick building that looked new. The university's main building was several stories high, earthen coloured and stylish. The trees and gardens around those buildings looked well taken care of. The couple had come early in the morning; they could hardly see any other visitors. The whole place was so clean and quiet. Even with some students playing on the sports ground, the serenity of the surroundings was not broken.

"It must be very nice to work here, so beautiful and peaceful," Meilin commented admiringly.

"Yes, if you have a nice job here," Jim agreed.

The couple visited the arts centre first. The two story building had housed an art gallery and a theatre. The long reception hall had a full glass windowed wall facing the gardens outside. Part of the hall was nicely decorated by large pieces of paintings and artworks. Inside the gallery, the couple saw quite some native artists' paintings and artistic crafts. In recent years, quite some Canadian native artists' works have been recognized nationally and internationally. The unique paintings by the northern aboriginal artists have aroused quite some attentions in the world. The couple were quite impressed by those paintings. In the cold Arctic areas, the snow and ice dominate the landscapes, yet the aboriginal artists have created colourful pictures to depicting their life and the northern world. Jim and Meilin felt that those colourful pictures were not only pleasing their senses, but also inspiring. To them, those bright colourful paintings showed the aboriginal artists' views of the relationship between man and nature, cheerful, positive, harmonious and interactively nurturing.

Besides science and technology, arts and literature are two important aspects that can well represent the culture and intelligence level of a people. The native peoples have sufficiently shown through their arts that they are equal human beings in every sense. They understand well themselves and the world around them. If given enough chances, they can conquer the difficulties and obstacles they are facing in their life in the modern world. Having lived very close to nature for thousands of years, they may find ways to live more harmoniously with nature, in spite of the tremendous changes in present and future times.

In addition to the native artworks, the gallery had quite some portraits of women. The portrayed women were ordinary folk, all in their fifties and a few were visible minorities. The portraits were very well done. The different faces with different expressions had well shown different characters, hard working, diligent, warm, caring, understanding, kind and motherly. Jim and Meilin were glad to see those ordinary women's faces being shown in the gallery. In addition to the artistic value of the portraits, it was good that some artist would take the time and efforts to show that ordinary simple women in their fifties could be beautiful with their loving characters and the ordinary good work they were doing.

Coming out of the gallery, the couple went into the garden. The garden looked orderly with trimmed low hedges, paved paths and large lawns. There were three large art pieces in the garden. They were symbolic modern arts. One was formed by different pieces of oddly shaped metals; another was a stone sculpture of a native woman. The couple could not well understand the artwork formed by the metal pieces; it might have symbolized the highly metallic machinery chaotic modern world. They liked the simple solemn sculpture of the native woman; it made them think of Mother Nature. The third piece of the artwork was located on the edge of the large lawn where some big evergreen trees stood. This artwork had the couple's special attention. It was formed by a few pieces of granite stone walls; each had a hollowed human shape in the centre. This art piece was named "Shadow". There were those descriptions for this piece of artwork:

> After the atomic bombing of Hiroshima, curious 'shadows' were noted on the walls facing the detonation point. They were all that remained of people who had been vaporized by the immense heat of the blast, their impressions burned onto the wall in front of which they had been standing.
>
> ....

This grim symbolic artwork was obviously intended to evoke strong emotions from the viewers. War is a terribly destructive human act. In modern times, war has become a more ominous monster because of the highly developed weaponries and arsenals epitomized by the nuclear weapons. In the recent two centuries, science and technology have greatly improved the quality of human life, but they have also created the weapons that can wipe out the whole human race and destroy the planet earth in a very short time. The arms races have been increasing speed and power between nations and countries. Some countries have announced that when perceiving immediate dangers, they will attack first, including the attack with nuclear weapons. Facing the tremendous instability of today's world situation, who will not tremble for the future of the human race and the world?

Bertrand Russell had said, "Most of the greatest evils that man has inflicted upon man have come through people feeling quite certain about something which, in fact, was false." Most wars through human histories have been started by certain races, nations or countries feeling that they are superior to other races, nations or countries and they have the right or duty to conquer, to control or to destroy other peoples, nations or countries. When some of those dark evil aggressors are at their powerful peak, many people have followed them and many have given their lives to fulfil their evil callings. But without exception, the cruel aggressions have been defeated by different peoples rising up and fighting for justice and peace. Many wars in human history have left ample lessons for peoples of the world to learn and to avoid repeating those tragic events. Some peoples, nations and countries have learnt from the histories, but there are always some that will not learn or do not want to learn. So the wars have continued to be part of human life. With the weaponry being highly developed in the modern world and wars being unavoidable, the human race looks heading to the ending of being swiftly and effectively extinguished.

Not too long ago, some scientific prophets had predicted that there might be a few thousand years left for the life span of the human race. In recent time, those prophets had drastically shortened the time to a few centuries. Now they have shortened it even further to probably a few decades. Seeing the more and more dangerous and unstable world situation with clear and scientific minds, some people are bound to feel the imminent doom that is hanging low over the human world. Many efforts and thinking have spun up, trying to avert or prevent the impending tragic ending for the human race and the world. The most significant among them has to be the call for all peoples of the world to fundamentally change their ways of thinking and even their consciousness. People have to see that on a deeper or a higher level, they are all related to each other and related to the natural world. Harming others and the earth is harming themselves. It looks that only by changing their ways of thinking and their consciousness, can the human race and the world be saved. Yet changing the ways of thinking and consciousness means changing human nature, which is almost impossible. The dark roots, such as selfishness, aggressiveness, greed, envy, prejudice, malice, hatred, suspicion, distrust and so on, have grown with the birth of human race; they have existed and seemed unchangeable through the whole human existence, and they have caused conflicts, abuses, killings, wars and all kinds of atrocities throughout human history. An idea or a calling is easy to make, but to have the whole world's peoples to act upon is a quite different story, which seems an illusion or a fantasy. So, is the human race fated to exist for a certain period of time and die with their world in the end like everything else in the universe? Of course, that is certain. The only thing the human beings can do is probably to avoid a sudden, total and too soon death. This again depends on whether most human beings can change their consciousness or their human nature. There is still hope and the hope lies in that, after all, unlike other living beings, human beings are with the abilities of thinking and reasoning, besides feeling.

The size of the stone walls for this artwork was varied; two were smaller and one larger. The illustration for the artwork was engraved on another piece of granite stone. Jim and Meilin had seen the stone walls with the hallowed human shapes first. They felt that those sculptures were peculiar. Jim went to the hallowed parts of the walls to have pictures taken. The smaller human shapes were relatively his size, but the human shape in the larger wall was much bigger than him. Afterwards, the couple found the stone with the description. Having read the engraved words, a chill shot through their spines. Now they could fully understand the symbolic meaning of this artwork. With the picture taken, they had realized the truth that today all the peoples, no matter they were in which corner of the world, were facing the danger of being evaporated by the powerful nuclear weapons. They could see that through the larger stone wall with a much larger hollowed human shape, the artist was trying to express the view of the horrible future that was waiting for the whole human race, gone, wiped out by powerful weapons and leaving only an empty space.

Jim and Meilin felt that the world needed more of the artists like this who could create gloomy images to show the reality faced by the world today, to toll the alarming bells and to shock the peoples of the world into some senses. Human beings are supposed to be rational beings, but many of their behaviours through the human history have been anything but rational.

Right now, with the sun shining brightly and their whole surrounding emitting beauty and peace, the couple tried to hold the belief that the physical ending of the human race might be far away yet.

Moreover, the material ending might not be the total ending either personally or universally, and the possibility of other levels of existence seemed remaining. This belief had kept them mentally balanced. The total definite annihilation either personally or universally was too starkly bleak and hard for them to accept. To them, that would mean that the human life and the whole world were meaningless.

After checking the art pieces in the garden, the couple walked to the edge of the hill. From the edge, they could see some part of Whitehorse down below. The city was definitely not large. After the Klondike Gold Rush, the population of Yukon plummeted and the later increases were slow. Today, the total population of Yukon is about 28,800 and most of Yukoners reside in Whitehorse. A city will grow in size only by the increase of its population. With the recent economic development in this area, Yukon may see some population increase in the future and Whitehorse will grow accordingly.

Jim and Meilin visited the Yukon Archives next. They were not going to check any specific materials, but having a brief look at the inside of the archives. The inside of the building was spacious, quiet, and good for people who were doing some researches. In addition to rooms with shelves of records and materials, there was a large reading area with chairs and tables for the guests. One of the rooms had caught the couple's attention. In this room, there was a display of some old photos, mainly photos concerning the construction of the Alaska Highway, the lives of the military personnel who were building this famous highway, the equipments they used and some other relevant facts.

During the World War II, events had led to the construction of Alaska Highway. In December 1941, the Japanese launched a surprise attack to American Navy fleet at Pearl Harbor; Japan had momentarily controlled the Pacific and even captured two western Aleutian Islands in Alaska. Before this time, Canada had already built some airfields to form a northwest air-staging route to Alaska. Those airfields became vitally important in the war. The Americans decided to build an immediate all-weather highway to supply the US forces in Alaska and to strengthen those Canadian airfields.

The construction of Alaska Highway started immediately in 1941, undertaken by the US Army with some help from the Canadian Army. The working condition in building a highway in the extreme north was gravely harsh, but the rough military road was completed in less than a year. The rushed road was about 2500 kilometers long, which started from Dawson Creek, British Columbia, and through Yukon in Canada to reach

Fairbanks in Alaska. The road was about 500 kilometers on the US soil and about 2000 kilometers on Canadian soil. As the road was built by the US and for Alaska, it has been called Alaska Highway. It was the only land route that had connected Alaska to the North American Continent. In 1942, Alaska Highway had been turned to the Public Road Administration, an American civilian agency, to transform the rough military road into a permanent civilian highway. The road had been widened and branched out to those airfields and a telephone line with posts had been built along the highway. The total cost for building this highway was 139 million dollars. In 1946, Canada took control the portion of Alaska Highway on Canadian soil after paying 120 million dollars for its installment and some other services. The gravel highway was for military use only until 1948 when it was opened to tourists. Today Alaska Highway is fully paved and it has extended on the Canadian side to Edmonton, Alberta.

Jim and Meilin were quite interested in those photos which showed some of the facts and reality of building Alaska Highway. Considering those photos were taken in the 1940s, the couple were amazed how well they had been done. The choice of the scenes, the lighting and the skill in presenting the reality at that time, all showed the talent of the photographer. The couple were no experts in photography, but those vivid pictures not only aroused their interest in the history of Alaska Highway construction, but also brought their attention to the photographer. The couple learned something about him from the brief introduction to the artist. Of course, the photographer being of Chinese origin had also much to do in the couple's focused attention.

James Quong was a self-taught photographer and artist. He was born in Lethbridge, Alberta in 1917, but spent most of his early years in Saskatchewan. He studied Engineering and gained a degree from University of Saskatchewan while working as a sign painter to help paying his tuition. After graduation, he found a job in the US Public Road Administration. His first job was designing and drafting temporary timber bridges for Alaska Highway. Two years later, Quong was involved in the design of 134 permanent bridges for the same highway. It was during this bridge building time, he had developed his interest in photography. He experimented with this art and his skills matured. The pictures taken by him had been noted for their technique and artistic values.

Quong worked for the Americans until 1946. After the portion of Alaska Highway on Canadian soil had been transferred to Canada, Quong moved to Canada's Department of Public Works. There he continued to work on Alaska Highway bridges and also design other bridges for other highways. Quong married Diamond Chan in 1944. After the wedding, he told his bride that they would go to the north for six months, but they stayed in Whitehorse for 37 years. The couple had three daughters and one son. The Quongs lived an active and happy life in Whitehorse. They had been well accepted by the locals and made many life-long friends there. Besides photography, Quong had quite a few other interests such as calligraphy and music. He was also very good in designing cake tops; many locals had enjoyed his designs for their wedding, anniversary and birthday cakes. Quong loved his family and had passed his interests to his children. On the whole, Quong lived a rich and fulfilling life. He died in Coquitlam, British Columbia at the age of 86.

Having viewed the photo display and read the introduction to James Quong, Jim and Meilin were struck by quite a few extraordinary things. In the early twentieth century, the Chinese descendents in Canada had much lower social status than today. Very few Chinese had a higher education. Until the mid-20th century, the Chinese in Canada had been forbidden to hold any public position or any socially considered decent profession. Quong was a rare exception to have gained a university degree, got a good job after the graduation and kept the good job until his retirement. This was hard to achieve by an engineering graduate of Chinese origin even today. Quong had developed different artistic interests during his lifetime. This was possible mainly because of his good and stable social status. If he had lived in poverty with little education, all his talents and interests would unlikely have been developed.

The levels of intelligence, talents, abilities, understanding or even perceptions vary greatly between people, but definitely not between races. There is definitely no race superior or inferior to other races. Peoples and races may have some different ways of thinking, believing, and doing things, but they are similar in human nature, capabilities and perceptions. After all, they all belong to the human race. The intelligence levels in human beings may in some part congenital, but are mainly developed in their lifetime by nurturing, education and life experiences. People's social status is a decisive condition in their developments of not only their intelligence but also many other aspects. In some societies, quite some people in the majority group will think that people in the ethnic minority groups are on the lower level of the society because they are inferior in intelligence. But the facts are that those minorities have been in the disadvantageous positions because they have been kept on a lower social level and there are not enough ideal conditions and opportunities for them to develop. Giving them equal opportunities and raising their social status, people will see that those minorities are the same human beings as themselves in every aspect.

Another thing struck Jim and Meilin about James Quong was that he and his family had been well accepted and loved by the white society in Whitehorse. This was shown by that years later after his death, Whitehorse still displayed Quong's artistic work in the Yukon Archives. The social status of the Chinese Canadians has been noted low in Canadian society. The situation had been worse in the old times. Chinatowns, the Chinese communities in Canada, had been historically singled out as being the nests of prostitution, gambling, drugs and some other crimes. In fact, Chinatowns might be much cleaner than some other parts of the society, because the Chinese people are soft in characters, naturally law-abiding, habitually humble in all kinds of situations and often go out of their ways to please the authorities. The soft humble timid Chinese characters and their lower social status had been the main cause for many blames of social evils being heaped onto Chinatowns. Even today, quite some white people have still kept those traditional prejudices against Chinatowns. Chinatowns may be visited by some white tourists from some other countries, but seldom visited by the local whites.

The social status of the Chinese Canadians has improved in recent years. This has been achieved by the country's establishment of charter of rights and freedom and the change of policies towards the ethnic minorities, and by some Chinese Canadians who have obtained higher education and some higher levels of professions in medicine, law, education, other scientific fields and even politics. Still those white-collar workers of Chinese origin today have to keep a low profile and to be most obedient to the authorities. The general population of the society still dislike to see the Chinese holding higher social or professional positions and try hard to keep the general Chinese population on the lower social level. The Chinese Canadians, even outstanding, have to be kept away from the public eyes. A few of them do occasionally pop up on the public scene and they are generally disliked intensely by some white people. There are standard behaviours and outward features expected of the Chinese Canadians from the general white population; they must look humble with their backs hunched and eyes downcast or something to show humility, and they should definitely not be forwardly outspoken. Many white people have been used to seeing the Chinese here as the servants; people's habit of enjoying the situation that the Chinese are lower than themselves is unlikely to change very soon. When some of the

Chinese Canadians today don't fit into those standard requirements for their behaviours or speeches, they will of course be considered uppity or cocky and disliked or even hated; they will have all kinds of difficulties and suffer all kinds of perils in their lives. Though improvements in Chinese Canadians' living and working conditions are great in recent time, the second-class citizen status is still sticking to the Chinese Canadians and they have not entirely gained the equal rights and equal treatments as normal Canadians. As there are still a large number of the Chinese Canadians on a lower social level and a few that have made it will be mostly busy in conforming with the will of the majority whites to protect themselves, the general population of the Chinese Canadians are still vulnerable from discriminations and maltreatments; there are not much they can do if being singled out for persecutions or abuses.

Jim and Meilin could see that all the components seemed present for James Quong to live a happy and fulfilling life in Canada. His life was extraordinary, because he was a Chinese descendent, living and working successfully in Canada from the early to the late twentieth century. Being a Chinese descendent to have lived a successful life during this period of time was quite exceptional. Many odds had been stacked against him, against his success in both living and working in a society that the Chinese had been kept at the bottom, but he had made it in both ways. Jim and Meilin could not decide whether the exceptional case of James Quong was resulted from his being especially capable, or his being especially lucky, or the society of Whitehorse being especially accommodating to the ethnic minorities. There were not many Chinese Canadians in Whitehorse even today. The white people here looked more accepting to the natives and other coloured people. Jim and Meilin were quite moved in seeing different kinds of people living and working together harmoniously here. This had made them like this city even more.

The couple finished the sightseeing for this day after checking out the Yukon Archives. Next day, they went to Yukon Beringia Interpretive Centre. The centre was actually a nature museum. The orange-coloured modern building with lots of colourful banners looked cheerfully attractive. The couple arrived at the centre too early; its door was not open yet. They walked in the wooded area at the back of the building while waiting for the door to open. The morning sun was shooting its rays through the trees and spreading fresh golden spots on the ground; the walk turned out to be very pleasant and refreshing. There were some sculpted Ice Age animals being placed in the woods and some open area. The couple were quite attracted by the Giant Beaver that might have lived in Beringia during the last Ice Age. All the sculptures were in their exact life sizes and looks in the Ice Age. The Giant Beaver was as big as a large black bear, about eight feet long and weighing about four hundred and eighty pounds. Imagine seeing a large beaver like this today! Obviously, the Giant Beaver was the favourite of many locals and tourists. It had some shiny polished spots on its body from many people's touches, and the ground around the sculpture was bare of grass from many people coming close to have their pictures taken with the beaver. Jim and Meilin admired the giant stand-up beaver and had some pictures taken with it too.

The sculptures of large woolly mammoths were placed on the open area close to the highway. The couple admired them from a distance. The walk did not last long. They went back to the museum when the door opened. Yukon Beringia Interpretive Centre was not too big; it had an exhibition hall and a fair-sized movie theater. The exhibition hall was very brightly lit, as a whole side of its walls was glass windows from the floor to the ceiling. Now the morning sun was shining through the windows and making the whole exhibition hall cheerfully sunny. The exhibits and the introductory illustrations in the hall showed the Beringia - a special historical geographic feature of Yukon, the origin of the aboriginals - the first people of North America and some special animals of this area during the Ice Age. Jim and Meilin felt that this interpretive centre, though not big, was of first class among natural museums. They had learnt quite a lot from not only the exhibits but also a film they had watched in the theater here.

About 20,000 years ago, the Northern Hemisphere was going through the Last Great Ice Age. The climate was much colder, glaciers grew and the sea level dropped 125 meters. The coastlines changed dramatically because of the much lower sea level. A land bridge appeared between North America and Asia, connecting these two continents. This land bridge was part of a larger unglaciated area called Beringia. The ice-free Beringia was about 1200 to 2000 kilometres wide, covering parts of Yukon, Alaska and Siberia. Beringia and much of Asia remained ice-free while much of North America and Europe were covered by ice. In some places, the ice was over 1 kilometer thick. This connection of the two continents existed until about 10,000 years ago. During this time, the aboriginals entered Beringia from Asia through this land bridge; they were the first people landing on North America. Also during this time, Beringia's grasslands flourished and quite some Ice Age mammals perished in other parts of Europe and North America, but survived here.

Although most of Beringia was semi-arid tundra, caribou and many other animals thrived on this land. The landed aboriginal peoples created new ways of hunting, preserving food and making clothes, which had allowed them to survive in Beringia. Their numbers soon grew and they started migrating to other parts of North America after the Ice Age. Some lived here for thousands of years until the Europeans started coming to this land a few hundred years ago. In the recent few hundred years, they experienced drastic changes in North America and suffered maltreatments, diseases and poverties. In Canada, the living conditions of the aboriginals had started seeing some positive changes after the World War II. The Canadians had realized the fallacy of some anthropologic theory about the aboriginal race being inferior; they had also seen the tragically impoverished living conditions of the aboriginal peoples.

During the 1940s, the Canadian federal government had taken quite some emergency measures to save the starving and diseased Inuit. With the pouring-in of the newcomers from other parts of the world, the activities of trapping and hunting had very much increased in North America. Seals were depleted and caribous failed to migrate to the areas where the natives and Inuit depended on those animals for their livelihood. Many Inuit were dying from starvation or tuberculosis. The federal government flew those widely spread Inuit family groups to the posts while there were food and they also sent the sick ones by planes or boats to the south where medical attentions were available. Then the government launched a campaign to combat tuberculosis. They X-rayed and immunized as many Inuit as possible with anti-tuberculosis vaccine. They built hospitals, living places and schools and brought in doctors and nurses to look after the Inuit refugees and the newcomers from the south. Soon the constructions went from semi permanent to permanent; power plants, water and sewer systems, roads, villages and towns had been built in the East Arctic areas. The instalments for military, sovereignty and government administration were also in place. By 1950s, the programs of the Department of Health and Welfare had lowered down the high mortality rate in this region.

In the recent half century, there have been many improvements in Canada's treatments towards the aboriginal peoples. Quite some native land issues have been looked at; some treaties or money compensations have been made to the native peoples' land claims and abuses they had suffered. Today, the status native peoples enjoy free medical care, free education on their reserves and subsidies for their housing and higher education. If they have earned money on their reserves, their earnings are exempt from taxation. In addition to their right for hunting and fishing, they are entitled for federal loans and grants to establish businesses on their reserves. However, the work to improve the native peoples' living and working conditions is far from being finished. The unemployment rate on quite some native reserves today is sometimes eighty percent high. When the unemployed native peoples come into cities, they will only be on welfare in cities. The native peoples in Canada are still ranked at the very bottom of the economic and social scales of the country. The income of an average native family is only half to two thirds of an average non-native Canadian family. The native peoples' life expectancy is statistically about ten years shorter than that of the average Canadians.

Jim and Meilin checked the exhibits and introductions in the exhibition hall. They were quite interested in the records about the early aboriginal peoples' life in this area, their stories, legends and beliefs. There were also quite a few fossil bone structures of Ice Age animals in display. They were the giant beaver, the woolly mammoth, the saber-toothed tiger and the short-faced bear. Then they watched a film about Beringia in the theater. After the film, a guide led the visitors to the backyard of the centre. There was a piece of beautiful native artwork in the backyard. On a concrete stand, a wood sculpture of a native man was sitting in and rowing a canoe. There was a circle of symbolic patterns around the man and his canoe. On the ground of the backyard, there were quite a few engraved metal plaques on posts. The illustrations on the plaques introduced the special geographic features of Beringia and some Ice Age plants. The guide was a middle-aged man. He explained the early geographic features in this area clearly and intelligently to the visitors.

According to the interpretations, the most prominent land feature of Beringia was the permafrost. Permafrost had shaped part of the whole northern Canada both in the past and at the present. Beringia was not totally ice free during the Ice Age, but relatively warmer than other areas. Permafrost is the land remaining permanently frozen and in most cases underneath a layer of unfrozen surface land. Part of Beringia with ice underneath cannot drain the water, so that the land is rather wet and good for the grass and some other shallow plants to grow. With the icy land below, the roots of the plants cannot reach deep and therefore not be able to grow big or tall. This land feature is typical of the tundra where dwarfed plants grow close to the surface of the land. When temperature rises, some of those frozen icy layers will thaw to form ponds and lakes. If the climate becomes too dry, some of the ponds will dry up to form a concaved land surface. With the seasonal thawing and freezing during the

Ice Age, the land had preserved quite some remains of the Ice Age animals, which have benefited the museums and knowledge-seeking people today.

After the interpretive explanations, the guide produced some javelins for the visitors to try them. There was a dried pond forming part of the backyard, which was the result of the land changes from permafrost. It was a relief for the visitors to know that the permafrost underneath Whitehorse no longer existed today. Right now some cardboard animals had been placed in or around this dried pond. The visitors were all in high spirits to throw the javelins at those cardboard bears, wolfs, foxes, hares and so on. The javelins here were not the same as those used in the Olympic Games. They were shorter and each set had two pieces. According to the guide, those javelins had been used by the aboriginals on Beringia in the ancient time. One piece of the javelin was used as a leverage to help them to shoot the other piece further and more forcefully. Every visitor had tried to shoot the cardboard animals with the javelins; some did better and some worse. There was a lot of laughter and shouting from the enthusiastic first-time javelin practitioners. The guide started calling people the bear or the hare person. Actually, the whole group of visitors could only be called grass persons. Being transported to any point in the ancient time, not one of them could kill a field mouse with the javelin, let alone a hare or any other big animals. It would be very lucky if they could survive on grass or some other vegetation.

The visit to the Beringia Centre ended in a cheerful atmosphere. Jim and Meilin then went directly to the Yukon Transportation Museum which was just a walking distance away from the interpretive centre. Like the Beringia Centre, the transportation museum was also not too big. But the couple found its exhibits quite comprehensive. Outside the museum, there was a twin-engine plane displayed as an exhibit on the spacious ground. The plane served in USAAF in the World War II, running transportation missions in India and China. After the war, she was sold for civilian use. She flew then as a bush plane, transporting goods to some remote places in Yukon. She had also flown chartered and scheduled routes from Yukon to some outside places. Now the plane was being set on a swirling pivot standing on a concrete mount about twenty feet high. She could turn with the wind, and her head was always against the wind. The war and peacetime veteran was hovering on the pivot here today, serving the museum and tourism.

The museum proper consisted of two large exhibition halls. One of them had all kinds of transportation devices used in Yukon in different times. They ranged from dog sled, horse-drawn cart, old motor car to a passenger car of an old train. From the tall ceilings of the large hall, hung some small planes; some of them were World War II planes. The other large hall was displaying the vehicles and equipments used in the construction and the maintenance of Alaska Highway. In this hall, the couple saw large vehicles and equipments, old and new. Some military heavy-duty trucks looked badly beaten by weather and usage; they showed what kind of hardships and difficulties both men and machines had gone through in building this highway. In this hall, there was a military tent set up in a corner. In the tent, a documentary film was showing on a TV screen. The film was telling the whole history of the Alaska Highway by showing the whole actual construction process and relevant events at that time. Jim and Meilin sat down on the wooden bench in the tent with a few other visitors and watched the film with great interest.

The visits to the natural centre and the transportation museum had taken the couple most of the day. Still, in the afternoon, they squeezed in more into their tour of the city. They had a quick visit to the McBride Museum of Yukon History and browsed through the exhibits that showed Yukon heritage from the prehistoric mammals to the Gold Rush. After buying a souvenir concerning Yukon's Gold Rush, they rushed to the Whitehorse Fishway. It was the first time that Meilin had seen a fish ladder. Whitehorse's fish ladder was believed to be the longest in the world. There was a dam built on the Yukon River in the spot. By the dam a long wooden ladder had been built to allow the Chinook salmon and other fish to bypass the Whitehorse Rapids Dam in their 3,000 kilometer migration from the Bering Sea to their spawning grounds in southern Yukon. The wooden ladder was built by large logs, more than a meter wide and had several turns. The couple were amazed by the fish ladder. After the whole day of visiting different attractions in Whitehorse, they felt that all the visits were educational and interests promoting. Now they were quite eager to see Yukon, its mountains and rivers, and of course, to drive through the famous Alaska Highway.

The couple had a good night's sleep. Next morning they started early on their way. Driving on the highway was one of their favorite enjoyments on the trip. Alaska Highway, though not a luxury four-lane highway, was wide enough with sufficient shoulder spaces. The couple had already driven some distance on Alaska Highway to reach Whitehorse; they knew the condition of the highway. Driving on Alaska Highway was definitely not a smooth ride all the time. There were quite some maintenance works going on in some spots. The maintenance for

Alaska Highway is an annual chore and sometimes this chore could get rather heavy. This highway is not heavily travelled by people or commercial vehicle drivers; the need to constantly maintain the road comes from the constant changes of the land. In quite some parts of Yukon, the land is still affected by permafrost. If the climate warms up to some unusual degrees, the icy land underneath will start to thaw. This thawing can inflate the land and push the surface up. If this kind of thawing inflation happens on the spots where the highway goes through, it will of course affect the condition of the highway and lead to the need for repair works.

The construction and maintenance of Alaska Highway is one of the great works that embodies the human will, drive and spirit to conquer, to achieve and to succeed. No matter in what kind of conditions, facing what kind of difficulties or obstacles, with the determination and perseverance, there seems nothing that the humans cannot get over to achieve their goals. If this kind of will, drive and spirit is used only to build and maintain the great projects for the welfare and well-being of the mankind, the world will be a totally different place. Hunger and poverty will definitely be the thing of the past. Without these two major miseries, peace and love among human beings will be easier to achieve. Unfortunately, since the existence of the human race, part of human will, drive and spirit have gone to some deadly destructive endeavours of fighting, conquering or destroying each other. After a few thousand years of evolution, the human beings seem still not progressed much in changing their will to power from dominating and controlling others to more efforts for the good of the whole human race and the world. With the quick progress of their science and technology, if the human beings continue their primitive aggressive ways of treating each other and the world with all its other living beings, their fate of doom will be sealed and the end will come in one way or another.

The couple drove on the smooth Alaska Highway. Never before, had they so keenly felt that every inch and foot of the highway had been built and maintained with tremendous efforts and labours. This feeling must be the result that they had just watched the documental film about how this highway was built in extremely harsh conditions. The struggles and tremendous efforts many people had gone through to build this road were still fresh in their minds.

People in modern time enjoy their travelling without much thought about those who have worked hard to bring the comfort and ease in all kinds of modern transportations. We drive through smooth highways or go across rivers through bridges, feeling great with the speed and comfort provided by the modern facilities. We ride in a train, going through dangerous terrains with the utmost sense of safety and freedom. Seldom will we think of those people who have worked hard and even given their lives in building and maintaining the roads, the bridges and the railways. Numerous modern facilities have indeed made human life more comfortable. It is high time that more thoughts and considerations be given to appreciating what we have, controlling our appetite and adjusting our attitudes towards others and the natural world.

On the way, the couple talked about the difficulties and hardships people had gone through in building this highway; they appreciated those who had made it possible for them to travel comfortably through the remote wilderness areas in this extreme northern region. They were much more patient now with the traffic interruptions and delays by the highway maintenance work. While driving and stopping to wait, they were deeply attracted by the sceneries along the highway. The vast wilderness of Yukon had very much reminded them of Newfoundland. However, the scenes in Yukon were different than that of Newfoundland, even though the landscapes had given them the same feeling of the vast openness of the terrains, the isolation of the land and the powerful beauty of unstained nature. The vast land rolled here, but it was not the rolling of hills; it was gigantic rolling of mountains. The giant rolling waves were green, but trees seemed scarce in some areas. However, along some rivers or around some lakes, the mountains would be attired in deep green with abundant trees.

Having driven for quite a long distance, the couple did not see any human residence or farmland; it seemed a vast wilderness everywhere. Like Newfoundland, Yukon has very little arable land. Agriculture here is in a very small scale and only serves the local. Traditionally, fur trapping is the main industry in this region and then mining. Today mining industry has developed to some extent and fur business has gone down. Yukon, to the couple, seemed to have great potential for tourism. The majestic land had so much awed them; they were sure that it would do the same to many others. The whole north close to the North Pole is the top part of the world. Yukon has many majestic mountains. Among them is Mount Logan, 6050 meters high, the highest peak in Canada. The more amazing scenes are the huge ice fields flanking the giant mountains and feeding many glaciers.

The couple were heading to the kluane National Park and Reserve which was by Alaska Highway. In the afternoon, they reached Haines

Junction, a small town just by the park. The name Haines Junction might have come from the famous explorer Samuel Hearnes. In 1760's, he was sent by Hudson's Bay Company to find the legendary copper mines in the Northwest Territories. On his first two trips, he was robbed and abandoned on the tundra by his guides. The first time, he came out on his own and the second time, he was saved by a Chipewyan native man named Matonabbee. Still he went the third time to find the mines. With the help and guidance of Matonabbee, he finally found the copper mines in 1770. Though the mines were shallow, Hearne had left a shining image of the early explorers who were full of adventurous spirit and invincible determination and perseverance.

As usual, when the couple arrived at Haines Junction, they went first to the gas station to gas up their van. Then from the information they got in the gas station, they found the visitor centre nearby. The visitor centre, though a wood structure, was of modern style. The reception hall had tall ceilings and large windows. Along the windows, there was a long wooden bench for the visitors to sit down and enjoy the outside view. Besides shelves full of brochures and pamphlets about traveling in Yukon, there were quite some exhibits in the center introducing the Kluane National Park and Reserve, some local birds and the mountainous terrains of the whole region. The clerk behind the information counter was a middle-aged native woman. She answered Jim's questions warmly and friendly. In no time, the couple got enough information and also found out there was a campground close by.

Kluane National Park and Reserve covers 22,015 square kilometers of wilderness and is dominated by Saint Elias Mountains and peaked by Mount Logan and Mount Saint Elias. During the years of building the Alaska Highway, the whole area was preserved as the Kluane Wild Game Sanctuary. In 1979, Kluane was declared a World Heritage Site because of its grand topographic features and massive nonpolar ice fields. The Saint Elias Mountains have extensive ice fields that dated from the last Ice Age, which form the world's largest nonpolar glacier systems. The ice fields and glaciers cover more than half of the park. Constant movements of the glaciers are leaving debris, forming sand dunes and even causing dust storms in the park. In the northern section of the park, the land has retained quite some tundra characters; everywhere Arctic flowers can be spotted. Along the rivers and in the valleys, the boreal forest covers some areas. In the southern section of the park, affected by the Pacific Ocean's climate, the vegetation is lusher. Many animals thrive in the park. Kluane has one of the largest populations of grizzly bears and moose in the world.

After checking out the introductions and model illustrations about the Kluane National Park and Reserve and the region, the couple spotted a deck outside the windows. They went out to the deck to enjoy the view and were immediately awed by what they saw. In a distance, Yukon was displaying her great beauty of a long range of magnificent Saint Elias Mountains. The green mountains with snow capped peaks were glowing under the sun. The couple had seen quite some snow-capped mountains in Canada, but this was the first time that they had seen so many of large high mountains forming such a gigantic panorama view. It was hard to describe the feelings when seeing nature displaying such grand beauty and power. They were completely overwhelmed, their breath had been taken away and they felt totally spellbound. For quite some time, they remained silent, totally lost in the majestic splendor. Then Jim took out the camera and they started taking pictures of the mountains and the pictures of themselves with the mountains. They knew that the pictures would never show the full reality of this kind of natural beauty, but they might jut their memories of what they had seen at this moment. There seemed a gigantic live or spirit in this beauty. At this moment, this spirit of nature was all harmonious, serene, vibrant, cheerful and even benevolent. Still it was easy to feel her power and indifference and to imagine her threatening grimace in a gloomy or stormy day. Under this kind of natural power and beauty, the humans and their noisy world seemed so remote and pitifully insignificant.

Having enjoyed enough of the mountain scene, the couple went to their vehicles and drove to find the campground which was quite close to the visitor centre. When they pulled into the campground, they were surprised to see a large campground in this remote place of Yukon. It was a big flat area at the foot of a mountain, one among a long range of snow-capped mountains. There were quite many RV lots on this open ground. It looked that most of the lots were fully serviced. If the couple were amazed by the mountain scene at the visitor centre, they were stunned and overpowered here by this even closer and larger panorama view of the colossal mountains that were all so tall and snow-capped. The couple were pleased beyond words. They could camp here with their trailer window facing this beautiful scenery and enjoy to their hearts' content. Jim pulled the trailer to the front of the office and the couple got out of their van. The office was a large residential house. The manager and his family seemed living in part of the house. There were a convenience store, a bathroom and a laundry on part of the main floor for the visitors.

The couple registered for two nights. Then they set their trailer on a lot with full service. After they had done everything, they had their late lunch and rest. While they were resting in their trailer, somebody came to knock on their trailer door. It was a young woman. She introduced herself as the park's tour guide. The park provided free guided hiking tour for the visitors to go through the woods of the mountains.

The young woman asked, "Would you like to go on a hiking trip tomorrow? I'll lead the hiking group."

Jim and Meilin were very interested. They had gone through quite some parks in Canada. This was the first time that a park's tour guide came to them to offer a guided hiking trip. The couple expressed their gratitude and then asked how long and how far the hiking trip would be and what kind of road conditions they would encounter. They found out that the trip was quite physically demanding. It was about fifteen to twenty kilometers long. Their neighbour now came over from his trailer and chatted about his experience on the hiking tour.

"It was a beautiful experience through the woods to know different plants, trees, birds and animals. We had seen black bears and some other animals. Well, some black bear had even come near to the campground the other day..." the middle-aged man chatted good-naturedly.

The hiking tour sounded very attractive, but Jim and Meilin had to turn it down. With their physical conditions, they had difficulties in handling a three-kilometer hiking. A fifteen-kilometer hiking plus or including the return trip was a long march to them. No matter how much they had coveted the experience of going through the pristine forest of Yukon mountains; they knew that they could not handle the trip.

Jim said to the young woman guide sincerely, "Thank you very much. It is a pity that our physical condition would not allow us to take this offer. The park here is the first that has given us such a kind and generous offer. Yukon is so beautiful and the park's service so good; I hope you'll see more tourists soon."

The young woman guide left with a broad smile on her face. The couple went back to their rest in the trailer. They talked about how good the hiking trip might be and how unfortunate that it was beyond their reach. They had to be satisfied with admiring the mountains in a distance, taking a full day tomorrow to rest at this beautiful spot and savoring the grand mountain-view from the campground. Anyway, the couple still felt quite fortunate. They had camped at the coast of Newfoundland and enjoyed the magnificent ocean; now they were camping in Yukon, soaking in the beauty of the majestic mountains. They doubted that the people who were living in places where the ocean or mountain views were a daily encounter would have enjoyed or felt so deeply the beauty of those natural scenes. People can get satiated with and tired of what is abundant to them, but they will highly appreciate and treasure what is scarce and hard to come by in their life.

After they had rested, the couple spent the rest of the afternoon walking around the campground. Side by side with the large open area for RVs, there was a large wooded area for tenting. The couple walked through the woods. The tall aspens with clean white trunks and shining leaves whispered gently in the wind. Among the light-coloured aspens, the few darker spruces and pines were quite eye-catching. Every tent lot was spaciously large. The paths through the tenting area were wide. Where the wide path parted the tall trees, the snow-capped mountains were displaying their beauty in a distance. The place was so peacefully beautiful and the air was so freshly clean, able to match up with the pure air in Newfoundland. The couple were entirely enchanted.

While enjoying the quiet walk through the woods, the couple were surprised to see that in such a big tenting area, there was only one lot occupied by a camper. Later that afternoon and evening, some RVs had pulled into the open area of the campground. Still, the few RVs on the large campground looked lost. The couple thought of those campgrounds near the large cities. In recent years, even though the fees charged by those campgrounds had soared, they became more and more crowded in summer time. Here, Yukon offered such grand natural beauty, but few visitors came. Obviously, Yukon was not for the faint hearts. The sparrow tourists kept close to large cities.

People in modern time are more and more used to crowded spaces and tremendous noises. Some people seem unable to live a normal life without them. One can often encounter some young people surrounding themselves with loud noises, imposing their presence on others and causing attention or disturbance all around. They must have felt that they themselves have actually become those loud noises. Camping becomes popular nowadays; lots of people have crowded the campgrounds near the cities, bringing with them their portable barbeques, portable generators and portable stereos. They even camp by some highways with heavy traffics going on all the time, walk in the small woods filled with smokes from firewood smouldering in the fire-pits of some campsites and sleep with their own or their neighbours' stereos blasting loud music all night long. Still, this kind of camping days and nights are enjoyable to them, because they mean parties. To many young people, anything if it is a party, it means leisure or recreation time and should be considered enjoyable and relaxing. Anyone thinks differently are considered not going with the flow and unable to enjoy a good time with the crowd. But for many normal adults, it is beyond their ability to appreciate or enjoy the loud music carried on in some youngsters' vehicles or on their campsites. Their music has no lyrics only one or two tunes which are constantly and repeatedly drumming the same monotonous notes; the booming noise will shake or vibrate the ground and drive other people around crazy. Under the hypnotic effect of this kind of music, the youngsters themselves look like in trance, their eyes almost crossed, their faces without any expression and their brains might have turned to oatmeal.

Music is the language of passion or the language of heart. It has the power and beauty to reach the inner most places of people's hearts, touching their souls and arousing their deepest feelings. Any sound that has the power and beauty to touch the chords of feelings can be called music. The sound that does not have this power and beauty fails to be music.

Jim and Meilin were now in the beautiful natural surrounding ruled by tranquility. The noises of human world were far away. At this peaceful and blissful moment, they pitied those crowd people. They knew that it might not be that those people were afraid of the efforts or difficulties of going to remote wilderness. The roads were smoothly paved and all had their vehicles to travel comfortably. The noise and crowds lovers might be actually afraid of the silence, the stillness and the solitude that go side by side with the wilderness. In the quiet solitude environment, they would be forced to face themselves and to think. For some people, all their life, they were afraid of these two things, to face or to be with themselves and to think.

After supper, the couple went to the office house to take a shower. The bathroom was of home style; the fair sized room had only one shower stall. Meilin went first. The bathroom was clean and comfortably spacious, but the shower was operated by coins. This was not a surprise. Throughout the country, many other campgrounds had their showers operated by coins. This campground had charged a moderate fee for the fully serviced RV lot, a little over thirty dollars; a fee for the shower looked not too bad. In recent years, almost all the campgrounds, either publicly or privately owned, had raised their fees. The publicly owned campgrounds around the place the couple were living now seemed in the very front to raise camping fees. Who can complain? The prices of commodities are naturally adjusted by the quantity of demands for them. Those camping sites in the campgrounds near the cities are hotly demanded nowadays. Comparing the camping fees with what they had experienced throughout the country, the couple were grateful for the moderate camping fees charged here at Kluane Park, so a coin operated shower became quite acceptable.

Meilin checked and found that she had a two-dollar coin and some smaller changes with her. She started showering. But in the middle of the shower, the two-dollar time ran out and the box would not accept the smaller coins. Some action had to be taken for her to finish her shower. She knocked the bathroom door from the inside. Soon she heard a knock from the outside and a woman's inquiring voice; she opened the door a crack and stuck her head at the crack. A young woman looking like a Métis was at the door. She must be the worker or the manager's wife. Meilin gave her a five-dollar bill and asked her to change it into some coins for her. The woman smiled and went away with the bill. She soon came back with the coins. After this interval, Meilin finished her shower. It was an enjoyable hot shower. The water pressure and water temperature were both good. Yukon's temperature in July was quite cool. The mirror in the bathroom was all steamed up.

When Meilin came back to the trailer, she told Jim to take two tunies for his shower. Jim went for his shower and came back satisfied with the four-dollar shower also. The couple settled comfortably in their trailer after the showers. The sun was now setting. Its rays had gilded the snow-capped mountains. The sky was glowing from rosy to crimson. The couple could not tear their eyes from such a glorious show of nature. Soon the show was finished. The sun dipped way down from the peaks of the mountains. Everything started to turn grey. With the time fleeting, the greyish colour was getting deeper and the mountains started looming dark. The couple stayed in and enjoyed the colour changes of the scenery from their trailer window. The sky was gradually changing from gray to dark, but it remained velvety. The mountains were getting more and more imposingly dark. When the darkness finally covered all, the stars started issuing their cool lights. It was true that in the wilderness, the stars in the velvet dark sky looked much bigger and shone much brighter. The moon too was glowing gently, but instead of covering everything with its silver rays, it only made the mountains showing more of their dark shadowy presence. Suddenly, somewhere in the deep of the mountains, a high pitched shrill came from some animal or bird. The piercing shrill tried to tear the dark stillness open, but was immediately swallowed up by it. The wind had totally died down. Darkness and stillness closed in with only the stars and the moon shining high in the sky and trying to lessen some of their power. The night in the wilderness was totally different than the night in a city. Here Nature reigned; when Nature went to sleep, everything quieted down.

Even with an electric light shining in front of the office house, the couple felt that they had been surrounded by the dark night. They went to sleep, feeling as if they had fallen into the immense womb of the earth. Next morning when they were awakened by the twilight, they felt thoroughly rested and refreshed. They reckoned that Mother Nature's embrace of a dark night must have great healing power for everything. They smiled and thought that they must be thinking like the natives now.

The couple spent their second day on the campground in utmost peace and contentment, enjoying and treasuring the beautiful mountain scenes which they knew would only last for them at this moment. Next day, they pressed on, driving on the Alaska Highway. Further north, the scenes along the highway became more mountainous. For some long stretch of the highway, the land seemed heaving more deeply. They felt like running on a huge rollercoaster. Only the up and down motion was largely scaled.

Having gone deep into Yukon, the couple then crossed the international border and went to Alaska. All along the highway, the scenes varied greatly. There were immense landscapes of high mountains, some covered by snows, some rocky and some green with plenty of trees. The ice fields along had covered huge areas of valleys and were trailed by glaciers. Tremendous areas were still dominated by tundra where the plants, vegetations and trees remained darkish colour, small and growing close to the surface of the land. Nowhere else, had the couple so deeply sensed the isolation of the wilderness and the immense size of the planet. In Alaska, the couple did not follow the Alaska Highway to Fairbanks, but turned onto a different highway and went to Anchorage, the capital city of Alaska. Anchorage was much bigger than Whitehorse and had plenty of public and cultural facilities. Though located in the extreme north, the city was full of flowers. The couple were quite impressed.

Coming back to Yukon, the couple decided to spend at least one night camping entirely in the wilderness. They chose Kluane Lake in Kluane National Park and Reserve for the wilderness camping. When they came to Kluane Lake on their trip in earlier time; they had encountered the most beautiful mystical scene in a grand scale. Kluane Lake was big. From one side of the lake, the view of the mountains on the other side looked rather remote. In this particular morning, heavy mist drifted and floated over the big lake. It was impossible to see where the lake started and where the land ended. The mountains over the other side of the lake and some small islands on the lake looked like some islands or mountains floating in the clouds of the sky. The whole scene was so surreally beautiful and made the couple feel that they were in heaven, seeing some heavenly places drifting in mist and clouds.

Having experienced the extraordinary scene of Kluane Lake, the couple now decided to camp by the lake to fully enjoy its mystic beauty. The lake was shaped oblong. They picked a spot at the head of the lake where they could see the mountains on both sides and the lake in front them was stretching towards the horizon. The spot was a large flat gravel area lower than the highway; it must have been made by the national park as a resting place for the travellers. There was a gravel path leading down from the highway to the area. The lake was lying lower than this open spot. The view of the lake and the surrounding area from this spot was spectacular. Though the highway was going through the area, there was no other human structure nearby. From this spot, the couple could see the highway with a bridge stretching on to a left bend of the lake. The place had given them the feeling of not being totally isolated from the human world.

Kluane Lake has always been the home of northern pike, Arctic grayling, lake trout and Kokanee salmon. For thousands of years, the native peoples have fished on the lake. In 1904, the North West Mounted Police set a post on the south shore of the lake. During the construction years of Alaska Highway, the lake was a meeting place for the construction crews. Right now, all was quiet. The only human activities were occasional vehicles running through the highway by the lake.

The couple pulled their van and trailer to the large gravel area. They were immediately enchanted by the beautiful lake. From the resting spot, the lake looked vast, reaching to the sky. The mountains on both sides were green, stretching along the lake, from big to small according to their distance from the spot. At the back of this open area, the mountains with sharp rocky peaks were thrusting into the sky. There was another motor home parked on this resting place. A family with children was playing at the shore. Two small kids were swimming in the lake and a few adults were enjoying the lake view. The spot must be a frequented scenery lookout.

Jim and Meilin were happy with the spot. They hoped that they would have some companies to spend the night here with them. After they had stabilized the trailer and settled down, they went to the shore. The day was sunny; everything looked so peaceful, bright and beautiful. The waves sparkled under the sun and were tapping the shore gently. The couple walked along the shore, soaking in the beauty provided by nature and picking up some good-looking pebbles. They could see some small rocks shooting out of the water at the spot where the family with kids were. The kids were jumping from the rocks into the water, shouting and laughing; and the adults chatted. Though they were some distance away, their cheerful voices were carried far and clear in the wide openness.

Time on this beautiful lakeside place passed most pleasantly. The couple felt fully relaxed and happy. In the late afternoon, the weather changed suddenly. The sky turned grey and all the brightness left quickly. Wind started gradually increasing power. The family with kids retreated to their motor home and drove away. Jim and Meilin decided to stay. No matter how the day was going to be, they were determined to see it out. They thought that since they were going to camp in the wilderness for a night, they might as well see what wilderness could present.

With the wind increasing power and speed, the couple were astonished to see that the lake was quickly stirred or agitated. A tide was coming in. From the map, the couple could not see any connection between the lake and the ocean. This was the first time in their life that they were going to see a tide coming in on a lake. They had seen tides coming in and going out on the ocean where the tides' coming and going seemed quiet with only the changes of the sea level. Here now, the tide was coming in on this lake accompanied by a coming storm. The sky was soon entirely overcast and the wind was blowing stronger by the minute.

The couple put on more clothes and stayed by the lake. They had always wished to see a high tide and now they got their wish. It was totally unexpected that they would see a high tide on a lake. Obviously; it showed that anything could happen with the weather and nature in Yukon. The wind started howling. Billows formed long layers of high waves, pounding the shore more and more urgently, one long layer of waves taking over by another; the intervals were getting shorter and shorter and the waves were getting higher and higher. The whole lake was now turned into a large cauldron with boiling water. The turquoise-coloured water under the sun soon changed into earthen colour. This change of the clear water into murky water started from along the shore and quickly spread to the whole lake. The billows soon looked full of sands. The lake looked being churned and stirred by a huge invisible staff; the very bottom of it had been turned up.

With the waves fiercely pounding, layer after layer in increasing speed and power, the couple saw the lake level quickly rising. The wind was blowing more and more violent. The chill it had brought was getting thicker. Soon the rain started. Jim went back to the trailer; Meilin stayed a little longer by the turbulent lake. She was trying to video-tape the whole violent natural scene. Soon she was also forced into the trailer. With the wind howling and the waves pounding, nature was amusing herself with a powerful symphony, a symphony with a strong rhythm unceasingly and relentlessly increasing the speed of the beats. To Jim and Meilin, this symphony was deafening and earth-shaking. Meilin continued to tape the scene from inside the trailer. The couple watched the boiling lake rising higher and higher. In a short time, the lake had risen about ten feet. The waves had started surging towards the flat open area where they had parked their van and trailer. Just when they started thinking of moving to avoid being pulled by the tide into the lake, the rhythm of the symphony seemed to have slowed down a little. Then they saw that the waves too slowed down the urgent beatings on the shore.

The couple knew that the waxing of the tide had reached its peak and the waning would start soon. They were glad that they did not have to move. Having been busy watching and feeling intensely nervous of the tide and the storm, they had forgotten their supper. Now with the situation calmed down a bit, they prepared their supper. The night had already set in and very soon everything would be engulfed by darkness. The couple had their supper with a small light in their trailer and did a little cleaning afterwards. There was not much else to do, but watching and listening in the trailer. Their lone trailer was by now surrounded by the impenetrable dark night. The rain was getting heavier. The beating sound of the rain on their trailer had changed into thunderous booming which had overpowered the sound of the pounding waves. There would be no living creatures venturing out in this dark stormy night. The couple knew that there was no danger camping in a trailer in the Canadian wilderness. Still, they were scared by the utter loneliness in this violent stormy dark night.

To divert themselves from the lonely scared feelings, Meilin tried to talk as calmly as possible, "With this kind of violent turbulence of the lake, some fish might have been beaten out their senses or even killed.

When the tide is out tomorrow morning, some of them might be beached; we can pick them up."

"Yes, we might have some fish for breakfast," Jim agreed readily with a smile.

The couple went to bed, fighting off their fear by holding the thought of a fish frying in their pan tomorrow morning. Strangely, the loud rainstorm soon lulled them to sleep and they had slept peacefully throughout the whole night.

Next morning, the couple woke up to a grey day. They found out that they were not alone last night. A big van had camped on the open area some distance away from them. On top of that van, there was a big canoe. Jim and Meilin had never heard anything of their neighbour's coming because of the fierce storm last night. They wondered whether the neighbour came with their canoe to pick up some fish, casualties of the violent storm. When they went to the lake to brush their teeth and wash their faces, they saw the lake water was no longer murky and the water level had lowered down, though not to the level when they first saw it. The water in the lake now was icy cold; the chilling air was absolutely clean and fresh. There was no fish lying anywhere on the shore; the fish here must have been used to this kind of violent turbulence. A drizzle was going on and the chill was heavy. The rocky mountain peaks behind the lookout spot had been covered with snow. Yesterday afternoon, children were swimming in the lake; overnight, the temperature had dropped drastically. This was in the middle of July. If the couple did not experience it personally, they would never have believed the fickleness of weather in Yukon.

After breakfast, the couple did not linger long by the lake, even though they still admired the scenery, grim and all. They thanked the lake and the whole place for giving them an amazing show of the powerful natural force, which they would never forget as long as they lived. Then they pulled up their trailer and went on their way.

The last place they had visited in Yukon was Watson Lake, a small city at the border of this province and British Columbia. There were two main attractions in this city. By the tourist centre of the city, there was a huge collection of city or town street-signs. Lanes after lanes of street-signs from different places of the world had covered a hill and a large area by the centre building. This collection of more than 60,000 street-signs was started in 1942 by a homesick soldier who was among the thousands of soldiers who were building the Alaska Highway. During the later years, the tourists from all over the world, who had travelled through Alaska

Highway, had contributed to this collection, bringing street-signs here from their own hometowns.

Jim and Meilin walked through the lanes of street-signs that had been stacked up to form walls for those sign alleys. Many of them came from the United States and some others were mostly from Europe. The couple were amazed and stunned. They could see that many people had traveled through Alaska Highway! Only a small portion of the travellers had contributed to this collection, but the street-signs had amounted to such an impressive number. Suddenly, they felt that they were not that different or alone for wanting to travel through the Alaska Highway and the remote northern regions were not that isolated from the world after all. Then they thought that if different peoples from all over the world could come together for a small collection like this, there should be nothing that they could not accomplish if they put down their hostilities and hatred against each other and do something constructive for the peace and well being of the world.

Walking through the lanes of street-signs, the couple felt as if the place was filled with different streets of the world. Reading the different names of those streets, they could not help thinking about the peoples who lived in those streets of different countries, what kind of houses or apartments they were in and what kind of life they had lived. They wondered whether those sign contributors had felt the isolation of the northern wilderness like themselves. Maybe for this feeling, they wanted to bring a piece of their hometowns to make them feel at home in the wild northern place. This exhibition of world street signs had also shown Canada's acceptance and tolerance to different peoples from the world bringing a piece of their hometowns here. The couple hoped that the Canadian society would eventually have the same kind of acceptance and tolerance towards different peoples from the world coming to Canada, bringing a piece of their origin hometowns, calling Canada their new home and building up their life and this country together with other Canadians.

The couple lingered and wandered through the numerous street-signs, wondering and imagining. This was definitely a site that would remain in their memory for a long time. The tourist centre had also a film theater that was showing the documentary film about the history of Alaska Highway construction. The couple had already watched this film in Whitehorse, so they moved on.

The other attraction of Watson Lake was its IMAX Theater. From late August on through the whole winter, people in Watson Lake and the whole northern region can sometimes enjoy the spectacular views of northern lights. Colourful simmering lights would show up in the northern skies in any night. Not many people in the world have had the luck in their life to see those spirit fires dancing in the dark sky. Jim and Meilin had very much wished to see the northern lights, but right now, it was in mid-July; they would not be that lucky to have this wish fulfilled. The IMAX Theater in Watson Lake had provided the show of northern lights to satisfy the visitors' wishes. The couple got two tickets and went to the theater to see the show. Besides the northern lights that had appeared in Watson Lake, they had watched also a show of a spaceship in space. The effects of the shows in the large domed theater were indeed amazing. Still, the couple thought that it was impossible to get the real feel of such a wondrous natural phenomenon from a theater.

The couple's trip to Yukon ended when they left Watson Lake. Overall, the trip and especially the drive through Alaska Highway were an unforgettable experience. At the start of the trip, they worried whether they could get fuels for their vehicle when they needed in the wilderness. They knew that Yukon and Alaska had large uninhabited areas. To prevent running out of gas on the way, they had brought two cans of fuels with them. But all the way through the thousands kilometers of travelling, they had always come to timely gas stations along the highway. The two cans of gas for emergency had come back home with them. Nonetheless, the northern regions were indeed very sparsely populated. For long stretches of vast wilderness, they saw no human habitations of any kind. One of the most important things for them to treasure in their memories for this trip was the feeling of peace and bliss in the wilderness when close to unmarred nature. They did not expect that they would feel this way so strongly, and therefore, the feeling was valued more. At the end of the trip, they felt sorry to say goodbye to Yukon, mainly because it meant that they were going back to the human world where the peace they had found in nature was hard to come by. At the thought of having to face what was waiting for them in their home city, the couple's peaceful and blissful minds were quickly disturbed. They had found peace in the fierce storm of nature, because they knew that there was no intentional malice from nature. In the human world, the man-made storms in people's life could be much worse, as those storms carried the force of hostilities and hatred.

It is getting harder for people living in the modern world to find peace. Besides the never ending conflicts or wars in some parts of the world, in any society, the rich worry about how to keep what they have and how to gain more; the poor worry about how to get enough to eat and how to keep a roof over their heads, and those in between are facing ever fiercer competitions in all aspects of life. All wish for more, more money, more power, more prestige and more everything. Thus the pace of life has increased so much that it is becoming more harmful to people physically and mentally. The frantic modern life has stretched nerves to the limit and caused more depressions and mental problems. Modern people desperately need fitful rest; they need peace and contentment. But all kinds of racings force them on. They are running to win all kinds of battles, to reach endless goals and to climb endless heights, without the slightest thought of their limitations. Because of the relentless drive, ambition and craving, the human world has developed to the amazing modern state in just a few hundred years. It is high time that the humans slow down a bit and advance with more caution. But the more the humans have got or achieved, the more they want. This crazed wanting, racing and achieving from the humans have pushed Mother Nature to a corner and started exhausting Her. The humans with their insatiable cravings are running right into the danger of shortening the life span of their own species after destroying many other species and shortening also the life span of Mother Nature.

Strangely, with more achievements and more wealth, human beings are feeling less peaceful and less secure. After thousands years of evolution, in every society, there are still discriminations, conflicts, and fights caused by peoples being of different skin colours, having different religions, different opinions, different ways of thinking and so on. When there is no peace among the people within one country, how can there be any hope for peace among all the different countries in the world? The human beings do live a better material life with all kinds of achievements they have made, but personally and countries wise, there seem less arms stretching out to help each other; and more claws aiming at each other's throat. With the high-speed development of science and technology, many more countries are sharpening their teeth, trying to look utmost puffed up and most threatening to others. They are indeed armed to their teeth and make the world situation critically unstable at any time. After the birth of civilization and thousands years of development in the human world, the human beings have not improved much their barbaric nature.

Many people have seen the problems; many have tried hard to find ways to save the human beings from themselves and to save the world. Through the human history, people have used religion, education, politics, science and technology, social and economical developments, increasing wealth or consuming to cure the problems or diseases that have plagued the human beings, their societies and the world. They have succeeded in solving some problems and curing some social and biological diseases, but there are always new problems and new diseases coming up. Some of the new problems and diseases seem more deadly and endangering the survival of the human race and the planet. In view of the successes and achievements from their struggles through the history, the majority of human beings are trying to keep the hope that the human race will keep on conquering whatever difficulties and threats lying ahead of them. But the realities are stubbornly showing negative signs; the human beings seem to have become more selfish, neurotic and easily provoked to kill each other. Besides the jumpiness, people are getting more and more indifferent to others' sufferings. They seem to feel more pains of a little hurt on their own baby fingers than thousands of people being killed in some parts of the world. With this kind of apathy, some people are ready to harm and kill for their own little gains. The development of this kind of human psyche makes it impossible to tell whether the human race and the world are heading for a better future or approaching a destructive ending.

Canada is a small country, population wise. The country may sometimes wish to have some influence in the world affairs, but can never dream of controlling other countries. This, of course, is good for both the Canadian people and the world peace. Compared with some other countries, Canada is relatively more peaceful and stable within the country. Since its birth, there have never been huge conflicts between the Canadians that had led to big bloodshed. The country has had political stability. Under the stable conditions, the country has developed industrially, economically, socially and culturally. However, human nature is similar everywhere. Like the whole world, Canada is not perfect and has its own problems. Its society is not entirely free from injustices, corruptions and conflicts among different people. Like in all other societies, people in Canada have also been ranked by classes, the haves and have-nots or have-less, the majorities and the minorities and so on. Being a multi-coloured country, Canada is bound to experience discriminations and inequalities among different races. There have always been efforts to improve the conditions of all the people, but obstacles exist and regressions happen even to some already gained progresses. To some people, they will rather see the social order remain the same forever. Of course, those are the ones who are on a higher level of the society. As for the people on the lower level of the society, most of them are content if their livelihood is secure, nobody bothers them and they can live a peaceful life. At the time when their livelihood becomes insecure and their peace is disturbed, they, of course, will have complaints and try to fight for their own rights. Thus the society will see some disturbances and even some conflicts.

In view of the country's wealth, large part of it is in the hands of the rich and the rich is the minority in any kind of society, even though they normally hold more power. Population wise in Canada, a white predominant country, the minority are the coloured people. The white majority are very much on the higher level of the society and control the political, social and economical powers. Everything goes with the power in any society. The group of people with power will enjoy more social privileges and have higher social status. In Canada, the working and living conditions of the visible minorities have improved to some extent in the recent half a century, but they are not up to the same level as that of the majority whites. Though there are a few of the visible minorities who have gone to a higher social level, the general population of the coloured has remained on a lower social level. The few successful ones have not fully changed the social perceptions and attitudes towards the visible minorities. The general white population refuses to admit that racial discrimination still exist in the country and in the meantime, has kept many visible minorities on a lower social level and in a lesser working and living conditions. For those in the visible minority groups, if they aspire to improve their own conditions and to raise their own social status, they have to work or struggle much harder to achieve their goals. Quite some white people consider that the visible minorities' lesser conditions are due to their lower intelligence or lack of certain abilities as the whites have. To make themselves feel better in the conspiracy of keeping the visible minorities on a lower social level, quite some whites put the responsibilities entirely to the coloured people for their disadvantageous conditions. In this way, they feel no obligation to do anything to improve the situation. Some whites with strong sense of racial superiority are accustomed to the situation of the whites on top in the society; they definitely don't want to see this order being disturbed. They are the ones that have disliked intensely seeing even a few coloured people gaining equal footage and equal social status as the whites.

Jim and Meilin happened to belong to the visible minorities in Canada. Though Jim was white, after his marriage to a Chinese woman, he was no longer considered belonging to the white society. Their marriage was disliked by quite some white people. After their privacy had totally gone, their private talks at home and Meilin's writings had been publicized. Those talks and writings had been considered as outrageous attacks to the society by quite some whites. Even though the reports about social ills and crimes were broadcasted almost daily over TV, the couple's frank talks and little criticisms at their own home could not be accepted or tolerated. Meilin came from China; to most white people, she remained a Chinese and not a Canadian. In spite of her being a Canadian citizen for more than two decades, she had been seen as a red Chinese. Her little criticisms were like some personal attacks from a red alien, burning some whites like fire. In their eyes, the Chinese woman should be greatly grateful for being accepted into Canada and not saying anything bad about the country. When people started reading what she wrote, some whites went crazy. In their eyes, attentions or any consideration should never be fallen to a Chinese woman to raise her status in any way. Whatever the couple had said and Meilin had written had hurt some white people's pride or vanity. There seemed no remedy to heal their hurts. They turned a total blind eye to the couple's good intention or wish that the country will be better for everybody. Frantic harassment, attacks and threats had been hurled onto the couple to vent those hurts. The couple had not only lost their privacy, but also their safety and peace in life.

The couple were ordinary folk. They knew their place in the society. Many times they had said or shown that they had neither ambition nor interest to get on top of anything or anyone. After quite some years of struggles, they had finally had financial security in their later life. What they wanted was only to finish their earthly time in peace. However, they strongly believed that they had every right to say or write their minds, especially at their own home, and they were not going to stop doing so. The couple were utterly tired of the task of constantly reassuring the hurt or jealous people that they were no threat to them and had no intention to get to any height. All the couple's efforts were in vain. They were besieged by hostilities and hatred. People around them at their home and anywhere they went tried to harass, insult and attack them, and eagerly to remind them that they were small, nothing, going to fall, going to die and so on.

What had happened to the couple had very well shown that the Canadian society had not come to the level that it would regard its coloured citizens equal in their abilities, intelligence and mental capacities. The majority whites not only wanted to keep their higher positions in the society, but were also afraid that the coloured people might try to get to the same height. The couple were not challenging them for whatever they held so dear, still they had scared and offended them. Right now, the only thing in the couple's minds was how to survive, transcend the terrible situation and have peace in the hostile environment.

Abbotsford to the couple had been a hostile place for years. Though there were good people in this city, they seemed to be without much power. The harassment, attacks and threats to the couple had been kept on for such a long time. The couple could find peace in a fierce natural storm, but they could not find peace in this small Canadian city. When they had perceived intentional malice and hatred from some of their neighbours and some store people whom they did not even know, the anger they felt sometimes was hard to control. For what they had done, they could not see why people should hate and treat them thus.

Like most ordinary people, the couple could be content, if their livelihood was secure and they had peace in their life. In their present situation, peace had been deprived from their life. They felt that they could handle those death threats better than they could handle their own angers. The fear of death had diminished in their minds for quite many years. To them, they would sooner or later leave this life; death was the equal end for everybody and there was no use or need to fear it. Moreover, the couple felt that death might not be the definite ending but a new beginning. They got this belief not entirely from some religious teachings, but from their own personal experiences. Those unexplainable experiences, though only a few in their life, had made them to see that their spirits or souls could exist and act without their physical bodies. Death might very well be just the threshold of shedding the physical body and releasing the imprisoned spirit, soul or consciousness to another level of existence. Scientists with their advanced modern sciences could not even explain effectively consciousness; they could not convince the couple with their definition of death. The couple preferred to believe their own instinct and experiences. As a matter of fact, many people had experienced the feeling that their passed loved-ones seemed still with them or existing in some other form somewhere. The conventional explanations for these feelings are that those passed loved-ones have lived in their memories and their hearts. However, there are still other explanations. Human beings have their instincts and intuitions. It is possible that they have instinctively felt the existence of their loved ones' souls, spirits or consciousness after their physical bodies have gone.

The fear of death had not much weight in the couple's minds, but the burning angers sometimes had weighed heavily and harmfully. They knew that to control their angers was the first step to master themselves, to deal with problems effectively and to live a peaceful life in a turbulent hostile situation. When leaving Yukon to go back to their own home, the couple felt that they were leaving the peaceful natural world to go back to the stormy human world where struggles, hostilities and hatred were waiting for them. They felt that they were not fully equipped to go through this human world storm and to pass the trial without suffering losses.

Anger is a major battle for many human beings to fight in their life. Because of anger, many problems cannot be dealt with rationally and effectively; situations can get more complicated and become worse. Actions taken with anger seldom achieve positive results. In addition to messing things up, anger will hurt mainly the angry people themselves physically and mentally. Theodor Roosevelt once quoted this saying, "Speak softly and carry a big stick; you will go far." This adage means that in life's situations, one should remain calm and civil, but ready with force to protect oneself and to fight against or beat down one's opponents or enemies. In the couple's situation, they had indeed to learn remaining calm and controlling their anger. However they would be delusional to use this wisdom word by word in their life. They might have offended some legitimate power and some illegitimate power. No matter how big of a stick they could carry, they would never be able to beat down any of the powers. Controlling anger meant for them to save their own peace of mind and their own physical and mental health.

In every era and every country, the powerful or the rulers have never liked people who will speak out to criticize their systems and they have disliked even more that people will think on their own. They have considered this kind of people hard to govern and dangerous to their ruling. In the old times, those outspoken people with their criticisms or their opinions contrary to that of the powerful would be killed. In the modern time, the situations have improved greatly, but not entirely. Canada, through one and half a centuries' democracy, has bred some people in power positions, who can be open to criticisms from all levels of the society and use those criticisms to see what need to be improved or changed in the system. Still there is a portion of people in power positions, who have kept the old rulers' mentality. Some members of the police force might very well represent this portion of power. Criticisms, especially criticisms from the lower level of the society will scare them and they have the urge to repress, to crush or to shut up those outspoken criticizers. They have the power and many ordinary people will do their biddings. Jim and Meilin's critical talks and writing might have offended this portion of the power and they had tasted this power being used through some ordinary people to harass and attack them.

Worse still, the couple's criticisms had touched the underground society. Canada is a peaceful and lawful country, but it is not free from criminal elements. Like every other country, Canada has its underground society. In recent years, the underground crime organizations seem gaining strength. When the couple's talks and writing criticized the social problems such as drugs, prostitution, child pornography, gang violence, the crime organizations' reaching ability to corrupt public law officers like the police and so on, they would inevitably offend the illegitimate power of the society. Consequently, the couple would receive death threats and their lives would be in danger.

More ridiculously, the couple's criticisms had offended the media. The media is definitely a power in the society. They have almost entire voice and exposure that can reach the general public. The couple's freak situation had touched a tender spot of the media. They were not only mad that the lowly couple dared to criticize them, but also furious that the couple had broken their monopoly in the media fields. They considered that their voice should be the only voice the public should listen to and they were the only authorities of information, news or criticisms the public should trust. Now the lowly couple's critical voice had been heard by the public; this had very much undermined their privilege and authority.

Many journalists, reporters and other workers working in the media fields are people who want to stick to the moral code of their profession, to be objective and to have integrity. Yet, the large media companies are owned by the rich, though they might be partially supported by the government. Those workers in the media business have, after all, to obey their bosses; this means to compromise or even sacrifice the objectiveness and integrity in order to satisfy their bosses' political, financial or some other personal needs. Some of the rich owners of the media business corrupted by their power will be arrogant enough to think that freedom of speech belongs to the media only.

Jim and Meilin had seen and experienced the reality that freedom of speech seemed entirely belongs to the rich media business owners. They did receive some sympathy from some of the workers in the media fields at earlier stage. But in later time, they saw that the bosses in this business might be very much offended by the couple. The rich and especially the very rich people are easily paranoid when there are some critical voices coming from the lower level of the society. They normally take those voices as personal attacks to themselves and will take actions to counterattack. The couple saw the TV media quickly turning hostile, first evasively and then openly. The media's changing of attitudes towards the couple had very much worsened the situation and brought more harassment and attacks on them in their life.

Even though the couple saw that they had offended quite some powers of the country, they did not have much fear. They were confident that if they were not physically removed from this life ahead of their time, they would eventually learn to be calm, to control anger and to be ready to face adversities with fortitude. They had no intention or capacity to beat down any of their opponents, but they could learn self-mastery to solve problems more effectively and to protect themselves the best way they could.

The couple were a tiny element in the big world. Though their troubles looked huge and hard to control to them, those troubles were very small compared to the countless big problems, miseries, sufferings and disasters peoples were going through daily in the world. The couple had been harassed and attacked, but their voice had also been heard in the public. They had been threatened and their lives were in danger, but they were still alive. This had given them confidence and hope for the country. They knew that there were no perfect political systems in the world, but they believed that the system in Canada was relatively sound, in spite of some glitches here and there, and the majority of Canadians were kind, loving and wishing things good for all the Canadians. On the whole, the couple were convinced that their personal and the country's situations were more optimistic than that of quite some other peoples and some other places in the world.

CHAPTER FOURTEEN

NORTHWEST TERRITORIES AND NUNAVUT

Another year had passed before Jim and Meilin took the last trip of their cross-country travels. This time they were going to the Northwest Territories. Their final destination for this trip was Yellowknife, the capital of this vast Canadian northern region. Whether Northwest Territories was a province, the couple had no idea. But they knew that the whole northern part which had all been called Northwest Territories before was the larger half of the whole Canadian soil. Now the old Northwest Territories had been divided into three parts: Yukon, Northwest Territories and Nunavut. Northwest Territories was the center part of these three vast northern areas of the country. There was a highway reaching Yellowknife. On the map, it was the only highway that led to this northern most city. As for Nunavut, there seemed no highway reaching any of the places there, though there were some towns or villages in that far north. Those places in or near the Arctic areas were mainly accessible by planes and ships.

The couple were not so ambitious to reach the farthest north, the Arctic Circle. They decided that the farthest north they would go to would be Yellowknife, as it was accessible by the highway. For this trip, they did not have the extensive preparation as they had for their Yukon trip and did not carry two extra cans of gas for emergency. All the convenient and easy accesses to gas stations along the highways throughout the whole country had relaxed them; they gave up their vigilance.

The couple started their trip to Yellowknife in July. They were prepared for the northern climate that might be cold even in summer, bringing enough clothing. The drive through both British Columbia and Alberta to reach Northwest Territories were quite pleasant. When passing through the mountainous terrain of British Columbia, they came across quite some fully loaded lumber trucks on the highway. The small cities and towns along the highway looked busy with their pulp and paper mills, lumber mills and some other plants. All along the highway of British Columbia, there were human residences and activities. When they were passing the prairie of Alberta, the temperature rose considerably. The couple felt pressed by the heat. The air conditioner in their van worked hard to cool them down, and the beautiful broad Alberta crop fields cheered them up. In this prime summer time, the vast canola fields were blooming with yellow flowers. The fresh yellow fields flanked the highway for miles and miles. The vast crop fields patterned by bright green and fresh yellow on both sides of the highway were sometimes reaching to the blue sky.

The couple admired the beautiful vast fields. Meilin was busy taking some pictures. They wondered who owned those massive well-cultivated farmlands. It looked impossible for small farmers to handle such huge scaled farming.

"It is strange. There are some nice residential houses here and there, but no sign of large machines anywhere and nobody works in those broad fields," Meilin muttered.

Jim took some glances and said, "There are some big barns. The farm machines might be stored away."

It was obvious that those vast fields could only be worked on by large farm machines. Meilin was not fully convinced that the few barns here and there could have stored all the machines. Then she suggested, "Maybe the fields are owned by some large agriculture corporations. Even if some farmers own those vast fields; they have to hire big machines to do the work."

The couple settled more on the idea that some large corporations owned and worked on those broad farm fields. They saw clusters of big shinning metal silos in some locations; this had further confirmed their belief. Individual farmers could not possibly need all those large storage silos for their harvests.

The couple were very much impressed by Alberta's giant fields thriving with crops and the numerous oil drilling machines operating right on some of those fields. Everywhere they looked, there was land being developed and worked on. It looked that Alberta was doing well in both agriculture and oil industry. It took two days for the couple to reach the border of Northwest Territories. Not long after they crossed the border, the landscape changed drastically. The couple felt that they were indeed entering true wilderness. The further they went, the less the land looked touched by humans. The vast land was quite even and trees dominated everywhere. Most of the trees were coniferous and some were broad-leafed. The further north they went, the less there were broad-leafed trees. For long stretches of drive, they could not see any human activity or inhabitation.

Highway here was as smooth as those in other parts of the country and traffic was very light. Not long after the couple crossed the provincial border, they saw a nice lookout. It was a stretch of paved road separated from the highway. Though the land was generally even, this lookout was on a high ground. The couple parked their van and trailer on this lookout. They tried to get out of their vehicle to relax and have a good look at the broad open land, but changed their minds promptly. There were quite some insects around. They decided to rest in the van while viewing the scene from the inside. The view was breathtakingly beautiful. The couple would never have dreamt that Northwest Territories would have such vast areas of forest. From this high lookout spot, they could see a sea of forest stretching far and wide. Though this sea was formed by myriads of green trees, its main colour was blue. The land looked waved a little, which made the forest-sea look in shades of different blues. The blue forest-sea stretched far to reach the horizon. At the point its border line touched the sky; its colour was faint blue and almost the same colour as the remote edge of the sky.

Jim and Meilin were both stunned and overwhelmed by such a broad view formed by a sea of forest. They had thought that the northern landscape would be dominated by desolate land deprived of trees because of the cold climate. Such a vast forest was indeed unexpected. They took out their camera, trying to capture this unexpected natural wonder. Knowing that the camera could never truthfully record this kind of natural beauty in such a gigantic scale did not deter them from snapping quite some pictures. In one way or another, those pictures might bring back some of their memories of this amazing moment.

The couple did not linger long at this lookout. The view was breathtaking, but sitting inside the van in the hot summer was not that pleasant, even though the temperature was only a little over twenty degrees Celsius. They had to turn off the engine to feel close to nature and close the van windows to prevent the invasion of the insects. Now the heat started building up and pressing on in the van. They started the engine and left this beautiful scenery spot, thinking that they would keep the scene in their mind for later reminiscence and enjoyment. Driving further on, they soon saw a large sign with white, green and blue words:

60th Parallel
Welcome to
Northwest Territories.

The background of those words was a compass with the needle pointing to the north.

60th parallel is a circle of altitude 60 degrees north of the earth equatorial plane. It crosses Europe, Asia, the Pacific Ocean, North America and the Atlantic Ocean. The length of this circle is only half of the length of the equator. This has clearly shown that the earth is shaped as a ball. Along the equator the earth is very much bulged in mass.

To Jim and Meilin who were crossing this line of 60th parallel, it meant that they were heading to the far north, the upper part of the globe, and approaching the Arctic and the North Pole. After the couple passed this informational welcome board, they saw a nice information centre by the highway. They pulled their van and trailer to the parking lot of the centre. Now they could stretch out to release some of the fatigue from the long distance drive and got some information from the centre. After the couple parked and got out of their van, they were immediately swarmed by quite some large horseflies. Meilin planned to take some pictures of themselves with the centre and some decorative artworks around, but the horseflies forced them running into the centre building as fast as they could.

The centre was a modern building in a traditional cabin style. It had two thick doors. The first door opened into a small coat-room and the second door opened to the centre proper. Obviously, this two-door design was to prevent the insects in summer and the cold in winter from entering the building. Still some large horseflies got into not only the coat-room, but also the building. In spite of a few horseflies flying around, the inside of the centre looked clean, bright and spacious with large open hall and high ceilings. The information counter was not big, but there were a large exhibition area and a nice classy sitting room for the visitors. A small coffee table was at the side of the sitting room. A coffee-pot with hot coffee, paper cups, milk and sugar were on the table. It looked that they were for both the workers here and the visitors.

Although the sitting room looked inviting, the couple were more attracted by the exhibition hall. On the walls of the exhibition hall, there were some brief introductions about Northwest Territories and the aboriginal peoples here. Standing on the floor, hanging from the wall and ceiling and climbing up the column of the hall were the exhibits of the regional fauna. They were stuffed life-like polar bear, musk ox, black bear, Arctic fox, timber wolf, caribou, wolverine and some smaller fur-bearing animals. This might be the closest the couple could get to see all those regional animals. They took some pictures of the animals and even asked the clerk to take a picture of them with the animals.

The clerk was a man in his thirties; he was either a white man or a Métis. The couple expected to see more natives and Métis in Northwest Territories, so they thought the man a Métis. Jim asked a lot of questions. The clerk was very helpful. The couple were glad that they had stopped at the information centre. Now they knew that the waterfalls they wanted to see were along the highway they were travelling on to get to Yellowknife and the good place to camp was not far. It was already afternoon. The couple soon had to settle for the night. Then, Jim got the information about the fishing and fishing license here. Though Meilin objected to Jim fishing during their short visit to Northwest Territories, Jim had smuggled his fishing gear in and was eager to fish in the northern waters.

"If you try fishing here, you will be made a pin-cushion by the insects," Meilin still objected and warned Jim.

Jim smiled. The clerk was a little curious about the couple. To him, the insects might have never been a problem for the fishermen or the anglers.

The couple left the centre with plenty of information from the clerk and the printed flyers. When they were walking towards their van accompanied by a cloud of horseflies, a big truck came in and parked not far from them. A big native man with his wife and son got out of the truck. Seeing the visiting couple, the native man greeted them friendly. Meilin ran into their van quickly after the greeting. Jim stayed among the horseflies to chat with the man for a while. It was amazing that the native man and his family seemed to have never noticed the horseflies and the horseflies did not go to bother them. Jim and Meilin knew that there would be quite some aboriginal peoples in Northwest Territories; still they were both surprised and glad to see this friendly native man with a hospitable host's attitude. Of course, the natives had lived here for thousands of years. Who would be better than them to be the host of this land?

The couple started driving again. They were a bit frustrated by the numerous insects, but still eager to see this northern land which must have many other things to offer. British Columbia had very little mosquitoes in summer. The couple had to admit that they were spoiled and had to have some time to get used to this bombardment of insects here.

"Oh, well. Once in a life, we should experience being swarmed by insects to know how the native peoples, the explorers and the early settlers had lived in the wilderness," Meilin commented with a resigned manner. Jim agreed.

Driving a little further on, the couple saw that the sky was suddenly darkened and then they smelt wood burning. Obviously, a forest fire was going on somewhere. The couple kept on driving. The further they went, the sky got darker and the burning smell got stronger. Nobody else was on the road. They were alone, driving right into this big dark smoky unknown ahead. This was the first time that the couple had personally encountered a forest fire. They had seen forest fires over TV often in British Columbia. Now in reality, the situation was truly scarier. Darkness covered everywhere and nobody around. The couple thought that other people might have got the fire warning and kept away from the highway. As there was no sight of fire, they kept on moving forward, thinking that they might be driving into the fire area or away from it. It was impossible to tell. The visibility of the highway however was still a little distance ahead. Though scared, the couple kept pressing on. Finally, they saw some road construction machines on the highway. They were glad to see that those machines were not abandoned by the workers and one was still working. Jim pulled up their vehicles to the machine that was running. They had to know whether the highway ahead was safe to pass.

"Hello, how are you?" Jim greeted the worker who was sitting high on the roller machine.

The worker was a stout native man in his thirties. He stopped the moving machine, but let the engine run and returned Jim's greeting. Jim then talked about the forest fire in a conversational manner.

"There is a forest fire?! The smoke is quite thick!"

"Oh, yes, the fire," the worker answered. His tune and manner showed that a forest fire was a very common thing and talking about a fire here was like talking about the weather. Then the man noticed the two travellers' worried looks. He smiled understandingly and said with a soothing manner, "The fire is some distance away. They are working on it. It's okay. You can drive on. It's safe."

The couple felt a relief. Jim thanked the worker and pulled the van and trailer away from the machine. While continuing on their way, the couple laughed at themselves a bit. They had really been spooked by the situation a moment ago. With the darkness everywhere and nobody else on the road, they thought that they were left alone and driving right towards the fire. After some further driving, the smoke thinned out some. Then a blue helicopter came flying low in front of them. There was a large carrier or a pouch hanging down through a long cable from the helicopter. The couple knew that the helicopter must have just come back from the fire site. Meilin took out the camera to snap some pictures of this working bird with its pouch hanging underneath. The helicopter hovered at the side of the highway and then landed. There were quite some people working intensely on the ground by some big barrels. Jim said that some chemicals were used in battling big fires on some occasions, which must be the case here now.

From fright to excitement, the couple had their first forest fire experience. Though they did not see the fire, they were thankful for that and satisfied that they had seen people who were fighting the fire. This experience had let them see how terribly scary a forest fire could be and how courageous those fire fighters were. The couple's feeling about the place changed. That the landscape looked void of human activities and inhabitation was only a surface image. It looked that if anything happened in this vast wilderness, the humans would come promptly to take care of it. Now the couple started paying closer attention along the highway. They noticed that sometimes there were some rough roads or trails branching out from the highway and reaching deep into the forests. Were those roads used by some explorers, miners, or some aboriginal peoples still living in the wilderness? The couple wondered and could not figure out.

After this fire scare, the couple started noticing some water signs appearing along the highway. According to the clerk of the information centre, those water signs would lead them to the waterfalls. Sure enough, when the first sign for the waterfalls showed up, they were approaching Alexandra Falls. To save time and efforts, the couple decided to see the waterfalls on their way. They pulled onto the side road leading to the waterfalls and were immediately arriving at a parking lot.

The insect situation was the same here. As soon as the couple got out of their van, the horseflies surrounded them. Jim had served in the military for many years. He had the foresight to buy two military-style hats from a store in their home city for this trip. Those hats had mosquito nets attached from the rims. The couple were fully prepared to venture into the woods. They put on their jackets and long trousers and covered their heads and faces by the hats with mosquito nets. The only vulnerable parts now were their hands which they could move constantly.

In spite of the numerous insects, the park looked nice. There were some big stone drums in front of a gate. On the faces of those drums were some introductory illustrations about the aboriginal peoples of Northwest Territories. The aboriginal peoples living in this region are the Dene. The Dene nations are formed by Gwich'in, Sahtu Dene, Tlicho, Akaitcho and Dehcho that reside in different areas of this region. According to the introduction on the stone drums, the Dene tribes are: South Slavey, North

Slavey, Chipewyan, Dogrib and Gwich'in. Through thousands of years they had existed here. The Dene nations had had peace treaties among themselves and peace had allowed them to prosper. As far as the Dene themselves are concerned, they believe that they have been created by the creator here and have always existed here. They had survived on this land through hunting, fishing, fur-trapping and gathering food from the wilderness. During winter, five or six families would stay together. Each family would have an area for trapping. Today some of those family trapping areas are still being recognized. During the more abundant times of summer and fall, large communities would gather together to share the harvests. Celebrations would be held normally near rivers where the fishing grounds were. During those festival celebrations, there would be marriages; decisions would be made and disputes resolved. The Dene had their own laws and health care. At some time in history, the Dene had amounted to 500,000 strong. They had accumulated intimate knowledge of this land, its animals, plants, waters and weather. The knowledge had been vital for their survival and prosperity in this northern region.

Besides the Dene, the Métis have also resided here from early time on. In this vast northern region, the Dene and the Métis have lived in the taiga, the coniferous forest areas. Beyond the tree line, there is the tundra, the Arctic areas where the Inuit call home. The Arctic areas have much less plant lives; the very far north is indeed a world of snow and ice. The Inuit had lived by sealing, fishing and hunting in the harsh far north areas. In the old days, during the winter, they lived in igloos, houses or huts built by snows, and during the summer, they lived in animal-skin tents. Their boats and clothing were all made from animal or fish skins. Their food was rather exclusively seal meat and fish. Even their lighting was produced by seal oil.

The Dene nations, the Inuit and the Métis in Northwest Territories are peoples who have their own traditions, their own cultures, their own languages and their own beliefs. Today, the native peoples still have their hunting and fishing rights on their traditional land. However, how many of them are still living entirely on hunting and fishing is a question. The natural resources the native peoples' livelihood has traditionally depended on have been gradually depleted. The native peoples have been going through great life transitions in the recent two or three centuries.

There are fundamental differences between the aboriginal way of life and the European way of life from the start. The aboriginal peoples had closely knit families and communities. They harvested natural resources and shared communal resources. In the early days, the aboriginal peoples had no concept of the ownership of land or private property. The European way of life had strong sense of ownership and private property. Individualism developed from the sense of ownership and personal possessions. They exploited and developed natural resources.

Starting from the time of the early European settlements on North America, the aboriginal way of life had been greatly impacted by the European way of life. The aboriginal peoples' life transitions had begun from those early days. To what extent this impact will affect the aboriginal peoples' traditions, cultures, beliefs and their life in a whole are still hard to see. Many good things have happened in the native peoples' life. Still, there are many negative effects that the European way of life has wrought on the native peoples' life and minds. Today, though the living standards of the native peoples have risen, the native families and communities have suffered disintegration. Quite some social ills of the larger Canadian society have spread to the native communities. The native communities have been experiencing alcoholic problems, substance abuse, domestic violence, prostitution and other crimes.

The good thing is that there is no longer language barrier between the natives and the non-natives. The new generations of the native peoples, though disconnected from their traditional way of life, are better educated, know what they want and will not hesitate to fight for their rights and for a better life. The pity is that quite many valuable things and knowledge in the aboriginal traditional way of life will be lost forever. But it is unrealistic and even cruel to ask the native peoples to go entirely back to their old way of life. While most of other non-native people are living in luxury and enjoying all the comfort provided by the modern facilities, there is no way that the native peoples should go back to live in igloos or animal-skin tepees. What should be preserved from the aboriginal way of life is their sense of community, their intimate knowledge of the land with all its animals and plants and their non-invasive way of harvesting natural resources. The developments of natural resources should go on and especially when those developments will also benefit the first nations. But those developments should be based on the knowledge of the land, the natural environment and the sustainability of natural resources, and not on the invasive exploitation that will take all and damage all.

Today, the Canadian cities are largely exclusive to the native peoples who sometimes come into the cities to find jobs and to live a life like other non-natives. The native reserves are underdeveloped and some are suffering poverties and all kinds of social ills. It will be much harder for the native peoples to get on the modern train of prosperity than other non-native Canadians. Still, the image of native peoples as the victims or the losers in the early colonization time is changing. With some help, the native peoples are going to make it and to be either integrated into the larger community of the country or a strong contributor to the national construction. For this to happen, the native peoples themselves have to work hard and to be strong in economic developments on their homelands. As the Canadian society is still discriminatory towards the visible minorities, some rules or regulations have to be set by the government not only to help the developments of the native reserves, but also to train the native peoples to be vocations ready and to make sure that companies or industries around the native communities will have a certain ratio of native employees. Isn't government set up to regulate, to help and to protect the weak?

Northwest Territories has vast minerals, oil and gas deposits. Serious developments of mining, oil and gas industries have only started here after the Second World War. From the early twentieth century on, petroleum, oil, gold, silver, zinc, lead, copper and platinum have been found in this region. Today, a brand new diamond mining industry has risen to occupy fifty percent of the region's economy. In the early days of industrial development here, the workers had been enrolled entirely from the south of the country. In recent years, the industries have started including some local native peoples in their crews. This is a good sign that the Dene, the Métis and the Inuit are to be benefited from the newly found riches of the land. For this trip, the couple wished to see that the native peoples were doing well in this northern region. So far, they were glad to see that the road construction here had employed native workers.

Jim and Meilin took some pictures of the stone drums and the park gate. After the gate, there was a boardwalk leading to the lookout. The distance from the gate to the lookout platform was not far. The waterfalls could be heard clearly from the gate. Close to the river, the horseflies had given way to mosquitoes. The walk through the woods would be more pleasant if there were not so many mosquitoes buzzing around. The couple were happy that they had their screen hats on. The mosquitoes could buzz as loud as they could, but they could not get to them. Very soon, the thunderous sound of waterfalls got louder. When the couple arrived at the lookout, the view of the waterfalls overpowered them. The colour of the soil in this region was yellow. The powerful rush of the river eroded the soil along the riverbanks. The waterfalls were golden coloured with a little brownish tint. The golden waters were plunging down from the cliff with tremendous force. Actually, the waterfalls started on the same level the couple were standing on. There were no hills around. The river after receiving the waterfalls cut deep into the earth and a canyon had formed by the powerful rush of the waters.

Whenever viewing waterfalls, the couple could not help feeling the tremendous force of nature. Like the native peoples, they could sense the powerful spirit behind the waterfalls. From the introduction of the stone drums, they knew that in the old times, the local native peoples had come to this very spot to hold ceremonies and offerings to the spirit of water. They asked to be cleansed by this powerful water. They believed that the animals were purer than the humans, and if they were cleansed by the spirit of this powerful water, they would be pure; being pure could make them invisible, and when they went hunting, some animals would sacrifice themselves to sustain their lives.

The Alexandra Falls was over a hundred metres wide and poured down about two hundred metres down into the Hay River. The splashing of the waters had formed a white mist at the bottom of the waterfalls. The tremendous force made the golden waterfalls look spectacular. No wonder the native peoples believed that there was a powerful spirit in this natural force. The waterfalls indeed looked alive, spirited and mysterious. The force of the waterfalls would definitely make anyone who was viewing it believe its power. The native peoples had believed its cleansing power. People of present time, on the other hand, might think of its infinite power to turn some turbines to produce electricity. Whether it could purify the humans or provide services for the humans, the humans seemed not being threatened by this powerful natural force, only feeling its benevolence. However, the humans were definitely becoming more utilitarian than spiritual towards any natural forces.

The couple had very much enjoyed the beauty and power of the waterfalls, but they did not linger long. They left the waterfalls with only a few mosquito bites on their hands and started driving again. It was already late afternoon. They decided to take the advice of the clerk in the information centre and camp in the park of Louise Falls. After a not too long drive, the sign of Louise Falls showed up by the highway. They followed the sign and pulled into the campground which was not far from the highway and situated in woods. As soon as they stopped their van in front of the campground office, a mob of horseflies took hold of their van. The insects were attracted by the heat of the metal vehicle and probably saw the hot van as a big live beast. Jim got out of the van and ran to the office to register; Meilin waited in the van.

The camping fees were not high, twenty-eight dollars a night. The camping lots were spacious and equipped with electricity. On the campground, there were public water taps in different locations and a bathroom with showers at the back. The couple chose a lot and pulled their van and trailer in. Jim plugged the trailer cable to the provided electric socket and stabilized the trailer; he was covered by his screen hat of course. Meilin quickly got into the trailer and decided not to come out again.

The couple rested in their trailer and had their supper. Towards evening, the temperature cooled down; the horseflies and mosquitoes gradually quieted down and stopped buzzing around. Still, the couple decided to spend the evening inside the trailer. There were a few other campers around. The wooded campground was serene. Five or six young people were cycling through the campground road in front of their lot. The couple were amazed to see that the cyclists seemed not afraid of the insects. They waited to see the group coming again, but they did not appear for a second run.

The night in this northern campground was peaceful and the temperature was nicely cool. The couple were tired of the day's travelling and had a good sleep. Still, they made sure to peek at the outside from their trailer window when they were awake in the middle of the night for a moment. They knew that in summer, parts of Northwest Territories would have a few months with daylights only. The couple did not see a mid-night sun, but they could see the woods clearly in the middle of the night. There was a white light, like a very strong moonlight that had turned the night into day. The woods in this white light looked eerily beautiful.

Next morning, before they drove to the highway, they went first to see the waterfalls which was by the campground. When they arrived at the sight, they saw a sign saying Twin Falls. The couple were confused. There was only one spot of waterfalls here. Where did the name of Twin Falls come from? They figured that the Louise Falls must also be called Twin Falls. It was nice to see another small park attached to this scenic place; a large parking lot and a children's playground were for this park. Again, the couple covered themselves up and ventured into the woods. Walking on the boardwalk that led to the waterfalls, the couple could see that down below, the river was gilded by the morning sun. They were walking high up on the riverbank. The landscape was similarly beautiful as that of the Alexandra Falls; the powerful rush of the river had cut deep into the earth to form a canyon. Twin Falls were bigger than Alexandra Falls, but also golden coloured and also tremendously forceful. Standing high at the lookout, the couple could see the waters running over two giant rocks before falling into the river. They realized that these two rocks must be the cause of the name Twin Falls. The waterfalls had been separated by the two rocks into two running forces; the two forces were still together, but one a little in front. The two giant rocks were perfectly square, one of them a little bigger and standing a little higher. From the lookout platform, they could see that the surface of the two giant rocks had been polished so smooth by the powerful rushing waters; they looked like two giant shining gold nuggets. The golden waters were rushing over the two giant gold nuggets and plunging into the river hundreds of feet below. The view was indeed magnificent. The couple took some pictures and then left the beautiful scene without lingering. The only regret for them was unable to stay long as the mosquitoes were quite vigorous. On the other hand, if they had stayed too long, their minds might be filled with gold, enchanted by the powerful spirited golden waterfalls and the giant gold nuggets.

Soon, the couple were on their way again. The last waterfalls they had visited along this highway were Lady Evelyn Falls. To go to see Lady Evelyn Falls, they had to get off the highway and drive on a side-road for five kilometers. It was worth their efforts. Lady Evelyn Falls were much wider than Alexandra and Twin Falls. Instead of showing fierce force, Lady Evelyn Falls looked gentler, showing an elegant beauty. All the three waterfalls were conveniently located by the highway leading to Yellowknife. The couple felt that they had had a feast of waterfalls. Though being bombarded by insects and mosquitoes, they felt the trip worthwhile.

Driving further on, the couple came to the new Deh Cho Bridge over the wide Mackenzie River. The steel bridge with strong triangular holders underneath and two A-shaped steel cable-holders above looked very modern and smartly neat. Having been driving through the vast wilderness, it was a surprise for the couple to see such a giant modern bridge here over the broad riverbed. Deh Cho Bridge was opened in 2012 and the bridge inaugural celebration was held in June this year, a month before the couple were driving over this brand new bridge. Deh Cho must be the native language for the name of this Mackenzie area. Mackenzie River is the longest river in Canada. It starts from the Great Slave Lake and runs through most part of Northwest Territories to reach the Arctic Ocean. It is named after the explorer Alexander Mackenzie who discovered this great river in 1789. Mackenzie had followed this river and reached the Arctic Ocean.

Though the aboriginal peoples have resided in this northern region for thousands of years, the known history of this region is largely related to the discoveries of the Arctic and the Subarctic by explorers. In 1570s, Martin Frobisher was the first to have sailed to Baffin Island. Then during the seventeenth century, there were quite some Arctic expeditions launched by explorers such as Henry Hudson, Thomas Button, Robert Bylot, William Baffin, Luke Foxe and Thomas James. All those dangerous early explorations were for the purpose of finding a northern route from Europe to the wealth of Orient. However, some of those voyages had carried out fur trade with the aboriginal peoples along the Hudson's Bay area. The furs they had brought back to England proved to be very lucrative. Thus a second source of interest for the northern expeditions began. In 1670, England granted by charter Hudson's Bay Company the monopoly of all the trade and all the lands within the drainage basin of the bay. Later on, when the North West Company was established, its Scottish personnel competed with the Hudson's Bay Company by establishing trading posts far inland and thus expanded the knowledge of the vast mainland of the western Arctic.

In 1870, Hudson's Bay Company's Rupert's Land and the Northwest Territories were transferred to Canada. Ten years later, the Arctic Archipelago to the north of the mainland was also transferred and thus Northwest Territories consist of the mainland region and the Arctic islands. During the 19th century, more geographic knowledge of the Northwest Territories had been gained indirectly by many searching expeditions to find Sir John Franklin who led a naval expedition in 1845 and disappeared. In 2014, the trace of Sir John Franklin's expedition team had finally been found. After Canada took control, extensive geological survey had been done to the vast expanse of the region with its natural resources and native inhabitants. However, it was after World War II, both Canada and the United States started to see the strategic and natural resource importance of the far north. In Canada, the mining industry and economic development in this region have started seriously from then on.

The couple drove through the smoothly paved bridge, thinking that only a year ago, all the travellers and their vehicles had to be carried over this broad riverbed by the ferry. They were grateful that many efforts had been made in building such a long bridge to provide the convenience for all who had to cross the river here. Close to the bridge, the couple had noticed a track by the river leading to a winter road. Before the bridge was built, in summer, the ferry carried people and vehicles over the river, and in winter when the river was frozen over, snows would be packed on the ice to make a road for people and vehicles to cross the river. Now the steel modern bridge had replaced both the ferry and the winter road here. However, there are not many paved highways in Northwest Territories. Some mines in this region still depend on winter roads for transportation. Those winter roads are built mainly on rivers. In winter, rivers here are frozen many feet down. The roads packed by snows on the rivers can carry heavy trucks with supplies and equipment.

Having crossed the river, the couple soon arrived at Fort Providence. Along the highway, there were a few towns or villages situated a little way off the highway. There would be a gas station with a few buildings by the highway and a side road leading to the small place. It was of no exception for Fort Providence. Shell, the gas station with a restaurant and a store, appeared by the highway, but Fort Providence and a native community were some distance away from the highway and accessible by a side road. The couple gassed up their van and got the information that the next gas station was in Yellowknife which was a little over three hundred kilometers away. This information made them worried. If they did not have the trailer, there would be no problem for their van with a tank of gas to reach Yellowknife. Towing the trailer, the van might not be able to cover the distance without gassing up in between.

The couple were soon on their way again. Being troubled by the thought of running out of gas mid-way, Meilin took out the map and started checking.

"There are still two places, Edzo and Rae, before we reach Yellowknife," Meilin announced, happy to tell Jim about her finding on the map. "The clerk might not know what he was talking about," she added.

The couple felt better. The tension or worry seemed released and they could get on their carefree drive again. After some time driving, they saw a large road sign showing that the area was a wood buffalo reservation, the "bison country". Now Jim and Meilin realized why there were so many horseflies around. In this area, the ground of the forest was covered with thick lush vegetations. With large mammals around, insects would naturally thrive. The horseflies here were much bigger than the normal horseflies. The couple decided that those horseflies should be called bison-flies. All along this stretch of the highway, there were some wooden signs of bison showing up. The signs were like some artworks.

The dark-coloured bison made by the wooden boards were the size of the real ones and life-like.

The couple started paying close attention, trying to spot some bison coming out of the woods. Sure enough, they soon spotted one. From a distance, the couple could see a dark-coloured bison walking on the shoulder of the highway. The big animal was twirling his tail and having a jolly jaunt on the highway. Meilin asked Jim to slow down the van, so that she could take a picture of the beautiful wild animal. When they got close, the couple were stunned to see that the bison, a big bull, was being swarmed by numerous bison-flies. The poor beast was in agony, frantically swinging his tail and trying to drive away the pests. Obviously, this large bull bison was driven out of the forest by those big flies. He was almost running on the shoulder of the highway, trying desperately to get away from the insects. Jim did not stop the van, afraid that the frantic bison might charge at their van or trailer. The couple drove slowly to approach the bison and then passed the poor animal in dilemma, feeling sorry for it.

"Maybe our van has attracted some of those bison-flies away from the bison and given him a little break," Jim said wishfully.

"I hope so. The poor animal looked at his wit's end," Meilin added hopefully.

Nature to the couple at this moment was not all that beautiful and harmonious. There were moments that all living beings had to face and suffer from the negative things which were also of nature. Mother Nature could be deadly harsh and destructive; all were powerless under her indifferent force and whim. Balance of all living things seemed to have come from chaotic imbalance; beautiful nature had its dark shadow of cruel ugliness.

Not long after this encounter, the couple saw a whole herd of bison. The herd seemed also being driven out of the forest by the too numerous insects. They walked at the edge of the woods close to the highway. Among the dark brown adult bison, there was a small calf that was orange colour. The day was quite hot and there was no wind. The air deep in the forest plus the blood-sucking insects must be too hard for the animals to bear. They came to the open area by the highway to have a break. The couple stopped by the highway to take some pictures of the beautiful herd. The bison, with the big humps on their back necks, looked strong and powerful. They walked along the edge of the woods in a single file; there were order and harmony in their community.

The couple had the luck to see another herd of bison along this stretch of the highway in the bison reservation. This herd had found a haven in an area where all the trees and bushes had been burnt out in a forest fire. There were not much insects in this area, as the insects' breeding grounds of the bushes and vegetations were burnt out. This herd of bison lay peacefully among the burnt stumps, not being bothered by the large flies. However, they would eventually have to go back to the green forests where their feeding grounds were. Besides the bison, the couple had spotted a strange animal in this area. It was a cat, orange-coloured, three times bigger than a normal cat and with a lanky body. The cat strolled over the highway softly and swiftly. Before Meilin could take out the camera to snap a picture, it had already disappeared into the forest. The couple wondered whether it was a lynx, but the lynx would not come out to stroll over the highway in daytime. Jim decided that it was a bobcat, but Meilin still thought that it was a small tiger.

In both Alberta and Northwest Territories, large areas have been reserved for wild buffaloes or bison. The bison reservation here spanned for miles and miles. It looked that the bison were thriving with a not too small number. The deeper the couple went into this region, the more insects there were. The collisions those insects had made on their moving van sounded like a rain storm the couple were driving through. Even with the loud sound from the engine and the air conditioner, they could still hear the collective buzzing of the insects; it sounded like a helicopter hovering around. In this kind of harsh condition, the couple were very much surprised to see some workers working on the highway and on some work sites by the highway. Further on, they saw a directing sign to an animal management office. Obviously, there were people not only working here, but also living here.

It was quite amazing to see wild animals thriving in this harsh natural condition, but even more amazing to see some humans living and working in this kind of harsh environment. It was summer time, the transportation artery that was vital for the economy of the region had to be maintained to ensure its normal function. The highway construction workers had not much protection against the numerous insects around. They gave the couple the impression that the bison-flies only bothered the bison, not the humans, or the workers had been used to the condition. Through the immense wilderness, the couple had thought that all the living beings here were at the mercy of nature. They were quite glad to see that there were actually humans living here to look after the wild animals. Jim talked about that the native peoples in the old times had to live close to the places where the large wild animals were. The caribous, the bison and the moose were the native peoples' livelihood and they had to live in places where those wild animals were or would migrate to. The couple now saw how harsh the natural world could be for both man and beasts. To survive, man and all other living beings had to struggle. It looked that the human beings came out to be the top winner, they had not only survived, but also greatly multiplied, and in some aspects, they had conquered nature.

After the bison country, the landscape started changing. The closer they got to Yellowknife, the more changes appeared. The highway was getting more and more affected by permafrost, the typical feature of tundra. The road became bumpy and wavy. Driving on the highway was becoming a ride on a rollercoaster. The thick forests along the highway disappeared. In their place, trees appeared sparsely dotting the vast even land. Those trees had thin dark trunks that were bare of leaves. The green leaves grew to form small balls hanging on the top of those trees. Obviously, the trees were stunned by the tundra condition. Lakes, ponds, and small bodies of waters were here and there; they were most probably the result of the thawing of permafrost. The land was vastly even and wide open, but the scenery turned to be rather desolate. This area had shown that there was not a clear line between the taiga and the tundra. The features of these two different lands could be interwoven for quite a large area.

The couple were affected by both the somber landscape and the dropping of the vehicle's indication needle reporting that their van was low on fuel. At this moment, they regretted greatly to have neglected bringing the two extra cans of gas with them. They were sure that they were not too far from Yellowknife now. But even with only a short distance left, if they ran out of gas, it would be very difficult to get help on this highway in the vast wilderness. The traffic on the highway remained light. The couple's minds now were filled with the worries of being stranded on the highway and the difficulties in getting help.

As if to save them from their troubled minds, Edzo appeared by the highway. The couple were overjoyed. They pulled into the small town or village, thinking that if there were people living here, there must be a gas station. The village was not far from the highway. They soon saw a fire-hall and a children's playground. The couple were happy. If there was a fire-hall, the place would not be too small and the possibility of a gas station here was large. They drove a little further and saw some residential houses, but there was no gas station in sight. They stopped the van and decided to ask for some information before going further in. The couple got out of the van and looked around. The place looked clean and peaceful. There were no bison-flies around. The residential houses looked nice just like the normal residential houses in other Canadian towns or villages, but there was nobody around. Down the hill, there were more residential houses and a garbage truck was taking garbage from some large bins. All those facilities and services indicated that the place was not small. The couple felt more hopeful about finding a gas station here.

Jim went down the hill to ask the driver of the garbage truck where the gas station was located here. It took some time for him to return. The information he brought back was not too good. There was no gas station here; people here had to go to Rae to gas up their vehicles. Rae had two gas stations, but it was ten kilometers off the highway. The shop assistant in the gas station of Fort Providence was right. Practically, the next gas station from Fort Providence was in Yellowknife.

There was no other way; the couple had to keep on driving. The side-road to reach Rae was further on by the highway. The couple thought over and over whether they should go to Rae to gas up. Maybe the gas left in the van was enough to carry them to Yellowknife, but there was the possibility that the gas could run out before they reached the destination. When the side-road to Rae appeared by the highway, the couple had made up their minds that they were going to Rae. Why should they run the risk of being stranded on the highway while they could run the extra miles to be safe? They had enough gas to get to Rae. The road to Rae was paved, which made it easier for them to make this decision.

The drive of the ten kilometers seemed a bit long. When they arrived at Rae, the first building they saw was the gas station. The couple were glad and pulled their van and trailer to the gas pump. Jim went to gas up the van and Meilin stayed in the van. The gas pump was crude and the ground of the gas station was not paved and full of potholes. It must have rained here a while ago; the ground was now strewn with large and small puddles. The gas station office was in a fair-sized wooden building that also hosted a store. In the store, there were groceries and some other goods for daily living. While Jim attended to filling up the gas tank and paying the bill in the office, Meilin looked around. The cars and trucks coming into the gas station were all operated by the native people. A teenage native boy came in, driving an ATV, All Terrain Vehicle, and carrying his sister with him. All the vehicles and the boy's ATV were in good shape. The place looked like a town and obviously a native community. Down through the paved street, there were quite some residential houses; some of them were fairly new and large. Further down, among the houses and buildings, there was a large building with a silver-coloured metal dome. The domed building might be a church or a community hall. Except the gas station ground that needed desperately a brushing up, the whole town looked as nice as any other Canadian towns.

Obviously, Rae had been a white settlement in the early time. For some period in the old days, a signal station had been set up here. When Yellowknife had been established to become the capital city, the signal station had moved there. The white settlers too had gradually moved to Yellowknife. After the white people had gone, the native people moved in. Now Rae was mainly a native community. In Canada today, the native peoples are no longer nomadic peoples. They have either had their own settlements or inherited some early European settlements that the white people had abandoned. The native settlements are normally lack of modern development. The streets and residences need badly improvement. Rae looked an exception. The street and houses the couple had seen were up to date and the native people's vehicles were in good conditions. This had indicated that the native peoples were doing well here and most probably having jobs in some companies or industrial sites around.

The couple soon gassed up their van and were on their way. They talked about Rae on their way and were glad to see that the living standards of the native people here seemed no different than that of other Canadians. Meilin complained about the puddle-ridden ground of the gas station; she could not understand why the services and public facilities in native communities could not come up to the same standards as that of other Canadian places. The couple thought that both Edzo and Rae were native communities. In fact, Edzo had remained largely a white community. After the bison reserve, they had seen a sign by the highway which had a native name to start and followed by "Corporates Limit" and "Alcohol Is Prohibited in This Area". The couple could not understand what the "Corporates Limit" meant. The sign looked like a landmark. Did it mean that this area belonged to the native peoples? Then the native peoples here might have turned their communities into corporations. It might be true that quite some native peoples in the northern region were working in mines and other construction sites nowadays. It looked that alcohol was a problem in the native communities; otherwise there would not be a sign even by the highway to forbid it. Anyhow, the couple were glad to see that the native people here lived a good life. Their vehicles and their houses showed that they were not poor. More importantly, the natives and the native children the couple had seen around the gas station all looked healthy.

The couple felt it worthwhile to have gone to Rae for gas, as they had seen a native community thriving here in this northern region. The ten kilometers seemed shorter on the return trip; they soon came to the highway again. There were still about sixty kilometers to reach Yellowknife. The road remained bumpy. When they got near Yellowknife, they could see a few houses, small trailers and even some chairs on some large rocks by the highway. It looked that some people were staking those big rocks to build their cottages on. In the harsh climate of the northern land, cottages or get-away cots probably could not be built too far away from the highway. There was also the problem of permafrost that prevented people to build on land. The freezing and thawing of the land could damage the structure of any building. The best location to build something that would stand up long would be on those big rocks. These rock-staking activities must be from some private small builders. In the far north where the Inuit were, innovative ways had already been found to build structures on permafrost land. Insulation materials separating the buildings, cables and pipes from the frozen ground had made those buildings stable and lasting. The new technology of building residential houses and public facilities on permafrost land today had allowed the Inuit to live in houses.

Besides those occupied rocks, there were also gravel sites showing up along the highway. The couple could see that some rocks by the highway had been crushed into gravels and the gravels had been used to build or repair the highway at some locations. The northern region was far away from other populated southern places; it was sensible that some industrial materials were better coming from local. For quite some distance, the highway here was red coloured as the local gravels were red. It gave the couple a different sensation while driving on a rosy highway.

In the afternoon, the couple arrived at Yellowknife. They tried to find the campground first, but had mistakenly turned into a street that might be the industrial section of the city. The city airport was along the highway and reaching into part of this industrial street. It looked like a large airport. A WWII transportation plane was mounted on a post at the city entrance that started this street. The couple could well sense and understand the importance of air transportation to this city. They drove quite some distance on this street before realizing that they had made a wrong turn. They had to turn back and go to the highway again to reach the campground. However, this wrong turn had given them a surprising impression of the city. They had only seen a little, but it had already told them that Yellowknife was not small and it had the scale and standards of a medium-sized modern city.

When the couple turned back and reached the campground, they first saw a path leading to a gate. There were some decorative ornaments along the path and a colourful wooden office building by the gate. A police car was parked by the office building. The nice gate indicated that the campground would be up to the modern standards, but the cop's car waiting at the gate gave them a bad signal. The couple had offended the police at their home city. They had suffered harassment all along their cross-country travels. A police car here at their arrival had run an alarm bell that, remote as the place was, harassment might be waiting for them in this city as well.

At this moment, the couple could not think too much else but to get a site and get settled down quickly. They needed a good rest after the long distance drive. Jim went to the office and came back with not so good news. They had been assigned a lot for only one night, because the campground was booked full. This was unexpected. All the while they were driving to come to Yellowknife, they did not see any other motor homes or camping trailers on the highway. From the tour book, the couple got to know that this campground by Yellowknife had 98 camping lots. How could the whole campground be booked full? Jim was informed that he had to go to the office tomorrow morning at ten o'clock to see if any lot would be vacant. The good news was that the office clerk had also talked about opening the overflow site for the situation. It looked that they would not be driven to the street after all.

The couple pulled their van and trailer to the assigned lot. The whole campground was situated in the woods and by a lake. Each lot was spacious and surrounded by trees and bushes. Yellowknife was only about 500 kilometers from the Arctic Circle. It was amazing to see so many trees, bushes and vegetations around here. The lot had electric power and no water or sewer drainage. There were public water taps and a large bathroom with showers on the campground. The couple soon settled in.

In order not to wait for a vacant lot tomorrow morning, after things settled, Meilin said to Jim, "Maybe we should ask the office to give us a lot on the overflow site now. We'll have two more nights after this one. In this way, we can start our city tour tomorrow without wasting a whole morning on the campground."

Jim agreed and went to the office again. When he came back, he asked his wife to go to see the overflow site. An office clerk would lead them to the site. The overflow site was on a rather large open area in front of the bathroom. There was a large lawn circled by large lying-down tree trunks. On one side of the lawn, there was a large white tepee and on one side of the circle, there were several posters artfully framed by small tree trunks. The posters introduced the history of local native peoples. The whole site looked open and naturally beautiful. The clerk showed the couple the place that they were going to park their van and trailer. Jim and Meilin were satisfied with the place. Their trailer window would face the open space and the trailer door would open to a path that led to an old cabin. The cabin was used by the prospectors in the Gold-Rush time. There was also a prospectors' trail starting from this path and meandering through the terrain for several kilometers, but the trail was closed now for some reason.

The couple had a good night's sleep on this campground and next morning they moved to the overflow site. The fees for the camping lot were thirty-two dollars per night but only fifteen dollars per night for the overflow site. This was the cheapest fees the couple had encountered through their camping across the country. The normal camping lots among the trees and bushes had some mosquitoes buzzing around. Here on the open overflow site, the mosquitoes were much less. The only thing lacking here was the electricity. For this shortcoming, the clerk had advised the couple to ask the neighbour who were camping on a normal lot not far from them to share their electricity, as each lot had two electric sockets.

The thrifty couple were more than satisfied with the overflow camping site. The bathroom was near them. It was a large grey wooden structure standing tall on a high foundation. It had a large wooden deck with a wide wooden staircase in front and a runway on the side of the building with another staircase. There were picnic tables with seats on the deck. For each bathroom, there were two thick doors, one leading to a small room and the other to the bathroom proper. Obviously, this was to prevent the insects getting into the bathroom in summer and cold in winter. The inside of the bathroom was spacious and clean. The tall ceiling had made the facility look very modern and comfortable. From the washing basins to showers, everything was shining, clean and up to the modern standards. More amazingly, the bathroom from inside out was thoroughly energy efficient and environmentally friendly. On the roof of the bathroom, there were quite some solar panels. Everything of the bathroom, from lighting, hot water, air conditioner to air-blow dryer, was all run by solar power. This was the first time that the couple had seen a public bathroom fully operated by solar power. They liked and admired it. The suspicion about the fully booked campground flew out of their minds. If some people booked the camping lots through the website, but not showing up; no matter what their motives were, the couple ended up with a better camping site; there was no more complaint from them.

The couple's tour of Yellowknife started early next morning. Yellowknife is located by the Great Slave Lake, the third largest freshwater lake in North America. Inside the city and the area, there are a few more other small lakes. Water is everywhere. As a matter of fact, the whole Northwest Territories is covered with large and small lakes and long and short rivers. The couple had to drive a little further on the highway to enter Yellowknife through another street instead of that industrial one. On this street, they first saw a direction sign for the city's museum and then a sign for the information centre. The couple went to the information centre first. The information centre was in a large grey-coloured wood and glass building of modern style. The building was partially sitting on tall cement pillars over a small lake. In front of the building, there were a small pavilion full of hanging flower-baskets, a place for bicycles to park, and an art ornament of a large metal-mesh insect, looking like a bison-fly. On the parking lot, there were some historical mining machines in display. By the building and the lake, there were garden and resting places for visitors to enjoy. The place looked beautifully peaceful and had no insects or mosquitoes around. It was quite strange. Yellowknife was located in the vast wilderness. While the wilderness was full of insects, Yellowknife City seemed entirely free of insects.

The couple took some pictures around and then entered the information center. The inside of the building was very spacious. There were a large information counter, a large exhibition hall and a gift store. Then, there was a second story in part of the building, which was also an exhibition area. From the exhibited items on the first and second levels, the couple got some information about the mining history of Yellowknife and Northwest Territories, the regional aboriginal peoples and a brief natural history of the region. On the second floor they had also seen a little artworks by some local artists.

The Dene had hunted and fished in Yellowknife area for thousands of years. The name of the city, Yellowknife, came from the copper knives worn by the Chipewyan tribe, one of the three aboriginal tribes that lived in this area. The non-native peoples came to this area during the 1930s when the Gold Rush took off. Large quantity of gold had been discovered by the Great Slave Lake in this area at that time and the population in Yellowknife exploded suddenly. When Yellowknife was built on this site, it was known as a city built on gold. Two large gold mines had been established, Con in 1938 and Giant Mines in 1984. The gold digging had lasted for about sixty years.

It was later on when Jim and Meilin got to know from a documentary film that the gold mines here had to be closed down because of the environmental damages done by them. The gold in the Great Slave Lake area was embedded in rocks. Large quantities of arsenic trioxide had been used to extract gold from the hard rocks. Arsenic trioxide was highly poisonous to the soil, the water, the air and all the living beings around. When the terrible environmental damages had been recognized, the mines had already generated 207 thousand tons of poisonous wastes that could kill the whole world population several times over. After the mines were closed down, the huge task of cleaning up the environmental damages began. The government had put the poisonous wastes underground and sealed them by freezing the rocks around them. Still, there were the contaminated mine structures, the grounds and the waters around the sites needed to be dealt with. The cost of the clean-up would mount to billions. The people and especially the aboriginal peoples in Yellowknife thought that to thoroughly clean up the environmental damages was impossible and they were highly worried that the pollution of the sites and the sealed wastes underground might leak out to poison the Great Slave Lake and even the Mackenzie River.

The environmental disaster caused by the gold mines in Yellowknife is just one of numerous environmental disasters caused by toxic industrial wastes in the world. The soils, waters and air of the planet have been polluted in an astronomical speed not only by the toxic industrial or other wastes, oil, chemical and radiation spills, but also by enormous emissions from burning fossil fuels by countless factories, plants and motor devices. The ozone layer has already suffered damages by the speedy industrial developments of the human world. The globe is already facing climate changes as the result. If the speedy industrial developments continue to ignore the protection of the natural environment, the planet will soon be ruined and uninhabitable to all the living beings. There is no doubt that developments are necessary. All the human beings, no matter in which corner of the world, wish, want or demand to live a good life. Good human lives depend on the developments of natural resources. But over developments or wrongful developments without sufficient researches, planning and precaution to ensure the safety of natural environment must be stopped as soon as possible.

Otherwise, planet earth will soon be ruined and all the living beings will be wiped out from this beautiful globe. If the human beings continue to ignore the dangerous environmental changes and other pollution signs caused by their wanton, selfish and irresponsible ways of exploiting, using and damaging the natural environment to satisfy their immediate, insatiable needs and wants, the world, the human race and all other living beings will have no future and the end for all will not be long to come.

When the gold mines in Yellowknife were closed, Yellowknife looked going to be a ghost town soon. Industrial and economical developments are indeed closely related to the developments of the human world; they are necessary for building countries, cities and communities. But the gold mines in Yellowknife had to be closed, as they had caused devastating environment damages. Perhaps the large quantities of gold can still be extracted from rocks when better ways can be found to extract them in the future. Now the Yellowknife people or practically Canada is facing the consequences from using the bad ways in industrial development and the huge task of cleaning up the mess.

However, life goes on and things are constantly evolving. When one door closes, another door will open. After the gold mines closed in 2003, large quantity of diamond had already been discovered in the farther north area to Yellowknife. Since 1998, three large mines, the Ekati, the Diavik and Snap Lake have been established and produced high quality diamonds. The boom of the city has thus continued. The people of Yellowknife now proudly call their city, the diamond capital of North America.

The information center had provided quite some information about the diamond mining industry here. Canada has two major geographic characteristics. One is the Canadian Shield formed by billowing ancient rocks covering about half of Canada. Some of those rocks are over 500 million years old and they are rich in minerals. The other is the boreal forests which are covering more than half of the country. Northwest Territories shares the two main geographic features of the country. Most of Northwest Territories is within the Canadian Shield and full of ancient rocks. Diamonds are imbedded in kimberlite, the molten rocks resulting from vocalic eruptions. Not all kimberlite hide diamonds, but finding kimberlite means the possibility of finding diamonds. In 1991, two Canadian geologists discovered the kimberlite that was rich with diamonds in Northwest Territories and the historical staking rush started then after. Today, the claim posts placed at every quarter mile in the relevant area have covered about 70 million acres.

Diamond mining industry is over half of Northwest Territories' economy today. It has provided jobs for the natives, the local non-natives and some people from other parts of the country. It is definitely important to the life of all the people in this region. The diamond mining process is using water to separate the diamonds from crushed rocks, which should be less dangerous to the nature environment.

The couple checked carefully about the information and displays about the diamond mining industry. They were impressed. Then they checked the information about the aboriginal peoples, their different tribes and their laws in the old time. Afterwards they went to the second floor to look at some paintings by the local artists and a small display of the natural history of the region. When they came out of the information centre, they felt that they knew a little better about this city and this region, and especially what were important to the people here.

Loaded with maps and brochures, the couple then went into the city centre. What they saw had surprised them. Yellowknife had always been a very remote small northern city in their minds. They had never expected to see such a beautiful modern city. The city center was around a lake. All the grand buildings were either by the lake or close to the lake. The couple had considered their home city Abbotsford a small city, while Abbotsford had a population of almost 150 thousand people. Here, Yellowknife's population was a little over 20 thousand. Yet the city centre of Yellowknife gave the couple an impression of a medium-sized city. The government buildings, the culture facilities and the city centre park had given the place a capital city status.

Around the lake, there was a beautiful paved path for people to walk and reach all the important buildings around. By one side of the lake there were wide cement staircases with large landings to reach the water. On top of the staircases, a large lawn was stretching to the city streets. Side by side with the staircase, there was a round concrete platform on the lake, with some metal benches for people to sit down and a beautiful abstract artwork in the center of the platform. The artwork was a sculpture of three human figures dancing together, which was formed by gentle metal frames. The fluid soft lines had set the dancing figures afloat and vividly alive. The name of this artwork was Unity. With the background of the lake and some small island, this piece of artwork had raised the artistic and ideological value of the city in the couple's eyes. On another side of the lake and in a corner of the park, there was a memorial garden for women who had suffered and died from breast cancer. In this summer time, the garden with its numerous hanging flower-baskets was blooming with different colours. Beside this garden, there was the display of old equipment for gold mining and a staking post which might be the very staking post that had started the gold mining here. On this visit, the couple had no knowledge of the environmental damages caused by the gold mining industry here and their minds were not disturbed by those sealed toxic wastes buried underground in this area. They enjoyed and admired this beautiful modern city wholeheartedly.

Right by the centre park was the large city hall which was a red brick building of several stories high. At the back of the city hall, there was another large red brick building which was the headquarters of RCMP. Close by the RCMP building, there was another large round building, looking most modern with full blue glass windows. This building was the headquarters of the military. Of course, in the whole remote northern region, the military was present in different posts. Across the lake, there was the domed building of the museum named Prince of Wales Northern Heritage Centre. Behind the museum, there was the building of the legislative assembly, which was of modern design, not the traditional classic or neoclassic style.

It took two days for the couple to check out the important sites of this city. They visited the museum. The fair-sized modern building housed the exhibits concerning the native peoples of this region, their culture, tradition and life. There was even a hall showing the native people's technique of building a large boat by using animal skins, tree trunks and wood beams. A big ready-made boat was in display and a video was showing the whole process of the native people making a same boat. The museum had also exhibited the history of transportation and communication carried out by bush planes in this region. In the far north, even today some communities have been connected to other parts of the region only by those bush planes. Those planes have been a very important part of the northern people's life. Of course, there were also exhibits and introductions about the history of the region and a big picture of Charles, the Prince of Wales who had opened this museum. The museum had a large restaurant which seemed to have customers all day long. The lunch menu included fresh fish. A lunch with fresh fish was only fourteen to sixteen dollars. The couple had heard about the high prices of food and other daily necessities in the far north before they came here; they now saw that those reports were exaggerated. However, they decided to go downtown to have their lunch in a fast food restaurant. The price of burger with fries in the fast food restaurant here was the same as that in any other cities.

The visit to the legislative assembly had also taken quite some of the couple's time. The grey coloured modern building looked simple but stylish. The grey colour came from the zinc metal sidings which were more endurable in the severe northern climate. There was a guide conducting a tour inside the legislative building. The guide was a willowy young girl with acne on her face. She looked like a high school girl, the type that often suffered bullying. It turned out that the girl was quite clear and fluent. The entrance hall of the legislative building was big with a long information counter. There were two assembly halls in the building, one small and one large. Jim and Meilin joined a small tourist group. The guide showed the group to the two assembly halls and the corridors. The couple were quite impressed by the paintings and stone carvings throughout the building; they were the works by some famous Canadian and northern artists. The paintings showed northern landscapes and the black marble or soapstone carvings depicted northern animals. The large assembly hall was quite different than the assembly halls of legislative buildings in other provinces. The domed ceiling of the hall was exceptionally high. The ceiling lights looked like the stars shining through an open observatory dome. Immediately beneath the vaulted ceiling, there was a whole ring of opaque glass with shadowy pictures of northern landscape. The hall looked like a round stadium with the centre ground arena and the audience seats circling around above. Sitting in the audience seats of this assembly hall, the couple felt like sitting inside a large spaceship. Only a big polar bear fur spreading in the center floor of the hall brought them down to this northern earth. The guide introduced many things from the flag of Northwest Territories, the beautiful paintings, native artworks to the big assembly hall. The last place the guide led the visitors to was a small room that had all the pictures of the legislative assembly members. The visitors had noticed that the members were all white in the early years, but from the 1970s on, there were a few native members appearing in the governing body. The government of Northwest Territories is very young. The federal government had governed this region for many early years. In 1967, the regional governing task had transferred from Ottawa to the local government now assembling in this legislative building. Today, of all the legislative assemblies in the country, Northwest Territories has the most native legislative members.

The couple were quite impressed by the museum and the legislative building. After visiting the two import buildings, they went to visit the headquarters of the military. A security guard stopped them at the door, but allowed them to stay at the entrance reception area. The security guard was in his late fifties. Jim chatted with him and found out that he was a military retiree. When the two talked some more and found out that they had served in the same squadron and on the same peace keeping duty in Cyprus, they were like two old friends meeting after a long time separation. In the reception area, there was a guest-waiting corner with some displays of old military communication equipment and a big life-like polar bear. The building was large. The guard told the couple that one side of the building was for the enlisted and the other side was for the officers. It looked that the building served as a small military base. The couple knew well how hard it was for the soldiers to guard the large Arctic areas. The border patrols sometimes were carried out in the coldest climate of minus fifty degrees Celsius. They hoped that, with the satellite and high-tech surveillance equipment today, the border guarding duties on the far north might be a bit easier. On their way in, the couple had seen a large military transportation plane in the airport. It looked that the military was vigilant and ready for any happening in the far north. The couple left the military headquarters after the guard's warm goodbye words. Though with quite some complaints, Jim still had a warm feeling towards the military. Having left the military headquarters, the couple passed by the headquarters of the RCMP. It was Sunday; the door of the RCMP headquarters was closed. The couple had a look at a small monument in front of the building. This monument was dedicated to some members of RCMP who had lost their lives while on duty. It must be quite hard even for the police to carry out their duties in this remote northern region.

The second day, the couple visited another important place, the old town of the city. Like all other cities, Yellowknife started from an old town. Today, there were still some old cabins and shacks left in this area, but beside those old small buildings there were some new cabins and houses built. The old town area had become a tourist attraction. There were some stores and restaurants which were the heritage from the old time. The Wildcat Cafe, a log cabin restaurant that had served the pilots, fishermen and miners in the old days had almost fallen apart, but was now renovated and carrying out business as usual. This old restaurant was a UN Heritage Site and the city's landmark now. The couple had a look at this important restaurant from inside out and had some pictures taken. The place looked practically rebuilt and like a new restaurant, all built by large wooden logs with a long wooden deck hugging the whole side of the building and dining tables and chairs on the deck as well.

The couple came to the old town early in the morning and waited at an old store for its opening. The store sold arts, crafts and souvenirs. They wanted to buy some soapstone carvings made by the Inuit. The store was a large log building. Around the building there were paintings, native artworks of the stone Man, the totem pole and a big bear sculpture with the famous street sign – Ragged Ass Road. All these decorations outside the store were already showing some northern arts. The paintings were of Arctic landscape, Inuit and their life. They looked done by professionals. The couple took some pictures with all of the artworks, especially the sign, Ragged Ass Road. This street name was given by the fishermen and miners who lived here in the beginning of the town, dirt poor, but in high spirit. Now the souvenir store was standing at the entrance of the Ragged Ass Road in the old time. When the store opened, the couple saw it is full of different goods, from diamond jewellery, clothing to all kinds of knickknacks. They bought some small souvenir; the soapstone carvings looked not from the Inuit and too expensive for them.

The high point of the old town visit was the Pilots' Monument on top of a large rock. The rock was on a hill, the highest point of Yellowknife. The rock itself was about six stories high. The couple climbed up the winding wooden staircase to reach the top. From this point, they could see the whole Yellowknife and part of the Great Slave Lake. The city, though with quite a few tall buildings, was not big; it was situated right by the Great Slave Lake. Under the summer sun, the great lake was blue and stretching to the horizon. On the lake along the city, there were some houseboats on the water. Those houseboats were actually normal wooden houses built on wood platforms or rafts. Some of those houses were two stories high, fair-sized and in different colours; they looked like colourful houses floating on the lake, very picturesque. Some fishing boats had anchored at part of the shore. Some sea-planes were taking off from the lake, leaving trails of white waves behind. The tourists could take those planes to have a look of the area from above. The huge lake, the city, the floating houses, the boats and the sea-planes formed a beautiful picture of the place, peaceful, yet full of vitality. The monument was a simple concrete spearing pillar with a small bush-plane model on top; it was erected to honour the pilots who had given their lives in building up the northern region. Those pilots were of both military and civilian air crews. Without the efforts and struggles of those military and civilian pilots flying under very harsh conditions, there would not be the existence of this northern region with a modern city and other communities connected with other parts of the country. It was quite fitting to have this monument here on this rock hill looking over Yellowknife and the Great Slave Lake.

Yellowknife had given the couple the impression of a wealthy city. Any place, if it is wealthy, its culture, arts and sports will flourish. Yellowknife's arts were indeed flourishing and of high quality. Even the street mural paintings here looked done by skilled professionals. The muskoxen with their manes flowing in the wind on one of the murals looked alive and full of courage. The residential houses in the city were rather new and comfortably sized. The couple could see that more condos were being built in some sub-division.

Yellowknife had amazed the couple with its beauty, modernness and wealth. However, there was another thing of the city that had also shocked the couple. It was the native people in this city. Before the couple visited Yellowknife, they had always thought that this northernmost city was occupied mainly by the native people. Now they saw that Yellowknife was mainly occupied by the white people. There were a few coloured people here. The couple had seen some coloured people working or having meals in the fast food restaurant and some even working in the museum, but they looked like the coloured people from the south of the country. Native people were visible in the city, but in a bad way. From their listless appearances and gaits, they were neither pleasure-seeking tourists nor leisure-seeking residents after their working hours. Those native people looked like jobless welfare recipients. The couple saw a few native people wandering aimlessly in the street and some small native groups gathering together to kill time in the garden of the information centre and the city centre park. The couple were saddened by the appearance of this kind of native people here. This was the old picture too familiar to the couple; they had seen them in other cities. Their hope to see at least one city in the country occupied mainly by the native people was dashed. Things here were the same as in all other cities. The native peoples had no place in any Canadian city and even in Yellowknife.

The beautiful sculpture named Unity now looked a pale decoration void of realistic value. Still the couple could see that there were some efforts being made in trying to bring the aboriginal peoples into the fold. Along one side of city centre lake, the walking path was connecting the city hall to the museum. This path was called Flag Walk. The walk was flanked on both sides by many flags. With the Canadian national, the regional and the municipal flags, there were many flags of the aboriginal tribes or communities in this region. To start this Flag Walk, there was a large paved circle with a fire pit. This round circle was for the locals and especially the aboriginal peoples to have their ceremonies. Then, the sculpture Unity did indicate the hope of different peoples living, working and playing together. The exhibits in the museum were mainly about the aboriginal peoples. The legislative assembly had some native members. Yellowknife was the only city in Canada that first had an Aboriginal Day. All these showed that efforts had been made to include the aboriginal peoples. But the reality showed that the result was far lacking in the city. Even though there was a native settlement right in the old town area; native people seemed living side by side, not together with or in the society of Yellowknife.

Many white Canadians believe or want to believe that the aboriginal peoples have refused to enter the Canadian society, but the reality shows that some of the native peoples have personally come into cities, but they are rejected and excluded from the life of those cities. The coloured people have a place in Canadian society, even though their place is at the bottom. The native peoples have been refused a place in the Canadian society. If there are some natives coming into cities, it shows that it is not the natives refusing to enter the Canadian society; it is the society that has rejected them. Those city-bound natives have suffered not only racial discriminations from some non-native citizens, but also much harsher treatments from the police. Still, some natives have kept on coming, hoping to live a good life like the city dwellers.

In Yellowknife, the native people lived so close to the non-natives and they naturally would wander into the city, but there was no place for them in the city. The mines might have employed some native peoples, but the city was off-limit to them. Yellowknife was the government, transportation and communication centre of this region. Not only the regional and municipal governments were here, but the headquarters of the RCMP, the military, the mines and some other industries' administrations were also here. The city provided all the administrations, services and supplies for the mines and fishery in this region. The unemployment rate in Yellowknife was the lowest and the average personal income of the city was the highest in the country. Still, the native people who lived right in the old town could not share the good life of the city. Being only two days in Yellowknife, the couple could sense the force of some citizens rejecting the native peoples and trying to rid the city of any aboriginal effect or influence. Some historical record had been changed to show that the city name Yellowknife was coming from the miners using copper-handle knives as a precaution. The small newsletter that was distributed freely to restaurants simply cut off "Yellow" to call the city "Knife". Obviously, those people wished that the native peoples would disappear from their life and their city. What a sharp contrast there was between the cultural and political efforts to include the native peoples and the actions of rejecting or excluding the native peoples by some racially discriminatory citizens! It looked that the winner was the later, as the inclusion was only formality, and the exclusion was the actual practice of the general public.

Yellowknife is not different than other cities of the country. The situation is the same in all other Canadian cities. Large or small, the cities either have no trace of native peoples or have a few listless native welfare recipients. The couple thought the situation highly unfair. The native peoples had shared their land and resources with the non-native later-comers, but the later-comers would not share a good life with them. Now the large native communities like Rae might be able to make it because of being adjacent to some industrial sites, but it would be hard for many other remote small native communities to make it. The urbanization, the industrial and economical developments, the pollution and over poaching and over fishing have affected and depleted natural resources that the native peoples' livelihood has been traditionally depended on. Trapping, hunting and fishing have been the native peoples' way of life. Now those natural resources are not entirely dependable for their livelihood. Quite some native reserves today have the highest unemployment rate. The statics shows that any place with an unemployment rate increasing one percent for a successive six years, the suicide and crime rates in that place will increase the same proportion. Some native reserves have over eighty percent unemployment rates for many years, which inevitably result in poverty, high suicide and high jail-mates rates, and other social ills.

In the beginning, the situations of the native peoples and the French Canadians had a lot in common. They were "conquered nations". However, what have consequently happened to them and the treatments they have received have been totally different. Through struggles in history, the French became the equal of the British and participated in the founding of Canada. Today, The French Canadians have the province of Quebec; they control their own affairs and their own future in Quebec. They have maintained their own language and developed their own culture in Quebec. The country recognizes French Quebec as a distinct society. The French Canadians have participated politically and economically in the life of Canada. There are quite some French Canadians in the federal government and a few of them had even become prime ministers. Outside Quebec, the French Canadians can reside in other cities of other provinces and they are treated the same as the other locals.

The native peoples have had very little of what the French Canadians have. Are the different fates of the native peoples and the French Canadians resulting from racial discrimination? It looks so. The French, after all, are the close relatives of the British; they are the same race. Through history, the native peoples had contributed to the birth or existence of Canada. In the very beginning, some aboriginal peoples had welcomed and helped some early European settlers to establish their homes on this northern land. Then some native peoples had helped the British during the era of the conflicts between Britain and France on this land. And in the War of 1812, some native peoples had fought side by side with the British to drive out the American invaders. Canada owes partially the native peoples for its existence. By all means, the native peoples should be treated the same as the French Canadians. With the example set up by the French Canadians, the native peoples should have the rights to control their own affairs and their own future on their reserves. They should be able to maintain their own languages and develop their own culture. Outside their reserves, they should be able to participate politically and economically in all aspects of the country's life. As for keeping their old way of life, after four hundred years' impact of the western way and with the environmental changes, the general population and especially the new generations of the native peoples are westernized. If some of them wish to come to cities, they should be welcomed and given equal rights and opportunities as other citizens to work and live a meaningful life in cities. The native peoples and their reserves are very much a part of the country. Only until the native peoples have the same living standards as other Canadians and enjoy all the rights and opportunities as other Canadians, can Canada be truly a first world country.

What had or have happened to the native peoples cannot stand any comparison with what have happened to the French Canadians. Through the history, Canada had done shameful injustices in its treatments towards the native peoples. Among many maltreatment and abuses, the most shocking one is the residential school system that was carried out from first half of the 19th century to the second half of the 20th century. In order to assimilate the native peoples, the Inuit and the Métis into the mainstay of the western culture and life, the residential schools had been set up to "educate" the native children. In the beginning, some of those schools were called industrial schools and had tried to teach the native children the skills of farming and some other trades. But as soon as some natives started to compete with the white settlers in farming and for the positions of some trades, the white settlers felt offended and threatened. The residential school system immediately changed the curriculum to teaching the native boys mainly manual labours to become farmhand and the native girls to be housekeepers. In late 19th century, the Canadian government struck an agreement with different churches to work together to set up the residential schools nationwide. The churches took over the actual work and the government set up the policy to ensure it compulsory for all the native children from 7 to 16 to attend those schools. The parents withholding their children would be punished by imprisonment.

By early 20th century, about 10 thousand native children had been herded into 60 residential schools all over the country, some as young as four years old. In those schools, the native children had suffered not only tremendous degradation, but also mental, physical, sexual and spiritual abuses. The hygiene and nutrition in some schools were atrociously poor, resulting in the death of some children. Those who had survived had been greatly damaged by different abuses.

Being gutted of their children, the native communities suffered greatly. On top of this, the native peoples were forbidden to practice their traditional dances and ceremonies. Their hereditary leadership system in their bands was also prohibited. Their reserves close to the towns with more than eight thousand inhabitants were moved away. In this period of time, while 160 acres land in the prairie provinces was given freely to any white man who would set up a homestead and cultivate 40 acres, some native peoples' land and even treaty land were sold to the white farmers or expropriated for the constructions of some public facilities. Some native reserves had been moved to give way to the constructions of some municipalities. Then the Indian Affairs department set the Indian Agents into all the native communities to govern their affairs.

After years of efforts and fighting from the native parents and different organizations, the situation started to change from the mid-20th century on. Extensive investigations had been made on the residential schools by the Royal Commission and then the Inquiry set up by the government. The result from the investigations and the recommendation from the Indian Affairs to abolish the residential school system had made the government part partnership with the churches and take control of those schools. Soon the residential schools had been closed down in different times and different provinces, and some schools had been transferred to the native bands. The last residential school was closed in Saskatchewan in 1996. In this time, some different churches had apologized to the native peoples for their participation in the residential school system. Also during this time, quite some injustices suffered by the native peoples had started to be addressed and dealt with by the country. In the early 21rst century, the Assembly of First Nations National Chief Phil Fontaine, a former residential school attendant, announced a class action lawsuit against the Government of Canada over the human rights violations and abuses suffered by the native peoples under the residential school system. Subsequently a settlement had been made to compensate all the residential school attendants. Also in this time, Prime Minister Stephen Harper finally gave the nation's apology to the native peoples, the Inuit and the Métis over the residential school system. The process of reconciliation, healing and rebuilding the relationship with the native peoples has then started.

The couple had no idea about the extensiveness and complexity of the native peoples' political and legal struggles for their rights, but they could see that the native peoples were taking actions to fight for and protect what lawfully belonged to them. They could see that the majority of the maltreatments that the native peoples had suffered could be categorized as coming from racism. From their own experiences, the couple knew how many sufferings racism could cause and how much racism could infuriate people and drive them to extremes. They could see the urgency of the native issues and things that had to be done to improve native peoples' conditions.

Understandably, it will be very hard on the native peoples' part for the reconciliation, healing and rebuilding relationship to work. All the maltreatment, abuses and especially the residential school system have had far reaching negative effects on native peoples' life. They have very much contributed to the disintegration of the native families and communities today. However, it is necessary for the native peoples to start the process of reconciliation, the healing and the rebuilding relationship with the rest of the country. It is the way for them to put the past behind and move forward. For the native peoples to achieve equality in all aspects of Canadian life, a large part depends on the native peoples themselves to stand up and fight to be strong. The victim mentality, the resentments and hostilities towards the large Canadian society will not help them. While it is important for them to fight to have the injustices recognized and redressed, it is also very important for them to address the present problems in the native communities. When the members from a few years old up in many native communities all drink alcohol, children grow up in adults' drunken ravings, and almost every family has had member committed suicide and member experienced being in jail, it is very obvious that serious energies have to be spend in dealing with those problems. When a man has been beaten down to the ground, no amount of external help can make the man stand up, unless the man himself has the will and confidence to stand up and to triumph over his defeat. The priority the native communities are facing today is to build up the confidence and self-esteem in their people and especially the young people, and to generate their will to stand up, to fight the adversities and to rebuild their nations strong. No poverty or discrimination can be more threatening to their survival as strong human beings than the loss of confidence and self-esteem in themselves and the loss of will to stand up.

Though the situations of the native communities looked grave today, Jim and Meilin had confidence that the native peoples would eventually work things out for themselves and to find ways to be strong. They had survived in very harsh natural conditions on this land for thousands of years; the couple believed that they could survive the modern world with all its problems and flourish in some way in the future.

Right now on this visit, though the couple were very much saddened by seeing the exclusiveness towards the native people even in Yellowknife, they had plenty of their own troubles to worry about. In a city where the racist force was strong, Jim and Meilin could not escape harassment and attacks. Yellowknife, though remote and seemingly isolated from other parts of the country, was a city with modern communication system for its citizens to be well informed of what were going on in the country and the world. It looked that some Yellowknifers had known the situation about the couple, in a prejudiced way of course, and they were ready to show their displeasure or hostilities towards the odd couple. Jim and Meilin had duly encountered harassment in this city. There were hostile shows put on for them, shows to say that the yellow Chinese woman had gone bananas, shows to indicate that the couple were bad and so on. The couple brushed them off. Meilin however commented a little about the racist harassers being dumb without creativity. The harassments put on by those Yellowknifers were the exact copies of what the couple had already encountered at their home city. The harassers here in Yellowknife were either under the instruction of the same dark power or they were simply thinking the same way.

It is a fact of life that the racially discriminatory people are not smart people. Truly intelligent and smart people have no need or urge to put down other kinds of people in order to raise themselves. Quite some racially discriminatory people are from some whites who are not sure about their own talents and their own abilities; some of them may truly be of a lower intelligence level or the best, mediocre. Those people are normally in some good social positions. They feel the need to stick to the concept of the superiority of their white race. In this way, they can convince themselves or prove to others that they deserve their higher social status and their good social positions. The couple had refuted the concept of white race superiority and asked for equal rights and equal opportunities for all the citizens and the native peoples. Their publicized bold speech had offended quite some of those racially discriminatory whites. Of course, in those whites' eyes, the couple were bad and had to be put down in whatever way possible. The couple had consequently encountered harassment, attacks and abuses from this type of whites and even from some coloured people who were under the control of this type whites.

Normally, the racially discriminatory whites consider themselves warriors or patriots who have to fight those radicals like the couple to protect the social order and their white race's top social positions. Patriotism is the last refuge of the racist scoundrels. In fact, this kind of racist elements are the true danger to the country. They divide the society by racial classes and cause conflicts, disturbances, sufferings and grieves in the country. Sooner or later the racist practices will fall. Like people, a country has also survival instinct. The country's survival instinct will demand its citizens to get rid of racial discrimination, so that the country can be strong and move forward.

Maybe it was because of the harassment they had received or the exclusiveness to the native peoples they had seen in this city, the couple felt that some Yellowknifers had excessive pride, pride that bordered on arrogance. Those Yellowknifers seemed to have inherited some traits of the gold diggers in the old time, secretive, suspicious and very protective of what they thought belonged to them only. Those traits were typically part of human nature. Not many people, when finding a pile of gold or diamonds, would like to share them with a whole lot of people. Jim and Meilin had respected and admired the Yellowknifers in the beginning. Those people had worked hard in the harsh natural conditions to achieve what they had today. Life here would not be all too easy and pleasant with some months of total darkness and some months of total daylight. And there was the extreme cold weather in winter to deal with. In the whole Northwest Territories, for any mineral or oil to be extracted from the earth, people had to work with the thick ice and hard rocks. It was amazing to see such a beautiful modern city built here in this northern region. Still, the couple disliked some Yellowknifers' arrogance. They could sense that their protectiveness and exclusiveness were coming from this arrogance. It would be highly ridiculous if the harassment to the couple coming from some Yellowknifers' fear that the couple might think of coming to Yellowknife to share their good fortune. The couple were neither young nor ambitious to dream of striking rich in some frontier, if there was any frontier left nowadays.

Pride can come from different things, some good and some bad. Wealth is definitely among those things that generate pride. Excessive wealth generates excessive pride which easily leads to arrogance. Arrogance elevates people's ego and isolates them from others. If pride can bring people sufferings, arrogance doubles pride in this aspect. Both pride and arrogance can blind people, so that they cannot see what is lacking in themselves, in their work and in their world. In the worst case, pride and arrogance can bring miseries and sufferings. Arrogance generated by wealth might be the least dangerous than arrogance generated by the sense of superiority or power. No matter this sense of superiority or power is being brought about racially, politically, religiously, scientifically or technologically; it can certainly bring miseries and sufferings and be dangerous to the arrogant people themselves and the people happen to be around them.

Yellowknife is a small and very remote city in the far north. The Canadians seldom think of this city, as they normally know very little about it. It was a big surprise for the couple to see the city so beautiful and modern, and even a bigger surprise for them to sense the arrogance of some Yellowknifers. Arrogance would not bring anything good to the city and its citizens. Yellowknife and the whole Northwest Territories had a small population. If the Yellowknifers did not want other people like Jim and Meilin to come into their community, they should at least embrace the native peoples who were living so close to them. The city and the region very much needed more people for their economical development and for a good future. Gold and diamonds could bring wealth, but they would eventually be exhausted. To insure that the city and the region would have lasting prosperity, the people in this region had to diversify their economy. To have the native peoples joining their work force and to have more people coming from other parts of the country to work here with them would be not only beneficial and advantageous, but also vital for the survival of the city and the development and prosperity of the region.

The couple stayed in Yellowknife for three nights and spent two days in the city. They left on the fourth day. The visit to Yellowknife was the last destination of the cross-country travels for them. Like their visits to other parts of the country, their visit to this northern region could only be considered as a browse, neither deep nor comprehensive. At their age and their energy level, the couple were satisfied with where they had reached, what they had seen and how they had felt. They felt that this far north trip like the whole cross-country travels was definitely a worthwhile life experience.

CHAPTER FIFTEEN

OH, CANADA

The couple arrived home safe and sound. Each time when they came back home after a long journey, they felt good. They started the trip enthusiastically in high spirit, but inevitably exhausted at the end. Home meant that they could rest and relief the fatigue generated by the long travelling to and touring the places. The soft big beds at home certainly felt most comfortable after days of sleeping in the small beds of the trailer. The home sleeping would be most sound after many nights of sleeping in different strange places. Home, after all, was still haven for the soundness of their body and mind. The restless and disturbed nights at home would come later on, as life without any trouble was impossible. Yet, at this moment when just coming back from a long trip, home seemed the most peaceful place on earth where they could be by themselves to rest, to think and to enjoy whatever they choose to enjoy.

The couple had finished their cross-country travels. Though they would still travel to different places in their later years, the cross-country travelling was ended for them. Intermittently, the cross-country travels had taken them five years to accomplish; it was indeed a big journey for them. Yet they had only covered the very basic parts of the country. Canada is a large country of about three million square kilometers. It has about one million kilometers of roads and highways; most of them are surfaced. With their return trips, the couple had traveled about thirty to forty thousand kilometers on the main highways throughout the country. The mileage they had covered in comparison to the total mileage of the country's roads showed that they had only touched the surface. However, the couple had gone through the main transportation arteries that had connected most capital cities of the ten provinces and the two northern territories.

Of course, after coming back home and even for the rest of their life, the couple would be reminiscent of their experiences from this cross-country journey. The places they had been, the things they had seen, the people they had met and what had happened to them on this journey would remain in their memories. As for what they had learnt and how they had felt from this journey, they could not clearly explain; some things were clear, some things were vague and then some other things were unexplainable. The beauty of the country had deeply touched them, but they could not definitely say that seeing the vast beautiful country had changed them. If they would boldly claim that seeing the beautiful country had changed them, they could not clearly answer in what way they had been changed. Jim was born in a poor Canadian family, had worked in lower level jobs and been a soldier for his working years. He had always simply thought himself as a Canadian and that was that. When seeing different beautiful places of the immense country, he would not be overwhelmed by pride to loudly exclaim or sing, "Oh, my country, my beautiful country!" To him, the country did not belong to him. Some high positioned politicians or wealthy people who owned a lot might be able to claim that the country belonged to them. But to Jim, from his life experiences, it was him who belonged to the country. He was a Canadian and that was that. He might have taken things granted, as a Canadian passport was highly coveted in the world and many people might like to trade place with him. Still, a not so easy life had made Jim feel that being a Canadian was ordinary and he himself but an ordinary human being. He loved Canada naturally, because it was his birthplace and his home, but there would be no exaggerations or flatteries coming from him.

Meilin, the intellectual type, was more sensitive or sentimental. The beauty of Canada had moved her deeply. The moments of viewing the magnificent snow-capped mountains, the majestic blue ocean, the fresh green rolling prairie fields, the broad ocean-like forests, the great rivers and gigantic lakes were very emotional moments for her. At those moments, she would very much like to be proud of this country and proud to be a Canadian. Yet, if she claimed that she had felt such pride, she would have to call herself a phony. After living in Canada for twenty-seven years and being a Canadian for twenty-one years, she had never felt being fully accepted as a Canadian citizen. Circumstances and certain realities of Canadian society had often made her feel like an outsider. Still, those moments of seeing the splendid beauty of the country, especially the glorious sunset and sunrise on the immense peaceful landscapes made her fall in love with this country. She had been moved so much that, in whatever small way, she wanted to know more of the country's past, was concerned about the country's present and future and even felt responsible for the country's well being. She knew that any normal Canadian, after travelling through this beautiful country, would feel the same way. Those feelings came from a normal human being's love for this earth he or she was dwelling on. The concerns and responsible feelings of a citizen of the world would inevitably be prompted when being moved by the beauty of the earth.

Of course, the couple had not only seen the natural beauty on their cross-country travels, they had gone through many Canadian cities to be dazzled by what had been created and built by the Canadians. Canada has Toronto, Montreal, Vancouver and now Calgary that are ranked among the largest modern cities in the world. Its Ottawa, Quebec and other capital cities are also first class cities and can compare with any other star cities in the world. In their visits to all those Canadian cities, the couple were deeply impressed by the museums displaying art treasures, different histories and cultures, and the various styles of grand architectures and arts decorations. They were overwhelmed by the achievements and wealth shown by those shining star cities of the country.

All those great Canadian achievements have been accomplished in just a couple of centuries. This northern half of North America Continent had been formerly resided by the aboriginal peoples for thousands of years. Then the Vikings discovered it in the end of the 10th century. 500 years after the Vikings' adventure, the European exploration of this land started. The very first official explorer to this land was John Cabot. He was authorized by King Henry VII in 1497 to claim any land he might find for England. Cabot was followed by Jacques Cartier commissioned by French King, Francis I in 1534 to find a passage to China. In those early days, the European economical activities on this land started from fishery and then went to fur trading. The immigration and settlements on this land started in the 1600s and went off in the 18th century after the British colonies replaced the French colony. After the birth of Canada in 1867, the country started forming in orderly steps. Starting from the mid-20th century, the population of the country has increased substantially resulting from the increase of immigration. With the increasing of the population, economic developments and productivities have increased in leaps and bounds. First, the agriculture developments have been achieved from the stable immigrants' settlements. Then in about a hundred years, the country has quickly developed from an agriculture country into an industrial one.

Today, Canada is among the highly developed countries of the world. Most Canadians have enjoyed high standards of living. Two thirds of Canadians own their own dwellings, even though the soaring real estate prices today have given quite some young people difficulties in gaining property ownership. Canadian homes are generally equipped with central heating, running water and electricity. Though with a moderate population, the Canadians are among the high consumers of the modern technology expressed by automobiles, home appliances, televisions, telephones and now cellular phones and computers. Of course, all these achievements and prosperity are closely related to the stable Canadian political system. Though the Canadian political system has modelled from British parliament system and American constitution, the Canadian political institutes have had their own characteristics. Canadian political policies have tended to be more conservative, and each term of Canadian government has strived for peace, order and good government.

Nonetheless, Canada is not perfect and there is no perfect country in the world. For some foreign tourists who had sporadically seen Canada, the country would be perfect, a paradise on earth. But for Jim and Meilin, the Canadians living here, they had not only seen the good, the beautiful and the shining side of the country, but also seen or were aware of the not so good or ugly side. There are still quite many native peoples in this country, whose living standards and conditions are that of the third world country. The rich beautiful Canadian cities still have homeless people shacking up in some tents in shadows or sleeping in the corners of some back streets. Quite some low income families have to depend on food banks. Like every other country of the world, crimes, social ills and activities of underground society are still going on in Canada.

Besides seeing both good and bad sides of the country, the couple, like most Canadians, were fully aware of the country's situation with its only neighbour, the world's super power- the United States. In the 20th century, large quantity of foreign and especially American capital had flown into Canada. It has helped Canadian economical development, but in the meantime, resulted in the American interests owning and controlling half of Canadian manufacturing industries and more than half of Canadian natural resource industries. The powerful American economy and culture have strongly affected Canada; the Canadians are becoming Americanized. Quite some Canadians have the sense of crises that Canada is being engulfed by the super power neighbour politically, economically and culturally, and that Canada has been out of being a British colony only to fall into a colonial dependency on the US. Yet the economists are not worried, saying that all foreign ownerships of industries in Canada are still under the control and regulations of the Canadian government, and besides, the Canadian investments are also in other countries. However, with the country's eighty percent international trading concentrated exclusively with the US, Canadian economy is vulnerable to the changes of American fiscal policies. It is understandable that there have been Canadian efforts throughout history to limit the US control and influence on Canadian economy, culture and politics, and to maintain Canadian identity and nationality, yet it is hard to see great success of those efforts.

However, what the couple most personally concerned about was the problem of racial discrimination in Canada, as they were the victims of this problem. The couple's present situation had put them in the spotlight. They had no more privacy. Their home talks and Meilin's writing had become the targets for attacks. The couple could see that their criticism on racial discrimination was the main thing disliked and hated by quite some white people. Through their cross-country travelling, the couple had been harassed and there were even a few attempts made to cause them bodily harm or even on their lives. For some foreign tourists, it was easy to have the impression that the Canadians were the nicest people in the world. The couple had also met quite some of those nicest Canadians along their way. They had been treated and helped by this type of Canadians with kindness, gentle help and polite manners. Yet, being an interracial couple in their present situation, they had also met some Canadians whose prejudice and even hostilities could be well sensed. Some racially discriminatory people's condescending, arrogant or indifferent manners had always hurt Meilin more than Jim. Jim normally ignored and advised his wife to do the same. Meilin tried to do so, but was not always successful. The harassments, hostile shows and malicious attempts the couple had come across on their way had made them see the wide spread and serious problems of racial discrimination in this country.

Social inequality exists in every country. Canada is of no exception. Canadian society is a classed society. The class system is strict and many efforts have been made to maintain this system, as it is perceived that the Canadian social order is based on this system. The top level of this system is formed by the elite who control the political and economical powers. Through the history, these elite are almost exclusively formed by the white and mainly the white males of British origin with the family background of the country's top rich and religious background of Anglican Church. Though Canada is a democratic country and its political positions are occupied by people who are elected by the public, the top level of the political positions are still being managed to be held mostly by those from the powerful directorship of large corporations, and those elite directorship are normally from the top rich. To view the Canadian social classes roughly, the next will be the rather large masses of middle class who are below the top class and ranked in different levels. There is probably an illusion nowadays that the middle class has the real power of the country because of being the largest number. In fact, the top class is still in control; the power still lies with the money. The corporate elite held the economic fate of the country. Their decisions and their money movements can make or break a country. With their economic power, they can make the political system or policies to serve their needs and choose the leaders of the country to suit their purposes. Of course, the bottom class of the country is formed by the poor, the native peoples and the coloured people. Those people's lives are largely controlled; they have less rights, opportunities and freedom and are often discriminated by different kinds of prejudices.

Through the Canadian history, many movements have been launched to iron out some of the inequalities caused by the classed social system. There has been the Quebec nationalist movement which has fought for the equal rights of the French Canadians and to protect their language and culture. The native peoples have had quite some battles to gain their lost land, to better their economic conditions, to strive for self-government and to maintain their languages and culture. There have been labour movements that have paved way for the country's universal health care, unemployment insurance and pension. The women's movements have fought to improve their lot, to control their own lives and to fight against discriminations and inequalities based on gender. The gays and lesbians have fought for their equal rights to choose their sex or marital partners and to enjoy the same treatment as the heterosexuals. All those movements have achieved substantial successes in Canada.

The problem of racial discrimination in Canada however has never met a large confrontational movement to diminish its damaging power. In the United States, the Civil War had been fought to liberate the black people from slavery and anti-racism movement has been fought for the equal rights of the blacks. Canada has never even experienced any significant demonstration against racism. Quite some white Canadians are complacent, thinking that this lack of movement against racism means that Canada is free of racism. But even those complacent whites know well that racism exists in Canada. This lack of fighting spirit against racism might mainly comes from that the complaints about racism have been suppressed. The situation of Jim and Meilin has best proven this. The white people can go to the street to put up a demonstration against being discriminated because of having red hair. The white people are bold enough to damage extensive public properties, because they are mad at the loss of some ball game. But the couple had been hated, harassed, attacked and their lives were even in danger, because they had uttered words of anti-racism at their own home. The white people are the majority of the country. With the example of what the couple had suffered, who, from the minority ethnical groups, would dare to say or do anything to change their discriminated conditions? They know well that the white people control their livelihood. If they complained about racism, their condition might be worsened; it would be even harder for them to find jobs or lose what they had already gained. The couple's situation has best shown that the coloured people in Canada do not have the same rights and opportunities as the whites; they are suppressed or scared to express their feelings openly and to expose some discriminatory treatments they have received.

Still, the couple could see that though Canada had not experienced anti-racism movement, the country had improved greatly in this aspect in the recent half century. Only about fifty or sixty years ago, very few coloured people could be seen holding any significant social position. Today more coloured people have moved up and gained some higher social status. This has shown that most Canadians are conscientious and know what is right and what is wrong. There is hope that the problem of racism can be solved gradually and peacefully in this country. Nevertheless, the recent improvements do not at all mean that Canada is already free of racism. No matter how much some white people want to turn a blind eye to this problem, racism is still racking havoc now and then in the society and in the life of the coloured people. Those coloured people who have moved up the social ladders are but a small number and it has not changed the low social status of the general population of the coloured. It has become a typical racist practice for some white people to use those coloured people who have made it to suppress and shut up the general population of the coloured and to claim that those coloured bottom liners are entirely responsible for their own disadvantaged conditions.

Canada is a democratic country. Democracy means that everyone can have a say in the destiny of the country. Unfortunately, the reality of the country is far from thus. The real situation is that the ordinary people, especially the coloured people, have not much say in matters concerning the country or themselves; their voices are hardly heard, and the media speak to the people and people cannot speak back to them. The media is owned or controlled by the top class, and therefore normally the top class has a voice, not the other classes. The couple's situation had turned the situation a bit upside down. What the couple had talked at their home had been heard in the public. The media were greatly offended by this situation, because their privileges were being invaded. Suddenly, a couple at the bottom of the society talked back at them and even criticised them. Others could hear what the couple had said and thus the couple had an equal voice in the public. This probably had never happened to the media before. Sure, there might be some individual criticisms towards them, but never so directly and so publicly. The media were used to their tyrannical position and could not tolerate this insult of being talked back by some nobody, and especially this nobody was an interracial couple at the bottom of the society.

As a matter of fact, the couple had never had any personal problems with the media. They had quite some problems with racial discrimination and expressed their indignations against racism. But some people in the media took upon themselves the task to protect those criticised by the couple and to use all their might to beat the couple down. This had inevitably created the problems between them and the couple. During the WWII, many white Canadians had lost their lives in fighting against the evils brought about by the sense or belief of race superiority. The sense of certain race superior was the main culprit that had caused so much destruction, miseries and death. If those who had sacrificed their lives to fight those evils could see some shows on TV today that had promoted race superiority and tried to beat down the coloured people who were speaking out against racism, they would turn in their graves, thinking that their sacrifices were in vain. In this period of time, some side shows from the TV media seemed trying to show that many in this country were sticking to the concept of white superiority. Though the couple were sometimes shocked and felt sad, they could not believe that this was true. They believed that it was only a small number of people who would follow the evil footsteps of fascists to raise the sense of white race superiority and their evil intention had been used to beat down Meilin, the Chinese woman who had got on top of the whites and had to be put down by any means. Meilin wrote at her own home. Though she expressed her opinions about quite some different things, she had never had any intention to get on top of anybody. What's more, her hard work and her good intention to make life better for the lower level people had brought nothing but troubles to her and her husband. All those jealousy, hostility and hatred towards the couple looked like that some people had gone insane. They forced the couple to see that racism was still a serious problem in Canada and some racially discriminatory people would try all kinds of ways to get support and followers from the general public.

The media are powerful tools of communication and education. What the media put on TV are greatly influential and educational to the general public. In any case, the TV media should be in the front, fighting against racism. But in this period of time, in trying to beat down a Chinese woman who could write and had her own opinions, some people had used racism and tried to arouse the sense of white race superiority, and often the insinuations had turned from attacking one Chinese woman to attacking the whole yellow race. The couple thought that this was deadly wrong, had to be stopped and not to appear in the future.

To know a country, besides reading the books about different aspects of the country, travelling through the country is another good way. The couple's travels across the country had opened their eyes to quite many different things about Canada. The traveling affirmed their sense of being the citizens of this country. Above all, the harassment and attacks on them had made them feel very much involved and hard to be outsiders any longer. They understood that for a country with such large land and diverse population and cultures, differences would inevitably occur; it was for the individuals to accept and adapt to the country's situations, and not for the country to suit every individual's demand or situation. However, this did not mean that nobody should do anything to help in making the country a good place to work and live for every citizen. Canada is a relatively peaceful country. There have been struggles and conflicts through history to achieve the present peaceful and stable national condition. If many people had let things staying in their established old ways, the country would not have developed to today's level to become one of the most advanced and developed countries in the world. Most people know that stagnancy causes decay and death; constant changes and improvements foster birth, rebirth and growth. Canada, like every other country, needs constant improvements and innovative changes in order to develop and to move forward. Every conscientious and capable Canadian has the duty to help in making those improvements and changes become reality and in building the country strong. The couple had no regret for what they had done in their present situation and no fear of whatever would happen to them because of the criticisms uttered by them.

In spite of some unpleasant things that had happened on their travels, the couple felt less anger towards their life's situation after they had returned home from the journey. Their home talks and Meilin's writing were no longer bending only on criticisms to vent their anger or to denounce injustice. Instead, they wished more that their opinions or criticisms would be helpful in making the country better for everybody. The traveling made them see the ridiculousness of over-seriousness about personal problems and negative things. In such a large country with numerous different people, they were but a tiny part of this large entity. If their efforts could make this large entity healthier and stronger, it would be good. If they were unable to change anything or anyone, over-seriousness or self-importance would only damage their own health.

Life goes on. Things move forward. Even with some bumps and downturns on the way. Canada has very much moved forward in all aspects including racial problems. Looking at the country's past and present, the couple could not help sensing great hope for the country's future. The moral principles and values are still held fast by the majority of Canadians. This may have resulted partially from religious beliefs. The western moral principles and values have been traditionally built on religion, mainly Christianity. Modern science has given the means for people to achieve their ends in the material world, but cannot provide any meaning or purpose for their life and the universe. It has successfully explained the natural world, but has not touched the spiritual side of things. Human beings are very much partially spiritual beings. To live a successful and fulfilling life, they need to know the purpose and meaning of things and their life. Though the influence of religious beliefs is diminishing in the modern time, the moral principles and values established by them are still upheld by many people.

Things are continuingly changing and evolving in the world. The more science has discovered, the more scientists have become humble and less assured that they have fathomed the whole reality of the universe. In recent times, the discoveries of quantum physics have pushed the scientists to the threshold of peeking into the deeper reality of the universe. On the side of religion, there are also changes for its survival. Modern religion has become more open minded and less hostile towards other beliefs and science. This has set up the first step for religion to evolve. All those changes have given hope that science and religion can work together in the future for the welfare and well being of mankind in both material and spiritual spheres. However, in time of transition for both science and religion, it is definitely a good thing to see that most Canadians are sticking to the moral principles and values, even though the foundation of those moral principles and values has shifted a bit from blind faith to personal moral and spiritual experiences. This upright character of the people was what gave the couple hope that the country would continue to move forward in the right direction and would have a bright future.

The couple had also based their hope for the country on their own life. They were an interracial couple. In spite of great differences between them in the aspects of race, background and others, they had made the union and a successful marriage. The love, understanding and trust they had formed in their marriage had brought them close and diminished their differences. Canada is a country that is becoming multi-coloured and will experience conflicts between different people. From their own experiences, the couple believed that this situation of living closely together would gradually diminish the differences and promote love, understanding and trust among different Canadians. This would be even more so with the younger generations, as they were growing up together. The couple hoped that the future generations of Canadians would be colour-blind in the aspect of their racial origins, and every citizen would be treated and feel just one of the Canadians.

In the world sphere, different peoples and different countries are getting closer. The highly developed technologies in communication and transportation and the closely interwoven global economy have brought peoples and countries together. The common concept or sense of the world becoming a global village is the reality today. Will this closeness bring more conflicts, hostilities and hatred among different peoples and countries, or will it bring more understanding, trust and cooperation that will lead to world peace? People can only wait and see. The peace-loving peoples will of course hope that the situation of living closely together will eventually diminish differences and bring the desperately needed peace in the world. The highly advanced weaponry and nuclear arsenals have put the whole world in grave danger today. Mankind is just coming of age, but already facing the very real danger of life being cut short or wiped out by what the human beings have created in order to protect themselves and to kill and destroy others. Misunderstanding, distrust, jealousy, aggressiveness, hostility or hatred, any one of them can trigger another big world war. In this modern time, human beings are capable of destroying the whole human race and the planet. If a large scaled world war happens again, the chance for either to survive is slim. The good thing is that more and more peoples in the world are seeing the dangers that humanity and the world are facing, they are joining in the world-wide struggles against violence and wars. Under the leadership of UN and some significant international organizations, many organized efforts have been in place to prevent war and to achieve world peace which is vital for the survival of the planet and all its living beings. The living togetherness might also make different peoples see that all of us are the same dwellers on this planet, our only home; we are all intricately connected and need each other; destroying others means destroying ourselves and only peace will save all and the world.

The couple's cross-country travels had very much reminded them of their life's journey. The two were quite similar. By all means, the journey, not the arrival, is all what the fuss is about. Through the journey, they experience different things, good or bad, pleasant or unpleasant, beautiful or ugly, true or false, joyous or grievous, blissful or miserable and so on. Consciously and unconsciously, they learn something from the journey and grow in knowledge and wisdom. In the end, the couple had to admit that their travels across Canada did broaden their minds.

REFERENCES

Introductory materials from:

British Columbia Legislative Buildings, Victoria
Reach Gallery, Abbotsford
Fort Edmonton, Edmonton
West Edmonton Mall, Edmonton
Manitoba Legislative Building, Winnipeg
Royal Canadian Mint, Winnipeg
Margaret Laurence Home, Neepawa
Ontario Legislative Buildings, Toronto
Royal Ontario Museum, Toronto
Casa Loma, Toronto
Parliament Buildings, Ottawa
Notre-Dame Cathedral Basilica, Ottawa
Canadian War Museum, Ottawa
National Gallery of Canada, Ottawa
Royal Canadian Museum of Civilization, Gatineau
Basilica of Notre Dame, Montreal
St. Joseph's Oratory, Montreal
University of New Brunswick, Fredericton
Indian Beach, North Sydney
The Rooms, St. John's
Johnson Geo Centre, St. John's
Signal Hill, St. John's
Cape St. Mary's Ecological Reserve, St. Bride's
The Archives of Yukon, Whitehorse
Yukon Beringia Interpretive Centre, Whitehorse
Yukon Transportation Museum, Whitehorse
Information Centre of Kluane National Park and Reserve, Yukon
Alexandra Falls, Northwest Territories
Northwest Territories Legislative Building, Yellowknife
Information Centre, Yellowknife
The Prince of Wales Northern Heritage Centre, Yellowknife

The Blue Book of Canadian Businesses. 2012. Canadian Newspaper Services International Ltd.

Canada, A Visual Journey. 2000. Prospro Books Inc.

Collier's Encyclopedia. 1981. Macmillan Educational Company

Tour Book. 2011. AAA Publishing

Leonard Roy Frank, Editor, 2000. Wit & Humor Quotationary. Random House

Kenneth G. Pryke and Walter C. Soderlund, Editors, 1992. Profiles of Canada. Copp Clark Pitman Ltd.

R. D. Lawrence, Text. William Curven and Nick Meers, Photography, 1983. Canada's National Parks. Collins Toronto

R. Douglas Francis/Richard Jones/Donald B. Smith 1992. Destinies, Canadian History Since Confederation. Harcourt Brace & Company Canada Inc.

Vic Satzewich 2011. Racism in Canada. Oxford University Press